CIVIL PROCEDURE
CASES AND MATERIALS

Compact Tenth Edition
for Shorter Courses

■ ■ ■

By
Jack H. Friedenthal
Edward F. Howrey Professor of Law
George Washington University

Arthur R. Miller
University Professor
New York University
Formerly Bruce Bromley Professor of Law
Harvard University

John E. Sexton
President and Benjamin Butler Professor of Law
New York University

Helen Hershkoff
Herbert M. and Svetlana Wachtell Professor of
Constitutional Law and Civil Liberties
New York University

AMERICAN CASEBOOK SERIES®

WEST®
A Thomson Reuters business

Mat #40918082

© 2010 Thomson Reuters

    610 Opperman Drive
    St. Paul, MN 55123
    1–800–313–9378

Printed in the United States of America

ISBN: 978–0–314–23291–5

For Jo Anne
    —Jack
In Ellen's Memory
    —Arthur
For Lisa
    —John
For my family
    —Helen

PREFACE

This Compact Tenth Edition is designed to meet the needs of those teaching Civil Procedure courses shorter than the traditional assignment of three hours for each of two semesters. It responds to suggestions and requests that a book of this type be made available. The shortening of the materials found in the larger Tenth Edition and the elimination of certain chapters reflect the authors' judgments concerning what should be the central themes of a Civil Procedure course. The authors continue to believe that the larger Tenth Edition will prove advantageous for many teachers who have shorter courses of four or even three hours because it provides the maximum flexibility in terms of an individual classroom's coverage, depth, sensibility, and emphasis.

Like the Tenth Edition from which it is adapted, the Compact Tenth Edition offers an up-to-date and accessible approach to the study of civil procedure. Students tend to find Civil Procedure the most mysterious of their law school courses. Our goal is to present the material in a clear and simple environment, yet one that challenges and stimulates the student toward increasing critical understanding. The Compact Tenth Edition reflects the restyled Federal Rules of Civil Procedure and covers important new Supreme Court cases on pleading, federal jurisdiction, summary judgment, due process, and res judicata. The edition addresses not simply doctrinal change, but also the still uncertain effects of new technology, globalism, and privatization on the system of civil justice. The edition also responds to the many helpful comments from judges, practitioners, colleagues, and students at the large number of schools in which earlier editions have been used. Our conversations confirm our own conclusion that the book is and will continue to be a highly successful teaching tool, and we have preserved in this compact edition the basic format of the Tenth Edition. Along with traditional material, we include contemporary cases in which the facts are interesting, in which the conflicting policies seem to be in a state of equilibrium or in which the context has extrinsic fascination, rather than materials that offer a tight monograph on various aspects of procedure. In addition, we have made room for cutting-edge issues—including the effect of the Internet on personal jurisdiction, the federalization of interstate, state law class actions, the relation between human rights litigation and forum non conveniens doctrine, the effect of pleading rules on corporate accountability and civil rights enforcement, and the incorporation of alternative dispute resolution techniques into judicial practice—which we believe will contribute in positive ways to a lively and engaged classroom discussion.

As has been the practice with all of the past editions, this Compact Tenth Edition offers substantial emphasis on the operation of the Federal Rules of Civil Procedure and draws comparisons with state and international practice.

The materials in this volume refer to and are augmented by a Supplement, which contains not only the federal statutes and rules governing procedure, but also selected state provisions for comparison. A number of other materials, such as Advisory Committee notes, proposed rule alterations, and local court rules, also are included. The Supplement contains a litigation timechart and an illustrative litigation problem, showing how a case develops in practice and samples of the documents that actually might have formed a portion of the record. These samples are not designed as models to be emulated. To the contrary, they often contain defects intended to encourage students to criticize them in light of knowledge they have obtained from the cases and classroom discussion. The Supplement also includes the complaint from a principal leading case and an important note case.

The cases and excerpts from other materials have been edited carefully in order to shorten them and clarify issues for discussion. With regard to footnotes, the same numbering appears in the casebook as appears in the original sources; our footnotes are indicated by letters. Omissions are indicated with asterisks.

The authors are deeply grateful to a host of people who have assisted us in the preparation of this volume, the earlier editions, and the Supplements. Among our students deserving special mention for the aid they have provided in preparing earlier editions of the book are Judge Prudence C. Beatty, Sam L. Abram, Kim Barry, James J. Beha, Jeffrey A. Benjamin, (Professor) Richard B. Bernstein, Michael Blasie, (Professor) Barry B. Boyer, (Professor) Michael Broyde, William M. Burns, Bertram Carp, (Professor) Sanford Caust–Ellenbogen, Anna L. Cavnar, Jeffrey J. Chapman, Daniel Chazin, Tan Yee Cheung, Caroline P. Cincotta, Adam S. Cohen, Stephanie Cohen, Steven Cohen, Diane Costa, Russell C. Crane, David Drueding, Gary Eisenberg, Seth K. Endo, Lisa Fair, David E. Firestone, (Judge) Raymond Fisher, Grant H. Franks, Kelly A. Frawley, Patrick P. Garlinger, Stacy Gershwind, Lisa E. Goldberg, Robert H. Goldman, Steven F. Goldman, Ashley K. Goodale, Amanda W. Goodin, Susanna R. Greenberg, Debra L. Greenberger, Kimberly M. Greene, Kevin A. Griffin, Edward Hartnett, Daniel M. Hennefeld, Wendy B. Jacobs, (Professor) Joe J. Kalo, (Dean) Mary Kay Kane, Lonnie Keene, Christopher D. Kercher, Tarek M. Khanachet, Amy Kimpel, Jessica M. Kumm, Pearline M. Kyi, Daniel Laguardia, Fredrick W. Lambert, Judyann M. Lee, Susan S. Lee, Kevin J. Lynch, Alexandra A. Magness, Christopher Mahon, Shirin Malkani, Maureen P. Manning, (Professor) John J. McGonagle, Matthew McGrath, Kiran H. Mehta, Lisabeth C. Meletta, Franklin N. Meyer, Gary Meyerhoff, Tara Mikkilineni, Joy E. Milligan, Jennifer Nevins, John Nichols, Greg G. Oehler, Marcy Oppenheimer, Jennifer Pariser, Dawn A. Pederson, Avi Perry, Kate Elizabeth Phillips, Norman A. Platt, Martin C. Recchuite, Christopher Reich, James E. Rossman, Beth A. Rotman, Gregory S. Schmolka, Marc Schuback, (Professor) Linda J. Silberman, Donna Silverberg, Robert Silvers, (Professor) William Slomanson, Roger D. Smith, David A. Stein, Brian A. Stern, Christopher M. Straw, Reuben B. Teague, Eva A. Temkin, Mara E. Trager, Lee Turner–Dodge, Jacqueline Veit, (Professor) Michael Vitiello, and Gail Zweig. For their help in preparing the Tenth

Edition and the Compact Tenth Edition, we thank the following students of New York University School of Law: Brandon Adoni, Gabriel Bedoya, Lina Bensman, John M. Bentil, Matt Brown, Stavan Shivrah Desai, Drew Johnson–Skinner, Xiang Li, Jeanette E. Markle, Claire Martirosian, Christen M. Martosella, Chris C. Morley, Benjamin M. Stoll, Robert M. Swan, Gregory Tuttle, Christopher R. Utecht, Ellison S. Ward, Lindsey Weinstock, and Nir Zicherman. We also thank Nancy Louise Hoffman and Tiffany Lee, students at The George Washington University Law School, for their help on the Compact Tenth Edition. Roxanne Birkel and Louis Higgins of Thomson–West deserve special mention. We also extend deep thanks to Jo Anne Friedenthal and Stephen Loffredo for personal encouragement and intellectual support; to Dan Evans, Stephen Wagner, Erica Tate, Michael Malavarca, John Easterbrook, Hetty Dekker, Bob Gatto, Silah Karim, Robert Anselmi, and Kristin Silberman for important work on this volume or prior editions; to Gretchen Feltes and Linda Ramsingh for exemplary library support; and to Rachel Jones for invaluable assistance on this volume.

Finally, we sincerely thank our many colleagues and students across the legal community for the countless excellent suggestions they have offered. Their contributions have been instrumental in the preparation of the Tenth Edition and this Compact Edition that is adapted from it.

J.H.F.

A.R.M.

J.E.S.

H.H.

February 2010

SUMMARY OF CONTENTS

———————

TABLE OF CONTENTS

_____

TABLE OF CASES

The principal cases are in bold type. Cases cited or discussed in the text are in roman type. References are to pages. Cases cited in principal cases and within other quoted materials are not included.

TABLE OF AUTHORITIES

References are to pages.

CIVIL PROCEDURE
CASES AND MATERIALS

**Compact Tenth Edition
for Shorter Courses**

CHAPTER 1

A SURVEY OF THE CIVIL ACTION

■ ■ ■

In this Chapter, we provide a thematic and doctrinal framework for studying civil procedure. Civil disputes in the United States typically are resolved by courts according to adversarial principles of justice. The adversarial ideal assumes that individual litigants have autonomy in shaping lawsuits and moving claims to their ultimate resolution. The materials examine how adversarial assumptions influence the design of judicial procedures and explore the ways in which adversarial decision making differs from other methods of resolving disputes. Another theme we consider is that of federalism: the relation between the federal government and the states. Federalism is important because the civil justice system in the United States comprises not a single set, but rather a multiplicity, of court systems. Civil procedure helps to coordinate the work of these courts; it also ensures that courts respect democratic processes. With these concepts in hand, the materials then offer a nuts-and-bolts picture of a civil action, tracing a lawsuit from the commencement of the suit and the service of the summons to the entry of judgment and subsequent appeals. As you read these materials, it is important to be alert to the historical context of your studies. Procedural doctrine has developed a great deal over the centuries, and in part reflects changes in social attitudes toward such matters as fairness, efficiency, participation, and justice. The materials invite you to take a critical view of civil procedure and to ask how the rules and doctrine that you study can be improved.

SECTION A. THE CONCERN AND CHARACTER OF CIVIL PROCEDURE

Courts exist to provide a decision "by an agent of state power, [of] a controversy existing between two individuals (or the State and an individual), by rational (not merely personal) considerations, purporting to rest on justice and law (i.e. the community's general sense of order)." Wigmore, The Judicial Function, in Science of Legal Method xxvi, xxviii

(1917). Although this definition contains some question-begging elements that need definition themselves, it provides a starting point for understanding the judicial system in the United States. For now, it will suffice to recognize the following points about courts:

(1) The judicial process deals with actual controversies between real parties and also helps to express abstract values for the society.

(2) Courts draw on public power to resolve controversies.

(3) This resolution proceeds not arbitrarily but according to some standards of general application.

(4) These standards are applied in a proceeding that follows some fixed lines set out by a system of rules known as procedure.

In resolving the legal disputes that are presented, courts apply two types of law—*substantive* and *procedural*. Other courses (such as Torts and Contracts) deal with the substantive rights and duties that regulate the everyday relationships among individuals and between individuals and institutions. The substantive law also defines the standard of liability in a particular case. This course, by contrast, will explore the procedures used by courts. Our focus will be on how attorneys in the United States frame their cases in order to bring them properly before a particular court, and how the case proceeds from its commencement until a judgment is reached and enforced.

It is interesting but sometimes frustrating that the line separating the substantive law from the procedural law is not clear in every instance. Certainly a requirement that all papers filed with a particular court be on 8 1/2 by 14-inch paper is a procedural rule. Equally certain is that the elements of the law of assault and battery are substantive. But not every legal rule can be so easily classified. For example, a statute of limitations (which determines the length of time a party has to sue on a claim) may appear at first glance to be purely procedural. But upon closer examination, it becomes clear that the length of a jurisdiction's statute of limitations is as much a product of public policy, and will affect the plaintiff's ability to recover, as any purely "substantive" provision of the jurisdiction's law. As a student of civil procedure, keep your eye on the substance-procedure dichotomy, but also remain wary of its rigid application.

This course deals with the procedural questions presented in *civil* suits; the procedures of *criminal* suits will not concern us. In analyzing questions of civil procedure, however, you should bear in mind the societal goals of civil suits as compared with those of criminal suits. The principal difference is that civil suits generally are initiated and litigated by private parties attempting to vindicate their legal rights vis-à-vis other private parties. The community thus is seeking to provide a method for resolving the disputes that arise out of the everyday interactions of private parties. Criminal suits, by contrast, are instituted and prosecuted by the government (on behalf of "the People") in an effort to punish those individuals whose conduct has violated the community's moral judgments as expressed in its penal law. Government involvement, however, is not always an indicator of a criminal suit since the government often is a party to civil suits, and can be either a plaintiff or a defendant.

The most distinctive element of United States procedure for resolving legal controversies is the *adversary system*. The central feature of this system is the almost total responsibility placed on the parties to the controversy for beginning suit, for shaping issues, and for producing evidence. However, commentators have observed that United States procedure is moving increasingly toward the authorization of measures that contemplate an affirmative or active function for the court. This is evidenced, for example, by the participation of judges in the settlement process, their active involvement during the pretrial conference stage, and their use of various management techniques to supervise discovery. See Rowe, *Authorized Managerialism Under the Federal Rules—And the Extent of Convergence with Civil-Law Judging*, 36 Sw. U. L. Rev. 191 (2007).

Despite criticisms of the adversary system, this mode of decision making persists in many parts of the world. Four explanations typically are put forward to explain its perseverance:

(1) A truer decision is reached as the result of a contest directed by interested parties.

(2) The parties, who after all are the ones principally interested in the controversy's resolution, should bear the major burden of the time and energy required.

(3) Although impartial investigation may be better when no final decision need be reached, setting up sides makes easier the type of yes-or-no decision that is thought to be necessary in most lawsuits.

(4) Since resort to law has replaced the resort to force that characterized primitive ages, the atavistic instinct to do battle is better satisfied by a means of settling disputes that is very much in the hands of the parties.

When one reflects on the fact that the adversary system often means that victory will turn on considerations other than the justice or true merits of the cause, there is reason to believe that we have permitted it to assume an exaggerated place in our civil dispute resolution scheme. But the system remains, and its presence will color every facet of this course. Full understanding of the materials in this book will require your constant attention to its existence, as well as critical analysis of its shortcomings.

What is the test of a good system of procedure? One answer is: *Does it tend to lead to the just and efficient determination of legal controversies?* In this regard, recognize that although this course is only an introduction to United States civil procedure, you are not to assume that your function simply is to digest uncritically the law that you read. Instead, this course will play an integral part in your process of learning to examine, to question, "to wash in cynical acid," each rule, each form, each principle you learn. But while doing so, keep in mind that many, diverse, and complex are the values that inform a procedural system.

NOTES AND QUESTIONS

1. Commentators offer differing perspectives on the goals and values of civil procedure. Professor Solum posits that concepts of procedural justice build on two principles:

> The Participation Principle requires that the arrangements for the resolution of civil disputes be structured to provide each interested party with a right to adequate participation. The Accuracy Principle requires that the arrangements for the resolution of civil disputes be structured to maximize the chances of achieving the legally correct outcome in each proceeding. Together, the two principles provide guidance where guidance is needed, both for the architects of procedural design and reform and for judges who apply general procedural rules to particular cases.

Solum, *Procedural Justice*, 78 S. Cal. L. Rev. 181, 321 (2004). Consider the importance of additional criteria for assessing the quality of a procedural system. What might those criteria be?

2. Commentators associate courts with various social goals. According to the Conflict Resolution Model, "in the interests of preserving the peace, society offers through the courts a mechanism for the impartial judgment of personal grievances, as an alternative to retaliation or forcible self-help." Courts do more, however, than simply resolve disputes. "A Behavior Modification Model * * * sees the courts and civil process as a way of altering behavior by imposing costs on a person. Not the resolution of the immediate dispute but its effect on the future conduct of others is the heart of the matter." Scott, *Two Models of the Civil Process*, 27 Stan. L. Rev. 937, 937–38 (1975). Courts also are associated with rulemaking, a function that is shared with legislatures and administrative agencies. See Sward, *Values, Ideology and the Evolution of the Adversary System*, 64 Ind. L.J. 301, 303 (1988/1989). What are the implications of each of these models for the design of a civil procedure system?

SECTION B.   AN OUTLINE OF THE PROCEDURE IN A CIVIL ACTION

Lawsuits do not begin themselves. Someone first must decide to sue someone else. If this decision is made intelligently, the person choosing to sue must have weighed several matters, among which at least three are basic.

A potential litigant obviously feels aggrieved or would not be thinking of a lawsuit. But he or she must further consider whether the grievance is one for which the law furnishes relief. There are a great many harms a person may feel that the law will not redress. She is offended by the paint on her neighbor's house; he has worked for weeks to persuade a distributor to buy his brand of digital recorder, and sees the sale go to a competitor; she has been holding a plot of ground for speculation, expecting industry to move in, and the area is zoned for residential use; he slips on a spot of grease in the county courthouse but the county is immune from suit. A potential litigant often must consult an attorney before deciding whether he or she "has a case."

Even if she concludes that the grievance is one for which the courts may grant relief, a potential litigant must consider the probability of winning a lawsuit. She must ask whether the person who has caused the injury can be found and brought into court; whether witnesses and documents will be available to support the claims being sued on; whether this proof will be believed; whether the potential adversary can justify its conduct or establish any defenses to the action; and whether an accurate assessment of the law can be made ahead of time.

Then, and perhaps most important of all, a potential litigant must consider whether what is won will be worth the time, the effort, and the expense it will cost, which most significantly includes the payment of fees to an attorney providing representation in the case. In the United States, each litigating party typically bears the full costs of these attorney's fees. These fees are calculated in several ways: by time (at an hourly rate); fixed (the attorney sets the fee prior to providing the services); by task (the attorney charges a fee based on the nature of the tasks she must provide for the client); and on contingency (the attorney is paid a portion of the ultimate judgment or settlement). Although it may seem natural that litigants pay their own way, the so-called "American Rule" stands in contrast to the more widely accepted "English Rule," which requires the losing party to pay the attorney's fees of the prevailing party. In certain kinds of cases, such as antitrust and civil rights, Congress has enacted statutes that mandate fee-shifting from the losing to the prevailing party.

A prospective litigant must weigh these costs against the alternatives to suit, among them settlement, arbitration, self-help, and letting matters rest. What form will the relief take? Most frequently it will be restricted to a judgment for damages. If this is true, the potential litigant must decide whether the injury is one for which a monetary payment will be satisfactory. Assuming it is, will defendant be rich enough to pay? How difficult will a judgment be to collect? How expensive? Will the recovery be enough to pay the lawyer's fees and the other litigation expenses that undoubtedly will be incurred? Even in a context in which the court may grant specific relief—for example, an order directing the opposing party to do something or to stop doing something—will compliance by defendant be possible? Worthwhile? Sufficient? In the same vein, a potential litigant also must consider whether there are risks not directly tied to the suit. Will he antagonize people whose goodwill he needs? Will the action publicize an error of judgment on her part or open her private affairs to public gaze?

Only after considerable thought has resolved questions about the utility and expense of litigation will the prospective plaintiff be ready for the steps that a litigant must take to bring a lawsuit. Let us now consider these steps in the light of a relatively uncluttered hypothetical case:

> Aikin, while crossing the street in front of her private home, was struck and seriously injured by an automobile driven by Beasley. On inquiry, Aikin found that the automobile was owned by Cecil and that Beasley apparently had been in Cecil's employ. Beasley was predictably without substantial assets and a judgment against him for Aikin's injuries promised little material compensation. But Cecil was wealthy, and Aikin was advised that if she could establish that Beasley had indeed been working for Cecil and had been negligent, she then could recover from Cecil. Aikin decided to sue Cecil for $500,000.

1. SELECTING A PROPER COURT

Aikin initially must determine in which court to bring the action. She might have some choice between filing her lawsuit in a state or a federal court, but her choice is not open-ended. This is because the court selected must have *jurisdiction over the subject matter* (that is, the constitution and statutes under which the court operates must have conferred upon it power to decide this type of case) and also must have *jurisdiction over the person* of Cecil (that is, Cecil must be subject or amenable to suit in the state in which the court is located so that a judgment may be entered against him).

Aikin probably will file suit in a state court, for, as we shall see shortly, the subject-matter jurisdiction of the federal courts is severely limited. If the court organization of Aikin's state is typical, there will be courts of *original jurisdiction* in which cases are brought and tried, and one court of *appellate jurisdiction* that sits, with rare exceptions, only to review the decisions of lower courts. (In most states there also will be a group of intermediate courts of appellate jurisdiction.) The courts of original jurisdiction probably consist of one set of courts of *general jurisdiction* and several sets of courts of *inferior jurisdiction*. The courts of general jurisdiction are organized into districts comprising for the most part several counties, although the largest or most populous counties each may constitute single districts. These district courts hear cases of many kinds and are competent to grant every kind of relief, but usually are authorized to hear claims for which the relief requested exceeds a statutorily fixed dollar amount. The courts of inferior jurisdiction will include municipal courts, whose jurisdiction resembles that of the district courts except that the claims are of smaller financial significance; justice-of-the-peace courts, which hear very minor matters; and specialized tribunals such as traffic courts. Since Aikin's injuries are quite serious and her claim correspondingly large, she will, if she sues in a state court, bring the action in one of the district courts.

The federal government also operates a system of courts. The principal federal courts are the United States District Courts, courts of original jurisdiction of which there is at least one in every state; the thirteen United States Courts of Appeals, each of which reviews the decisions of federal district courts in the several states within its circuit (with the exception of the Courts of Appeals for the District of Columbia Circuit and the Federal Circuit); and the Supreme Court of the United States, which reviews the decisions of federal courts and state-court judgments that involve a question of federal law.

The jurisdiction over the subject matter of the United States District Courts extends to many, but by no means all, cases involving federal law and also to many cases, similar to Aikin's, that do not involve federal law, but where there is *diversity of citizenship* (the parties are citizens of different states or one of them is a citizen of a foreign country) and the required *amount in controversy* (currently more than $75,000) is at stake. Diversity jurisdiction, in common with most of the federal courts' jurisdiction, is not *exclusive*; the state courts also are competent to hear these cases and have *concurrent jurisdiction* with the United States District Courts. If Cecil is not a citizen of Aikin's state, Aikin may bring an action for $500,000 in a federal court even though Aikin asserts only state law claims. Indeed, in these circumstances, if Aikin sued Cecil in a state court in Aikin's home state, Cecil could *remove* the action from the state court in which it was commenced to the federal district court in that state.[a]

It is not enough that the court selected by Aikin has jurisdiction over the subject matter, however. That court, whether state or federal, must be one in which Cecil can be required to appear so that it is appropriate for the legal system to enter a judgment against him. Traditionally, a court could enter a judgment only against a defendant who resides in the state or is physically in the state, even if temporarily. However, constitutional restrictions on a court's jurisdiction over the person have diminished in recent decades, and if Cecil is not present in Aikin's state but he directed Beasley to drive there, Aikin probably will be able to bring the action in that state because of Cecil's prior contact with the state and the benefits that those contacts have brought him, assuming that a statute authorizes the court to exercise personal jurisdiction in these circumstances.

Not every court that has jurisdiction over the subject matter and jurisdiction over the person of the defendant will hear a case. It also is necessary that an action be brought in a court having proper *venue*. Thus, although every court in Aikin's state could assert personal jurisdiction over Cecil if he was within its boundaries, that state's statutes typically will provide that the case should be brought in a court whose district includes the county in which either Aikin or Cecil lives. Similarly, if Aikin decides to sue in federal court based on diversity of citizenship, she must bring suit in a district that has venue as defined by federal statute

---

a. If Cecil is not a citizen of Aikin's state and Beasley is, then one of the considerations Aikin will have in deciding whether to join Beasley as a defendant is the effect on the availability of subject-matter jurisdiction in the federal courts. If Aikin wants to be in the federal court, she should not join Beasley; if Aikin wants to begin and stay in a state court, she should join him. In the latter case, there will not be complete diversity of citizenship between plaintiff and defendants.

(currently, the district in which Cecil resides, or in a district where a substantial part of the events giving rise to the claim occurred, or in any district where Cecil is subject to personal jurisdiction if there is no district in which the action otherwise may be brought).

Jurisdiction over the subject matter cannot be waived by the parties. If Aikin and Cecil are both citizens of the same state, a federal court will refuse to hear the action even if both are anxious that it do so. Jurisdiction over the person and venue, on the other hand, essentially are protections for the defendant, who may waive them if he wishes.

Note and Questions

Plaintiff, having decided to sue, must determine in which court to bring the action. A court must be chosen that has jurisdiction over the subject matter of the suit and over the person of the defendant. In the following case, consider which of these two types of jurisdiction the Supreme Court is addressing in the context of a lawsuit filed in federal court. In reading the case, notice that the word "jurisdiction" is used without a modifier. But from the context and from the information you have been given above, you should be able to identify the kind of jurisdiction involved.

———

CAPRON v. VAN NOORDEN

Supreme Court of the United States, 1804.
6 U.S. (2 Cranch) 126, 2 L.Ed. 229.

Error to the [United States] circuit court of North Carolina. The proceedings stated Van Noorden to be late of Pitt county [in North Carolina], but did not allege Capron, the plaintiff, to be an alien, nor a citizen of any state, nor the place of his residence.

Upon the general issue, in an action of trespass on the case, a verdict was found for the defendant, Van Noorden, upon which judgment was rendered.

The writ of error was sued out by Capron, the plaintiff below, who assigned for error, among other things, first, "that the circuit court aforesaid is a court of limited jurisdiction, and that by the record aforesaid it doth not appear, as it ought to have done, that either the said George Capron, or the said Hadrianus Van Noorden, was an alien at the time of the commencement of said suit, or at any other time, or that one of the said parties was at that or any other time, a citizen of the state of North Carolina where the suit was brought, and the other a citizen of another state; or that they the said George and Hadrianus were, for any cause whatever, persons within the jurisdiction of the said court, and capable of suing and being sued there." And, secondly, "that by the record aforesaid it manifestly appeareth that the said circuit court had not any jurisdiction of the cause aforesaid, nor ought to have held plea thereof or given judgment therein, but ought to have dismissed the same, whereas the said court hath proceeded to final judgment therein."

Harper, for the plaintiff in error, stated the only question to be whether the plaintiff had a right to assign for error the want of jurisdiction in that court to which he had chosen to resort. * * *

Here it was the duty of the Court to see that they had jurisdiction, for the consent of parties could not give it. * * *

The defendant in error did not appear, but the citation having been duly served, the judgment was reversed.

NOTES AND QUESTIONS

1. The Supreme Court regarded the defect in this case as extremely serious. Does the fact that it was the plaintiff who brought the case to the Supreme Court make this particularly clear? Why? Why is such significance attached to this error?

2. Read Article III, Section 2, of the United States Constitution, which is set out in the Supplement. What specific language in that Section is pertinent to the Supreme Court's opinion in *Capron?*

3. The Supreme Court reversed the judgment of the lower court. What was the effect of this reversal? Does it mean that Capron wins the lawsuit? If not, why had he sought review in the appellate court?

2. COMMENCING THE ACTION

Aikin must give Cecil notice of the commencement of the action by *service of process*. The process typically consists of a *summons*, which directs defendant to appear and defend under penalty of *default*; that is, unless defendant answers the summons, a judgment will be entered against him. Service of process generally is achieved by *personal service*; the summons is physically delivered to defendant or is left at his home, sometimes by plaintiff or her attorney, sometimes by a public official such as a sheriff or a United States marshal. If Cecil lives in another state, but the circumstances are such that a court in Aikin's state may assert jurisdiction over Cecil, the summons may be personally delivered to him, or some form of *substituted service*, such as sending the papers by registered mail or delivering the summons to his agent within Aikin's state, may be employed. Even if Cecil cannot be located, service in yet another form, usually by *publication* in a newspaper for a certain length of time, may be allowed, although the validity of this kind of service in the type of case Aikin is bringing against Cecil is unlikely to be upheld. The United States Supreme Court repeatedly has emphasized that service must be of a kind reasonably calculated to bring the action to defendant's notice. But service is effective only if the court has power to require the defendant to appear in the action. In the next case, the court must decide whether it has that power, and whether it will exercise it.

TICKLE v. BARTON

Supreme Court of Appeals of West Virginia, 1956.
142 W.Va. 188, 95 S.E.2d 427.

HAYMOND, JUDGE. The plaintiff, Richard Tickle, an infant, who sues by his next friend, instituted this action of trespass on the case in the Circuit Court of McDowell County in March, 1955, to recover damages from the defendants, Raymond Barton, a resident of Austinville, Virginia, and Lawrence Coleman, for personal injuries inflicted upon him by a motor vehicle, owned by the defendant Raymond Barton and operated by his agent the defendant Lawrence Coleman, on private property instead of a public highway, in that county which the plaintiff alleges were caused by the negligence of the defendants.

* * * [A first attempt to serve Barton had been made under a statute relating to actions by or against nonresident drivers involved in accidents on a public highway, and the validity of this service was still undecided at the time the instant decision was rendered.]

On December 5, 1955, one of the attorneys for the plaintiff caused an alias process to be issued against the defendants * * * and delivered it to a deputy sheriff for service upon the defendant Barton in McDowell County; and in the evening of December 6, 1955, that process was served by the deputy upon the defendant Barton in person at the War Junior High School in the town of War in that county where he appeared to attend a banquet which was held there at that time.

By his amended plea in abatement No. 2, the defendant Barton challenged the validity of the service of the alias process upon him on the ground that he had been induced to come to that place in McDowell County by trickery, artifice and deceit practiced upon him by the attorney for the plaintiff.

The circuit court overruled the demurrer of the plaintiff to the amended plea in abatement and * * * certified its ruling upon the demurrer to this Court on the joint application of the plaintiff and the defendant Barton.

* * * [T]he amended plea in abatement alleges in substance that after procuring alias process for the purpose of causing it to be served upon the defendant Barton in McDowell County, and inducing him to come to the Junior High School in the town of War in that county, an attorney representing the plaintiff in this action, in the evening of December 5, 1955, called by telephone the defendant Barton at his home in Austinville, Virginia, and wrongfully and deceitfully represented that, in behalf of the sponsors of a banquet honoring a championship high school football team to be held at the Junior High School in the town of War, in McDowell County * * *, he extended an invitation to the defendant Barton, whose son had been a member of an earlier football team of that school, to attend the banquet; that during that telephone conversation between them the attorney, though requested to do so by the defendant Barton, did not disclose his identity except to say that he called him in behalf of the sponsors to extend the defendant Barton a special invitation to attend the banquet; that the defendant Barton before being so invited did not know that the banquet would be held and did not intend to attend it; that he did not know or suspect the identity of the attorney, or realize that the telephone call was a trick or device to entice, induce and inveigle him to come into McDowell County to be served with process in this action; that the attorney was not connected with any of the sponsors of the banquet and was not authorized by them to invite the defendant Barton to attend it; that the attorney called the defendant Barton and invited him to the banquet solely for the purpose of tricking, deceiving and inveigling him to come to the town of War in order to obtain personal service * * * upon him * * *; that the defendant Barton, believing that the invitation was extended in good faith, by a person authorized to extend it, and not suspecting the real purpose of the telephone call, accepted the invitation and informed the attorney that he would be present at the banquet and on December 6, 1955, left Austinville, Virginia, and went to the town of War with the intention of attending it; that, when he entered the high school where the banquet was held * * * he was served by the deputy sheriff with the alias process * * *; that the service of the alias process upon the defendant Barton, having been procured by trickery, deceit and subterfuge which was not realized or suspected by him, is, for that reason, null and void and of no force or effect and does not confer upon the Circuit Court of McDowell County jurisdiction of the person of the defendant Barton in this action.

The amended plea in abatement also alleges, on information and belief, that after the defendant Barton had left his home * * * the attorney for the plaintiff * * * made a telephone call to the residence of the defendant Barton, or caused some other person to make such call, and inquired of the wife of the defendant Barton if he intended to attend the banquet and was informed by her that he had left his home to attend it and was then on his way to the town of War for that purpose.

The amended plea in abatement further avers that after the defendant Barton had been served with the alias process his attorney inquired of the attorney for the plaintiff if he had made either of the two telephone calls or had procured some person to make the second telephone call and that the attorney for the plaintiff denied that he had made, or procured any person to make, either of the foregoing telephone calls, and denied that he had any knowledge whatsoever of either of them.

The question certified to this Court for decision is whether the allegations of the amended plea in abatement, which insofar as they are material and are well pleaded must be considered as true upon demurrer, are sufficient to render invalid the personal service of process upon the defendant Barton in McDowell County because his presence in that county at the time of such service of process was induced or procured by trickery, artifice, or deceit practiced upon him by an attorney representing the plaintiff in this action.

* * *

* * * In 42 Am. Jur., Process, Section 35, the general principle is stated thus:

> * * * "[I]f a person resident outside the jurisdiction of the court and the reach of its process is inveigled, enticed, or induced, by any false representation, deceitful contrivance, or wrongful device for which the plaintiff is responsible, to come within the jurisdiction of the court for the purpose of obtaining service of process on him in an action brought against him in such court, process served upon him through such improper means is invalid, and upon proof of such fact the court will, on motion, set it aside." * * *

The foregoing principle applies to the party when such service is procured by his agent or by someone acting for and in his behalf. * * *

In Economy Electric Company v. Automatic Electric Power and Light Plant, 185 N.C. 534, 118 S.E. 3, the court, discussing service of process by fraudulent means, used this language: "Where service of process is procured by fraud, that fact may be shown, and, if shown seasonably, the court will refuse to exercise its jurisdiction and turn the plaintiff out of court. The law will not lend its sanction or support to an act, otherwise lawful, which is accomplished by unlawful means. * * * Such a fraud is one affecting the court itself and the integrity of its process. * * * The objection, strictly, is not that the court is without jurisdiction, but that it ought not, by reason of the alleged fraud, to take or to hold jurisdiction of the action. * * * "

Under the material allegations of the amended plea in abatement which, as already indicated, must be considered as true upon demurrer, the defendant Barton was induced or enticed to come into McDowell County by the unauthorized invitation extended to him by the attorney for the plaintiff whose purpose at the time was to obtain personal service upon the defendant Barton * * *; the defendant Barton knew that the present action against him was pending in the circuit court by reason of the service of the original process upon him * * * but he did not suspect or realize that he would be served with process while present in McDowell County to attend the banquet; he was induced to come into that county by the invitation to the banquet; and he would not have come into that jurisdiction if the attorney for the plaintiff had disclosed his identity and his real purpose in extending the invitation, all of which he concealed from the defendant Barton.

* * *

The amended plea in abatement is sufficient on demurrer and the action of the circuit court in overruling the demurrer was correct.

It should perhaps be emphasized that, as the factual allegations of the amended plea in abatement have not been denied at this stage of this action by any pleading filed by the plaintiff, the question of the truth or the falsity of those allegations is not before this Court * * *.

Ruling affirmed.

GIVEN, JUDGE (dissenting).

My disagreement with the majority is not as to the rule of law laid down. I think the rule a salutary one, and masterfully stated. I do not believe, however, that the facts properly pleaded, and the inferences which may be rationally drawn therefrom, bring the facts of this case within the influence of the rule.

Stripped of all explanatory language, and of many allegations of conclusions of fact, * * * the plea in abatement charges no more than that the attorney, by telephone, inquired at defendant's home whether defendant intended to attend a certain social function to be held in McDowell County, to which defendant was then invited by the attorney; that the attorney, though requested to give his name, did not do so; that the attorney later, or someone for him, again by telephone, inquired whether defendant had decided to attend the social function, and was advised that defendant had made arrangements to attend; and that the attorney caused process to be served on defendant while attending the social function. * * * The principal, if not only, fact of wrongdoing, if wrongdoing, alleged against the attorney was his failure to inform defendant of the identity of the telephone caller. * * * It seems to me that the facts properly alleged can not be held to establish fraud or wrongdoing. At most, they would simply show that the attorney took advantage of an opportunity, the holding of the social function in McDowell County and the interest of defendant's son in the holding of the function, to try to obtain proper service of process, which was no more than a duty owed his client. In considering the questions arising, it should be kept in mind that defendant had full knowledge of the institution of the action against him in McDowell County, of the fact that he had questioned the validity of the service of other process issued in that action, and of the fact that the alleged cause of action arose in McDowell County, where ordinarily it would have been triable.

* * *

NOTES AND QUESTIONS

1. Did the court in this case decide that West Virginia courts did not have jurisdiction over the person of defendant (assuming his story were true), or that those courts should not exercise jurisdiction in these circumstances even though they had it?

2. In thinking about the cases you read, try to consider how the court might approach the problem presented by a particular case with certain facts

changed. For example, should service in West Virginia in the following situations be treated in the same way as it was under the facts alleged in the principal case?

(a) Tickle had asked Barton to appear as a witness in a suit against a third party involved in the accident;

(b) Tickle had asked Barton to come to West Virginia to discuss settling the case;

(c) Tickle had telephoned Barton and falsely told him that his son lay critically injured in a West Virginia hospital;

(d) Tickle (like the Sheriff of Nottingham) had scheduled a football banquet in West Virginia that he knew Barton (like Robin Hood) would be unable to resist attending, although he did not personally invite him.

3. When the case is reconsidered by the West Virginia Circuit Court on remand, Barton's lawyer must prove his allegations if Barton is to avoid trial in West Virginia. What problems do you foresee in his being able to prove them, and how should he attempt to do so?

3. PLEADING AND PARTIES

With the summons, Aikin usually will serve on Cecil the first of the *pleadings*, commonly called the *complaint*. This is a written statement that will contain Aikin's claim against Cecil. What should be required of such a statement? It may vary from a simple assertion that Cecil owes her $500,000, to a second-by-second narration of the accident, closely describing the scene and the conduct of each party, followed by a gruesome recital of Aikin's medical treatment and her prognosis for recovery. No procedural system insists upon either of these extremes, but systems do vary greatly in the detail required depending on the purposes that the pleadings are expected to serve. These purposes are many, but three objectives are particularly relevant, and to the extent that a procedural system regards one rather than another as crucial, we may expect to find differing amounts of detail required.

First, the system may desire the pleadings to furnish a basis for identifying and separating the legal and factual contentions involved so that the legal issues—and hopefully through them the entire case—may be disposed of at an early stage. Thus, suppose that Cecil's liability for Beasley's driving depends upon the degree of independence with which Beasley was working at the time of the accident. A dispute on this issue might exist on either or both of two elements. The parties might disagree as to what Beasley's duties were, and they might disagree as to whether those duties put Beasley so much under the control of Cecil that the law will impose liability on Cecil for Beasley's actions. The first disagreement would be a question of fact, and there would be no alternative to trying the suit and letting the finder of fact (usually the jury) decide the truth. But if there was agreement on that first element, a question of law would be presented by the second issue, which could be determined by the judge without a trial. The objective of identifying the legal question is served in such a case only if the pleadings set forth exactly what Beasley's job required him to do. It would be served very inadequately if the complaint stated only that "Beasley was driving the car on Cecil's business."

Second, the pleadings may be intended to establish in advance what a party proposes to prove at trial so that his opponent will know what contentions he must prepare to meet. If this objective is regarded as very important, it will not be enough for the complaint to state that Beasley was negligent or that Aikin suffered serious bodily injuries. It must say that Beasley was speeding, or was not keeping a proper look-out, or had inadequate brakes, or describe some other act of negligence and say that Aikin suffered a concussion, or a broken neck, or fractures of three ribs, or other injuries.

Third, the pleadings may be intended to give each party only a general notice of his opponent's contentions, in which event the system would rely upon subsequent stages of the lawsuit to identify the legal and factual contentions of the parties and to enable each to prepare to meet the opponent's case. In such a case a complaint similar to that in Form 11 of the Federal Rules of Civil Procedure should be sufficient.

Obviously each of the first two objectives is desirable. It is a waste of everybody's time to try lawsuits when the underlying legal claim is inadequate to support a judgment, and it is only fair that a person called upon to defend a judicial proceeding should know what he is alleged to have done. But to achieve the first objective fully may require pleading after pleading in order to expose and sharpen the issues; if detail is insisted upon, a long time may be consumed in producing it. Moreover, a single pleading oversight may eliminate a contention necessary to one party's case that easily could have been proven, but that will be held to have been waived. To achieve the second objective through the pleadings will mean that the parties must take rigid positions as to their factual contentions at the very beginning when they do not know what they will learn about their cases by the time trial begins. Either the first or second objective, if fully pursued, requires that the parties adhere to the positions taken in the pleadings. They could not be permitted to introduce evidence in conflict with the pleadings or to change them. To the extent that *variances* between pleading and proof or *amendments* to the pleadings are permitted, the objectives will be lost. The court frequently will find itself forced either to depart from these objectives or to tolerate cases turning on the skill of the lawyers rather than on the merits of the controversy.

The third objective, insofar as it allows the parties to use the later stages of the lawsuit to identify and flesh out the issues in the case, avoids the delays and potential injustices created by trying to decide the case based only on the pleadings. However, simple notice pleading may be used to harass defendant when plaintiff has no real claim. More often, though, plaintiff will use notice pleading to subject defendant to pretrial discovery (discussed more fully below), and, in the process, to reveal information so that plaintiff can determine or confirm whether a bona fide claim actually exists. Discovery may be essential if defendant controls access to the information that plaintiff needs to establish her claim. Lawyers often refer to such use of the pleadings as a "fishing expedition," or alternatively as a "springboard into litigation." One way that courts have dealt with these problems is to sanction parties and lawyers who bring baseless claims.

4. THE RESPONSE

Following the service of Aikin's complaint, Cecil must respond. He may challenge the complaint by a *motion to dismiss*. This motion may challenge the court's jurisdiction over the subject matter or Cecil's person, the service of process, or venue. It also may be a *motion to dismiss for failure to state a claim or cause of action* (the older term for this motion is a *demurrer*). For the purpose of this motion, the facts alleged in the complaint are accepted as true, and the court considers whether, on this assumption, plaintiff has shown that she is entitled to legal relief.

There are three general situations in which such a motion might be granted. First, the complaint may clearly show that the injury is one for which the law furnishes no redress; for example, when plaintiff simply alleges that "defendant has made faces at me." Second, plaintiff may have failed to include an allegation on a necessary part of the case; for example, Aikin might have alleged the accident, her injuries, and Beasley's negligence, but have forgotten to allege that Beasley was Cecil's servant. Third, the complaint may be so general or so confused that the court finds that it does not give adequate notice of what plaintiff's claim is or does not support a plausible inference of injury; this would be true, for example, of a complaint in which Aikin merely said, "Cecil injured me and owes me $500,000," although complaints far more specific have been dismissed on this ground. Obviously, the extent to which motions to dismiss will be granted on the second and third grounds will vary with the degree of detail that the particular system requires of its pleadings. A court generally has power to allow the plaintiff an opportunity to amend her pleading to cure certain kinds of defects.

If the motion to dismiss is denied, or if none is made, Cecil must file an *answer*. In this pleading, he must admit or deny the factual allegations made by Aikin in the complaint. Moreover, if Cecil wishes to rely on certain legal contentions called *affirmative defenses*, he must plead them in the answer. Thus, if he wishes to contend that Aikin was negligent in the manner in which she tried to cross the street and that this negligence was also a cause of the accident, he must in many states plead this in the answer; if the answer only denied the allegations in Aikin's complaint, Cecil may not advance at trial the contention that Aikin's negligence caused the accident.

There may be further pleadings, particularly a *reply* by Aikin. But the tendency today is to close the pleadings after the answer, and if Cecil has raised new matters in his answer, they automatically are taken as denied by Aikin. There is one major exception: if Cecil has a claim against Aikin, particularly one that arises out of the same occurrence being sued upon by Aikin, Cecil may plead this claim as a *counterclaim* as part of the answer. This is in essence a complaint by Cecil, and Aikin will have to respond to it just as Cecil had to respond to the original complaint.

The original action between Aikin and Cecil may expand in terms of the number of parties, and this frequently will occur at the pleading stage. For example, although Aikin decided not to sue Beasley, Cecil might *implead* Beasley, asking that Beasley be held liable to him for whatever amount he may be found liable to Aikin, since his liability depends upon Beasley having been at fault. Cecil will decide whether to do this in light of a number of practical concerns, including the effect Beasley's presence will have on the jury in the Aikin v. Cecil suit.

5.   OBTAINING INFORMATION PRIOR TO TRIAL

Pretrial discovery is the procedure currently designed to allow the parties to exchange information about their claims and defenses and to prepare for trial. At earlier periods in history, the pleadings served this purpose.

The chief method for obtaining information is to take *depositions* of parties and witnesses. In this procedure, the person whose deposition is to be taken is questioned by lawyers for each side through direct and cross-examination; the *deponent's* statements are taken down and transcribed. This device is useful for finding information that is relevant to the case, including unearthing leads as to other witnesses or documents; it also is useful for laying a basis for impeaching a witness who attempts to change his story at trial. The two parties almost certainly will want depositions taken of each other, as well as of Beasley; the depositions of Aikin and Cecil will be particularly important because they are treated as admissions and can be used by their adversaries as evidence at trial. In some circumstances, even the deposition of a nonparty witness who will be unavailable at trial may be used in place of live testimony.

Another device especially adapted to probing the content of an opponent's case is *written interrogatories*, which usually may be addressed only to a party to the suit. (The availability of interrogatories may be one reason why Aikin might join Beasley as a defendant with Cecil or why Cecil might implead Beasley.) These interrogatories are answered by the party with counsel's aid, and the answers will not be as spontaneous as they would be in a deposition; on the other hand, interrogatories will require him to supply some information that he does not carry in his head but can get, and may be even more valuable than the deposition in finding out what he will try to prove. Thus, information regarding Beasley's employment that Cecil cannot be expected to have in his mind may best be exposed in this way.

Other discovery devices include *the production of documents*, such as the service record of Cecil's automobile, and *requests for admissions*, which will remove uncontested issues from the case. A particularly useful device for Cecil will be a court order directing Aikin to submit to a *physical examination* by a physician of Cecil's choice to determine the real extent of Aikin's alleged injuries.

The availability of discovery, which is now common throughout the country, has had its effect on judicial approaches toward the pleadings. This is not simply because it enables parties to prepare for trial better than pleadings ever did. Of more significance perhaps is the fact that if broad discovery is allowed, it is senseless to make parties take rigid positions with respect to the issues at the very beginning of the lawsuit before they have had the chance to utilize these very useful devices for obtaining information. In addition, the availability of discovery does much to make summary judgment, which is discussed below, a viable and fair procedure, since it enables a party to ascertain those issues on which the opposing party has no evidence, and it also gives the opponent a real chance to develop such evidence. On the other hand, if the costs of discovery are excessive, a defendant may be motivated to settle a lawsuit that satisfies a weak pleading standard yet would lack sufficient proof at trial. Courts and commentators disagree considerably on the extent to which these issues ought to shape the governing pleading standard.

Amendments to the Federal Rules of Civil Procedure were promulgated in recent years that, in time, may revolutionize the way in which litigants conduct pretrial discovery. They require both parties—automatically in most cases—to identify individuals "likely to have discoverable information" and to provide copies of documents "that the disclosing party may use to support its claims or defenses." See Federal Rule 26(a). This mandatory self-disclosure procedure theoretically should decrease considerably the amount of time and resources that the judicial system expends in overseeing the discovery process, but in practice courts sometimes are called upon to define the scope of mandatory disclosure and to enforce its terms, undermining the efficiency of the procedure.

6. SUMMARY JUDGMENT

One of the basic difficulties with attempting to resolve cases at the pleading stage is that the allegations of the parties must be accepted as true for the purpose of ruling on a motion to dismiss. Thus, if plaintiff tells a plausible story in the complaint, the court cannot dismiss the action even though it does not believe the allegations or think that the plaintiff will be able to prove the tale. The pleading stage is not the time to resolve questions of fact.

But in some cases it will be possible to supplement the pleadings with additional documents to show that an apparent decisive issue is spurious. This is done by a motion for *summary judgment*. This motion can be supported by demonstrating that the crucial issue will have to be resolved in the movant's favor at trial because the opposing party will be unable to produce any admissible evidence in support of her position on the issue. For example, suppose that it is Cecil's position that prior to the accident he had fired Beasley, but that Beasley had secreted keys to Cecil's automobile and had taken Cecil's car without permission shortly before the accident. On the face of the pleadings, we have only an allegation that Beasley was Cecil's employee and a denial of that allegation; thus, the pleadings seem to present a question of credibility that cannot be resolved at this stage. Cecil now moves for summary judgment, alleging that this issue is not a genuine one, and he accompanies his motion with affidavits of his own and two other witnesses that he had fired Beasley; a deposition of the garage attendant indicating that he had been instructed not to allow Beasley to have the car and that it was taken without Cecil's knowledge; and a deposition of Beasley to the effect that he had been fired, but wanted to use the car once more for his own purposes. It is now incumbent upon Aikin to show that the issue is genuine; Aikin cannot rely simply upon her own assertion that all this is not so; after all, she has no personal knowledge of the facts. Aikin must convince the court that she has admissible evidence that Beasley still was acting as Cecil's employee in driving the car at the time of the accident. If Aikin fails to do so, judgment will be entered against her.

It should be noted that in ruling on a summary judgment motion the judge does not decide which party is telling the truth. If Aikin presents an affidavit of a witness who claims to have been present when Cecil allegedly fired Beasley, and says that Cecil told Beasley that this was only a subterfuge and that he wanted him to continue to work for him but to pretend to steal the car, summary judgment will not be appropriate even though the judge is firmly convinced that Aikin's affiant is lying.

7.   SETTING THE CASE FOR TRIAL

After discovery is completed, and if the case has not been terminated by dismissal, summary judgment, or settlement, it must be set for *trial*. Most cases already will have been disposed of prior to trial. If Aikin's lawsuit has not yet been resolved, typically either party may file a *note of issue*, at which time the case will be given a number and placed on a *trial calendar*. These calendars have become extremely long in many courts, and the case may have to wait a year, three years, or more before it is called for trial, especially if a jury trial has been requested.

8.   THE JURY AND ITS SELECTION

In most actions for damages, the parties have a right to have the facts tried by a *jury*. This right is assured in the federal courts by the Seventh Amendment to the Constitution, and it is protected in the courts of most states by similar state constitutional provisions. If there is a right to a trial by jury, either party may assert it, but if neither wishes to do so, a judge will try the facts as well as the law. Largely for historical reasons growing out of a division of authority in the English court structure, there are many civil actions in which neither party has a right to a jury trial; these include most cases in which plaintiff wants an order directing or prohibiting specified action by defendant rather than a judgment for damages—a so-called *equitable* remedy.

If a jury has been demanded, the first order of business at trial will be to impanel the jurors. A large number of people, selected in an impartial manner from various lists, tax rolls, or street directories, will have been ordered to report to the courthouse for jury duty at a given term of court. The prospective jurors will be questioned—usually by the judge but sometimes by the lawyers—as to their possible biases. If one of the persons called has prior knowledge of the case or is a personal friend of one of the parties, he or she probably will be successfully *challenged for cause* and excused. But suppose Aikin is an architect and her lawyer finds that one of the jury panel has recently constructed a house and believes that he was greatly overcharged for its design and construction; this likely will not be enough to persuade the judge to excuse him, but fearing the juror may be prejudiced against her client, Aikin's lawyer probably will exercise one of the small number of *peremptory challenges* a party is allowed for which no reason need be given. Ultimately, a panel of between six and twelve hopefully unbiased jurors will be selected.

9. THE TRIAL

After the jurors have been sworn, plaintiff's lawyer will make an *opening statement*, in which she will describe for the jury what the case is about, what contentions she will make, and how she will prove them. Defendant's lawyer also may make an opening statement at this time, but he may reserve the right to do so until he is ready to present his own case. Following the opening statement, plaintiff's lawyer calls her witnesses one by one. Each witness is first questioned by the lawyer who has called that witness—this is the *direct examination*; then the lawyer for the other side has the opportunity to *cross-examine* the same witness; this may be followed by *re-direct* and *re-cross* examination, and even further stages. The judge maintains some control over the length and tenor of the examination, and in particular will see to it that the stages beyond cross-examination are not prolonged.

Just as the primary responsibility for introducing evidence is on the lawyers, so too is the responsibility for objecting to evidence that is thought to be inadmissible under the rules of evidence. Suppose that Aikin's lawyer asks: "What happened while you were lying on the ground after the accident?" To which Aikin replies: "The driver of the car came over and said that he had been going too fast and he was sorry." Aikin's answer is objectionable because it contains *hearsay evidence*; that is, it repeats what someone else has said for the purpose of proving the truth of the matter asserted. The judge will not raise this issue herself, however; it is up to Cecil's counsel to object, and then the judge must rule on the objection. This particular issue is not an easy one, for Aikin's answer may well come within one of the exceptions to the rule excluding hearsay evidence. Evidentiary issues will recur continually throughout the trial and the judge must be prepared to make instantaneous rulings if the trial is to proceed with dispatch. Small wonder that evidentiary rulings form a major source of the errors raised on appeal, but at the same time appellate courts are very reluctant to disturb the trial judge's determination. What happens if the judge rules that Aikin's answer is inadmissible? She will instruct the jury to disregard it. Can a juror who has heard such an important confession totally drive it from his or her mind?

Documents, pictures, and other tangible items may be put into evidence, but unless their admissibility has been stipulated to in advance, they will be introduced through witnesses. For example, if Aikin's lawyer has had pictures taken of the accident scene and wishes to get them to the jury, she will call the photographer as a witness, have him testify that he took pictures of the scene, and then show them to the photographer who will identify them as the pictures he took. At this point, they may be formally introduced into evidence.

When plaintiff's lawyer has called all of her witnesses, and their examinations are over, plaintiff will *rest*. At this point, defendant's lawyer may ask for a *directed verdict* (in federal practice now called a judgment as a matter of law) for defendant on the ground that plaintiff has not established a prima facie case; the thrust of the motion is that plaintiff has not introduced enough evidence to permit the jury to find in her favor. If the motion is denied, defendant may rest and choose to rely on the jury's agreeing with him, but in almost all cases he will proceed to present witnesses of his own, and these witnesses will be exposed to the same process of direct and cross-examination. When defendant has rested, plaintiff may present additional evidence to meet any new matter raised by defendant's witnesses. In turn, defendant, after plaintiff rests, may meet any new matter presented by plaintiff. This procedure will continue until both parties rest. Again, the trial judge will maintain considerable control to prevent the protraction of these latter stages.

When both parties have rested, either or both may move for a directed verdict. Again, this motion asks the trial judge to rule that under the evidence presented, viewed most favorably to the nonmoving party, the jury cannot reasonably find in his or her favor. If these motions are denied, the case must be submitted to the jury.

10. SUBMITTING THE CASE TO THE JURY

At this stage the judge and the lawyers will confer out of the jury's hearing with regard to the content of the judge's *instructions* or *charge* to the jury. Each lawyer may submit proposed instructions, which the trial judge will grant or deny, but the judge is under a duty to charge the jury on the basic aspects of the case in any event. If a party's lawyer has neither requested a particular instruction nor objected to the judge's charge, however, a claim that the charge was erroneous generally will not be upheld on appeal.

Ordinarily the lawyers will make their final arguments to the jury before the judge delivers the charge. The lawyers will review the evidence from their own points of view, and may suggest how the jury should weigh certain items and resolve specific issues, but it is improper for the lawyers to discuss a matter that has been excluded or never has been introduced. In other words, they are arguing, not testifying.

In the instructions the judge will summarize the facts and issues, tell the jury about the substantive law to be applied on each issue, give general information on determining the credibility of witnesses, and state who has the *burden of persuasion* on each issue of fact. The burden of persuasion in a civil case ordinarily requires that one party prove her contention on a given issue by a preponderance of the evidence. On most issues, Aikin will carry this burden, but on an affirmative defense such as contributory negligence the burden probably will be on Cecil. What the burden means is that if a juror is unable to resolve an issue in his mind, he should find on that issue against the party who has the burden. In the federal courts and in some states, the judge may comment on the evidence, as long as she emphasizes that her comments represent her own opinion and that the jurors should not feel bound by it; judicial comment is rare, however, and in many states it is not permitted at all.

Following the charge, the jury retires to reach its *verdict*. The verdict, the jury's decision, will be of a type chosen by the judge. There are three types, of which by far the most common is the *general verdict*. This verdict permits the jurors to determine the facts and apply the law on which they have been charged to those facts; it is simple in form in that only the conclusion as to who prevails, and the amount of the damages, if that party is a claimant, is stated. A second type is the *general verdict with interrogatories*, which combines the form of the general verdict with several key questions that are designed to test the jury's understanding of the issues. Suppose that the accident occurred five miles away from Beasley's appointed route. Aikin's evidence is that Beasley detoured to have the vehicle's brakes fixed; Cecil's is that Beasley was going to visit his friend. The judge might charge the jury that in the former event, but not in the latter, Beasley was acting within the scope of his employment and Cecil would be liable for his negligence. The judge might direct the jury, in addition to rendering a verdict for Aikin or for Cecil, to answer the question, "Why did Beasley depart from his route?" If the general verdict was for Aikin, but the jury's answer was that Beasley was driving to his friend's home, the judge would order judgment for Cecil, for if the answer is inconsistent with the verdict, the answer controls. The third type of verdict is the *special verdict*, in which all of the factual issues in the case are submitted to the jury as questions without instructions as to their legal effect; the judge applies the law to the jury's answers and determines which party prevails.

Traditionally, only a unanimous jury verdict has been effective. In many states, and by consent of the parties in the federal courts, a nonunanimous verdict by the jurors may stand in a civil action. If the minimum number of jurors required for a verdict are unable to reach agreement, the jury is said to be *hung*, and a new trial before a different jury is necessary.

11. POST-TRIAL MOTIONS

After the jury has returned its verdict, judgment will be entered thereon, but the losing party will have an opportunity to make certain post-trial motions. There may be a motion for a *judgment notwithstanding the verdict* (commonly called a motion for a *judgment n.o.v.*, from the Latin non obstante veredicto, but now in federal practice called a renewed motion for judgment as a matter of law; this motion raises the same question as a motion for a directed verdict). The losing party also may move for a *new trial*; the grounds for this motion are many, and may include assertions that the judge erred in admitting certain evidence, that the charge was defective, that attorneys, parties, or jurors have been guilty of misconduct, that the damages awarded are excessive, or that the jury's verdict is against the clear weight of the evidence. Should these motions fail, it sometimes is possible to reopen a judgment, even several months after the trial, on the grounds of clerical mistake, newly discovered evidence, or fraud, but the occasions on which relief is granted are very rare.

12. THE JUDGMENT AND ITS ENFORCEMENT

The *judgment* is the final determination of the lawsuit, absent an appeal. Judgment may be rendered on default when the defendant does not appear; or following the granting of a demurrer, a motion to dismiss, or a motion for summary judgment; or based on a settlement agreement of the parties; or upon the jury's verdict; or the findings of fact and conclusions of law of the trial judge in a nonjury case. The judgment may be in the form of an award of money to plaintiff, a declaration of rights between the parties, specific recovery of property, or an order requiring or prohibiting some future activity. When defendant has prevailed, the judgment generally will not be "for" anything nor will it order anything; it simply will provide that plaintiff takes nothing by her complaint.

In most cases, a judgment for plaintiff will not order defendant to do anything; typically it will simply state that plaintiff shall recover a sum of money from defendant. This does not necessarily mean that defendant will pay. It is up to plaintiff to collect the money. *Execution* is the common method of forcing the losing party to satisfy a money judgment, if the loser does not do so voluntarily. A *writ of execution* is issued by the court commanding an officer—usually the sheriff—to seize property of the losing party and, if necessary, to sell it at public sale and use the proceeds to satisfy plaintiff's judgment.

When plaintiff's recovery takes the form of an *injunction* requiring defendant to do something or to stop doing something, the judgment (in this context typically called the *decree*) is said to operate against defendant's person (in personam). Its sanction is direct, and if defendant fails to obey, he may be held in *contempt of court* and punished by fine or imprisonment.

Costs provided by statute and certain out-of-pocket disbursements are awarded to the prevailing party and included in the judgment. Usually, these costs are nominal in relation to the total expense of litigation and include only such items as the clerk's fee and witnesses' mileage. As previously mentioned, in the United States, in contrast to England, attorney's fees are not recoverable as costs in ordinary litigation.

13.   APPEAL

Every judicial system in the United States provides for review by an appellate court of the decisions of the trial court. Generally a party has the right to appeal any judgment to at least one higher court. When the system contains two levels of appellate courts, appeal usually lies initially to one of the intermediate courts, and review at the highest level is only at the discretion of that court except in certain classes of cases. Thus, in the federal courts, district court decisions are reviewed by the courts of appeals, but review in the United States Supreme Court currently must be sought in most cases by a *petition for a writ of certiorari*, which that Court may deny as a matter of discretion without reaching any conclusion as to the merits of the case. (In a few cases, a direct appeal lies from the United States District Court to the Supreme Court.) The discretion of a higher-level appellate court generally is exercised so that only cases with legal issues of broad importance are taken.

The *record* on appeal will contain the pleadings, at least a portion of the *transcript of the trial* (the court reporter's verbatim record of the trial), and the orders and rulings relevant to the appeal. The parties present their contentions to the appellate court by written *briefs* and in addition, in most cases, by *oral argument*. The appellate court may review any ruling of law by the trial judge, although frequently it will limit the scope of its review by holding that particular matters were within the trial judge's discretion or that the error, if any, was not prejudicial—that is, it did not substantially affect the outcome of the case. There are constitutional limits to the review of a jury's verdict, but even when these limits do not apply—for example, when the judge has tried the case without a jury—an appellate court rarely will re-examine a question of fact because a cold record does not convey the nuances of what the trier observed, notably the demeanor of the witnesses.

The appellate court has the power to *affirm*, *reverse*, or *modify* the judgment of the trial court. If it reverses, it may order that a new judgment be entered or it may *remand* the case to the trial court for a new trial or other proceedings not inconsistent with its decision. The decision of an appellate court usually is accompanied by a written *opinion*, signed by one of a panel of judges hearing the appeal, there always being more than one judge deciding an appeal. Concurring and dissenting opinions also may be filed. The opinions of a court are designed to set forth the reasons for a decision and to furnish guidance to lower courts, lawyers, and the public. You will spend much of your time in law school—and afterwards—reading the opinions of appellate courts. Although trial courts frequently deliver opinions when ruling on motions or sitting without a jury, they rarely are published except for decisions by the federal trial courts.

There is an important distinction between the *reviewability* of a particular ruling of a trial judge and its *appealability*. For example, a trial judge's ruling excluding certain evidence at trial as hearsay is reviewable; that is, when the judgment is appealed, that ruling may be assigned as error and the appellate court will consider whether it was correct. But trial would be impossible if an appeal could be taken from every ruling. Thus, appeals lie only from judgments and from certain orders made in the course of litigation when immediate review is deemed so important that a delay in the action during appeal can be tolerated. Judicial systems differ in the extent to which *interlocutory orders* can be appealed. In the federal system, very little other than a final judgment can be taken to the courts of appeals; in some states, on the other hand, many kinds of orders can be appealed even before a final judgment is entered.

A good example of the contrast between the two approaches can be seen by looking at the consequences of an order denying a motion to dismiss. Suppose that Cecil moves to dismiss Aikin's complaint on the grounds that even on Aikin's view of the facts, Cecil is not responsible for the conduct of Beasley, and this motion is denied. In the federal courts, such an order would not be appealable, since it does not terminate the lawsuit. Indeed, the disposition of the motion means that the action will continue. In some states, however, this question could be taken immediately to a higher court for a ruling, while the other stages of the litigation wait.

The question as to which system is better is not easy to answer. One may argue in favor of the federal practice that everything should be done at one level before going to the next, that too much time is taken in waiting for appellate courts to decide these questions serially, and that no appeal may ever be necessary, since Cecil may prevail anyway. On the other hand, if the appellate court holds at this early stage that Aikin has no claim against Cecil, we will save the time necessary for discovery and trial.

One point worth noting is that the resolution of the question of the appealability of interlocutory orders has an important bearing on the procedural developments within a given system. In the case of motions to dismiss, for example, if denials are not appealable, the law on this subject will be made largely in the trial courts. The trial judge who is in doubt may tend to deny such motions rather than to grant them, and her decision generally will not be disturbed; even though the ruling theoretically is reviewable after final judgment, by that time the significance of the ruling on the pleadings may have been displaced by more substantive questions. If the denial is appealable, a tactical consideration is added and such motions will be resorted to more frequently, inasmuch as they will afford defendant an additional opportunity to delay trial and thus to wear down his opponent. With respect to other procedural rulings—as in the discovery area—the absence of an interlocutory appeal will strengthen the hand of the trial judge; she will in fact, if not in theory, be given a wider discretion because fewer of her rulings will come before the appellate courts and when they do they will be enmeshed in a final judgment, which will make it easy to conclude that any error was not prejudicial.

14. THE CONCLUSIVENESS OF JUDGMENTS

After the appeal and whatever further proceedings may take place, or, if no appeal is taken, when the time for appeal expires, the judgment is final. With very rare exceptions, the judgment cannot be challenged in another proceeding. It is *res judicata*, a thing decided, and now at rest. Defining the scope and effect of this finality principle is one of the most complex tasks in the entire law of procedure.

SECTION C. A NOTE ON MOTION PRACTICE

Throughout the previous Section, the term "motion" is used frequently, and for good reason. What a motion is, how one makes a motion, and when one should make a motion are all questions of "motion practice." A motion is the procedural device by which a litigant asks a court for an order. For example, a request for an order to dismiss a complaint for failure to state a claim, a request for an order granting a summary judgment, and a request for an order granting a new trial all are made formally to a court through a motion.

A litigant generally must make a motion in writing. Two exceptions to this rule are when the court is recording a hearing verbatim or when a trial is taking place. A motion generally must state with particularity the reasons or grounds supporting the motion and the relief sought. The written motion also must appear in a proper form, which usually is determined by local court rules.

The litigant also must serve the motion on her adversary. In addition, a notice of hearing regarding the motion, a brief or memorandum of law in support of the motion, a proposed order, and affidavits, if necessary, generally accompany a motion. Briefs usually have a maximum page limit (and quite often are not brief). Not all courts require the movant to submit a proposed order. Only certain motions require affidavits.

All motions in federal court require the signature of the litigant's attorney or the litigant. The signature attests that the attorney or litigant has read the motion papers and that the motion has sufficient grounds and is made in good faith. If a court decides that any of these are not true, the court may sanction the attorney or the litigant. Sanctions have been imposed more frequently in recent years.

A party served with a motion may answer and usually must do so within a time period specified by the rules. A party also may move for an extension of time, either to make a cross-motion, to extend the time to respond to the motion, or both. In addition, making a motion may defer the next stage of litigation. Finally, making a particular motion may preserve other legal rights.

It is the interrelationship among motions, their intended effects, their secondary effects, and their effects on the opposing party that determine how a party utilizes motion practice. A motion such as summary judgment usually is designed to win the lawsuit. A successful motion to exclude certain material from discovery may convince an adversary that he cannot obtain the information necessary to establish his case and thus may induce him to end the lawsuit early to avoid an unfavorable judgment. A motion to bring a third party into the lawsuit may help convince an adversary that the lawsuit will be more time consuming and costly than expected. A lawyer deciding to make a motion must consider carefully what benefits will accrue to the movant and what obstacles will be imposed on her adversary as a result of the motion.

But a motion may have negative aspects. One of the drawbacks may be the time and expense of making the motion, including drafting and serving multiple copies of papers, spending hours preparing the brief in support of the motion, and taking resources from other more fruitful pursuits. Repeated, unsuccessful motions will result in expense and delay that may reduce client satisfaction.

In addition, poor motion practice may leave the judge with the impression that the lawyer is sloppy, shoddy, and disorganized. Arguing motions at a hearing that the attorneys could have settled without a hearing may convince the judge that the movant is contentious by nature. In short, an unwise use of a motion may do more harm in the long run than not making the motion at all, even if the motion is granted.

In sum, motion practice is a central part of a litigator's arsenal. When a particular motion can be made, how it must be made, and what its effect will be are questions that can be answered by studying the applicable procedural rules. When a motion *should* be made and how it can affect the course of the lawsuit are matters of judgment and experience.

SECTION D. A NOTE ON REMEDIES

The remedies that may be obtained in a modern civil action should be viewed principally as a part of the substantive law: contract law, tort law, commercial law, labor law, and so forth. Yet, because the goal of a lawsuit is the remedy and the means of securing it is procedural, there necessarily is a close relationship between them. For example, the range of available remedies in a case may be limited by the manner in which plaintiff has pleaded, and, on the other hand, certain procedural aspects of the case, such as whether it is tried to a judge or a jury, may be determined by the remedy that is being sought; again, whether a person may be joined as a party may depend on the relief that is being sought, and conversely certain remedies may be available only if all interested persons can be joined.

Without question, the most important relationship between procedure and remedies grows out of the existence in English law of two great branches of jurisprudence administered in different courts: common law and equity; the latter was envisioned as complementary to the former. There are two special facts about equity that are important for our purpose. First, already alluded to, courts of equity had no jury. Second, the injunction was a creature of equity and remained in its sole custody when the two branches remained distinct.

From this heritage, two consequences of immense significance for the law of procedure result. One, the right of a trial by jury in the United States today, especially in the federal courts, is determined by inquiring whether the matter in question was a subject of legal or equitable cognizance in 1791—the date of the Seventh Amendment—and to some extent this question depends on the remedy sought, since the availability of injunctive relief was one form of equity's jurisdiction. Two, just as equity was regarded as a special kind of law to be resorted to only when the common law was inadequate, so too the injunction—and most forms of specific relief, even in those limited circumstances in which it is available at law—has been and still is regarded as a form of exceptional relief, to be allowed only when the ordinary remedy of damages is inadequate.

The most important types of relief that a court may award in a civil action fall into three categories: *declarative*, *specific*, and *compensatory*. Declarative relief consists simply in a court's defining the rights and duties of the parties in a particular legal context. Suppose a person believes that an agreement she has entered into is not a valid contract and that she is under no obligation to perform it; however, she is afraid to act on this belief in the face of another's insistence that she perform, because if the contract is enforceable the damages for the nonperformance will be great. In these circumstances, she may seek a declaratory judgment asking the court to determine whether she is under a duty to perform. This type of relief is not as common as those discussed below, and its availability often is limited by statute. In numerous situations, however, it is invaluable.

Specific relief consists generally of an order directing conduct. Defendant may be commanded to return a jewel he has taken from plaintiff, to stop operating a pig farm in a residential neighborhood, to deliver a car she has contracted to sell, or to refrain from opening a barbershop next door to a person to whom he has just sold his former barbershop. Obviously, specific relief is not possible in all cases. For example, no kind of specific relief will compensate or cure Aikin in our hypothetical case; Beasley cannot be ordered retroactively not to run into her. On the other hand, in some kinds of cases specific relief is available almost as a matter of course. A person who has contracted to sell a house or a piece of land ordinarily will be ordered to perform the agreement, for the law regards each bit of real property as unique. But beyond the real-property context, specific relief will be given only if damages would be completely inadequate. Thus, if you order a tuxedo from a tailor who fails to perform his promise to deliver it, it is unlikely that any remedy except damages will be forthcoming. The reasons for this are not purely historical. There is a burden on the court in ordering and supervising performance of a decree of specific performance that is avoided if a simple judgment for money damages is entered; moreover, specific performance might impose a hardship or at least an indignity on the tailor not commensurate with the advantage to be gained by your receiving this tailor's garment rather than one from another tailor. But it may well be asked whether our courts today are not being too reluctant to grant that form of relief that will most adequately redress plaintiff's grievance.

Compensatory relief calls for a judgment that defendant pay plaintiff a certain sum of money. But you should recognize that when we speak of compensation—of the remedy of damages—although we are speaking of one form of relief, it can be computed in accordance with many measures. In your action against the tailor, for example, if you had struck a good bargain, you might claim the difference between the price you agreed to pay and the value the tuxedo would have had if the tailor had performed the promise; or you might claim only the money you had advanced as a down payment; or you might claim the amount you paid for opera tickets you were unable to use without the tuxedo. The difference in amount that could be collected under these theories might be very substantial.

There is a final point to be considered in evaluating the adequacy of any judicial remedy: How much of it will be consumed by the cost of litigation? As we have noted, the costs awarded to a successful plaintiff will not, in most cases, reimburse her for the fees of her lawyer or for many other substantial costs of a suit, such as the expense of investigation or the fees of expert witnesses. It is not possible to give any meaningful figure for the cost of an average trial, but it can be assumed that as the stakes rise the fees will be correspondingly higher and indeed, some top attorneys charge upward of $800 an hour for their services.

In most personal injury and in many other types of damages actions, plaintiff's cost of recovery must be computed differently because the attorney will be litigating the case under a contingent-fee agreement; that is, the attorney will receive a percentage—one-third is common—of plaintiff's judgment. Thus, in a real sense, an adequate legal remedy is one that not simply compensates plaintiff for a loss but is one that covers both the loss and the cost of recovering it. This distinction has not been ignored by many triers of fact. Indeed, it has been suggested that if damages for pain and suffering ever are abolished, defendants should be required explicitly to pay prevailing plaintiffs' legal fees.

SECTION E.   A NOTE ON PROCEDURAL RULES IN THE FEDERAL AND STATE COURTS

Federal and state rules of procedure derive from constitutional authority, statute, and judicial decision. The Federal Rules of Civil Procedure owe their genesis to the Rules Enabling Act, 28 U.S.C. § 2072, enacted in 1934, which vests power in the United States Supreme Court to promulgate rules of procedure for the district courts and to combine law and equity into one civil action. In 1935, the Supreme Court appointed an Advisory Committee composed of lawyers, judges, and law professors to draft federal procedural rules. The Advisory Committee proposed rules that the Court approved in 1937, and the Federal Rules of Civil Procedure became law on September 16, 1938. See Burbank, *The Rules Enabling Act of 1934*, 130 U. Pa. L. Rev. 1015 (1982). Amending the Federal Rules follows a seven-step process that usually runs between two and three years. The process requires giving notice to the public and allowing individuals an opportunity to comment; approval by multiple committees; and final review by the Court and Congress.

An important hallmark of the Federal Rules is their trans-substantivity. The Rules apply to all causes of action no matter how complex or simple. Some commentators regard trans-substantivity as essential to maintaining the neutrality and impartiality of the civil process. See, e.g., Carrington, *Making Rules to Dispose of Manifestly Unfounded Assertions: An Exorcism of the Bogy of Non-Trans-Substantive Rules of Civil Procedure*, 137 U. Pa. L. Rev. 2067, 2068 (1989). The alternative point of view questions whether trans-substantivity is practical or even desirable, arguing, for example, that a large antitrust case requires different procedural treatment than that of a simple negligence case. See, e.g., Cover, *For James Wm. Moore: Some Reflections on a Reading of the Rules*, 84 Yale L.J. 718, 732, 739–40 (1975). As your study of procedure goes forward, consider whether procedural developments such as the adoption of local court rules, the negotiation of customized procedural rules, and the enactment of statutory "carve-outs" from particular procedures for discrete areas of the law are compatible with the principle of trans-substantivity. See Tobias, *The Transformation of Trans-Substantivity*, 49 Wash. & Lee L. Rev. 1501 (1992).

The Federal Rules generally do not bind state judicial systems, and currently no state's procedures completely track the federal courts', although some come close. See Oakley, *A Fresh Look at the Federal Rules in State Courts*, 3 Nev. L.J. 354, 354–55 (2003). States typically use one of two models to adopt procedural rules: in the first, the state constitution grants exclusive rulemaking power to the state judiciary; in the second, state courts exercise inherent rulemaking authority but share such authority with the legislature. For a collection of state constitutional provisions as they bear on state rulemaking authority, see Main, *Reconsidering Procedural Conformity Statutes*, 35 W. St. U. L. Rev. 75, 84–85 (2007).

CHAPTER 2

JURISDICTION OVER THE PARTIES
OR THEIR PROPERTY

■ ■ ■

This Chapter explores some of the principles that affect where a lawsuit can be filed and entertained. The materials focus on the doctrine of personal jurisdiction: the power of a court to enter a judgment against a defendant. A court can assert personal jurisdiction only if power is authorized by statute and its exercise does not exceed the limitations of the Due Process Clause of the United States Constitution. The earliest basis for a court's assertion of personal jurisdiction over a person or a thing was the presence of defendant within the territory of the tribunal. As the national economy developed and technology fostered the movement of goods and people across state boundaries, the doctrine of personal jurisdiction underwent evolution. Under contemporary doctrine, the question of a court's power is analyzed in functional terms, "based upon a review of the relationship that exists among the place where the underlying transaction took place, the parties, and the territory of the state where suit is brought." Friedenthal, Kane & Miller, Civil Procedure § 3.1 (4th ed. 2005). The Digital Revolution—with its virtual world of emails, hyperlinks, and software—has created new and difficult issues for personal jurisdiction doctrine. Even before these developments, one federal judge likened the question of a court's power over a defendant to "a riddle wrapped in a mystery inside an enigma." Donatelli v. National Hockey League, 893 F.2d 459, 462 (1st Cir. 1990).

SECTION A. THE TRADITIONAL
BASES FOR JURISDICTION

PENNOYER v. NEFF

Supreme Court of the United States, 1877.
95 U.S. (5 Otto) 714, 24 L.Ed. 565.

Error to the Circuit Court of the United States for the District of Oregon.

MR. JUSTICE FIELD delivered the opinion of the court.

This is an action to recover the possession of a tract of land, of the alleged value of $15,000, situated in the State of Oregon. The plaintiff asserts title to the premises by a patent of the United States issued to him in [March] 1866, under the Act of Congress of September 27th, 1850, 9 Stat. at L., 496, usually known as the Donation Law of Oregon. The defendant claims to have acquired the premises under a sheriff's deed, made upon a sale of the property on execution issued upon a judgment recovered against the plaintiff in one of the circuit courts of the State. The case turns upon the validity of this judgment.

It appears from the record that the judgment was rendered in February, 1866, in favor of J.H. Mitchell, for less than $300, including costs, in an action brought by him upon a demand for services as an attorney; that, at the time the action was commenced and the judgment rendered, the defendant therein, the plaintiff here, was a non-resident of the State; that he was not personally served with process, and did not appear therein; and that the judgment was entered upon his default in not answering the complaint, upon a constructive service of summons by publication.

The Code of Oregon provides for such service when an action is brought against a non-resident and absent defendant, who has property within the State. It also provides, where the action is for the recovery of money or damages, for the attachment of the property of the non-resident. And it also declares that no natural person is subject to the jurisdiction of a court of the State, "unless he appear in the court, or be found within the State, or be a resident thereof, or have property therein; and in the last case, only to the extent of such property at the time the jurisdiction attached." Construing this latter provision to mean that, in an action for money or damages where a defendant does not appear in the court, and is not found within the State, and is not a resident thereof, but has property therein, the jurisdiction of the court extends only over such property, the declaration expresses a principle of general, if not universal, law. The authority of every tribunal is necessarily restricted by the territorial limits of the State in which it is established. Any attempt to exercise authority beyond those limits would be deemed in every other forum, as has been said by this court, an illegitimate assumption of power, and be resisted as mere abuse. * * * In the case against the plaintiff, the property here in controversy sold under the judgment rendered was not attached, nor in any way brought under the jurisdiction of the court. Its first connection with the case was caused by a levy of the execution. It was not, therefore, disposed of pursuant to any adjudication, but only in enforcement of a personal judgment, having no relation to the property, rendered against a non-resident without service of process upon him in the action, or his appearance therein. The court below did not consider that an attachment of the property was essential to its jurisdiction or to the validity of the sale, but held that the judgment was invalid from defects in the affidavit upon which the order of publication was obtained, and in the affidavit by which the publication was proved.

There is some difference of opinion among the members of this court as to the rulings upon these alleged defects. The majority are of opinion that, inasmuch as the statute requires, for an order of publication, that certain facts shall appear by affidavit *to the satisfaction of the court or judge,* defects in such affidavit can only be taken advantage of on appeal, or by some other direct proceeding, and cannot be urged to impeach the judgment collaterally. The majority of the court are also of opinion that the provision of the statute requiring proof of the publication in a newspaper to be made by the "affidavit of the printer, or his foreman, or his principal clerk," is satisfied when the affidavit is made by the editor of the paper. The term "printer," in their judgment, is there used not to indicate the person who sets up the type—he does not usually have a foreman or clerks—it is rather used as synonymous with publisher. * * *

If, therefore, we were confined to the rulings of the court below upon the defects in the affidavits mentioned, we should be unable to uphold its decision. But it was also contended in that court, and is insisted upon here, that the judgment in the State Court against the plaintiff was void for want of personal service of process on him, or of his appearance in the action in which it was rendered, and that the premises in controversy could not be subjected to the payment of the demand of a resident creditor except by a proceeding *in rem;* that is, by a direct proceeding against the property for that purpose. If these positions are sound, the ruling of the Circuit Court as to the invalidity of that judgment must be sustained, notwithstanding our dissent from the reasons upon which it was made. And that they are sound would seem to follow from two well established principles of public law respecting the jurisdiction of an independent State over persons and property. The several States of the Union are not, it is true, in every respect independent, many of the rights and powers which originally belonged to them being now vested in the government created by the Constitution. But, except as restrained and limited by that instrument, they possess and exercise the authority of independent States, and the principles of public law to which we have referred are applicable to them. One of these principles is, that every State possesses exclusive jurisdiction and sovereignty over persons and property within its territory. As a consequence, every State has the power to determine for itself the civil *status* and capacities of its inhabitants; to prescribe the subjects upon which they may contract, the forms and solemnities with which their contracts shall be executed, the rights and obligations arising from them, and the mode in which their validity shall be determined and their obligations enforced; and also to regulate the manner and conditions upon which property situated within such territory, both personal and real, may be acquired, enjoyed and transferred. The other principle of public law referred to follows from the one mentioned; that is, that no State can exercise direct jurisdiction and authority over persons or property without its territory. * * * The several States are of equal dignity and authority, and the independence of one implies the exclusion of power from all others. And so it is laid down by jurists, as an elementary principle, that the laws of one State have no operation outside of its territory, except so far as is allowed by comity; and that no tribunal established by it can extend its process beyond that territory so as to subject either persons or property to its decisions. * * *

But as contracts made in one State may be enforceable only in another State, and property may be held by non-residents, the exercise of the jurisdiction which every State is admitted to possess over persons and property within its own territory will often affect persons and property without it. To any influence exerted in this way by a State affecting persons resident or property situated elsewhere, no objection can be justly taken; whilst any direct exertion of authority upon them, in an attempt to give ex-territorial operation to its laws, or to enforce an ex-territorial jurisdiction by its tribunals, would be deemed an encroachment upon the independence of the State in which the persons are domiciled or the property is situated, and be resisted as usurpation.

Thus the State, through its tribunals, may compel persons domiciled within its limits to execute, in pursuance of their contracts respecting property elsewhere situated, instruments in such form and with such solemnities as to transfer the title, so far as such formalities can be complied with; and the exercise of this jurisdiction in no manner interferes with the supreme control over the property by the State within which it is situated. * * *

So the State, through its tribunals, may subject property situated within its limits owned by non-residents to the payment of the demand of its own citizens against them; and the exercise of this jurisdiction in no respect infringes upon the sovereignty of the State where the owners are domiciled. Every State owes protection to its own citizens; and, when non-residents deal with them, it is a legitimate and just exercise of authority to hold and appropriate any property owned by such non-residents to satisfy the claims of its citizens. It is in virtue of the State's jurisdiction over the property of the non-resident situated within its limits that its tribunals can inquire into that non-resident's obligations to its own citizens, and the inquiry can then be carried only to the extent necessary to control the disposition of the property. If the non-resident has no property in the State, there is nothing upon which the tribunals can adjudicate.

* * * If, without personal service, judgments *in personam,* obtained *ex parte* against non-residents and absent parties, upon mere publication of process, which, in the great majority of cases, would never be seen by

the parties interested, could be upheld and enforced, they would be the constant instruments of fraud and oppression. Judgments for all sorts of claims upon contracts and for torts, real or pretended, would be thus obtained, under which property would be seized, when the evidence of the transactions upon which they were founded, if they ever had any existence, had perished.

Substituted service by publication, or in any other authorized form, may be sufficient to inform parties of the object of proceedings taken where property is once brought under the control of the court by seizure or some equivalent act. The law assumes that property is always in the possession of its owner, in person or by agent; and it proceeds upon the theory that its seizure will inform him, not only that it is taken into the custody of the court, but that he must look to any proceedings authorized by law upon such seizure for its condemnation and sale. * * * In other words, such service may answer in all actions which are substantially proceedings *in rem*. But where the entire object of the action is to determine the personal rights and obligations of the defendants, that is, where the suit is merely *in personam*, constructive service in this form upon a non-resident is ineffectual for any purpose. Process from the tribunals of one State cannot run into another State, and summon parties there domiciled to leave its territory and respond to proceedings against them. Publication of process or notice within the State where the tribunal sits cannot create any greater obligation upon the non-resident to appear. Process sent to him out of the State, and process published within it, are equally unavailing in proceedings to establish his personal liability.

The want of authority of the tribunals of a State to adjudicate upon the obligations of non-residents, where they have no property within its limits, is not denied by the court below; but the position is assumed that, where they have property within the State, it is immaterial whether the property is in the first instance brought under the control of the court by attachment or some other equivalent act, and afterwards applied by its judgment to the satisfaction of demands against its owner; or such demands be first established in a personal action, and the property of the non-resident be afterwards seized and sold on execution. But the answer to this position has already been given in the statement, that the jurisdiction of the court to inquire into and determine his obligations at all is only incidental to its jurisdiction over the property. Its jurisdiction in that respect cannot be made to depend upon facts to be ascertained after it has tried the cause and rendered the judgment. If the judgment be previously void, it will not become valid by the subsequent discovery of property of the defendant, or by his subsequent acquisition of it. The judgment, if void when rendered, will always remain void; it cannot occupy the doubtful position of being valid if property be found, and void if there be none. Even if the position assumed were confined to cases where the non-resident defendant possessed property in the State at the commencement of the action, it would still make the validity of the proceedings and judgment depend upon the question whether, before the levy of the execution, the defendant had or had not disposed of the property. If, before the levy, the property should be sold, then, according to this position, the judgment would not be binding. This doctrine would introduce a new element of uncertainty in judicial proceedings. The contrary is the law; the validity of every judgment depends upon the jurisdiction of the court before it is rendered, not upon what may occur subsequently. * * *

The force and effect of judgments rendered against non-residents without personal service of process upon them, or their voluntary appearance, have been the subject of frequent consideration in the courts of the United States and of the several States, as attempts have been made to enforce such judgments in States other than those in which they were rendered, under the provision of the Constitution requiring that "Full faith and credit shall be given in each State to the public Acts, records and judicial proceedings of every other State;" and the Act of Congress providing for the mode of authenticating such Acts, records and proceedings, and declaring that, when thus authenticated, "They shall have such faith and credit given to them in every court within the United States as they have by law or usage in the courts of the State from which they are or shall be taken." In the earlier cases, it was supposed that the Act gave to all judgments the same effect in other States which they had by law in the State where rendered. But this view was afterwards qualified so as to make the Act applicable only when the court rendering the judgment had jurisdiction of the parties and of the subject-matter, and not to preclude an inquiry into the jurisdiction of the court in which the judgment was rendered, or the right of the State itself to exercise authority over the person or the subject-matter. * * *

Since the adoption of the 14th Amendment to the Federal Constitution, the validity of such judgments may be directly questioned, and their enforcement in the State resisted, on the ground that proceedings in a court of justice to determine the personal rights and obligations of parties over whom that court has no jurisdiction do not constitute due process of law. Whatever difficulty may be experienced in giving to those terms a definition which will embrace every permissible exertion of power affecting private rights, and exclude such as is forbidden, there can be no doubt of their meaning when applied to judicial proceedings. They then mean a course of legal proceedings according to those rules and principles which have been established in our systems of jurisprudence for the protection and enforcement of private rights. To give such proceedings any validity, there must be a tribunal competent by its constitution—that is, by the law of its creation—to pass upon the subject-matter of the suit; and, if that involves merely a determination of the personal liability of the defendant, he must be brought within its jurisdiction by service of process within the State, or his voluntary appearance.

Except in cases affecting the personal *status* of the plaintiff, and cases in which that mode of service may be considered to have been assented to in advance as hereinafter mentioned, the substituted service of process by publication allowed by the law of Oregon and by similar laws in other States, where actions are brought against non-residents, is effectual only where, in connection with process against the person for commencing the action, property in the State is brought under the control of the court, and subjected to its disposition by process adapted to that purpose, or where the judgment is sought as a means of reaching such property or affecting some interest therein; in other words, where the action is in the nature of a proceeding *in rem.* * * *

It is true that, in a strict sense, a proceeding *in rem* is one taken directly against property, and has for its object the disposition of the property, without reference to the title of individual claimants; but, in a larger and more general sense, the terms are applied to actions between parties, where the direct object is to reach and dispose of property owned by them, or of some interest therein. Such are cases commenced by attachment against the property of debtors, or instituted to partition real estate, foreclose a mortgage, or enforce a lien. So far as they affect property in the State, they are substantially proceedings *in rem* in the broader sense which we have mentioned.

* * *

It follows from the views expressed that the personal judgment recovered in the State Court of Oregon against the plaintiff herein, then a non-resident of the State, was without any validity, and did not authorize a sale of the property in controversy.

To prevent any misapplication of the views expressed in this opinion, it is proper to observe that we do not mean to assert, by anything we have said, that a State may not authorize proceedings to determine the *status* of one of its citizens towards a non-resident, which would be binding within the State, though made without service of process or personal notice to the non-resident. The jurisdiction which every State possesses to determine the civil *status* and capacities of all its inhabitants involves authority to prescribe the conditions on which proceedings affecting them may be commenced and carried on within its territory. The State, for example, has absolute right to prescribe the conditions upon which the marriage relation between its own citizens shall be created, and the causes for which it may be dissolved. One of the parties guilty of acts for which, by the law of the State, a dissolution may be granted, may have removed to a State where no dissolution is permitted. The complaining party would, therefore, fail if a divorce were sought in the State of the defendant; and if application could not be made to the tribunals of the complainant's domicil in such case, and proceedings be there instituted without personal service of process or personal notice to the offending party, the injured citizen would be without redress. * * *

Neither do we mean to assert that a State may not require a non-resident entering into a partnership or association within its limits, or making contracts enforceable there, to appoint an agent or representative in the State to receive service of process and notice in legal proceedings instituted with respect to such partnership, association or contracts, or to designate a place where such service may be made and notice given, and provide, upon their failure, to make such appointment or to designate such place that service may be made upon a public officer designated for that purpose, or in some other prescribed way, and that judgments rendered upon such service may not be binding upon the non-residents both within and without the State. * * * Nor do we doubt that a State, on creating corporations or other institutions for pecuniary or charitable purposes, may provide a mode in which their conduct may be investigated, their obligations enforced, or their charters revoked, which shall require other than personal service upon their officers or members. * * *

In the present case, there is no feature of this kind and, consequently, no consideration of what would be the effect of such legislation in enforcing the contract of a non-resident can arise. * * *

Judgment affirmed.

[The dissenting opinion of JUSTICE HUNT is omitted.]

NOTES AND QUESTIONS

1.   The colorful characters and scandalous facts surrounding Pennoyer v. Neff have been chronicled by Professor Perdue:

Our story begins with a young man, Marcus Neff, heading across the country by covered wagon train, presumably to seek his fortune. Neff left Iowa in early 1848 * * * [and] was one of the earliest settlers to claim land under the Oregon Donation Act. * * *

Early in 1862 Neff made the unfortunate decision to consult a local Portland attorney, J.H. Mitchell. * * * Neff may have consulted Mitchell in an attempt to expedite the paperwork concerning his land patent. * * * "J.H. Mitchell" was actually the Oregon alias of one John Hipple. Hipple had been a teacher in Pennsylvania who, after being forced to marry the 15–year-old student whom he seduced, left teaching and took up law. * * * [I]n 1860 Hipple headed west taking with him four thousand dollars of client money and his then current paramour, a local school teacher. They made their way to California where Hipple abandoned the teacher * * * and moved on to Portland, Oregon. There, using the name John H. Mitchell, he quickly established himself as a successful lawyer, specializing in land litigation and railroad right-of-way cases. He also remarried without bothering to divorce his first wife. * * *

On November 3, 1865, Mitchell filed suit against Neff in Oregon state court [seeking payment for the legal services that had been rendered]. * * * A default judgment * * * was entered against Neff on February 19, 1866. Although Mitchell had an immediate right to execute on the judgment, he waited until early June 1866 to seek a writ of execution, possibly waiting for the arrival of Neff's land patent. * * * On August 7, 1866, the property was sold at a sheriff's auction * * *. Notably, the buyer was not Sylvester Pennoyer, as the Supreme Court opinion and commentators have implied. The property was purchased by none other than J. H. Mitchell, who three days later assigned the property to Sylvester Pennoyer. * * *

Following the litigation, Neff disappeared into obscurity; not so Pennoyer and Mitchell. Pennoyer went on to be Governor of Oregon * * *. Mitchell * * * was elected to the United States Senate in 1872, [but] lost his senate seat in 1879 * * *. * * * Shortly before the 1885 election, Judge Deady, the lower court judge in *Pennoyer v. Neff*, came into possession of a set of love letters which Mitchell had written to Mitchell's second wife's younger sister during the five years that he carried on an affair with her. Deady turned the love letters over to a newspaper, the *Oregonian* * * *. [However, in spite of] the scandal, Mitchell was [re]elected four days later * * *. In July of 1905, while still serving in the United States Senate, Mitchell was convicted [of land fraud] and sentenced to six months in jail, a $1,000 fine, and complete disbarment from public office.

Perdue, *Sin, Scandal and Substantive Due Process: Personal Jurisdiction and Pennoyer Reconsidered*, 62 Wash. L. Rev. 479, 481–90 (1987).

2. Traditional analysis distinguishes three types of jurisdiction. In a proceeding *in personam*, the court exercises its power to render a judgment for or against a person by virtue of his presence within the state's territory or his citizenship there. In a proceeding *in rem*, the court exercises its power to determine the status of property located within its territory, and the determination of the court is binding with respect to all possible interest holders in that property. In a proceeding *quasi in rem*, the court renders a judgment for or against a person, but recovery is limited to the value of property that is within the jurisdiction and thus subject to the court's authority. The dispute that gives rise to an action quasi in rem may be related to the property or unrelated to it. In an action quasi in rem, the property may be used to satisfy any judgment assessed in the action.

3. The concepts of jurisdiction found in the *Pennoyer* opinion were derived from nineteenth-century international law. In the traditional international model, a citizen of Country A might have been injured by a citizen of Country B in Country A. The citizen of Country A seeking relief had three options: proceed against the citizen of Country B in personam in Country A (with the likelihood that the paper called a judgment would be worthless because the courts of Country B would not enforce it against citizens of Country B); proceed against the citizen of Country B quasi in rem in Country A (with the advantage that the property of the citizen of Country B in Country A would be available to satisfy at least part (possibly all) of the judgment); or proceed against the citizen of Country B in the courts of Country B (in the hope of winning a judgment enforceable in Country B). Given these choices, it is understandable that the citizen of Country A probably would prefer the courts of Country A to the courts of Country B, the latter being farther away and possibly more disposed to find in favor of its own citizens, and would sue quasi in rem in Country A, so at least partial payment would be assured.

How much weight ought to be given to the international model in the context of the American federal system? Does the Full Faith and Credit Clause of the federal Constitution require states to recognize and enforce valid judgments by other states? Do the states have the same kind of interest in adjudicating claims brought by their citizens when the stake is state sovereignty rather than national sovereignty? Are there analogous grounds for concern that state courts may be unduly disposed to find in favor of citizens of their own state?

4.   According to the territorial principle identified in *Pennoyer*, does the length of time the defendant is in the jurisdiction matter in an in personam action? Does the reason for the person's presence in the jurisdiction make a difference? In GRACE v. MACARTHUR, 170 F.Supp. 442 (E.D.Ark. 1959), service of the complaint was made on the defendant while he was a passenger on a commercial flight from Tennessee to Texas when the plane was over Arkansas. The court upheld the exercise of jurisdiction by the federal district court sitting in Arkansas. The Supreme Court has reaffirmed the continuing vitality of this traditional form of personal jurisdiction. See Burnham v. Superior Court of California, p. 107, infra.

5.   Can a court assert jurisdiction over a citizen who is absent from the country? In BLACKMER v. UNITED STATES, 284 U.S. 421, 52 S.Ct. 252, 76 L.Ed. 375 (1932), petitioner, an American citizen, sought reversal of a contempt conviction resulting from his refusal to comply with a subpoena issued by an American court and served upon him in France in connection with a proceeding that grew out of the Teapot Dome Scandal during President Harding's administration. Service was authorized by federal statute. The Supreme Court concluded that no violation of due process had taken place. The *Blackmer* principle was applied to state-court litigation in MILLIKEN v. MEYER, 311 U.S. 457, 462–63, 61 S.Ct. 339, 342–43, 85 L.Ed. 278, 283 (1940), where Milliken sued Meyer, a Wyoming resident, in a Wyoming state court. Personal service was effected in Colorado under a Wyoming statute that permitted such service, in lieu of service by publication, on absent residents. Meyer did not appear and an in personam judgment was entered against him. Four years later, Meyer asked a Colorado court to restrain Milliken's enforcement of the Wyoming judgment. The United States Supreme Court held the Wyoming judgment valid and entitled to full faith and credit. According to the Court:

> * * * Domicile in the state is alone sufficient to bring an absent defendant within the reach of the state's jurisdiction for purposes of a personal judgment by means of appropriate substituted service. * * * [T]he authority of a state over one of its citizens is not terminated by the mere fact of his absence from the state. The state which accords him privileges and affords protection to him and his property by virtue of his domicile may also exact reciprocal duties.

What factors are relevant in deciding whether defendant's relationship with the forum state is sufficient to invoke the *Milliken* doctrine? Do *Blackmer* and *Milliken* fall within the scope of the statement in *Pennoyer* that "every State has the power to determine for itself the civil *status* and capacities of its inhabitants," or do they involve a different basis of jurisdiction?

6.   Suppose a plaintiff brings suit in a forum with which she has no other connection. Should that forum be able to entertain a suit *against* the plaintiff if the claim is asserted as a part of the same proceeding? Consider the Court's

analysis ADAM v. SAENGER, 303 U.S. 59, 67–68, 58 S.Ct. 454, 458, 82 L.Ed. 649, 654–55 (1938):

> There is nothing in the Fourteenth Amendment to prevent a state from adopting a procedure by which a judgment *in personam* may be rendered in a cross-action against a plaintiff in its courts, upon service of process or of appropriate pleading upon his attorney of record. The plaintiff having, by his voluntary act in demanding justice from the defendant, submitted himself to the jurisdiction of the court, there is nothing arbitrary or unreasonable in treating him as being there for all purposes for which justice to the defendant requires his presence. It is the price which the state may exact as the condition of opening its courts to the plaintiff.

Would it matter whether the later action is between the same two parties? Suppose a third party had instituted suit in California against the plaintiff in an action unrelated to the pending suit. Would the California court have jurisdiction? If there was jurisdiction, would it be based on plaintiff's presence in the state or on some other notion? Should a state be permitted to condition the use of its courts on consent to the jurisdiction of those courts in actions unrelated to the initial lawsuit? See generally 4 Wright & Miller, Federal Practice and Procedure: Civil 3d § 1064.

7.   The expanding global economy has encouraged efforts to define an international law of jurisdiction, but agreement has proved difficult to reach. See Oestreicher, *"We're on a Road to Nowhere"—Reasons for the Continuing Failure to Regulate Recognition and Enforcement of Foreign Judgments*, 42 Int'l Law. 59 (2008). Although the cornerstone of the British and American common law concept of jurisdiction historically has been defendant's presence, domicile has been the key in the Netherlands and Switzerland, plaintiff's nationality has been of great importance in France, and domicile and the situs of property have been of major significance in Germany. See Juenger, *Judicial Jurisdiction in the United States and in the European Communities: A Comparison*, 82 Mich. L. Rev. 1195 (1984). Commentators emphasize that "[i]n this area of law, differences among civil-law countries are as great as differences between given civil-law and common-law countries." de Vries & Lowenfeld, *Jurisdiction in Personal Actions—A Comparison of Civil Law Views*, 44 Iowa L. Rev. 306, 344 (1959).

SECTION B.   EXPANDING THE BASES OF PERSONAL JURISDICTION

Increased interstate travel in the early twentieth century, particularly as a result of the growing popularity of the automobile, brought with it increased interstate litigation. In order to ensure that transient drivers not be beyond jurisdiction when they drove into another state, some states came to condition the use of their roads by out-of-state drivers on consent to the jurisdiction of the state's courts over matters arising from a party's activity within the state. In KANE v. NEW JERSEY, 242 U.S. 160, 37 S.Ct. 30, 61 L.Ed. 222 (1916), the Supreme Court held that New Jersey could require an out-of-state motorist to file a formal instrument appointing a New Jersey agent to receive process prior to using the state's highways. Eventually, some states moved beyond the nonresident's express consent to in-state service as a basis for asserting jurisdiction.

In HESS v. PAWLOSKI, 274 U.S. 352, 47 S.Ct. 632, 71 L.Ed. 1091 (1927), the Court upheld service on a nonresident automobile driver pursuant to chapter 90, General Laws of Massachusetts, as amended by Stat. 1923, c. 431, § 2, the material parts of which follow:

> The acceptance by a nonresident of the rights and privileges conferred by section three or four, as evidenced by his operating a motor vehicle thereunder, or the operation by a nonresident of a motor vehicle on a public way in the commonwealth other than under said sections, shall be deemed equivalent to an appointment by such nonresident of the registrar or his successor in office, to be his true and lawful attorney upon whom may be served all lawful processes in any action or proceeding against him, growing out of any accident or collision in which said nonresident may be involved while operating a motor vehicle on such a way, and said acceptance or operation shall be a signification of his agreement that any such process against him which is so served shall be of the same legal force and validity as if served on him personally. Service of such process shall be made by leaving a copy of the process with a fee of two dollars in the hands of the registrar, or in his office, and such service shall be sufficient service upon the said nonresident: Provided, that notice of such service and a copy of the process are forthwith sent by registered mail by the plaintiff to the defendant, and the defendant's return receipt and the plaintiff's affidavit of compliance herewith are appended to the writ and entered with the declaration. * * *

The Court explained in its opinion:

> The process of a court of one state cannot run into another and summon a party there domiciled to respond to proceedings against him. Notice sent outside the state to a nonresident is unavailing to give jurisdiction in an action against him personally for money recovery. Pennoyer v. Neff * * *. There must be actual service within the state of notice upon him or upon some one authorized to accept service for him. * * * A personal judgment rendered against a nonresident, who has neither been served with process nor appeared in the suit, is without validity. * * * The mere transaction of business in a state by nonresident natural persons does not imply consent to be bound by the process of its courts. * * * The power of a state to exclude foreign corporations, although not absolute, but qualified, is the ground on which such an implication is supported as to them. * * * But a state may not withhold from nonresident individuals the right of doing business therein. The privileges and immunities clause of the Constitution (section 2, art. 4), safeguards to the citizens of one state the right "to pass through, or to reside in any other state for

purposes of trade, agriculture, professional pursuits, or otherwise.'' And it prohibits state legislation discriminating against citizens of other states. * * *

Motor vehicles are dangerous machines, and, even when skillfully and carefully operated, their use is attended by serious dangers to persons and property. In the public interest the state may make and enforce regulations reasonably calculated to promote care on the part of all, residents and nonresidents alike, who use its highways. The measure in question operates to require a nonresident to answer for his conduct in the state where arise causes of action alleged against him, as well as to provide for a claimant a convenient method by which he may sue to enforce his rights. Under the statute the implied consent is limited to proceedings growing out of accidents or collisions on a highway in which the nonresident may be involved. It is required that he shall actually receive and receipt for notice of the service and a copy of the process. And it contemplates such continuances as may be found necessary to give reasonable time and opportunity for defense. It makes no hostile discrimination against nonresidents, but tends to put them on the same footing as residents. Literal and precise equality in respect of this matter is not attainable; it is not required. * * * The state's power to regulate the use of its highways extends to their use by nonresidents as well as by residents. * * * And, in advance of the operation of a motor vehicle on its highway by a nonresident, the state may require him to appoint one of its officials as his agent on whom process may be served in proceedings growing out of such use. Kane v. New Jersey * * *. That case recognizes power of the state to exclude a nonresident until the formal appointment is made. And, having the power so to exclude, the state may declare that the use of the highway by the nonresident is the equivalent of the appointment of the registrar as agent on whom process may be served. * * * The difference between the formal and implied appointment is not substantial, so far as concerns the application of the due process clause of the Fourteenth Amendment.

274 U.S. at 353–57, 47 S.Ct. at 632–34, 71 L.Ed. at 1093–95.

NOTE AND QUESTIONS

What are the limits to the theory of jurisdiction expressed in *Hess*? Would a nonresident-motorist statute that purported to assert jurisdiction over any cause of action that arises out of the presence of defendant's vehicle within the state, or over people other than the driver of the vehicle, be constitutional? Could the implied consent to jurisdiction created by driving within a state be employed to support jurisdiction over a nonresident in a matter unrelated to her conduct within the state?

SECTION C.   A NEW THEORY
OF JURISDICTION

The jurisdictional bases developed in *Pennoyer*—presence and citizenship—were not easily applied to corporations. A corporation, after all, is a fiction. It exists on paper and acts through its employees, directors, and shareholders. It generally was accepted well into the nineteenth century that a "corporation can have no legal existence out of the boundaries of the sovereignty by which it is created." Bank of Augusta v. Earle, 38 U.S. (13 Pet.) 519, 588, 10 L.Ed. 274, 308 (1839) (Taney, J.). Nonetheless, as corporations grew beyond those boundaries, courts were forced to develop ways to apply the jurisdictional principles of *Pennoyer* to them.

The courts first developed the "consent" theory, which presupposed that a foreign corporation could transact business in a state only with that state's consent. Under this theory, a foreign corporation could be required to consent to service of process by appointing an agent to receive process within the state, as a condition of obtaining permission to do business there. The courts soon began to apply this principle both when the corporation actually designated an agent to receive process and when it did not appoint an agent and, thus, could be said only to have granted implied consent to in-state service.

As the courts became increasingly disenchanted with the unrealistic nature of the "consent" theory, they developed the "presence" theory premised on the notion that: "A foreign corporation is amenable to process * * * if it is doing business within the State in such manner and to such extent as to warrant the inference that it is present there." Philadelphia & Reading Ry. Co. v. Mckibbin, 243 U.S. 264, 265, 37 S.Ct. 280, 61 L.Ed. 710, 711–12 (1917) (Brandeis, J.). This doctrine measured the propriety of a state's assertion of jurisdiction over a foreign corporation in terms of the actual activities of the corporation in the state. Under the presence theory, however, a court lost its adjudicatory authority over a corporation once it ceased doing business in the state. In addition, "presence" is a conclusory term, and all too often was used by the courts without any meaningful analysis.

Under both the implied consent and the presence theories, the first question to be asked was whether the corporation was "doing business" within the state. As the number of cases making this factual inquiry multiplied, "doing business" gradually came to be a test in and of itself. The cases became cluttered with refined and often senseless distinctions that sought to measure the quantity of defendant's activities within the state, but paid little or no attention to the burden imposed on the corporation by asserting jurisdiction over it or the overall desirability of litigating in the particular forum.

With doctrine in so bad a state of disrepair, the time had long since passed for the Supreme Court to acknowledge the truth of Holmes' dictum that "[t]he Constitution is not to be satisfied with a fiction." International Shoe Co. v. Washington afforded the Court an opportunity to begin to set its house in order in this field.

Kurland, *The Supreme Court, the Due Process Clause and the In Personam Jurisdiction of State Courts—From* Pennoyer *to* Denckla: *A Review*, 25 U. Chi. L. Rev. 569, 586 (1958).

INTERNATIONAL SHOE CO. v. WASHINGTON

Supreme Court of the United States, 1945.
326 U.S. 310, 66 S.Ct. 154, 90 L.Ed. 95.

Appeal from the Supreme Court of the State of Washington.

MR. CHIEF JUSTICE STONE delivered the opinion of the Court.

The questions for decision are (1) whether, within the limitations of the due process clause of the Fourteenth Amendment, appellant, a Delaware corporation, has by its activities in the State of Washington rendered itself amenable to proceedings in the courts of that state to recover unpaid contributions to the state unemployment compensation fund exacted by state statutes * * * and (2) whether the state can exact those contributions consistently with the due process clause of the Fourteenth Amendment.

The statutes in question set up a comprehensive scheme of unemployment compensation, the costs of which are defrayed by contributions required to be made by employers to a state unemployment compensation fund. The contributions are a specified percentage of the wages payable annually by each employer for his employees' services in the state. The assessment and collection of the contributions and the fund are administered by respondents. Section 14(c) of the Act, Wash. Rev. Stat. 1941 Supp., § 9998–114c, authorizes respondent Commissioner to issue an order and notice of assessment of delinquent contributions upon prescribed personal service of the notice upon the employer if found within the state, or, if not so found, by mailing the notice to the employer by registered mail at his last known address. That section also authorizes the Commissioner to collect the assessment by distraint if it is not paid within ten days after service of the notice. * * *

In this case notice of assessment for the years in question was personally served upon a sales solicitor employed by appellant in the State of Washington, and a copy of the notice was mailed by registered mail to appellant at its address in St. Louis, Missouri. Appellant appeared specially before the office of unemployment and moved to set aside the order and notice of assessment on the ground that the service upon appellant's salesman was not proper service upon appellant; that appellant was not a corporation of the State of Washington and was not doing business within the state; that it had no agent within the state upon whom service could be made; and that appellant is not an employer and does not furnish employment within the meaning of the statute.

The motion was heard on evidence and a stipulation of facts by the appeal tribunal which denied the motion and ruled that respondent Commissioner was entitled to recover the unpaid contributions. That action was affirmed by the Commissioner; both the Superior Court and the Supreme Court affirmed. * * * Appellant in each of these courts assailed the statute as applied, as a violation of the due process clause of the Fourteenth Amendment, and as imposing a constitutionally prohibited burden on interstate commerce.

* * * Appellant is a Delaware corporation, having its principal place of business in St. Louis, Missouri, and is engaged in the manufacture and sale of shoes and other footwear. It maintains places of business in several states, other than Washington, at which its manufacturing is carried on and from which its merchandise is distributed interstate through several sales units or branches located outside the State of Washington.

Appellant has no office in Washington and makes no contracts either for sale or purchase of merchandise there. It maintains no stock of merchandise in that state and makes there no deliveries of goods in intrastate commerce. During the years from 1937 to 1940, now in question, appellant employed eleven to thirteen salesmen under direct supervision and control of sales managers located in St. Louis. These salesmen resided in Washington; their principal activities were confined to that state; and they were compensated by commissions based upon the amount of their sales. The commissions for each year totaled more than $31,000. Appellant supplies its salesmen with a line of samples, each consisting of one shoe of a pair, which they display to prospective purchasers. On occasion they rent permanent sample rooms, for exhibiting samples, in business buildings, or rent rooms in hotels or business buildings temporarily for that purpose. The cost of such rentals is reimbursed by appellant.

The authority of the salesmen is limited to exhibiting their samples and soliciting orders from prospective buyers, at prices and on terms fixed by appellant. The salesmen transmit the orders to appellant's office in St. Louis for acceptance or rejection, and when accepted the merchandise for filling the orders is shipped f.o.b. from points outside Washington to the purchasers within the state. All the merchandise shipped into Washington is invoiced at the place of shipment from which collections are made. No salesman has authority to enter into contracts or to make collections.

The Supreme Court of Washington was of opinion that the regular and systematic solicitation of orders in the state by appellant's salesmen, resulting in a continuous flow of appellant's product into the state, was sufficient to constitute doing business in the state so as to make appellant amenable to suit in its courts. But it was also of opinion that there were sufficient additional activities shown to bring the case within the rule frequently stated, that solicitation within a state by the agents of a foreign corporation plus some additional activities there are sufficient to render the corporation amenable to suit brought in the courts of the state to enforce an obligation arising out of its activities there. * * * The court found such additional activities in the salesmen's display of samples sometimes in permanent display rooms, and the salesmen's residence within the state, continued over a period of years, all resulting in a substantial volume of merchandise regularly shipped by appellant to purchasers within the state. * * *

Appellant * * * insists that its activities within the state were not sufficient to manifest its "presence" there and that in its absence the state courts were without jurisdiction, that consequently it was a denial of due process for the state to subject appellant to suit. It refers to those cases in which it was said that the mere solicitation of orders for the purchase of goods within a state, to be accepted without the state and filled by shipment of the purchased goods interstate, does not render the corporation seller amenable to suit within the state. * * * And appellant further argues that since it was not present within the state, it is a denial of due process to subject it to taxation or other money exaction. It thus denies the power of the state to lay the tax or to subject appellant to a suit for its collection.

Historically the jurisdiction of courts to render judgment in personam is grounded on their de facto power over the defendant's person. Hence his presence within the territorial jurisdiction of a court was prerequisite to its rendition of a judgment personally binding him. Pennoyer v. Neff * * *. But now that the capias ad respondendum has given way to personal service of summons or other form of notice, due process requires only that in order to subject a defendant to a judgment in personam, if he be not present within the territory of the forum, he have certain minimum contacts with it such that the maintenance of the suit does not offend "traditional notions of fair play and substantial justice." Milliken v. Meyer, [Note 5, p. 41, supra]. * * *

Since the corporate personality is a fiction, although a fiction intended to be acted upon as though it were a fact * * *, it is clear that unlike an individual its "presence" without, as well as within, the state of its origin can be manifested only by activities carried on in its behalf by those who are authorized to act for it. To say that the corporation is so far "present" there as to satisfy due process requirements, for purposes of taxation or the maintenance of suits against it in the courts of the state, is to beg the question to be decided. For the terms "present" or "presence" are used merely to symbolize those activities of the corporation's agent within the state which courts will deem to be sufficient to satisfy the demands of due process. * * * Those demands may be met by such contacts of the corporation with the state of the forum as make it reasonable, in the context of our federal system of government, to require the corporation to defend the particular suit which is brought there. An "estimate of the inconveniences" which would result to the corporation from a trial away from its "home" or principal place of business is relevant in this connection. * * *

"Presence" in the state in this sense has never been doubted when the activities of the corporation there have not only been continuous and systematic, but also give rise to the liabilities sued on, even though no consent to be sued or authorization to an agent to accept service of process has been given. * * * Conversely it has been generally recognized that the casual presence of the corporate agent or even his conduct of single or isolated items of activities in a state in the corporation's behalf are not enough to subject it to suit on causes of action unconnected with the activities there. * * * To require the corporation in such circumstances to defend the suit away from its home or other jurisdiction where it carries on more substantial activities has been thought to lay too great and unreasonable a burden on the corporation to comport with due process.

While it has been held in cases on which appellant relies that continuous activity of some sorts within a state is not enough to support the demand that the corporation be amenable to suits unrelated to that activity * * * there have been instances in which the continuous corporate operations within a state were thought so substantial and of such a nature as to justify suit against it on causes of action arising from dealings entirely distinct from those activities. * * *

Finally, although the commission of some single or occasional acts of the corporate agent in a state sufficient to impose an obligation or liability on the corporation has not been thought to confer upon the state authority to enforce it, Rosenberg Bros. & Co. v. Curtis Brown Co., 260 U.S. 516, 43 S. Ct. 170, 67 L. Ed. 372, other such acts, because of their nature and quality and the circumstances of their commission, may be deemed sufficient to render the corporation liable to suit. Cf. Kane v. New Jersey * * *; Hess v. Pawloski, [p. 43, supra] * * *. True, some of the decisions holding the corporation amenable to suit have been supported by resort to the legal fiction that it has given its consent to service and suit, consent being implied from its presence in the state through the acts of its authorized agents. * * * But more realistically it may be said that those authorized acts were of such a nature as to justify the fiction. * * *

It is evident that the criteria by which we mark the boundary line between those activities which justify the subjection of a corporation to suit, and those which do not, cannot be simply mechanical or quantitative. The test is not merely, as has sometimes been suggested, whether the activity, which the corporation has seen fit to procure through its agents in another state, is a little more or a little less. * * * Whether due process is satisfied must depend rather upon the quality and nature of the activity in relation to the fair and orderly administration of the laws which it was the purpose of the due process clause to insure. That clause does not contemplate that a state may make binding a judgment in personam against an individual or corporate defendant with which the state has no contacts, ties, or relations. * * *

But to the extent that a corporation exercises the privilege of conducting activities within a state, it enjoys the benefits and protection of the laws of that state. The exercise of that privilege may give rise to obligations; and, so far as those obligations arise out of or are connected with the activities within the state, a procedure which requires the corporation to respond to a suit brought to enforce them can, in most instances, hardly be said to be undue. * * *

Applying these standards, the activities carried on in behalf of appellant in the State of Washington were neither irregular nor casual. They were systematic and continuous throughout the years in question. They resulted in a large volume of interstate business, in the course of which appellant received the benefits and protection of the laws of the state, including the right to resort to the courts for the enforcement of its rights. The obligation which is here sued upon arose out of those very activities. It is evident that these operations establish sufficient contacts or ties with the state of the forum to make it reasonable and just according to our traditional conception of fair play and substantial justice to permit the state to enforce the obligations which appellant has incurred there. Hence we cannot say that the maintenance of the present suit in the State of Washington involves an unreasonable or undue procedure.

We are likewise unable to conclude that the service of the process within the state upon an agent whose activities establish appellant's "presence" there was not sufficient notice of the suit, or that the suit was so unrelated to those activities as to make the agent an inappropriate vehicle for communicating the notice. It is enough that appellant has established such contacts with the state that the particular form of substituted service adopted there gives reasonable assurance that the notice will be actual. * * *

Appellant having rendered itself amenable to suit upon obligations arising out of the activities of its salesmen in Washington, the state may maintain the present suit in personam to collect the tax laid upon the exercise of the privilege of employing appellant's salesmen within the state. For Washington has made one of those activities, which taken together establish appellant's "presence" there for purposes of suit, the taxable event by which the state brings appellant within the reach of its taxing power. The state thus has constitutional power to lay the tax and to subject appellant to a suit to recover it. The activities which establish its "presence" subject it alike to taxation by the state and to suit to recover the tax. * * *

Affirmed.

MR. JUSTICE JACKSON took no part in the consideration or decision of this case.

MR. JUSTICE BLACK delivered the following opinion.

* * *

I believe that the Federal Constitution leaves to each State, without any "ifs" or "buts," a power to tax and to open the doors of its courts for its citizens to sue corporations whose agents do business in those States. Believing that the Constitution gave the States that power, I think it a judicial deprivation to condition its exercise upon this Court's notion of "fair play," however appealing that term may be. Nor can I stretch the meaning of due process so far as to authorize this Court to deprive a State of the right to afford judicial protection to its citizens on the ground that it would be more "convenient" for the corporation to be sued somewhere else.

There is a strong emotional appeal in the words "fair play," "justice," and "reasonableness." But they were not chosen by those who wrote the original Constitution or the Fourteenth Amendment as a measuring rod for this Court to use in invalidating State or Federal laws passed by elected legislative representatives. No one, not even those who most feared a democratic government, ever formally proposed that courts should be given power to invalidate legislation under any such elastic standards. Express prohibitions against certain types of legislation are found in the Constitution, and under the long settled practice, courts invalidate laws found to conflict with them. This requires interpretation, and interpretation, it is true, may result in extension of the Constitution's purpose. But that is no reason for reading the due process clause so as to restrict a State's power to tax and sue those whose activities affect persons and businesses within the State, provided proper service can be had. * * *

NOTES AND QUESTIONS

1. In its argument before the United States Supreme Court, International Shoe insisted that it would be imprudent to link the company's amenability to suit in a tax-enforcement action with service on salesmen who happened to work in the state: "It would be manifestly impolitic to uphold service upon a salesman in a case not involving a sale. It would require of mere soliciting salesmen, notoriously happy-go-lucky fellows, good mixers, a higher degree of judgment and responsibility than that for which they are selected." For more of the facts of *International Shoe* and a discussion of how the company litigated the question of personal jurisdiction, see Cameron & Johnson, *Death of a Salesman? Forum Shopping and Outcome Determination Under International Shoe*, 28 U.C. Davis L. Rev. 769 (1995).

2. *International Shoe* uses contacts with the forum in two different ways. First, a defendant may have sufficient contact with the forum to warrant asserting jurisdiction over it for all matters. This is termed "general jurisdiction," and we will return to study it in more detail later in this Chapter. Second, a defendant may have sufficient contact with the forum to warrant asserting jurisdiction over it for matters related to its activity in the forum without having sufficient contact with the forum to warrant general jurisdiction. In such a case, the jurisdiction is termed "specific jurisdiction." Whether a corporation is subject to specific or general jurisdiction depends on the nature and number of contacts it has with the forum. Determining what

constitutes sufficient business within the state, or what matters are related to activity within it, often are uncertain questions that may blur the distinction between general and specific jurisdiction. See Brilmayer, *Related Contacts and Personal Jurisdiction*, 101 Harv. L. Rev. 1444 (1988).

SECTION D. SPECIFIC JURISDICTION AND STATE LONG–ARM LAWS

Read the selected state jurisdiction statutes in the Supplement.

1. THE DEVELOPMENT OF LONG–ARM LAWS

The Supreme Court's decision in Hess v. Pawloski, p. 43, supra, encouraged states to utilize their police powers to enact statutes asserting jurisdiction based on the operation of automobiles within a state and a variety of other hazardous activities or enterprises. As time progressed and liberal judicial construction and emboldened state legislatures gave broader scope to these statutes, the usefulness of the technique suggested by the nonresident motorist statutes became even more apparent.

The Court's decision in *International Shoe*—with its emphasis on contacts with the forum state—further encouraged states to expand their jurisdictional reach and led to efforts on the part of many state legislatures to conform their statutory pattern to the Supreme Court's latest view as to when personal jurisdiction could be asserted consistently with the Constitution. This spate of legislative activity came largely in the form of "long-arm" or "single-act" statutes, which seek to provide personal jurisdiction over nonresidents who cannot be found and served in the forum. These statutes predicate jurisdiction over nonresidents upon the defendant's general activity in the state, or the commission of any one of a series of enumerated acts within the jurisdiction, or, in some cases, the commission of a certain act outside the jurisdiction causing consequences within it. The theory supporting the assertion of jurisdiction in these circumstances flows naturally from the Court's decision in *International Shoe* and its emphasis on the quantum and quality of the defendant's activity in the forum state.

The first truly comprehensive long-arm statute was enacted in Illinois, and it was used as a model by a number of states. Under the Illinois act, an individual or a corporation, whether a citizen or noncitizen of Illinois, is said to be amenable to the jurisdiction of the state's courts if he transacts any business within the state; commits a tort within the state; owns, uses, or possesses any real estate within the state; or contracts to insure any person, property, or risk located within the state. Several years after its enactment, the Illinois statute was amended to include jurisdiction over claims involving alimony, support, and property division against former residents. Other states soon followed Illinois's lead in expanding the jurisdictional reach of their courts.

Contemporary long-arm statutes run the gamut from very broad ones that permit states to assert jurisdiction up to the limits allowed by the Constitution, to narrow ones that only carve out small parts of their constitutionally permitted authority. One limitation that generally is placed on the use of long-arm statutes is that they apply only to suits brought in the courts of the state in which the jurisdictional act occurs or in the federal courts sitting in that state. Long-arm statutes are set out in the Supplement. Which of the statutes are most limited in application? In what ways? As you read the following case, consider whether the state court could exercise personal jurisdiction assuming the same facts, if the applicable long-arm statute were that of New York or California. Despite the textual similarities of many of these statutes, judicial construction of them often differs.

GRAY v. AMERICAN RADIATOR & STANDARD SANITARY CORP.

Supreme Court of Illinois, 1961.
22 Ill.2d 432, 176 N.E.2d 761.

KLINGBIEL, JUSTICE. Phyllis Gray appeals from a judgment of the circuit court of Cook County dismissing her action for damages. The issues are concerned with the construction and validity of our statute providing for substituted service of process on nonresidents. Since a constitutional question is involved, the appeal is direct to this court.

The suit was brought against the Titan Valve Manufacturing Company and others, on the ground that a certain water heater had exploded and injured the plaintiff. The complaint charges, *inter alia*, that the Titan company, a foreign corporation, had negligently constructed the safety valve; and that the injuries were suffered as a proximate result thereof. Summons issued and was duly served on Titan's registered agent in Cleveland, Ohio. The corporation appeared specially, filing a motion to quash on the ground that it had not committed a tortious act in Illinois. Its affidavit stated that it does no business here; that it has no agent physically present in Illinois; and that it sells the completed valves to defendant, American Radiator & Standard Sanitary Corporation, outside Illinois. The American Radiator & Standard Sanitary Corporation (also made a defendant) filed an answer in which it set up a cross claim against Titan, alleging that Titan made certain warranties to American Radiator, and that if the latter is held liable to the plaintiff it should be indemnified and held harmless by Titan. The court granted Titan's motion, dismissing both the complaint and the cross claim.

Section 16 of the Civil Practice Act provides that summons may be personally served upon any party outside the State; and that as to nonresidents who have submitted to the jurisdiction of our courts, such service has the force and effect of personal service within Illinois. (Ill. Rev. Stat. 1959, chap. 110, par. 16.) Under section 17(1)(b) a nonresident who, either in person or through an agent, commits a tortious act within this State submits to jurisdiction. * * * The questions in this case are (1) whether a tortious act was committed here, within the meaning of the statute, despite the fact that the Titan corporation had no agent in Illinois; and (2) whether the statute, if so construed, violates due process of law.

The first aspect to which we must direct our attention is one of statutory construction. Under section 17(1)(b) jurisdiction is predicated on the committing of a tortious act in this State. It is not disputed, for the purpose of this appeal, that a tortious act was committed. The issue depends on whether it was committed in Illinois, so as to warrant the assertion of personal jurisdiction by service of summons in Ohio.

The wrong in the case at bar did not originate in the conduct of a servant physically present here, but arose instead from acts performed at the place of manufacture. Only the consequences occurred in Illinois. It is well established, however, that in law the place of a wrong is where the last event takes place which is necessary to render the actor liable. Restatement, Conflict of Laws, sec. 377. A second indication that the place of injury is the determining factor is found in rules governing the time within which an action must be brought. In applying statutes of limitation our court has computed the period from the time when the injury is done. * * * We think it is clear that the alleged negligence in manufacturing the valve cannot be separated from the resulting injury; and that for present purposes, like those of liability and limitations, the tort was committed in Illinois.

Titan seeks to avoid this result by arguing that instead of using the word "tort," the legislature employed the term "tortious act"; and that the latter refers only to the act or conduct, separate and apart from any consequences thereof. We cannot accept the argument. To be tortious an act must cause injury. The concept of injury is an inseparable part of the phrase. In determining legislative intention courts will read words in their ordinary and popularly understood sense. * * * We think the intent should be determined less from technicalities of definition than from considerations of general purpose and effect. To adopt the criteria urged by defendant would tend to promote litigation over extraneous issues concerning the elements of a tort and the territorial incidence of each, whereas the test should be concerned more with those substantial elements of convenience and justice presumably contemplated by the legislature. As we observed in Nelson v. Miller, 11 Ill. 2d 378, 143 N.E.2d 673, the statute contemplates the exertion of jurisdiction over nonresident defendants to the extent permitted by the due-process clause.

The Titan company contends that if the statute is applied so as to confer jurisdiction in this case it violates the requirement of due process of law. The precise constitutional question thus presented has not heretofore been considered by this court. * * *

[The court's discussion of the constitutional question is omitted.]

NOTE AND QUESTIONS

As *Gray* illustrates, the application of long-arm statutes often entails difficult questions of statutory construction. In GREEN v. ADVANCE ROSS ELECTRONICS CORP., 86 Ill.2d 431, 437–40, 56 Ill.Dec. 657, 660–62, 427 N.E.2d 1203, 1206–08 (1981), the issue was whether Advance Ross, a Delaware corporation with headquarters in Illinois, in an action claiming breach of fiduciary duty, could assert jurisdiction over Green, a Texas resident, who once served as president of two of its affiliates. All of Green's corporate responsibilities, including the acts that allegedly injured the corporation, were performed outside Illinois. Nonetheless, Advance Ross argued that, under Section 17(1)(b) of Illinois's long-arm statute, an out-of-state resident submits to the jurisdiction of the Illinois courts when he commits a tort that causes a diminution of the funds of a corporation organized or headquartered in Illinois. The Illinois Supreme Court, distinguishing *Gray*, refused to read Section 17(1)(b) to establish jurisdiction:

> As in *Gray* * * * for the purpose of disposing of the propriety of long-arm jurisdiction there is no dispute that tortious acts were committed. To be resolved is whether their commission was "within this State" as those words are used in section 17(1)(b).
>
> * * * [Advance Ross's] theory is that although the misconduct of Green, Sr., took place outside Illinois, the consequences of his misconduct were felt in Illinois. They * * * contend that the misconduct alleged resulted in a drain upon those assets in Illinois. But the consequences upon which [Advance Ross relies] are too remote from the misconduct of Green, Sr., to support the conclusion that the tortious acts complained of were committed in Illinois. The situs of the last event whose happening was necessary to hold Green, Sr., liable was in Texas.

In support of its conclusion, the Illinois court noted:

> [A]cceptance of the theory of long-arm jurisdiction advanced by [Advance Ross] would be tantamount to permitting a corporation operating nationwide to sue employees, suppliers, customers and perhaps others, at the company's State of incorporation or at its headquarters no matter how far away they lived and worked or their contact with the corporation was. Any interpretation of the Illinois long-arm statute which would permit that result is neither fair nor wise as a matter of policy. The meaning [which Advance Ross] ask[s] us to give the words "within this State" takes us too easily out of this State to be acceptable. * * *

Illinois's long-arm statute, 735 ILCS 5/2–209, formerly cited as Ill. Rev. Stat. ch. 110, ¶ 2–209(a), was amended in 1989 to give the Illinois state courts jurisdiction over any cause of action arising out of:

* * *

(7) The making or performance of any contract or promise substantially connected with this State; * * *

(11) The breach of any fiduciary duty within this State;

(12) The performance of duties as a director or officer of a corporation organized under the laws of this State or having its principal place of business within this State * * *.

If these provisions had been in effect, would the Illinois Supreme Court have decided *Advance Ross* the same way? In this regard, consider whether *Gray* and *Advance Ross* are applicable only to cases asserting jurisdiction based on a "tortious act within this State," or whether they apply equally to all assertions of jurisdiction under Illinois's long-arm statute.

2. DUE PROCESS AND LONG–ARM STATUTES

Interpreting the relevant long-arm statute is only half the job in determining whether a court can exercise jurisdiction over a defendant. Once the meaning of the statute has been determined, we must ask whether the statute, as interpreted, is consistent with the Due Process Clause of the Constitution.

———

McGEE v. INTERNATIONAL LIFE INSURANCE CO., 355 U.S. 220, 222–24, 78 S.Ct. 199, 200–01, 2 L.Ed.2d 223, 225–26 (1957). The plaintiff, McGee, was the beneficiary of a life insurance policy issued by the Empire Mutual Insurance Co., an Arizona corporation, to one Lowell Franklin, a resident of California. In 1948, the defendant, International Life Insurance Co., assumed Empire Mutual's insurance obligations. Franklin and International Life transacted business by mail until Franklin's death in 1950. Neither Empire Mutual nor International Life ever had any office or agent in California, and, as far as the record disclosed, International Life had never solicited or done any insurance business in California other than the policy with Franklin.

When International Life refused to pay McGee upon Franklin's death, she sued in a California state court, basing jurisdiction on the California Unauthorized Insurer's Process Act. The Act subjects foreign corporations to suit on insurance contracts with in-state residents. After recovering a judgment in California, McGee sought to enforce the judgment in Texas. The Texas court refused to enforce the judgment, holding it to be void under the Fourteenth Amendment on the ground that the California courts could not assume jurisdiction over International Life without service of process within its boundaries. The Supreme Court held that the exercise of jurisdiction by California was proper.

The Court noted that, with increased "nationalization of commerce," the tremendous growth "in the amount of business conducted by mail across state lines," and the frequency with which "commercial transactions touch two or more States," there had developed "a trend * * * clearly discernible toward expanding the permissible scope of state jurisdiction over foreign corporations and other nonresidents."

> * * * [W]e think it apparent that the Due Process Clause did not preclude the California court from entering a judgment binding on respondent. It is sufficient * * * that the suit was based on a contract which had substantial connection with that State. * * * The contract was delivered in California, the premiums were mailed from there and the insured was a resident of that State when he died. * * * California has a manifest interest in providing effective means of redress for its residents when their insurers refuse to pay claims. These residents would be at a severe disadvantage if they were forced to follow the insurance company to a distant State in order to hold it legally accountable. When claims were small or moderate individual claimants frequently could not afford the cost of bringing an action in a foreign forum—thus in effect making the company judgment proof. Often the crucial witnesses—as here on the company's defense of suicide—will be found in the insured's locality. Of course there may be inconvenience to the insurer if it is held amenable to suit in California * * * but certainly nothing which amounts to a denial of due process. * * * There is no contention that respondent did not have adequate notice of the suit or sufficient time to prepare its defenses and appear.

NOTES AND QUESTIONS

1. The Court said in *McGee* that improvements in transportation and communication make it less burdensome for out-of-state litigants to defend suits. Did the *McGee* Court modify the *International Shoe* test? Is *McGee* consistent with *International Shoe*?

2. Does *McGee* support the Illinois court's exercise of power in *Gray*, p. 53, supra?

———

HANSON v. DENCKLA, 357 U.S. 235, 78 S.Ct. 1228, 2 L.Ed.2d 1283 (1958). Dora Donner, a resident of Pennsylvania, established a trust in Delaware, naming a Delaware bank as trustee. By the terms of the trust, during her lifetime the income from the trust would go to her and, upon her death, the remainder would pass to whomever she had appointed as beneficiaries. Donner retained the power to change the appointed beneficiaries at any time.

Later, Donner moved to Florida, and, several years before her death, she executed her last will and testament, leaving most of her estate to two of her daughters, Katherine and Dorothy. On the same day, she executed (for the last time) her power to change the appointed beneficiaries under the Delaware trust—this time, she designated two of her grandchildren (the children of a third daughter, Elizabeth) the beneficiaries of a significant portion of the trust's assets, with the remainder going to her estate.

After Donner's death, Katherine and Dorothy, the two daughters named in the will, brought an action in Florida claiming that the appointment of their sister's children as beneficiaries of the trust had been ineffective. If that were true, the assets of the trust would pass under the will to the two daughters, as legatees.

The trust beneficiaries argued that the suit could not go forward because the Florida court could not assert jurisdiction over the Delaware trustee, an indispensable party under Florida law.

The Florida court found that it had jurisdiction over the trustee, concluded that the trust was invalid and that the exercise of the power of appointment was ineffective to pass title, and held that the trust property therefore passed under the will. Before the Florida judgment was rendered, Elizabeth, as executrix of the estate, commenced an action in Delaware to determine who was entitled to share the trust assets, which were situated in Delaware. With minor exceptions, the parties were the same as in the Florida action. When the Florida judgment was rendered, the legatees under the will unsuccessfully urged it as res judicata of the Delaware action. The Delaware court ultimately held the trust and the exercise of the power of appointment valid under Delaware law.

Accepting both cases for review, a divided Supreme Court found that because the trustee's contacts with Florida had been less than minimal, that state could not assert personal jurisdiction over it. Since Florida had not obtained personal jurisdiction over the trustee, an indispensable party to the action, Delaware was justified in refusing full faith and credit to the Florida decree. Writing for a majority of five, Chief Justice Warren explained that:

> * * * [T]he requirements for personal jurisdiction over nonresidents have evolved from the rigid rule of Pennoyer v. Neff * * * to the flexible standard of International Shoe Co. v. State of Washington * * *. But it is a mistake to assume that this trend heralds the eventual demise of all restrictions on the personal jurisdiction of state courts. * * * Those restrictions are more than a guarantee of immunity from inconvenient or distant litigation. They are a consequence of territorial limitations on the power of the respective States. However minimal the burden of defending in a foreign tribunal, a defendant may not be called upon to do so unless he has had the "minimal contacts" with that State that are a prerequisite to its exercise of power over him. * * *

> We fail to find such contacts in the circumstances of this case. The defendant trust company has no office in Florida, and transacts no business there. None of the trust assets has ever been held or administered in Florida, and the record discloses no solicitation of business in that State either in person or by mail. * * *

The cause of action in this case is not one that arises out of an act done or transaction consummated in the forum State. * * * From Florida Mrs. Donner carried on several bits of trust administration that may be compared to the mailing of premiums in *McGee*. But the record discloses no instance in which the trustee performed any acts in Florida that bear the same relationship to the agreement as the solicitation in *McGee*. Consequently, this suit cannot be said to be one to enforce an obligation that arose from a privilege the defendant exercised in Florida. * * *

* * * The unilateral activity of those who claim some relationship with a nonresident defendant cannot satisfy the requirement of contact with the forum State. The application of that rule will vary with the quality and nature of the defendant's activity, but it is essential in each case that there be some act by which the defendant purposefully avails itself of the privilege of conducting activities within the forum State, thus invoking the benefits and protections of its laws. * * *

* * * As we understand [Florida's] law, the trustee is an indispensable party over whom the court must acquire jurisdiction before it is empowered to enter judgment in a proceeding affecting the validity of a trust. It does not acquire that jurisdiction by being the "center of gravity" of the controversy, or the most convenient location for litigation. The issue is personal jurisdiction, not choice of law. * * *

Id. at 251–54, 78 S.Ct. at 1238–40, 2 L.Ed.2d at 1296–98.

Justice Black dissented:

In light of the * * * circumstances it seems quite clear to me that there is nothing in the Due Process Clause which denies Florida the right to determine whether [the] appointment was valid as against its statute of wills. * * * Not only was the appointment made in Florida by a domiciliary of Florida, but the primary beneficiaries also lived in that State. In my view it could hardly be denied that Florida had sufficient interest so that a court with jurisdiction might properly apply Florida law, if it chose, to determine whether the appointment was effectual. * * * True, the question whether the law of a State can be applied to a transaction is different from the question whether the courts of that State have jurisdiction to enter a judgment, but the two are often closely related and to a substantial degree depend upon similar considerations. It seems to me that where a transaction has as much relationship to a State as * * * [this] appointment had to Florida its courts ought to have power to adjudicate controversies arising out of that transaction, unless litigation there would impose such a heavy and disproportionate burden on a nonresident defendant that it would offend what this Court has referred to as "traditional notions of fair play and substantial justice." * * * Florida, the home of the principal contenders * * *, was a reasonably convenient forum for all. Certainly there is nothing fundamentally unfair in subjecting the corporate trustee to the jurisdiction of the Florida courts. It chose to maintain business relations with [the settlor] in that State for eight years, regularly communicating with her with respect to the business of the trust including the very appointment in question.

Florida's interest in the validity of [the] appointment is made more emphatic by the fact that her will is being administered in that State. It has traditionally been the rule that the State where a person is domiciled at the time of his death is the proper place to determine the validity of his will, to construe its provisions and to marshal and distribute his personal property. Here Florida was seriously concerned with winding up [this] estate and with finally determining what property was to be distributed under her will. * * *

Id. at 258–59, 78 S.Ct. at 1242–43, 2 L.Ed.2d at 1300–01.

NOTES AND QUESTIONS

1.   Under the last appointment of the trust, the children of Donner's third daughter Elizabeth would have received about $400,000 from the trust. Donner's other two daughters, the residual legatees under the will, would have received over $1,000,000 from the estate. The Florida decision would have invalidated the last appointment over the trust, defeated Donner's estate plan, and added $400,000 to the amount received by Elizabeth's sisters at the expense of Elizabeth's family.

2.   When can a state assert a sufficient "interest" in a dispute to support the exercise of jurisdiction over a nonresident defendant? Could the *Hanson* decision be justified on the ground that Delaware, as the state where the trust was validly established (at least under Delaware law), had a stronger interest in the disposition of the trust's funds than Florida? Delaware's interest certainly is sufficient to support jurisdiction in Delaware, but was it sufficient to preclude jurisdiction in Florida? Compare California's interests in *McGee*, in which jurisdiction was upheld, with Florida's interests in *Hanson*, in which jurisdiction was denied. What defines a state "interest" sufficient to support jurisdiction?

3.   In their opinions in *Hanson*, the Chief Justice and Justice Black agree that the question whether a court may apply its own law to a controversy is to be decided by a standard that differs from that used to decide the question whether the court can adjudicate the controversy at all. That is, the constitutional power to apply local law is of a different dimension from the constitutional power to assert jurisdiction.

4.   Do you think it appropriate to allow a court to adjudicate any controversy to which it might apply local law under the applicable choice-of-law rule? In ALLSTATE INSURANCE CO. v. HAGUE, 449 U.S. 302, 312–13, 101 S.Ct. 633, 640, 66 L.Ed.2d 521, 531 (1981), the plurality opinion held that "for a State's substantive law to be selected in a constitutionally permissible manner, that State must have a significant contact or significant aggregation of contacts, creating state interests, such that choice of its law is neither arbitrary nor fundamentally unfair." Under this test, the plurality upheld Minnesota's decision to apply its own law in an action by a former Wisconsin

resident who moved to Minnesota just prior to filing suit to collect proceeds under an automobile insurance policy made in Wisconsin covering vehicles owned by a Wisconsin resident who had been killed in an accident in Wisconsin. After *Hague* it seems clear that the Due Process Clause allows states extraordinary latitude in developing and applying choice-of-law rules. The due process restrictions on state jurisdiction are considerably greater than those on choice of law.

5.   Does *Hanson* support the exercise of personal jurisdiction in *Gray*, p. 53, supra?

_____

WORLD-WIDE VOLKSWAGEN CORP. v. WOODSON

Supreme Court of the United States, 1980.
444 U.S. 286, 100 S.Ct. 559, 62 L.Ed.2d 490.

Certiorari to the Supreme Court of Oklahoma.

MR. JUSTICE WHITE delivered the opinion of the Court.

The issue before us is whether, consistently with the Due Process Clause of the Fourteenth Amendment, an Oklahoma court may exercise *in personam* jurisdiction over a nonresident automobile retailer and its wholesale distributor in a products liability action, when the defendants' only connection with Oklahoma is the fact that an automobile sold in New York to New York residents became involved in an accident in Oklahoma.

I

Respondents Harry and Kay Robinson purchased a new Audi automobile from petitioner Seaway Volkswagen, Inc. (Seaway) in Massena, N.Y., in 1976. The following year the Robinson family, who resided in New York, left that State for a new home in Arizona. As they passed through the State of Oklahoma, another car struck their Audi in the rear, causing a fire which severely burned Kay Robinson and her two children.

The Robinsons subsequently brought a products liability action in the District Court for Creek County, Okla., claiming that their injuries resulted from defective design and placement of the Audi's gas tank and fuel system. They joined as defendants the automobile's manufacturer, Audi NSU Auto Union Aktiengesellschaft (Audi); its importer, Volkswagen of America, Inc. (Volkswagen); its regional distributor, petitioner World-Wide Volkswagen Corporation (World-Wide); and its retail dealer, petitioner Seaway. Seaway and World-Wide entered special appearances, claiming that Oklahoma's exercise of jurisdiction over them would offend the limitations on the State's jurisdiction imposed by the Due Process Clause of the Fourteenth Amendment.

The facts presented to the District Court showed that World–Wide is incorporated and has its business office in New York. It distributes vehicles, parts, and accessories, under contract with Volkswagen, to retail dealers in New York, New Jersey, and Connecticut. Seaway, one of these retail dealers, is incorporated and has its place of business in New York. Insofar as the record reveals, Seaway and World-Wide are fully independent corporations whose relations with each other and with Volkswagen and Audi are contractual only. Respondents adduced no evidence that either World-Wide or Seaway does any business in Oklahoma, ships or sells any products to or in that State, has an agent to receive process there, or purchases advertisements in any media calculated to reach Oklahoma. In fact, * * * there was no showing that any automobile sold by World-Wide or Seaway has ever entered Oklahoma with the single exception of the vehicle involved in the present case.

Despite the apparent paucity of contacts between petitioners and Oklahoma, the District Court rejected their constitutional claim and reaffirmed that ruling in denying petitioners' motion for reconsideration. Petitioners then sought a writ of prohibition in the Supreme Court of Oklahoma to restrain the District Judge, respondent Charles S. Woodson, from exercising *in personam* jurisdiction over them. They renewed their contention that, because they had no "minimal contacts" * * * with the State of Oklahoma, the actions of the District Judge were in violation of their rights under the Due Process Clause.

The Supreme Court of Oklahoma denied the writ, * * * holding that personal jurisdiction over petitioners was authorized by Oklahoma's "long-arm" statute, Okla. Stat. Tit. 12, § 1701.03(a)(4) (1971).[7] Although the court noted that the proper approach was to test jurisdiction against both statutory and constitutional standards, its analysis did not distinguish these questions, probably because § 1701.03(a)(4) has been interpreted as conferring jurisdiction to the limits permitted by the United States Constitution. The court's rationale was contained in the following paragraph * * *:

> In the case before us, the product being sold and distributed by the petitioners is by its very design and purpose so mobile that petitioners can foresee its possible use in Oklahoma. This is especially true of the distributor, who has the exclusive right to distribute such automobile in New York, New Jersey and Connecticut. The evidence presented below demonstrated that goods sold and distributed by the petitioners were used in the State of Oklahoma, and under the facts we believe it reasonable to infer, given the retail value of the automobile, that the petitioners derive substantial income from automobiles which from time to time are used in the State of Oklahoma. This being the case, we hold that under the facts presented, the trial court was justified in

---

7. This subsection provides:

"A court may exercise personal jurisdiction over a person, who acts directly or by an agent, as to a cause of action or claim for relief arising from the person's * * * causing tortious injury in this state by an act or omission outside this state if he regularly does or solicits business or engages in any other persistent course of conduct, or derives substantial revenue from goods used or consumed or services rendered, in this state * * *." * * *

concluding that the petitioners derive substantial revenue from goods used or consumed in this State.

We granted certiorari * * * to consider an important constitutional question with respect to state-court jurisdiction and to resolve a conflict between the Supreme Court of Oklahoma and the highest courts of at least four other States. We reverse.

II

* * *

As has long been settled, and as we reaffirm today, a state court may exercise personal jurisdiction over a nonresident defendant only so long as there exist "minimum contacts" between the defendant and the forum State. International Shoe Co. v. Washington, [p. 46, supra,] * * *. The concept of minimum contacts, in turn, can be seen to perform two related, but distinguishable, functions. It protects the defendant against the burdens of litigating in a distant or inconvenient forum. And it acts to ensure that the States, through their courts, do not reach out beyond the limits imposed on them by their status as coequal sovereigns in a federal system.

The protection against inconvenient litigation is typically described in terms of "reasonableness" or "fairness." We have said that the defendant's contacts with the forum State must be such that maintenance of the suit "does not offend 'traditional notions of fair play and substantial justice.' " * * * The relationship between the defendant and the forum must be such that it is "reasonable * * * to require the corporation to defend the particular suit which is brought there." * * * Implicit in this emphasis on reasonableness is the understanding that the burden on the defendant, while always a primary concern, will in an appropriate case be considered in light of other relevant factors, including the forum State's interest in adjudicating the dispute * * *; the plaintiff's interest in obtaining convenient and effective relief, * * * at least when that interest is not adequately protected by the plaintiff's power to choose the forum * * *; the interstate judicial system's interest in obtaining the most efficient resolution of controversies; and the shared interest of the several States in furthering fundamental substantive social policies * * *.

The limits imposed on state jurisdiction by the Due Process Clause, in its role as a guarantor against inconvenient litigation, have been substantially relaxed over the years.* * * Nevertheless, we have never accepted the proposition that state lines are irrelevant for jurisdictional purposes, nor could we, and remain faithful to the principles of interstate federalism embodied in the Constitution. * * *

* * *

* * * Even if the defendant would suffer minimal or no inconvenience from being forced to litigate before the tribunals of another State; even if the forum State has a strong interest in applying its law to the controversy; even if the forum State is the most convenient location for litigation,

the Due Process Clause, acting as an instrument of interstate federalism, may sometimes act to divest the State of its power to render a valid judgment. Hanson v. Denckla, [p. 57, supra] * * *.

III

Applying these principles to the case at hand, we find in the record before us a total absence of those affiliating circumstances that are a necessary predicate to any exercise of state-court jurisdiction. Petitioners carry on no activity whatsoever in Oklahoma. They close no sales and perform no services there. They avail themselves of none of the privileges and benefits of Oklahoma law. They solicit no business there either through salespersons or through advertising reasonably calculated to reach the State. Nor does the record show that they regularly sell cars at wholesale or retail to Oklahoma customers or residents or that they indirectly, through others, serve or seek to serve the Oklahoma market. In short, respondents seek to base jurisdiction on one, isolated occurrence and whatever inferences can be drawn therefrom: the fortuitous circumstance that a single Audi automobile, sold in New York to New York residents, happened to suffer an accident while passing through Oklahoma.

It is argued, however, that because an automobile is mobile by its very design and purpose it was "foreseeable" that the Robinsons' Audi would cause injury in Oklahoma. Yet "foreseeability" alone has never been a sufficient benchmark for personal jurisdiction under the Due Process Clause. In Hanson v. Denckla * * * it was no doubt foreseeable that the settlor of a Delaware trust would subsequently move to Florida and seek to exercise a power of appointment there; yet we held that Florida courts could not constitutionally exercise jurisdiction over a Delaware trustee that had no other contacts with the forum State. * * *

If foreseeability were the criterion, a local California tire retailer could be forced to defend in Pennsylvania when a blowout occurs there, * * * a Wisconsin seller of a defective automobile jack could be haled before a distant court for damage caused in New Jersey, * * * or a Florida soft-drink concessionaire could be summoned to Alaska to account for injuries happening there * * *. Every seller of chattels would in effect appoint the chattel his agent for service of process. His amenability to suit would travel with the chattel. * * *

This is not to say, of course, that foreseeability is wholly irrelevant. But the foreseeability that is critical to due process analysis is not the mere likelihood that a product will find its way into the forum State. Rather, it is that the defendant's conduct and connection with the forum State are such that he should reasonably anticipate being haled into court there. * * * The Due Process Clause, by ensuring the "orderly administration of the laws," * * * gives a degree of predictability to the legal system that allows potential defendants to structure their primary conduct with some minimum assurance as to where that conduct will and will not render them liable to suit.

When a corporation "purposefully avails itself of the privilege of conducting activities within the forum State," * * * it has clear notice that it is subject to suit there, and can act to alleviate the risk of burdensome litigation by procuring insurance, passing the expected costs on to customers, or, if the risks are too great, severing its connection with the State. Hence if the sale of a product of a manufacturer or distributor such as Audi or Volkswagen is not simply an isolated occurrence, but arises from the efforts of the manufacturer or distributor to serve, directly or indirectly, the market for its product in other States, it is not unreasonable to subject it to suit in one of those States if its allegedly defective merchandise has there been the source of injury to its owner or to others. The forum State does not exceed its powers under the Due Process Clause if it asserts personal jurisdiction over a corporation that delivers its products into the stream of commerce with the expectation that they will be purchased by consumers in the forum State. * * *

But there is no such or similar basis for Oklahoma jurisdiction over World-Wide or Seaway in this case. Seaway's sales are made in Massena, N.Y. World-Wide's market, although substantially larger, is limited to dealers in New York, New Jersey, and Connecticut. There is no evidence of record that any automobiles distributed by World-Wide are sold to retail customers outside this tristate area. It is foreseeable that the purchasers of automobiles sold by World-Wide and Seaway may take them to Oklahoma. But the mere "unilateral activity of those who claim some relationship with a nonresident defendant cannot satisfy the requirement of contact with the forum State." Hanson v. Denckla * * *.

In a variant on the previous argument, it is contended that jurisdiction can be supported by the fact that petitioners earn substantial revenue from goods used in Oklahoma. * * * While this inference seems less than compelling on the facts of the instant case, we need not question the court's factual findings in order to reject its reasoning.

This argument seems to make the point that the purchase of automobiles in New York, from which the petitioners earn substantial revenue, would not occur *but for* the fact that the automobiles are capable of use in distant States like Oklahoma. Respondents observe that the very purpose of an automobile is to travel, and that travel of automobiles sold by petitioners is facilitated by an extensive chain of Volkswagen service centers throughout the country, including some in Oklahoma. However, financial benefits accruing to the defendant from a collateral relation to the forum State will not support jurisdiction if they do not stem from a constitutionally cognizable contact with that State. * * * In our view, whatever marginal revenues petitioners may receive by virtue of the fact that their products are capable of use in Oklahoma is far too attenuated a contact to justify that State's exercise of *in personam* jurisdiction over them.

Because we find that petitioners have no "contacts, ties, or relations" with the State of Oklahoma, International Shoe Co. v. Washington, * * * the judgment of the Supreme Court of Oklahoma is

Reversed.

[The dissenting opinions of JUSTICE MARSHALL and JUSTICE BLACKMUN are omitted.]

MR. JUSTICE BRENNAN, dissenting.

* * *

I

The Court's opinions focus tightly on the existence of contacts between the forum and the defendant. In so doing, they accord too little weight to the strength of the forum State's interest in the case and fail to explore whether there would be any actual inconvenience to the defendant. The essential inquiry in locating the constitutional limits on state-court jurisdiction over absent defendants is whether the particular exercise of jurisdiction offends " 'traditional notions of fair play and substantial justice.' " * * * The clear focus in *International Shoe* was on fairness and reasonableness. * * * The Court specifically declined to establish a mechanical test based on the quantum of contacts between a State and the defendant * * *. The existence of contacts, so long as there were some, was merely one way of giving content to the determination of fairness and reasonableness.

Surely *International Shoe* contemplated that the significance of the contacts necessary to support jurisdiction would diminish if some other consideration helped establish that jurisdiction would be fair and reasonable. The interests of the State and other parties in proceeding with the case in a particular forum are such considerations. McGee v. International Life Ins. Co. * * *, for instance, accorded great importance to a State's "manifest interest in providing effective means of redress" for its citizens. * * *

Another consideration is the actual burden a defendant must bear in defending the suit in the forum. * * * Because lesser burdens reduce the unfairness to the defendant, jurisdiction may be justified despite less significant contacts. The burden, of course, must be of constitutional dimension. Due process limits on jurisdiction do not protect a defendant from all inconvenience of travel * * *. Instead, the constitutionally significant "burden" to be analyzed relates to the mobility of the defendant's defense. For instance, if having to travel to a foreign forum would hamper the defense because witnesses or evidence or the defendant himself were immobile, or if there were a disproportionately large number of witnesses or amount of evidence that would have to be transported at the defendant's expense, or if being away from home for the duration of the trial would work some special hardship on the defendant, then the Constitution would require special consideration for the defendant's interests.

That considerations other than contacts between the forum and the defendant are relevant necessarily means that the Constitution does not require that trial be held in the State which has the "best contacts" with the defendant. * * * The defendant has no constitutional entitlement to the best forum or, for that matter, to any particular forum. Under even the most restrictive view of *International Shoe*, several States could have jurisdiction over a particular cause of action. We need only determine whether the forum States in these cases satisfy the constitutional minimum.

II

* * * I would find that the forum State has an interest in permitting the litigation to go forward, the litigation is connected to the forum, the defendant is linked to the forum, and the burden of defending is not unreasonable. Accordingly, I would hold that it is neither unfair nor unreasonable to require these defendants to defend in the forum State.

* * *

* * * [T]he interest of the forum State and its connection to the litigation is strong. The automobile accident underlying the litigation occurred in Oklahoma. The plaintiffs were hospitalized in Oklahoma when they brought suit. Essential witnesses and evidence were in Oklahoma. * * * The State has a legitimate interest in enforcing its laws designed to keep its highway system safe, and the trial can proceed at least as efficiently in Oklahoma as anywhere else.

The petitioners are not unconnected with the forum. Although both sell automobiles within limited sales territories, each sold the automobile which in fact was driven to Oklahoma where it was involved in an accident. It may be true, as the Court suggests, that each sincerely intended to limit its commercial impact to the limited territory, and that each intended to accept the benefits and protection of the laws only of those States within the territory. But obviously these were unrealistic hopes that cannot be treated as an automatic constitutional shield.

An automobile simply is not a stationary item or one designed to be used in one place. An automobile is *intended* to be moved around. Someone in the business of selling large numbers of automobiles can hardly plead ignorance of their mobility or pretend that the automobiles stay put after they are sold. It is not merely that a dealer in automobiles foresees that they will move. * * * The dealer actually intends that the purchasers will use the automobiles to travel to distant States where the dealer does not directly "do business." The sale of an automobile does *purposefully* inject the vehicle into the stream of interstate commerce so that it can travel to distant States. * * *

The Court accepts that a State may exercise jurisdiction over a distributor which "serves" that State "indirectly" by "deliver[ing] its products into the stream of commerce with the expectation that they will be purchased by consumers in the forum State." * * * It is difficult to see why the Constitution should distinguish between a case involving goods which reach a distant State through a chain of distribution and a case involving goods which reach the same State because a consumer, using them as the dealer knew the customer would, took them there. In each case the seller purposefully injects the goods into the stream of commerce and those goods predictably are used in the forum State. * * *

* * *

III

It may be that affirmance of the judgments in these cases would approach the outer limits of *International Shoe*'s jurisdictional principle. But that principle, with its almost exclusive focus on the rights of defendants, may be outdated. * * *

International Shoe inherited its defendant focus from Pennoyer v. Neff * * * and represented the last major step this Court has taken in the long process of liberalizing the doctrine of personal jurisdiction. Though its flexible approach represented a major advance, the structure of our society has changed in many significant ways since *International Shoe* was decided in 1945. * * * As the Court acknowledges, * * * both the nationalization of commerce and the ease of transportation and communication have accelerated in the generation since 1957. The model of society on which the *International Shoe* Court based its opinion is no longer accurate. Business people, no matter how local their businesses, cannot assume that goods remain in the business' locality. Customers and goods can be anywhere else in the country usually in a matter of hours and always in a matter of a very few days.

In answering the question whether or not it is fair and reasonable to allow a particular forum to hold a trial binding on a particular defendant, the interests of the forum State and other parties loom large in today's world and surely are entitled to as much weight as are the interests of the defendant. The "orderly administration of the laws" provides a firm basis for according some protection to the interests of plaintiffs and States as well as of defendants. Certainly, I cannot see how a defendant's right to due process is violated if the defendant suffers no inconvenience. * * *

The conclusion I draw is that constitutional concepts of fairness no longer require the extreme concern for defendants that was once necessary. Rather, * * * minimum contacts must exist "among the *parties*, the contested transaction, and the forum State."[15] The contacts between any two of these should not be determinative. * * *

In effect the Court is allowing defendants to assert the sovereign rights of their home States. The expressed fear is that otherwise all limits on personal jurisdiction would disappear. But the argument's premise is wrong. I would not abolish limits on jurisdiction or strip state boundaries of all significance * * *; I would still require the plaintiff to demonstrate

---

15. In some cases, the inquiry will resemble the inquiry commonly undertaken in determining which State's law to apply. That it is fair to apply a State's law to a nonresident defendant is clearly relevant in determining whether it is fair to subject the defendant to jurisdiction in that State. * * *

sufficient contacts among the parties, the forum, and the litigation to make the forum a reasonable State in which to hold the trial.

I would also, however, strip the defendant of an unjustified veto power over certain very appropriate fora—a power the defendant justifiably enjoyed long ago when communication and travel over long distances were slow and unpredictable and when notions of state sovereignty were impractical and exaggerated. * * *

NOTES AND QUESTIONS

1. At the time the suit was filed, Kay Robinson and her two children, Sam and Eva, were hospitalized with severe burns:

> Since Kay Robinson had been trapped in the burning car the longest, her burns were the most horrible of all. She had burns on forty-eight percent of her body—thirty-five percent of which were third degree. Kay was in the intensive care unit for seventy-seven days and was hospitalized in Tulsa for another several months. She underwent thirty-four operations, all but two of which were under general anesthetic, for skin grafts and other reconstructive surgery. Most of her fingers were amputated, and she had severe scarring over the entire part of her body. Eva and Kay also suffered severe psychological trauma both from the ordeal and from their permanent disfigurement.

See Adams, World-Wide Volkswagen v. Woodson—*The Rest of the Story*, 72 Neb. L. Rev. 1122, 1127 (1993).

2. In the course of its *World-Wide Volkswagen* opinion, the Court employed notions of sovereignty and of convenience. Is there a tension between these two notions? Is the Court promulgating a two-part test with a "sovereignty branch" and a "convenience branch"? Is this a new test or a refinement of the "minimum contacts" test announced in *International Shoe*?

3. How might *World-Wide Volkswagen* have been decided if the Robinsons had been Oklahoma residents and had purchased the ill-fated car while in New York on vacation? Would the Justices in the majority have given more weight to plaintiff's foreseeability argument? What if the driver of the other car sued World-Wide and Seaway for injuries resulting from the exploding gas tank? What if that driver never had been outside the state of Oklahoma?

4. In KEETON v. HUSTLER MAGAZINE, INC., 465 U.S. 770, 104 S.Ct. 1473, 79 L.Ed.2d 790 (1984), Kathy Keeton, a resident of New York, brought a libel suit against Hustler Magazine, an Ohio corporation, in federal district court in New Hampshire. Keeton chose the New Hampshire court because New Hampshire was the only state where the action was not time-barred by a statute of limitations when it was filed. She argued that jurisdiction existed under New Hampshire's long-arm statute because Hustler sold 10,000 to 15,000 magazines a month in the state. Keeton herself had only one connection to New Hampshire: a magazine that she helped to produce was circulated there.

The District Court dismissed Keeton's suit for lack of jurisdiction, and the First Circuit affirmed, holding that Keeton's lack of contacts with New

Hampshire rendered the state's interest in redressing the libel to the plaintiff too attenuated to support jurisdiction over a suit necessarily involving nationwide damages.

The Supreme Court unanimously reversed, saying:

> [R]egular monthly sales of thousands of magazines cannot by any stretch of the imagination be characterized as random, isolated, or fortuitous. It is, therefore, unquestionable that New Hampshire jurisdiction over a complaint based on those contacts could ordinarily satisfy the requirement of the Due Process Clause that a State's assertion of personal jurisdiction over a nonresident defendant be predicated on "minimum contacts" between the defendant and the State. And, as the Court of Appeals acknowledged, New Hampshire has adopted a "long-arm" statute authorizing service of process on nonresident corporations whenever permitted by the Due Process Clause. Thus, all the requisites for personal jurisdiction over Hustler Magazine, Inc., in New Hampshire are present.

Id. at 774–75, 104 S.Ct. at 1478, 79 L.Ed.2d at 797. Is the key to the Court's decision in *Keeton* that the defendants intentionally acted in the forum?

5.   In CALDER v. JONES, 465 U.S. 783, 104 S.Ct. 1482, 79 L.Ed.2d 804 (1984), Shirley Jones, an actress who lived and worked in California, brought suit in California Superior Court, claiming that she had been libeled in an article published in the National Enquirer, a national magazine having its largest circulation in California. Plaintiff sued the writer and editor of the article, both residents of Florida, as well as the magazine. The writer and the editor moved to quash service of process for lack of personal jurisdiction, and the Superior Court granted the motion on the ground that the First Amendment imposed a significant limitation upon the exercise of jurisdiction over defendants whose rights of expression might thereby be compromised. Ultimately, the United States Supreme Court disagreed, saying, "We * * * reject the suggestion that First Amendment concerns enter into jurisdictional analysis." Given that the writer and editor had acted intentionally to produce an article for dissemination in California, the Court had no trouble finding that they could foresee being haled into court there. The Court explained:

> The allegedly libelous story concerned the California activities of a California resident. It impugned the professionalism of an entertainer whose television career was centered in California. The article was drawn from California sources, and the brunt of the harm, in terms both of respondent's emotional distress and the injury to her professional reputation, was suffered in California. In sum, California, is the focal point both of the story and of the harm suffered. Jurisdiction over petitioners is therefore proper in California based on the "effects" of their Florida conduct in California.

Id. at 788–91, 104 S.Ct. at 1486–88, 79 L.Ed.2d at 812–13.

———

KULKO v. SUPERIOR COURT, 436 U.S. 84, 98 S.Ct. 1690, 56 L.Ed.2d 132 (1978), was a suit for modification of a child support agreement by a California citizen against her ex-husband, a New Yorker. Under the couple's separation agreement, the father had custody of their two children in New York. However, when the daughter told defendant that she wanted to live with her mother, he assented and bought her a one-way plane ticket to California. Later, the son joined his mother in California, without defendant's knowledge.

The California Supreme Court upheld jurisdiction over the defendant husband under the California long-arm statute, which authorized the exercise of jurisdiction "on any basis not inconsistent with the Constitution." The court concluded that it was "fair and reasonable" for the New York defendant to be subject to personal jurisdiction in California because by purchasing his daughter's airline ticket, he had committed a "purposeful act" outside the state that caused an effect within the state. The United States Supreme Court reversed:

> * * * We cannot accept the proposition that appellant's acquiescence in * * * [his daughter's] desire to live with her mother conferred jurisdiction over appellant in the California courts in this action. A father who agrees, in the interests of family harmony and his children's preferences, to allow them to spend more time in California than was required under a separation agreement can hardly be said to have "purposefully availed himself" of the "benefits and protections" of California's laws. * * *

> Nor can we agree with the assertion of the court below that the exercise of *in personam* jurisdiction here was warranted by the financial benefit appellant derived from his daughter's presence in California for nine months of the year. * * * [T]his circumstance, even if true, does not support California's assertion of jurisdiction here. Any diminution in appellant's household costs resulted, not from the child's presence in California, but rather from her absence from appellant's home.

Id. at 94–95, 98 S.Ct. at 1698, 56 L.Ed.2d at 142–43.

The Court also noted that the California court's reliance on the "effects" test was misplaced because that approach applies only to wrongful activity done outside the state causing injury inside the state, or to commercial activity affecting state residents. Moreover, the Court emphasized that in the circumstances of this case it would be unreasonable to assert jurisdiction based on the effects of the nonresident defendant's out-of-state acts in California for defendant had not purposefully availed himself of the benefit of the forum state's laws. Do you agree with the Court's analysis?

NOTE AND QUESTION

The Ninth Circuit has applied a three-prong "effects" test, under which minimum contacts may be found "if the defendant is alleged to have (1) committed an intentional act; (2) expressly aimed at the forum state; (3) causing harm, the brunt of which is suffered—and which the defendant knows is likely to be suffered—in the forum state." HARRIS RUTSKY & CO. INS. SERVS., INC. v. BELL & CLEMENTS LTD., 328 F.3d 1122 (9th Cir. 2003). Can you reconcile this approach with the purposeful availment requirement articulated in Hanson v. Denckla, p. 57, supra?

BURGER KING CORP. v. RUDZEWICZ

Supreme Court of the United States, 1985.
471 U.S. 462, 105 S.Ct. 2174, 85 L.Ed.2d 528.

[Burger King is a Florida corporation whose principal offices are in Miami. Franchisees are licensed to use its trademarks and service marks in leased standardized restaurant facilities for a period of twenty years. The governing contracts provide that the franchise relationship is established in Miami and governed by Florida law and call for payment of all required monthly fees and forwarding of all relevant notices to the Miami headquarters. The Miami headquarters sets policy and works directly with the franchisees in attempting to resolve major problems. Day-to-day monitoring of franchisees, however, is conducted through district offices that in turn report to the Miami headquarters. John Rudzewicz is a Michigan resident who, along with another Michigan resident (Brian MacShara), entered into a twenty-year franchise contract with Burger King to operate a restaurant in Michigan. Subsequently, when the restaurant's patronage declined, the franchisees fell behind in their monthly payments. Burger King then brought a diversity action in federal District Court in Florida, alleging that the franchisees had breached their franchise obligations and requesting damages and injunctive relief. The franchisees claimed that, because they were Michigan residents and because Burger King's claim did not "arise" within Florida, the District Court lacked personal jurisdiction over them. But the court held that the franchisees were subject to personal jurisdiction pursuant to Florida's long-arm statute, which extends jurisdiction to any person, whether or not a citizen or resident of the State, who breaches a contract in the State by failing to perform acts that the contract requires to be performed there. Thereafter, the court entered judgment against the franchisees on the merits. The Court of Appeals reversed, holding that "[j]urisdiction under these circumstances would offend the fundamental fairness which is the touchstone of due process," but the Supreme Court disagreed.]

Appeal from the United States Court of Appeals for the Eleventh Circuit.

Justice Brennan delivered the opinion of the Court.

[Part I of the opinion includes a lengthy recitation of the facts and is omitted.]

II

A

* * *

Th[e] "purposeful availment" requirement ensures that a defendant will not be haled into a jurisdiction solely as a result of "random," "fortuitous," or "attenuated" contacts, * * * or of the "unilateral activity of another party or a third person" * * *. Jurisdiction is proper, however, where the contacts proximately result from actions by the defendant *himself* that create a "substantial connection" with the forum State. * * * Thus where the defendant "deliberately" has engaged in significant activities within a State, * * * or has created "continuing obligations" between himself and residents of the forum, * * * he manifestly has availed himself of the privilege of conducting business there, and because his activities are shielded by "the benefits and protections" of the forum's laws it is presumptively not unreasonable to require him to submit to the burdens of litigation in that forum as well. * * *

Once it has been decided that a defendant purposefully established minimum contacts within the forum State, these contacts may be considered in light of other factors to determine whether the assertion of personal jurisdiction would comport with "fair play and substantial justice." * * *

B

(1)

Applying these principles to the case at hand, we believe there is substantial record evidence supporting the District Court's conclusion that the assertion of personal jurisdiction over Rudzewicz in Florida for the alleged breach of his franchise agreement did not offend due process. At the outset, we note a continued division among lower courts respecting whether and to what extent a contract can constitute a "contact" for purposes of due process analysis. If the question is whether an individual's contract with an out-of-state party *alone* can automatically establish sufficient minimum contacts in the other party's home forum, we believe the answer clearly is that it cannot. The Court long ago rejected the notion that personal jurisdiction might turn on "mechanical" tests, or on "conceptualistic * * * theories of the place of contracting or of performance" * * *. Instead, we have emphasized the need for a "highly realistic" approach that recognizes that a "contract" is "ordinarily but an intermediate step serving to tie up prior business negotiations with future consequences which themselves are the real object of the business transaction." * * * It is these factors—prior negotiations and contemplated future consequences, along with the terms of the contract and the parties' actual course of dealing—that must be evaluated in determining whether the defendant purposefully established minimum contacts within the forum.

In this case, no physical ties to Florida can be attributed to Rudzewicz other than MacShara's brief training course in Miami. * * * Rudzewicz did not maintain offices in Florida and, for all that appears from the record, has never even visited there. Yet this franchise dispute grew directly out of "a contract which had a *substantial* connection with that State." McGee, [p. 56, supra]. * * *. Eschewing the option of operating an independent local enterprise, Rudzewicz deliberately "reach[ed] out beyond" Michigan and negotiated with a Florida corporation for the purchase of a long-term franchise and the manifold benefits that would derive from affiliation with a nationwide organization. * * * Upon approval, he entered into a carefully structured 20–year relationship that envisioned continuing and wide-reaching contacts with Burger King in Florida. In light of Rudzewicz's voluntary acceptance of the long-term and exacting regulation of his business from Burger King's Miami headquarters, the "quality and nature" of his relationship to the company in Florida can in no sense be viewed as "random," "fortuitous," or "attenuated." * * * Rudzewicz's refusal to make the contractually required payments in Miami, and his continued use of Burger King's trademarks and confidential business information after his termination, caused foreseeable injuries to the corporation in Florida. * * *

* * * Rudzewicz most certainly knew that he was affiliating himself with an enterprise based primarily in Florida. The contract documents themselves emphasize that Burger King's operations are conducted and supervised from the Miami headquarters, that all relevant notices and payments must be sent there, and that the agreements were made in and enforced from Miami. * * * Moreover, the parties' actual course of dealing repeatedly confirmed that decisionmaking authority was vested in the Miami headquarters and that the district office served largely as an intermediate link between the headquarters and the franchisees. * * *

Moreover, * * * provisions in the various franchise documents provid[ed] that all disputes would be governed by Florida law. * * * The Court of Appeals reasoned that choice-of-law provisions are irrelevant to the question of personal jurisdiction, relying on Hanson v. Denckla [p. 57, supra,] for the proposition that "the center of gravity for choice-of-law purposes does not necessarily confer the sovereign prerogative to assert jurisdiction." * * * This reasoning misperceives the import of the quoted proposition. The Court in *Hanson* and subsequent cases has emphasized that choice-of-law *analysis*—which focuses on all elements of a transaction, and not simply on the defendant's conduct—is distinct from minimum-contacts jurisdictional analysis—which focuses at the threshold solely on the defendant's purposeful connection to the forum. Nothing in our cases, however, suggests that a choice-of-law *provision* should be ignored in considering whether a defendant has "purposefully invoked the benefits and protections of a State's laws" for jurisdictional purposes. Although such a provision standing alone would be insufficient to confer jurisdiction, we believe that, when combined with the 20–year interdependent relationship Rudzewicz established with Burger King's Miami headquarters, it reinforced his deliberate affiliation with the forum State and the reasonable foreseeability of possible litigation there. * * *

(2)

Nor has Rudzewicz pointed to other factors that can be said persuasively to outweigh the considerations discussed above and to establish the *unconstitutionality* of Florida's assertion of jurisdiction. We cannot conclude that Florida had no "legitimate interest in holding [Rudzewicz] answerable on a claim related to" the contacts he had established in that State. * * * Moreover, although Rudzewicz has argued at some length that Michigan's Franchise Investment Law * * * governs many aspects of this franchise relationship, he has not demonstrated how Michigan's acknowledged interest might possibly render jurisdiction in Florida *unconstitutional.* * * * Finally, the Court of Appeals' assertion that the Florida litigation "severely impaired [Rudzewicz's] ability to call Michigan witnesses who might be essential to his defense and counterclaim" * * * is wholly without support in the record. * * * Although the Court has suggested that inconvenience may at some point become so substantial as to achieve *constitutional* magnitude, * * * this is not such a case.

The Court of Appeals also concluded, however, that the parties' dealings involved "a characteristic disparity of bargaining power" and "elements of surprise," and that Rudzewicz "lacked fair notice" of the potential for litigation in Florida because the contractual provisions suggesting to the contrary were merely "boilerplate declarations in a lengthy printed contract." * * * After a 3-day bench trial, the District Court found that Burger King had made no misrepresentations, that * * * [defendants] "were and are experienced and sophisticated businessmen," and that "at no time" did they "ac[t] under economic duress or disadvantage imposed by" Burger King. * * * Federal Rule of Civil Procedure 52(a) [now Rule 52(a)(6)] requires that "[f]indings of fact shall not be set aside unless clearly erroneous," and neither Rudzewicz nor the Court of Appeals have pointed to record evidence that would support a "definite and firm conviction" that the District Court's findings are mistaken. * * *

III

Notwithstanding these considerations, the Court of Appeals apparently believed that it was necessary to reject jurisdiction in this case as a prophylactic measure, reasoning that an affirmance of the District Court's judgment would result in the exercise of jurisdiction over "out-of-state consumers to collect payments due on modest personal purchases" and would "sow the seeds of default judgments against franchisees owing smaller debts." * * * We share the Court of Appeals' broader concerns and therefore reject any talismanic jurisdictional formulas; "the facts of each case must [always] be weighed" in determining whether personal jurisdiction would comport with "fair play and substantial justice." * * *

* * * Because Rudzewicz established a substantial and continuing relationship with Burger King's Miami headquarters, received fair notice from the contract documents and the course of dealing that he might be subject to suit in Florida, and has failed to demonstrate how jurisdiction in that forum would otherwise be fundamentally unfair, we conclude that the District Court's exercise of jurisdiction * * * did not offend due process. The judgment of the Court of Appeals is accordingly reversed, and the case is remanded for further proceedings consistent with this opinion.

JUSTICE POWELL took no part in the consideration or decision of this case.

JUSTICE STEVENS, with whom JUSTICE WHITE joins, dissenting.

In my opinion there is a significant element of unfairness in requiring a franchisee to defend a case of this kind in the forum chosen by the franchisor. It is undisputed that respondent maintained no place of business in Florida, that he had no employees in that State, and that he was not licensed to do business there. Respondent did not prepare his french fries, shakes, and hamburgers in Michigan, and then deliver them into the stream of commerce "with the expectation that they [would] be purchased by consumers in" Florida. * * * To the contrary, respondent did business only in Michigan, his business, property, and payroll taxes were payable in that State, and he sold all of his products there.

Throughout the business relationship, respondent's principal contacts with petitioner were with its Michigan office. Notwithstanding its disclaimer, * * * the Court seems ultimately to rely on nothing more than standard boilerplate language contained in various documents * * * to establish that respondent " 'purposefully availed himself of the benefits and protections of Florida's laws.' " * * * Such superficial analysis creates a potential for unfairness not only in negotiations between franchisors and their franchisees but, more significantly, in the resolution of the disputes that inevitably arise from time to time in such relationships.

* * *

Accordingly, I respectfully dissent.

NOTES AND QUESTIONS

1. The First Circuit has described the Supreme Court's decision in *Burger King* as mandating a "contract-plus" analysis: "[A] court is to look at all of the communications and transactions between the parties, before, during and after the consummation of the contract, to determine the degree and type of contacts the defendant has with the forum, apart from the contract alone." Ganis Corp. of Cal. v. Jackson, 822 F.2d 194, 197–98 (1st Cir. 1987). What purpose is served by this "plus" analysis? Is it constitutionally compelled? Should a contract standing alone ever be enough to subject a defendant to jurisdiction?

2. How important to the decision in *Burger King* was the inclusion of the choice-of-law provision in the franchise agreement? Is that type of provision appropriately considered a "contact" with the chosen forum? Is it a "plus" factor? What if the forum has no interest in the contract other than the parties' agreement to be bound by the law of that state?

ASAHI METAL INDUSTRY CO. v. SUPERIOR COURT

Supreme Court of the United States, 1987.
480 U.S. 102, 107 S.Ct. 1026, 94 L.Ed.2d 92.

Certiorari to the Supreme Court of California.

JUSTICE O'CONNOR announced the judgment of the Court and delivered the unanimous opinion of the Court with respect to Part I, the opinion of the Court with respect to Part II–B, in which THE CHIEF JUSTICE, JUSTICE BRENNAN, JUSTICE WHITE, JUSTICE MARSHALL, JUSTICE BLACKMUN, JUSTICE POWELL, and JUSTICE STEVENS join, and an opinion with respect to Parts II–A and III, in which THE CHIEF JUSTICE, JUSTICE POWELL, and JUSTICE SCALIA join.

This case presents the question whether the mere awareness on the part of a foreign defendant that the component it manufactured, sold, and delivered outside the United States would reach the forum state in the stream of commerce constitutes "minimum contacts" between the defendant and the forum state such that the exercise of jurisdiction "does not offend 'traditional notions of fair play and substantial justice.'" * * *

I

On September 23, 1978, on Interstate Highway 80 in Solano County, California, Gary Zurcher lost control of his Honda motorcycle and collided with a tractor. Zurcher was severely injured, and his passenger and wife, Ruth Ann Moreno, was killed. In September 1979, Zurcher filed a product liability action in the Superior Court of the State of California in and for the County of Solano. Zurcher alleged that the 1978 accident was caused by a sudden loss of air and an explosion in the rear tire of the motorcycle, and alleged that the motorcycle tire, tube, and sealant were defective. Zurcher's complaint named, *inter alia*, Cheng Shin Rubber Industrial Co., Ltd. (Cheng Shin), the Taiwanese manufacturer of the tube. Cheng Shin in turn filed a cross-complaint seeking indemnification from its codefendants and from petitioner, Asahi Metal Industry Co., Ltd. (Asahi), the manufacturer of the tube's valve assembly. Zurcher's claims against Cheng Shin and the other defendants were eventually settled and dismissed, leaving only Cheng Shin's indemnity action against Asahi.

California's long-arm statute authorizes the exercise of jurisdiction "on any basis not inconsistent with the Constitution of this state or of the United States." * * * Asahi moved to quash Cheng Shin's service of summons arguing the State could not exert jurisdiction over it consistent with the Due Process Clause of the Fourteenth Amendment.

In relation to the motion, the following information was submitted by Asahi and Cheng Shin. Asahi is a Japanese corporation. It manufactures tire valve assemblies in Japan and sells the assemblies to Cheng Shin, and to several other tire manufacturers, for use as components in finished tire tubes. Asahi's sales to Cheng Shin took place in Taiwan. The shipments from Asahi to Cheng Shin were sent from Japan to Taiwan. Cheng Shin bought and incorporated into its tire tubes 150,000 Asahi valve assemblies in 1978; 500,000 in 1979; 500,000 in 1980; 100,000 in 1981; and 100,000 in 1982. Sales to Cheng Shin accounted for 1.24 percent of Asahi's income in 1981 and 0.44 percent in 1982. Cheng Shin alleged that approximately 20 percent of its sales in the United States are in California. Cheng Shin purchases valve assemblies from other suppliers as well, and sells finished tubes throughout the world.

In 1983 an attorney for Cheng Shin conducted an informal examination of the valve stems of the tire tubes sold in one cyclery in Solano County. The attorney declared that of the approximately 115 tire tubes in the store, 97 were purportedly manufactured in Japan or Taiwan, and of those 97, 21 valve stems were marked with the circled letter "A", apparently Asahi's trademark. Of the 21 Asahi valve stems, 12 were incorporated into Cheng Shin tire tubes. The store contained 41 other Cheng Shin tubes that incorporated the valve assemblies of other manufacturers. * * * An affidavit of a manager of Cheng Shin whose duties included the purchasing of component parts stated: " 'In discussions with Asahi regarding the purchase of valve stem assemblies the fact that my Company sells tubes throughout the world and specifically the United States has been discussed. I am informed and believe that Asahi was fully aware that valve stem assemblies sold to my Company and to others would end up throughout the United States and in California.' " * * * An affidavit of the president of Asahi, on the other hand, declared that Asahi " 'has never contemplated that its limited sales of tire valves to Cheng Shin in Taiwan would subject it to lawsuits in California.' " * * * The record does not include any contract between Cheng Shin and Asahi. * * *

Primarily on the basis of the above information, the Superior Court denied the motion to quash summons, stating that "Asahi obviously does business on an international scale. It is not unreasonable that they defend claims of defect in their product on an international scale." * * *

The Court of Appeal of the State of California issued a peremptory writ of mandate commanding the Superior Court to quash service of summons. The court concluded that "it would be unreasonable to require Asahi to respond in California solely on the basis of ultimately realized foreseeability that the product into which its component was embodied would be sold all over the world including California." * * *

The Supreme Court of the State of California reversed and discharged the writ issued by the Court of Appeal. * * * The court observed that "Asahi has no offices, property or agents in California. It solicits no business in California and has made no direct sales [in California]." * * * Moreover, "Asahi did not design or control the system of distribution that carried its valve assemblies into California." * * * Nevertheless, the court found the exercise of jurisdiction over Asahi to be consistent with the Due Process Clause. It concluded that Asahi knew that some of the valve assemblies sold to Cheng Shin would be incorporated into tire tubes sold in California, and that Asahi benefited indirectly from the sale in California of products incorporating its components. The court considered Asahi's intentional act of placing its components into the stream of commerce—that is, by delivering the components to Cheng Shin in Taiwan—coupled with Asahi's awareness that some of the components would eventually find their way into California, sufficient to form the basis for state court jurisdiction under the Due Process Clause.

We granted certiorari * * * and now reverse.

II

A

* * *

Applying the principle that minimum contacts must be based on an act of the defendant, the Court in World-Wide Volkswagen Corp. v. Woodson * * * rejected the assertion that a *consumer's* unilateral act of bringing the defendant's product into the forum State was a sufficient constitutional basis for personal jurisdiction over the defendant. It had been argued in *World-Wide Volkswagen* that because an automobile retailer and its wholesale distributor sold a product mobile by design and purpose, they could foresee being haled into court in the distant States into which their customers might drive. The Court rejected this concept of foreseeability as an insufficient basis for jurisdiction under the Due Process Clause. * * * The Court disclaimed, however, the idea that "foreseeability is wholly irrelevant" to personal jurisdiction, concluding that "[t]he forum State does not exceed its powers under the Due Process Clause if it asserts personal jurisdiction over a corporation that delivers its products into the stream of commerce with the expectation that they will be purchased by consumers in the forum State." * * *

* * *

In *World-Wide Volkswagen* itself, the state court sought to base jurisdiction not on any act of the defendant, but on the foreseeable unilateral actions of the consumer. Since *World-Wide Volkswagen*, lower courts have been confronted with cases in which the defendant acted by placing a product in the stream of commerce, and the stream eventually swept defendant's product into the forum State, but the defendant did nothing else to purposefully avail itself of the market in the forum state.

Some courts have understood the Due Process Clause, as interpreted in *World-Wide Volkswagen*, to allow an exercise of personal jurisdiction to be based on no more than the defendant's act of placing the product in the stream of commerce. Other courts have understood the Due Process Clause and the above-quoted language in *World-Wide Volkswagen* to require the action of the defendant to be more purposefully directed at the forum State than the mere act of placing a product in the stream of commerce.

The reasoning of the Supreme Court of California in the present case illustrates the former interpretation of *World-Wide Volkswagen*. The Supreme Court of California held that, because the stream of commerce eventually brought some valves Asahi sold Cheng Shin into California, Asahi's awareness that its valves would be sold in California was sufficient to permit California to exercise jurisdiction over Asahi consistent with the requirements of the Due Process Clause. The Supreme Court of California's position was consistent with those courts that have held that mere foreseeability or awareness was a constitutionally sufficient basis for personal jurisdiction if the defendant's product made its way into the forum State while still in the stream of commerce. * * *

Other courts, however, have understood the Due Process Clause to require something more than that the defendant was aware of its product's entry into the forum State through the stream of commerce in order for the state to exert jurisdiction over the defendant. In the present case, for example, the State Court of Appeal did not read the Due Process Clause, as interpreted by *World-Wide Volkswagen*, to allow "mere foreseeability that the product will enter the forum state [to] be enough by itself to establish jurisdiction over the distributor and retailer." * * *

We now find this latter position to be consonant with the requirements of due process. The "substantial connection" * * * between the defendant and the forum State necessary for a finding of minimum contacts must come about by *an action of the defendant purposefully directed toward the forum State.* * * * The placement of a product into the stream of commerce, without more, is not an act of the defendant purposefully directed toward the forum State. Additional conduct of the defendant may indicate an intent or purpose to serve the market in the forum State, for example, designing the product for the market in the forum State, advertising in the forum State, establishing channels for providing regular advice to customers in the forum State, or marketing the product through a distributor who has agreed to serve as the sales agent in the forum State. But a defendant's awareness that the stream of commerce may or will sweep the product into the forum State does not convert the mere act of placing the product into the stream into an act purposefully directed toward the forum State.

Assuming, *arguendo*, that respondents have established Asahi's awareness that some of the valves sold to Cheng Shin would be incorporated into tire tubes sold in California, respondents have not demonstrated any action by Asahi to purposefully avail itself of the California market. Asahi does not do business in California. It has no office, agents, employees, or property in California. It does not advertise or otherwise solicit business in California. It did not create, control, or employ the distribution system that brought its valves to California. * * * There is no evidence that Asahi designed its product in anticipation of sales in California. * * * On the basis of these facts, the exertion of personal jurisdiction over Asahi by the Superior Court of California exceeds the limits of due process.

B

* * *

We have previously explained that the determination of the reasonableness of the exercise of jurisdiction in each case will depend on an evaluation of several factors. A court must consider the burden on the defendant, the interests of the forum state, and the plaintiff's interest in obtaining relief. It must also weigh in its determination "the interstate judicial system's interest in obtaining the most efficient resolution of controversies; and the shared interest of the several States in furthering fundamental substantive social policies." * * *

A consideration of these factors in the present case clearly reveals the unreasonableness of the assertion of jurisdiction over Asahi, even apart from the question of the placement of goods in the stream of commerce.

Certainly the burden on the defendant in this case is severe. Asahi has been commanded by the Supreme Court of California not only to traverse the distance between Asahi's headquarters in Japan and the Superior Court of California in and for the County of Solano, but also to submit its dispute with Cheng Shin to a foreign nation's judicial system. The unique burdens placed upon one who must defend oneself in a foreign legal system should have significant weight in assessing the reasonableness of stretching the long arm of personal jurisdiction over national borders.

When minimum contacts have been established, often the interests of the plaintiff and the forum in the exercise of jurisdiction will justify even the serious burdens placed on the alien defendant. In the present case, however, the interests of the plaintiff and the forum in California's assertion of jurisdiction over Asahi are slight. All that remains is a claim for indemnification asserted by Cheng Shin, a Taiwanese corporation, against Asahi. The transaction on which the indemnification claim is based took place in Taiwan; Asahi's components were shipped from Japan to Taiwan. Cheng Shin has not demonstrated that it is more convenient for it to litigate its indemnification claim against Asahi in California rather than in Taiwan or Japan.

Because the plaintiff is not a California resident, California's legitimate interests in the dispute have considerably diminished. The Supreme Court of California argued that the State had an interest in "protecting its consumers by ensuring that foreign manufacturers comply with the state's safety standards." * * * The State Supreme Court's definition of California's interest, however, was overly broad. The dispute between Cheng Shin and Asahi is primarily about indemnification rather than safety standards. Moreover, it is not at all clear at this point that California law should govern the question whether a Japanese corporation should indemnify a Taiwanese corporation on the basis of a sale made in Taiwan and a shipment of goods from Japan to Taiwan. * * * The possibility of being haled into a California court as a result of an accident involving Asahi's components undoubtedly creates an additional deterrent to the manufacture of unsafe components; however, similar pressures will be placed on Asahi by the purchasers of its components as long as those who use Asahi components in their final products, and sell those products in California, are subject to the application of California tort law.

World-Wide Volkswagen also admonished courts to take into consideration the interests of the "several States," in addition to the forum state, in the efficient judicial resolution of the dispute and the advancement of substantive policies. In the present case, this advice calls for a court to consider the procedural and substantive policies of other *nations* whose interests are affected by the assertion of jurisdiction by the California court. The procedural and substantive interests of other nations in a state court's assertion of jurisdiction over an alien defendant will differ from case to case. In every case, however, those interests, as well as the Federal interest in its foreign relations policies, will be best served by a careful inquiry into the reasonableness of the assertion of jurisdiction in the particular case, and an unwillingness to find the serious burdens on an alien defendant outweighed by minimal interests on the part of the plaintiff or the forum State. "Great care and reserve should be exercised when extending our notions of personal jurisdiction into the international field." * * *

Considering the international context, the heavy burden on the alien defendant, and the slight interests of the plaintiff and the forum State, the exercise of personal jurisdiction by a California court over Asahi in this instance would be unreasonable and unfair.

III

Because the facts of this case do not establish minimum contacts such that the exercise of personal jurisdiction is consistent with fair play and substantial justice, the judgment of Supreme Court of California is reversed, and the case is remanded for further proceedings not inconsistent with this opinion.

It is so ordered.

JUSTICE BRENNAN, with whom JUSTICE WHITE, JUSTICE MARSHALL, and JUSTICE BLACKMUN join, concurring in part and concurring in the judgment.

I do not agree with the interpretation in Part II–A of the stream-of-commerce theory, nor with the conclusion that Asahi did not "purposely avail itself of the California market." * * * I do agree, however, with the Court's conclusion in Part II–B that the exercise of personal jurisdiction over Asahi in this case would not comport with "fair play and substantial justice" * * *. This is one of those rare cases in which "minimum requirements inherent in the concept of 'fair play and substantial justice' ... defeat the reasonableness of jurisdiction even [though] the defendant has purposefully engaged in forum activities." * * * I therefore join Parts I and II–B of the Court's opinion, and write separately to explain my disagreement with Part II–A.

Part II–A states that "a defendant's awareness that the stream of commerce may or will sweep the product into the forum State does not convert the mere act of placing the product into the stream into an act purposefully directed toward the forum State." * * * Under this view, a plaintiff would be required to show "[a]dditional conduct" directed toward the forum before finding the exercise of jurisdiction over the defendant to be consistent with the Due Process Clause. * * * I see no need for such a showing, however. The stream of commerce refers not to unpredictable currents or eddies, but to the regular and anticipated flow of products from manufacture to distribution to retail sale. As long as a participant in this process is aware that the final product is being marketed in the forum State, the possibility of a lawsuit there cannot come as a surprise. Nor will the litigation present a burden for which there is no corresponding benefit. A defendant who has placed goods in the stream of commerce benefits economically from the retail sale of the final product in the forum State, and indirectly benefits from the State's laws that regulate and facilitate commercial activity. These benefits accrue regardless of whether that participant directly conducts business in the forum State, or engages in additional conduct directed toward that State. Accordingly, most courts and commentators have found that jurisdiction premised on the placement of a product into the stream of commerce is consistent with the Due Process Clause, and have not required a showing of additional conduct.

* * *

JUSTICE STEVENS, with whom JUSTICE WHITE and JUSTICE BLACKMUN join, concurring in part and concurring in the judgment.

The judgment of the Supreme Court of California should be reversed for the reasons stated in Part II–B of the Court's opinion. While I join Parts I and II–B, I do not join Part II–A for two reasons. First, it is not necessary to the Court's decision. An examination of minimum contacts is not always necessary to determine whether a state court's assertion of personal jurisdiction is constitutional. * * * Part II–B establishes, after considering the factors set forth in World-Wide Volkswagen Corp. v. Woodson, * * * that California's exercise of jurisdiction over Asahi in this case would be "unreasonable and unfair." * * * This finding alone requires reversal; this case fits within the rule that "minimum requirements inherent in the concept of 'fair play and substantial justice' may defeat the reasonableness of jurisdiction even if the defendant has purposefully engaged in forum activities." * * * Accordingly, I see no reason in this case for the plurality to articulate "purposeful direction" or any other test as the nexus between an act of a defendant and the forum State that is necessary to establish minimum contacts.

Second, even assuming that the test ought to be formulated here, Part II–A misapplies it to the facts of this case. The plurality seems to assume that an unwavering line can be drawn between "mere awareness" that a component will find its way into the forum State and "purposeful avail- ment" of the forum's market. * * *. Over the course of its dealings with Cheng Shin, Asahi has arguably engaged in a higher quantum of conduct than "[t]he placement of a product into the stream of commerce, without more ...." * * * Whether or not this conduct rises to the level of purposeful availment requires a constitutional determination that is af- fected by the volume, the value, and the hazardous character of the components. In most circumstances I would be inclined to conclude that a regular course of dealing that results in deliveries of over 100,000 units annually over a period of several years would constitute "purposeful availment" even though the item delivered to the forum State was a standard product marketed throughout the world.

NOTES AND QUESTIONS

1.   There was no majority opinion in *Asahi*. Given the division among the Justices, which opinion states the law as it now stands?

2.   The Supreme Court did not disturb the California court's finding that "Asahi knew that some of the valve assemblies sold to Cheng Shin would be incorporated into tire tubes sold in California." Under Part II–A of Justice O'Connor's opinion, this knowledge alone could not serve as a basis for jurisdiction unless Asahi had taken some further action "purposefully directed toward the forum state." Does this approach allow the nonresident manufac- turer of a component part to avoid the safety standards of states in which the final product is sold? How would the *Asahi* plurality respond to this concern?

3.   Should the plurality's approach in *Asahi* be applied only to foreign defendants? Does it affect your view that some American bases of jurisdiction are regarded as "exorbitant" from an international perspective? See Clermont & Palmer, *Exorbitant Jurisdiction*, 58 Me. L. Rev. 474 (2006).

SECTION E.   GENERAL JURISDICTION AND STATE LONG–ARM LAWS

PERKINS v. BENGUET CONSOLIDATED MINING CO., 342 U.S. 437, 445–48, 72 S.Ct. 413, 418–20, 96 L.Ed. 485, 492–94 (1952). The defendant, a Philippine corporation, was sued by a nonresident of Ohio in an Ohio state court on two causes of action arising from activities conducted by defendant outside of Ohio. Plaintiff claimed $68,400 in dividends due her as a stockholder and $2,500,000 in damages due to defendant's failure to issue to her certificates for 120,000 shares of its stock. The Ohio state courts granted defendant's motion to quash the service of summons. The Supreme Court addressed the issue of whether or not the Due Process Clause of the Fourteenth Amendment prohibited Ohio from exercising jurisdiction:

> * * * The corporate activities of a foreign corporation which, under state statute, make it necessary for it to secure a license and to designate a statutory agent upon whom process may be served provide a helpful but not a conclusive test. * * * [I]f the same corporation carries on, in that state, other continuous and systematic corporate activities as it did here—consisting of directors' meetings, business correspondence, banking, stock transfers, payment of salaries, purchasing of machinery, etc.—those activities are enough to make it fair and reasonable to subject that corporation to proceedings *in personam* in that state, at least insofar as the proceedings *in personam* seek to enforce causes of action relating to those very activities or to other activities of the corporation within the state.

> The instant case takes us one step further to a proceeding *in personam* to enforce a cause of action not arising out of the corporation's activities in the state of the forum. * * * [W]e find no requirement of federal due process that either *prohibits* Ohio from opening its courts to the cause of action here presented or *compels* Ohio to do so. * * *

> It remains only to consider * * * whether, as a matter of federal due process, the business done in Ohio by the respondent mining company was sufficiently substantial and of such a nature to *permit* Ohio to entertain a cause of action against a foreign corporation, where the cause of action arose from activities entirely distinct from its activities in Ohio. * * *

> * * * [T]he following facts are substantially beyond controversy: The company's mining properties were in the Philippine Islands. Its operations there were completely halted during the occupation of the Islands by the Japanese. During that interim the president, who was also the general manager and principal stockholder of the company, returned to his home in Clermont County, Ohio. There he maintained an office in which he conducted his personal affairs and did many things on behalf of the company. He kept there office files of the company. He carried on there correspondence relating to the business of the company and to its employees. He drew and distributed there salary checks on behalf of the company, both in his own favor as president and in favor of two company secretaries who worked there with him. He used and maintained in Clermont County, Ohio, two active bank accounts carrying substantial balances of company funds. A bank in Hamilton County, Ohio, acted as transfer agent for the stock of the company. Several directors' meetings were held at his office or home in Clermont County. From that office he supervised policies dealing with the rehabilitation of the corporation's properties

in the Philippines and he dispatched funds to cover purchases of machinery for such rehabilitation. Thus he carried on in Ohio a continuous and systematic supervision of the necessarily limited wartime activities of the company. * * * While no mining properties in Ohio were owned or operated by the company, many of its wartime activities were directed from Ohio and were being given the personal attention of its president in that State at the time he was served with summons. * * * [W]e conclude that, under the circumstances above recited, it would not violate federal due process for Ohio either to take or decline jurisdiction of the corporation in this proceeding.

On remand the Ohio courts refused to quash the summons. 158 Ohio St. 145, 107 N.E.2d 203 (1952).

NOTES AND QUESTIONS

1. The dispute in *Perkins* can be traced back to the marriage of Eugene and Idonah Slade Perkins in Manila under authority granted by the United States Military Occupation of the Philippines. Husband and wife were both United States citizens. Beginning in 1916, the wife used her personal funds to purchase stock in the Benguet Consolidated Mining Co., a Philippine corporation. Later, the husband also purchased stock in the company and gave the shares to his wife as a Christmas present. In 1930, the couple separated and a messy divorce followed. The husband claimed a right to his wife's stock under the community property laws of the Philippines, and lawsuits followed in the courts of the Philippines, New York, and California. By the time the United States Supreme Court entered the picture, a New York court had declared the wife the owner of the stock, and she had recovered some of the cash dividends from the Benguet company. However, the company refused to deliver the stock dividends that she claimed to be owed, and in 1947 she sued the company in state court in Ohio, where the company had relocated temporarily during World War II. Does this procedural history help to explain why the Supreme Court said that the cause of action in *Perkins* did not arise "out of the corporation's activities in the state of the forum"?

2. In the wake of *Perkins*, lower courts expressed difficulty in determining when contacts with the forum were "continuous and systematic" and so "sufficiently substantial" as to permit the exercise of personal jurisdiction in an action where the cause of action did not arise out of defendant's "activities in the state of the forum." E.g., Aquascutum of London, Inc. v. S.S. American Champion, 426 F.2d 205, 211 (2d Cir. 1970) ("The problem of what contacts with the forum state will suffice to subject a foreign corporation to suit there on an unrelated cause of action is such that the formulation of useful general standards is almost impossible and even an examination of the multitude of decided cases can give little assistance.").

3. In FISHER GOVERNOR CO. v. SUPERIOR COURT, 53 Cal.2d 222, 225, 1 Cal.Rptr. 1, 3, 347 P.2d 1, 3 (1959), a wrongful death action growing out of an explosion in Idaho, plaintiffs served defendant, an Iowa corporation, by delivering the papers to a California manufacturers' agent who sold

defendant's products. The California Supreme Court ordered the process quashed. In his opinion for the court, Justice Traynor said:

> Although a foreign corporation may have sufficient contacts with a state to justify an assumption of jurisdiction over it to enforce causes of action having no relation to its activities in that state * * *, more contacts are required for the assumption of such extensive jurisdiction than sales and sales promotion within the state by independent nonexclusive sales representatives. * * * To hold otherwise would subject any corporation that promotes the sales of its goods on a nationwide basis to suit anywhere in the United States without regard to other considerations bearing on "the fair and orderly administration of the laws which it was the purpose of the due process clause to insure." * * * Accordingly, we must look beyond defendant's sales activities in this state to determine whether jurisdiction may constitutionally be assumed.

4. In FRUMMER v. HILTON HOTELS INTERNATIONAL, INC., 19 N.Y.2d 533, 281 N.Y.S.2d 41, 227 N.E.2d 851, certiorari denied 389 U.S. 923, 88 S.Ct. 241, 19 L.Ed.2d 266 (1967), a New York tourist who fell and injured himself while taking a shower in the London Hilton brought a personal injury action against the hotel (an English corporation) in New York. Jurisdiction was upheld on the basis of the activities of the Hilton Reservation Service, a separate corporation. Although separate, the interlocking ownership of the two corporations and other facts persuaded New York's highest court that an agency relationship existed between them. It thus held that London Hilton did business in New York by "do[ing] all the business which [the principal] could do were it [in New York] by its own officials."

HELICOPTEROS NACIONALES DE COLOMBIA, S.A. v. HALL

Supreme Court of the United States, 1984.
466 U.S. 408, 104 S.Ct. 1868, 80 L.Ed.2d 404.

Certiorari to the Supreme Court of Texas.

JUSTICE BLACKMUN delivered the opinion of the Court.

We granted certiorari in this case * * * to decide whether the Supreme Court of Texas correctly ruled that the contacts of a foreign corporation with the State of Texas were sufficient to allow a Texas state court to assert jurisdiction over the corporation in a cause of action not arising out of or related to the corporation's activities within the State.

I

Petitioner Helicopteros Nacionales de Colombia, S.A., (Helicol) is a Colombian corporation with its principal place of business in the city of Bogota in that country. It is engaged in the business of providing helicopter transportation for oil and construction companies in South America. On January 26, 1976, a helicopter owned by Helicol crashed in Peru. Four

United States citizens were among those who lost their lives in the accident. Respondents are the survivors and representatives of the four decedents.

At the time of the crash, respondents' decedents were employed by Consorcio, a Peruvian consortium, and were working on a pipeline in Peru. Consorcio is the alter-ego of a joint venture named Williams-Sedco-Horn (WSH). The venture had its headquarters in Houston, Texas. Consorcio had been formed to enable the venturers to enter into a contract with Petro Peru, the Peruvian state-owned oil company. Consorcio was to construct a pipeline for Petro Peru running from the interior of Peru westward to the Pacific Ocean. Peruvian law forbade construction of the pipeline by any non-Peruvian entity.

Consorcio/WSH needed helicopters to move personnel, materials, and equipment into and out of the construction area. In 1974, upon request of Consorcio/WSH, the chief executive officer of Helicol, Francisco Restrepo, flew to the United States and conferred in Houston with representatives of the three joint venturers. At that meeting, there was a discussion of prices, availability, working conditions, fuel, supplies, and housing. Restrepo represented that Helicol could have the first helicopter on the job in 15 days. The Consorcio/WSH representatives decided to accept the contract proposed by Restrepo. Helicol began performing before the agreement was formally signed in Peru on November 11, 1974. The contract was written in Spanish on official government stationery and provided that the residence of all the parties would be Lima, Peru. It further stated that controversies arising out of the contract would be submitted to the jurisdiction of Peruvian courts. In addition, it provided that Consorcio/WSH would make payments to Helicol's account with the Bank of America in New York City. * * *

Aside from the negotiation session in Houston between Restrepo and the representatives of Consorcio/WSH, Helicol had other contacts with Texas. During the years 1970–1977, it purchased helicopters (approximately 80% of its fleet), spare parts, and accessories for more than $4 million from Bell Helicopter Company in Fort Worth. In that period, Helicol sent prospective pilots to Fort Worth for training and to ferry the aircraft to South America. It also sent management and maintenance personnel to visit Bell Helicopter in Fort Worth during the same period in order to receive "plant familiarization" and for technical consultation. Helicol received into its New York City and Panama City, Florida, bank accounts over $5 million in payments from Consorcio/WSH drawn upon First City National Bank of Houston.

Beyond the foregoing, there have been no other business contacts between Helicol and the State of Texas. Helicol never has been authorized to do business in Texas and never has had an agent for the service of process within the State. It never has performed helicopter operations in Texas or sold any product that reached Texas, never solicited business in Texas, never signed any contract in Texas, never had any employee based there, and never recruited an employee in Texas. In addition, Helicol never has owned real or personal property in Texas and never has maintained an office or establishment there. Helicol has maintained no records in Texas and has no shareholders in that State. None of the respondents or their decedents were domiciled in Texas, * * *[5] but all of the decedents were hired in Houston by Consorcio/WSH to work on the Petro Peru pipeline project.

Respondents instituted wrongful-death actions in the District Court of Harris County, Texas, against Consorcio/WSH, Bell Helicopter Company, and Helicol. Helicol filed special appearances and moved to dismiss the actions for lack of *in personam* jurisdiction over it. The motion was denied. After a consolidated jury trial, judgment was entered against Helicol on a jury verdict of $1,141,200 in favor of respondents.[6] * * *

The Texas Court of Civil Appeals, Houston, First District, reversed the judgment of the District Court, holding that *in personam* jurisdiction over Helicol was lacking. * * * The Supreme Court of Texas * * * reversed the judgment of the intermediate court. * * * In ruling that the Texas courts had *in personam* jurisdiction, the Texas Supreme Court first held that the State's long-arm statute reaches as far as the Due Process Clause of the Fourteenth Amendment permits. * * *[7] Thus, the only question remaining for the court to decide was whether it was consistent with the Due Process Clause for Texas courts to assert *in personam* jurisdiction over Helicol. * * *

II

* * *

Even when the cause of action does not arise out of or relate to the foreign corporation's activities in the forum State, due process is not offended by a State's subjecting the corporation to its *in personam* jurisdiction when there are sufficient contacts between the State and the foreign corporation. * * *

All parties to the present case concede that respondents' claims against Helicol did not "arise out of," and are not related to, Helicol's activities within Texas.[10] We thus must explore the nature of Helicol's

---

5. Respondents' lack of residential or other contacts with Texas of itself does not defeat otherwise proper jurisdiction. * * * We mention respondents' lack of contacts merely to show that nothing in the nature of the relationship between respondents and Helicol could possibly enhance Helicol's contacts with Texas. The harm suffered by respondents did not occur in Texas. Nor is it alleged that any negligence on the part of Helicol took place in Texas.

6. Defendants Consorcio/WSH and Bell Helicopter Company were granted directed verdicts with respect to respondents' claims against them. Bell Helicopter was granted a directed verdict on Helicol's cross-claim against it. * * * Consorcio/WSH, as cross-plaintiff in a claim against Helicol, obtained a judgment in the amount of $70,000. * * *

7. * * * It is not within our province, of course, to determine whether the Texas Supreme Court correctly interpreted the State's long-arm statute. We therefore accept that court's holding that the limits of the Texas statute are coextensive with those of the Due Process Clause.

10. * * * Because the parties have not argued any relationship between the cause of action and Helicol's contacts with the State of Texas, we, contrary to the dissent's implication, * * * assert no "view" with respect to that issue.

contacts with the State of Texas to determine whether they constitute the kind of continuous and systematic general business contacts the Court found to exist in *Perkins*. We hold that they do not.

It is undisputed that Helicol does not have a place of business in Texas and never has been licensed to do business in the State. Basically, Helicol's contacts with Texas consisted of sending its chief executive officer to Houston for a contract-negotiation session; accepting into its New York bank account checks drawn on a Houston bank; purchasing helicopters, equipment, and training services from Bell Helicopter for substantial sums; and sending personnel to Bell's facilities in Fort Worth for training.

The one trip to Houston by Helicol's chief executive officer for the purpose of negotiating the transportation-services contract with Consorcio/WSH cannot be described or regarded as a contact of a "continuous and systematic" nature, as *Perkins* described it, * * * and thus cannot support an assertion of *in personam* jurisdiction over Helicol by a Texas court. Similarly, Helicol's acceptance from Consorcio/WSH of checks drawn on a Texas bank is of negligible significance for purposes of determining whether Helicol had sufficient contacts in Texas. There is no indication that Helicol ever requested that the checks be drawn on a Texas bank or that there was any negotiation between Helicol and Consorcio/WSH with respect to the location or identity of the bank on which checks would be drawn. Common sense and everyday experience suggest that, absent unusual circumstances, the bank on which a check is drawn is generally of little consequence to the payee and is a matter left to the discretion of the drawer. Such unilateral activity of another party or a third person is not an appropriate consideration when determining whether a defendant has sufficient contacts with a forum State to justify an assertion of jurisdiction. * * *

The Texas Supreme Court focused on the purchases and the related training trips in finding contacts sufficient to support an assertion of jurisdiction. We do not agree with that assessment, for the Court's opinion in Rosenberg Bros. & Co. v. Curtis Brown Co., 260 U.S. 516 (1923) (Brandeis, J., for a unanimous tribunal), makes clear that purchases and

---

The dissent suggests that we have erred in drawing no distinction between controversies that "relate to" a defendant's contacts with a forum and those that "arise out of" such contacts. * * * This criticism is somewhat puzzling, for the dissent goes on to urge that, for purposes of determining the constitutional validity of an assertion of specific jurisdiction, there really should be no distinction between the two. * * *

We do not address the validity or consequences of such a distinction because the issue has not been presented in this case. Respondents have made no argument that their cause of action either arose out of or is related to Helicol's contacts with the State of Texas. Absent any briefing on the issue, we decline to reach the questions (1) whether the terms "arising out of" and "related to" describe different connections between a cause of action and a defendant's contacts with a forum, and (2) what sort of tie between a cause of action and a defendant's contacts with a forum is necessary to a determination that either connection exists. Nor do we reach the question whether, if the two types of relationship differ, a forum's exercise of personal jurisdiction in a situation where the cause of action "relates to," but does not "arise out of," the defendant's contacts with the forum should be analyzed as an assertion of specific jurisdiction.

related trips, standing alone, are not a sufficient basis for a State's assertion of jurisdiction.

* * *

* * * In accordance with *Rosenberg*, we hold that mere purchases, even if occurring at regular intervals, are not enough to warrant a State's assertion of *in personam* jurisdiction over a nonresident corporation in a cause of action not related to those purchase transactions. Nor can we conclude that the fact that Helicol sent personnel into Texas for training in connection with the purchase of helicopters and equipment in that State in any way enhanced the nature of Helicol's contacts with Texas. The training was a part of the package of goods and services purchased by Helicol from Bell Helicopter. The brief presence of Helicol employees in Texas for the purpose of attending the training sessions is no more a significant contact than were the trips to New York made by the buyer for the [Oklahoma] retail store in *Rosenberg*. * * *

III

We hold that Helicol's contacts with the State of Texas were insufficient to satisfy the requirements of the Due Process Clause of the Fourteenth Amendment. Accordingly, we reverse the judgment of the Supreme Court of Texas.

It is so ordered.

JUSTICE BRENNAN, dissenting.

* * *

* * * I believe that the undisputed contacts in this case between petitioner Helicol and the State of Texas are sufficiently important, and sufficiently related to the underlying cause of action, to make it fair and reasonable for the State to assert personal jurisdiction over Helicol for the wrongful-death actions filed by the respondents. * * * I therefore dissent.

I

* * * As active participants in interstate and foreign commerce take advantage of the economic benefits and opportunities offered by the various States, it is only fair and reasonable to subject them to the obligations that may be imposed by those jurisdictions. And chief among the obligations that a nonresident corporation should expect to fulfill is amenability to suit in any forum that is significantly affected by the corporation's commercial activities.

As a foreign corporation that has actively and purposefully engaged in numerous and frequent commercial transactions in the State of Texas, Helicol clearly falls within the category of nonresident defendants that may be subject to the forum's general jurisdiction. Helicol not only purchased helicopters and other equipment in the State for many years, but also sent pilots and management personnel into Texas to be trained in the use of this equipment and to consult with the seller on technical matters. Moreover, negotiations for the contract under which Helicol provided transportation services to the joint venture that employed the respondents' decedents also took place in the State of Texas. Taken together, these contacts demonstrate that Helicol obtained numerous benefits from its transaction of business in Texas. In turn, it is eminently fair and reasonable to expect Helicol to face the obligations that attach to its participation in such commercial transactions. Accordingly, on the basis of continuous commercial contacts with the forum, I would conclude that the Due Process Clause allows the State of Texas to assert general jurisdiction over petitioner Helicol.

II

The Court also fails to distinguish the legal principles that controlled our prior decisions in *Perkins* and *Rosenberg*. In particular, the contacts between petitioner Helicol and the State of Texas, unlike the contacts between the defendant and the forum in each of those cases, are significantly related to the cause of action alleged in the original suit filed by the respondents. Accordingly, in my view, it is both fair and reasonable for the Texas courts to assert specific jurisdiction over Helicol in this case.

By asserting that the present case does not implicate the specific jurisdiction of the Texas courts, * * * the Court necessarily removes its decision from the reality of the actual facts presented for our consideration. Moreover, the Court refuses to consider any distinction between contacts that are "related to" the underlying cause of action and contacts that "give rise" to the underlying cause of action. In my view, however, there is a substantial difference between these two standards for asserting specific jurisdiction. Thus, although I agree that the respondents' cause of action did not formally "arise out of" specific activities initiated by Helicol in the State of Texas, I believe that the wrongful-death claim filed by the respondents is significantly related to the undisputed contacts between Helicol and the forum. On that basis, I would conclude that the Due Process Clause allows the Texas courts to assert specific jurisdiction over this particular action.

* * *

Limiting the specific jurisdiction of a forum to cases in which the cause of action formally arose out of the defendant's contacts with the State would subject constitutional standards under the Due Process Clause to the vagaries of the substantive law or pleading requirements of each State. For example, the complaint filed against Helicol in this case alleged negligence based on pilot error. Even though the pilot was trained in Texas, the Court assumes that the Texas courts may not assert jurisdiction over the suit because the cause of action "did not 'arise out of,' and [is] not related to," that training. * * * If, however, the applicable substantive law required that negligent training of the pilot was a necessary element of a cause of action for pilot error, or if the respondents had simply added an allegation of negligence in the training provided for the

Helicol pilot, then presumably the Court would concede that the specific jurisdiction of the Texas courts was applicable.

Our interpretation of the Due Process Clause has never been so dependent upon the applicable substantive law or the State's formal pleading requirements. * * * [T]he principal focus when determining whether a forum may constitutionally assert jurisdiction over a nonresident defendant has been on fairness and reasonableness to the defendant. To this extent, a court's specific jurisdiction should be applicable whenever the cause of action arises out of *or* relates to the contacts between the defendant and the forum. It is eminently fair and reasonable, in my view, to subject a defendant to suit in a forum with which it has significant contacts directly related to the underlying cause of action. Because Helicol's contacts with the State of Texas meet this standard, I would affirm the judgment of the Supreme Court of Texas.

NOTES AND QUESTIONS

1. The terminology "general jurisdiction" and "specific jurisdiction" was developed by Professors von Mehren and Trautman. See Von Mehren & Trautman, *Jurisdiction to Adjudicate: A Suggested Analysis*, 79 Harv. L. Rev. 1121 (1966). In their article, the authors explained:

> [A]ffiliations between the forum and the underlying controversy normally support only the power to adjudicate * * * issues deriving from, or connected with, the very controversy that establishes jurisdiction * * *. This we call specific jurisdiction. On the other hand, American practice for the most part is to exercise power to adjudicate any kind of controversy when jurisdiction is based on relationships, direct or indirect, between the forum, and the person or persons whose legal rights are to be affected. This we call general jurisdiction.

Id. at 1136. Which of the traditional bases of jurisdiction already examined in this Chapter ought to support a court's exercise of general jurisdiction?

2. What purpose does the distinction between general and specific jurisdiction serve? Has the expansion of specific jurisdiction rendered the concept of general jurisdiction obsolete? Some commentators have argued that the concept of general jurisdiction ensures the availability of at least one state in which "a defendant may be sued on any cause of action." Twitchell, *The Myth of General Jurisdiction*, 101 Harv. L. Rev. 610, 632, 667 (1988). See also Borchers, *The Problem with General Jurisdiction*, 2001 U. Chi. Legal F. 119, 139 (describing general jurisdiction as "an imperfect safety valve that sometimes allows plaintiffs access to a reasonable forum in a case when specific jurisdiction would deny it").

3. Should general and specific jurisdiction be viewed as two separate categories or as two ends of a continuum? Professor Richman has urged replacing the binary distinction with a "sliding scale model" that looks at "the extent of the defendant's forum contacts on the one hand and the proximity of the connection between those contacts and the plaintiff's claim on the other." According to this view, "as the quantity and quality of the

defendant's forum contacts increase, a weaker connection between the plaintiff's claim and those contacts is permissible; as the quantity and quality of the defendant's forum contacts decrease, a stronger connection between the plaintiff's claim and those contacts is required." Richman, *Review Essay, Part II: A Sliding Scale to Supplement the Distinction Between General and Specific Jurisdiction*, 72 Cal. L. Rev. 1328, 1345 (1984).

4.   Justice Brennan's dissent in *Helicopteros* argued that specific jurisdiction is implicated whenever the defendant's contacts with the forum "relate to" the cause of action; he expressed concern that the Court had defined specific jurisdiction to require the cause of action to "arise out of" the defendant's forum contacts and, as such, to entangle personal jurisdiction with the substantive law of the case. Professor Brilmayer has proposed just such a "substantive relevance" standard:

> Substantive relevance provides a natural test. A contact is related to the controversy if it is the geographical qualification of a fact relevant to the merits. A forum occurrence which would ordinarily be alleged as part of a comparable domestic complaint is a related contact. In contrast, an occurrence in the forum State of no relevance to a totally domestic cause of action is an unrelated contact, a purely jurisdictional allegation with no substantive purpose. If a fact is irrelevant in a purely domestic dispute, it does not suddenly become related to the controversy simply because there are multistate elements.

Brilmayer, *How Contacts Count: Due Process Limitations on State Court Jurisdiction*, 1980 Sup. Ct. Rev. 77, 82–83. Professor Brilmayer later defended the test of "substantive relevance" on the view that it helps to identify cases in which the exercise of jurisdiction "would further the state's legitimate interests in local regulation." Brilmayer, Haverkamp & Logan, *A General Look at General Jurisdiction*, 66 Texas L. Rev. 721, 740 (1988). Do you agree with that analysis?

5.   The *Helicopteros* decision provided the lower courts with little guidance in determining when general jurisdiction may be exercised in the individual case. Many questions about the doctrine still remain unanswered. In METROPOLITAN LIFE INSURANCE CO. v. ROBERTSON-CECO CORP., 84 F.3d 560 (2d Cir.), certiorari denied 519 U.S. 1006, 117 S.Ct. 508, 136 L.Ed.2d 398 (1996), the Second Circuit held that the exercise of general jurisdiction over defendant was unreasonable in light of the five-factor reasonableness test endorsed in *Asahi* and *World-Wide Volkswagen*. Other courts, however, have not embraced this approach. See Cebik, *"A Riddle Wrapped in a Mystery Inside an Enigma": General Personal Jurisdiction and Notions of Sovereignty*, 1998 Ann. Surv. Am. L. 1, 10.

SECTION F.   INTERNET AND OTHER TECHNOLOGICAL CONTACTS

Technological change unquestionably has affected jurisdictional doctrine. Telephone calls, faxes, and emails sent by businesses or individuals and directed at a recipient in a forum state today may be considered as contacts that count for jurisdictional purposes. The Supreme Court has yet to consider the issue of personal jurisdiction based upon Internet contacts. Websites often are not targeted at a particular state, but rather at all online users. Do the operators of those websites have contacts wherever the Internet is available, i.e., everywhere? As you read this Section, ask yourself what factors should matter in assessing whether a website and other virtual activity are to be treated as a contact with the forum state. Should the answer depend on the kind of harm that plaintiff alleges?

NOTE ON THE INTERNET

One of the first cases to deal with the question of personal jurisdiction and the Internet was INSET SYSTEMS, INC. v. INSTRUCTION SET, INC., 937 F.Supp. 161 (D.Conn. 1996), in which the court found that an Internet website advertisement operated by a nonresident, although not directed at any state in particular, was sufficient to support personal jurisdiction in Connecticut under the purposeful availment test. In CYBERSELL, INC. v. CYBERSELL, INC., 130 F.3d 414, 418 (9th Cir. 1997), the court held that "something more" than the mere maintenance of a website is required to show that the defendant purposefully directed its activities at the forum. A district court expanded upon this notion in ZIPPO MANUFACTURING CO. v. ZIPPO DOT COM, INC., 952 F.Supp. 1119, 1124 (W.D.Pa. 1997). In *Zippo*, the court articulated a "sliding scale" test, which places at one end of the scale "active" websites that businesses use to carry out transactions with residents of a forum state. At the other end of the scale are "passive" websites, which do little more than make information available to those who choose to visit the website. The "active" websites almost always provide for an exercise of personal jurisdiction; the "passive" websites rarely can be used alone to establish personal jurisdiction. In the middle are "interactive" websites, which permit a user to exchange information with the business; it is in these cases that the sliding scale of commercial activity becomes relevant.

Courts almost immediately recognized *Zippo* as a leading case, but applied it in an inconsistent manner. Some courts found that an interactive website alone is sufficient to establish minimum contacts; others required additional non-Internet activity in the forum, regardless of whether it was related to the underlying claim. Finally, some courts looked for additional conduct in the forum that is related to the plaintiff's cause of action. Courts and commentators increasingly have criticized the *Zippo* test. In HY CITE CORP. v. BADBUSINESSBUREAU.COM, L.L.C., 297 F.Supp.2d 1154, 1160 (W.D.Wis. 2004), the District Court declined to follow *Zippo*:

> First, it is not clear why a website's level of interactivity should be determinative on the issue of personal jurisdiction. As even courts adopting the *Zippo* test have recognized, a court cannot determine whether personal jurisdiction is appropriate simply by deciding whether a website is "passive" or "interactive" (assuming that websites can be readily classified into one category or the other). * * *

> Second, * * * [t]he Supreme Court has never held that courts should apply different standards for personal jurisdiction depending on the type of contact involved.

Many courts today have begun to move away from *Zippo*, either replacing it entirely with *Calder*'s "effects test," p. 70, supra, or combining the two standards. Another proposed approach emphasizes a state's interest in regulating Internet activity, rather than defendant's interest in not litigating in the state's forum. See Stein, *Personal Jurisdiction and the Internet: Seeking Due Process Through the Lens of Regulatory Precision*, 98 Nw. U. L. Rev. 411 (2004). What difficulties do you anticipate with this approach?

SECTION G. JURISDICTION BASED UPON POWER OVER PROPERTY

PENNINGTON v. FOURTH NATIONAL BANK, 243 U.S. 269, 271– 72, 37 S.Ct. 282, 282–83, 61 L.Ed. 713, 714–15 (1917). Petitioner challenged the garnishment of his bank account to pay alimony. Although petitioner did not reside in the forum state, the Court held that attachment of his in-state bank account satisfied due process. Justice Brandeis explained in his opinion for the Court:

> The 14th Amendment did not, in guarantying due process of law, abridge the jurisdiction which a state possessed over property within its borders, regardless of the residence or presence of the owner. That jurisdiction extends alike to tangible and to intangible property. Indebtedness due from a resident to a nonresident—of which bank deposits are an example—is property within the state. * * * It is, indeed, the species of property which courts of the several states have most frequently applied in satisfaction of the obligations of absent debtors. * * * Substituted service on a nonresident by publication furnishes no legal basis for a judgment in personam. * * * But garnishment or foreign attachment is a proceeding quasi in rem. * * * The thing belonging to the absent defendant is seized and applied to the satisfaction of his obligation. The Federal Constitution presents no obstacle to the full exercise of this power.

NOTE AND QUESTION

What is the situs of corporate stock for purposes of attachment—the corporation's place of incorporation, the domicile of the shareholder, or the state in which the stock certificates actually are located? See generally Note, *Attachment of Corporate Stock: The Conflicting Approaches of Delaware and the Uniform Stock Transfer Act*, 73 Harv. L. Rev. 1579 (1960).

HARRIS v. BALK, 198 U.S. 215, 25 S.Ct. 625, 49 L.Ed. 1023 (1905). Harris, a citizen of North Carolina, owed Balk, also of North Carolina, $180. Epstein, a Maryland citizen, claimed that Balk owed him $344. On

August 6, 1896, while Harris was visiting Baltimore, Epstein instituted a garnishee proceeding in a Maryland court, attaching the debt due Balk from Harris. Harris was personally served with the writ of attachment and summons, and notice of the suit was posted at the courthouse door, as required by Maryland law. Harris consented to the entry of judgment against him and paid the $180 to Epstein. On August 11, 1896, Balk commenced an action against Harris in a North Carolina court to recover the $180. Harris asserted that he no longer owed Balk the $180, having paid that sum to Epstein in partial satisfaction of Balk's debt to Epstein, since the Maryland judgment and his payment thereof was valid in Maryland, and was therefore entitled to full faith and credit in the courts of North Carolina. The trial court ruled in favor of Balk, and the North Carolina Supreme Court affirmed on the ground that the Maryland court had no jurisdiction over Harris to attach the debt because Harris was only temporarily in the state, and the situs of the debt was in North Carolina. The Supreme Court reversed:

> * * * We do not see how the question of jurisdiction *vel non* can properly be made to depend upon the so-called original situs of the debt, or upon the character of the stay of the garnishee, whether temporary or permanent, in the state where the attachment is issued. Power over the person of the garnishee confers jurisdiction on the courts of the state where the writ issues. * * * If, while temporarily there, his creditor might sue him there and recover the debt, then he is liable to process of garnishment, no matter where the situs of the debt was originally. We do not see the materiality of the expression "situs of the debt," when used in connection with attachment pro-ceedings. If by situs is meant the place of the creation of the debt, that fact is immaterial. If it be meant that the obligation to pay the debt can only be enforced at the situs thus fixed, we think it plainly untrue. The obligation of the debtor to pay his debt clings to and accompanies him wherever he goes. He is as much bound to pay his debt in a foreign state when therein sued upon his obligation by his creditor, as he was in the state where the debt was contracted. * * * It would be no defense to such suit for the debtor to plead that he was only in the foreign state casually or temporarily. * * * It is nothing but the obligation to pay which is garnished or attached. This obli-gation can be enforced by the courts of the foreign state after personal service of process therein, just as well as by the courts of the domicil of the debtor. * * *

Id. at 222, 25 S.Ct. at 626, 49 L.Ed. at 1026. The Court indicated in dictum that the result might have been different had Balk not been given notice of the attachment and an opportunity to defend in the Maryland action.

NOTES AND QUESTIONS

1. Professor Lowenfeld provides the following interesting information concerning Harris, Balk, and Epstein. Epstein was an importer of goods who regularly did business with Balk, a retailer. The $344 debt was for money owed on shipments of goods by Epstein to Balk. Harris was a dry goods merchant from the same town as Balk, and had borrowed money from Balk on several occasions, including a $10 loan just before the fateful trip to Baltimore. Harris carried with him on that trip a message from Balk to Epstein saying that Balk would be coming to Baltimore soon. See Lowenfeld, *In Search of the Intangible: A Comment on* Shaffer v. Heitner, 53 N.Y.U. L. Rev. 102, 104–06 (1978).

2. If the events leading up to Harris v. Balk were to occur today, could Epstein have sued Balk in personam, assuming a long-arm statute similar to Rhode Island's? Could Epstein have served Harris as Balk's agent?

———

SHAFFER v. HEITNER

Supreme Court of the United States, 1977.
433 U.S. 186, 97 S.Ct. 2569, 53 L.Ed.2d 683.

On Appeal from the Supreme Court of Delaware.

MR. JUSTICE MARSHALL delivered the opinion of the Court.

* * *

I

Appellee Heitner, a nonresident of Delaware, is the owner of one share of stock in the Greyhound Corp., a business incorporated under the laws of Delaware with its principal place of business in Phoenix, Ariz. On May 22, 1974, he filed a shareholder's derivative suit in the Court of Chancery for New Castle County, Del., in which he named as defendants Greyhound, its wholly owned subsidiary Greyhound Lines, Inc.,[1] and 28 present or former officers or directors of one or both of the corporations. In essence, Heitner alleged that the individual defendants had violated their duties to Greyhound by causing it and its subsidiary to engage in actions that resulted in the corporations being held liable for substantial damages in a private antitrust suit and a large fine in a criminal contempt action. The activities which led to these penalties took place in Oregon.

Simultaneously with his complaint, Heitner filed a motion for an order of sequestration of the Delaware property of the individual defendants pursuant to Del.Code Ann., Tit. 10, § 366 (1975). This motion was accompanied by a supporting affidavit of counsel which stated that the individual defendants were nonresidents of Delaware. The affidavit identi-

---

1. Greyhound Lines, Inc., is incorporated in California and has its principal place of business in Phoenix, Ariz.

fied the property to be sequestered as [shares of Greyhound Corp. stock and stock options] * * *. The requested sequestration order was signed the day the motion was filed. Pursuant to that order, the sequestrator "seized" approximately 82,000 shares of Greyhound common stock belonging to 19 of the defendants, and options belonging to another 2 defendants. These seizures were accomplished by placing "stop transfer" orders or their equivalents on the books of the Greyhound Corp. So far as the record shows, none of the certificates representing the seized property was physically present in Delaware. The stock was considered to be in Delaware, and so subject to seizure, by virtue of Del. Code Ann., Tit. 8, § 169 (1975), which makes Delaware the situs of ownership of all stock in Delaware corporations.

All 28 defendants were notified of the initiation of the suit by certified mail directed to their last known addresses and by publication in a New Castle County newspaper. The 21 defendants whose property was seized (hereafter referred to as appellants) responded by entering a special appearance for the purpose of moving to quash service of process and to vacate the sequestration order. They contended that the *ex parte* sequestration procedure did not accord them due process of law and that the property seized was not capable of attachment in Delaware. In addition, appellants asserted that under the rule of International Shoe Co. v. Washington, * * * [p. 46, supra], they did not have sufficient contacts with Delaware to sustain the jurisdiction of that State's courts.

The Court of Chancery rejected these arguments * * *.

On appeal, the Delaware Supreme Court affirmed the judgment of the Court of Chancery.

* * *

Appellants' claim that the Delaware courts did not have jurisdiction to adjudicate this action received * * * cursory treatment. * * *[12] We reverse.

II

The Delaware courts rejected appellants' jurisdictional challenge by noting that this suit was brought as a *quasi in rem* proceeding. Since *quasi in rem* jurisdiction is traditionally based on attachment or seizure of property present in the jurisdiction, not on contacts between the defendant and the State, the courts considered appellants' claimed lack of contacts with Delaware to be unimportant. This categorical analysis assumes the continued soundness of the conceptual structure founded on the century-old case of Pennoyer v. Neff, * * * [p. 33, supra].

[The Court's description of *Pennoyer* is omitted.] * * *

* * *

---

12. Under Delaware law, defendants whose property has been sequestered must enter a general appearance, thus subjecting themselves to *in personam* liability, before they can defend on the merits. * * *

* * * As we have noted, under *Pennoyer* state authority to adjudicate was based on the jurisdiction's power over either persons or property. This fundamental concept is embodied in the very vocabulary which we use to describe judgments. If a court's jurisdiction is based on its authority over the defendant's person, the action and judgment are denominated *"in personam"* and can impose a personal obligation on the defendant in favor of the plaintiff. If jurisdiction is based on the court's power over property within its territory, the action is called *"in rem"* or *"quasi in rem."* The effect of a judgment in such a case is limited to the property that supports jurisdiction and does not impose a personal liability on the property owner, since he is not before the court. * * * In *Pennoyer*'s terms, the owner is affected only "indirectly" by an *in rem* judgment adverse to his interest in the property subject to the court's disposition.

* * *

* * * Well-reasoned lower court opinions have questioned the proposition that the presence of property in a State gives that State jurisdiction to adjudicate rights to the property regardless of the relationship of the underlying dispute and the property owner to the forum. * * * The overwhelming majority of commentators have also rejected *Pennoyer*'s premise that a proceeding "against" property is not a proceeding against the owners of that property. Accordingly, they urge that the "traditional notions of fair play and substantial justice" that govern a State's power to adjudicate *in personam* should also govern its power to adjudicate personal rights to property located in the State. * * *

* * *

* * * We think that the time is ripe to consider whether the standard of fairness and substantial justice set forth in *International Shoe* should be held to govern actions *in rem* as well as *in personam.*

III

The case for applying to jurisdiction *in rem* the same test of "fair play and substantial justice" as governs assertions of jurisdiction *in personam* is simple and straightforward. It is premised on recognition that "[t]he phrase, 'judicial jurisdiction over a thing', is a customary elliptical way of referring to jurisdiction over the interests of persons in a thing." Restatement (Second) of Conflict of Laws § 56, Introductory Note * * *. This recognition leads to the conclusion that in order to justify an exercise of jurisdiction *in rem*, the basis for jurisdiction must be sufficient to justify exercising "jurisdiction over the interests of persons in a thing." The standard for determining whether an exercise of jurisdiction over the interests of persons is consistent with the Due Process Clause is the minimum-contacts standard elucidated in *International Shoe*.

This argument, of course, does not ignore the fact that the presence of property in a State may bear on the existence of jurisdiction by providing contacts among the forum State, the defendant, and the litigation. For example, when claims to the property itself are the source of the underlying controversy between the plaintiff and the defendant, it would be unusual for the State where the property is located not to have jurisdiction. In such cases, the defendant's claim to property located in the State would normally indicate that he expected to benefit from the State's protection of his interest. The State's strong interests in assuring the marketability of property within its borders and in providing a procedure for peaceful resolution of disputes about the possession of that property would also support jurisdiction, as would the likelihood that important records and witnesses will be found in the State. The presence of property may also favor jurisdiction in cases, such as suits for injury suffered on the land of an absentee owner, where the defendant's ownership of the property is conceded but the cause of action is otherwise related to rights and duties growing out of that ownership.

It appears, therefore, that jurisdiction over many types of actions which now are or might be brought *in rem* would not be affected by a holding that any assertion of state-court jurisdiction must satisfy the *International Shoe* standard. For the type of *quasi in rem* action typified by Harris v. Balk and the present case, however, accepting the proposed analysis would result in significant change. These are cases where the property which now serves as the basis for state-court jurisdiction is completely unrelated to the plaintiff's cause of action. Thus, although the presence of the defendant's property in a State might suggest the existence of other ties among the defendant, the State, and the litigation, the presence of the property alone would not support the State's jurisdiction. If those other ties did not exist, cases over which the State is now thought to have jurisdiction could not be brought in that forum.

Since acceptance of the *International Shoe* test would most affect this class of cases, we examine the arguments against adopting that standard as they relate to this category of litigation. Before doing so, however, we note that this type of case also presents the clearest illustration of the argument in favor of assessing assertions of jurisdiction by a single standard. For in cases such as *Harris* and this one, the only role played by the property is to provide the basis for bringing the defendant into court. Indeed, the express purpose of the Delaware sequestration procedure is to compel the defendant to enter a personal appearance. In such cases, if a direct assertion of personal jurisdiction over the defendant would violate the Constitution, it would seem that an indirect assertion of that jurisdiction should be equally impermissible.

The primary rationale for treating the presence of property as a sufficient basis for jurisdiction to adjudicate claims over which the State would not have jurisdiction if *International Shoe* applied is that a wrongdoer

> should not be able to avoid payment of his obligations by the expedient of removing his assets to a place where he is not subject to an in personam suit. Restatement [(Second) of Conflicts] § 66, Comment a.

* * * This justification, however, does not explain why jurisdiction should be recognized without regard to whether the property is present in the State because of an effort to avoid the owner's obligations. Nor does it support jurisdiction to adjudicate the underlying claim. At most, it suggests that a State in which property is located should have jurisdiction to attach that property, by use of proper procedures, as security for a judgment being sought in a forum where the litigation can be maintained consistently with *International Shoe*. * * * Moreover, we know of nothing to justify the assumption that a debtor can avoid paying his obligations by removing his property to a State in which his creditor cannot obtain personal jurisdiction over him. The Full Faith and Credit Clause, after all, makes the valid *in personam* judgment of one State enforceable in all other States.

It might also be suggested that allowing *in rem* jurisdiction avoids the uncertainty inherent in the *International Shoe* standard and assures a plaintiff of a forum.[37] * * * We believe, however, that the fairness standard of *International Shoe* can be easily applied in the vast majority of cases. Moreover, when the existence of jurisdiction in a particular forum under *International Shoe* is unclear, the cost of simplifying the litigation by avoiding the jurisdictional question may be the sacrifice of "fair play and substantial justice." That cost is too high.

We are left, then, to consider the significance of the long history of jurisdiction based solely on the presence of property in a State. Although the theory that territorial power is both essential to and sufficient for jurisdiction has been undermined, we have never held that the presence of property in a State does not automatically confer jurisdiction over the owner's interest in that property. This history must be considered as supporting the proposition that jurisdiction based solely on the presence of property satisfies the demands of due process * * *, but it is not decisive. * * * The fiction that an assertion of jurisdiction over property is anything but an assertion of jurisdiction over the owner of the property supports an ancient form without substantial modern justification. Its continued acceptance would serve only to allow state-court jurisdiction that is fundamentally unfair to the defendant.

We therefore conclude that all assertions of state-court jurisdiction must be evaluated according to the standards set forth in *International Shoe* and its progeny.

IV

The Delaware courts based their assertion of jurisdiction in this case solely on the statutory presence of appellants' property in Delaware. Yet that property is not the subject matter of this litigation, nor is the underlying cause of action related to the property. Appellants' holdings in Greyhound do not, therefore, provide contacts with Delaware sufficient to

---

37. This case does not raise, and we therefore do not consider, the question whether the presence of a defendant's property in a State is a sufficient basis for jurisdiction when no other forum is available to the plaintiff.

support the jurisdiction of that State's courts over appellants. If it exists, that jurisdiction must have some other foundation.

Appellee Heitner did not allege and does not now claim that appellants have ever set foot in Delaware. Nor does he identify any act related to his cause of action as having taken place in Delaware. Nevertheless, he contends that appellants' positions as directors and officers of a corporation chartered in Delaware provide sufficient "contacts, ties, or relations" * * * with that State to give its courts jurisdiction over appellants in this stockholder's derivative action. This argument is based primarily on what Heitner asserts to be the strong interest of Delaware in supervising the management of a Delaware corporation. That interest is said to derive from the role of Delaware law in establishing the corporation and defining the obligations owed to it by its officers and directors. In order to protect this interest, appellee concludes, Delaware's courts must have jurisdiction over corporate fiduciaries such as appellants.

This argument is undercut by the failure of the Delaware Legislature to assert the state interest appellee finds so compelling. Delaware law bases jurisdiction, not on appellants' status as corporate fiduciaries, but rather on the presence of their property in the State. Although the sequestration procedure used here may be most frequently used in derivative suits against officers and directors, * * * the authorizing statute evinces no specific concern with such actions. Sequestration can be used in any suit against a nonresident * * * and reaches corporate fiduciaries only if they happen to own interests in a Delaware corporation, or other property in the State. But as Heitner's failure to secure jurisdiction over seven of the defendants named in his complaint demonstrates, there is no necessary relationship between holding a position as a corporate fiduciary and owning stock or other interests in the corporation. If Delaware perceived its interest in securing jurisdiction over corporate fiduciaries to be as great as Heitner suggests, we would expect it to have enacted a statute more clearly designed to protect that interest.

* * *

Appellee suggests that by accepting positions as officers or directors of a Delaware corporation, appellants performed the acts [sufficient to justify the assertion of jurisdiction by Delaware courts under] Hanson v. Denckla. He notes that Delaware law provides substantial benefits to corporate officers and directors, and that these benefits were at least in part the incentive for appellants to assume their positions. It is, he says, "only fair and just" to require appellants, in return for these benefits, to respond in the State of Delaware when they are accused of misusing their power. * * *

But like Heitner's first argument, this line of reasoning establishes only that it is appropriate for Delaware law to govern the obligations of appellants to Greyhound and its stockholders. It does not demonstrate that appellants have "purposefully avail[ed themselves] of the privilege of conducting activities within the forum State," Hanson v. Denckla * * *, in a way that would justify bringing them before a Delaware tribunal. Appellants have simply had nothing to do with the State of Delaware. Moreover, appellants had no reason to expect to be haled before a Delaware court. Delaware, unlike some States, has not enacted a statute that treats acceptance of a directorship as consent to jurisdiction in the State. And "[i]t strains reason ... to suggest that anyone buying securities in a corporation formed in Delaware 'impliedly consents' to subject himself to Delaware's * * * jurisdiction on any cause of action." Folk & Moyer, [*Sequestration in Delaware: A Constitutional Analysis*, 73 Colum. L. Rev. 749, 785 (1973)] .... Appellants, who were not required to acquire interests in Greyhound in order to hold their positions, did not by acquiring those interests surrender their right to be brought to judgment only in States with which they had had "minimum contacts."

* * * Delaware's assertion of jurisdiction over appellants in this case is inconsistent with that constitutional limitation on state power. The judgment of the Delaware Supreme Court must, therefore, be reversed.

It is so ordered.

MR. JUSTICE REHNQUIST took no part in the consideration or decision of this case.

MR. JUSTICE POWELL, concurring.

* * *

I would explicitly reserve judgment * * * on whether the ownership of some forms of property whose situs is indisputably and permanently located within a State may, without more, provide the contacts necessary to subject a defendant to jurisdiction within the State to the extent of the value of the property. In the case of real property, in particular, preservation of the common law concept of *quasi in rem* jurisdiction arguably would avoid the uncertainty of the general *International Shoe* standard without significant cost to " 'traditional notions of fair play and substantial justice.' " * * *

Subject to the foregoing reservation, I join the opinion of the Court.

MR. JUSTICE STEVENS, concurring in the judgment.

* * *

One who purchases shares of stock on the open market can hardly be expected to know that he has thereby become subject to suit in a forum remote from his residence and unrelated to the transaction. As a practical matter, the Delaware sequestration statute creates an unacceptable risk of judgment without notice. Unlike the 49 other States, Delaware treats the place of incorporation as the situs of the stock, even though both the owner and the custodian of the shares are elsewhere. Moreover, Delaware denies the defendant the opportunity to defend the merits of the suit unless he subjects himself to the unlimited jurisdiction of the court. Thus, it coerces a defendant either to submit to personal jurisdiction in a forum which could not otherwise obtain such jurisdiction or to lose the securities which have been attached. If its procedure were upheld, Delaware would, in effect, impose a duty of inquiry on every purchaser of securities in the national market. For unless the purchaser ascertains both the State of incorporation of the company whose shares he is buying, and also the idiosyncrasies of its law, he may be assuming an unknown risk of litigation. I therefore agree with the Court that on the record before us no adequate basis for jurisdiction exists and that the Delaware statute is unconstitutional on its face.

How the Court's opinion may be applied in other contexts is not entirely clear to me. I agree with MR. JUSTICE POWELL that it should not be read to invalidate *in rem* jurisdiction where real estate is involved. I would also not read it as invalidating other long-accepted methods of acquiring jurisdiction over persons with adequate notice of both the particular controversy and the fact that their local activities might subject them to suit. My uncertainty as to the reach of the opinion, and my fear that it purports to decide a great deal more than is necessary to dispose of this case, persuade me merely to concur in the judgment.

MR. JUSTICE BRENNAN, concurring in part and dissenting in part.

I join Parts I–III of the Court's opinion. I fully agree that the minimum-contacts analysis * * * represents a far more sensible construct for the exercise of state-court jurisdiction than the patchwork of legal and factual fictions that has been generated from the decision in Pennoyer v. Neff * * *. It is precisely because the inquiry into minimum contacts is now of such overriding importance, however, that I must respectfully dissent from Part IV of the Court's opinion.

* * *

II

* * * While evidence derived through discovery might satisfy me that minimum contacts are lacking in a given case, I am convinced that as a general rule a state forum has jurisdiction to adjudicate a shareholder derivative action centering on the conduct and policies of the directors and officers of a corporation chartered by that State. Unlike the Court, I therefore would not foreclose Delaware from asserting jurisdiction over appellants were it persuaded to do so on the basis of minimum contacts.

It is well settled that a derivative lawsuit as presented here does not inure primarily to the benefit of the named plaintiff. Rather, the primary beneficiaries are the corporation and its owners, the shareholders. * * *

* * *

* * * Certainly nothing said by the Court persuades me that it would be unfair to subject appellants to suit in Delaware. The fact that the record does not reveal whether they "set foot" or committed "acts related to [the] cause of action" in Delaware * * * is not decisive, for jurisdiction can be based strictly on out-of-state acts having foreseeable effects in the forum State. * * * I have little difficulty in applying this principle to

nonresident fiduciaries whose alleged breaches of trust are said to have substantial damaging effect on the financial posture of a resident corporation. Further, I cannot understand how the existence of minimum contacts in a constitutional sense is at all affected by Delaware's failure statutorily to express an interest in controlling corporate fiduciaries. * * * To me this simply demonstrates that Delaware did not elect to assert jurisdiction to the extent the Constitution would allow. Nor would I view as controlling or even especially meaningful Delaware's failure to exact from appellants their consent to be sued. * * * Once we have rejected the jurisdictional framework created in Pennoyer v. Neff, I see no reason to rest jurisdiction on a fictional outgrowth of that system such as the existence of a consent statute, expressed or implied.

I, therefore, would approach the minimum-contacts analysis differently than does the Court. Crucial to me is the fact that appellants voluntarily associated themselves with the State of Delaware, "invoking the benefits and protections of its laws," * * * by entering into a long-term and fragile relationship with one of its domestic corporations. They thereby elected to assume powers and to undertake responsibilities wholly derived from that State's rules and regulations, and to become eligible for those benefits that Delaware law makes available to its corporations' officials. E.g., Del. Code Ann., Tit. 8, § 143 (1975) (interest-free loans); § 145 (1975 ed. and Supp. 1976) (indemnification). While it is possible that countervailing issues of judicial efficiency and the like might clearly favor a different forum, they do not appear on the meager record before us; and, of course, we are concerned solely with "minimum" contacts, not the "best" contacts. * * *

NOTES AND QUESTIONS

1. Within thirteen days after the decision in *Shaffer*, the Delaware legislature amended its laws to provide that every nonresident who is elected or appointed a director of a Delaware corporation after September 1, 1977, shall "be deemed" to have consented to the appointment of the corporation's registered agent in Delaware, or, if there is no registered agent, of the Secretary of State of Delaware, as his agent for service of process in any Delaware action based on violation of the director's duties as director after September 1, 1977. 10 Del. Code § 3114. The constitutionality of the section was upheld by the Supreme Court of Delaware in Armstrong v. Pomerance, 423 A.2d 174 (Del. 1980), a suit against nonresidents whose sole contact with Delaware was their status as directors of a Delaware corporation. See also Stearn v. Malloy, 89 F.R.D. 421 (E.D.Wis. 1981) (reaching same conclusion under similar Wisconsin statute). See Comment, *Constitutional Analysis of the New Delaware Director–Consent-to-Service Statute*, 70 Geo. L.J. 1209 (1983). In 2004, the Delaware consent-to-service statute was extended to high officers of Delaware corporations (such as the president, treasurer, or CEO).

2. How does *Shaffer* affect a court's power to enter a judgment in an action where the cause of action relates to property that defendant owns and is located in the forum state?

3.   In RUSH v. SAVCHUK, 444 U.S. 320, 100 S.Ct. 571, 62 L.Ed.2d 516 (1980), the Supreme Court settled the question of whether an insurance obligation can be attached to effect quasi in rem jurisdiction. In finding such an attachment unconstitutional, the Court separated the contacts of the defendant with the forum from those of the insurer with the forum. Having done so, the Court held that sufficient contacts between the defendant and the forum did not exist and that the Due Process Clause forbade the assertion of jurisdiction.

SECTION H.   TRANSIENT PRESENCE IN THE FORUM

BURNHAM v. SUPERIOR COURT

Supreme Court of the United States, 1990.
495 U.S. 604, 110 S.Ct. 2105, 109 L.Ed.2d 631.

Certiorari to the Court of Appeal of California, First Appellate District.

JUSTICE SCALIA announced the judgment of the Court and delivered an opinion in which THE CHIEF JUSTICE and JUSTICE KENNEDY join, and in which JUSTICE WHITE joins with respect to Parts I, II–A, II–B, and II–C.

The question presented is whether the Due Process Clause of the Fourteenth Amendment denies California courts jurisdiction over a nonresident, who was personally served with process while temporarily in that State, in a suit unrelated to his activities in the State.

I

Petitioner Dennis Burnham married Francie Burnham in 1976 in West Virginia. In 1977 the couple moved to New Jersey, where their two children were born. In July 1987 the Burnhams decided to separate. They agreed that Mrs. Burnham, who intended to move to California, would take custody of the children. Shortly before Mrs. Burnham departed for California that same month, she and petitioner agreed that she would file for divorce on grounds of "irreconcilable differences."

In October 1987, petitioner filed for divorce in New Jersey state court on grounds of "desertion." Petitioner did not, however, obtain an issuance of summons against his wife and did not attempt to serve her with process. Mrs. Burnham, after unsuccessfully demanding that petitioner adhere to their prior agreement to submit to an "irreconcilable differences" divorce, brought suit for divorce in California state court in early January 1988.

In late January, petitioner visited southern California on business, after which he went north to visit his children in the San Francisco Bay area, where his wife resided. He took the older child to San Francisco for the weekend. Upon returning the child to Mrs. Burnham's home on January 24, 1988, petitioner was served with a California court summons and a copy of Mrs. Burnham's divorce petition. He then returned to New Jersey.

Later that year, petitioner made a special appearance in the California Superior Court, moving to quash the service of process on the ground that the court lacked personal jurisdiction over him because his only contacts with California were a few short visits to the State for the purposes of conducting business and visiting his children. The Superior Court denied the motion, and the California Court of Appeal denied mandamus relief, rejecting petitioner's contention that the Due Process Clause prohibited California courts from asserting jurisdiction over him because he lacked "minimum contacts" with the State. The court held it to be "a valid jurisdictional predicate for *in personam* jurisdiction" that the "defendant [was] present in the forum state and personally served with process." * * * We granted certiorari. * * *

II

* * *

To determine whether the assertion of personal jurisdiction is consistent with due process, we have long relied on the principles traditionally followed by American courts in marking out the territorial limits of each State's authority. * * * In what has become the classic expression of the criterion, we said in International Shoe Co. v. Washington, * * * that a state court's assertion of personal jurisdiction satisfies the Due Process Clause if it does not violate " 'traditional notions of fair play and substantial justice.' " * * * Since *International Shoe*, we have only been called upon to decide whether these "traditional notions" permit States to exercise jurisdiction over absent defendants in a manner that deviates from the rules of jurisdiction applied in the 19th century. We have held such deviations permissible, but only with respect to suits arising out of the absent defendant's contacts with the State. * * * The question we must decide today is whether due process requires a similar connection between the litigation and the defendant's contacts with the State in cases where the defendant is physically present in the State at the time process is served upon him.

B

Among the most firmly established principles of personal jurisdiction in American tradition is that the courts of a State have jurisdiction over nonresidents who are physically present in the State. * * *

* * *

Decisions in the courts of many States in the 19th and early 20th centuries held that personal service upon a physically present defendant sufficed to confer jurisdiction, without regard to whether the defendant was only briefly in the State or whether the cause of action was related to his activities there. * * * Although research has not revealed a case deciding the issue in every State's courts, that appears to be because the issue was so well settled that it went unlitigated. * * * Particularly striking is the fact that, as far as we have been able to determine, *not one* American case from the period (or, for that matter, not one American case until 1978) held, or even suggested, that in-state personal service on an individual was insufficient to confer personal jurisdiction. Commentators were also seemingly unanimous on the rule. * * *

This American jurisdictional practice is, moreover, not merely old; it is continuing. It remains the practice of, not only a substantial number of the States, but as far as we are aware *all* the States and the Federal Government—if one disregards (as one must for this purpose) the few opinions since 1978 that have erroneously said, on grounds similar to those that petitioner presses here, that this Court's due process decisions render the practice unconstitutional. * * * We do not know of a single state or federal statute, or a single judicial decision resting upon state law, that has abandoned in-state service as a basis of jurisdiction. Many recent cases reaffirm it. * * *

C

Despite this formidable body of precedent, petitioner contends, in reliance on our decisions applying the *International Shoe* standard, that in the absence of "continuous and systematic" contacts with the forum, * * * a nonresident defendant can be subjected to judgment only as to matters that arise out of or relate to his contacts with the forum. This argument rests on a thorough misunderstanding of our cases.

The view of most courts in the 19th century was that a court simply could not exercise *in personam* jurisdiction over a nonresident who had not been personally served with process in the forum. * * *

* * *

Nothing in *International Shoe* or the cases that have followed it, however, offers support for the very different proposition petitioner seeks to establish today: that a defendant's presence in the forum is not only unnecessary to validate novel, nontraditional assertions of jurisdiction, but is itself no longer sufficient to establish jurisdiction. That proposition is unfaithful to both elementary logic and the foundations of our due process jurisprudence. The distinction between what is needed to support novel procedures and what is needed to sustain traditional ones is fundamental * * *. The short of the matter is that jurisdiction based on physical presence alone constitutes due process because it is one of the continuing traditions of our legal system that define the due process standard of "traditional notions of fair play and substantial justice." That standard was developed by *analogy* to "physical presence," and it would be perverse to say it could now be turned against that touchstone of jurisdiction.

D

Petitioner's strongest argument, though we ultimately reject it, relies upon our decision in Shaffer v. Heitner * * *.

It goes too far to say, as petitioner contends, that *Shaffer* compels the conclusion that a State lacks jurisdiction over an individual unless the litigation arises out of his activities in the State. *Shaffer*, like *International Shoe,* involved jurisdiction over an *absent defendant*, and it stands for nothing more than the proposition that when the "minimum contact" that is a substitute for physical presence consists of property ownership it must, like other minimum contacts, be related to the litigation. * * * The logic of *Shaffer*'s holding—which places all suits against absent nonresidents on the same constitutional footing, regardless of whether a separate Latin label is attached to one particular basis of contact—does not compel the conclusion that physically present defendants must be treated identically to absent ones. As we have demonstrated at length, our tradition has treated the two classes of defendants quite differently, and it is unreasonable to read *Shaffer* as casually obliterating that distinction. *International Shoe* confined its "minimum contacts" requirement to situations in which the defendant "be not present within the territory of the forum," * * * and nothing in *Shaffer* expands that requirement beyond that.

It is fair to say, however, that while our holding today does not contradict *Shaffer*, our basic approach to the due process question is different. We have conducted no independent inquiry into the desirability or fairness of the prevailing in-state service rule, leaving that judgment to the legislatures that are free to amend it; for our purposes, its validation is its pedigree, as the phrase *"traditional notions* of fair play and substantial justice" makes clear. *Shaffer* did conduct such an independent inquiry, asserting that " 'traditional notions of fair play and substantial justice' can be as readily offended by the perpetuation of ancient forms that are no longer justified as by the adoption of new procedures that are inconsistent with the basic values of our constitutional heritage." * * * Perhaps that assertion can be sustained when the "perpetuation of ancient forms" is engaged in by only a very small minority of the States. Where, however, as in the present case, a jurisdictional principle is both firmly approved by tradition and still favored, it is impossible to imagine what standard we could appeal to for the judgment that it is "no longer justified." * * * For new procedures, hitherto unknown, the Due Process Clause requires analysis to determine whether "traditional notions of fair play and substantial justice" have been offended. * * * But a doctrine of personal jurisdiction that dates back to the adoption of the Fourteenth Amendment and is still generally observed unquestionably meets that standard.

III

* * *

The difference between us and Justice Brennan has nothing to do with whether "further progress [is] to be made" in the "evolution of our legal system." * * * It has to do with whether changes are to be adopted as progressive by the American people or decreed as progressive by the Justices of this Court. Nothing we say today prevents individual States from limiting or entirely abandoning the in-state-service basis of jurisdiction. And nothing prevents an overwhelming majority of them from doing so, with the consequence that the "traditional notions of fairness" that this Court applies may change. But the States have overwhelmingly declined to adopt such limitation or abandonment, evidently not considering it to be progress. The question is whether, armed with no authority other than individual Justices' perceptions of fairness that conflict with both past and current practice, this Court can compel the States to make such a change on the ground that "due process" requires it. We hold that it cannot.

Because the Due Process Clause does not prohibit the California courts from exercising jurisdiction over petitioner based on the fact of in-state service of process, the judgment is

Affirmed.

JUSTICE WHITE, concurring in part and concurring in the judgment.

I join Parts I, II–A, II–B, and II–C of Justice Scalia's opinion and concur in the judgment of affirmance. The rule allowing jurisdiction to be obtained over a nonresident by personal service in the forum State, without more, has been and is so widely accepted throughout this country that I could not possibly strike it down, either on its face or as applied in this case, on the ground that it denies due process of law guaranteed by the Fourteenth Amendment. * * *

JUSTICE BRENNAN, with whom JUSTICE MARSHALL, JUSTICE BLACKMUN, and JUSTICE O'CONNOR join, concurring in the judgment.

I agree with Justice Scalia that the Due Process Clause of the Fourteenth Amendment generally permits a state court to exercise jurisdiction over a defendant if he is served with process while voluntarily present in the forum State. I do not perceive the need, however, to decide that a jurisdictional rule that " 'has been immemorially the actual law of the land,' " * * * automatically comports with due process simply by virtue of its "pedigree." * * * Unlike Justice Scalia, I would undertake an "independent inquiry into the … fairness of the prevailing in-state service rule." * * * I therefore concur only in the judgment.

I

I believe that the approach adopted by Justice Scalia's opinion today—reliance solely on historical pedigree—is foreclosed by our decisions in International Shoe Co. v. Washington * * * and Shaffer v. Heitner * * *. The critical insight of *Shaffer* is that all rules of jurisdiction, even ancient ones, must satisfy contemporary notions of due process. * * * I agree with this approach and continue to believe that "the minimum-contacts analysis developed in *International Shoe* … represents a far more sensible construct for the exercise of state-court jurisdiction than the patchwork of legal and factual fictions that has been generated from the decision in Pennoyer v. Neff." * * * [Shaffer v. Heitner, p. 98, supra].

While our *holding* in *Shaffer* may have been limited to *quasi in rem* jurisdiction, our mode of analysis was not. * * * Notwithstanding the nimble gymnastics of JUSTICE SCALIA's opinion today, it is not faithful to our decision in *Shaffer*.

II

Tradition, though alone not dispositive, is of course *relevant* to the question whether the rule of transient jurisdiction is consistent with due process. * * *

* * * I find the historical background relevant because, however murky the jurisprudential origins of transient jurisdiction, the fact that American courts have announced the rule for perhaps a century * * * provides a defendant voluntarily present in a particular State *today* "clear notice that [he] is subject to suit" in the forum. * * * [Thus, t]he transient rule is consistent with reasonable expectations and is entitled to a strong presumption that it comports with due process. * * *

By visiting the forum State, a transient defendant actually "avail[s]" himself * * * of significant benefits provided by the State. His health and safety are guaranteed by the State's police, fire, and emergency medical services; he is free to travel on the State's roads and waterways; he likely enjoys the fruits of the State's economy as well. Moreover, the Privileges and Immunities Clause of Article IV prevents a state government from discriminating against a transient defendant by denying him the protections of its law or the right of access to its courts. * * * Without transient jurisdiction, an asymmetry would arise: A transient would have the full benefit of the power of the forum State's courts as a plaintiff while retaining immunity from their authority as a defendant. * * *

The potential burdens on a transient defendant are slight. * * * Finally, any burdens that do arise can be ameliorated by a variety of procedural devices. For these reasons, as a rule the exercise of personal jurisdiction over a defendant based on his voluntary presence in the forum will satisfy the requirements of due process. * * *

In this case, it is undisputed that petitioner was served with process while voluntarily and knowingly in the State of California. I therefore concur in the judgment.

JUSTICE STEVENS, concurring in the judgment.

As I explained in my separate writing, I did not join the Court's opinion in Shaffer v. Heitner * * * because I was concerned by its unnecessarily broad reach. * * * The same concern prevents me from joining either Justice Scalia's or Justice Brennan's opinion in this case. For me, it is sufficient to note that the historical evidence and consensus identified by Justice Scalia, the considerations of fairness identified by

Justice Brennan, and the common sense displayed by Justice White, all combine to demonstrate that this is, indeed, a very easy case.* Accordingly, I agree that the judgment should be affirmed.

NOTES AND QUESTIONS

1.   The Justices agreed on the result in *Burnham,* but could not agree on its theoretical underpinnings. Which opinion states the law of transient personal jurisdiction as it now stands? Which approach do you find to be more persuasive? Is the intense debate in *Burnham* evidence of a deeper disagreement between Justice Scalia and Justice Brennan? If so, what is it?

2.   Has Justice Scalia correctly interpreted the word "traditional" in the phrase "traditional notions of fair play and substantial justice"? See Greenberger, *Justice Scalia's Due Process Traditionalism Applied to Territorial Jurisdiction: The Illusion of Adjudication Without Judgment,* 33 B.C. L. Rev. 981 (1992). If he has not, what is its intended meaning? Similarly, what significance ought to attach to the statement in Shaffer v. Heitner that: "all assertions of state-court jurisdiction must be evaluated according to the standards set forth in *International Shoe* and its progeny"?

3.   Are there special factors in a case brought against a foreign defendant that would argue in favor of adopting Justice Brennan's, rather than Justice Scalia's, approach? See Hay, *Transient Jurisdiction, Especially Over International Defendants: Critical Comments on* Burnham v. Superior Court of California, 1990 U. Ill. L. Rev. 593.

4.   Should a "virtual" contact with the forum be treated as transient presence for jurisdictional purposes? If so, what types of virtual contacts should qualify?

SECTION I.   ANOTHER BASIS OF JURISDICTION: CONSENT

1.   CONSENT BY APPEARANCE IN COURT

Defendant may choose to waive objections to the court's exercise of personal jurisdiction. Defendant also may forfeit the opportunity to raise objections. Rule 12(h)(1) of the Federal Rules provides that a defendant who fails to raise an objection to personal jurisdiction in the answer or in an initial motion under Rule 12 is precluded from raising the issue. Must defendant assist the court in determining whether a basis for personal jurisdiction exists?

———

INSURANCE CORP. OF IRELAND, LTD. v. COMPAGNIE DES BAUXITES DE GUINEE, 456 U.S. 694, 102 S.Ct. 2099, 72 L.Ed.2d 492 (1982). The plaintiff, Compagnie des Bauxites de Guinee (CBG), a bauxite

———

* Perhaps the adage about hard cases making bad law should be revised to cover easy cases.

producer incorporated in Delaware but doing business only in the Republic of Guinea, purchased business-interruption insurance from a domestic insurer in Pennsylvania and from a group of foreign insurance companies through a London brokerage house. When a mechanical failure forced a halt in production, CBG filed a multi-million dollar claim, which the insurers refused to pay. CBG then sued in federal court in Pennsylvania, but most of the foreign insurance companies contested personal jurisdiction. CBG attempted to use discovery to establish the essential jurisdictional facts. After the companies failed to comply with the court's orders for production of the requested information and after repeated warnings, the District Court, pursuant to Federal Rule 37(b)(2)(A)(i), imposed a sanction consisting of a presumptive finding that the insurers were subject to the jurisdiction of the court because of their business contacts in Pennsylvania. The Supreme Court upheld the sanction in an opinion by Justice White.

> Because the requirement of personal jurisdiction represents first of all an individual right, it can, like other such rights, be waived. * * *
>
> * * * By submitting to the jurisdiction of the court for the limited purpose of challenging jurisdiction, the defendant agrees to abide by that court's determination on the issue of jurisdiction * * * [and] the manner in which the court determines whether it has personal jurisdiction may include a variety of legal rules and presumptions, as well as straightforward factfinding. * * *
>
> CBG was seeking through discovery to respond to [the insurers'] contention that the District Court did not have personal jurisdiction. Having put the issue in question, [the insurers] did not have the option of blocking the reasonable attempt of CBG to meet its burden of proof. * * * [They] surely did not have this option once the court had overruled [their] objections. Because of [the insurers'] failure to comply with the discovery orders, CBG was unable to establish the full extent of the contacts between [the insurers] and Pennsylvania, the critical issue in proving personal jurisdiction. * * * [Their] failure to supply the requested information as to [their] contacts with Pennsylvania supports "the presumption that the refusal to produce evidence ... was but an admission of the want of merit in the asserted defense." * * * The sanction took as established the facts—contacts with Pennsylvania—that CBG was seeking to establish through discovery.

Id. at 702–09, 102 S.Ct. at 2104–08, 72 L.Ed.2d at 501–05.

2. CONSENT BY REGISTRATION IN STATE

Most states have statutes that require a foreign corporation to register as a condition of doing business in the forum state. Would it be constitutional for a court to exercise general jurisdiction based solely on a nonresident company's compliance with a registration statute on the view that the act of registration manifests consent to jurisdiction in the forum? Should it be relevant that a registration statute also requires appointment of an in-state agent for service of process? Compare Knowlton v. Allied Van Lines, Inc., 900 F.2d 1196, 1200 (8th Cir. 1990) ("[A]ppointment of an agent for service of process * * * gives consent to the jurisdiction of Minnesota courts for any cause of action, whether or not arising out of activities within the state."), with Wenche Siemer v. Learjet Acquisition Corp., 966 F.2d 179, 183 (5th Cir. 1992) ("[T]he mere act of registering an agent * * * does not act as consent.").

Why isn't this "consent," as Justice Holmes observed, a "mere fiction," Flexner v. Farson, 248 U.S. 289, 39 S.Ct. 97, 63 L.Ed. 250 (1919), that should not be invoked unless the requisite "minimum contacts" exist? In RATLIFF v. COOPER LABORATORIES, INC., 444 F.2d 745 (4th Cir.), certiorari denied 404 U.S. 948, 92 S.Ct. 271, 30 L.Ed.2d 265 (1971), the Court of Appeals held that a foreign corporation that had qualified to do business in South Carolina and regularly sent salesmen into the state could not be sued in South Carolina by plaintiffs from Florida and Indiana that had purchased and consumed in their home states drugs manufactured by the defendant, and sued in South Carolina because of that state's relatively long statute of limitations: "Applying for the privilege of doing business is one thing, but the actual exercise of that privilege is quite another. * * * The principles of due process require a firmer foundation than mere compliance with state domestication statutes." Id. at 748.

3. CONSENT BY CONTRACT

Defendant may consent to the court's exercise of personal jurisdiction by agreeing to a contract that includes a forum-selection clause. Such a clause can apply to a dispute that already exists or to one that later may arise between the parties. Courts traditionally did not give effect to forum-selection clauses, on the view that they impermissibly oust a court of power. Consider how the following cases affect the parties' ability to contract for a jurisdiction they prefer.

M/S BREMEN v. ZAPATA OFF-SHORE CO., 407 U.S. 1, 92 S.Ct. 1907, 32 L.Ed.2d 513 (1972). Plaintiff Zapata, a Houston-based American corporation, contracted with Unterweser, a German corporation, to tow Zapata's drilling rig from Louisiana to Italy. The contract contained a provision that all disputes were to be litigated before the "London Court of Justice." In the course of the towing, the rig was damaged in a storm off Florida and was towed to Tampa. Zapata commenced suit against Unterweser in a federal court in Florida. Unterweser, citing the forum-selection clause in the contract, moved to dismiss or, alternatively, to stay the action pending the submission of the dispute to the High Court of

Justice in London. Simultaneously, Unterweser sued Zapata for breach of contract in the English court.

The District Court refused to dismiss or stay the American action, and the Court of Appeals affirmed. But the Supreme Court reversed:

> We hold * * * that far too little weight and effect were given to the forum clause in resolving this controversy. * * * The expansion of American business and industry will hardly be encouraged if, notwithstanding solemn contracts, we insist on a parochial concept that all disputes must be resolved under our laws and in our courts. * * * We cannot have trade and commerce in world markets and international waters exclusively on our terms, governed by our laws, and resolved in our courts.

Id. at 8–9, 92 S.Ct. at 1912–13, 32 L.Ed.2d at 519–20.

———

CARNIVAL CRUISE LINES, INC. v. SHUTE, 499 U.S. 585, 111 S.Ct. 1522, 113 L.Ed.2d 622 (1991). Plaintiffs, Eulala and Russel Shute, purchased passage for a seven-day cruise on defendant's ship, the Tropicale, through a Washington State travel agent. Plaintiffs paid the fare to the agent who forwarded the payment to defendant's headquarters in Florida. Defendant then prepared the tickets and sent them to plaintiffs in Washington. The ticket included a provision stating that:

> 8. It is agreed by and between the passenger and the Carrier that all disputes and matters whatsoever arising under, in connection with or incident to this Contract shall be litigated, if at all, in and before a Court located in the State of Florida, U.S.A., to the exclusion of the Courts of any other state or country.

Plaintiffs boarded the Tropicale in Los Angeles, California and sailed for Puerto Vallarta, Mexico. Off the coast of Mexico, Mrs. Shute slipped on a deck mat and was injured. Plaintiffs filed suit in federal district court in Washington, claiming that the negligence of defendant and its employees had caused Mrs. Shute's injuries. The District Court held that defendant's contacts with Washington were constitutionally insufficient to exercise personal jurisdiction; the Ninth Circuit Court of Appeals declined to enforce the forum-selection clause, but concluded that defendant did have sufficient contacts with Washington, and reversed the lower court.

The Supreme Court did not consider defendant's "minimum contacts" argument; instead, it addressed the enforceability of the forum-selection clause. Rejecting the argument that *Zapata* was limited to contracts between two business corporations, the Court stated:

> * * * Including a reasonable forum clause in a form contract of this kind well may be permissible for several reasons: First, a cruise line has a special interest in limiting the fora in which it potentially could be subject to suit. Because a cruise ship typically carries passengers

from many locales, it is not unlikely that a mishap on a cruise could subject the cruise line to litigation in several different fora. * * * Additionally, a clause establishing *ex ante* the forum for dispute resolution has the salutary effect of dispelling any confusion about where suits arising from the contract must be brought and defended, sparing litigants the time and expense of pretrial motions to determine the correct forum, and conserving judicial resources that otherwise would be devoted to deciding those motions. * * * Finally, it stands to reason that passengers who purchase tickets containing a forum clause like that at issue in this case benefit in the form of reduced fares reflecting the savings that the cruise line enjoys by limiting the fora in which it may be sued. * * *

Id. at 593, 111 S.Ct. at 1527, 113 L.Ed.2d at 632.

NOTE AND QUESTIONS

M/S Bremen held that forum-selection clauses "are prima facie valid" and "should be enforced" by federal courts sitting in admiralty "unless enforcement is shown by the resisting party to be 'unreasonable' under the circumstances." 407 U.S. at 9, 92 S.Ct. at 1913, 32 L.Ed.2d at 520. Applying this test, *Carnival Cruise* emphasized that "forum-selection clauses contained in form passage contracts are subject to judicial scrutiny for fundamental fairness." 499 U.S. at 595, 111 S.Ct. at 1528, 113 L.Ed.2d at 633. What factors are relevant in determining whether a forum-selection clause is "unreasonable" or meets "fundamental fairness"? Are you convinced that the *Carnival Cruise* Court engaged in the appropriate level of scrutiny?

SECTION J.   JURISDICTIONAL REACH OF THE FEDERAL DISTRICT COURTS

———

Read Federal Rule of Civil Procedure 4 and the accompanying materials in the Supplement.

———

NOTE ON FEDERAL RULE 4

A federal court, like any court in the United States, can exercise personal jurisdiction over a defendant only if that power is authorized by statute and comports with due process. Conventionally, discussions about personal jurisdiction in the federal courts focus on Rule 4, but it is important to remember that Rule 4 is a service-of-process rule. "The court's jurisdictional power comes from the legal sources that are incorporated by reference in Rule 4." 4 Wright & Miller, Federal Practice and Procedure: Civil 3d § 1063.

Rule 4 sets out different service rules that you must be able to distinguish:

Rule 4(k)(1)(A) is a general service rule that the federal court may use when a federal statute does not otherwise authorize jurisdiction. Under the Rule, the federal court "piggy-backs" on the long-arm statute of the state in which it sits.

Rule 4(k)(1)(B) is a special service rule that applies to parties joined under Rules 14 and 19 and allows for service "within a judicial district of the United States and not more than 100 miles from where the summons was issued."

Rule 4(k)(1)(C) permits service when authorized by a federal statute (for example, the Anti–Terrorism Act allows for service "in any district where the defendant resides, is found, or has an agent," 18 U.S.C. §§ 2300, 2334(a)).

By contrast, Rule 4(k)(2) is a limited federal long-arm provision that establishes personal jurisdiction "for a claim that arises under federal law" if the "defendant is not subject to jurisdiction in any state's courts of general jurisdiction" and "exercising jurisdiction is consistent with the United States Constitution and laws."

Do you agree that the *International Shoe* standard applies when a federal court, pursuant to Rule 4(k)(1)(A), resorts to the law of the forum state to serve process on an out-of-state defendant? This means that a federal court can use the forum state's long-arm statute only to reach those parties whom a court of the state also could reach. Does the Fifth Amendment also require the application of the "minimum contacts" standard? How would the due process inquiry differ when a federal court exercises power under Federal Rule 4(k)(2)?

SECTION K. CHALLENGING A COURT'S EXERCISE OF JURISDICTION OVER THE PERSON OR PROPERTY

Read Federal Rules of Civil Procedure 12(b), (g), and (h) and the accompanying material in the Supplement.

1. RAISING THE JURISDICTIONAL ISSUE DIRECTLY

The term "special appearance" refers to the procedure at common law by which a defendant presented a challenge to the court's exercise of personal jurisdiction without submitting to the court's jurisdiction for any other purpose. The rules varied from state to state on the technical requirements for making a special appearance. A defendant generally had to designate the appearance "special" and limit himself to raising the jurisdictional defense. If he did anything else, such as argue the merits in any way, the defendant would be deemed to have made a "general appearance," constituting a voluntary submission to the court's jurisdiction and a waiver of any defects in the court's jurisdiction. Although substantial variation still may be encountered among different systems of state procedure, the general rules regarding objections to personal jurisdiction are illustrated by the federal scheme.

2. COLLATERAL ATTACK ON PERSONAL JURISDICTION

If a defendant contests a court's exercise of personal jurisdiction and loses, may he challenge jurisdiction again in a later action to enforce the judgment? Consider BALDWIN v. IOWA STATE TRAVELING MEN'S ASS'N, 283 U.S. 522, 51 S.Ct. 517, 75 L.Ed. 1244 (1931), in which respondent attempted to attack a judgment rendered against it in a Missouri federal district court. The company had made a special appearance in the prior suit and had moved to set aside service and dismiss the case for a lack of personal jurisdiction. In rejecting the respondent's attempt to attack the first judgment collaterally, the Supreme Court stated:

> Public policy dictates that there be an end of litigation; that those who have contested an issue shall be bound by the result of the contest; and that matters once tried shall be considered forever settled as between parties. We see no reason why this doctrine should not apply in every case where one voluntarily appears, presents his case and is fully heard, and why he should not, in the absence of fraud, be thereafter concluded by the judgment of the tribunal to which he has submitted his cause.

Id. at 524–26, 51 S.Ct. at 517–18, 75 L.Ed. at 1245. The *Baldwin* opinion repeats the established rule that a defendant who makes no appearance whatsoever remains free to challenge collaterally a default judgment for want of personal jurisdiction. The principle that a court has power to determine its own personal jurisdiction is limited to defendants who submit the question for resolution in that court. Would it be unthinkable to require a defendant to raise the jurisdictional objection in the initial forum or lose the opportunity to contest personal jurisdiction?

3. THE LIMITED–APPEARANCE PROBLEM

A "limited appearance" allows a defendant in an action commenced on a quasi in rem basis to appear for the limited purpose of defending his interest in the attached property without submitting to the full in personam jurisdiction of the court. See, e.g., Dry Clime Lamp Corp. v. Edwards, 389 F.2d 590 (5th Cir. 1968); Harvard Trust Co. v. Bray, 138 Vt. 199, 413 A.2d 1213 (1980). Without provision for such a limited appearance, a defendant must choose between appearing, and thereby risking the possibility of an in personam judgment in excess of the value of the attached property, or not appearing, thereby, as a practical matter, suffering the forfeiture of his property. See *Developments in the Law—State Court Jurisdiction*, 73 Harv. L. Rev. 909, 954 (1960). Does the limited appearance have a constitutional basis after Shaffer v. Heitner, p. 98, supra?

CHAPTER 3

PROVIDING NOTICE AND AN OPPORTUNITY TO BE HEARD

■ ■ ■

In this Chapter, we continue to examine the Due Process Clause and the several conditions it defines that must exist before a court may render a valid judgment. The concept of "due process of law" traces back to the Magna Carta: "No freemen shall be taken, or imprisoned, or disseized, or outlawed, or banished, or in anywise destroyed; nor will the king pass upon him, or commit him to prison, save by the lawful judgment of his peers, or the law of the land." See Russell, *Due Process of Law*, 14 Yale L.J. 322, 325–26 (1905). The Due Process Clause assures that the parties receive adequate notice of the commencement of the action and the issues involved in it. Yet another condition imposed by the Due Process Clause is that the parties have an adequate opportunity at an appropriate time to present their side of the dispute. These constitutional requirements, essential to the well-functioning of an adversarial system, are well-settled but generate disagreement as to their scope and content.

SECTION A.   THE VALUE OF DUE PROCESS

AVISTA MANAGEMENT, INC. v. WAUSAU UNDERWRITERS INSURANCE CO.

United States District Court, Middle District of Florida, 2006.
2006 WL 1562246.

PRESNELL, J.

This matter comes before the Court on Plaintiff's Motion to designate location of a Rule 30(b)(6) deposition (Doc. 105). Upon consideration of the Motion—the latest in a series of Gordian knots that the parties have been unable to untangle without enlisting the assistance of the federal courts—it is

ORDERED that said Motion is DENIED. Instead, the Court will fashion a new form of alternative dispute resolution, to wit: at 4:00 P.M. on Friday, June 30, 2006, counsel shall convene at a neutral site agreeable to both parties. If counsel cannot agree on a neutral site, they shall meet on the front steps of the Sam M. Gibbons U.S. Courthouse, 801 North Florida Ave., Tampa, Florida 33602. Each lawyer shall be entitled to be accompanied by one paralegal who shall act as an attendant and witness. At that time and location, counsel shall engage in one (1) game of "rock, paper, scissors." The winner of this engagement shall be entitled to select the location for the 30(b)(6) deposition to be held somewhere in Hillsborough County during the period July 11–12, 2006. If either party disputes the outcome of this engagement, an appeal may be filed and a hearing will be held at 8:30 A.M. on Friday, July 7, 2006 before the undersigned in Courtroom 3, George C. Young United States Courthouse and Federal Building, 80 North Hughey Avenue, Orlando, Florida 32801.

DONE and ORDERED.

NOTES AND QUESTIONS

1. Is it appropriate for a court to resolve a discovery dispute through a children's game such as "rock, paper, scissors"? Why or why not? Would it have been appropriate to resolve the discovery dispute in *Avista Management* through the drawing of lots in chambers? See Brown, *Casting Lots: The Illusion of Justice and Accountability in Property Allocation*, 53 Buff. L. Rev. 65 (2005).

2. What are the values that a system of civil procedure ought to serve? Commentators take very different approaches in answering this question. Professor Michelman, for example, has argued that civil process implicates and ought to serve "four discrete, though interrelated" values:

> *Dignity values* reflect concern for the humiliation or loss of self-respect which a person might suffer if denied an opportunity to litigate. *Participation values* reflect an appreciation of litigation as one of the modes in which persons exert influence, or have their wills "counted," in societal decisions they care about. *Deterrence values* recognize the instrumentality of litigation as a mechanism for influencing or constraining individual behavior in ways thought socially desirable. *Effectuation values* see litigation as an important means through which persons are enabled to get, or are given assurances of having, whatever we are pleased to regard as rightfully theirs.

Michelman, *The Supreme Court and Litigation Access Fees: The Right to Protect One's Rights*, 1973 Duke L.J. 1153, 1172 (1973). Judge Posner, by contrast, has emphasized efficiency as the touchstone of a sound system of procedure, and he sees the goal of process "as being the minimization of the sum of error and direct costs." Posner, Economic Analysis of Law § 21.1, at 549 (4th ed. 1992). As you read the cases and materials in this Chapter, consider how these competing values are reflected in the procedures under review.

SECTION B. THE REQUIREMENT OF REASONABLE NOTICE

MULLANE v. CENTRAL HANOVER BANK & TRUST CO.

Supreme Court of the United States, 1950.
339 U.S. 306, 70 S.Ct. 652, 94 L.Ed. 865.

Appeal from the Court of Appeals of New York.

MR. JUSTICE JACKSON delivered the opinion of the Court.

This controversy questions the constitutional sufficiency of notice to beneficiaries on judicial settlement of accounts by the trustee of a common trust fund established under the New York Banking Law * * *. The New York Court of Appeals considered and overruled objections that the statutory notice contravenes requirements of the Fourteenth Amendment * * *. The case is here on appeal * * *.

Common trust fund legislation is addressed to a problem appropriate for state action. Mounting overheads have made administration of small trusts undesirable to corporate trustees. In order that donors and testators of moderately sized trusts may not be denied the service of corporate fiduciaries, the District of Columbia and some thirty states other than New York have permitted pooling small trust estates into one fund for investment administration. The income, capital gains, losses and expenses of the collective trust are shared by the constituent trusts in proportion to their contribution. By this plan, diversification of risk and economy of management can be extended to those whose capital standing alone would not obtain such advantage.

Statutory authorization for the establishment of such common trust funds is provided in the New York Banking Law, § 100–c * * *. Under this Act a trust company may, with approval of the State Banking Board, establish a common fund and, within prescribed limits, invest therein the assets of an unlimited number of estates, trusts or other funds of which it is trustee. Each participating trust shares ratably in the common fund, but exclusive management and control is in the trust company as trustee, and neither a fiduciary nor any beneficiary of a participating trust is deemed to have ownership in any particular asset or investment of this common fund. The trust company must keep fund assets separate from its own, and in its fiduciary capacity may not deal with itself or any affiliate. Provisions are made for accountings twelve to fifteen months after the establishment of a fund and triennially thereafter. The decree in each such judicial settlement of accounts is made binding and conclusive as to any matter set forth in the account upon everyone having any interest in the common fund or in any participating estate, trust or fund.

In January, 1946, Central Hanover Bank and Trust Company established a common trust fund in accordance with these provisions, and in March, 1947, it petitioned the Surrogate's Court for settlement of its first account as common trustee. During the accounting period a total of 113 trusts, approximately half *inter vivos* and half testamentary, participated in the common trust fund, the gross capital of which was nearly three million dollars. The record does not show the number or residence of the beneficiaries, but they were many and it is clear that some of them were not residents of the State of New York.

The only notice given beneficiaries of this specific application [for judicial settlement of the account] was by publication in a local newspaper [for four successive weeks] in strict compliance with the minimum requirements of N.Y. Banking Law § 100–c(12) * * *. Thus the only notice required, and the only one given, was by newspaper publication setting forth merely the name and address of the trust company, the name and the date of establishment of the common trust fund, and a list of all participating estates, trusts or funds.

At the time the first investment in the common fund was made on behalf of each participating estate, however, the trust company, pursuant to the requirements of § 100–c(9), had notified by mail each person of full age and sound mind whose name and address was then known to it and who was "entitled to share in the income therefrom * * * [or] * * * who would be entitled to share in the principal if the event upon which such estate, trust or fund will become distributable should have occurred at the time of sending such notice." Included in the notice was a copy of those provisions of the Act relating to the sending of the notice itself and to the judicial settlement of common trust fund accounts.

Upon the filing of the petition for the settlement of accounts, appellant was, by order of the court pursuant to § 100–c(12), appointed special guardian and attorney for all persons known or unknown not otherwise appearing who had or might thereafter have any interest in the income of the common trust fund; and appellee Vaughan was appointed to represent those similarly interested in the principal. There were no other appearances on behalf of any one interested in either interest or principal.

Appellant appeared specially, objecting that notice and the statutory provisions for notice to beneficiaries were inadequate to afford due process under the Fourteenth Amendment, and therefore that the court was without jurisdiction to render a final and binding decree. Appellant's objections were entertained and overruled [by] the Surrogate * * *. A final decree accepting the accounts has been entered, affirmed by the Appellate Division of the Supreme Court * * * and by the Court of Appeals of the State of New York * * *.

The effect of this decree, as held below, is to settle "all questions respecting the management of the common fund." We understand that every right which beneficiaries would otherwise have against the trust company, either as trustee of the common fund or as trustee of any individual trust, for improper management of the common trust fund during the period covered by the accounting is sealed and wholly terminated by the decree. * * *

* * *

* * * Many controversies have raged about the cryptic and abstract words of the Due Process Clause but there can be no doubt that at a minimum they require that deprivation of life, liberty or property by adjudication be preceded by notice and opportunity for hearing appropriate to the nature of the case.

In two ways this proceeding does or may deprive beneficiaries of property. It may cut off their rights to have the trustee answer for negligent or illegal impairments of their interests. Also, their interests are presumably subject to diminution in the proceeding by allowance of fees and expenses to one who, in their names but without their knowledge, may conduct a fruitless or uncompensatory contest. Certainly the proceeding is one in which they may be deprived of property rights and hence notice and hearing must measure up to the standards of due process.

Personal service of written notice within the jurisdiction is the classic form of notice always adequate in any type of proceeding. But the vital interest of the State in bringing any issues as to its fiduciaries to a final settlement can be served only if interests or claims of individuals who are outside of the State can somehow be determined. A construction of the Due Process Clause which would place impossible or impractical obstacles in the way could not be justified.

Against this interest of the State we must balance the individual interest sought to be protected by the Fourteenth Amendment. This is defined by our holding that "The fundamental requisite of due process of law is the opportunity to be heard." Grannis v. Ordean, 234 U.S. 385, 394, 34 S. Ct. 779, 783, 58 L. Ed. 1363 [(1914)]. This right to be heard has little reality or worth unless one is informed that the matter is pending and can choose for himself whether to appear or default, acquiesce or contest.

The Court has not committed itself to any formula achieving a balance between these interests in a particular proceeding or determining when constructive notice may be utilized or what test it must meet. Personal service has not in all circumstances been regarded as indispensable to the process due to residents, and it has more often been held unnecessary as to nonresidents. * * *

An elementary and fundamental requirement of due process in any proceeding which is to be accorded finality is notice reasonably calculated, under all the circumstances, to apprise interested parties of the pendency of the action and afford them an opportunity to present their objections. * * * The notice must be of such nature as reasonably to convey the required information * * * and it must afford a reasonable time for those interested to make their appearance * * *. But if with due regard for the practicalities and peculiarities of the case these conditions are reasonably met the constitutional requirements are satisfied. * * *

But when notice is a person's due, process which is a mere gesture is not due process. The means employed must be such as one desirous of actually informing the absentee might reasonably adopt to accomplish it. The reasonableness and hence the constitutional validity of any chosen method may be defended on the ground that it is in itself reasonably certain to inform those affected * * *, or, where conditions do not reasonably permit such notice, that the form chosen is not substantially less likely to bring home notice than other of the feasible and customary substitutes.

It would be idle to pretend that publication alone, as prescribed here, is a reliable means of acquainting interested parties of the fact that their rights are before the courts. It is not an accident that the greater number of cases reaching this Court on the question of adequacy of notice have been concerned with actions founded on process constructively served through local newspapers. Chance alone brings to the attention of even a local resident an advertisement in small type inserted in the back pages of a newspaper, and if he makes his home outside the area of the newspaper's normal circulation the odds that the information will never reach him are large indeed. The chance of actual notice is further reduced when as here the notice required does not even name those whose attention it is supposed to attract, and does not inform acquaintances who might call it to attention. In weighing its sufficiency on the basis of equivalence with actual notice we are unable to regard this as more than a feint.

Nor is publication here reinforced by steps likely to attract the parties' attention to the proceeding. It is true that publication traditionally has been acceptable as notification supplemental to other action which in itself may reasonably be expected to convey a warning. The ways of an owner with tangible property are such that he usually arranges means to learn of any direct attack upon his possessory or proprietary rights. Hence, libel of a ship, attachment of a chattel or entry upon real estate in the name of law may reasonably be expected to come promptly to the owner's attention. When the state within which the owner has located such property seizes it for some reason, publication or posting affords an additional measure of notification. A state may indulge the assumption that one who has left tangible property in the state either has abandoned it, in which case proceedings against it deprive him of nothing * * *, or that he has left some caretaker under a duty to let him know that it is being jeopardized. * * *

In the case before us there is, of course, no abandonment. On the other hand these beneficiaries do have a resident fiduciary as caretaker of their interest in this property. But it is their caretaker who in the accounting becomes their adversary. Their trustee is released from giving notice of jeopardy, and no one else is expected to do so. Not even the special guardian is required or apparently expected to communicate with his ward and client, and, of course, if such a duty were merely transferred from the trustee to the guardian, economy would not be served and more likely the cost would be increased.

This Court has not hesitated to approve of resort to publication as a customary substitute in another class of cases where it is not reasonably possible or practicable to give more adequate warning. Thus it has been recognized that, in the case of persons missing or unknown, employment of an indirect and even a probably futile means of notification is all that the situation permits and creates no constitutional bar to a final decree foreclosing their rights. * * *

Those beneficiaries represented by appellant whose interests or whereabouts could not with due diligence be ascertained come clearly within this category. As to them the statutory notice is sufficient. However great the odds that publication will never reach the eyes of such unknown parties, it is not in the typical case much more likely to fail than any of the choices open to legislators endeavoring to prescribe the best notice practicable.

Nor do we consider it unreasonable for the State to dispense with more certain notice to those beneficiaries whose interests are either conjectural or future or, although they could be discovered upon investigation, do not in due course of business come to knowledge of the common trustee. Whatever searches might be required in another situation under ordinary standards of diligence, in view of the character of the proceedings and the nature of the interests here involved we think them unnecessary. We recognize the practical difficulties and costs that would be attendant on frequent investigations into the status of great numbers of beneficiaries, many of whose interests in the common fund are so remote as to be ephemeral; and we have no doubt that such impracticable and extended searches are not required in the name of due process. The expense of keeping informed from day to day of substitutions among even current income beneficiaries and presumptive remaindermen, to say nothing of the far greater number of contingent beneficiaries, would impose a severe burden on the plan, and would likely dissipate its advantages. These are practical matters in which we should be reluctant to disturb the judgment of the state authorities.

Accordingly, we overrule appellant's constitutional objections to published notice insofar as they are urged on behalf of any beneficiaries whose interests or addresses are unknown to the trustee.

As to known present beneficiaries of known place of residence, however, notice by publication stands on a different footing. Exceptions in the name of necessity do not sweep away the rule that within the limits of practicability notice must be such as is reasonably calculated to reach interested parties. Where the names and post office addresses of those affected by a proceeding are at hand, the reasons disappear for resort to means less likely than the mails to apprise them of its pendency.

The trustee has on its books the names and addresses of the income beneficiaries represented by appellant, and we find no tenable ground for dispensing with a serious effort to inform them personally of the accounting, at least by ordinary mail to the record addresses. * * * Certainly sending them a copy of the statute months and perhaps years in advance does not answer this purpose. The trustee periodically remits their income to them, and we think that they might reasonably expect that with or apart from their remittances word might come to them personally that steps were being taken affecting their interests.

We need not weigh contentions that a requirement of personal service of citation on even the large number of known resident or nonresident beneficiaries would, by reasons of delay if not of expense, seriously interfere with the proper administration of the fund. Of course personal service even without the jurisdiction of the issuing authority serves the end of actual and personal notice, whatever power of compulsion it might lack. However, no such service is required under the circumstances. This type of trust presupposes a large number of small interests. The individual interest does not stand alone but is identical with that of a class. The rights of each in the integrity of the fund and the fidelity of the trustee are shared by many other beneficiaries. Therefore notice reasonably certain to reach most of those interested in objecting is likely to safeguard the interests of all, since any objections sustained would inure to the benefit of all. We think that under such circumstances reasonable risks that notice might not actually reach every beneficiary are justifiable. * * *

The statutory notice to known beneficiaries is inadequate, not because in fact it fails to reach everyone, but because under the circumstances it is not reasonably calculated to reach those who could easily be informed by other means at hand. However it may have been in former times, the mails today are recognized as an efficient and inexpensive means of communication. Moreover, the fact that the trust company has been able to give mailed notice to known beneficiaries at the time the common trust fund was established is persuasive that postal notification at the time of accounting would not seriously burden the plan.

We hold the notice of judicial settlement of accounts required by the New York Banking Law § 100–c(12) is incompatible with the requirements of the Fourteenth Amendment as a basis for adjudication depriving known persons whose whereabouts are also known of substantial property rights. * * *

Reversed.

MR. JUSTICE DOUGLAS took no part in the consideration or decision of this case.

[The dissenting opinion of JUSTICE BURTON is omitted.]

NOTES AND QUESTIONS

1. *Mullane* seems to require notice that is reasonably calculated to succeed. Does this mean that the method *most likely* to succeed is not required? How does *Mullane* justify this? What role should cost play in determining what is reasonable? Does *Mullane* justify applying different notice requirements for small claims than for large claims?

2.   In WUCHTER v. PIZZUTTI, 276 U.S. 13, 48 S.Ct. 259, 72 L.Ed. 446 (1928), the Supreme Court invalidated a New Jersey nonresident-motorist statute similar to the one involved in Hess v. Pawloski, p. 43, supra, because it did not expressly require the Secretary of State to communicate notice of the commencement of the action to the nonresident. In fact, notice actually was given by the Secretary of State. According to the Supreme Court: "Every statute of this kind * * * should require the plaintiff bringing the suit to show in the summons to be served the post office address or residence of the defendant being sued, and should impose either on the plaintiff himself or upon the official receiving service or some other, the duty of communication by mail or otherwise with the defendant."

Why would the Supreme Court have invalidated service even though the defendant received actual notice of the action? One commentator has suggested the following explanation: "Apart from the defendant's personal constitutional right to notice, the due process clause also imposes restrictions on how a state must act when it imposes unique burdens on persons. One such restriction, *Wuchter* seems to say, is that the steps that can lead to the imposition of such a burden must be formally and officially predetermined and declared rather than determined ad hoc." Casad, *Book Review*, 80 Mich. L. Rev. 664, 670 (1982). Does this explanation convince you? Would the result of *Wuchter* be the same after *Mullane*?

3.   The Court has held repeatedly that constructive notice does not satisfy *Mullane*'s due-process mandate if the name and address of the defendant is known or available from public records. For example, the Court has held that notice by publication in a local newspaper does not meet due process requirements in state condemnation proceedings. E.g., Walker v. City of Hutchinson, 352 U.S. 112, 77 S.Ct. 200, 1 L.Ed.2d 178 (1956). In this setting, the Court also has rejected publication coupled with signs posted on trees, see Schroeder v. City of New York, 371 U.S. 208, 83 S.Ct. 279, 9 L.Ed.2d 255 (1962).

In MENNONITE BOARD OF MISSIONS v. ADAMS, 462 U.S. 791, 103 S.Ct. 2706, 77 L.Ed.2d 180 (1983), the Court held that notice by publication and posting did not provide a mortgagee of real property with adequate notice of a proceeding to sell the mortgaged property for nonpayment of taxes. The Court emphasized that personal service or mailed notice is required even though a mortgagee may know of the delinquency in the payment of taxes or had the means to discover that the taxes had not been paid and that a tax sale proceeding was therefore likely to be initiated.

The Court also found constructive notice constitutionally deficient in TULSA PROFESSIONAL COLLECTION SERVICES, INC. v. POPE, 485 U.S. 478, 108 S.Ct. 1340, 99 L.Ed.2d 565 (1988). Under the nonclaim provision of Oklahoma's probate code, creditors' claims against an estate generally are barred unless presented to the executor or executrix within two months of the publication of notice of the commencement of probate proceedings. Jeanne Pope, an executrix, published the required notice in compliance with the terms of the nonclaim statute and a probate court order, but Tulsa Professional Collection Services, Inc. failed to file a timely claim, and application for payment was rejected. The United States Supreme Court reversed, holding that if Tulsa Professional's identity as a creditor was known or "reasonably ascertainable" by Pope (a fact the Court said could not be determined from the record before it), due process required that the creditor defendant be given notice by mail or such other means as is reasonably certain to ensure actual notice. See Waterbury, *Notice to Decedents' Creditors*, 73 Minn. L. Rev. 763 (1989); Note, *New Requirements of Creditor Notice in Probate Proceedings*, 54 Mo. L. Rev. 189 (1989).

4.   In GREENE v. LINDSEY, 456 U.S. 444, 102 S.Ct. 1874, 72 L.Ed.2d 249 (1982), the Supreme Court held that posting notice of eviction on a tenant's door does not satisfy due process. Plaintiffs, tenants in public housing who had been sued in a forcible entry and detainer action, brought a declaratory judgment action challenging the application of a Kentucky statute that permitted service by posting a summons on the door of a tenant's apartment. Plaintiffs claimed never to have seen the posted summonses, and that they did not learn of the eviction proceedings until they were served with writs of possession, executed after default judgments had been entered against them and after their opportunity for appeal had lapsed. The District Court granted summary judgment for defendants, and the Court of Appeals reversed. The Supreme Court affirmed in an opinion written by Justice Brennan:

> The empirical basis of the presumption that notice posted upon property is adequate to alert the owner or occupant of property of the pendency of legal proceedings would appear to make the presumption particularly well-founded where notice is posted at a residence. * * *

> But whatever the efficacy of posting in many cases, it is clear that, in the circumstances of this case, merely posting notice on an apartment door does not satisfy minimum standards of due process. In a significant number of instances, reliance on posting pursuant to the provisions of * * * [the statute] results in a failure to provide actual notice to the tenant concerned. Indeed, appellees claim to have suffered precisely such a failure of actual notice. As the process servers were well aware, notices posted on apartment doors in the area where these tenants lived were "not infrequently" removed by children or other tenants before they could have their intended effect. Under these conditions, notice by posting on the apartment door cannot be considered a "reliable means of acquainting interested parties of the fact that their rights are before the courts."

Id. at 452–54, 102 S.Ct. at 1879–80, 72 L.Ed.2d at 257–58.

Justice Brennan concluded that, in these circumstances, the Due Process Clause required that the posting be supplemented by notice through the mails. Justice O'Connor, joined by Chief Justice Burger and Justice Rehnquist, dissented:

> The Court * * * holds that notice via the mails is so far superior to posted notice that the difference is of constitutional dimension. How the Court reaches this judgment remains a mystery, especially since the Court is unable, on the present record, to evaluate the risks that notice mailed to public housing projects might fail due to loss, misdelivery, lengthy delay, or theft. Furthermore, the advantages of the mails over

posting, if any, are far from obvious. It is no secret, after all, that unattended mailboxes are subject to plunder by thieves. Moreover, unlike the use of the mails, posting notices at least gives assurance that the notice has gotten as far as the tenant's door.

Id. at 459–60, 102 S.Ct. at 1883, 72 L.Ed.2d at 261.

5. Does the government's use of mail service for the purpose of giving notice satisfy due process? Consider the following pair of cases.

DUSENBERY v. UNITED STATES, 534 U.S. 161, 122 S.Ct. 694, 151 L.Ed.2d 597 (2002), involved the adequacy of notice given to a prisoner by the Federal Bureau of Investigation prior to forfeiting property seized under the Controlled Substances Act, 21 U.S.C. § 801 (1988). The property consisted of about $30,000 and a car registered in his step-mother's name. The FBI published notice in a newspaper, and it also sent letters by certified mail addressed to petitioner in care of the federal prison where he was incarcerated; to his residence at the time of arrest; and to an address where his step-mother lived. In challenging the forfeiture, Dusenbery claimed he never received notice. A prison mailroom officer testified by telephone deposition that the officer had signed the certified mail receipt and that "the procedure would have been for him to log the mail in, for petitioner's 'Unit Team' to sign for it, and for it then to be given to petitioner." However, "a paper trail no longer existed because the Bureau of Prisons (BOP) had a policy of holding prison logbooks for only one year after they were closed." Applying *Mullane*, the Court held that the government's use of certified mail satisfied the Due Process Clause and that additional steps would demand "heroic efforts" and were not required. 534 U.S. at 170–71, 122 S.Ct. at 701, 151 L.Ed.2d at 606–07. Justice Ginsburg dissented, joined by Justices Stevens, Souter, and Breyer, criticizing the prison's mail-delivery procedure as "too lax to reliably ensure that a prisoner will receive a legal notice sent to him," and emphasizing "the evident feasibility of tightening the notice procedure 'as [would] one desirous of actually informing [the prisoner].' " Id. at 173, 122 S.Ct. at 702, 151 L.Ed.2d at 608.

JONES v. FLOWERS, 547 U.S. 220, 126 S.Ct. 1708, 164 L.Ed.2d 415 (2006), addressed whether the government's sending of notice by mail satisfies the Due Process Clause, this time in a case involving a homeowner who had failed to pay property taxes. The government notified the taxpayer by certified mail of an impending sale of his property and made no further efforts to contact the taxpayer even when the notice was returned unclaimed. The Court held that in these circumstances the government must take "additional reasonable steps * * *, if it is practicable to do so," id. at 225, 126 S.Ct. at 1713, 164 L.Ed. 2d at 425, to ensure that the taxpayer receives notice before forfeiting his property. Writing for the Court, Chief Justice Roberts explained:

We do not think that a person who actually desired to inform a real property owner of an impending tax sale of a house he owns would do nothing when a certified letter sent to the owner is returned unclaimed. If the Commissioner prepared a stack of letters to mail to delinquent taxpayers, handed them to the postman, and then watched as the departing postman accidentally dropped the letters down a storm drain, one would certainly expect the Commissioner's office to prepare a new stack of letters and send them again. No one "desirous of actually informing" the owners would simply shrug his shoulders as the letters disappeared and say "I tried." Failure to follow up would be unreasonable, despite the fact that the letters were reasonably calculated to reach their intended recipients when delivered to the postman.

Id. at 229, 126 S.Ct. at 1716, 164 L.Ed.2d at 427–28.

The Court identified a number of "reasonable additional steps" that the government could have taken once it knew that the notice had been returned unclaimed:

The return of the certified letter marked "unclaimed" meant either that Jones still lived at 717 North Bryan Street, but was not home when the postman called and did not retrieve the letter at the post office, or that Jones no longer resided at that address. One reasonable step primarily addressed to the former possibility would be for the State to resend the notice by regular mail, so that a signature was not required. The Commissioner says that use of certified mail makes actual notice more likely, because requiring the recipient's signature protects against misdelivery. But that is only true, of course, when someone is home to sign for the letter, or to inform the mail carrier that he has arrived at the wrong address. * * * [T]he use of certified mail might make actual notice less likely in some cases—the letter cannot be left like regular mail to be examined at the end of the day, and it can only be retrieved from the post office for a specified period of time. * * * Even occupants who ignored certified mail notice slips addressed to the owner (if any had been left) might scrawl the owner's new address on the notice packet and leave it for the postman to retrieve, or notify Jones directly.

Id. at 234–35, 126 S.Ct. at 1718–19, 164 L.Ed.2d at 431.

The Court found it would be unjustified, however, to require the government to search the phonebook or public records, such as the tax rolls, to locate the taxpayer's new address.

Justice Thomas in a dissent, joined by Justices Scalia and Kennedy, emphasized that the meaning of the Due Process Clause "should not turn on the antics of tax evaders and scofflaws." Id. at 248, 126 S.Ct. at 1727, 164 L.Ed.2d at 440. He insisted that the government's sending notice by certified mail to the taxpayer's "record address" is constitutionally sufficient and that the state had exceeded due process requirements by publishing additional notice in a local newspaper. Underscoring "the well-established presumption that individuals, especially those owning property, act in their own interest" to guard that interest, the dissent criticized the Court for assessing the government's method of notice from an ex-post, and not from an ex-ante perspective:

First, whether a method of notice is reasonably calculated to notify the interested party is determined *ex ante*, *i.e.*, from the viewpoint of the government agency at the time its notice is sent. * * * [In] *Mullane*, * * * this Court rested its analysis on the information the sender had "at hand" when its notice was sent. * * * Relatedly, we have refused to evaluate the reasonableness of a particular method of notice by comparing it to alternative methods that are identified after the fact. * * *

Second, implicit in our holding that due process does not require "actual notice," * * * is that when the "government becomes aware ... that its attempt at notice has failed," * * * it is not required to take additional steps to ensure that notice has been received. * * * Under the majority's logic, each time a doubt is raised with respect to whether notice has reached an interested party, the State will have to consider additional means better calculated to achieve notice. Because this rule turns on speculative, newly acquired information, it has no natural end point, and, in effect, requires the States to achieve something close to actual notice.

Id. at 243–44, 126 S.Ct. at 1723–24, 164 L.Ed.2d at 436–37.

What do you think is more significant about *Flowers*: that the Court required the government to take additional reasonable steps to ensure notice, or that the Court looked to regular mail as an acceptable method of providing notice? See Note, *Tax Sales of Real Property—Notice and Opportunity to Be Heard*, 120 Harv. L. Rev. 233 (2006).

6.   *Dusenbery* involved the adequacy of notice given to an incarcerated individual whose access to mail is carefully regulated by the government. One commentator has raised concerns that *Dusenbery* "could impact any group of people whose location, travel, and mail are controlled by the government," and includes in this category members of the military, certain law enforcement agents, and some federal employees. Burnett, Dusenbery v. United States: *Setting the Standard for Adequate Notice*, 37 U. Rich. L. Rev. 613, 635 (2003). How does *Flowers* affect this concern?

7.   The question of what methods for communicating notice are acceptable is different from the question of what the content of the notice should be. In AGUCHAK v. MONTGOMERY WARD CO., INC., 520 P.2d 1352 (Alaska 1974), Montgomery Ward, the plaintiff, sold a snowmobile and freezer to the Aguchaks, which they took to a remote area where they lived. When the Aguchaks allegedly did not pay, Montgomery Ward sent a summons to which the Aguchaks did not respond and a default judgment of $988.22 plus costs was entered against them. The summons did not inform the Aguchaks that they could appear by a written pleading, nor did it inform them that they had a right to request a change of venue. In order to appear in person at the court, the defendants would have had to fly at a cost of $186 with at least one night stopover. On appeal, the Supreme Court of Alaska held that the summons in small claims cases had to include this information, and it set aside the default judgment.

8.   In FINBERG v. SULLIVAN, 634 F.2d 50 (3d Cir. 1980), the Third Circuit, sitting en banc, held that Pennsylvania's post-judgment garnishment procedure violated the Due Process Clause. Finberg was a sixty-eight year old widow entirely dependent on Social Security for her income. A discount company obtained a default judgment against her and sought to execute the judgment pursuant to Pennsylvania practice permitting the seizure of assets, without notice or opportunity for a hearing, upon a judgment creditor's petition (to a clerk or magistrate) for a writ of execution. Under this procedure, the plaintiff garnished Finberg's bank accounts, which contained

the proceeds of her Social Security benefits. The critical fact was that all of the garnished money was exempt from seizure because federal law proscribes the seizure of Social Security benefits and Pennsylvania law provides a $300 cash exemption to debtors in Finberg's position. The *Finberg* court held the Pennsylvania practice unconstitutional, among other reasons, because it failed to require the creditor to inform the debtor of existing exemptions. Other courts also have found notice to be unconstitutional if it lacks "a detailed individualized explanation of the reason(s) for the action being taken * * * in terms comprehensible to the claimant." Ortiz v. Eichler, 794 F.2d 889, 892 (3d Cir. 1986). The content of the government's notice is implicated in the administration of a broad range of benefit programs. For examples, see Hershkoff & Loffredo, The Rights of the Poor 94 (Supplemental Security Income benefits), 252 (public housing) (1997).

SECTION C. THE MECHANICS OF GIVING NOTICE

Read Federal Rule of Civil Procedure 4 and the comparable state statutes set out in the Supplement.

----

1. INTRODUCTION

Notice of a suit is given by the service of process upon the defendant. Each jurisdiction has a set of rules governing the correct methods of making service. Traditionally, process consists of a copy of the plaintiff's complaint, together with a summons directing the defendant to answer. Service of process is made by personal delivery of the summons and complaint to the defendant. Other methods of service, such as delivery by mail, have assumed greater importance since the advent of long-arm statutes.

The procedure governing service of process in federal actions was changed significantly in 1983, and again in 1993. In 1982, the Supreme Court proposed but Congress rejected an amendment to the Rules that would have permitted service by registered or certified mail, return receipt, with delivery restricted to the addressee. It was asserted that the use of certified mail causes problems when, for example, the signature on the return receipt is illegible or the name signed differs somewhat from that of the defendant, or when it is difficult to determine whether mail has been "refused" or "unclaimed." It also was argued that the result of relying on the mail for service of process would be the entry of many more unnecessary and unfair default judgments that would have to be reopened when challenged. Another objection raised the concern that mail carriers might deliver process to the wrong person or fail to make the necessary inquiries to find the proper person. See 128 Cong. Rec. H9848, H9856 (daily ed. Dec. 15, 1982). In 1983, Congress chose a system of service by mail modeled after the one used in California. See Cal. Code Civ. Proc. § 415.30. The summons and complaint could be sent by ordinary first class mail, together with a form for acknowledging receipt of service. If the acknowledgment form was not returned, plaintiff had to effect service through some other means authorized by the Rules. In order to encourage defendants to execute and return the form, the Rule directed the court to order a defendant who did not cooperate to pay the costs incurred by the plaintiff in making personal service unless the defendant could show good cause for failing to return the acknowledgment form.

This system was not always successful because it relied on the defendant's cooperation in returning the acknowledgment form. Thus, after a decade of use, Rule 4 was revised again in 1993. The most significant change was that the "service by mail" provision was replaced by Rule 4(d), which strongly encourages waiver of formal service. Under this modification, an action commences when the plaintiff sends a form (Official Form 5) entitled "Notice of a Lawsuit and Request to Waive Service of a Summons," or similar document, by mail or some other "reliable" means. Domestic defendants have thirty days from the date on which the waiver was sent to return the waiver; otherwise they will be charged with the costs associated with providing formal service. Along with the threat of paying for the costs of service, defendants receive a positive incentive in that they are allowed sixty days after the date on which the waiver was sent to answer the complaint if the waiver is returned in a timely fashion. Note that even under the amended rule, if a plaintiff is confronting a statute of limitations deadline in a state in which the statute continues to run until a defendant is served, formal service sometimes still may be the wisest course of action, because the defendant may refuse to waive service.

Rule 4, in several subdivisions, sets forth specific means of making personal service on, among others, individuals, corporations, partnerships, and other associations subject to suit under a common name. In addition, Rule 4(e)(1) provides an alternative to these methods by broadly authorizing the use in federal courts of the procedures governing the manner of service prescribed by the law of the state in which the District Court is sitting. And Rule 4(e) specifically provides that state procedures to serve a party "may be served in a judicial district of the United States," thus enabling federal courts to take advantage of the reach of state long-arm statutes. See 4B Wright & Miller, Federal Practice and Procedure: Civil 3d §§ 1112–16, 1119–23; Foster, *Long-Arm Jurisdiction in Federal Courts*, 1969 Wis. L. Rev. 9; Foster, *Judicial Economy; Fairness and Convenience of Place of Trial: Long-Arm Jurisdiction in District Courts*, 47 F.R.D. 73 (1969).

2. SPECIFIC APPLICATIONS OF
THE SERVICE PROVISIONS

a. Federal Rule 4(d): "Waiving Service"

NOTES AND QUESTIONS

1.   The "waiving service" provision of Federal Rule 4 replaced an earlier version that provided for service by mail. Does the "waiving service" provision excuse the requirement of notice or simply waive various formal attributes of notice? What purpose does the "waiving service" provision serve? What are the procedures for requesting and effecting waiver of service? Can a request for waiver be effected through electronic means, such as email or facsimile? What is the effective date of a request for "waiving service"?

2.   The Advisory Committee has emphasized that litigants seeking to commence actions for which the statute of limitations might soon expire ought not use the provisions of Federal Rule 4(d). What is the rationale behind this advice?

b. Federal Rule 4(e): Personal Delivery on Natural Persons

McKELWAY, PROFILES—PLACE AND LEAVE WITH, New Yorker, August 24, 1935, at 23–26:

* * * In a little frame house near the intersection of Rogers and Flatbush Avenues in Brooklyn there lived until a few years ago an old lady named Mrs. Katherina Schnible. She was seventy-two and a little lame. She owned the house and rented out the first two floors as apartments, but there were mortgages and she had not met the payments. She knew the bank that held the mortgages was about to foreclose * * *. Her son, who lived with her, went out to work at eight in the morning and did not return until six, so from eight till six every day, except Sunday, Mrs. Schnible stayed in her room on the third floor and refused to open the door, no matter who knocked. Came a day when she heard a heavy footfall on the first landing, heard somebody running frantically up the first flight of stairs, heard a man's voice shouting something. Then the footsteps came closer, up the second flight of stairs, and right outside her door she heard yelled the word "Fire!" Mrs. Schnible opened her door and hobbled hurriedly into the hall. "Hello, Mrs. Schnible," said a man standing there. "Here's a summons for you." He handed her the papers, and the proceedings were begun which eventually put Mrs. Schnible out of her house.

Harry Grossman, who was the man in the hall, is regarded by those who employ him as the champion process-server of the day. He is an instrument of justice and his profession is a corner-stone of civil law, but not many of the people he serves appreciate that. * * * Grossman has been cursed by hundreds of defendants, many of them distinguished citizens. Defendants have thrown him down flights of stairs and shoved him off porches. He has been pinched, slapped, punched, and kicked by scores of individuals, and he was beaten up one time by a family of seven.

* * *

"Place and leave with" is the legal phrase for what a process-server must do with a summons when he goes out to serve papers on a defendant, but the courts never have explained precisely what that means. Where the process-server must place the papers is still a nice legal question. A process-server once threw a summons-and-complaint at James Gordon Bennett and hit him in the chest with it, but the courts held that this was not a proper service. Another famous case in the lawbooks tells of a defendant named Martin, who in 1893 hid himself under his wife's petticoats and refused to receive the papers. The process-server saw him crouching there, so he put the papers on what seemed to be the defendant's shoulder, and went away. The Supreme Court rendered a decision which held that "where a person, to avoid service of summons, shelters himself in his wife's petticoats, the laying of the papers on his shoulder will be a sufficient service." * * *

Grossman has never bothered to look up legal precedents for his actions; he simply places the papers in the hands of the defendant and leaves them there. On innumerable occasions he has had to use ingenuity in order to get close enough to the defendant to do this, and only once has he been forced to depart from a literal interpretation of the legal phrase. That was in the case of an elderly lady, who, like Mrs. Schnible, was trying to hide from him. This lady, whose name was Mrs. Mahoney, refused to leave her apartment in the East Side tenement she owned, and Grossman's routine tricks * * * failed to budge her. He knew she was there, because he had wheedled his way into a flat across the court from her and had seen her sitting at her kitchen table in front of an open window, peeling potatoes. Grossman went home to his own apartment in Brooklyn and thought for a while, and then began to practice throwing the summons. He put rubber bands around the paper to make it compact, placed a salad bowl on the dining-room table, and practiced all that afternoon, throwing the subpoena into the bowl from the middle of the living-room. He went back next morning to the flat across the court from Mrs. Mahoney's kitchen. She came into the kitchen a little before noon, puttered around for a while, and then sat down at the table with a bowl of potatoes in front of her and began placidly to peel them. Grossman leaned out of his window and tossed the subpoena. The papers landed in the bowl just as the old lady reached into it. "There you are, Mrs. Mahoney!" Grossman shouted. "There's a foreclosure paper for you!" The courts never questioned his method of placing these papers, and Mrs. Mahoney lost her property.

Tens of thousands of papers have to be served in the course of a year in this city, and the majority of them are handled for the law firms by process-serving agencies, which rely for their profits on quantity and a quick turnover. * * * Cases involving expert dodgers or stubborn hug-the-hearths usually are turned over to private detective agencies, and the detective agencies usually hire Grossman to serve the papers. When the Electrical Research Product Institute sued the Fox Film Corporation for $15,000,000 in 1930, the lawyers for the plaintiff, naturally, surmised that it would be difficult to "place and leave with" William Fox, Winfield Sheehan, and other defendants, the papers summoning them to come to court. Grossman received the assignment through a detective agency. He got in to see Fox by having a telegram sent from Boston saying that Mr. Grossman had "closed the theatre deal" and would call on Fox at eleven o'clock the next morning. When Grossman reached Fox's office, the film executive's secretary told him Mr. Fox had received the wire but was not sure what deal it was that had been closed. "My God," said Grossman, "the theatre deal—that's what deal! If this is the way I am to be received, never mind—to hell with it!" He started out, and the secretary called him back. "Just wait one moment," she said. "I'll tell Mr. Fox" She opened a door marked "Private" and went into an inner office. Grossman followed her and handed Fox the subpoena. Fox started up from his desk indignantly, but Grossman's indignation expressed itself first. "You, a multi-millionaire!" Grossman shouted. "Is it decent, is it nice, for a multi-millionaire who can be sued for fifteen million dollars to hide from me? Why don't you take the papers like a man?" This so flabbergasted Fox that he sank back in his chair, and Grossman went through the corporation's offices unimpeded and served papers on Sheehan, two vice-presidents, the secretary, and the treasurer.

Harry established a reputation as an adroit private detective before he was old enough to serve subpoenas. * * * But after he had passed his eighteenth birthday and had begun to serve summonses and subpoenas, it was evident to his employer, and to everybody else who knew him, that he had found a vocation in which he might expect to excel. During his first year he served Maude Adams by posing as a youthful adorer. When she came out of the stage entrance at the Empire Theatre after a performance one evening, Grossman stepped in front of her holding in his left hand a bouquet of jonquils. "Are you Maude Adams?" he asked. "Oh, are those really for me?" she exclaimed, reaching for the flowers, "No, but this is," said Grossman, jerking back the bouquet. With his right hand he served her with a summons. He still remembers that he had paid fifty cents for the jonquils and that he was able to sell them back to the florist for twenty.

His ability to become more indignant at the attitude of defendants than defendants are at his actions has saved Grossman from bodily injury on many occasions. One of his early triumphs involved Gutzon Borglum. The sculptor was at that time modelling life-size figures in a studio in the Gramercy Park section. Grossman entered by means of what he calls the rush act. A maid opened the door and Grossman rushed past her, saying perfunctorily "Is Mr. Borglum in?" Borglum was chipping stone on a nearly completed nude. "Here's a summons for you, Mr. Borglum," said Grossman. "Of all the effrontery," began the sculptor. "You * * * you

* * * you ought to be * * *." Then Grossman began to shout. "How about you?" he asked. "Shouldn't you maybe be ashamed of yourself? You and your naked women!" He went out spluttering with indignation, leaving Borglum speechless, clutching the summons in his hand.

c.   Rule 4(e)(2)(B): Service on a Person Residing in Defendant's Dwelling or Usual Place of Abode

As an alternative to personal delivery, Rule 4(e)(2)(B) permits service of process to be made upon an individual by leaving a copy of the summons and complaint at his "dwelling or usual place of abode with someone of suitable age and discretion who resides there." The facts of a particular case often prove to be crucial.

Notes and Questions

1.   In NATIONAL DEVELOPMENT CO. v. TRIAD HOLDING CORP., 930 F.2d 253, 258 (2d Cir.), certiorari denied 502 U.S. 968, 112 S.Ct. 440, 116 L.Ed.2d 459 (1991), defendant was a wealthy, globe-trotting Saudi businessman. Service was made by leaving a copy of the summons with defendant's housekeeper at an apartment he maintained in New York. Defendant testified that the apartment, valued at $20–$25 million, was one of twelve residences around the world in which he spent his time; service was upheld because "Khashoggi [the defendant] was actually living in [the apartment when service was effected], service there on that day was, if not the most likely method of ensuring that he received the summons and complaint, reasonably calculated to provide actual notice."

2.   To what extent should it be relevant that a defendant actually received the summons and complaint at the particular place where it was served? In KARLSSON v. RABINOWITZ, 318 F.2d 666, 668 (4th Cir. 1963), the Fourth Circuit validated service that was left with the defendant's wife in Maryland even though the family was in the process of moving, and the defendant already had left for Arizona, with no intent ever to return. On facts similar to *Karlsson,* the District of Columbia Circuit held that service was invalid because the papers were left with defendant's estranged wife, and he did not receive the summons and complaint until three years after a default judgment was entered against him. Williams v. Capital Transit Co., 215 F.2d 487 (D.C. Cir. 1954). Does this insistence on actual receipt of service create a "double" standard for construing the language of Rule 4(e)(2)(B)? Does this make sense?

d.   Rule 4(e)(2)(C): Delivery to an Agent Authorized by Appointment

Rule 4(e)(2)(c) permits a third method of effecting personal service on an individual: by delivering a copy of the summons and complaint to an agent of the defendant who is "authorized by appointment or by law" to receive process. The cases dealing with agency by appointment indicate that an actual appointment for the specific purpose of receiving process normally is expected. Consistent with this judicial construction of "appointment," the courts have held that claims by an agent that he has authority to receive process or the fact that an agent actually accepts process is not enough to bind defendant; there must be evidence that defendant himself intended to confer such authority upon the agent.

NATIONAL EQUIPMENT RENTAL, LTD. v. SZUKHENT

Supreme Court of the United States, 1964.
375 U.S. 311, 84 S.Ct. 411, 11 L.Ed.2d 354.

Certiorari to the United States Court of Appeals for the Second Circuit.

MR. JUSTICE STEWART delivered the opinion of the Court.

* * * The petitioner is a corporation with its principal place of business in New York. It sued the respondents, residents of Michigan, in a New York federal court, claiming that the respondents had defaulted under a farm equipment lease. The only question now before us is whether the person upon whom the summons and complaint were served was "an agent authorized by appointment" to receive the same, so as to subject the respondents to the jurisdiction of the federal court in New York.

The respondents obtained certain farm equipment from the petitioner under a lease executed in 1961. The lease was on a printed form less than a page and a half in length, and consisted of 18 numbered paragraphs. The last numbered paragraph, appearing just above the respondents' signatures and printed in the same type used in the remainder of the instrument, provided that "the Lessee hereby designates Florence Weinberg, 47–21 Forty-first Street, Long Island City, N.Y., as agent for the purpose of accepting service of any process within the State of New York." The respondents were not acquainted with Florence Weinberg.

In 1962 the petitioner commenced the present action by filing in the federal court in New York a complaint which alleged that the respondents had failed to make any of the periodic payments specified by the lease. The Marshal delivered two copies of the summons and complaint to Florence Weinberg. That same day she mailed the summons and complaint to the respondents, together with a letter stating that the documents had been served upon her as the respondents' agent for the purpose of accepting service of process in New York, in accordance with the agreement contained in the lease. The petitioner itself also notified the respondents by certified mail of the service of process upon Florence Weinberg.

Upon motion of the respondents, the District Court quashed service of the summons and complaint, holding that, although Florence Weinberg had promptly notified the respondents of the service of process and mailed copies of the summons and complaint to them, the lease agreement itself had not explicitly required her to do so, and there was therefore a "failure

of the agency arrangement to achieve intrinsic and continuing reality."
* * * The Court of Appeals affirmed * * * and we granted certiorari
* * *.

We need not and do not in this case reach the situation where no
personal notice has been given to the defendant. Since the respondents did
in fact receive complete and timely notice of the lawsuit pending against
them, no due process claim has been made. The case before us is therefore
quite different from cases where there was no actual notice * * *. Similarly, as the Court of Appeals recognized, this Court's decision in Wuchter v.
Pizzutti, [p. 129, supra,] * * * is inapposite here. * * * *Wuchter* dealt
with the limitations imposed by the Fourteenth Amendment upon a
statutory scheme by which a State attempts to subject nonresident individuals to the jurisdiction of its courts. The question presented here, on
the other hand, is whether a party to a private contract may appoint an
agent to receive service of process within the meaning of Federal Rule
* * * [4(e)(2)(C)], where the agent is not personally known to the party,
and where the agent has not expressly undertaken to transmit notice to
the party.

The purpose underlying the contractual provision here at issue seems
clear. The clause was inserted by the petitioner and agreed to by the
respondents in order to assure that any litigation under the lease should
be conducted in the State of New York. The contract specifically provided
that "This agreement shall be deemed to have been made in Nassau
County, New York, regardless of the order in which the signatures of the
parties shall be affixed hereto, and shall be interpreted, and the rights and
liabilities of the parties here determined, in accordance with the laws of
the State of New York." And it is settled, as the courts below recognized,
that parties to a contract may agree in advance to submit to the jurisdiction of a given court, to permit notice to be served by the opposing party,
or even to waive notice altogether. * * *

Under well-settled general principles of the law of agency, Florence
Weinberg's prompt acceptance and transmittal to the respondents of the
summons and complaint pursuant to the authorization was itself sufficient to validate the agency, even though there was no explicit previous
promise on her part to do so. * * *

We deal here with a Federal Rule, applicable to federal courts in all 50
States. But even if we were to assume that this uniform federal standard
should give way to contrary local policies, there is no relevant concept of
state law which would invalidate the agency here at issue. In Michigan,
where the respondents reside, the statute which validates service of
process under the circumstances present in this case contains no provision
requiring that the appointed agent expressly undertake to notify the
principal of the service of process. Similarly, New York law, which it was
agreed should be applicable to the lease provisions, does not require any
such express promise by the agent in order to create a valid agency for
receipt of process. * * *

It is argued, finally, that the agency sought to be created in this case was invalid because Florence Weinberg may have had a conflict of interest. This argument is based upon the fact that she was not personally known to the respondents at the time of her appointment and upon a suggestion in the record that she may be related to an officer of the petitioner corporation. But such a contention ignores the narrowly limited nature of the agency here involved. Florence Weinberg was appointed the respondents' agent for the single purpose of receiving service of process. An agent with authority so limited can in no meaningful sense be deemed to have had an interest antagonistic to the respondents, since both the petitioner and the respondents had an equal interest in assuring that, in the event of litigation, the latter be given that adequate and timely notice which is a prerequisite to a valid judgment.

A different case would be presented if Florence Weinberg had not given prompt notice to the respondents, for then the claim might well be made that her failure to do so had operated to invalidate the agency. We hold only that, prompt notice to the respondents having been given, Florence Weinberg was their "agent authorized by appointment" to receive process within the meaning of Federal Rule * * * [4(e)(2)(C)].

* * *

Judgment of Court of Appeals reversed and case remanded.

MR. JUSTICE BLACK, dissenting.

* * * I disagree with * * * [the Court's] holding, believing that (1) whether Mrs. Weinberg was a valid agent upon whom service could validly be effected under Rule * * * [4(e)(2)(C)] should be determined under New York law and that we should accept the holdings of the federal district judge and the Court of Appeals sitting in New York that under that State's law the purported appointment of Mrs. Weinberg was invalid and ineffective; (2) if however, Rule * * * [4(e)(2)(C)] is to be read as calling upon us to formulate a new federal definition of agency for purposes of service of process, I think our formulation should exclude Mrs. Weinberg from the category of an "agent authorized by appointment * * * to receive service of process"; and (3) upholding service of process in this case raises serious questions as to whether these Michigan farmers have been denied due process of law in violation of the Fifth and Fourteenth Amendments.

* * *

The end result of today's holding is not difficult to foresee. Clauses like the one used against the Szukhents—clauses which companies have not inserted, I suspect, because they never dreamed a court would uphold them—will soon find their way into the "boilerplate" of everything from an equipment lease to a conditional sales contract. Today's holding gives a green light to every large company in this country to contrive contracts which declare with force of law that when such a company wants to sue someone with whom it does business, that individual must go and try to defend himself in some place, no matter how distant, where big business enterprises are concentrated, like, for example, New York, Connecticut, or Illinois, or else suffer a default judgment. In this very case the Court holds that by this company's carefully prepared contractual clause the Szukhents must, to avoid a judgment rendered without a fair and full hearing, travel hundreds of miles across the continent, probably crippling their defense and certainly depleting what savings they may have, to try to defend themselves in a court sitting in New York City. I simply cannot believe that Congress, when by its silence it let Rule * * * [4(e)(2)(C)] go into effect, meant for that rule to be used as a means to achieve such a far-reaching, burdensome, and unjust result. Heretofore judicial good common sense has, on one ground or another, disregarded contractual provisions like this one, not encouraged them. It is a long trip from San Francisco—or from Honolulu or Anchorage—to New York, Boston, or Wilmington. And the trip can be very expensive, often costing more than it would simply to pay what is demanded. The very threat of such a suit can be used to force payment of alleged claims, even though they be wholly without merit. This fact will not be news to companies exerting their economic power to wangle such contracts. * * *

MR. JUSTICE BRENNAN, with whom THE CHIEF JUSTICE and MR. JUSTICE GOLDBERG join, dissenting.

I would affirm. In my view, federal standards and not state law must define who is "an agent authorized by appointment" within the meaning of Rule * * * [4(e)(2)(C)]. * * * In formulating these standards I would, *first*, construe Rule * * * [4(e)(2)(C)] to deny validity to the appointment of a purported agent whose interests conflict with those of his supposed principal * * *. *Second*, I would require that the appointment include an explicit condition that the agent after service transmit the process forthwith to the principal. Although our decision in Wuchter v. Pizzutti * * * dealt with the constitutionality of a state statute, the reasoning of that case is persuasive that, in fashioning a federal agency rule, we should engraft the same requirement upon Rule * * * [4(e)(2)(C)]. *Third*, since the corporate plaintiff prepared the printed form contract, I would not hold the individual purchaser bound by the appointment without proof, in addition to his mere signature on the form, that the individual understandingly consented to be sued in a State not that of his residence. * * * It offends common sense to treat a printed form which closes an installment sale as embodying terms to all of which the individual knowingly assented. The sales pitch aims solely at getting the signature on the form and wastes no time explaining or even mentioning the print. * * *

NOTE AND QUESTIONS

Like personal jurisdiction, notice and service-of-process requirements may be waived by a party at trial or even in advance of litigation. For example, under the provisions of a cognovit note, a debtor may agree to submit to the jurisdiction of any court chosen by the creditor for an action to collect the debt and may even empower the creditor or any attorney to appear in the suit and confess judgment, typically waiving any objection to jurisdiction, notice, or service of process. In D.H. OVERMYER CO., INC. v. FRICK CO., 405 U.S. 174, 92 S.Ct. 775, 31 L.Ed.2d 124 (1972), the Supreme Court considered the constitutionality of cognovit provisions and ruled that they were not per se violative of the Due Process Clause. Such agreements must be judged on a case-by-case basis, with particular sensitivity to whether there was inequality of bargaining power or lack of consideration. See, e.g., Atl. Leasing & Fin., Inc. v. IPM Tech., Inc., 885 F.2d 188 (4th Cir. 1989) (holding that guarantor's assent to confessed-judgment provision was voluntarily, knowingly, and intelligently made). Many state courts have invalidated cognovit notes and other "consent to judgment" provisions. See, e.g., Isbell v. County of Sonoma, 21 Cal.3d 61, 145 Cal.Rptr. 368, 577 P.2d 188, certiorari denied 439 U.S. 996, 99 S.Ct. 597, 58 L.Ed.2d 669 (1978).

e.   Federal Rule 4(h): Serving a Corporation, Partnership, or Association

Rule 4(h) authorizes service upon corporations, partnerships, and unincorporated associations that are subject to suit under a common name. The most frequently invoked portion of the rule permits service by delivery of process to an officer, a managing agent, or a general agent.

———

In INSURANCE CO. OF NORTH AMERICA v. S/S "HELLENIC CHALLENGER," 88 F.R.D. 545 (S.D.N.Y. 1980), a United States Marshal deposited the summons and complaint with a claims adjuster at the office of defendant. The complaint stated an admiralty and maritime claim for nondelivery, shortage, loss, and damage relating to pickled sheepskins shipped to New York aboard defendant's vessel.

The adjuster who had accepted service of the summons and complaint was not expressly authorized by defendant to accept process; the only employees endowed with express authority to do so on behalf of defendant were the titled officers and the claims manager. At the time of service of the summons and complaint, the claims manager was absent due to illness and the adjuster, an assistant to the claims manager, accepted service.

Since the adjuster misplaced the summons and complaint, defendant remained unaware of the pendency of the lawsuit until its bank informed it that its account had been attached by the plaintiff. Only then did the defendant learn that the plaintiff's counsel had filed a default judgment and that a writ of execution had been issued. The court denied the defendant's motion to set aside the judgment on the basis of improper service of process:

> Rule * * * [4(h)] has been liberally construed by the courts and, as interpreted, does not require rigid formalism. To be valid, service of process is not limited solely to officially designated officers, managing

agents or agents appointed by law for the receipt of process. Rather, "[r]ules governing service of process [are] to be construed in a manner reasonably calculated to effectuate their primary purpose: to give the defendant adequate notice that an action is pending. * * * [T]he rule does not require that service be made solely on a restricted class of formally titled officials, but rather permits it to be made 'upon a representative so integrated with the organization that he will know what to do with the papers. Generally, service is sufficient when made upon an individual who stands in such a position as to render it fair, reasonable and just to imply the authority on his part to receive services.' " * * *

Plaintiff's method of service of the summons and complaint was indeed "reasonably calculated" to alert defendants to the initiation of the suit. * * * [T]he adjuster served with the summons and complaint, can be categorized as a representative of defendant "well-integrated" into the organization and quite familiar with the formalities associated with the receipt of service of summonses and complaints. He had accepted service of summonses and complaints on behalf of defendant on at least two previous occasions * * * in connection with his ordinary duties of receiving and investigating new claims against defendant. Furthermore, it may be inferred from the facts presented on this motion that [the adjuster] had easy access to * * * the claims manager officially authorized to accept service of process, since the two men are separated from each other only by [the claims manager's] glass-walled office. [The adjuster's] familiarity with service of process negates any and all suspicion that the U.S. Marshal delivered the summons and complaint to a representative of defendant who had infrequent contact with summonses and complaints and whose unfamiliarity with service of process increased the risk of careless or improper handling. * * *

In the case at hand, the * * * adjuster's loss of the summons and complaint is a mistake in the ordinary course of the internal operations of defendant's business and thus does not merit remedial relief * * *.

Id. at 547–48.

NOTE AND QUESTIONS

Is the court's willingness to disregard labels and conclusory terms such as "general" and "managing" agent consistent with the clear requirements of Rule 4(h)(1)(B)? Should the court simply have held that the claims adjuster could be regarded as a "managing agent" of the defendant? Could the court reasonably have reached the same result by finding that the claims adjuster was an agent authorized by appointment to receive process? What factors ought a court to consider in determining whether an entity permissibly may receive service on behalf of a corporation?

f.   Rule 4(f): Serving an Individual in a Foreign Country

Federal Rule 4(f) makes provision for service of process in a foreign country, affording American attorneys with a flexible framework to permit accommodation of the widely divergent procedures for service of process employed by the various nations of the world. This accommodation is necessary in order to avoid violating the sovereignty of other countries by committing acts within their borders that they may consider to be "official" and to maximize the likelihood that the judgment rendered in an action in this country will be recognized and enforced abroad. Service of process in a foreign country and other procedural aspects of civil litigation having multi-national incidents are discussed in Baumgartner, *Is Transnational Litigation Different?*, 25 U. Pa. J. Int'l Econ. L. 1297 (2004). See also Miller, *International Cooperation in Litigation Between the United States and Switzerland: Unilateral Procedural Accommodation in a Test Tube*, 49 Minn. L. Rev. 1069, 1075–86 (1965).

Rule 4(f)(1) now expressly provides that "any internationally agreed means of service that is reasonably calculated to give notice, such as those authorized by the Hague Convention on the Service Abroad of Judicial and Extrajudicial Documents" may be used to effect service on those outside the United States. The Hague Convention contains the most important internationally agreed means of service of process, and so far it has been adopted by 65 countries. See Convention on the Service Abroad of Judicial and Extrajudicial Documents in Civil or Commercial Matters, The Hague, 1965, 20 U.S.T. 361, T.I.A.S. No. 6638, 658 U.N.T.S. 163, reproduced (with declarations by the contracting states) in 28 U.S.C.A. following Fed. R. Civ. P. 4; see also Status Table, available at http://www.hcch.net (last visited Jan. 4, 2010). The heart of the Convention is a requirement that each Contracting State establish a Central Authority, which will receive and execute requests for service from judicial authorities in other Contracting States and will see that a certification that service has been effected is returned to the court of origin. Service may be made either in accordance with the law of the nation in which service is to be made or (unless incompatible with that law) by a particular method requested by the applicant. 1 Ristau, International Judicial Assistance (Civil and Commercial) § 4–3–1 (rev. ed. 1990); see Tamayo, *Catch Me If You Can: Serving United States Process on an Elusive Defendant Abroad*, 17 Harv. J.L. & Tech. 211 (2003).

There are, however, several circumstances involving foreign defendants not governed by the Hague Convention. Most significantly, the Convention does not govern in those countries that are not Contracting States. Furthermore, the United States Supreme Court held in VOLKSWAGENWERK AKTIENGESELLSCHAFT v. SCHLUNK, 486 U.S. 694, 108 S.Ct. 2104, 100 L.Ed.2d 722 (1988), that the Convention applies only if service actually is made *abroad*, rather than on the domestic subsidiary of a foreign corporation deemed to be the corporation's involuntary agent for service of process. Moreover, as a result of the 1993 change in Rule 4(d), from "service by agreement" to "waiver of service" (renamed "waiving service" in 2007), the Hague Convention appears to be inapplicable when the defendant takes advantage of the waiver procedure. Because the Convention is only invoked by "service" abroad, an agreement to waive service, if voluntary and private, may be regarded as not implicating the Convention, although some other nations might well take a contrary position. Foreign defendants, like domestic defendants, are given incentives by Rule 4(d) to waive service in the form of longer times to respond, but they are not to be charged with the costs for formal service should they refuse to return the waiver; otherwise, the waiver could be deemed compulsory and thus might violate the Convention. See Born & Vollmer, *The Effect of the Revised Federal Rules of Civil Procedure on Personal Jurisdiction, Service and Discovery in International Cases*, 150 F.R.D. 221, 230–41 (1993).

Rule 4(f)(3) authorizes forms of service "by other means not prohibited by international agreement, as the court orders." Rule 4(f)(3) is regarded as a flexible provision so that the "use of a court-directed means for service of process under Rule 4(f)(3) is not a disfavored process and should not be considered extraordinary relief." 4B Wright & Miller, Federal Practice and Procedure: Civil 3d § 1134. Trial courts have authorized "a wide variety of alternative methods of service including publication, ordinary mail, mail to the defendant's last known address, delivery to the defendant's attorney, telex, and most recently, email." Rio Properties, Inc. v. Rio Int'l Interlink, 284 F.3d 1007, 1016 (9th Cir. 2002). In approving the use of email, the Ninth Circuit has explained that "when faced with an international e-business scofflaw, playing hide-and-seek with the federal court, email may be the only means of effecting service of process." Id. at 1018.

NOTE AND QUESTIONS

New forms of technology continue to affect the forms of process that are considered permissible. In MKM Capital Pty Ltd. v. Corbo, A.C.T. Sup. Ct. No. SC608–2008 (Dec. 16, 2008), a loan default case, plaintiffs repeatedly but unsuccessfully attempted to serve defendants. The Supreme Court of the Australian Capital Territory finally allowed plaintiffs to effect service through the sending of "a private message via computer to the Facebook page" of the named defendants. What kind of showing should be required before granting permission to effect service by means of Facebook? What problems do you see with this form of service?

3. RETURN OF SERVICE

After the process-server has delivered the papers, she must file a return, which should disclose enough facts to demonstrate that defendant actually has been served and given notice that he is required to appear in court. Thus, although the actual service of process and not the proof of that act is a prerequisite to the court's assuming jurisdiction, it has been held that a proper return ordinarily is necessary to enable the trial court to conclude it has jurisdiction. The specific form that proof of service must take varies from state to state, as well as according to the method of service used. An affidavit executed by the person who performed the acts constituting service, or the sworn statement of the officer—the marshal, sheriff, or deputy—who made the service, is the usual proof.

Should the process-server's return of service be considered conclusive or merely presumptive evidence that service has been effected? In MIEDR-EICH v. LAUENSTEIN, 232 U.S. 236, 34 S.Ct. 309, 58 L.Ed. 584 (1914), plaintiff sought to vacate a mortgage foreclosure judgment rendered in a prior suit. She was not a resident of the county in which the action was brought, was not served with process, and had no knowledge of the prior proceeding; the sheriff had made a false return of summons. The Supreme Court upheld the prior judgment:

> In the present case the * * * original party in the foreclosure proceeding did all that the law required in the issue of and attempt to serve process; and, without fraud or collusion, the sheriff made a return to the court that service had been duly made. * * * [A]lthough contrary to the fact, in the absence of any attack upon it, the court was justified in acting upon such return as upon a true return. If the return is false the law of the State * * * permitted a recovery against the sheriff upon his bond. We are of the opinion that this system of jurisprudence, with its provisions for safeguarding the rights of litigants, is due process of law.

Id. at 246, 34 S.Ct. at 312, 58 L.Ed. at 591. Is it significant that *Miedreich* involved a collateral attack on the sheriff's return? Would the result have been the same if it were a direct attack in the original proceeding?

In most American jurisdictions, the return of service is considered strong evidence of the facts stated, but it is not conclusive and may be controverted by proof that the return is inaccurate. However, the defendant's own testimony generally will not be sufficient to impeach the return unless it is corroborated by other evidence. See, e.g., Trustees of Local Union No. 727 Pension Fund v. Perfect Parking, Inc., 126 F.R.D. 48 (N.D. Ill. 1989) (requiring "strong and convincing evidence" to overcome return of private process-server). See generally 4B Wright & Miller, Federal Practice and Procedure: Civil 3d § 1130.

4. IMMUNITY FROM PROCESS

A court sometimes will immunize a party from service of process, despite the fact that the constitutional and statutory conditions governing personal jurisdiction and service of process have been met. In such cases, the grant of immunity usually is justified as promoting the administration of justice. Thus, although the doctrine may help a party avoid suit, it does so not for the benefit of the party, but for the benefit of the court. For example, witnesses, parties, and attorneys who come to a state to participate in a lawsuit often are granted immunity from service of process in other suits.

In many instances, immunity from process is governed by statute. For example, federal law grants immunity to certain representatives of foreign governments, their families, and members of their households. What justification is there for giving these people immunity? KADIC v. KARAD-ZIC, 70 F.3d 232 (2d Cir. 1995), involved the question of whether defendant Karadzic, president of the break-away Bosnian-Serb republic, was entitled to immunity from service in a federal court action by Croat and Muslim citizens of Bosnia-Herzegovina alleging genocide, torture, rape, and other atrocities. Plaintiffs served defendant while he was in the United States as an invitee of the United Nations. The question of immunity under the United Nations "Headquarters Agreement" turned, in part, on whether service was affected in an area "bounded by Franklin D. Roosevelt Drive, 1st Avenue, 42nd Street, and 48th Street." The court explained:

> In the *Doe* action, the affidavits detail that on February 11, 1993, process servers approached Karadzic in the lobby of the Hotel Inter-continental at 111 East 48th St. in Manhattan, called his name and identified their purpose, and attempted to hand him the complaint from a distance of two feet, that security guards seized the complaint papers, and that the papers fell to the floor. * * * In the *Kadic* action, the plaintiffs obtained from Judge Owen an order for alternative means of service, directing service by delivering the complaint to a member of defendant's State Department security detail, who was ordered to hand the complaint to the defendant. The security officer's affidavit states that he received the complaint and handed it to Karadzic outside the Russian Embassy in Manhattan. * * * Appellants also allege that during his visits to New York City, Karadzic stayed at hotels outside the "headquarters district" of the United Nations and engaged in non-United Nations-related activities such as fundraising.

Id. at 246–47. The court held that immunity from service is confined to the headquarters district itself, and also declined to treat Karadzic as an accredited diplomatic envoy because he was only an invitee, and not a designated representative of the United Nations. Defendant argued that the court's approach would undermine the important work of the United Nations. Do you agree or not?

SECTION D.　OPPORTUNITY TO BE HEARD

The Due Process Clause requires that parties have a "right to be heard" before the government effects a deprivation of their liberty or property. Recall that in *Mullane*, Justice Jackson stated: "Many controversies have raged about the cryptic and abstract words of the Due Process Clause but there can be no doubt that at a minimum they require that deprivation of life, liberty or property by adjudication *be preceded* by notice and opportunity for hearing appropriate to the nature of the case" (emphasis added), p. 125, supra. In simple terms, a defendant has an adequate opportunity to be heard when—in light of the interests at stake in the litigation—she is able to develop the facts and legal issues in the case and present her position to the court. Depending on the interests involved, a full trial may be required or something less formal may pass muster. One common requirement is that the defendant must be informed of the action (that is, must receive notice) long enough in advance of the time when she is required to respond so as to allow her to obtain counsel and prepare a defense.

In a series of important cases, the Court has considered whether the Due Process Clause always requires a hearing before the state effects a deprivation of property or liberty, or whether a hearing after the fact may sometimes suffice. At stake in the resolution of this question is the scope and effect of many provisional remedies, which include such devices as sequestration, temporary restraining orders, and pre-action attachments. At common law, provisional remedies represented an important exception to the requirement of providing a pre-deprivation hearing, and traditionally were justified by the need for expedition and summary action.

NOTES AND QUESTIONS

1. By virtue of Federal Rule 64, a federal court may use the provisional remedies available to the courts of the state in which it is sitting to the extent that these state remedies are not inconsistent with any other federal rule or statute. See 11A Wright, Miller & Kane, Federal Practice and Procedure: Civil 2d §§ 2931–36. Provisional remedies primarily are a creature of statute, and their character and effectiveness vary considerably from state to state. For a general discussion of provisional remedies, see Miller, Civil Procedure of the Trial Court in Historical Perspective 481–515 (1952). For an illustrative example of state practice, see Articles 60 through 65 of New York's Civil Practice Law and Rules, which provide a claimant with the remedies of attachment and garnishment of property and debts, injunction, receivership, and notice of pendency. See 12 & 13 Weinstein, Korn & Miller, New York Civil Practice ¶¶ 6001.01–6515.07 (2d ed. 2004).

2. In a series of cases, the Supreme Court has subjected provisional remedies to the constraints of the Due Process Clause. See Countryman, *The Bill of Rights and the Bill Collector*, 15 Ariz. L. Rev. 521 (1973).

In SNIADACH v. FAMILY FINANCE CORP. OF BAY VIEW, 395 U.S. 337, 89 S.Ct. 1820, 23 L.Ed.2d 349 (1969), the Court struck down a Wisconsin prejudgment wage garnishment procedure as violative of due process guarantees. The statute authorized a summons to issue at the request of the creditor's lawyer who served the garnishee in order to freeze the debtor's wages during the period before trial of the main suit; the wage earner had no opportunity to be heard prior to the creditor's garnishment of his wages. The Court explained:

> A prejudgment garnishment of the Wisconsin type is a taking which may impose tremendous hardship on wage earners with families to support. Until a recent act of Congress, * * * which forbids discharge of employees on the ground that their wages have been garnished, garnishment often

meant the loss of a job. Over and beyond that was the great drain on family income.

Id. at 340–42, 89 S.Ct. at 1822–23, 23 L.Ed.2d at 353–54. Justice Harlan, in concurrence, stated:

> * * * Apart from special situations, * * * I think that due process is afforded only by the kinds of "notice" and "hearing" which are aimed at establishing the validity, or at least the probable validity of the underlying claim against the alleged debtor *before* he can be deprived of his property or its unrestricted use.

Id. at 343, 89 S.Ct. at 1823, 23 L.Ed.2d at 354–55.

3. Initially, the effect of *Sniadach* on other provisional remedies was unclear. However, in FUENTES v. SHEVIN, 407 U.S. 67, 92 S.Ct. 1983, 32 L.Ed.2d 556, rehearing denied 409 U.S. 902, 93 S.Ct. 177, 34 L.Ed.2d 165 (1972), the Court held that a state statute authorizing the replevin of property without a pre-seizure hearing was unconstitutional. The property seized in *Fuentes* consisted of consumer goods—an oven and a stereo—purchased on credit and paid for in installments. As the Court explained,

> There is no requirement that the applicant [for the writ of replevin] make a convincing showing before the seizure that the goods are, in fact, "wrongfully detained." Rather, Florida law * * * requires only that the applicant file a complaint, initiating a court action for repossession and reciting in conclusory fashion that he is "lawfully entitled to the possession" of the property, and that he file a security bond * * *.
>
> On the sole basis of the complaint and bond, a writ is issued "command[ing] the officer to whom it may be directed to replevy the goods and chattels in possession of defendant * * * and to summon the defendant to answer the complaint." * * * If the goods are "in any dwelling house or other building or enclosure," the officer is required to demand their delivery; but if they are not delivered, "he shall cause such house, building or enclosure to be broken open and shall make replevin according to the writ * * *." Fla. Stat. § 78.10.
>
> Thus, at the same moment that the defendant receives the complaint seeking repossession of property through court action, the property is seized from him. He is provided no prior notice and allowed no opportunity whatever to challenge the issuance of the writ. *After* the property has been seized, he will eventually have an opportunity for a hearing, as the defendant in the trial of the court action for repossession, which the plaintiff is required to pursue. And he is also not wholly without recourse in the meantime. For under the Florida statute, the officer who seizes the property must keep it for three days, and during that period the defendant may reclaim possession of the property by posting his own security bond in double its value. But if he does not post such a bond, the property is transferred to the party who sought the writ, pending a final judgment in the underlying action for repossession. * * *

Id. at 73–75, 93 S.Ct. at 1991, 34 L.Ed.2d at 566–67. The Court emphasized the importance of affording the consumer an opportunity to be heard before, rather than after, the seizure of her property:

The constitutional right to be heard is a basic aspect of the duty of government to follow a fair process of decisionmaking when it acts to deprive a person of his possessions. The purpose of this requirement is not only to ensure abstract fair play to the individual. Its purpose, more particularly, is to protect his use and possession of property from arbitrary encroachment—to minimize substantively unfair or mistaken deprivations of property, a danger that is especially great when the State seizes goods simply upon the application of and for the benefit of a private party. * * *

The requirement of notice and an opportunity to be heard raises no impenetrable barrier to the taking of a person's possessions. But the fair process of decision-making that it guarantees works, by itself, to protect against arbitrary deprivation of property. For when a person has an opportunity to speak up in his own defense, and when the State must listen to what he has to say, substantively unfair and simply mistaken deprivations of property interests can be prevented. * * *

If the right to notice and a hearing is to serve its full purpose, then, it is clear that it must be granted at a time when the deprivation can still be prevented. At a later hearing, an individual's possessions can be returned to him if they were unfairly or mistakenly taken in the first place. Damages may even be awarded to him for the wrongful deprivation. But no later hearing and no damage award can undo the fact that the arbitrary taking that was subject to the right of procedural due process has already occurred. * * *

* * *

* * * To be sure, the requirements that a party seeking a writ must first post a bond, allege conclusorily that he is entitled to specific goods, and open himself to possible liability in damages if he is wrong, serve to deter wholly unfounded applications for a writ. But those requirements are hardly a substitute for a prior hearing, for they test no more than the strength of the applicant's own belief in his rights.* * * Since his private gain is at stake, the danger is all too great that his confidence in his cause will be misplaced. * * *

The minimal deterrent effect of a bond requirement is, in a practical sense, no substitute for an informed evaluation by a neutral official. * * * While the existence of these other, less effective, safeguards may be among the considerations that affect the form of hearing demanded by due process, they are far from enough by themselves to obviate the right to a prior hearing of some kind.

Id. at 80–84, 93 S.Ct. at 1994–96, 34 L.Ed.2d at 570–72. The Court also criticized the state's relying on a clerk, rather than a judge, to oversee the summary action:

[The Florida statute] * * * abdicate[s] effective state control over state power. Private parties, serving their own private advantage, may unilaterally invoke state power to replevy goods from another. No state official participates in the decision to seek a writ; no state official reviews the basis for the claim to repossession; and no state official evaluates the need for immediate seizure. There is not even a requirement that the plaintiff provide any information to the court on these matters. The State acts largely in the dark.

Id. at 93, 93 S.Ct. at 2001, 34 L.Ed.2d at 577. The Court rejected the contention that consumers "who signed conditional sales contracts thereby waived their basic procedural due process rights":

> The contract signed by Mrs. Fuentes provided that "in the event of default of any payment or payments, Seller at its option may take back the merchandise * * *." The contracts signed by the Pennsylvania appellants similarly provided that the seller "may retake" or "repossess" the merchandise in the event of a "default in any payment." These terms were parts of printed form contracts, appearing in relatively small type and unaccompanied by any explanations clarifying their meaning.

> * * * [A] waiver of constitutional rights in any context must, at the very least, be clear. We need not concern ourselves with the involuntariness or unintelligence of a waiver when the contractual language relied upon does not, on its face, even amount to a waiver.

> The conditional sales contracts here simply provided that upon a default the seller "may take back," "may retake" or "may repossess" merchandise. The contracts included nothing about the waiver of a prior hearing. They did not indicate *how* or *through what process*—a final judgment, self-help, prejudgment replevin with a prior hearing, or prejudgment replevin without a prior hearing—the seller could take back the goods. Rather, the purported waiver provisions here are no more than a statement of the seller's right to repossession upon occurrence of certain events. * * *

Id. at 94, 93 S.Ct. at 2001, 34 L.Ed.2d at 578. Finally, although the Court recognized that "extraordinary situations" might exist to "justify postponing notice and opportunity for a hearing," these situations "must be truly unusual" for the exception to be constitutional:

> Only in a few limited situations has this Court allowed outright seizure * * * without opportunity for a prior hearing. First, in each case, the seizure has been directly necessary to secure an important governmental or general public interest. Second, there has been a special need for very prompt action. Third, the State has kept strict control over its monopoly of legitimate force; the person initiating the seizure has been a government official responsible for determining, under the standards of a narrowly drawn statute, that it was necessary and justified in the particular instance. Thus, the Court has allowed summary seizure of property to collect the internal revenue of the United States, to meet the needs of a national war effort, to protect against the economic disaster of a bank failure, and to protect the public from misbranded drugs and contaminated food.

Id. at 90–91, 93 S.Ct. at 1999, 34 L.Ed.2d at 575–76. See also Clark & Landers, Sniadach, Fuentes *and Beyond: The Creditor Meets the Constitution*, 59 Va. L. Rev. 355 (1973); Note, *Procedural Due Process—The Prior Hearing Rule and the Demise of Ex Parte Remedies*, 53 B.U. L. Rev. 41 (1973).

4. Uncertainty about the requirements of due process surfaced after the Court in MITCHELL v. W.T. GRANT CO., 416 U.S. 600, 94 S.Ct. 1895, 40 L.Ed.2d 406 (1974), upheld the Louisiana sequestration statute permitting the creditor to obtain the writ on an ex-parte application without giving the debtor either notice or a prior opportunity for a hearing. The Court reasoned that the risk of a wrongful taking was minimized by the creditor's interest in the property prior to the lawsuit, the judicial authorization of the writ, and the immediate availability of a post-seizure hearing.

5. In NORTH GEORGIA FINISHING, INC. v. DI–CHEM, INC., 419 U.S. 601, 95 S.Ct. 719, 42 L.Ed.2d 751 (1975), the Court relied on *Fuentes* to invalidate the Georgia garnishment statute, which permitted the writ to be issued on the basis of conclusory allegations by the plaintiff without providing the defendant with an opportunity for an "early" hearing "or other safeguard against mistaken repossession." The opinion for the Court stressed the need for statutes to guard against the risk of initial error resulting in irreparable injury to the defendant even when the debt arises in a commercial context between parties of equal bargaining power, two corporations in this case.

6. The Court also has considered whether the government must provide notice and an opportunity to be heard when it decides to terminate or deny publicly-funded benefits, such as public assistance, to an individual who claims eligibility under the statutory criteria. In GOLDBERG v. KELLY, 397 U.S. 254, 90 S.Ct. 1011, 25 L.Ed.2d 287 (1970), the Court held that the recipient of government funded public assistance is entitled to "the opportunity for an evidentiary hearing prior to termination of benefits" given the importance of the property interest at stake: "termination of aid pending resolution of a controversy over eligibility may deprive an *eligible* recipient of the very means by which to live while he waits." Id. at 264, 90 S.Ct. at 1018, 25 L.Ed.2d 297. However, in MATHEWS v. ELDRIDGE, 424 U.S. 319, 96 S.Ct. 893, 47 L.Ed.2d 18 (1976), the Court appeared to retreat from this principle, and held that the Due Process Clause does not require a hearing before the termination of Social Security disability benefits. A post-termination hearing is constitutionally sufficient, the Court explained, given the balance of three factors:

> First, the private interest that will be affected by the official action; second, the risk of an erroneous deprivation of such interest through the procedures used, and the probable value, if any, of additional or substitute procedural safeguards; and finally, the Government's interest, including the function involved and the fiscal and administrative burdens that the additional or substitute procedural requirement would entail.

Id. at 335, 96 S.Ct. at 903, 47 L.Ed.2d at 33. In the case that follows, the Supreme Court adapted the *Mathews* factors to a dispute between two private parties. Would application of the *Mathews* factors have changed the outcome in Fuentes v. Shevin?

———

CONNECTICUT v. DOEHR

Supreme Court of the United States, 1991.
501 U.S. 1, 111 S.Ct. 2105, 115 L.Ed.2d 1.

Certiorari to the United States Court of Appeals for the Second Circuit.

JUSTICE WHITE delivered an opinion, Parts I, II, and III of which are the opinion of the Court.*

This case requires us to determine whether a state statute that authorizes prejudgment attachment of real estate without prior notice or hearing, without a showing of extraordinary circumstances, and without a requirement that the person seeking the attachment post a bond, satisfies the Due Process Clause of the Fourteenth Amendment. We hold that, as applied to this case, it does not.

I

On March 15, 1988, Petitioner John F. DiGiovanni submitted an application to the Connecticut Superior Court for an attachment in the amount of $75,000 on respondent Brian K. Doehr's home in Meridan, Connecticut. DiGiovanni took this step in conjunction with a civil action for assault and battery that he was seeking to institute against Doehr in the same court. The suit did not involve Doehr's real estate nor did DiGiovanni have any pre-existing interest either in Doehr's home or any of his other property.

Connecticut law authorizes prejudgment attachment of real estate without affording prior notice or the opportunity for a prior hearing to the individual whose property is subject to the attachment. The State's prejudgment remedy statute provides, in relevant part:

> "The court or a judge of the court may allow the prejudgment remedy to be issued by an attorney without hearing * * * upon verification by oath of the plaintiff or of some competent affiant, that there is probable cause to sustain the validity of the plaintiff's claims and * * * that the prejudgment remedy requested is for an attachment of real property . . . ." Conn. Gen. Stat. § 52–278e (1991).

The statute does not require the plaintiff to post a bond to insure the payment of damages that the defendant may suffer should the attachment prove wrongfully issued or the claim prove unsuccessful.

As required, DiGiovanni submitted an affidavit in support of his application. In five one-sentence paragraphs, DiGiovanni stated that the facts set forth in his previously submitted complaint were true; that "I was willfully, wantonly and maliciously assaulted by the defendant, Brian K. Doehr"; that "[s]aid assault and battery broke my left wrist and further caused an ecchymosis to my right eye, as well as other injuries";

---

* The Chief Justice, Justice Blackmun, Justice Kennedy, and Justice Souter join Parts I, II, and III of this opinion, and Justice Scalia joins Parts I and III.

and that "I have further expended sums of money for medical care and treatment." The affidavit concluded with the statement, "In my opinion, the foregoing facts are sufficient to show that there is probable cause that judgment will be rendered for the plaintiff."

On the strength of these submissions the Superior Court judge * * * found "probable cause to sustain the validity of the plaintiff's claim" and ordered the attachment on Doehr's home "to the value of $75,000." The sheriff attached the property four days later * * *. Only after this did Doehr receive notice of the attachment. He also had yet to be served with the complaint * * *. As the statute further required, the attachment notice informed Doehr that he had the right to a hearing: (1) to claim that no probable cause existed to sustain the claim; (2) to request that the attachment be vacated, modified, or that a bond be substituted; or (3) to claim that some portion of the property was exempt from execution. * * *

Rather than pursue these options, Doehr filed suit against DiGiovanni in Federal District Court, claiming that [the statute] was unconstitutional under the Due Process Clause of the Fourteenth Amendment. The District Court upheld the statute and granted summary judgment in favor of DiGiovanni. * * * On appeal, a divided panel of the United States Court of Appeals for the Second Circuit reversed. * * *

* * *

II

With this case we return to the question of what process must be afforded by a state statute enabling an individual to enlist the aid of the State to deprive another of his or her property by means of the prejudgment attachment or similar procedure. * * * In [Mathews v. Eldridge, Note 6, p. 154, supra,] * * * we drew upon * * * [these] decisions to determine what process is due when the government itself seeks to effect a deprivation on its own initiative. * * * That analysis resulted in * * * [a] threefold inquiry requiring consideration of "the private interest that will be affected by the official action"; "the risk of an erroneous deprivation of such interest through the procedures used, and the probable value, if any, of additional or substitute safeguards"; and lastly "the Government's interest, including the function involved and the fiscal and administrative burdens that the additional or substitute procedural requirement would entail." * * *

Here the inquiry is similar but the focus is different. Prejudgment remedy statutes ordinarily apply to disputes between private parties rather than between an individual and the government. * * * For this type of case, therefore, the relevant inquiry requires, as in *Mathews,* first, consideration of the private interest that will be affected by the prejudgment measure; second, an examination of the risk of erroneous deprivation through the procedures under attack and the probable value of additional or alternative safeguards; and third, in contrast to *Mathews,* principal attention to the interest of the party seeking the prejudgment remedy, with, nonetheless, due regard for any ancillary interest the government may have in providing the procedure or forgoing the added burden of providing greater protections.

We now consider the *Mathews* factors in determining the adequacy of the procedures before us, first with regard to the safeguards of notice and a prior hearing, and then in relation to the protection of a bond.

III

We agree with the Court of Appeals that the property interests that attachment affects are significant. For a property owner like Doehr, attachment ordinarily clouds title; impairs the ability to sell or otherwise alienate the property; taints any credit rating; reduces the chance of obtaining a home equity loan or additional mortgage; and can even place an existing mortgage in technical default where there is an insecurity clause. * * *

* * * [Connecticut] correctly points out that these effects do not amount to a complete, physical, or permanent deprivation of real property; their impact is less than the perhaps temporary total deprivation of household goods or wages. * * * But the Court has never held that only such extreme deprivations trigger due process concern. * * * To the contrary, our cases show that even the temporary or partial impairments to property rights that attachments, liens, and similar encumbrances entail are sufficient to merit due process protection. * * *

* * * [The] risk of erroneous deprivation that the State permits here is substantial. By definition, attachment statutes premise a deprivation of property on one ultimate factual contingency—the award of damages to the plaintiff which the defendant may not be able to satisfy. * * * For attachments before judgment, Connecticut mandates that this determination be made by means of a procedural inquiry that asks whether "there is probable cause to sustain the validity of the plaintiff's claim." Conn. Gen. Stat. § 52–278e(a). * * * What probable cause means in this context, however, remains obscure. The State initially took the position * * * that the statute requires a plaintiff to show the objective likelihood of the suit's success. * * * DiGiovanni * * * reads the provision as requiring no more than that a plaintiff demonstrate a subjective good faith belief that the suit will succeed. * * * At oral argument, the State shifted its position to argue that the statute requires something akin to the plaintiff stating a claim with sufficient facts to survive a motion to dismiss.

We need not resolve this confusion since the statute presents too great a risk of erroneous deprivation under any of these interpretations. If the statute demands inquiry into the sufficiency of the complaint, or, still less, the plaintiff's good-faith belief that the complaint is sufficient, requirement of a complaint and a factual affidavit would permit a court to make these minimal determinations. But neither inquiry adequately reduces the risk of erroneous deprivation. Permitting a court to authorize attachment merely because the plaintiff believes the defendant is liable, or because the plaintiff can make out a facially valid complaint, would permit the deprivation of the defendant's property when the claim would fail to convince a jury, when it rested on factual allegations that were sufficient to state a cause of action but which the defendant would dispute, or in the case of a mere good-faith standard, even when the complaint failed to state a claim upon which relief could be granted. The potential for unwarranted attachment in these situations is self-evident and too great to satisfy the requirements of due process absent any countervailing consideration.

Even if the provision requires the plaintiff to demonstrate, and the judge to find, probable cause to believe that judgment will be rendered in favor of the plaintiff, the risk of error was substantial in this case. As the record shows, and as the State concedes, only a skeletal affidavit need be and was filed. The State urges that the reviewing judge normally reviews the complaint as well, but concedes that the complaint may also be conclusory. It is self-evident that the judge could make no realistic assessment concerning the likelihood of an action's success based upon these one-sided, self-serving, and conclusory submissions. And as the Court of Appeals said, in a case like this involving an alleged assault, even a detailed affidavit would give only the plaintiff's version of the confrontation. Unlike determining the existence of a debt or delinquent payments, the issue does not concern "ordinarily uncomplicated matters that lend themselves to documentary proof." * * *

What safeguards the State does afford do not adequately reduce this risk. Connecticut points out that the statute also provides an "expeditiou[s]" postattachment adversary hearing * * *; notice for such a hearing * * *; judicial review of an adverse decision * * *; and a double damages action if the original suit is commenced without probable cause * * *. [The Court noted that factors that might diminish the need for a predeprivation hearing, such as the existence of a vendor's lien, whether liability is likely to turn on documentary proof, and the requirement that plaintiff put up a bond, are not present.] It is true that a later hearing might negate the presence of probable cause, but this would not cure the temporary deprivation that an earlier hearing might have prevented. * * *

Finally, we conclude that the interests in favor of an *ex parte* attachment, particularly the interests of the plaintiff, are too minimal to supply such a consideration here. Plaintiff had no existing interest in Doehr's real estate when he sought the attachment. His only interest in attaching the property was to ensure the availability of assets to satisfy his judgment if he prevailed on the merits of his action. Yet there was no allegation that Doehr was about to transfer or encumber his real estate or take any other action during the pendency of the action that would render his real estate unavailable to satisfy a judgment. Our cases have recognized such a properly supported claim would be an exigent circumstance permitting postponing any notice or hearing until after the attachment is effected. * * * Absent such allegations, however, the plaintiff's interest in attaching the property does not justify the burdening of Doehr's owner-ship rights without a hearing to determine the likelihood of recovery.

No interest the government may have affects the analysis. The State's substantive interest in protecting any rights of the plaintiff cannot be any more weighty than those rights themselves. Here the plaintiff's interest is *de minimis*. Moreover, the State cannot seriously plead additional finan-cial or administrative burdens involving predeprivation hearings when it already claims to provide an immediate post-deprivation hearing. * * *

* * *

IV

A

Although a majority of the Court does not reach the issue, Justices Marshall, Stevens, O'Connor, and I deem it appropriate to consider whether due process also requires the plaintiff to post a bond or other security in addition to requiring a hearing or showing of some exigency.

As noted, the impairments to property rights that attachments affect merit due process protection. Several consequences can be severe, such as the default of a homeowner's mortgage. In the present context, it need only be added that we have repeatedly recognized the utility of a bond in protecting property rights affected by the mistaken award of prejudgment remedies. * * *

Without a bond, at the time of attachment, the danger that these property rights may be wrongfully deprived remains unacceptably high even with such safeguards as a hearing or exigency requirement. The need for a bond is especially apparent where extraordinary circumstances justify an attachment with no more than the plaintiff's *ex parte* assertion of a claim. * * * Until a postattachment hearing * * *, a defendant has no protection against damages sustained where no extraordinary circum-stance in fact existed or the plaintiff's likelihood of recovery was nil. Such protection is what a bond can supply. Both the Court and its individual members have repeatedly found the requirement of a bond to play an essential role in reducing what would have been too great a degree of risk in precisely this type of circumstance. * * *

But the need for a bond does not end here. A defendant's property rights remain at undue risk even when there has been an adversarial hearing to determine the plaintiff's likelihood of recovery. At best, a court's initial assessment of each party's case cannot produce more than an educated prediction as to who will win. This is especially true when, as here, the nature of the claim makes any accurate prediction elusive. * * * In consequence, even a full hearing under a proper probable-cause stan-dard would not prevent many defendants from having title to their homes impaired during the pendency of suits that never result in the contingency that ultimately justifies such impairment, namely, an award to the plain-tiff. Attachment measures currently on the books reflect this concern. All but a handful of States require a plaintiff's bond despite also affording a hearing either before, or (for the vast majority, only under extraordinary circumstances) soon after, an attachment takes place. * * *

The State stresses its double damages remedy for suits that are commenced without probable cause. * * * This remedy, however, fails to make up for the lack of a bond. As an initial matter, the meaning of "probable cause" in this provision is no more clear here than it was in the attachment provision itself. Should the term mean the plaintiff's good faith or the facial adequacy of the complaint, the remedy is clearly insufficient. A defendant who was deprived where there was little or no likelihood that the plaintiff would obtain a judgment could nonetheless recover only by proving some type of fraud or malice or by showing that the plaintiff had failed to state a claim. * * *

Nor is there any appreciable interest against a bond requirement. * * * [A] plaintiff [is not required] to show exigent circumstances nor any pre-existing interest in the property facing attachment. A party must show more than the mere existence of a claim before subjecting an opponent to prejudgment proceedings that carry a significant risk of erroneous deprivation. * * *

B

Our foregoing discussion compels the four of us to consider whether a bond excuses the need for a hearing or other safeguards altogether. If a bond is needed to augment the protections afforded by preattachment and postattachment hearings, it arguably follows that a bond renders these safeguards unnecessary. That conclusion is unconvincing, however, for it ignores certain harms that bonds could not undo but that hearings would prevent. The law concerning attachments has rarely, if ever, required defendants to suffer an encumbered title until the case is concluded without any prior opportunity to show that the attachment was unwarranted. Our cases have repeatedly emphasized the importance of providing a prompt postdeprivation hearing at the very least. * * *

* * *

V

Because Connecticut's prejudgment remedy provision * * * violates the requirements of due process * * *, the judgment of the Court of Appeals is affirmed, and the case is remanded to that court for further proceedings consistent with this opinion.

It is so ordered.

CHIEF JUSTICE REHNQUIST with whom JUSTICE BLACKMUN joins, concurring.

* * *

* * * The Court's opinion is, in my view, ultimately correct * * *. But I do not believe that the result follows so inexorably as the Court's

opinion suggests. All of the * * * [prior] cases dealt with personalty—bank deposits or chattels—and each involved the physical seizure of the property itself, so that the defendant was deprived of its use. * * * [I]n all of them the debtor was deprived of the use and possession of the property. In the present case, on the other hand, Connecticut's prejudgment attachment on real property statute, which secures an incipient lien for the plaintiff, does not deprive the defendant of the use or possession of the property.

The Court's opinion therefore breaks new ground * * *. * * * I agree with the Court, however, that upon analysis the deprivation here is a significant one, even though the owner remains in undisturbed possession. * * *

* * *

It is both unwise and unnecessary, I believe, for the Court to proceed, as it does in Part IV, from its decision of the case before it to discuss abstract and hypothetical situations not before it. * * * The two elements of due process with which the Court concerns itself in Part IV—the requirement of a bond, and of "exigent circumstances"—prove to be upon analysis so vague that the discussion is not only unnecessary, but not particularly useful. * * * We should await concrete cases which present questions involving bonds and exigent circumstances before we attempt to decide when and if the Due Process Clause of the Fourteenth Amendment requires them as prerequisites for a lawful attachment.

[The concurring opinion of JUSTICE SCALIA is omitted.]

NOTES AND QUESTIONS

1.   SHAUMYAN v. O'NEILL, 987 F.2d 122 (2d Cir. 1993), a challenge to the application of the same statute at issue in *Doehr,* involved a contract dispute between a homeowner and a contractor hired to do repairs. The home owner questioned the quality of the repair work and refused to pay the remainder of the bill. The contractor, ex parte, obtained a prejudgment attachment against the owner's home. While the state court action was pending, the homeowner sued in federal court to enjoin application of the attachment statute, and the District Court upheld the constitutionality of the statute as applied. Relying on *Mathews,* the Court of Appeals affirmed. Although the home owner had a strong private interest, the likelihood of an erroneous deprivation was not high because the evidence largely involved written documentation; moreover, the contractor "had a substantial pre-existing interest" in the property once his labor and materials were incorporated into plaintiff's home. Id. at 217. See Alquist, *Balancing the Checklist: Connecticut's Legislative Response to* Connecticut v. Doehr, 26 Conn. L. Rev. 721 (1994).

2.   In *Doehr,* defendant continued to possess and in fact reside in his home, even after the court's entry of the prejudgment attachment. The Court found that defendant was entitled to due process protection even though the

attachment caused only a "temporary or partial" impairment of Doehr's property right. In the wake of *Doehr*, commentators raised questions about the constitutionality of lis pendens statutes, which permit a plaintiff who claims an interest in real property to file a "notice of pendency" that alerts potential buyers of the claim, without affording the property owner an opportunity to contest imposition of the notice. See Levy, *Lis Pendens and Procedural Due Process: A Closer Look After* Connecticut v. Doehr, 51 Md. L. Rev. 1054 (1992). In DIAZ v. PATERSON, 547 F.3d 88 (2d Cir. 2008), a federal appeals court upheld the constitutionality of New York's lis pendens statute, applying the *Mathews* factors as construed in *Doehr*. Should the property owner be given any opportunity to challenge the notice after it has been imposed?

3. In UNITED STATES v. JAMES DANIEL GOOD REAL PROPERTY, 510 U.S. 43, 114 S.Ct. 492, 126 L.Ed.2d 490 (1993), the government filed an in rem action seeking civil forfeiture of a property owner's home four years after he had pled guilty to drug charges under state law. Pursuant to the seizure warrant, the government seized the home and ordered tenants living in the property to pay rent to the government rather than to the homeowner. The Supreme Court held that in the absence of exigent circumstances, the government was required to afford the homeowner notice and an opportunity to be heard before seizing real property that may be subject to civil forfeiture.

CHAPTER 4

JURISDICTION OVER THE SUBJECT MATTER OF THE ACTION—THE COURT'S COMPETENCY

■ ■ ■

This Chapter considers subject-matter jurisdiction: the court's power to hear a case because of the nature of the dispute. The topic of subject-matter jurisdiction in the United States is a complex one that reflects the division of authority between the federal judiciary and the court systems of the fifty states. "Each of the fifty states and the District of Columbia has its own judicial system. In addition, there is a separate federal court system, as well as courts for each of the United States territories and possessions." Friedenthal, Kane & Miller, Civil Procedure § 1.2 (4th ed. 2005). The subject-matter jurisdiction of the state courts is determined largely by state constitutions, state statutes, and judicial decisions; the subject-matter jurisdiction of the federal courts is determined by Article III of the federal Constitution, federal statutes, and judicial decisions. State and federal courts share overlapping jurisdiction in certain areas, and this concurrent authority creates strategic opportunities for both plaintiff and defendant.

SECTION A. THE SUBJECT–MATTER JURISDICTION OF THE STATE COURTS

State courts are considered to be courts of general jurisdiction, meaning their power is plenary and inherent; they have authority to hear cases on any subject matter unless they are ousted of such power by state or federal law. The jurisdiction of most state courts is distributed among a variety of courts. In many instances this is accomplished by segregating certain types of controversies from the mainstream of litigation and giving special courts subject-matter jurisdiction over them, as usually is done with domestic relations and probate matters, and formerly was true of "actions at law" and "suits in equity." Probably the most common method of limiting judicial power is by providing that the court can adjudicate only controversies involving more than a certain minimum or less than a stated maximum amount of money, or its equivalent.

NOTES AND QUESTIONS

1. A state court of general jurisdiction is permitted, and may be under a constitutional duty, to hear a cause of action arising under the laws of another state. In HUGHES v. FETTER, 341 U.S. 609, 71 S.Ct. 980, 95 L.Ed. 1212 (1951), the Supreme Court held that the Full Faith and Credit Clause, U.S. Const. Art. IV, § 1, precluded Wisconsin from closing its courts to a suit under the Illinois wrongful-death act in the absence of a valid Wisconsin policy to weigh against the national interest favoring the availability of a Wisconsin forum. *Hughes* has not been construed as barring a state from applying its own procedural law when adjudicating a sister state's cause of action in its own courts. For example, a state may apply its own statute of limitations even though the claim would be timely under the law of the state under which the cause of action arose. Conversely, a state may apply its own longer statute of limitations even though the claim would have been time-barred under the law of the state under which the cause of action arose. See Sun Oil Co. v. Wortman, 486 U.S. 717, 108 S.Ct. 2117, 100 L.Ed.2d 743 (1988).

2. When Congress enacts a federal statute, the presumption is that a state court has concurrent jurisdiction with the federal courts to decide claims based entirely on federal law. The presumption of concurrent jurisdiction is rooted in a "system of dual sovereignty":

> * * * This deeply rooted presumption in favor of concurrent state court jurisdiction is, of course, rebutted if Congress affirmatively ousts the state courts of jurisdiction over a particular claim. * * * "Thus, the presumption of concurrent jurisdiction can be rebutted by an explicit statutory directive, by unmistakable implication from legislative history, or by a clear incompatibility between state-court jurisdiction and federal interests." * * *

TAFFLIN v. LEVITT, 493 U.S. 455, 458–59, 110 S.Ct. 792, 795, 107 L.Ed.2d 887, 894 (1990).

3. If a state court can hear a case arising under federal law, must it do so? In HOWLETT v. ROSE, 496 U.S. 356, 110 S.Ct. 2430, 110 L.Ed.2d 332 (1990), a unanimous Supreme Court held that a Florida court could not decline to hear a federal civil rights claim under 42 U.S.C. § 1983 on the ground of sovereign immunity when that defense would not bar a similar state-law claim. Noting that the Florida court's holding "raises the concern that the state court may be evading federal law and discriminating against federal causes of action," the Court explained:

> A state policy that permits actions against state agencies for the failure of their officials to adequately police a parking lot and for the negligence of such officers in arresting a person on a roadside, but yet declines jurisdiction over federal actions for constitutional violations by the same persons can be based only on the rationale that such persons should not be liable for § 1983 violations in the courts of the State. That reason,

whether presented in terms of direct disagreement with substantive federal law or simple refusal to take cognizance of the federal cause of action, flatly violates the Supremacy Clause.

Id. at 380–81, 110 S.Ct. at 2445, 110 L.Ed.2d at 356. The Court also has held that a state court cannot eliminate jurisdiction to avoid hearing a federal claim. See HAYWOOD v. DROWN, ___ U.S. ___, 129 S.Ct. 2108, 173 L.Ed.2d 920 (2009).

SECTION B. THE SUBJECT–MATTER JURIS-DICTION OF THE FEDERAL COURTS—DIVERSITY OF CITIZENSHIP

———

Read Article III, § 2 of the United States Constitution and 28 U.S.C. §§ 1332, 1359, and 1369 in the Supplement.

———

Article III, Section 2 of the United States Constitution extends the judicial power of the federal courts to controversies "between Citizens of different States * * * and between a State, or the Citizens thereof, and Foreign States, Citizens or Subjects." The current scope of the diversity jurisdiction that Congress has granted to the federal courts is set out in 28 U.S.C. § 1332. The practical implications of diversity jurisdiction are significant: "diversity" jurisdiction allows the federal courts to hear cases in which the claims arise solely under *state* law, so long as constitutional and statutory requirements are satisfied (controversies between a citizen of a state and an alien are denominated "alienage cases"). Diversity jurisdiction thus raises important theoretical questions about federalism and the appropriate relation between unelected federal judges and the states.

One of the most important limitations on federal diversity jurisdiction is the rule of "complete diversity" announced by Chief Justice Marshall in STRAWBRIDGE v. CURTISS, 7 U.S. (3 Cranch) 267, 2 L.Ed. 435 (1806). The rule provides that there is no diversity jurisdiction if any plaintiff is a citizen of the same state as any defendant, no matter how many parties are involved in the litigation. The precise status of the complete diversity doctrine has been a subject of considerable debate because until quite recently it was not clear that the *Strawbridge* decision was an interpretation of the diversity statute at the time rather than a constitutional limitation on federal court jurisdiction.

The origin and purposes of diversity-of-citizenship jurisdiction have long been the subject of vigorous debate. The most widely accepted rationale—the desire to avoid discrimination against out-of-state residents in state courts—was offered by Chief Justice Marshall in BANK OF THE

UNITED STATES v. DEVEAUX, 9 U.S. (5 Cranch) 61, 87, 3 L.Ed. 38, 45 (1809):

> However true the fact may be, that the tribunals of the states will administer justice as impartially as those of the nation, * * * it is not less true that the constitution itself either entertains apprehensions on this subject, or views with such indulgence the possible fears and apprehensions of suitors, that it has established national tribunals for the decision of controversies * * * between citizens of different states.

Another argument of longstanding vintage is that the availability of a federal tribunal during the nation's formative period afforded some measure of security to investors developing the southern and western portions of the country. Analyses of the historical origins of diversity jurisdiction can be found in Frank, *Historical Bases of the Federal Judicial System*, 13 Law & Contemp. Prob. 1 (1948); Friendly, *The Historic Basis of the Diversity Jurisdiction*, 41 Harv. L. Rev. 483 (1928); and Phillips & Christenson, *The Historical and Legal Background of the Diversity Jurisdiction*, 46 A.B.A. J. 959 (1960). Recent research suggests that the grant of diversity jurisdiction protected creditors because federal officials could channel important litigation into the federal courts, where they were able to control the composition of federal juries. See Jones, *Finishing a Friendly Argument: The Jury and the Historical Origins of Diversity Jurisdiction*, 82 N.Y.U. L. Rev. 997 (2007).

Assuming that diversity jurisdiction was created to protect out-of-state litigants against local prejudice and that it has helped speed the economic growth of the country, are these meaningful bases for continuing diversity jurisdiction today? Statistical data on the actual existence of local prejudice in the states against out-of-state parties, and on whether an attorney's belief in the existence of such prejudice is a factor influencing forum choice, is sparse and inconclusive.

More than 72,000 diversity cases were filed in the federal district courts in 2007. This figure represents approximately 28 percent of the total number of federal civil cases filed during that year. By contrast only about 57,000 diversity cases were filed in the federal district courts in 1990, representing about 26 percent of the total cases filed. Some commentators have questioned whether the current utility of diversity jurisdiction justifies the federal resources devoted to the diversity docket. Indeed, proposals to curtail or abolish diversity jurisdiction have been made in Congress since the 1920s.

The Terms of the Debate

Critics of diversity jurisdiction concentrate primarily on five problems. The first, often noted by Justice Frankfurter, is the congestion diversity cases allegedly cause in the federal courts. Second, the rule of Erie Railroad Co. v. Tompkins, p. 234, infra, which requires the application of state law to substantive issues in diversity cases, has been thought by many to make the handling of diversity cases by federal judges unnecessary, wasteful, and inappropriate. The reasoning behind this argument is that only the state courts are considered to be authoritative on matters of substantive law, and the federal courts therefore are unable to exercise their creative function and are performing an unneeded service in avowedly aiming to follow state court decisions. Third, it is argued that judicial and legislative authority should be coextensive and that federal courts' deciding cases arising under state law is an undesirable interference with state autonomy. A fourth and related problem is the effect that the diversion of litigation to federal courts may have in retarding the development of state law. Fifth, and finally, it is said that the continuation of diversity jurisdiction diminishes the incentives for state court reform by those influential professional groups who, by virtue of diversity jurisdiction, are able to avoid litigation in the state courts.

Those who seek to retain diversity jurisdiction contend that state court prejudice against out-of-state parties still exists and that provincial attitudes, especially among jurors, can interfere with the administration of justice. Opponents counter that in today's mobile and wired society, such fears are unfounded. State judges and jurors alike are much more likely to have been exposed to citizens of other states, and, indeed, to have visited those states themselves. In the United States today, is prejudice attributable to race, gender, or sexual orientation likely to be more significant than bias attributable to state citizenship?

Another argument in favor of the status quo is that diversity jurisdiction implements the constitutional guarantee that the citizens of each state shall be entitled to all the privileges and immunities of citizens of the several states. See U.S. Const. Art. IV, § 2. However, abridgement of the Privileges and Immunities Clause is in itself sufficient for federal question jurisdiction under 28 U.S.C. § 1331, see p. 180, infra, and therefore diversity jurisdiction is not needed to provide a federal forum for this purpose.

A further argument in favor of diversity jurisdiction focuses on the purported institutional superiority of the federal courts and contends that it is desirable to channel as many cases as possible away from the state courts, or at least that out-of-state litigants, who have no opportunity to work for the improvement of the state courts, should be spared exposure to them. This argument builds, in part, on structural distinctions between the federal and state courts. Federal judges enjoy life tenure and sit with juries selected from a broader geographical area than most state tribunals. Most importantly, federal judges are appointed; since many state judges are elected, state judges are thought to be more susceptible to political pressure and local biases than federal judges. The idea of federal court superiority also rests on empirical factors, such as court resources, procedural rules, and judicial background, which change over time. Not all lawyers would agree that differences between the state and federal systems inevitably lead to better justice in the federal courts. Although the prestige of the federal courts generally has been high, there have been long periods when federal courts were perceived to be rich people's courts or defendants' courts.

A related argument in favor of diversity jurisdiction posits that the existence of concurrent state and federal jurisdiction to resolve state-law disputes creates a competition between the two systems that acts as a spur to higher standards of justice in terms of substantive law and procedural improvement. The metaphor typically used to express this rationale is that of the "cross-pollination" of ideas across courts. See Redish, *Reassessing the Allocation of Judicial Business Between State and Federal Courts: Federal Jurisdiction and "The Martian Chronicles,"* 78 Va. L. Rev. 1769, 1785 (1992).

Critics further argue that parties use the choice of forum made available through the grant of diversity jurisdiction for tactical purposes in order to gain an advantage from one forum or another in a particular case. To the extent that forum shopping exists, as it surely does, how much should it impact our consideration of a grant of power that is authorized by Article III of the federal Constitution? Professor Purcell has documented the extreme forum-shopping tactics of large corporations at the end of the nineteenth-century and the beginning of the twentieth-century, a period in which federal courts were perceived to be partial to commercial interests. See Purcell, Litigation and Inequality: Federal Diversity Jurisdiction in Industrial America, 1870–1958 (1992).

Some commentators justify diversity jurisdiction by pointing to the fear of investors that local prejudice may exist. This argument at one time was endorsed by the Judicial Conference of the United States. In considering this argument, the key question is not whether out-of-state investors in fact will receive fair treatment from state courts, but whether they *think* they will. If the abolition, or significant curtailment, of diversity jurisdiction would inhibit the willingness of investors to enter markets in different parts of the country, then diversity may serve a useful purpose. However, United States investors may now be sufficiently national-minded, and accustomed enough to investing abroad where they enjoy no protection from the federal courts, that they no longer fear state courts.

Finally, those favoring an expansion of diversity jurisdiction argue that it is an important institutional tool for solving problems of national significance in areas that traditionally are governed by state law. Diversity jurisdiction thus is associated with national debates about consumer protection, medical malpractice, and corporate accountability—areas of tort law that typically are regulated by the states. In addition, supporters see jurisdictional reform as a way to deal with large or complex disputes that straddle multiple states, comprise multiple state-law claims, and include multiple parties residing in different states. See Rowe & Sibley, *Beyond Diversity: Federal Multiparty, Multiforum Jurisdiction*, 135 U. Pa. L. Rev. 7 (1986).

New Developments

Congress has expanded the reach of diversity jurisdiction to provide a federal forum to certain large scale, state law, multiparty actions in which one plaintiff is a citizen of a state different from that of one defendant—so-called "minimal diversity." See Class Action Fairness Act of 2005, 28 U.S.C. §§ 1332(d), 1453; Multiparty, Multiforum Trial Jurisdiction Act of 2002, 28 U.S.C. §§ 1369, 1441(e)(5). Supporters of these statutes have argued that a federal forum is appropriate because the cases that will be heard are of interstate importance, and so should be determined from a national perspective. Critics have warned that opening the federal courthouse to complex state law cases will increase judicial workloads dramatically, unnecessarily nationalize local concerns, and undermine democracy by permitting unelected federal judges to decide state law issues. For an overview of these arguments, see Marcus, *Assessing CAFA's Stated Jurisdictional Policy*, 156 U. Pa. L. Rev. 1765 (2008). Other commentators have criticized this use of minimal diversity as result-driven and reflecting a pro-business bias. See Lind, *"Procedural Swift": Complex Litigation Reform, State Tort Law, and Democratic Values*, 37 Akron L. Rev. 717, 718 (2004). Still others have acknowledged the special problems of multistate class actions, in which the law of a single state "can bind the nation," but urge a solution drawn from choice-of-law principles. Miller & Crump, *Jurisdiction and Choice of Law in Multistate Class Actions After* Phillips Petroleum Co. v. Shutts, 96 Yale L.J. 1, 57 (1986).

The Multiparty, Multiforum Act, or Section 1369, deals with the problem of catastrophic mass accidents that involve the deaths of many people. Section 1369 authorizes original federal jurisdiction in any civil action arising "from a single accident, when at least 75 natural persons have died in the accident at a discrete location" provided "minimal diversity exists between adverse parties" and other conditions are satisfied. The statute reflects the view that consolidation of mass accident cases in a single forum will reduce expenses and avoid inconsistent judgments. Other jurisdictional conditions that must be met include the requirement that "substantial parts of the accident took place in different States"; and "a defendant resides in a State and substantial part of the accident took place in another State." 28 U.S.C. § 1369 (a)(1)-(3). Why do you think Congress imposed these additional conditions?

The Class Action Fairness Act, or CAFA, deals with big dollar class actions (although the individual claims may be small). CAFA makes federal district courts available for any class action in which the aggregate amount in controversy exceeds $5 million and in which any plaintiff "is a citizen of a State different from any defendant." CAFA gives the district court discretion, "in the interests of justice and looking at the totality of the circumstances," to decline jurisdiction over any lawsuit "in which greater than one-third but less than two-thirds of the members of all proposed plaintiff classes and the primary defendants are citizens of the State in which the action was originally filed," based on a consideration of listed factors, such as the national importance of the asserted claims and the "distinct nexus" between the forum and the parties or injuries. CAFA also provides for two jurisdictional exceptions. The district court "shall decline to exercise jurisdiction" over an action in which more than two-thirds of the putative class members are citizens of the state in which the action originally was filed, and over cases involving federal securities claims or claims related to corporate governance. Why do you think Congress included these exceptions? See Resnik, *Class Action Lessons in Federalism*, 156 U. Pa. L. Rev. 1929 (2008).

Some commentators have raised questions about this use of minimal diversity and suggested that limits be placed on it. See Lloyd, *The Limits of Minimal Diversity*, 55 Hastings L.J. 613 (2004). Should Congress develop these limits? What statistics and empirical data would be relevant to the reform process? How much weight should be given to federalism? To the differing interests of plaintiffs and defendants? What role should the federal courts have in the process? To what extent should the judiciary retain discretion to interpret jurisdictional provisions in light of changing conditions and evolving social needs? For a discussion of these and other issues, see Burbank, *The Class Action Fairness Act of 2005 in Historical Context: A Preliminary View*, 156 U. Pa. L. Rev. 1439 (2008).

––––––

Assessing whether the federal court may exercise diversity jurisdiction requires a determination of (1) the citizenship of the parties and (2) the amount in controversy in the dispute. Both requirements of 28 U.S.C. § 1332 must be met.

1. DETERMINING CITIZENSHIP

––––––

MAS v. PERRY

United States Court of Appeals, Fifth Circuit, 1974.
489 F.2d 1396, certiorari denied 419 U.S. 842, 95 S.Ct. 74, 42 L.Ed.2d 70.

AINSWORTH, CIRCUIT JUDGE.

* * *

Appellees Jean Paul Mas, a citizen of France, and Judy Mas were married at her home in Jackson, Mississippi. Prior to their marriage, Mr. and Mrs. Mas were graduate assistants, pursuing coursework as well as performing teaching duties, for approximately nine months and one year, respectively, at Louisiana State University in Baton Rouge, Louisiana. Shortly after their marriage, they returned to Baton Rouge to resume their duties as graduate assistants at LSU. They remained in Baton Rouge for approximately two more years, after which they moved to Park Ridge, Illinois. At the time of the trial in this case, it was their intention to return to Baton Rouge while Mr. Mas finished his studies for the degree of Doctor of Philosophy. Mr. and Mrs. Mas were undecided as to where they would reside after that.

Upon their return to Baton Rouge after their marriage, appellees rented an apartment from appellant Oliver H. Perry, a citizen of Louisiana. This appeal arises from a final judgment entered on a jury verdict awarding $5,000 to Mr. Mas and $15,000 to Mrs. Mas for damages incurred by them as a result of the discovery that their bedroom and bathroom contained "two-way" mirrors and that they had been watched through them by the appellant during three of the first four months of their marriage.

At the close of the appellees' case at trial, appellant made an oral motion to dismiss for lack of jurisdiction. The motion was denied by the district court. Before this Court, appellant challenges the final judgment below solely on jurisdictional grounds, contending that appellees failed to prove diversity of citizenship among the parties and that the requisite jurisdictional amount is lacking with respect to Mr. Mas. Finding no merit to these contentions, we affirm. Under section 1332(a)(2), the federal judicial power extends to the claim of Mr. Mas, a citizen of France, against the appellant, a citizen of Louisiana. Since we conclude that Mrs. Mas is a citizen of Mississippi for diversity purposes, the district court also properly had jurisdiction under section 1332(a)(1) of her claim.

It has long been the general rule that complete diversity of parties is required in order that diversity jurisdiction obtain; that is, no party on one side may be a citizen of the same State as any party on the other side. Strawbridge v. Curtiss * * *. This determination of one's State citizenship for diversity purposes is controlled by federal law, not by the law of any State. * * * As is the case in other areas of federal jurisdiction, the diverse citizenship among adverse parties must be present at the time the complaint is filed. * * * Jurisdiction is unaffected by subsequent changes in the citizenship of the parties. * * * The burden of pleading the diverse citizenship is upon the party invoking federal jurisdiction * * * and if the diversity jurisdiction is properly challenged, that party also bears the burden of proof.

To be a citizen of a State within the meaning of section 1332, a natural person must be both a citizen of the United States * * * and a domiciliary of that State. * * * For diversity purposes, citizenship means domicile; mere residence in the State is not sufficient. * * *

A person's domicile is the place of "his true, fixed, and permanent home and principal establishment, and to which he has the intention of returning whenever he is absent therefrom ...." * * * A change of domicile may be effected only by a combination of two elements: (a) taking up residence in a different domicile with (b) the intention to remain there. * * *

It is clear that at the time of her marriage, Mrs. Mas was a domiciliary of the State of Mississippi. While it is generally the case that the domicile of the wife—and, consequently, her State citizenship for purposes of diversity jurisdiction—is deemed to be that of her husband, * * * we find no precedent for extending this concept to the situation here, in which the husband is a citizen of a foreign state but resides in the United States. Indeed, such a fiction would work absurd results on the facts before us. If Mr. Mas were considered a domiciliary of France—as he would be since he had lived in Louisiana as a student-teaching assistant prior to filing this suit * * *—then Mrs. Mas would also be deemed a domiciliary, and thus, fictionally at least, a citizen of France. She would not be a citizen of any State and could not sue in a federal court on that basis; nor could she invoke the alienage jurisdiction to bring her claim in federal court, since she is not an alien. * * * On the other hand, if Mrs. Mas's domicile were Louisiana, she would become a Louisiana citizen for diversity purposes and could not bring suit with her husband against appellant, also a Louisiana citizen, on the basis of diversity jurisdiction. These are curious results under a rule arising from the theoretical identity of person and interest of the married couple. * * *

An American woman is not deemed to have lost her United States citizenship solely by reason of her marriage to an alien. 8 U.S.C. § 1489. Similarly, we conclude that for diversity purposes a woman does not have her domicile or State citizenship changed solely by reason of her marriage to an alien.

Mrs. Mas's Mississippi domicile was disturbed neither by her year in Louisiana prior to her marriage nor as a result of the time she and her husband spent at LSU after their marriage, since for both periods she was a graduate assistant at LSU. * * * Though she testified that after her marriage she had no intention of returning to her parents' home in Mississippi, Mrs. Mas did not effect a change of domicile since she and Mr. Mas were in Louisiana only as students and lacked the requisite intention to remain there. Until she acquires a new domicile, she remains a domiciliary, and thus a citizen of Mississippi. * * *

[The court's discussion of the jurisdictional amount is omitted.]

Thus the power of the federal district court to entertain the claims of appellees in this case stands on two separate legs of diversity jurisdiction: a claim by an alien against a State citizen; and an action between citizens of different States. We also note, however, the propriety of having the federal district court entertain a spouse's action against a defendant, where the district court already has jurisdiction over a claim, arising from the same transaction, by the other spouse against the same defendant. * * * In the case before us, such a result is particularly desirable. The claims of Mr. and Mrs. Mas arise from the same operative facts, and there was almost complete interdependence between their claims with respect to the proof required and the issues raised at trial. Thus, since the district court had jurisdiction of Mr. Mas's action, sound judicial administration militates strongly in favor of federal jurisdiction of Mrs. Mas's claim.

Affirmed.

NOTES AND QUESTIONS

1. In DRED SCOTT v. SANDFORD, 60 U.S. (19 How.) 393, 15 L.Ed. 691 (1856), the Supreme Court held that persons descended from African slaves were excluded from citizenship and could not invoke diversity jurisdiction. The Citizenship Clause of the Fourteenth Amendment overruled this holding. See U.S. Const. amend. XIV, § 1.

2. Can a United States citizen who is domiciled abroad invoke diversity jurisdiction? See Cresswell v. Sullivan & Cromwell, 922 F.2d 60, 68 (2d Cir. 1990).

3. *Mas* equates state citizenship with state domicile for purposes of diversity jurisdiction, but distinguishes domicile from residence. How does the court define domicile? If the goal of diversity jurisdiction is to protect out-of-staters from bias in suits against in-staters, does it make sense to disregard residence in defining citizenship for diversity purposes?

4. Under Section 1332, a corporation, unlike a natural person, can be a citizen of more than one state, but is deemed to have only one principal place of business. How should a court determine where a corporation has its principal place of business? What factors might be relevant?

Currently, three different tests are used to locate a corporation's principal place of business:

> The first test is the "nerve center" test. * * * Under this test, "the locus of corporate decision-making authority and overall control constitutes a corporation's principal place of business for diversity purposes." * * *

> The second test is referred to as the "corporate activities" or "operating assets" test. Greater weight is attached to the location of a corporation's production or service activities in determining the principal place of business under this test. * * *

> The third test is known as the "total activity" test. This test is a hybrid of the "nerve center" and "corporate activities" tests and considers all the circumstances surrounding a corporation's business to discern its principal place of business. "The 'total activity' test provides a realistic, flexible and nonformalistic approach to determining a corporation's principal place of business through a balancing of all relevant factors." * * *

WHITE v. HALSTEAD INDUSTRIES, INC., 750 F.Supp. 395, 397 (E.D.Ark. 1990). Is any one of these tests significantly more reasonable than the others? Or should the circumstances of the individual case dictate which test is applied? See 13F Wright & Miller, Federal Practice and Procedure: Jurisdiction and Related Matters 3d § 3625.

5. In determining the citizenship of an unincorporated association for diversity jurisdiction, courts look to the citizenship of each of the association's members, rather than the state under whose laws the association is created. Unincorporated associations include such entities as partnerships, labor unions, and charitable organizations. (Note the special rule for determining the citizenship of an unincorporated association under the Class Action Fairness Act, 28 U.S.C. § 1332(d)(10).)

6. In addition to conferring jurisdiction over controversies between "citizens of different states," Section 1332(a) authorizes jurisdiction over controversies that involve state citizens and "citizens or subjects of a foreign state"—often referred to as "alienage" jurisdiction. Do you agree that a federal forum is needed to protect foreign litigants against bias? See Johnson, *Why Alienage Jurisdiction? Historical Foundations and Modern Justifications for Federal Jurisdiction Over Disputes Involving Noncitizens*, 21 Yale J. Int'l L. 1, 2 (1996). Compare Clermont & Eisenberg, *Xenophilia in American Courts*, 109 Harv. L. Rev. 1120 (1996), with Moore, *Xenophobia in American Courts*, 97 Nw. U. L. Rev. 1497 (2003).

7. "Stateless" sometimes refers to an individual who is not a citizen of any country. How should a "stateless" alien be treated for purposes of determining whether jurisdiction exists under Section 1332? In BLAIR HOLDINGS CORP. v. RUBINSTEIN, 133 F.Supp. 496 (S.D.N.Y. 1955), the defendant was described in the complaint as "not [being] a citizen of the United States." The court interpreted 28 U.S.C. § 1332(a)(2) to require a showing that the defendant was a citizen of a foreign state. Since that showing had not been made, suit could not be maintained in federal court. Professor Chemerinsky questions this rule on the ground that "individuals who are not citizens of any state seem to be the most vulnerable to potential discrimination." Chemerinsky, Federal Jurisdiction § 5.3 (5th ed. 2007).

8. Plaintiffs who prefer to litigate in federal court as opposed to state court may attempt to create diversity of citizenship to accomplish their goal. In KRAMER v. CARIBBEAN MILLS, INC., 394 U.S. 823, 89 S.Ct. 1487, 23 L.Ed.2d 9 (1969), a Panamanian corporation assigned its interest under a contract with a Haitian corporation to Kramer, a Texas attorney, for $1. By a separate agreement, Kramer reassigned 95 percent of any net recovery on the assigned cause of action to the Panamanian company. Kramer then commenced suit against the Haitian company on the basis of diversity of citizenship. The District Court denied defendant's motion to dismiss for want of jurisdiction. The Court of Appeals reversed, holding that the assignment was "improperly or collusively made" within the meaning of 28 U.S.C. § 1359. The Supreme Court affirmed, holding that:

> If federal jurisdiction could be created by assignments of this kind, which are easy to arrange and involve few disadvantages for the assignor, then a vast quantity of ordinary contract and tort litigation could be channeled into the federal courts at the will of one of the parties. Such "manufacture of Federal jurisdiction" was the very thing which Congress intended to prevent when it enacted § 1359 and its predecessors.

Id. at 828–29, 89 S.Ct. at 1490, 23 L.Ed.2d at 14.

Would it have made a difference if the assignment had been made for a valid business reason? Note that Section 1359 prohibits only the creation of diversity jurisdiction and says nothing about its destruction. Is such a "one-way street" consistent with the purposes that diversity jurisdiction is intended to serve? See Grassi v. Ciba–Geigy, Ltd., 894 F.2d 181 (5th Cir. 1990) (holding that assignments that destroy diversity and those that create diversity should be analyzed under same standard).

9.   In 1988, as part of the Judicial Improvements and Access to Justice Act, Pub. L. No. 100–702, 102 Stat. 4642 (1988), Congress amended Section 1332(a) to provide that for purposes of diversity jurisdiction "an alien admitted to the United States for permanent residence shall be deemed a citizen of the State in which such alien is domiciled." Would this provision have changed the outcome in Mas v. Perry? Does the deeming provision authorize federal court jurisdiction in an action between two aliens, assuming one party is a permanent resident alien and so deemed to be "a citizen of the State" in which he or she is domiciled? Would this reading of the statute go beyond the limits of Article III? The circuits are divided on this question. In SINGH v. DAIMLER–BENZ AG, 9 F.3d 303 (3d Cir. 1993), the Third Circuit held that jurisdiction under Section 1332 was available in a state-law action brought by a permanent-resident-alien residing in Virginia against a nonresident alien and citizen of a state other than Virginia.

The District of Columbia Circuit rejected this reasoning in SAADEH v. FAROUKI, 107 F.3d 52 (D.C. Cir. 1997), holding instead that "Congress intended to contract diversity jurisdiction through the 1988 amendment to § 1332(a), not to expand it by abrogating the longstanding rule that complete diversity is destroyed in lawsuits between aliens." Id. at 52. However, in CHINA NUCLEAR ENERGY INDUSTRY CORP. v. ANDERSEN, LLP, 11 F.Supp.2d 1256 (D.Colo. 1998), the District Court followed the *Saadeh* approach and dismissed a federal-court action by an alien corporation against a partnership made up of both United States citizens and permanent-resident aliens.

The Seventh Circuit addressed the effect of the deeming provision of Section 1332(a) in INTEC USA, LLC v. ENGLE, 467 F.3d 1038 (7th Cir. 2006), rejecting *Singh*'s holding that a permanent-resident alien should be deemed a citizen only of the state of domicile, but questioning *Saadeh*'s suggestion that a permanent-resident-alien retains only foreign citizenship. Instead, Judge Easterbrook concluded that for purposes of Section 1332, "permanent-resident aliens have both state and foreign citizenship," and that this "dual citizenship" sometimes will defeat, but sometimes support, diversity jurisdiction depending on the citizenship of the other parties to the litigation. Id. at 1043.

10.   In 1988, Congress added to Section 1332(c) a provision that "the legal representative of the estate of a decedent shall be deemed to be a citizen only of the same State as the decedent, and the legal representative of an infant or incompetent shall be deemed to be a citizen only of the same State as the infant or incompetent." In so doing, Congress articulated a rule that prevents the appointment of administrators to create (or destroy) diversity. See Mullenix, *Creative Manipulation of Federal Jurisdiction: Is There Diversity After Death?*, 70 Cornell L. Rev. 1011 (1985).

11.   Plaintiffs who prefer to litigate in state court rather than in federal court may attempt to destroy diversity of citizenship to make it impossible for defendant to remove the action to federal court. In ROSE v. GIAMATTI, 721 F.Supp. 906 (S.D.Ohio 1989), plaintiff, Pete Rose, was the manager of the Cincinnati Reds baseball team. The Commissioner of Baseball, A. Bartlett Giamatti, was conducting an investigation into allegations that Rose had

wagered on major league baseball games in violation of the Rules of Major League Baseball. Rose filed suit in an Ohio state court seeking a temporary restraining order and preliminary injunction against pending disciplinary proceedings on the ground that he was being denied his right to a fair hearing because Giamatti was a biased decisionmaker. Rose named Giamatti, Major League Baseball, and the Cincinnati Reds as defendants. Giamatti removed the action to federal district court in Ohio. Rose, a citizen of Ohio, sought to have the case remanded to the Ohio state court arguing that diversity was lacking between himself, and both the Cincinnati Reds and Major League Baseball (an unincorporated association), who he alleged were also citizens of Ohio. Giamatti, a citizen of New York, argued that the citizenship of the other defendants should be ignored. The District Court noted:

> * * * [I]t is * * * a long-established doctrine that a federal court in its determination of whether there is diversity of citizenship between the parties, must disregard nominal or formal parties to the action, and determine jurisdiction based solely upon the citizenship of the real parties to the controversy. * * * A real party in interest defendant is one who, by the substantive law, has the duty sought to be enforced or enjoined. * * * [A] formal or nominal party is one who, in a genuine legal sense, has no interest in the result of the suit, * * * or no actual interest or control over the subject matter of the litigation. * * *

The court then concluded:

> [T]he controversy in this case is between plaintiff Rose and defendant Giamatti; that they are the real parties in interest in this case; that the Cincinnati Reds and Major League Baseball, are, at best, nominal parties in this controversy; and that, consequently, the citizenship of the Cincinnati Reds and Major League Baseball may be disregarded for diversity of citizenship purposes. The Court determines that diversity of citizenship exists between Rose, * * * and Commissioner Giamatti, * * * and that the Court has diversity subject matter jurisdiction over this action.

Id. at 914, 923–24.

Is it right for a court to disregard parties it determines to be "formal or nominal"? Do you agree that the Cincinnati Reds and Major League Baseball were "nominal" parties? Why was Rose so anxious to keep the case in state court? Is *Rose* the prototypical case in which diversity jurisdiction serves to protect an out-of-state defendant against local prejudice? See Case Note, *"Root, Root, Root for the Home Team": Pete Rose, Nominal Parties and Diversity Jurisdiction*, 66 N.Y.U. L. Rev. 148 (1991).

2. AMOUNT IN CONTROVERSY

Congress consistently has imposed an amount-in-controversy requirement on the grant of diversity jurisdiction. Congress raised the jurisdictional amount to its current level in 1996, and the diversity power can be invoked only if "the matter in controversy exceeds the sum or value of $75,000." See 28 U.S.C. § 1332(a). The test for determining whether the plaintiff has met the requirement is well settled: "The rule * * * is that,

* * * the sum claimed by the plaintiff controls if the claim is apparently made in good faith. It must appear to a legal certainty that the claim is really for less than the jurisdictional amount to justify dismissal." ST. PAUL MERCURY INDEMNITY CO. v. RED. CAB CO., 303 U.S. 283, 288–89, 58 S.Ct. 586, 589, 82 L.Ed. 845, 848 (1938) (footnotes omitted). The Court has emphasized that "[t]he inability of plaintiff to recover an amount adequate to give the court jurisdiction does not show his bad faith or oust the jurisdiction," and that "events occurring subsequent to the institution of suit which reduce the amount recoverable below the statutory limit do not oust jurisdiction." Id. at 289–90, 58 S.Ct. at 590–91, L.Ed. at 848–49.

NOTE ON AGGREGATION OF CLAIMS

The Federal Rules of Civil Procedure allow parties to join multiple claims in one action. See Chapter 8, infra. Should parties be permitted to "aggregate" the value of claims to meet the amount-in-controversy requirement for federal diversity jurisdiction? Courts have developed a number of rules to govern the variety of situations that typically arise.

Generally, one plaintiff can aggregate all of her claims against one defendant to meet the amount-in-controversy requirement, "even when those claims share nothing in common besides the identity of the parties." Everett v. Verizon Wireless, Inc., 460 F.3d 818, 822 (6th Cir. 2006). Thus, a plaintiff can satisfy the amount-in-controversy requirement by alleging a number of small claims against one defendant, assuming the total value satisfies the statutory requirement and citizenship is diverse. By contrast, multiple plaintiffs who join together in one lawsuit may not aggregate their claims to meet the jurisdictional requirement if the claims are separate and distinct. Rather, multiple plaintiffs may aggregate their claims only when they seek "to enforce a single title or right, in which they have a common and undivided interest." Troy Bank of Troy, Ind. v. G.A. Whitehead & Co., 222 U.S. 39, 40–41, 32 S.Ct. 9, 9, 56 L.Ed. 81, 82 (1911).

Given the current amount-in-controversy requirement of more than $75,000, and assuming citizenship is satisfied, consider whether diversity jurisdiction is available in the following cases:

(a) One plaintiff sues one defendant, claiming $40,000 in property damage and $45,000 for personal injury resulting from the same accident.

(b) One plaintiff sues one defendant on two unrelated claims, one for $40,000 and the other for $45,000.

(c) Two plaintiffs sue one defendant, each seeking $40,000 in damages.

(d) Two plaintiffs sue one defendant, jointly seeking $80,000 in damages.

(e) One plaintiff sues two defendants, seeking $40,000 from each defendant.

(f) Two plaintiffs sue one defendant on the same issue. One plaintiff seeks $45,000 in damages; the other seeks $35,000.

NOTE ON INJUNCTIVE RELIEF

Injunctions raise additional questions for the amount-in-controversy requirement of diversity jurisdiction. How should a court determine the value of the equitable relief that plaintiff seeks? At least three different approaches have emerged. As explained in McCARTY v. AMOCO PIPELINE CO., 595 F.2d 389, 392–93 (7th Cir. 1979):

> * * * Some courts have resolved the difficulty by adopting the rule that only the value to the plaintiff may be used to determine the jurisdictional amount. Support for this interpretation is principally garnered from the Supreme Court's opinion in Glenwood Light & Water Co. v. Mutual Light, Heat & Power Co., 239 U.S. 121, 36 S.Ct. 30, 60 L.Ed. 174 (1915). * * *

> Although supportive of the "plaintiff viewpoint" rule, the holding in *Glenwood* is only that jurisdiction is present if the value to the plaintiff exceeds the required amount regardless of the value to the defendant. The *Glenwood* case does not exclude the possibility that jurisdiction would be present in a case where the value required was present from the defendant's viewpoint but not from the plaintiff's. * * *

> Another approach taken by some courts is to view the amount in controversy from the point of view of the party seeking to invoke federal jurisdiction. * * * Under this rule, the court would look to the plaintiff's viewpoint in a case brought originally in federal court and to the defendant's viewpoint in a case removed to federal court from a state court.

> Although this rule has certain attractive features such as tying the controlling viewpoint to the burden of proof as to jurisdiction, two problems with it arise. The first is the possibility of anomalous results. Under the rule, if a case originally brought in federal court were dismissed for failure to meet the jurisdictional amount from the plaintiff's viewpoint, it could yet end up in federal court if the plaintiff reinstituted the case in state court and the defendant—from whose point of view the required amount was present—then removed it. * * *

> There is yet a third rule which a number of courts have adopted and which may be termed the "either viewpoint" rule. Under this rule * * *:

>> In determining the matter in controversy, we may look to the object sought to be accomplished by the plaintiffs' complaint; the test for determining the amount in controversy is the pecuniary result to either party which the judgment would directly produce.

> Although there are no Supreme Court cases directly on point, some support for this third rule can be found in the Court's opinions. * * *

Which approach best promotes the purposes of diversity jurisdiction and the principle of limited federal jurisdiction? See McInnis, *The $75,000.01 Ques-*

tion: What is the Value of Injunctive Relief?, 6 Geo. Mason L. Rev. 1013 (1998).

3. JUDICIALLY CREATED EXCEPTIONS TO DIVERSITY JURISDICTION

Even if the requirements of diversity jurisdiction are met, a federal court generally will decline to hear probate matters and domestic relations cases and instead dismiss for lack of subject-matter jurisdiction. See 13E Wright, Miller & Cooper, Federal Practice and Procedure: Jurisdiction and Related Matters 3d §§ 3609–10. These judicially created exceptions to diversity jurisdiction were first developed at a time when the diversity statute granted jurisdiction over "suits of a civil nature in law or in equity," and it was thought that probate and domestic-relations cases, being matters that would have been heard in the ecclesiastical courts, did not fit this description. The 1948 Judicial Code substituted the term "civil action" for the phrase used in the older statutes, but the exceptions have persisted.

The Supreme Court addressed the domestic-relations exception in ANKENBRANDT v. RICHARDS, 504 U.S. 689, 112 S.Ct. 2206, 119 L.Ed.2d 468 (1992), in which plaintiff invoked diversity jurisdiction to assert claims of physical and sexual abuse on behalf of her daughters against the children's father and his female companion. The Court found that a domestic-relations exception does exist, but the exception reaches only cases involving the issuance of a divorce, alimony, or a child custody decree, and that the exclusion is not constitutionally mandated. As a result, the Supreme Court upheld the District Court's jurisdiction over this tort action and ordered it to proceed. Is this distinction reasonable? Appropriate?

The Supreme Court clarified the limited nature of the probate exception in MARSHALL v. MARSHALL, 547 U.S. 293, 126 S.Ct. 1735, 164 L.Ed.2d 480 (2006), a dispute involving bankruptcy jurisdiction and concerning the estate of J. Howard Marshall II. Marshall died in 1994 and left his entire estate to his son, leaving nothing to his widow to whom he had been married for little more than one year. Two years later, while the estate was subject to proceedings in a Texas probate court, the widow filed for bankruptcy in the Federal Bankruptcy Court of Central California. In that latter case, the son filed a claim, asserting that the widow had defamed him. The widow counterclaimed, alleging that the son tortiously had interfered to prevent her husband from making her a substantial gift of money he had promised. Justice Ginsburg, writing for a unanimous Court, held that the widow's claim, seeking damages for a "widely recognized tort," id. at 312, 126 S.Ct. at 1748, 164 L.Ed.2d at 498, did not interfere with the state probate proceeding and was within the subject-matter jurisdiction of the Bankruptcy Court. Justice Stevens concurred in a separate opinion advocating the elimination of the probate exception as historically unjustified.

SECTION C. THE SUBJECT–MATTER JURISDICTION OF THE FEDERAL COURTS—FEDERAL QUESTIONS

————

Read Article III, § 2 of the United States Constitution and 28 U.S.C. §§ 1331 and 1441 in the Supplement.

————

Article III, § 2 of the United States Constitution extends the judicial power of the United States "to all Cases, in Law and Equity, arising under this Constitution, the Laws of the United States, and Treaties made, or which shall be made under their Authority." The current grant of "federal question" jurisdiction is set out in 28 U.S.C. § 1331. Although the grant of diversity jurisdiction dates to the Judiciary Act of 1789, Congress did not enact federal question jurisdiction until the Midnight Judges Act of 1801, which was repealed the next year when the Federalists lost power and Thomas Jefferson became President. The current statute traces back to the jurisdictional grant made in 1875. Commentators ascribe three purposes to Section 1331 jurisdiction: to promote uniformity of federal law; to develop judicial expertise in interpreting federal law; and to protect against possible state-court hostility to claims arising under federal law. See Shapiro, *Reflections on the Allocation of Jurisdiction Between State and Federal Courts: A Response to "Reassessing the Allocation of Judicial Business Between State and Federal Courts,"* 78 Va. L. Rev. 1839, 1842 (1992).

————

MISHKIN, THE FEDERAL "QUESTION" IN THE DISTRICT COURTS, 53 Colum. L. Rev. 157, 157–59 (1953):

Although the framers of our Constitution could not agree upon whether there should be any federal trial courts at all, it was generally conceded at the Convention that the national judicial power should, in some form, extend to cases arising under the laws of the new government. However, though the first Congress did exercise its option to establish a system of "inferior" national tribunals, it did not assign to them general jurisdiction over cases of that type. With the exception of an extremely shortlived statute enacted just after the end of the eighteenth century, it was not until 1875 that the federal courts were given initial cognizance of all types of federal question cases. * * *

Whatever may have been the circumstances and needs during the first century of our country's history, there seems to be little doubt that today, with the expanding scope of federal legislation, the exercise of power over cases of this sort constitutes one of the major purposes of a full independent system of national trial courts. The alternative would be to rely entirely upon United States Supreme Court review of state court decisions. But, at least in our present judicial system, Supreme Court pronouncements as to any particular segment of national law are comparatively few. Consequently, sympathetic handling of the available Supreme Court rulings assumes a role of substantial importance in achieving widespread, uniform effectuation of federal law. Presumably judges selected and paid by the central government, with tenure during good behavior—and that determined by the Congress—and probably even somewhat insulated by a separate building, are more likely to give full scope to any given Supreme Court decision, and particularly ones unpopular locally, than are their state counterparts. By the same token, should a district judge fail, or err, a more sympathetic treatment of Supreme Court precedents can be expected from federal circuit judges than from state appellate courts.

Thus, the exercise of federal question jurisdiction by lower federal tribunals presumably permits the Supreme Court to confine itself (insofar as any such distinction can be drawn) to the solving of new problems rather than the policing of old solutions, without the loss that might otherwise be entailed in the effectuation of national rights. Further, the fact that the lower federal bench is chosen by officials of the national government under the same procedure as the members of the high Court suggests a greater similarity in the interpretation of national law, even on first impression, among the several parts of the national system than between the Supreme Court and any state system, or among the various state tribunals themselves. Insofar as this is true, it also promotes a more uniform, correct application of federal law in that significant group of cases where, either because of the novelty of the question, disproportionate expense or for other reasons, recourse to the Supreme Court has previously either not been attempted or been precluded. Finally, it might even be argued that the very existence of an alternative forum stimulates state courts to give a more attentive treatment to claims of federal right.

These factors suggest that it is desirable that Congress be competent to bring to an initial national forum all cases in which the vindication of federal policy may be at stake. However, it does not follow from this that at any given time all such cases should in fact be brought before the federal courts. There are other considerations which must enter into any decision as to the actual use of the national judiciary. For example, there are limits on the volume of litigation which they can handle without an expansion which might not be warranted by the advantages to be gained; the hardships which the geographic location of these courts may impose on the litigants and a willingness to trust that a party's self-interest will lead him to bring or remove an appropriate case to the federal courts might well justify the current rule that federal question jurisdiction is, for the most part, shared by the local courts; in some circumstances, such as where the validity of state action may be at issue, it may avoid friction and wasted effort, without sacrificing national authority, to allow the initial adjudication to be made by the state's tribunals subject to ultimate review by the United States Supreme Court. Other factors could easily be added. * * *

OSBORN v. BANK OF THE UNITED STATES, 22 U.S. (9 Wheat.) 738, 6 L.Ed. 204 (1824). The Bank of the United States brought suit in federal court to enjoin the state auditor of Ohio from collecting from it a tax alleged to be unconstitutional. The court granted a temporary injunction restraining the state auditor from collecting the tax. The state auditor, however, forcibly entered the bank and took the money he claimed the state was owed. The court ordered the state officials to return the money that had been taken from the bank. The officials appealed on the grounds that the federal court lacked subject-matter jurisdiction over the case.

The congressional act chartering the bank authorized it "to sue and be sued * * * in any Circuit Court of the United States." First, Chief Justice Marshall held that this authorization was a grant by Congress to the federal courts of jurisdiction in all cases to which the bank was a party. He then considered whether Congress had the constitutional power to confer jurisdiction over these cases pursuant to the "arising under" language of Article III, § 2. That power clearly existed in the actual case, since the bank was alleging that Ohio's attempt to tax it violated the federal Constitution. The Chief Justice, however, undertook to support the validity of the jurisdictional grant in all cases to which the bank was a party. In particular, he discussed the situation presented if the bank asserted a claim under state law arising out of a contract:

> When [the] Bank sues, the first question which presents itself, and which lies at the foundation of the cause, is, has this legal entity a right to sue? Has it a right to come, not into this Court particularly, but into any Court? This depends on a law of the United States. The next question is, has this being a right to make this particular contract? If this question be decided in the negative, the cause is determined against the plaintiff; and this question, too, depends entirely on a law of the United States. These are important questions, and they exist in every possible case. The right to sue, if decided once, is decided for ever; but the power of Congress was exercised antecedently to the first decision on that right, and if it was constitutional then, it cannot cease to be so, because the particular question is decided. It may be revived at the will of the party, and most probably would be renewed, were the tribunal to be changed. But the question respecting the right to make a particular contract, or to acquire a particular property, or to sue on account of a particular injury, belongs to every particular case, and may be renewed in every case.

The question forms an original ingredient in every cause. Whether it be in fact relied on or not, in the defence, it is still a part of the cause, and may be relied on. The right of the plaintiff to sue, cannot depend on the defence which the defendant may choose to set up. His right to sue is anterior to that defence, and must depend on the state of things when the action is brought. The questions which the case involves, then, must determine its character, whether those questions be made in the cause or not.

The appellants say, that the case arises on the contract; but the validity of the contract depends on a law of the United States, and the plaintiff is compelled, in every case, to show its validity. The case arises emphatically under the law. The act of Congress is its foundation. The contract could never have been made, but under the authority of that act. The act itself is the first ingredient in the case, is its origin, is that from which every other part arises. That other questions may also arise, as the execution of the contract, or its performance, cannot change the case, or give it any other origin than the charter of incorporation. The action still originates in, and is sustained by, that charter.

Id. at 823–25, 6 L.Ed. at 224–25.

NOTE AND QUESTIONS

Some commentators read *Osborn* as permitting federal jurisdiction in "all cases where issues of federal law might possibly be an issue." Cohen, *The Broken Compass: The Requirement that a Case Arise "Directly" Under Federal Law*, 115 U. Pa. L. Rev. 890, 891 (1967). Consistent with this broad reading, *Osborn* is said to support the exercise of "protective jurisdiction," a species of federal question jurisdiction that permits "federal courts to hear state law claims, even though the claims themselves neither incorporate an original federal ingredient nor seek to enforce rights conferred by federal law." Pfander, *Protective Jurisdiction, Aggregate Litigation, and the Limits of Article III*, 95 Cal. L. Rev. 1423 (2007). Why might a federal forum be needed to protect federal interests even where the lawsuit involves only state claims? Justice Frankfurter criticized the concept of protective jurisdiction in TEXTILE WORKERS UNION v. LINCOLN MILLS, 353 U.S. 448, 471, 77 S.Ct. 912, 928–29, 1 L.Ed.2d 972, 989 (1957), and the Court has not explicitly ratified the exercise of this power. Would the exercise of protective jurisdiction be consistent with Article III?

––––––––

The *Osborn* decision took on added importance after an 1875 statute (the predecessor to 28 U.S.C. § 1331) gave the federal courts jurisdiction over cases arising under federal law. Although Section 1331 uses the same language as Article III, § 2, "the statutory language * * * has been more narrowly construed than its constitutional counterpart." Currie, *The Federal Courts and the American Law Institute, Part II*, 36 U. Chi. L. Rev.

268, 268–69 (1969). As you read the cases that follow, be clear on when the Court is interpreting Article III and when it is construing the statutory grant of jurisdiction under Section 1331.

————

LOUISVILLE & NASHVILLE R. CO. v. MOTTLEY

Supreme Court of the United States, 1908.
211 U.S. 149, 29 S.Ct. 42, 53 L.Ed. 126.

Appeal from the Circuit Court of the United States for the Western District of Kentucky * * *.

* * *

The bill alleged that in September, 1871, plaintiffs, while passengers upon the defendant railroad, were injured by the defendant's negligence, and released their respective claims for damages in consideration of the agreement for transportation during their lives, expressed in the contract. It is alleged that the contract was performed by the defendant up to January 1, 1907, when the defendant declined to renew the passes. The bill then alleges that the refusal to comply with the contract was based solely upon that part of the act of Congress of June 29, 1906, 34 Stat. 584, which forbids the giving of free passes or free transportation. The bill further alleges: First, that the act of Congress referred to does not prohibit the giving of passes under the circumstances of this case; and, second, that, if the law is to be construed as prohibiting such passes, it is in conflict with the 5th Amendment of the Constitution, because it deprives the plaintiffs of their property without due process of law. The defendant demurred to the bill. The judge of the circuit court overruled the demurrer, entered a decree for the relief prayed for, and the defendant appealed directly to this court.

MR. JUSTICE MOODY, after making the foregoing statement, delivered the opinion of the court:

Two questions of law were raised by the demurrer to the bill, were brought here by appeal, and have been argued before us. They are, first, whether * * * the act of Congress of June 29, 1906 * * * makes it unlawful to perform a contract for transportation of persons who, in good faith, before the passage of the act, had accepted such contract in satisfaction of a valid cause of action against the railroad; and, second, whether the statute, if it should be construed to render such a contract unlawful, is in violation of the 5th Amendment of the Constitution of the United States. We do not deem it necessary, however, to consider either of these questions, because, in our opinion, the court below was without jurisdiction of the cause. Neither party has questioned that jurisdiction, but it is the duty of this court to see to it that the jurisdiction of the circuit court, which is defined and limited by statute, is not exceeded. * * *

There was no diversity of citizenship, and it is not and cannot be suggested that there was any ground of jurisdiction, except that the case was a "suit ... arising under the Constitution or laws of the United States." Act of August 13, 1888, c.866, 25 Stat. 433, 434. It is the settled interpretation of these words, as used in this statute, conferring jurisdiction, that a suit arises under the Constitution and laws of the United States only when the plaintiff's statement of his own cause of action shows that it is based upon those laws or that Constitution. It is not enough that the plaintiff alleges some anticipated defense to his cause of action, and asserts that the defense is invalidated by some provision of the Constitution of the United States. Although such allegations show that very likely, in the course of the litigation, a question under the Constitution would arise, they do not show that the suit, that is, the plaintiff's original cause of action, arises under the Constitution. * * *

* * *

* * * The application of this rule to the case at bar is decisive against the jurisdiction of the circuit court.

It is ordered that the judgment be reversed and the case remitted to the circuit court with instructions to dismiss the suit for want of jurisdiction.

NOTES AND QUESTIONS

1.   Under *Mottley*, can jurisdiction under 28 U.S.C. § 1331 be based on defendant's affirmative defense or counterclaim? Consider the proposal of the American Law Institute, Study of the Division of Jurisdiction Between State and Federal Courts § 1312(d) (1969), which provides that a federal court may retain subject-matter jurisdiction even when the complaint does not present a claim within its original jurisdiction if defendant introduces a federal defense or counterclaim. Do you see any advantages to this reform?

2.   The Declaratory Judgment Act, 28 U.S.C. §§ 2201–02, allows the federal court to issue a declaration of "rights and other legal relations" to an "interested party" in "a case of actual controversy within its jurisdiction." Would there have been jurisdiction in the principal case if the railroad had sought, as it can today, a judicial declaration that the 1906 Act had rendered the passes invalid? See SKELLY OIL CO. v. PHILLIPS PETROLEUM CO., 339 U.S. 667, 673–74, 70 S.Ct. 876, 880, 94 L.Ed. 1194, 1200–01 (1950), in which suit was brought under the Declaratory Judgment Act for a declaration that certain contracts had not been terminated. Had the plaintiff (who also was the party who initiated the declaratory action) simply sued to enforce the contract, the complaint would not have raised a federal question; in defending against the breach of contract complaint, however, the defendant would have argued termination, and the effectiveness of an attempted termination turned on a federal question. The Court held that federal question jurisdiction was not present, explaining that "[t]o sanction suits for declaratory relief as within the jurisdiction of the District Courts merely because, as in this case, artful pleading anticipates a defense based on federal law would contravene

the whole trend of jurisdictional legislation by Congress, disregard the effective functioning of the federal judicial system and distort the limited procedural purposes of the Declaratory Judgment Act." How would the assertion of jurisdiction in *Skelly* have done all of these things?

3. Should all causes of action created by federal law confer federal question jurisdiction? Consider this question in light of SHOSHONE MINING CO. v. RUTTER, 177 U.S. 505, 20 S.Ct. 726, 44 L.Ed. 864 (1900). Congress established a system allowing miners to file land patents on claims and to settle conflicting claims. The federal statute provided that the right to possession was to be determined by the "local customs or rules of miners in the several mining districts, so far as the same are applicable and not inconsistent with the laws of the United States." The Court determined:

> Inasmuch * * * as the "adverse suit" to determine the right of possession may not involve any question as to the construction or effect of the Constitution or laws of the United States, but may present simply a question of fact as to the time of the discovery of mineral, the location of the claim on the ground, or a determination of the meaning and effect of certain local rules and customs prescribed by the miners of the district, or the effect of state statutes, it would seem to follow that it is not one which necessarily arises under the Constitution and laws of the United States.

Id. at 509, 20 S.Ct. at 727, 44 L.Ed. at 866.

4. Conversely, should all causes of action created by state law be outside Section 1331? SMITH v. KANSAS CITY TITLE & TRUST CO., 255 U.S. 180, 41 S.Ct. 243, 65 L.Ed. 577 (1921), provides an example of a claim that, although created by state law, was found to arise under a law of the United States. In *Smith*, a shareholder sued to enjoin the Trust Company, a Missouri corporation, from investing in certain federal bonds on the ground that the Act of Congress authorizing their issuance was unconstitutional. The plaintiff claimed that under Missouri law an investment in securities the issuance of which had not been authorized by a valid law was *ultra vires* and enjoinable. The cause of action was thus created by the state. Nonetheless, the Supreme Court held that the action arose under federal law:

> The general rule is that where it appears from the bill or statement of the plaintiff that the right to relief depends upon the construction or application of the Constitution or laws of the United States, and that such federal claim is not merely colorable, and rests upon a reasonable foundation, the District Court has jurisdiction. * * *

Id. at 199, 41 S.Ct. at 245, 65 L.Ed. at 585. Justice Holmes dissented on the ground that because state and not federal law created the cause of action, the case did not arise under the federal law for purposes of Section 1331:

> It is evident that the cause of action arises not under any law of the United States but wholly under Missouri law. The defendant is a Missouri corporation and the right claimed is that of a stockholder to prevent the directors from doing an act, that is, making an investment, alleged to be contrary to their duty. But the scope of their duty depends upon the charter of their corporation and other laws of Missouri. If those laws had

authorized the investment in terms the plaintiff would have no case, and this seems to me to make manifest what I am unable to deem even debatable, that, as I have said, the cause of action arises wholly under Missouri law. If the Missouri law authorizes or forbids the investment according to the determination of this Court upon a point under the Constitution or acts of Congress, still that point is material only because the Missouri law saw fit to make it so. The whole foundation of the duty is Missouri law, which at its sole will incorporated the other law as it might incorporate a document. The other law or document depends for its relevance and effect not on its own force but upon the law that took it up, so I repeat once more the cause of action arises wholly from the law of the State.

Id. at 214, 41 S.Ct. at 250, 65 L.Ed. at 591 (Holmes, J., dissenting).

The holding of *Smith* appeared to be contradicted by the Court's later decision in MOORE v. CHESAPEAKE & OHIO RAILWAY CO., 291 U.S. 205, 54 S.Ct. 402, 78 L.Ed. 755 (1934). In *Moore*, plaintiff brought an action under Kentucky's Employer Liability Act, which provided that a plaintiff could not be held responsible for contributory negligence or assumption of risk if defendant violated state or federal employee-safety laws. The Supreme Court found that federal question jurisdiction did not exist, holding that:

> [A] suit brought under the state statute which defines liability to employees who are injured while engaged in intrastate commerce, and brings within the purview of the statute a breach of the duty imposed by the federal statute, should [not] be regarded as a suit arising under the laws of the United States and cognizable in the federal court in the absence of diversity of citizenship.

Id. at 214–15, 54 S.Ct. at 406, 78 L.Ed. at 762.

In MERRELL DOW PHARMACEUTICALS INC. v. THOMPSON 478 U.S. 804, 106 S.Ct. 3229, 92 L.Ed.2d 650 (1986), the Court again faced the question of whether jurisdiction is available under Section 1331 to hear a state law cause of action that incorporates a federal issue. Plaintiff sued a drug manufacturer in state court under a state statute that made the violation of a health or safety requirement per se negligence; plaintiff alleged that defendant failed to comply with labeling requirements under a federal statute. Defendant removed. Emphasizing that Congress had not created a private right of action to enforce the labeling requirement, the Supreme Court reversed, holding that the federal interest in the suit was too insubstantial to support jurisdiction under Section 1331. The Court explained:

> We * * * conclude that the congressional determination that there should be no federal remedy for the violation of this federal statute is tantamount to a congressional conclusion that the presence of a claimed violation of the statute as an element of a state cause of action is insufficiently "substantial" to confer federal-question jurisdiction. * * *

In a footnote, the Court elaborated on the significance of "the *nature* of the federal interest at stake":

> Focusing on the nature of the federal interest, moreover, suggests that the widely perceived "irreconcilable" conflict between the finding of

federal jurisdiction in Smith v. Kansas City Title & Trust Co., * * * and the finding of no jurisdiction in Moore v. Chesapeake & Ohio R. Co. * * * is far from clear. For the difference in result can be seen as manifestations of the differences in the nature of the federal issues at stake. In *Smith,* as the Court emphasized, the issue was the constitutionality of an important federal statute. * * * In *Moore,* in contrast, the Court emphasized that the violation of the federal standard as an element of state tort recovery did not fundamentally change the state tort nature of the action. * * *

The importance of the nature of the federal issue in federal-question jurisdiction is highlighted by the fact that, despite the usual reliability of the Holmes test as an inclusionary principle, this Court has sometimes found that formally federal causes of action were not properly brought under federal-question jurisdiction because of the overwhelming predominance of state-law issues. See * * * Shoshone Mining Co. v. Rutter * * *.

Id. at 814, 106 S.Ct. at 3235, 92 L.Ed.2d at 662.

————

After *Merrell Dow* the circuits were divided on whether Section 1331 jurisdiction exists where a state-law claim incorporates a federal issue. Some courts interpreted *Merrell Dow* as treating federal issues that were not enforceable through a federal right of action as too insubstantial to support federal question jurisdiction. The Supreme Court addressed this question in the pair of cases that follow.

————

GRABLE & SONS METAL PRODUCTS, INC. v. DARUE ENGINEERING & MANUFACTURING

Supreme Court of the United States, 2005.
545 U.S. 308, 125 S.Ct. 2363, 162 L.Ed.2d 257.

Certiorari to the United States Court of Appeals for the Sixth Circuit.

JUSTICE SOUTER delivered the opinion of the Court.

The question is whether want of a federal cause of action to try claims of title to land obtained at a federal tax sale precludes removal to federal court of a state action with nondiverse parties raising a disputed issue of federal title law. We answer no, and hold that the national interest in providing a federal forum for federal tax litigation is sufficiently substantial to support the exercise of federal question jurisdiction over the disputed issue on removal, which would not distort any division of labor between the state and federal courts, provided or assumed by Congress.

I

In 1994, the Internal Revenue Service seized Michigan real property belonging to petitioner Grable & Sons Metal Products, Inc., to satisfy

Grable's federal tax delinquency. Title 26 U.S.C. § 6335 required the IRS to give notice of the seizure, and there is no dispute that Grable received actual notice by certified mail before the IRS sold the property to respondent Darue Engineering & Manufacturing. Although Grable also received notice of the sale itself, it did not exercise its statutory right to redeem the property within 180 days of the sale, § 6337(b)(1), and after that period had passed, the Government gave Darue a quitclaim deed, § 6339.

Five years later, Grable brought a quiet title action in state court, claiming that Darue's record title was invalid because the IRS had failed to notify Grable of its seizure of the property in the exact manner required by § 6335(a), which provides that written notice must be "given by the Secretary to the owner of the property [or] left at his usual place of abode or business." Grable said that the statute required personal service, not service by certified mail.

Darue removed the case to Federal District Court as presenting a federal question, because the claim of title depended on the interpretation of the notice statute in the federal tax law. The District Court declined to remand the case at Grable's behest after finding that the "claim does pose a 'significant question of federal law,' " * * * and ruling that Grable's lack of a federal right of action to enforce its claim against Darue did not bar the exercise of federal jurisdiction. On the merits, the court granted summary judgment to Darue, holding that although § 6335 by its terms required personal service, substantial compliance with the statute was enough. * * *

The Court of Appeals for the Sixth Circuit affirmed. * * * On the jurisdictional question, the panel thought it sufficed that the title claim raised an issue of federal law that had to be resolved, and implicated a substantial federal interest (in construing federal tax law). The court went on to affirm the District Court's judgment on the merits. We granted certiorari on the jurisdictional question alone * * * to resolve a split within the Courts of Appeals on whether *Merrell Dow* * * * always requires * * * a federal cause of action as a condition for exercising federal-question jurisdiction. We now affirm.

II

Darue was entitled to remove the quiet title action if Grable could have brought it in federal district court originally, 28 U.S.C. § 1441(a), as a civil action "arising under the Constitution, laws, or treaties of the United States," § 1331. This provision for federal-question jurisdiction is invoked by and large by plaintiffs pleading a cause of action created by federal law (e.g., claims under 42 U.S.C. § 1983). There is, however, another longstanding, if less frequently encountered, variety of federal "arising under" jurisdiction, this Court having recognized for nearly 100 years that in certain cases federal-question jurisdiction will lie over state-law claims that implicate significant federal issues. * * * The doctrine captures the commonsense notion that a federal court ought to be able to hear claims recognized under state law that nonetheless turn on substantial questions of federal law, and thus justify resort to the experience, solicitude, and hope of uniformity that a federal forum offers on federal issues, see ALI, Study of the Division of Jurisdiction Between State and Federal Courts 164–166 (1968).

The classic example is *Smith* * * *. Although Missouri law provided the cause of action, the Court recognized federal-question jurisdiction because the principal issue in the case was the federal constitutionality of the bond issue. * * *

* * * *Smith* * * * has been subject to some trimming to fit earlier and later cases recognizing the vitality of the basic doctrine, but shying away from the expansive view that mere need to apply federal law in a state-law claim will suffice to open the "arising under" door. * * * [Justice Cardozo explained] that a request to exercise federal-question jurisdiction over a state action calls for a "common-sense accommodation of judgment to [the] kaleidoscopic situations" that present a federal issue, in "a selective process which picks the substantial causes out of the web and lays the other ones aside." *Gully v. First Nat. Bank in Meridian*, 299 U.S. 109, 117–118, 81 L. Ed. 70, 57 S. Ct. 96 (1936). It has in fact become a constant refrain in such cases that federal jurisdiction demands not only a contested federal issue, but a substantial one, indicating a serious federal interest in claiming the advantages thought to be inherent in a federal forum. * * *

But even when the state action discloses a contested and substantial federal question, the exercise of federal jurisdiction is subject to a possible veto. For the federal issue will ultimately qualify for a federal forum only if federal jurisdiction is consistent with congressional judgment about the sound division of labor between state and federal courts governing the application of § 1331. * * * Because arising-under jurisdiction to hear a state-law claim always raises the possibility of upsetting the state-federal line drawn (or at least assumed) by Congress, the presence of a disputed federal issue and the ostensible importance of a federal forum are never necessarily dispositive; there must always be an assessment of any disruptive portent in exercising federal jurisdiction. * * *

These considerations have kept us from stating a "single, precise, all-embracing" test for jurisdiction over federal issues embedded in state-law claims between nondiverse parties. *Christianson v. Colt Industries Operating Corp.*, 486 U.S. 800, 821, 100 L. Ed. 2d 811, 108 S. Ct. 2166 (1988) (Stevens, J., concurring). We have not kept them out simply because they appeared in state raiment, as Justice Holmes would have done * * * [dissenting in *Smith*], but neither have we treated "federal issue" as a password opening federal courts to any state action embracing a point of federal law. Instead, the question is, does a state-law claim necessarily raise a stated federal issue, actually disputed and substantial, which a federal forum may entertain without disturbing any congressionally approved balance of federal and state judicial responsibilities.

III

A

This case warrants federal jurisdiction. Grable's state complaint must specify "the facts establishing the superiority of [its] claim," Mich. Ct. Rule 3.411(B)(2)(c) (West 2005), and Grable has premised its superior title claim on a failure by the IRS to give it adequate notice, as defined by federal law. Whether Grable was given notice within the meaning of the federal statute is thus an essential element of its quiet title claim, and the meaning of the federal statute is actually in dispute; it appears to be the only legal or factual issue contested in the case. The meaning of the federal tax provision is an important issue of federal law that sensibly belongs in a federal court. The Government has a strong interest in the "prompt and certain collection of delinquent taxes," *United States v. Rodgers*, * * * and the ability of the IRS to satisfy its claims from the property of delinquents requires clear terms of notice to allow buyers like Darue to satisfy themselves that the Service has touched the bases necessary for good title. The Government thus has a direct interest in the availability of a federal forum to vindicate its own administrative action, and buyers (as well as tax delinquents) may find it valuable to come before judges used to federal tax matters. Finally, because it will be the rare state title case that raises a contested matter of federal law, federal jurisdiction to resolve genuine disagreement over federal tax title provisions will portend only a microscopic effect on the federal-state division of labor. * * *

* * *

B

Merrell Dow * * *, on which Grable rests its position, is not to the contrary. * * * The Court assumed that federal law would have to be applied to resolve the claim, but after closely examining the strength of the federal interest at stake and the implications of opening the federal forum, held federal jurisdiction unavailable. * * *

Because federal law provides for no quiet title action that could be brought against Darue, Grable argues that there can be no federal jurisdiction here, stressing some broad language in *Merrell Dow* * * * that on its face supports Grable's position * * *. But an opinion is to be read as a whole, and *Merrell Dow* cannot be read whole as overturning decades of precedent, as it would have done by effectively adopting the Holmes dissent in *Smith* * * * and converting a federal cause of action from a sufficient condition for federal-question jurisdiction into a necessary one.

In the first place, *Merrell Dow* disclaimed the adoption of any bright-line rule, as when the Court reiterated that "in exploring the outer reaches of § 1331, determinations about federal jurisdiction require sensitive judgments about congressional intent, judicial power, and the federal system." * * * The opinion included a lengthy footnote explaining that questions of jurisdiction over state-law claims require "careful judgments," * * * about the "nature of the federal interest at stake," * * * (emphasis deleted). And as a final indication that it did not mean to make a federal right of action mandatory, it expressly approved the exercise of jurisdiction sustained in *Smith*, despite the want of any federal cause of action available to *Smith*'s shareholder plaintiff. * * * *Merrell Dow* then, did not toss out, but specifically retained, the contextual enquiry that had been *Smith*'s hallmark for over 60 years. At the end of *Merrell Dow*, Justice Holmes was still dissenting.

Accordingly, *Merrell Dow* should be read in its entirety as treating the absence of a federal private right of action as evidence relevant to, but not dispositive of, the "sensitive judgments about congressional intent" that § 1331 requires. The absence of any federal cause of action affected *Merrell Dow*'s result two ways. The Court saw the fact as worth some consideration in the assessment of substantiality. But its primary importance emerged when the Court treated the combination of no federal cause of action and no preemption of state remedies for misbranding as an important clue to Congress's conception of the scope of jurisdiction to be exercised under § 1331. The Court saw the missing cause of action not as a missing federal door key, always required, but as a missing welcome mat, required in the circumstances, when exercising federal jurisdiction over a state misbranding action would have attracted a horde of original filings and removal cases raising other state claims with embedded federal issues. For if the federal labeling standard without a federal cause of action could get a state claim into federal court, so could any other federal standard without a federal cause of action. And that would have meant a tremendous number of cases.

One only needed to consider the treatment of federal violations generally in garden variety state tort law. "The violation of federal statutes and regulations is commonly given negligence per se effect in state tort proceedings." Restatement (Third) of Torts § 14 Reporters' Note, Comment *a*, p. 195 (Tent. Draft No. 1, March 28, 2001). * * * A general rule of exercising federal jurisdiction over state claims resting on federal mislabeling and other statutory violations would thus have heralded a potentially enormous shift of traditionally state cases into federal courts. Expressing concern over the "increased volume of federal litigation," and noting the importance of adhering to "legislative intent," *Merrell Dow* thought it improbable that the Congress, having made no provision for a federal cause of action, would have meant to welcome any state-law tort case implicating federal law "solely because the violation of the federal statute is said to [create] a rebuttable presumption [of negligence] . . . under state law." * * * [brackets in original]. In this situation, no welcome mat meant keep out. *Merrell Dow*'s analysis thus fits within the framework of examining the importance of having a federal forum for the issue, and the consistency of such a forum with Congress's intended division of labor between state and federal courts.

As already indicated, however, a comparable analysis yields a different jurisdictional conclusion in this case. Although Congress also indicated ambivalence in this case by providing no private right of action to Grable, it is the rare state quiet title action that involves contested issues of federal law * * *. * * * Consequently, jurisdiction over actions like Grable's would not materially affect, or threaten to affect, the normal currents of litigation. Given the absence of threatening structural consequences and the clear interest the Government, its buyers, and its delinquents have in the availability of a federal forum, there is no good reason to shirk from federal jurisdiction over the dispositive and contested federal issue at the heart of the state-law title claim.

IV

The judgment of the Court of Appeals * * * is affirmed.

It is so ordered.

[A concurring opinion by Justice Thomas stated that "[i]n an appropriate case, I would be willing to consider * * * limiting § 1331 jurisdiction to cases in which federal law creates the cause of action pleaded on the face of the plaintiff's complaint * * *."]

————

EMPIRE HEALTHCHOICE ASSURANCE, INC. v. McVEIGH, 547 U.S. 677, 126 S.Ct. 2121, 165 L.Ed.2d 131 (2006). Joseph McVeigh, a federal employee, was injured and eventually died, allegedly as a result of acts of a third party. Empire Healthchoice Assurance, McVeigh's private insurance carrier, paid substantial sums for McVeigh's medical care. After McVeigh's death, the administrator of McVeigh's estate sued the third party and received a large monetary settlement. Empire then sued McVeigh's estate in federal court to recoup amounts Empire had paid for McVeigh's medical expenses. Empire is under contract with the federal Office of Personnel Management (OPM) to provide insurance coverage to federal workers like McVeigh. The Federal Employees Health Benefits Act of 1959, the federal statute regulating health-benefit plans for federal employees, is silent on whether private carriers can recoup third-party medical payments. However, OPM's contract with Empire requires the carrier to take reasonable steps to make such recoupment, and enrolled employees are informed that if they recover medical expenses from an outside party, they must reimburse the private carrier. The District Court dismissed the case for lack of federal question jurisdiction, and the Court of Appeals for the Second Circuit, by divided vote, affirmed. The Supreme Court granted certiorari on the subject-matter jurisdiction question, and affirmed.

Justice Ginsburg, writing for the Court, observed that Congress had not created a federal right of action allowing insurance carriers to seek reimbursement from beneficiaries in federal court. The Court declined to characterize the insurer's claim as federal, despite "distinctly federal interests," such as negotiation of the OPM master contract by a federal agency, the effect of the contract on the interests of federal employees, and the crediting of reimbursements to a federal fund. Rather, the Court wrote, "countervailing considerations control"—in particular, Congress's conferring of federal jurisdiction over suits involving benefits against the United States, but not over carrier reimbursement claims. "Had Congress found it necessary or proper to extend federal jurisdiction * * *," the Court explained, "it would have been easy enough for Congress to say so." Id. at 696, 126 S.Ct. at 2134–35, 165 L.Ed.2d at 147.

The Court further declined to characterize the claim as arising under federal law simply because federal law forms a necessary element of the claim for relief. To the contrary, the Court emphasized, Empire's claim "does not fit within the special and small category" of state-law claims cognizable in federal court under *Grable*. First, the dispute in *Grable* "centered on the action of a federal agency (IRS) and its compatibility with a federal statute, the question qualified as 'substantial,' and its resolution was both dispositive of the case and would be controlling in numerous other cases." By contrast, Empire's "reimbursement claim was triggered, not by the action of any federal department, agency, or service, but by the settlement of a personal-injury action launched in state court." Second, "*Grable* presented a nearly 'pure issue of law,'" one 'that could be settled once and for all and thereafter would govern numerous tax sale cases.'" Empire's claim "is fact-bound and situation-specific," involving such matters as whether there were overcharges or duplicative charges. Finally, even if Empire's claim might raise the legal issue of whether to account for the beneficiary's attorney's fees expended for recovery, "it is hardly apparent why a proper 'federal-state balance' * * * would place such a nonstatutory issue under the complete governance of federal law, to be declared in a federal forum." Id. at 700–01, 126 S.Ct. at 2137, 165 L.Ed.2d at 150.

[Justice Breyer's dissenting opinion, in which Justices Kennedy, Souter, and Alito joined, is omitted.]

NOTES AND QUESTIONS

1. *Grable* upheld federal jurisdiction over a state cause of action that involved an important issue of federal law and affected the interests of the United States. The carrier's reimbursement claim in *Empire Healthchoice* likewise affected significant federal interests, including the treatment of federal employees and protection of the federal fisc. Why did the Court nevertheless withhold federal question jurisdiction from the reimbursement claim?

2. The dissent in *Empire Healthchoice* emphasized the role of federal common law in resolving the carrier's reimbursement claim. The topic of federal common law is a complex one and is taken up Chapter 6, infra.

3. Professor Cohen has argued that the search for "a single, all-purpose, neutral analytical concept which marks out federal question jurisdiction" is futile. He suggests a "pragmatic" test that would include consideration of the extent of the effect on judicial caseload if jurisdiction is recognized, the extent

to which a class of cases is likely to turn on issues of state or federal law, the extent to which the federal courts would have expertise in the area, and the extent to which a sympathetic tribunal is necessary. Cohen, *The Broken Compass: The Requirement that a Case Arise "Directly" Under Federal Law*, 115 U. Pa. L. Rev. 890 (1967). See also Shapiro, *Jurisdiction and Discretion*, 60 N.Y.U. L. Rev. 543 (1985). Is this approach consistent with the Court's approach in *Grable* and *Empire Healthchoice*?

SECTION D. THE SUBJECT–MATTER JURISDICTION OF THE FEDERAL COURTS— SUPPLEMENTAL CLAIMS AND PARTIES

———

Read Article III, § 2 of the United States Constitution and 28 U.S.C. § 1367 in the Supplement.

———

Sometimes a federal court may decide matters that, if presented independently, would not provide a basis for federal subject-matter jurisdiction. The judicially created doctrines of pendent and ancillary jurisdiction describe two such situations. The term "pendent jurisdiction" has been used when plaintiff, in her complaint, appends a claim lacking an independent basis for federal jurisdiction to a claim possessing such a basis. The term "ancillary jurisdiction" has been used when either a plaintiff or a defendant injects a claim lacking an independent basis for federal jurisdiction by way of a counterclaim, cross-claim, or third-party complaint. Although the doctrines of ancillary and pendent jurisdiction were spawned from two separate lines of authorities, they became two species of the same generic phenomenon. In 1990, when Congress undertook to codify these doctrines, it gave them the collective name of "supplemental jurisdiction." 28 U.S.C. § 1367. In analyzing these doctrines, consider how Article III limits the scope of supplemental jurisdiction and the policies that ought to govern its exercise.

———

UNITED MINE WORKERS OF AMERICA v. GIBBS
Supreme Court of the United States, 1966.
383 U.S. 715, 86 S.Ct. 1130, 16 L.Ed.2d 218.

Certiorari to the United States Court of Appeals for the Sixth Circuit.

MR. JUSTICE BRENNAN delivered the opinion of the Court.

Respondent Paul Gibbs was awarded compensatory and punitive damages in this action against petitioner United Mine Workers of America (UMW) for alleged violations of § 303 of the Labor Management Relations

Act, 1947, and of the common law of Tennessee. The case grew out of the rivalry between the United Mine Workers and the Southern Labor Union over representation of workers in the southern Appalachian coal fields. Tennessee Consolidated Coal Company, not a party here, laid off 100 miners of the UMW's Local 5881 when it closed one of its mines in southern Tennessee during the spring of 1960. Late that summer, Grundy Company, a wholly owned subsidiary of Consolidated, hired respondent as mine superintendent to attempt to open a new mine on Consolidated's property at nearby Gray's Creek through use of members of the Southern Labor Union. As part of the arrangement, Grundy also gave respondent a contract to haul the mine's coal to the nearest railroad loading point.

On August 15 and 16, 1960, armed members of Local 5881 forcibly prevented the opening of the mine, threatening respondent and beating an organizer for the rival union. The members of the local believed Consolidated had promised them the jobs at the new mine; they insisted that if anyone would do the work, they would. * * * George Gilbert, the UMW's field representative for the area including Local 5881, * * * [had] explicit instructions from his international union superiors to establish a limited picket line, to prevent any further violence, and to see to it that the strike did not spread to neighboring mines. There was no further violence at the mine site * * *.

Respondent lost his job as superintendent, and never entered into performance of his haulage contract. He testified that he soon began to lose other trucking contracts and mine leases he held in nearby areas. Claiming these effects to be the result of a concerted union plan against him, he sought recovery not against Local 5881 or its members, but only against petitioner, the International. The suit was brought in the United States District Court for the Eastern District of Tennessee, and jurisdiction was premised on allegations of secondary boycotts under § 303. The state law claim, for which jurisdiction was based upon the doctrine of pendent jurisdiction, asserted "an unlawful conspiracy and an unlawful boycott aimed at him and [Grundy] to maliciously, wantonly and willfully interfere with his contract of employment and with his contract of haulage."

* * * The jury's verdict was that the UMW had violated both § 303 and state law. Gibbs was awarded $60,000 as damages under the employment contract and $14,500 under the haulage contract; he was also awarded $100,000 punitive damages. On motion, the trial court set aside the award of damages with respect to the haulage contract on the ground that damage was unproved. It also held that union pressure on Grundy to discharge respondent as supervisor would constitute only a primary dispute with Grundy, as respondent's employer, and hence was not cognizable under § 303. Interference with employment was cognizable as a state claim, however, and a remitted award was sustained on the state law claim. * * * The Court of Appeals for the Sixth Circuit affirmed. * * * We granted certiorari. * * *

I

A threshold question is whether the District Court properly entertained jurisdiction of the claim based on Tennessee law. * * *

* * * The Court held in Hurn v. Oursler, 289 U.S. 238, 53 S.Ct. 586, 77 L.Ed. 1148, that state law claims are appropriate for federal court determination if they form a separate but parallel ground for relief also sought in a substantial claim based on federal law. The Court distinguished permissible from non-permissible exercises of federal judicial power over state law claims by contrasting "a case where two distinct grounds in support of a single cause of action are alleged, one only of which presents a federal question, and a case where two separate and distinct causes of action are alleged, one only of which is federal in character. In the former, where the federal question averred is not plainly wanting in substance, the federal court, even though the federal ground be not established, may nevertheless retain and dispose of the case upon the nonfederal *ground*; in the latter it may not do so upon the nonfederal *cause of action*." 289 U.S., at 246, 53 S.Ct., at 589. The question is into which category the present action fell.

Hurn was decided in 1933, before the unification of law and equity by the Federal Rules of Civil Procedure. At the time, the meaning of "cause of action" was a subject of serious dispute * * *.

* * *

With the adoption of the Federal Rules of Civil Procedure and the unified form of action * * * much of the controversy over "cause of action" abated. The phrase remained as the keystone of the *Hurn* test, however, and * * * has been the source of considerable confusion. Under the Rules, the impulse is toward entertaining the broadest possible scope of action consistent with fairness to the parties; joinder of claims, parties and remedies are strongly encouraged. Yet because the *Hurn* question involves issues of jurisdiction as well as convenience, there has been some tendency to limit its application to cases in which the state and federal claims are, as in *Hurn*, "little more than the equivalent of different epithets to characterize the same group of circumstances." 289 U.S., at 246, 53 S.Ct. at 590.

This limited approach is unnecessarily grudging. Pendent jurisdiction, in the sense of judicial *power*, exists whenever there is a claim "arising under [the] Constitution, the Laws of the United States, and Treaties made, or which shall be made, under their Authority * * *," U.S. Const., Article III, § 2, and the relationship between that claim and the state claims made in the complaint permits the conclusion that the entire action before the court comprises but one constitutional "case." The federal claim must have substance sufficient to confer subject matter jurisdiction on the court. * * * The state and federal claims must derive from a common nucleus of operative fact. But if, considered without regard for their federal or state character, a plaintiff's claims are such that he would ordinarily be expected to try them all in one judicial proceeding, then, assuming substantiality of the federal issues, there is *power* in federal courts to hear the whole.

That power need not be exercised in every case in which it is found to exist. It has consistently been recognized that pendent jurisdiction is a doctrine of discretion, not of plaintiff's right. Its justification lies in considerations of judicial economy, convenience and fairness to litigants; if these are not present a federal court should hesitate to exercise jurisdiction over state claims, even though bound to apply state law to them, * * *. Needless decisions of state law should be avoided both as a matter of comity and to promote justice between the parties, by procuring for them a surer-footed reading of applicable law. Certainly, if the federal claims are dismissed before trial, even though not insubstantial in a jurisdictional sense, the state claims should be dismissed as well. Similarly, if it appears that the state issues substantially predominate, whether in terms of proof, of the scope of the issues raised, or of the comprehensiveness of the remedy sought, the state claims may be dismissed without prejudice and left for resolution to state tribunals. There may, on the other hand, be situations in which the state claim is so closely tied to questions of federal policy that the argument for exercise of pendent jurisdiction is particularly strong. In the present case, for example, the allowable scope of the state claim implicates the federal doctrine of preemption; while this interrelationship does not create statutory federal question jurisdiction, Louisville & N.R. Co. v. Mottley, [p. 184, supra,] * * * its existence is relevant to the exercise of discretion. Finally, there may be reasons independent of jurisdictional considerations, such as the likelihood of jury confusion in treating divergent legal theories of relief that would justify separating state and federal claims for trial, Fed. Rule Civ. Proc. 42(b). If so, jurisdiction should ordinarily be refused.

The question of power will ordinarily be resolved on the pleadings. But the issue whether pendent jurisdiction has been properly assumed is one which remains open throughout the litigation. Pretrial procedures or even the trial may reveal a substantial hegemony of state law claims, or likelihood of jury confusion, which could not have been anticipated at the pleading stage. Although it will of course be appropriate to take account in this circumstance of the already completed course of the litigation, dismissal of the state claim might even then be merited. For example, it may appear that the plaintiff was well aware of the nature of his proofs and the relative importance of his claims; recognition of a federal court's wide latitude to decide ancillary questions of state law does not imply that it must tolerate a litigant's effort to impose upon it what is in effect only a state law case. Once it appears that a state claim constitutes the real body of a case, to which the federal claim is only an appendage, the state claim may fairly be dismissed.

We are not prepared to say that in the present case the District Court exceeded its discretion in proceeding to judgment on the state claim. * * *

It is true that the § 303 claims ultimately failed and that the only recovery allowed respondent was on the state claim. We cannot confidently say, however, that the federal issues were so remote or played such a minor role at the trial that in effect the state claim only was tried. Although the District Court dismissed as unproved the claims that petitioner's secondary activities included attempts to induce coal operators other than Grundy to cease doing business with respondent, the court submitted the § 303 claims relating to Grundy to the jury. The jury returned verdicts against petitioner on those § 303 claims, and it was only on petitioner's motion for a directed verdict and a judgment *n.o.v.* that the verdicts on those claims were set aside. * * * Although there was some risk of confusing the jury in joining the state and federal claims—especially since, as will be developed, differing standards of proof of UMW involvement applied—the possibility of confusion could be lessened by employing a special verdict form, as the District Court did. * * *

[The Court went on to hold that the plaintiff could not recover damages for conspiracy under Tennessee common law on the basis of the record.]

Reversed.

THE CHIEF JUSTICE took no part in the decision of this case.

[A concurring opinion by JUSTICE HARLAN, joined by JUSTICE CLARK, is omitted.]

NOTE AND QUESTIONS

Under *Gibbs*, the power to exercise pendent jurisdiction exists wherever the relation between the federal and nonfederal claims "permits the conclusion that the entire action * * * comprises but one constitutional 'case.' " See p. 197, supra. How does the Court determine whether the requisite relation exists? Is this approach consistent with the limited subject-matter jurisdiction of the federal courts?

NOTE ON PENDENT AND ANCILLARY JURISDICTION FOLLOWING GIBBS

In the years following *Gibbs*, the expansion of federal substantive law placed similar pressures on pendent and ancillary jurisdiction. In *Gibbs*, plaintiff joined related federal and state claims against a single nondiverse defendant, and pendent jurisdiction was exercised over the state-law claim. After *Gibbs*, courts began to consider whether pendent jurisdiction could be justified in cases where plaintiff filed a federal claim against one defendant and a state claim against a different nondiverse defendant. In a series of cases, the Supreme Court considered the propriety of "pendent party" jurisdiction.

In ALDINGER v. HOWARD, 427 U.S. 1, 96 S.Ct. 2413, 49 L.Ed.2d 276 (1976), an action alleging violations of the federal Civil Rights Act, 42 U.S.C. § 1983, the Court, exercising subject-matter jurisdiction under 28 U.S.C. § 1343, held that pendent party jurisdiction would not support the joinder of a nondiverse municipal county defendant, emphasizing that under the construction given the federal civil rights statute at the time, counties were not considered to be subject to it. The Court declined to lay down any "sweeping pronouncement upon the existence or exercise of [pendent party] jurisdiction," and instead instructed district courts to consider whether "Congress in the statutes conferring jurisdiction has not expressly or by implication negated its existence." Id. at 18, 96 S.Ct. at 2422, 49 L.Ed.2d at 289.

In OWEN EQUIPMENT & ERECTION CO. v. KROGER, 437 U.S. 365, 98 S.Ct. 2396, 57 L.Ed.2d 274 (1978), Kroger, a citizen of Iowa, sued Omaha Public Power District (OPPD), a Nebraska corporation, for the wrongful death of her husband, who had been electrocuted while walking next to the beam of a steel crane that came too close to a high-tension electric line. Kroger brought the action in federal district court in Nebraska based on diversity of citizenship, alleging that OPPD's negligent operation of the power line had caused her husband's death. OPPD, in turn, filed a third-party complaint pursuant to Federal Rule 14(a) against Owen Equipment and Erection Company, alleging that the crane was owned and operated by Owen, and that it was Owen's negligence that had been the proximate cause of the decedent's death.

Plaintiff was allowed to amend her complaint to name Owen as a defendant, which she alleged was a Nebraska corporation with its principal place of business in Nebraska. OPPD requested, and was granted, summary judgment, leaving Owen as the sole defendant. During the course of the trial, it was discovered that Owen's principal place of business was actually in Iowa,[a] and, Owen moved to dismiss the case based on a lack of subject-matter jurisdiction. The District Court denied the motion and the Court of Appeals affirmed. The Supreme Court reversed:

> It is apparent that *Gibbs* delineated the constitutional limits of judicial power. * * *
>
> That statutory law as well as the Constitution may limit a federal court's jurisdiction over nonfederal claims is well illustrated by * * * Aldinger v. Howard * * *. * * * The *Aldinger* * * * [case] make[s] clear that a finding that federal and nonfederal claims arise from a "common nucleus of operative fact," the test of *Gibbs*, does not end the inquiry into whether a federal court has power to hear the nonfederal claims along with the federal ones. Beyond this constitutional minimum, there must be an examination of the posture in which the nonfederal claim is asserted and of the specific statute that confers jurisdiction over the federal claim, in order to determine whether "Congress in [that statute] has ... expressly or by implication negated" the exercise of jurisdiction over the particular nonfederal claim." * * *
>
> The relevant statute in this case, 28 U.S.C. § 1332(a)(1), * * * and its predecessors have consistently been held to require complete diversity of

---

a. The problem concerned the Missouri River, which generally marks the boundary between Iowa and Nebraska. Carter Lake, Iowa, where the accident occurred and where Owen had its main office, lies west of the river, adjacent to Omaha, Nebraska. Apparently, the river had avulsed at one of its bends, cutting Carter Lake off from the rest of Iowa. See Oakley, *The Story of* Owen Equipment v. Kroger: *A Change in the Weather of Federal Jurisdiction*, in Civil Procedure Stories 81–134 (Clermont ed., 2d ed. 2008.)

citizenship. * * * Over the years Congress has repeatedly re-enacted or amended the statute conferring diversity jurisdiction, leaving intact this rule of complete diversity. Whatever may have been the original purposes of diversity-of-citizenship jurisdiction, this subsequent history clearly demonstrates a congressional mandate that diversity jurisdiction is not to be available when any plaintiff is a citizen of the same State as any defendant. * * *

Thus it is clear that the respondent could not originally have brought suit in federal court naming Owen and OPPD as codefendants, since citizens of Iowa would have been on both sides of the litigation. Yet the identical lawsuit resulted when she amended her complaint. Complete diversity was destroyed just as surely as if she had sued Owen initially. * * *

* * *

It is not unreasonable to assume that, in generally requiring complete diversity, Congress did not intend to confine the jurisdiction of federal courts so inflexibly that they are unable to protect legal rights or effectively to resolve an entire, logically entwined lawsuit. Those practical needs are the basis of the doctrine of ancillary jurisdiction. But neither the convenience of litigants nor considerations of judicial economy can suffice to justify extension of the doctrine of ancillary jurisdiction to a plaintiff's cause of action against a citizen of the same State in a diversity case. Congress has established the basic rule that diversity jurisdiction exists * * * only when there is complete diversity of citizenship. * * * To allow the requirement of complete diversity to be circumvented as it was in this case would simply flout the congressional command.

Id. at 371–74, 98 S.Ct. at 2401–03, 2404, 57 L.Ed.2d at 280–82, 284.

FINLEY v. UNITED STATES, 490 U.S. 545, 109 S.Ct. 2003, 104 L.Ed.2d 593 (1989), addressed the availability of pendent party jurisdiction where one of the claims was within the exclusive jurisdiction of the federal court and the other was a state-law claim against a nondiverse defendant. Plaintiff's husband and two of her children were killed when their plane struck electric power lines on its approach to a city-run airfield in San Diego, California. Plaintiff alleged that the Federal Aviation Administration had been negligent in its operation and maintenance of the runway lights and in its performance of air traffic control functions, and her complaint invoked federal jurisdiction under 28 U.S.C. § 1346(b). Later, plaintiff was allowed to amend her complaint to include state-law tort claims against both the city of San Diego and the utility company that maintained the power lines. The Court of Appeals reversed the District Court's decision to allow the amendment, and the Supreme Court affirmed in a five-to-four opinion:

> * * * It remains rudimentary law that "[a]s regards all courts of the United States inferior to this tribunal, two things are necessary to create jurisdiction, whether original or appellate. The Constitution must have given to the court the capacity to take it, *and an act of Congress must have supplied it* * * *. To the extent that such action is not taken, the power lies dormant." The Mayor v. Cooper, 73 U.S. (6 Wall.) 247, 252, 18 L. Ed. 851 (1867) (emphasis added) * * *.

Despite this principle, in a line of cases by now no less well established we have held, without specific examination of jurisdictional statutes, that federal courts have "pendent" claim jurisdiction * * * to the full extent permitted by the Constitution. Mine Workers v. Gibbs * * *. * * * Analytically, petitioner's case is fundamentally different from *Gibbs* in that it brings into question what has become known as pendent-*party* jurisdiction, that is, jurisdiction over parties not named in any claim that is independently cognizable by the federal court. We may assume, without deciding, that the constitutional criterion for pendent-party jurisdiction is analogous to the constitutional criterion for pendent-claim jurisdiction, and that petitioner's state-law claims pass that test. Our cases show, however, that with respect to the addition of parties, as opposed to the addition of only claims, we will not assume that the full constitutional power has been congressionally authorized, and will not read jurisdictional statutes broadly. * * *

* * *

* * * The FTCA, § 1346(b), confers jurisdiction over "civil actions on claims against the United States." It does not say "civil actions on claims that include requested relief against the United States," nor "civil actions in which there is a claim against the United States"—formulations one might expect if the presence of a claim against the United States constituted merely a minimum jurisdiction requirement, rather than a definition of the permissible scope of FTCA actions. Just as the statutory provision "between * * * citizens of different States" has been held to mean citizens of different States and no one else, * * * so also here we conclude that "against the United States" means against the United States and no one else. * * *

* * *

As we noted at the outset, our cases do not display an entirely consistent approach with respect to the necessity that jurisdiction be explicitly conferred. The *Gibbs* line of cases was a departure from prior practice, and a departure that we have no intent to limit or impair. But *Aldinger* indicated that the *Gibbs* approach would not be extended to the pendent-party field, and we decide today to retain that line. Whatever we say regarding the scope of jurisdiction conferred by a particular statute can of course be changed by Congress. What is of paramount importance is that Congress be able to legislate against a background of clear interpretive rules, so that it may know the effect of the language it adopts. All our cases * * * have held that a grant of jurisdiction over claims involving particular parties does not itself confer jurisdiction over additional claims by or against different parties. Our decision today reaffirms that interpretive rule; the opposite would sow confusion.

Id. at 547–49, 552, 556, 109 S.Ct. at 2005–07, 2008, 2010, 104 L.Ed.2d at 600–01, 603–04, 606.

NOTES AND QUESTIONS

1.　Commentators generally state that Congress intended the *Gibbs* test to define whether a federal and nonfederal claim "form part of the same case or controversy" under Section 1367. However, the statute does not refer to the "common nucleus of operative fact" which is central to the *Gibbs* inquiry, and so other interpretations of the statute remain possible.

2.　Before the enactment of Section 1367, courts assumed that a permissive counterclaim—which, by definition, is not transactionally related to the original claim—requires an independent basis of subject-matter jurisdiction. See Federal Rule 13. Some circuit courts have continued to apply this same limitation to Section 1367. The First Circuit in IGLESIAS v. MUTUAL LIFE INSURANCE CO. OF NEW YORK, 156 F.3d 237, 241 (1st Cir. 1998), emphasized that "[o]nly compulsory counterclaims can rely upon supplemental jurisdiction; permissive counterclaims require their own jurisdictional basis." However, in JONES v. FORD MOTOR CREDIT CO., 358 F.3d 205 (2d Cir. 2004), the Court of Appeals for the Second Circuit held that Section 1367 "displaced, rather than codified, * * * the earlier view * * * that a permissive counterclaim requires independent jurisdiction (in the sense of federal question or diversity jurisdiction)." Id. at 213–14. In *Jones*, the complaint alleged racially discriminatory lending practices in violation of federal law. Defendant counterclaimed to recover the plaintiffs' unpaid state-law loans. The Court of Appeals found that Section 1367(a) was satisfied, but remanded to let the District Court decide whether to exercise its discretion under Section 1367(c). Are you convinced that Article III supports this exercise of power? See Floyd, *Three Faces of Supplemental Jurisdiction After the Demise of* United Mine Workers v. Gibbs, 60 Fla. L. Rev. 277 (2008).

3.　Section 1367(b) restricts supplemental jurisdiction in diversity cases when plaintiff seeks to assert claims against nondiverse parties. If P, from Virginia, sues D, from Texas, can D implead a third-party defendant from Texas? From Virginia? Can P assert claims against a third-party defendant from Virginia? See Oakley, Kroger *Redux*, 51 Duke L.J. 663 (2001).

4.　Section 1367(b), which applies when the District Court exercises original jurisdiction under the diversity jurisdiction statute, 28 U.S.C. § 1332, generated a number of questions involving application of the amount-in-controversy requirement to supplemental claims and parties. In particular, courts and commentators disagreed as to whether Section 1367(b) codified or changed the judicial rules that had developed governing the aggregation of claims for diversity jurisdiction. In EXXON MOBIL CORP. v. ALLAPATTAH SERVICES, INC., 545 U.S. 546, 125 S.Ct. 2611, 162 L.Ed.2d 502 (2005), the Court held that "a federal court in a diversity action may exercise supplemental jurisdiction over additional plaintiffs whose claims do not satisfy the minimum amount-in-controversy requirement, provided the claims are part of the same case or controversy as the claims of plaintiffs who do allege a sufficient amount in controversy * * *." Assuming complete diversity of citizenship, if plaintiff's claim meets the amount-in-controversy requirement, does the court have power under Section 1367(b) to hear a supplemental claim that is alleged to be $75,000 or less? Does *Allapattah* allow the exercise of supplemental jurisdiction if the original claim is alleged to be $75,000 or less?

5.   On what basis may a district court decline to exercise jurisdiction under Section 1367 and remand supplemental claims? Courts have adopted two approaches to this question:

> One group of appellate courts gives the district courts unlimited discretion to decline supplemental jurisdiction despite the mandatory grant of supplemental jurisdiction in § 1367(a). This group views § 1367 as a codification of *Gibbs* with no change to the law occurring with the enactment of the statute. * * *

> The other group of appellate courts fall into the category of severely constrained discretion. This group views § 1367 as narrowing the district courts' discretion from the *Gibbs* standard.

Hinkle, *The Revision of 28 U.S.C. § 1367(c) and the Debate over the District Court's Discretion To Decline Supplemental Jurisdiction*, 69 Tenn. L. Rev. 111, 120 (2001).

6.   Does the enactment of Section 1367 mean that there no longer can be any judicially created jurisdiction not provided for by statute? In KOKKO-NEN v. GUARDIAN LIFE INSURANCE CO. OF AMERICA, 511 U.S. 375, 114 S.Ct. 1673, 128 L.Ed.2d 391 (1994), plaintiff sued in federal court to enforce a settlement agreement that resolved a prior federal action. Defendant challenged jurisdiction on the ground that the District Court lost jurisdiction after it entered an order dismissing the prior litigation. The Supreme Court, without citing Section 1367, held that federal courts have "ancillary jurisdiction" to enforce their decrees and orders; however, in this particular case, the Court agreed with defendant that jurisdiction was lacking because the District Court had not made compliance with the settlement agreement a condition of dismissal. A number of lower courts have followed *Kokkonen* in locating an ancillary enforcement jurisdiction in equity and common law. See Alexandria Resident Council, Inc. v. Alexandria Redevelopment & Housing Authority, 218 F.3d 307 (4th Cir. 2000) (discussing distinction between statutory supplemental jurisdiction and equitable ancillary jurisdiction). For a discussion of *Kokkonen*, see Green, *Justice Scalia and Ancillary Jurisdiction: Teaching a Lame Duck New Tricks in* Kokkonen v. Guardian Life Insurance Company of America, 81 Va. L. Rev. 631 (1995).

7.   Section 1367 has generated criticism and suggested revisions. In 2004, the American Law Institute, as part of the Federal Judicial Code Project, approved a final draft of an amendment to the statute. See ALI, Federal Code Revision Project, Tent. Draft No. 2. Professor Shapiro has argued that the scope of supplemental jurisdiction is "a matter best left to 'common law' development" and that Congress simply should "enact a statute establishing the principle of supplemental jurisdiction, and then * * * leave all or most of the details to be worked out by the courts." See Shapiro, *Supplemental Jurisdiction: A Confession, An Avoidance, and a Proposal*, 74 Ind. L.J. 211, 218 (1998). What are the advantages and disadvantages of this approach?

SECTION E. THE SUBJECT–MATTER JURIS- DICTION OF THE FEDERAL COURTS— REMOVAL JURISDICTION

———

Read 28 U.S.C. § 1441 in the Supplement.

———

Removal jurisdiction gives a defendant who has been sued in a state court the right to transfer the action to federal court, if the federal court would have had jurisdiction over the case had plaintiff filed it there originally. Article III of the federal Constitution does not explicitly refer to removal jurisdiction, but Congress has authorized this power since the First Judiciary Act of 1789. The current removal statute, 28 U.S.C. § 1441, traces back to the Judiciary Act of 1875 and amendments enacted in 1887. In addition to the general removal statute, Congress has enacted specific removal statutes to deal with particular federal claims or federal parties. See, e.g., 28 U.S.C. § 1442 (removal of actions by federal officers); 28 U.S.C. § 1443 (removal of civil rights cases); 28 U.S.C. § 1453 (removal of interstate class actions). Congress also has provided that certain claims may not be removed to the federal courts. See, e.g., 28 U.S.C. § 1445 (no federal jurisdiction for actions against railroads under the Federal Employers' Liability Act).

NOTES AND QUESTIONS

1. What motivates defendants to remove cases? An empirical study by Professors Clermont and Eisenberg finds that plaintiffs win less often in cases that are removed to federal court than in cases which the plaintiff chooses to file in federal court as an original matter. See Clermont & Eisenberg, *Do Case Outcomes Really Reveal Anything About the Legal System? Win Rates and Removal Jurisdiction*, 83 Cornell L. Rev. 581, 581 (1998). What factors other than forum selection might explain a win-loss disparity?

2. SHAMROCK OIL & GAS CORP. v. SHEETS, 313 U.S. 100, 105–09, 61 S.Ct. 868, 871–72, 85 L.Ed. 1214, 1217–19 (1941), presented the question of whether plaintiff can remove a state-court action on the basis of defendant's asserting a federal-law counterclaim. Justice Stone, writing for a unanimous Court, held no. Can you explain this result?

———

Section 1441(c) has provoked considerable discussion among courts and commentators. AMERICAN FIRE & CAS. CO. v. FINN, 341 U.S. 6, 71 S.Ct. 534, 95 L.Ed. 702 (1951), an insurance dispute, involved the assertion of state law claims against multiple defendants. Some of the defendants were diverse from plaintiff, but others were not. The requirement of complete diversity barred Section 1332 jurisdiction as an original matter. However, two of the "diverse" defendants successfully removed to federal court. One of the defendants lost and moved to vacate the judgment on the ground that the matter should not have been removed because original jurisdiction was lacking. The Supreme Court agreed. Looking to an earlier version of Section 1441(c), the Court first found that the claim against the losing defendant was not "separate and independent." The Court found only a "single wrong": "the failure to pay compensation for the loss on the property." The Court thus concluded that removal was improper, explaining that "where there is a single wrong to plaintiffs, for which relief is sought, arising from an interlocked series of transactions, there is no separate and independent claim or cause of action under § 1441(c)." Id. at 14, 71 S.Ct. at 540, 95 L.Ed. at 708–09. This statement has been applied by many courts to determine whether Section 1441(c) is applicable. See McFarland, *The Unconstitutional Stub of Section 1441(c)*, 54 Ohio St. L.J. 1059 (1993).

NOTE AND QUESTION

What is the constitutional basis for a court's exercise of power under Section 1414(c)? Can a claim that is "separate and independent" from the original federal claim nevertheless be so "related" as to form part of the "same case or controversy" under Section 1367(a)?

SECTION F. CHALLENGING THE SUBJECT–MATTER JURISDICTION OF THE COURT

1. DIRECT ATTACK ON A COURT'S LACK OF SUBJECT–MATTER JURISDICTION

———

Read Federal Rules of Civil Procedure 8(a)(1), 12(b)(1) and (h)(3), and 60(b)(4), Official Form 40, and 28 U.S.C. § 1653 in the Supplement.

———

A lack of subject-matter jurisdiction may be asserted at any time by any interested party, either in the answer, or in the form of a suggestion to the court prior to final judgment, or on appeal, and also may be raised by the court sua sponte. Moreover, the parties may not create the jurisdiction of a federal court by agreement or by consent. See, e.g., Mansfield, C. & L.M. Ry. Co. v. Swan, 111 U.S. 379, 4 S.Ct. 510, 28 L.Ed. 462 (1884).

NOTES AND QUESTIONS

1. In RUHRGAS AG v. MARATHON OIL CO., 526 U.S. 574, 119 S.Ct. 1563, 143 L.Ed.2d 760 (1999), the defendant removed the case to federal court, and the plaintiff moved to remand for lack of subject-matter jurisdiction. The defendant then moved to dismiss for lack of personal jurisdiction, and the District Court granted the motion and dismissed the action for lack of personal jurisdiction without deciding the subject-matter jurisdiction question. The Supreme Court unanimously held that because both subject-matter and personal jurisdiction are required by the Constitution and affect a federal court's power to adjudicate a case, there is no reason to require a district court to decide subject-matter jurisdiction first:

> Where * * * a district court has before it a straightforward personal jurisdiction issue presenting no complex question of state law, and the alleged defect in subject-matter jurisdiction raises a difficult and novel question, the court does not abuse its discretion by turning directly to personal jurisdiction.

Id. at 588, 119 S.Ct. at 1572, 143 L.Ed.2d at 773. How far does the Supreme Court's approach go? May a court decide a statute of limitations issue or some aspect of the merits when the case may be disposed of more efficiently on one of those grounds than by grappling with a difficult question of jurisdiction? See Friedenthal, *The Crack in the Steel Case*, 68 Geo. Wash. L. Rev. 258 (2000). We revisit this issue in Chapter 5, see Note 4, p. 230, infra.

2. In GRUPO DATAFLUX v. ATLAS GLOBAL GROUP, L.P., 541 U.S. 567, 124 S.Ct. 1920, 158 L.Ed.2d 866 (2004), a partnership sued a Mexican corporation in federal district court under diversity jurisdiction. After three years of pretrial motions and discovery, followed by a six-day trial, the jury returned a verdict in favor of the partnership. Before entry of judgment, however, defendant filed a motion to dismiss for lack of subject-matter jurisdiction. At the time the complaint was filed, the parties were not diverse, because two of plaintiff's partners were Mexican citizens. Yet for all practical purposes, diversity did exist during the trial because the Mexican partners had left the partnership a month before the trial's commencement. In a five-to-four decision, with Justice Scalia writing for the majority, the Court held that in a diversity action, a party's post-filing change in citizenship cannot cure a lack of subject-matter jurisdiction which existed at the time of the filing. Do you agree with this result?

2. COLLATERAL ATTACK ON A JUDGMENT FOR LACK OF SUBJECT–MATTER JURISDICTION

If both the parties and the court fail to notice the absence of subject-matter jurisdiction at any time during the original proceeding, can defendant successfully raise the lack of jurisdiction as a defense to a subsequent proceeding by plaintiff to enforce the judgement? Would it make any difference for purposes of collateral attack if the issue of jurisdiction had been raised and litigated in the original action and it had been decided that the court did have power to proceed?

Section 10 of the first Restatement of Judgments analyzed the question of the availability of collateral attack in terms of balancing the policies underlying res judicata and finality of judgments, which are treated in detail in Chapter 15, infra, against the policy of prohibiting a court from exceeding the powers conferred upon it by the legislature or the jurisdiction's organic law. It stated that if the court in the original action determined that it had subject-matter jurisdiction, the permissibility of collateral attack depends on weighing a non-exclusive list of factors:

(a) the lack of jurisdiction over the subject matter was clear;

(b) the determination as to jurisdiction depended upon a question of law rather than of fact;

(c) the court was one of limited and not of general jurisdiction;

(d) the question of jurisdiction was not actually litigated;

(e) the policy against the court's acting beyond its jurisdiction is strong.

The Restatement (Second) Judgments §§ 12, 69 (1982) takes the approach that the judgment in a contested action, whether or not the question of subject-matter jurisdiction actually was litigated, is beyond collateral attack unless there are no justifiable interests of reliance that must be protected, and:

(1) The subject matter of the action was so plainly beyond the court's jurisdiction that its entertaining the action was a manifest abuse of authority; or

(2) Allowing the judgment to stand would substantially infringe the authority of another tribunal or agency of government; or

(3) The judgment was rendered by a court lacking capability to make an adequately informed determination of a question concerning its own jurisdiction and as a matter of procedural fairness the party seeking to avoid the judgment should have opportunity belatedly to attack the court's subject matter jurisdiction.

In addition, the Restatement (Second) of Judgments generally permits collateral attack on the original court's subject-matter jurisdiction, as well as on personal jurisdiction and inadequate notice, in default judgment situations. Id. § 65. Does this approach go far enough, or too far, toward giving preclusive effect to the original court's judgment? See generally Moore, *Collateral Attack on Subject-Matter Jurisdiction: A Critique of the Restatement (Second) of Judgments*, 66 Cornell L. Rev. 534 (1981).

The Supreme Court has had to deal with problems of collateral attack on numerous occasions. In CHICOT COUNTY DRAINAGE DISTRICT v. BAXTER STATE BANK, 308 U.S. 371, 60 S.Ct. 317, 84 L.Ed. 329 (1940), parties who had notice but chose not to appear in the original action attempted to attack collaterally a judgment rendered by a district court sitting as a court of bankruptcy under a statute that was later declared unconstitutional. The Supreme Court refused to allow the attack. However, collateral attack was allowed by the Court in KALB v. FEUERSTEIN, 308 U.S. 433, 60 S.Ct. 343, 84 L.Ed. 370 (1940), decided the same day as *Chicot*. A fuller discussion of *Chicot* and *Kalb* can be found in Boskey & Braucher, *Jurisdiction and Collateral Attack: October Term, 1939*, 40 Colum. L. Rev. 1006 (1940). See generally 18A Wright, Miller & Cooper, Federal Practice and Procedure: Jurisdiction and Related Matters § 4428. In TRAVELERS INDEMNITY CO. v. BAILEY, 557 U.S. ___, 129 S.Ct. 2195, 174 L.Ed.2d 99 (2009), the Court relied on *Chicot* to bar a collateral challenge to a Bankruptcy Court's order.

CHAPTER 5

VENUE, TRANSFER, AND FORUM NON CONVENIENS

■ ■ ■

Another doctrine that affects where a lawsuit can be filed and entertained is venue, which serves to allocate cases within a given judicial system. Unlike personal jurisdiction or subject-matter jurisdiction, the venue of a civil action does not raise a constitutional question, but rather relates primarily to the convenience of the parties and to concerns of judicial economy.

SECTION A. VENUE

1. GENERAL PRINCIPLES

STEVENS, VENUE STATUTES: DIAGNOSIS AND PROPOSED CURE, 49 Mich. L. Rev. 307, 307–15 (1951):

Venue * * * means the place of trial in an action within a state. Given a cause of action, and having decided what court has jurisdiction over the subject matter, the lawyer must lay the venue, that is, select the place of trial. In making this decision, the lawyer in every state of the United States turns in the first instance, not to common law, but to statute, constitutional provision or rule of court. And he finds that the "proper" venue of his action depends upon the theory of his claim, the subject matter of his claim, the parties involved, or a combination of these factors.

Most codes make provision for the place of trial in local actions, and all codes provide in one way or another for venue in transitory actions arising both within and without the state. Many states make special provision for divorce actions, actions against executors, and actions for the specific recovery of personal property. Most states also provide for venue in actions against residents, against nonresidents, against corporations, domestic and foreign, against partnerships, associations and individuals doing business in the state, and against the state, or a county, or a city or public officers generally or specifically. The nature of the plaintiff, as a resident or nonresident, corporation, domestic or foreign, or political entity, is another factor frequently considered and provided for. * * *

A comparative study of contemporary venue provisions reveals some thirteen different fact situations upon which venue statutes are predicated.

A. *Where the subject of action or part thereof is situated.* The common law concept of actions which were local because the facts could have occurred only in a particular place still persists. As might well be expected, the proper venue for such actions is the county where the subject of the action is situated. There is, however, considerable variation from state to state as to what types of cases are local and fall into this category. * * *

This type of venue * * * is based upon the idea that the court of the county in which the res, which is the subject matter of the suit, is located is best able to deal with the problem. The local sheriff can attach, deliver or execute upon the property. The local clerk can make the necessary entries with a minimum of red tape where title to land is affected. Trial convenience is served where "a view" is necessary or of value in reaching a determination. Third parties can readily ascertain, at a logical point of inquiry, the status of a res in which they may be interested.

It is submitted that these factors are of sufficient importance in this type of case to outweigh other considerations such as convenience of parties or witnesses in the selection of place of trial. * * *

B. *Where the cause of action, or part thereof, arose or accrued.* Convenience of witnesses is the most logical reason for venue provisions allowing the action to be brought in the county where the cause of action, or part thereof, arose or accrued. And since convenience of witnesses is a very practical problem in the trial of a law suit, one would expect to find venue based upon the place where the cause of action arose or accrued a rather common, and general, provision. * * *

The idea behind this type of venue provision * * * is sound and popular. * * * However, its usefulness has been somewhat impaired by difficulties arising out of problems of statutory interpretation. First, what do the words "arose" and "accrued" mean? Second, what is the difference, if any, between: "arose" and "accrued"? And, third, what is the meaning of the phrase "or part thereof"? * * *

C. *Where some fact is present or happened.* There is a sizeable group of statutes which provide for trial of the action in the county where some particular fact or fact situation related to, but no part of, the cause of action is present or happened. * * *

If the purpose of venue is trial convenience, either of parties, or witnesses, or the court or court officials, then it is hard to find any real justification for this group of venue provisions. Most if not all of them are examples of singling out certain specific types of actions for special treatment where a need for special treatment is not or at least no longer [is] apparent. * * *

D. *Where the defendant resides.* Convenience of the defendant is the reason usually given for venue statutes which provide for the place of trial in the county where the defendant resides—the theory probably being, as suggested by Professor E.R. Sunderland, "that since the plaintiff controls the institution of the suit he might behave oppressively toward the defendant unless restrained." * * *

E. *Where the defendant is doing business.* * * * Convenience of the defendant, and of witnesses, appears to be the reason behind such provisions where they are tied to causes of action arising out of the doing of business in the state. Convenience of the defendant, and even more clearly, convenience of the plaintiff, by providing a county in which to lay the venue against a nonresident individual, partnership, company or corporation without undue inconvenience to defendant, is served by the broader type of provision—against certain classes of defendants generally. * * *

F. *Where defendant has an office or place of business, or an agent, or representative, or where an agent or officer of defendant resides.* [These venue statutes] * * * are quite common where a corporation, company or some other type of business organization is the defendant. Convenience of the plaintiff, rather than the defendant, is the moving consideration behind such statutes in most instances. * * *

G. *Where the plaintiff resides.* * * *

Convenience of the plaintiff is the obvious reason behind venue statutes of this nature. Convenience of plaintiff's witnesses may or may not be served, depending upon the nature of the action. * * * In certain types of cases against certain classes of defendants—such as an action on a foreign cause of action against a nonresident—this type of provision is both logical and practical. * * *

H. *Where the plaintiff is doing business.* * * * Obviously the convenience of the plaintiff is the sole consideration behind such a provision. It is submitted that other factors of trial convenience such as convenience of witnesses and of the defendant are more important, and that in view of the number of adherents to this ground of venue, it would be wise to advocate its abandonment. * * *

I. *Where the defendant may be found.* Venue based upon the county where the defendant may be found is in accord with the common law doctrine that the right of action follows the person. * * *

It is difficult to find any sound reason for venue based upon where the defendant may be found. It serves no useful purpose—no trial convenience of either witnesses or parties. It is a good example of a historical hangover—a type of provision which has long since outlived its usefulness. The problem which this type of provision was designed to solve was and is not one of venue but of service of process. * * *

J. *Where the defendant may be summoned or served.* Another group of statutes, also based upon the common law doctrine that the right of action follows the person, provides that venue may be laid in the county where the defendant may be summoned, or served with process. * * *

The comments which were made with respect to venue based upon where the defendant may be found apply with equal force to this type of provision. * * *

K. *In the county designated in the plaintiff's complaint.* * * *

Venue provisions of this type give the plaintiff an unnecessary economic advantage not warranted by convenience of parties or witnesses. In the interests of justice and trial convenience they should be eliminated.

L. *In any county.* The broadest venue provision on the books is that which provides that the plaintiff may lay the venue in any county. * * *

M. *Where the seat of government is located.* * * *

Statutes of this sort have a sound and practical reason behind them. With one exception, this type of provision is reserved for actions by or against governmental units or agencies. Convenience of the government appears to be the controlling factor. * * *

NOTES AND QUESTIONS

1. Venue refers to "the place where a lawsuit should be heard" and is distinct from a court's authority to adjudicate a case. See 14D Wright, Miller & Cooper, Federal Practice and Procedure: Jurisdiction and Related Matters 3d § 3801. A state venue rule allocates judicial business within a state. A federal venue rule allocates judicial business within the nation. What should be the underlying goals of a venue system? In what ways should the venue system for the federal courts differ from how a state allocates business among its courts?

2. Is it really necessary to superimpose notions of venue on a soundly conceived jurisdictional system, especially one with a long-arm statute? Indeed, do we need venue provisions at all, given the kind of convenience analysis that *World-Wide Volkswagen*, p. 61, supra, requires as a matter of due process? See Clermont, *Refuting Territorial Jurisdiction and Venue for State and Federal Courts*, 66 Cornell L. Rev. 411 (1981). What additional protection is provided through well-considered venue rules?

2. LOCAL AND TRANSITORY ACTIONS

REASOR-HILL CORP. v. HARRISON

Supreme Court of Arkansas, 1952.
220 Ark. 521, 249 S.W.2d 994.

GEORGE ROSE SMITH, JUSTICE. Petitioner asks us to prohibit the circuit court of Mississippi County from taking jurisdiction of a cross-complaint filed by D.M. Barton. In the court below the petitioner moved to dismiss the cross-complaint for the reason that it stated a cause of action for injury to real property in the state of Missouri. When the motion to dismiss was overruled the present application for prohibition was filed in this court.

The suit below was brought by the Planters Flying Service to collect an account for having sprayed insecticide upon Barton's cotton crop in Missouri. In his answer Barton charged that the flying service had damaged his growing crop by using an adulterated insecticide, and by cross-complaint he sought damages from the petitioner for its negligence in putting on the market a chemical unsuited to spraying cotton. The petitioner is an Arkansas corporation engaged in manufacturing insecticides and is not authorized to do business in Missouri.

The question presented is one of first impression: May the Arkansas courts entertain a suit for injuries to real property situated in another State? For the respondent it is rightly pointed out that if the suit is not maintainable Barton has no remedy whatever. The petitioner cannot be served with summons in Missouri; so unless it is subject to suit in Arkansas it can escape liability entirely by staying out of Missouri until the statute of limitations has run. * * * The petitioner answers this argument by showing that with the exception of the Supreme Court of Minnesota every American court that has passed upon the question (and there have been about twenty) has held that jurisdiction does not exist.

We agree that the weight of authority is almost unanimously against the respondent, although in some States the rule has been changed by statute and in others it has been criticized by the courts and restricted as narrowly as possible. But before mechanically following the majority view we think it worthwhile to examine the origin of the rule and the reasons for its existence.

The distinction between local and transitory actions was recognized at the beginning of the fourteenth century in the common law of England. Before then all actions had to be brought where the cause of action arose, because the members of the jury were required to be neighbors who would know something of the litigants and of the dispute as well. But when cases were presented that involved separate incidents occurring in different communities the reason for localizing the action disappeared, for it was then impossible to obtain a jury who knew all the facts. Consequently the courts developed the distinction between a case that might have arisen anywhere, which was held to be transitory, and one that involved a particular piece of land, which was held to be local. * * *

As between judicial districts under the same sovereign the rule has many advantages and has been followed in America. As between counties our statutes in Arkansas require that actions for injury to real estate be brought where the land lies. * * * But we permit the defendant to be served anywhere in the State * * *; so the plaintiff is not denied a remedy even though the defendant is a resident of another county.

The English courts, in developing the law of local and transitory actions, applied it also to suits for injuries to real property lying outside England. If, for example, there had been a trespass upon land in France, the courts would not permit the plaintiff to bring suit in England, even though the defendant lived in England and could not be subjected to liability in France. The American courts, treating the separate States as independent sovereigns, have followed the English decisions.

In the United States the leading case is unquestionably Livingston v. Jefferson * * *. That suit was a part of the famous litigation between Edward Livingston and Thomas Jefferson * * *. The case was heard by Marshall as circuit justice and Tyler as district judge. Both agreed that the suit, which was for a wrongful entry upon land in Louisiana, could not be maintained in Virginia. In Marshall's concurring opinion he examined the English precedents and concluded that the law was so firmly established that the court was bound to follow it, though Marshall expressed his dissatisfaction with a rule which produced "the inconvenience of a clear right without a remedy."

Since then the American courts have relied almost uniformly upon the Livingston case in applying the rule to interstate litigation in this country. At least three reasons have been offered to justify the rule, but it is easy to show that each reason is more applicable to international controversies than to interstate disputes.

First, the ground most frequently relied upon is that the courts are not in a position to pass upon the title to land outside the jurisdiction. As between nations this reasoning may be sound. The members of this court have neither the training nor the facilities to investigate questions involving the ownership of land in France, in Russia, or in China. But the same difficulties do not exist with respect to land in another State. In our library we have the statutes and decisions of every other State, and it seldom takes more than a few hours to find the answer to a particular question. Furthermore, the American courts do not hesitate to pass upon an out-of-state title when the issue arises in a transitory action. If, for example, Barton had charged that this petitioner converted a mature crop in Missouri and carried it to Arkansas, our courts would decide the case even though it became necessary to pass upon conflicting claims of title to the land in Missouri. Again, a suit for damages for nonperformance of a contract to purchase land is transitory and may be maintained in another State, even though the sole issue is the validity of the seller's title. To put an extreme example, suppose that two companion suits, one local and one transitory, were presented to the same court together. In those States where the courts disclaim the ability to pass upon questions of title in local actions it might be necessary for the court to dismiss the local action for that reason and yet to decide the identical question in the allied transitory case.

Second, it has been argued that since the tort must take place where the land is situated the plaintiff should pursue his remedy before the defendant leaves the jurisdiction. This argument, too, has merit when nations are concerned. A sovereign, by its control of passports and ports of entry, may detain those who wish to cross its borders. But the citizens of the various States have a constitutional right to pass freely from one jurisdiction to another. * * * In the case at bar * * * Barton could hardly be expected to discover the damage and file an attachment suit before the pilot returned to his landing field in Arkansas.

Third, there is an understandable reluctance to subject one's own citizens to suits by aliens, especially if the other jurisdiction would provide no redress if the situation were reversed. * * * One may have some sympathy for this position in international disputes, but it has no persuasive effect when the States are involved. We do not feel compelled to provide a sanctuary in Arkansas for those who have willfully and wrongfully destroyed property, torn down houses, uprooted crops, polluted streams, and inflicted other injuries upon innocent landowners in our sister States. Yet every jurisdiction which follows the rule of the Livingston case affords that refuge to any person—whether one of its citizens or not—who is successful in fleeing from the scene of such misdeeds.

The truth is that the majority rule has no basis in logic or equity and rests solely upon English cases that were decided before America was discovered and in circumstances that are not even comparable to those existing in our Union. Basic principles of justice demand that wrongs should not go unredressed. * * * Under the majority rule we should have to tell Barton that he would have been much better off had the petitioner stolen his cotton outright instead of merely damaging it. And the only reason we could give for this unfortunate situation would be that English juries in the thirteenth century were expected to have personal knowledge of the disputes presented to them. We prefer to afford this litigant his day in court.

Writ denied.

GRIFFIN SMITH, C.J., concurs.

McFADDIN and WARD, JJ., dissent.

McFADDIN, JUSTICE (dissenting).

* * *

In the first place, the majority says that we have ample facilities to determine the land laws of other States in the United States. * * * This statement about the size of the law library seems rather weak, because land actions are tried in lower courts and not in the Supreme Court library. Just because we have a fine law library does not mean that we are prepared to determine the title to lands in Texas,[1] Missouri, Vermont, or any other State. But if we have the jurisdiction which the majority claims, then we could determine ejectment actions involving ownership of lands in other States. We might undertake to do this, but the Full Faith and Credit clause of the U.S. Constitution would not require the Sister State to recognize our judgment. * * *

---

1. The writer knows by experience that only one skilled in Texas Land Law can successfully handle an action of Trespass to Try Title in the State of Texas.

Secondly, the majority says that the rule, requiring that an action be brought in the jurisdiction in which the land is situated, is a good rule between Nations, but is not good as between States in the American Union. For answer to this, I say: I have always understood that each of the American States is Sovereign; that the Federal Government is a government of delegated powers; and that all powers not delegated to the Federal Government are retained by the States and the People. Surely the majority is not attempting to reduce our American States to the level of mere local administrative units. Yet such, unfortunately, is the natural conclusion to which the majority opinion would carry us, when it concedes one rule for Nations and another for States.

Thirdly, the majority says that it does not desire to afford Arkansas Citizens a sanctuary from damage actions by citizens of other States. This is an argument that should be made—if at all—in the Legislative branch of Government, rather than in a judicial opinion. It is for the Legislative Department to determine when and where actions may be prosecuted. * * *

* * * [M]any, many cases * * * have considered the question here involved; and each Court—with the sole exception of Minnesota—has seen fit to follow the great weight of authority which has come down to us from the common law. In matters affecting real property particularly, we should leave undisturbed the ancient landmarks. * * *

NOTE AND QUESTIONS

In those jurisdictions following the "majority" or "local action" rule, can the parties consent to a waiver of the venue objection in actions involving foreign land? Parties can waive a defect in venue, but not of subject-matter jurisdiction. Is this why the dissenting opinion in *Reasor-Hill* says that a judgment in ejectment rendered by the Arkansas courts involving lands in other states would not be entitled to full faith and credit? "To this day it is unclear whether the local action rule is jurisdictional or merely a venue rule." Friedenthal, Kane & Miller, Civil Procedure § 2.16 (4th ed. 2005).

3. VENUE IN THE FEDERAL COURTS

———

Read 28 U.S.C. § 1391 in the Supplement.

———

NOTES AND QUESTIONS

1. Venue in the federal system is governed by a general venue statute, 28 U.S.C. § 1391, which was extensively amended in 1990 and then modestly revised in 1992 and 1995. Venue also is governed by specialized statutes that

apply to particular federal claims such as antitrust, bankruptcy, employment discrimination, and patent. E.g., 28 U.S.C. § 1400 (copyright and patent litigation).

2. The general federal venue statute relies on two important criteria: the residence of the defendants and the location of the transaction that gives rise to the dispute. The majority of courts treat an individual's citizenship for determining diversity jurisdiction the same as residence for venue purposes. See 14D Wright, Miller & Cooper, Federal Practice and Procedure: Jurisdiction and Related Matters 3d § 3805. However, the residence of an unincorporated association for venue purposes differs from its citizenship under the diversity statute, and is "determined by looking to the residence of the association itself rather than that of its individual members." DENVER & R.G.W.R. CO. v. BROTHERHOOD OF RAILROAD TRAINMEN, 387 U.S. 556, 559–62, 87 S.Ct. 1746, 1748–50, 18 L.Ed.2d 954, 958–59 (1967). As the Court explained:

> Otherwise, § 1391(b) would seem to require either holding the association not suable at all where its members are residents of different States, or holding that the association "resides" in any State in which any of its members resides. The first alternative * * * removes federal-question litigation from the federal courts unnecessarily; the second is patently unfair to the association when it is remembered that venue is primarily a matter of convenience of litigants and witnesses.

To complicate matters more, Section 1391(c) places corporate residence for venue purposes "in any judicial district in which it is subject to personal jurisdiction at the time the action is commenced." See 14D Wright, Miller & Cooper, Federal Practice and Procedure: Jurisdiction and Related Matters 3d § 3811.1. In a state with more than one judicial district, a corporation is deemed to reside in any district within which its contacts would be sufficient to subject it to personal jurisdiction if that district were a separate state. Do the considerations that justify the "minimum contacts" test for personal jurisdiction apply with equal force to venue?

3. Congress amended the transactional-venue provision of Section 1391 to make clear that venue may be proper in more than one district. See, e.g., Gulf Insurance Co. v. Glasbrenner, 417 F.3d 353 (2d Cir. 2005). Transactional-venue does not simply fill a venue "gap," but rather may be used in any appropriate case.

4. Section 1391 contains a "fallback" provision for cases in which venue cannot be based on defendant's residence or the location of the transaction. What is the fallback rule for diversity jurisdiction cases? How does if differ from the rule for federal question cases? Can you explain the difference between the two rules? An important commentary characterizes the distinction as one that "seems to be a clear act of drafting inadvertence" and that lacks any "logical or policy justification." 14D Wright, Miller & Cooper,

Federal Practice and Procedure: Jurisdiction and Related Matters 3d § 3806.2.

SECTION B. TRANSFER OF VENUE IN THE FEDERAL COURTS

———

Read 28 U.S.C. §§ 1404, 1406, and 1407 in the Supplement.

———

NOTES AND QUESTIONS

1. When may a court authorize a transfer of venue under 28 U.S.C. § 1404? When would the court instead rely on Section 1406?

2. In HOFFMAN v. BLASKI, 363 U.S. 335, 80 S.Ct. 1084, 4 L.Ed.2d 1254 (1960), the Court construed the statutory language "where it might have been brought" to bar the transfer of a case to a district that lacks personal jurisdiction over defendant even if defendant is willing to waive objections to the forum. Do you agree with this result?

3. Why do parties care about venue? According to an empirical study, "[T]he plaintiff wins in 58% of the nontransferred cases that go to judgment for one side or the other, but wins in only 29% of such cases in which a transfer occurred." Clermont & Eisenberg, *Exorcising the Evil of Forum–Shopping*, 80 Cornell L. Rev. 1507 (1995). Can you think of reasons other than venue that might explain these differences in win rates?

4. To what extent should the transferee court attempt to reach the same result on the merits that the transferor court would have reached? Must the transferee court apply the law of the transferor court? Is the fact that an action would be barred by the statute of limitations in the transferee district relevant to the decision of a motion under Section 1404(a)? In VAN DUSEN v. BARRACK, 376 U.S. 612, 639, 84 S.Ct. 805, 821, 11 L.Ed.2d 945, 962–63 (1964), the Supreme Court held that, in diversity cases, the law applicable in the transferor forum follows the transfer and must be applied by the transferee forum.

5. Can a clever plaintiff intentionally bring suit in an inconvenient forum with favorable law and then move for transfer under Section 1404(a), ending up with both the forum and law of her choice?

In FERENS v. JOHN DEERE CO., 494 U.S. 516, 110 S.Ct. 1274, 108 L.Ed.2d 443 (1990), plaintiff, a citizen of Pennsylvania, lost a hand when it allegedly became caught in a harvester manufactured by defendant, a Delaware corporation. Plaintiff failed to file suit within Pennsylvania's two-year tort limitations period. But, in the third year, plaintiff filed one suit in federal court in Pennsylvania, raising contract and warranty claims that were not yet time-barred, and a second suit in federal court in Mississippi, alleging tort claims. Mississippi had a six-year tort statute of limitations, which the federal court was required to apply. The federal court in Mississippi then granted plaintiff's motion to transfer the tort action to the Pennsylvania court under Section 1404(a). The Pennsylvania court, however, refused to apply Mississippi's statute of limitations and dismissed the tort claims as time-barred under Pennsylvania's statute of limitations. The Court of Appeals affirmed. Relying on *Van Dusen,* Note 4, p. 219, supra, the Supreme Court reversed, holding that in a diversity suit the transferee forum is required to apply the law of the transferor court, regardless of who initiates the transfer. Is this a sound result? See Bassett, *The Forum Game,* 84 N.C. L. Rev. 333, 352–70 (2006).

6. One significant development in federal venue procedure has been the enactment of 28 U.S.C. § 1407, which provides for the temporary transfer to one district of related complex cases such as multidistrict antitrust actions and authorizes consolidation of cases for pretrial purposes only. Transfer is appropriate when the cases involve common questions of fact and law and when it would be for the convenience of the parties and witnesses and in the interests of justice. This provision has been used frequently to take advantage of coordinated pretrial discovery, for example. A Panel on Multidistrict Litigation, composed of seven Court of Appeals and District Court judges appointed by the Chief Justice, makes decisions on whether or not cases should be transferred. In LEXECON INC. v. MILBERG WEISS BERSHAD HYNES & LERACH, 523 U.S. 26, 118 S.Ct. 956, 140 L.Ed.2d 62 (1998), the Supreme Court held that the panel on multidistrict litigation is required to remand cases consolidated under Section 1407 to their original courts for trial. Prior to this ruling, it was common practice for transferee courts to transfer cases to themselves rather than to the original transferor court for trial under Section 1404(a). Given that the intent of Section 1407 is to allow federal courts to handle complex cases more efficiently, what purposes are served by returning cases to their original districts for trial? Should the parties to the litigation be allowed to consent to having the case tried in the transferee court? Does the Court's reading of the statute properly balance efficiency concerns with traditional deference to plaintiff's choice of forum? Should Congress amend Section 1407 and overrule *Lexecon*? See 15 Wright, Miller & Cooper, Federal Practice and Procedure: Jurisdiction and Related Matters 3d § 3861; Marcus, *Cure-All For an End of Dispersed Litigation? Toward a Maximalist Use of the Multidistrict Litigation Panel's Transfer Power,* 82 Tul. L. Rev. 2245 (2009).

SECTION C.   FORUM NON CONVENIENS

GULF OIL CORP. v. GILBERT, 330 U.S. 501, 67 S.Ct. 839, 91 L.Ed. 1055 (1947), delineated the factors to be considered in deciding a motion based upon the principle of forum non conveniens:

> The principle of *forum non conveniens* is simply that a court may resist imposition upon its jurisdiction even when jurisdiction is authorized by the letter of a general venue statute. These statutes are drawn with a necessary generality and usually give a plaintiff a choice of courts, so that he may be quite sure of some place in which to pursue his remedy. But the open door may admit those who seek not simply justice but perhaps justice blended with some harassment. A plaintiff sometimes is under temptation to resort to a strategy of forcing the trial at a most inconvenient place for an adversary, even at some inconvenience to himself.

Many of the states have met misuse of venue by investing courts with a discretion to change the place of trial on various grounds, such as the convenience of witnesses and the ends of justice. The federal law contains no such express criteria to guide the district court in exercising its power. But the problem is a very old one affecting the administration of the courts as well as the rights of litigants, and both in England and in this country the common law worked out techniques and criteria for dealing with it.

* * *

If the combination and weight of factors requisite to given results are difficult to forecast or state, those to be considered are not difficult to name. An interest to be considered, and the one likely to be most pressed, is the private interest of the litigant. Important considerations are the relative ease of access to sources of proof; availability of compulsory process for attendance of unwilling, and the cost of obtaining attendance of willing witnesses; possibility of view of premises, if view would be appropriate to the action; and all other practical problems that make trial of a case easy, expeditious and inexpensive. There may also be questions as to the enforcibility [sic] of a judgment if one is obtained. The court will weigh relative advantages and obstacles to fair trial. It is often said that the plaintiff may not, by choice of an inconvenient forum, "vex," "harass," or "oppress" the defendant by inflicting upon him expense or trouble not necessary to his own right to pursue his remedy. But unless the balance is strongly in favor of the defendant, the plaintiff's choice of forum should rarely be disturbed.

Factors of public interest also have place in applying the doctrine. Administrative difficulties follow for courts when litigation is piled up in congested centers instead of being handled at its origin. Jury duty is a burden that ought not to be imposed upon the people of a community which has no relation to the litigation. In cases which touch the affairs of many persons, there is reason for holding the trial in their view and reach rather than in remote parts of the country where they can learn of it by report only. There is a local interest in having localized controversies decided at home. There is an appropriateness, too, in having the trial of a diversity case in a forum that is at home with the state law that must govern the case, rather than having a court in some other forum untangle problems in conflict of laws, and in law foreign to itself.

Id. at 507–09, 67 S.Ct. at 842–43, 91 L.Ed. at 1062–63.

PIPER AIRCRAFT CO. v. REYNO

Supreme Court of the United States, 1981.
454 U.S. 235, 102 S.Ct. 252, 70 L.Ed.2d 419.

Certiorari to the United States Court of Appeals for the Third Circuit.

JUSTICE MARSHALL delivered the opinion of the Court.

* * *

I

A

In July 1976, a small commercial aircraft crashed in the Scottish highlands during the course of a charter flight from Blackpool to Perth. The pilot and five passengers were killed instantly. The decedents were all Scottish subjects and residents, as are their heirs and next of kin. There were no eyewitnesses to the accident. At the time of the crash the plane was subject to Scottish air traffic control.

The aircraft, a twin-engine Piper Aztec, was manufactured in Pennsylvania by petitioner Piper Aircraft Co. (Piper). The propellers were manufactured in Ohio by petitioner Hartzell Propeller, Inc. (Hartzell). At the time of the crash the aircraft was registered in Great Britain and was owned and maintained by Air Navigation and Trading Co., Ltd. (Air Navigation). It was operated by McDonald Aviation, Ltd. (McDonald), a Scottish air taxi service. Both Air Navigation and McDonald were organized in the United Kingdom. The wreckage of the plane is now in a hangar in Farnsborough, England.

The British Department of Trade investigated the accident several months after it occurred. A preliminary report found that the plane crashed after developing a spin, and suggested that mechanical failure in the plane or the propeller was responsible. At Hartzell's request, this report was reviewed by a three-member Review Board, which held a 9–day adversary hearing attended by all interested parties. The Review Board found no evidence of defective equipment and indicated that pilot error may have contributed to the accident. The pilot, who had obtained his commercial pilot's license only three months earlier, was flying over high ground at an altitude considerably lower than the minimum height required by his company's operations manual.

In July 1977, a California probate court appointed respondent Gaynell Reyno administratrix of the estates of the five passengers. Reyno is not related to and does not know any of the decedents or their survivors; she was a legal secretary to the attorney who filed this lawsuit. Several days after her appointment, Reyno commenced separate wrongful death actions against Piper and Hartzell in the Superior Court of California, claiming negligence and strict liability. Air Navigation, McDonald, and the estate of the pilot are not parties to this litigation. The survivors of the five passengers whose estates are represented by Reyno filed a separate action in the United Kingdom against Air Navigation, McDonald, and the pilot's estate. Reyno candidly admits that the action against Piper and Hartzell was filed in the United States because its laws regarding liability, capacity to sue, and damages are more favorable to her position than are those of Scotland. Scottish law does not recognize strict liability in tort. Moreover, it permits wrongful death actions only when brought by a decedent's relatives. The relatives may sue only for "loss of support and society."

On petitioners' motion, the suit was removed to the United States District Court for the Central District of California. Piper then moved for transfer to the United States District Court for the Middle District of Pennsylvania, pursuant to 28 U.S.C. § 1404(a). Hartzell moved to dismiss for lack of personal jurisdiction, or in the alternative, to transfer.[5] In December 1977, the District Court quashed service on Hartzell and transferred the case to the Middle District of Pennsylvania. Respondent then properly served process on Hartzell.

B

In May 1978, after the suit had been transferred, both Hartzell and Piper moved to dismiss the action on the ground of *forum non conveniens.* The District Court granted these motions in October 1979. It relied on the balancing test set forth by this Court in Gulf Oil Corp. v. Gilbert * * *.

* * * [T]he District Court analyzed the facts of [this case]. It began by observing that an alternative forum existed in Scotland; Piper and Hartzell had agreed to submit to the jurisdiction of the Scottish courts and to waive any statute of limitations defense that might be available. It then stated that plaintiff's choice of forum was entitled to little weight. The court recognized that a plaintiff's choice ordinarily deserves substantial deference. It noted, however, that Reyno "is a representative of foreign citizens and residents seeking a forum in the United States because of the more liberal rules concerning products liability law," and that "the courts have been less solicitous when the plaintiff is not an American citizen or resident, and particularly when the foreign citizens seek to benefit from the more liberal tort rules provided for the protection of citizens and residents of the United States." * * *

The District Court next examined several factors relating to the private interests of the litigants, and determined that these factors strongly pointed towards Scotland as the appropriate forum. Although evidence concerning the design, manufacture, and testing of the plane and propeller is located in the United States, the connections with Scotland are otherwise "overwhelming." * * * The real parties in interest are citizens of Scotland, as were all the decedents. Witnesses who could testify regarding the maintenance of the aircraft, the training of the pilot, and the investigation of the accident—all essential to the defense—are in Great Britain.

---

5. The District Court concluded that it could not assert personal jurisdiction over Hartzell consistent with due process. However, it decided not to dismiss Hartzell because the corporation would be amenable to process in Pennsylvania.

Moreover, all witnesses to damages are located in Scotland. Trial would be aided by familiarity with Scottish topography, and by easy access to the wreckage.

The District Court reasoned that because crucial witnesses and evidence were beyond the reach of compulsory process, and because the defendants would not be able to implead potential Scottish third-party defendants, it would be "unfair to make Piper and Hartzell proceed to trial in this forum." * * * The survivors had brought separate actions in Scotland against the pilot, McDonald, and Air Navigation. "[I]t would be fairer to all parties and less costly if the entire case was presented to one jury with available testimony from all relevant witnesses." * * * Although the court recognized that if trial were held in the United States, Piper and Hartzell could file indemnity or contribution actions against the Scottish defendants, it believed that there was a significant risk of inconsistent verdicts.

The District Court concluded that the relevant public interests also pointed strongly towards dismissal. The court determined that Pennsylvania law would apply to Piper and Scottish law to Hartzell if the case were tried in the Middle District of Pennsylvania.[8] As a result, "trial in this forum would be hopelessly complex and confusing for a jury." * * * In addition, the court noted that it was unfamiliar with Scottish law and thus would have to rely upon experts from that country. The court also found that the trial would be enormously costly and time-consuming; that it would be unfair to burden citizens with jury duty when the Middle District of Pennsylvania has little connection with the controversy; and that Scotland has a substantial interest in the outcome of the litigation.

In opposing the motions to dismiss, respondent contended that dismissal would be unfair because Scottish law was less favorable. The District Court explicitly rejected this claim. * * *

C

On appeal, the * * * Third Circuit reversed and remanded for trial. The decision to reverse appears to be based on two alternative grounds. First, the Court held that the District Court abused its discretion in conducting the *Gilbert* analysis. Second, the Court held that dismissal is never appropriate where the law of the alternative forum is less favorable to the plaintiff.

---

8. Under Klaxon Co. v. Stentor Electric Mfg. Co., 313 U.S. 487, 61 S. Ct. 1020, 85 L. Ed. 1477 (1941), [p. 265, infra], a court ordinarily must apply the choice-of-law rules of the State in which it sits. However, where a case is transferred pursuant to 28 U.S.C. § 1404(a), it must apply the choice-of-law rules of the State from which the case was transferred. Van Dusen v. Barrack, [Note 4, p. 219, supra] * * *. Relying on these two cases, the District Court concluded that California choice-of-law rules would apply to Piper, and Pennsylvania choice-of-law rules would apply to Hartzell. It further concluded that California applied a "governmental interests" analysis in resolving choice-of-law problems, and that Pennsylvania employed a "significant contacts" analysis. The court used the "governmental interests" analysis to determine that Pennsylvania liability rules would apply to Piper, and the "significant contacts" analysis to determine that Scottish liability rules would apply to Hartzell.

The Court of Appeals began its review of the District Court's *Gilbert* analysis by noting that the plaintiff's choice of forum deserved substantial weight, even though the real parties in interest are nonresidents. It then rejected the District Court's balancing of the private interests. It found that Piper and Hartzell had failed adequately to support their claim that key witnesses would be unavailable if trial were held in the United States: they had never specified the witnesses they would call and the testimony these witnesses would provide. The Court of Appeals gave little weight to the fact that Piper and Hartzell would not be able to implead potential Scottish third-party defendants, reasoning that this difficulty would be "burdensome" but not "unfair" * * *. Finally, the court stated that resolution of the suit would not be significantly aided by familiarity with Scottish topography, or by viewing the wreckage.

The Court of Appeals also rejected the District Court's analysis of the public interest factors. It found that the District Court gave undue emphasis to the application of Scottish law: "the fact that the court is called upon to determine and apply foreign law does not present a legal problem of the sort which would justify the dismissal of a case otherwise properly before the court." * * * In any event, it believed that Scottish law need not be applied. After conducting its own choice-of-law analysis, the Court of Appeals determined that American law would govern the actions against both Piper and Hartzell. The same choice-of-law analysis apparently led it to conclude that Pennsylvania and Ohio, rather than Scotland, are the jurisdictions with the greatest policy interests in the dispute, and that all other public interest factors favored trial in the United States.

In any event, it appears that the Court of Appeals would have reversed even if the District Court had properly balanced the public and private interests. * * * [T]he court decided that dismissal is automatically barred if it would lead to a change in the applicable law unfavorable to the plaintiff.

We granted certiorari * * *.

II

The Court of Appeals erred in holding that plaintiffs may defeat a motion to dismiss on the ground of *forum non conveniens* merely by showing that the substantive law that would be applied in the alternative forum is less favorable to the plaintiffs than that of the present forum. The possibility of a change in substantive law should ordinarily not be given conclusive or even substantial weight in the *forum non conveniens* inquiry.

* * *

In fact, if conclusive or substantial weight were given to the possibility of a change in law, the *forum non conveniens* doctrine would become virtually useless. Jurisdiction and venue requirements are often easily satisfied. As a result, many plaintiffs are able to choose from among several forums. Ordinarily, these plaintiffs will select that forum whose choice-of-law rules are most advantageous. Thus, if the possibility of an unfavorable change in substantive law is given substantial weight in the *forum non conveniens* inquiry, dismissal would rarely be proper.

* * *

The Court of Appeals' approach is not only inconsistent with the purpose of the *forum non conveniens* doctrine, but also poses substantial practical problems. If the possibility of a change in law were given substantial weight, deciding motions to dismiss on the ground of *forum non conveniens* would become quite difficult. Choice-of-law analysis would become extremely important, and the courts would frequently be required to interpret the law of foreign jurisdictions. First, the trial court would have to determine what law would apply if the case were tried in the chosen forum, and what law would apply if the case were tried in the alternative forum. It would then have to compare the rights, remedies, and procedures available under the law that would be applied in each forum. Dismissal would be appropriate only if the court concluded that the law applied by the alternative forum is as favorable to the plaintiff as that of the chosen forum. The doctrine of *forum non conveniens,* however, is designed in part to help courts avoid conducting complex exercises in comparative law. As we stated in *Gilbert,* the public interest factors point towards dismissal where the court would be required to "untangle problems in conflict of laws, and in law foreign to itself." * * *

Upholding the decision of the Court of Appeals would result in other practical problems. At least where the foreign plaintiff named an American manufacturer as defendant, a court could not dismiss the case on grounds of *forum non conveniens* where dismissal might lead to an unfavorable change in law. The American courts, which are already extremely attractive to foreign plaintiffs, would become even more attractive. The flow of litigation into the United States would increase and further congest already crowded courts.

* * *

We do not hold that the possibility of an unfavorable change in law should *never* be a relevant consideration in a *forum non conveniens* inquiry. Of course, if the remedy provided by the alternative forum is so clearly inadequate or unsatisfactory that it is no remedy at all, the unfavorable change in law may be given substantial weight; the district court may conclude that dismissal would not be in the interests of justice.[22] In these cases, however, the remedies that would be provided by the Scottish courts do not fall within this category. Although the relatives

---

22. At the outset of any *forum non conveniens* inquiry, the court must determine whether there exists an alternative forum. Ordinarily, this requirement will be satisfied when the defendant is "amenable to process" in the other jurisdiction. *Gilbert* * * *. In rare circumstances, however, where the remedy offered by the other forum is clearly unsatisfactory, the other forum may not be an adequate alternative, and the initial requirement may not be satisfied. Thus, for example, dismissal would not be appropriate where the alternative forum does not permit litigation of the subject matter of the dispute. * * *

of the decedents may not be able to rely on a strict liability theory, and although their potential damages award may be smaller, there is no danger that they will be deprived of any remedy or treated unfairly.

III

The Court of Appeals also erred in rejecting the District Court's *Gilbert* analysis. The Court of Appeals stated that more weight should have been given to the plaintiff's choice of forum, and criticized the District Court's analysis of the private and public interests. However, the District Court's decision regarding the deference due plaintiff's choice of forum was appropriate. Furthermore, we do not believe that the District Court abused its discretion in weighing the private and public interests.

A

The District Court acknowledged that there is ordinarily a strong presumption in favor of the plaintiff's choice of forum, which may be overcome only when the private and public interest factors clearly point towards trial in the alternative forum. It held, however, that the presumption applies with less force when the plaintiff or real parties in interest are foreign.

The District Court's distinction between resident or citizen plaintiffs and foreign plaintiffs is fully justified * * * When the home forum has been chosen, it is reasonable to assume that this choice is convenient. When the plaintiff is foreign, however, this assumption is much less reasonable. Because the central purpose of any *forum non conveniens* inquiry is to ensure that the trial is convenient, a foreign plaintiff's choice deserves less deference.

B

The *forum non conveniens* determination is committed to the sound discretion of the trial court. It may be reversed only when there has been a clear abuse of discretion; where the court has considered all relevant public and private interest factors, and where its balancing of these factors is reasonable, its decision deserves substantial deference. * * * Here, the Court of Appeals expressly acknowledged that the standard of review was one of abuse of discretion. In examining the District Court's analysis of the public and private interests, however, the Court of Appeals seems to have lost sight of this rule, and substituted its own judgment for that of the District Court.

(1)

In analyzing the private interest factors, the District Court stated that the connections with Scotland are "overwhelming." * * * This characterization may be somewhat exaggerated. Particularly with respect to the question of relative ease of access to sources of proof, the private interests point in both directions. As respondent emphasizes, records concerning the design, manufacture, and testing of the propeller and plane are located in the United States. She would have greater access to sources of proof relevant to her strict liability and negligence theories if trial were held here. However, the District Court did not act unreasonably in concluding that fewer evidentiary problems would be posed if the trial were held in Scotland. A large proportion of the relevant evidence is located in Great Britain.

The Court of Appeals found that the problems of proof could not be given any weight because Piper and Hartzell failed to describe with specificity the evidence they would not be able to obtain if trial were held in the United States. It suggested that defendants seeking *forum non conveniens* dismissal must submit affidavits identifying the witnesses they would call and the testimony these witnesses would provide if the trial were held in the alternative forum. Such detail is not necessary. Piper and Hartzell have moved for dismissal precisely because many crucial witnesses are located beyond the reach of compulsory process, and thus are difficult to identify or interview. Requiring extensive investigation would defeat the purpose of their motion. Of course, defendants must provide enough information to enable the District Court to balance the parties' interests. Our examination of the record convinces us that sufficient information was provided here. Both Piper and Hartzell submitted affidavits describing the evidentiary problems they would face if the trial were held in the United States.

The District Court correctly concluded that the problems posed by the inability to implead potential third party defendants clearly supported holding the trial in Scotland. Joinder of the pilot's estate, Air Navigation, and McDonald is crucial to the presentation of petitioners' defense. If Piper and Hartzell can show that the accident was caused not by a design defect, but rather by the negligence of the pilot, the plane's owners, or the charter company, they will be relieved of all liability. It is true, of course, that if Hartzell and Piper were found liable after a trial in the United States, they could institute an action for indemnity or contribution against these parties in Scotland. It would be far more convenient, however, to resolve all claims in one trial. The Court of Appeals rejected this argument. Forcing petitioners to rely on actions for indemnity or contributions would be "burdensome" but not "unfair." * * * Finding that trial in the plaintiff's chosen forum would be burdensome, however, is sufficient to support dismissal on grounds of *forum non conveniens*.

(2)

The District Court's review of the factors relating to the public interest was also reasonable. On the basis of its choice-of-law analysis, it concluded that if the case were tried in the Middle District of Pennsylvania, Pennsylvania law would apply to Piper and Scottish law to Hartzell. It stated that a trial involving two sets of laws would be confusing to the jury. It also noted its own lack of familiarity with Scottish law. Consideration of these problems was clearly appropriate under *Gilbert*; in that case we explicitly held that the need to apply foreign law pointed towards dismissal. The Court of Appeals found that the District Court's choice-of-law analysis was incorrect, and that American law would apply to both Hartzell and Piper. Thus, lack of familiarity with foreign law would not be a problem. Even if the Court of Appeals' conclusion is correct, however, all other public interest factors favored trial in Scotland.

Scotland has a very strong interest in this litigation. The accident occurred in its airspace. All of the decedents were Scottish. Apart from Piper and Hartzell, all potential plaintiffs and defendants are either Scottish or English. As we stated in *Gilbert,* there is "a local interest in having localized controversies decided at home." * * * Respondent argues that American citizens have an interest in ensuring that American manufacturers are deterred from producing defective products, and that additional deterrence might be obtained if Piper and Hartzell were tried in the United States, where they could be sued on the basis of both negligence and strict liability. However, the incremental deterrence that would be gained if this trial were held in an American court is likely to be insignificant. The American interest in this accident is simply not sufficient to justify the enormous commitment of judicial time and resources that would inevitably be required if the case were to be tried here.

* * *

Reversed.

[JUSTICE POWELL and JUSTICE O'CONNOR took no part in the decision of this case. JUSTICE WHITE concurred in part and dissented in part. JUSTICE STEVENS, with whom JUSTICE BRENNAN joined, dissented.]

NOTES AND QUESTIONS

1.   Lord Denning famously said: "As a moth is drawn to the light, so is a litigant drawn to the United States." Smith Kline & French Labs. Ltd. v. Bloch, [1983] 2 All E.R. 72, 72 (Eng. C.A. 1982). Why is the American legal system so attractive to foreign litigants?

2.   Courts may choose to condition a forum non conveniens dismissal on defendant's waiver of a defense to being sued in the foreign forum. For example, a court may require a defendant to waive an objection to personal jurisdiction, or waive a defense that the statute of limitations in the foreign forum has run. E.g., In re Union Carbide Corp. Gas Plant Disaster at Bhopal, India in Dec., 1984, 809 F.2d 195 (2d Cir. 1987), certiorari denied 484 U.S. 871, 108 S.Ct. 199, 98 L.Ed.2d 150 (1987). Are these conditions sufficient to ensure that the foreign plaintiff has an adequate remedy abroad? What if plaintiff demonstrates that the alternative forum is subject to corruption or political pressure?

3.   Under what circumstances might an international tribunal—such as the International Court of Justice, the World Trade Organization, or the United Nations Compensation Commission—be an acceptable alternative forum to support a dismissal on grounds of forum non conveniens? In NEMARIAM v. FEDERAL DEMOCRATIC REPUBLIC OF ETHIOPIA, 315 F.3d 390

(D.C. Cir. 2003), certiorari denied 540 U.S. 877, 124 S.Ct. 278, 157 L.Ed.2d 141 (2003), the D.C. Circuit considered whether a dismissal on grounds of forum non conveniens was proper where the alternative forum was a special Claims Commission designed to resolve war-related suits between Ethiopia and Eritrea. Any relief that plaintiff might secure in the Claims Commission would be subject to offset by amounts due from one nation to the other. The Court of Appeals found that "it would be peculiar indeed to dismiss Nemarian's claim in the United States District Court—a forum in which * * * she is certain to be awarded full relief if she wins on the merits of her claim—in favor of a forum in which she has no certainty of getting relief for a meritorious claim." Id. at 395.

4. Must a district court first determine that it can assert personal jurisdiction before dismissing an action on forum non conveniens grounds? In SINOCHEM INTERNATIONAL CO. LTD. v. MALAYSIA INTERNATIONAL SHIPPING CORP., 549 U.S. 422, 127 S.Ct. 1184, 167 L.Ed.2d 15 (2007), Malaysia International brought suit in federal district court against Sinochem, a Chinese company, alleging fraudulent misrepresentation in connection with the shipment of steel coils from a United States port to China. The District Court dismissed the case on forum non conveniens grounds without first establishing personal jurisdiction over Sinochem. The District Court noted that even if, after lengthy and costly discovery, it found that Sinochem had minimum contacts with the United States, the case ultimately would be dismissed on forum non conveniens grounds because China was undoubtedly the more convenient forum for litigation. The Supreme Court held that a district court has the authority "to respond at once to a defendant's *forum non conveniens* plea, and need not take up first any other threshold objection." Id. at 425, 127 S.Ct. at 1188, 167 L.Ed.2d at 2.

CHAPTER 6

ASCERTAINING THE APPLICABLE LAW

■ ■ ■

This Chapter focuses on the ways in which federalism and separation of powers affect choice of law in United States courts. Civil actions involving citizens of a single state and a transaction that occurred entirely within the boundaries of that state do not present any problems of choosing the proper body of substantive law to be applied in determining the rights and liabilities of the parties. However, as soon as the litigation touches two or more states, one is likely to be confronted with the serious question of choosing between two or more sources of law. For example, suppose plaintiff and defendant, both citizens of State X, are involved in an automobile accident or agree to perform a contract or engage in a sale of property in State Y. Should questions pertaining to defendant's alleged negligence or failure to perform the contract or transfer the ownership of the property be decided under the law of State X or the law of State Y? Should the choice be made in the same way in tort, contract, and property actions? The complexity of these questions increases if plaintiff and defendant are citizens of different states and the event, relationship, or property that forms the predicate of the controversy can be traced to a third, or perhaps even a fourth or fifth state. You will be exposed to problems of this type on numerous occasions. Formal education in the philosophy of choosing among the laws of two or more states is the focus of a course in Conflict of Laws. This Chapter is devoted to choice-of-law problems of a somewhat different dimension. Let us suppose that plaintiff is a citizen of State X and defendant is a citizen of State Y, and plaintiff has decided to litigate a tort or contract claim against defendant in a federal district court in State Y. What law should the federal court apply to adjudicate this action? The law of State X? Of State Y? Federal law? Would the answer be different if, assuming personal jurisdiction could be acquired, the action were commenced in a federal district court in State X? Conversely, the problem of choosing between federal and state law is present when a state court is called upon to decide cases arising under federal statutes or cases in which federal rights and liabilities are in issue. As one might surmise, the processes of choosing between the law of two states and that of choosing between federal and state law are analogous, but also involve important differences. This Chapter will explore some of the problems that are raised in these various situations.

SECTION A.   STATE LAW IN THE FEDERAL COURTS

1.   THE RULE IN SWIFT v. TYSON

Although Article III of the Constitution sets limits on the jurisdiction of those federal court systems, it does not specify the law that is to be applied in the lower federal courts that are established. The Judiciary Act of 1789, which established a lower federal court system, promulgated rules governing those courts' jurisdiction and operation. Among those rules, in Section 34 of the Judiciary Act, was the so-called Rules of Decision Act. The modern version of this Act is found at 28 U.S.C. § 1652 and reads:

> The laws of the several states, except where the Constitution or treaties of the United States or Acts of Congress otherwise require or provide, shall be regarded as rules of decision in civil actions in the courts of the United States, in cases where they apply.

For nearly one hundred years, the Supreme Court's decision in SWIFT v. TYSON, 41 U.S. (16 Pet.) 1, 10 L.Ed. 865 (1842), provided the basic interpretation of the language of the Rules of Decision Act. In *Swift,* Maine land speculators sold land that they did not own to New Yorkers. The principal question before the court was whether the case should be governed by New York commercial law, as set out in state decisional law, or whether the federal court, sitting in diversity, could devise its own common-law rule.

Whether New York law applied or not turned upon the meaning of the phrase "laws of the several states" in the Rules of Decision Act. If the phrase encompassed both the statutory and the decisional law of the states (that is, if the Act commanded federal courts to follow both state statutes and state court decisions in cases in which they covered the controversy), then the New York rule (which was judge-made, not part of a statute) had to be applied. If, on the other hand, the phrase encompassed only statutory law (that is, if the Act commanded federal courts to follow the state rule *only* if it was in a state statute), then the federal court in *Swift* was free to use the emerging rule or any other rule deemed appropriate. Justice Story, writing for a unanimous Court, concluded that the Act commanded federal courts to follow only the statutory law of the states:

It is observable that the courts of New York do not found their decisions upon this point upon any local statute, or positive, fixed, or ancient local usage: but they deduce the doctrine from the general principles of commercial law. It is, however, contended, that the thirty-fourth section of the judiciary act of 1789, ch. 20, furnishes a rule obligatory upon this court to follow the decisions of the state tribunals in all cases to which they apply. * * * In order to maintain the argument, it is essential, therefore, to hold, that the word "laws," in this section, includes within the scope of its meaning the decisions of the local tribunals. In the ordinary use of language it will hardly be contended that the decisions of courts constitute laws. They are, at most, only evidence of what the laws are, and are not of themselves laws. They are often reexamined, reversed, and qualified by the courts themselves, whenever they are found to be either defective, or ill-founded, or otherwise incorrect. The laws of a state are more usually understood to mean the rules and enactments promulgated by the legislative authority thereof, or long established local customs having the force of laws. In all the various cases, which have hitherto come before us for decision, this court have uniformly supposed, that the true interpretation of the thirty-fourth section limited its application to state laws strictly local, that is to say, to the positive statutes of the state, and the construction thereof adopted by the local tribunals, and to rights and titles to things having a permanent locality, such as the rights and titles to real estate, and other matters immovable and intraterritorial in their nature and character. It never has been supposed by us, that the section did apply, or was designed to apply, to questions of a more general nature, not at all dependent upon local statutes or local usages of a fixed and permanent operation, as, for example, to the construction of ordinary contracts or other written instruments and especially to questions of general commercial law, where the state tribunals are called upon to perform the like functions as ourselves, that is, to ascertain upon general reasoning and legal analogies, what is the true exposition of the contract or instrument, or what is the just rule furnished by the principles of commercial law to govern the case. And we have not now the slightest difficulty in holding, that this section, upon its true intendment and construction, is strictly limited to local statutes and local usages of the character before stated, and does not extend to contracts and other instruments of a commercial nature, the true interpretation and effect whereof are to be sought, not in the decisions of the local tribunals, but in the general principles and doctrines of commercial jurisprudence. * * *

Id. at 18–19, 10 L.Ed. at 871.

2. THE *ERIE* DOCTRINE: THE RULES OF DECISION ACT AND THE RULES ENABLING ACT

———

ERIE R. CO. v. TOMPKINS
Supreme Court of the United States, 1938.
304 U.S. 64, 58 S.Ct. 817, 82 L.Ed. 1188.

[Slightly after midnight on July 27, 1934, Harry James Tompkins was walking home along a well-trodden footpath running parallel to the Erie Railroad tracks in Hughestown, Pennsylvania, when he was struck by "a black object that looked like a door" protruding from a passing train. Tompkins' right arm was severed.

Under Pennsylvania law, a traveler like Tompkins on a parallel (or "longitudinal") path was regarded as a trespasser to whom the railroad merely owes a duty to avoid wanton negligence. The majority rule in most states, however, was that a railroad owes a duty of ordinary care to a traveler on a parallel footpath.

Tompkins' lawyers were well aware of the rule in *Swift* that, absent state statutory law, federal courts apply "general law," and thus they tried to avoid the harsh Pennsylvania rule by suing the New York-based railroad in federal court. As anticipated, the District Court applied "general law," the majority rule, and the jury awarded Tompkins $30,000 in damages.

The Court of Appeals affirmed, holding that:

[U]pon questions of general law the federal courts are free, in absence of a local statute, to exercise their independent judgment as to what the law is; and it is well settled that the question of the responsibility of a railroad for injuries caused by its servants is one of general law. * * * Where the public has made open and notorious use of a railroad right of way for a long period of time and without objection, the company owes to persons on such permissive pathway a duty of care in the operation of its trains. * * * It is likewise generally recognized law that a jury may find that negligence exists toward a pedestrian using a permissive path on the railroad right of way if he is hit by some object projecting from the side of the train.

The Supreme Court granted certiorari. After hearing the opening arguments, Chief Justice Hughes declared: "If we wish to overrule Swift v. Tyson, here is our opportunity."]

Certiorari to the Circuit Court of Appeals for the Second Circuit.

MR. JUSTICE BRANDEIS delivered the opinion of the Court.

* * *

First. Swift v. Tyson * * * held that federal courts exercising jurisdiction on the ground of diversity of citizenship need not, in matters of general jurisprudence, apply the unwritten law of the state as declared by its highest court; that they are free to exercise an independent judgment as to what the common law of the state is—or should be * * *.

* * * The federal courts assumed, in the broad field of "general law," the power to declare rules of decision which Congress was confessedly without power to enact as statutes. Doubt was repeatedly expressed as to the correctness of the construction given section 34, and as to the soundness of the rule which it introduced. But it was the more recent research of a competent scholar, who examined the original document, which established that the construction given to it by the Court was erroneous; and that the purpose of the section was merely to make certain that, in all matters except those in which some federal law is controlling, the federal courts exercising jurisdiction in diversity of citizenship cases would apply as their rules of decision the law of the state, unwritten as well as written.[5]

Criticism of the doctrine became widespread after the decision of Black & White Taxicab & Transfer Co. v. Brown & Yellow Taxicab & Transfer Co., 276 U.S. 518, 48 S.Ct. 404, 72 L.Ed. 681, 57 A.L.R. 426. There, Brown & Yellow, a Kentucky corporation owned by Kentuckians, and the Louisville & Nashville Railroad, also a Kentucky corporation, wished that the former should have the exclusive privilege of soliciting passenger and baggage transportation at the Bowling Green, Ky., railroad station; and that the Black & White, a competing Kentucky corporation, should be prevented from interfering with that privilege. Knowing that such a contract would be void under the common law of Kentucky, it was arranged that the Brown & Yellow reincorporate under the law of Tennessee, and that the contract with the railroad should be executed there. The suit was then brought by the Tennessee corporation in the federal court for Western Kentucky to enjoin competition by the Black & White; an injunction issued by the District Court was sustained by the Court of Appeals; and this Court, citing many decisions in which the doctrine of Swift v. Tyson had been applied, affirmed the decree.

Second. Experience in applying the doctrine of Swift v. Tyson, had revealed its defects, political and social; and the benefits expected to flow from the rule did not accrue. Persistence of state courts in their own opinions on questions of common law prevented uniformity; and the impossibility of discovering a satisfactory line of demarcation between the province of general law and that of local law developed a new well of uncertainties.

On the other hand, the mischievous results of the doctrine had become apparent. Diversity of citizenship jurisdiction was conferred in order to prevent apprehended discrimination in state courts against those not citizens of the state. Swift v. Tyson introduced grave discrimination by noncitizens against citizens. It made rights enjoyed under the unwritten "general law" vary according to whether enforcement was sought in the state or in the federal court; and the privilege of selecting the court in which the right should be determined was conferred upon the noncitizen.

---

5. Charles Warren, New Light on the History of the Federal Judiciary Act of 1789 (1923) 37 Harv.L.Rev. 49, 51–52, 81–88, 108.

Thus, the doctrine rendered impossible equal protection of the law. In attempting to promote uniformity of law throughout the United States, the doctrine had prevented uniformity in the administration of the law of the state.

The discrimination resulting became in practice far-reaching. This resulted in part from the broad province accorded to the so-called "general law" as to which federal courts exercised an independent judgment. In addition to questions of purely commercial law, "general law" was held to include the obligations under contracts entered into and to be performed within the state, the extent to which a carrier operating within a state may stipulate for exemption from liability for his own negligence or that of his employee; the liability for torts committed within the state upon persons resident or property located there, even where the question of liability depended upon the scope of a property right conferred by the state; and the right to exemplary or punitive damages. Furthermore, state decisions construing local deeds, mineral conveyances, and even devises of real estate, were disregarded.

In part the discrimination resulted from the wide range of persons held entitled to avail themselves of the federal rule by resort to the diversity of citizenship jurisdiction. Through this jurisdiction individual citizens willing to remove from their own state and become citizens of another might avail themselves of the federal rule. And, without even change of residence, a corporate citizen of the state could avail itself of the federal rule by reincorporating under the laws of another state, as was done in the Taxicab Case.

The injustice and confusion incident to the doctrine of Swift v. Tyson have been repeatedly urged as reasons for abolishing or limiting diversity of citizenship jurisdiction. Other legislative relief has been proposed. If only a question of statutory construction were involved, we should not be prepared to abandon a doctrine so widely applied throughout nearly a century. But the unconstitutionality of the course pursued has now been made clear, and compels us to do so.

Third. Except in matters governed by the Federal Constitution or by acts of Congress, the law to be applied in any case is the law of the state. And whether the law of the state shall be declared by its Legislature in a statute or by its highest court in a decision is not a matter of federal concern. There is no federal general common law. Congress has no power to declare substantive rules of common law applicable in a state whether they be local in their nature or "general," be they commercial law or a part of the law of torts. And no clause in the Constitution purports to confer such a power upon the federal courts. * * *

The fallacy underlying the rule declared in Swift v. Tyson is made clear by Mr. Justice Holmes. The doctrine rests upon the assumption that there is "a transcendental body of law outside of any particular State but obligatory within it unless and until changed by statute," that federal courts have the power to use their judgment as to what the rules of common law are; and that in the federal courts "the parties are entitled to an independent judgment on matters of general law":

> But law in the sense in which courts speak of it today does not exist without some definite authority behind it. The common law so far as it is enforced in a State, whether called common law or not, is not the common law generally but the law of that State existing by the authority of that State without regard to what it may have been in England or anywhere else. * * *

> The authority and only authority is the State, and if that be so, the voice adopted by the State as its own [whether it be of its Legislature or of its Supreme Court] should utter the last word.

Thus the doctrine of Swift v. Tyson is, as Mr. Justice Holmes said, "an unconstitutional assumption of powers by the Courts of the United States which no lapse of time or respectable array of opinion should make us hesitate to correct." In disapproving that doctrine we do not hold unconstitutional section 34 of the Federal Judiciary Act of 1789 or any other act of Congress. We merely declare that in applying the doctrine this Court and the lower courts have invaded rights which in our opinion are reserved by the Constitution to the several states.

Fourth. The defendant contended that by the common law of Pennsylvania * * * the only duty owed to the plaintiff was to refrain from willful or wanton injury. The plaintiff denied that such is the Pennsylvania law. In support of their respective contentions the parties discussed and cited many decisions of the Supreme Court of the State. The Circuit Court of Appeals ruled that the question of liability is one of general law; and on that ground declined to decide the issue of state law. As we hold this was error, the judgment is reversed and the case remanded to it for further proceedings in conformity with our opinion.

Reversed.

MR. JUSTICE CARDOZO took no part in the consideration or decision of this case.

[The dissenting opinion of MR. JUSTICE BUTLER is omitted.]

MR. JUSTICE REED (concurring in part).

I concur in the conclusion reached in this case, in the disapproval of the doctrine of *Swift v. Tyson*, and in the reasoning of the majority opinion except in so far as it relies upon the unconstitutionality of the "course pursued" by the federal courts.

* * *

To decide the case now before us and to "disapprove" the doctrine of Swift v. Tyson requires only that we say that the words "the laws" include in their meaning the decisions of the local tribunals. As the majority opinion shows, by its reference to Mr. Warren's researches and the first quotation from Mr. Justice Holmes, that this Court is now of the view that "laws" includes "decisions," it is unnecessary to go further and declare that the "course pursued" was "unconstitutional," instead of merely erroneous.

The "unconstitutional" course referred to in the majority opinion is apparently the ruling in Swift v. Tyson that the supposed omission of Congress to legislate as to the effect of decisions leaves federal courts free to interpret general law for themselves. I am not at all sure whether, in the absence of federal statutory direction, federal courts would be compelled to follow state decisions. There was sufficient doubt about the matter in 1789 to induce the first Congress to legislate. No former opinions of this Court have passed upon it. * * * If the opinion commits this Court to the position that the Congress is without power to declare what rules of substantive law shall govern the federal courts, that conclusion also seems questionable. The line between procedural and substantive law is hazy, but no one doubts federal power over procedure. * * * The Judiciary Article, 3, and the "necessary and proper" clause of article 1, § 8, may fully authorize legislation, such as this section of the Judiciary Act.

NOTES AND QUESTIONS

1. Is *Erie* a constitutional decision or does it rest on other grounds? What constitutional provision could provide the basis for Justice Brandeis's opinion? The Commerce Clause of the Constitution, Article I, § 8, certainly allows Congress to regulate interstate railroads. If Congress can legislate in this area, why can't the courts act as well? The constitutional discussion in *Erie* is sometimes referred to as dicta. Is Justice Brandeis's reference to the Constitution merely a way of bolstering his interpretation of the Rules of Decision Act? See Clark, *State Law in the Federal Courts: The Brooding Omnipresence of Erie v. Tompkins*, 55 Yale L.J. 267, 278 (1946).

2. The *Erie* decision relied on research that revealed a previously unknown draft of what became the Rules of Decision Act of 1789. The draft read:

> And be it further enacted, That the Statute law of the several States in force for the time being and their unwritten or common law now in use, whether by adoption from the common law of England, the ancient statutes of the same or otherwise, except where the Constitution, treaties or statutes of the United States shall otherwise require or provide, shall be regarded as rules of decision in the trials at common law in the courts of the United States in cases where they apply.

Warren, *New Light on the History of the Federal Judiciary Act of 1789*, 37 Harv. L. Rev. 49 (1923). Did Justice Brandeis properly interpret the Rules of Decision Act given this legislative history? Or, did the shorter final version reflect congressional intent to limit the definition of "laws of the several states" to statutory laws, thus expanding the federal common law lawmaking power of the federal courts in diversity cases? Subsequent scholarship casts doubt on the Warren interpretation of the Judiciary Act of 1789. See Ritz,

Rewriting the History of the Judiciary Act, in Rewriting the History of the Judiciary Act of 1789: Exposing Myths, Challenging Premises, and Using New Evidence (Ritz, Holt & LaRue eds., 1990).

3. Professors Wright and Kane have said: "It is impossible to overstate the importance of the *Erie* decision." Wright & Kane, Federal Courts § 55 (6th ed. 2002). As you read the cases that follow, consider why this might be so. For an analysis of the social and political context of the decision, as well as its jurisprudential underpinnings, see Purcell, The Story of *Erie*: How Litigants, Lawyers, Judges, Politics, and Social Change Reshape the Law, in Civil Procedure Stories 21 (Clermont ed., 2d ed. 2008).

———

GUARANTY TRUST CO. v. YORK

Supreme Court of the United States, 1945.
326 U.S. 99, 65 S.Ct. 1464, 89 L.Ed. 2079.

[The Guaranty Trust Company served as trustee for some of the noteholders of Van Sweringen Corporation. In October 1930, Guaranty loaned money to corporations affiliated with and controlled by Van Sweringen. By October 1931, it was evident that Van Sweringen was having trouble meeting its financial obligations. Guaranty and several other banks worked out a plan by which Guaranty would offer to purchase the notes by paying $500 and twenty shares of Van Sweringen stock for each $1,000 note.

Respondent York received $6,000 of the notes from a donor who had not accepted Guaranty's offer. York brought a diversity suit alleging that Guaranty had breached its fiduciary duties. York's complaint involved allegations of fraud and misrepresentation, relief for which was governed by equitable principles. On appeal, the Circuit Court of Appeals, one judge dissenting, found that in a suit brought in equity the federal court was not required to apply the state statute of limitations that would govern similar suits in state courts, even though the exclusive basis of federal jurisdiction was diversity of citizenship. The Supreme Court granted review in order to decide whether federal courts should apply state statutes of limitations in such cases.]

Certiorari to the Circuit Court of Appeals for the Second Circuit.

MR. JUSTICE FRANKFURTER delivered the opinion of the Court.

* * *

In exercising their jurisdiction on the ground of diversity of citizenship, the federal courts, in the long course of their history, have not differentiated in their regard for State law between actions at law and suits in equity. * * *

Partly because the States in the early days varied greatly in the manner in which equitable relief was afforded and in the extent to which it was available, * * * Congress provided that "the forms and modes of proceeding in suits * * * of equity" would conform to the settled uses of courts of equity. * * * But this enactment gave the federal courts no power that they would not have had in any event when courts were given "cognizance," by the first Judiciary Act, of suits "in equity." * * * In giving federal courts "cognizance" of equity suits in cases of diversity jurisdiction, Congress never gave, nor did the federal courts ever claim, the power to deny substantive rights created by State law or to create substantive rights denied by State law.

This does not mean that whatever equitable remedy is available in a State court must be available in a diversity suit in a federal court, or conversely, that a federal court may not afford an equitable remedy not available in a State court. * * * State law cannot define the remedies which a federal court must give simply because a federal court in diversity jurisdiction is available as an alternative tribunal to the State's courts. Contrariwise, a federal court may afford an equitable remedy for a substantive right recognized by a State even though a State court cannot give it. Whatever contradiction or confusion may be produced by a medley of judicial phrases severed from their environment, the body of adjudications concerning equitable relief in diversity cases leaves no doubt that the federal courts enforced State-created substantive rights if the mode of proceeding and remedy were consonant with the traditional body of equitable remedies, practice and procedure, and in so doing they were enforcing rights created by the States and not arising under any inherent or statutory federal law.

* * *

And so this case reduces itself to the narrow question whether, when no recovery could be had in a State court because the action is barred by the statute of limitations, a federal court in equity can take cognizance of the suit because there is diversity of citizenship between the parties. Is the outlawry, according to State law, of a claim created by the States a matter of "substantive rights" to be respected by a federal court of equity when that court's jurisdiction is dependent on the fact that there is a State-created right, or is such statute of "a mere remedial character," * * * which a federal court may disregard?

Matters of "substance" and matters of "procedure" are much talked about in the books as though they defined a great divide cutting across the whole domain of law. But, of course, "substance" and "procedure" are the same keywords to very different problems. Neither "substance" nor "procedure" represents the same invariants. Each implies different variables depending upon the particular problem for which it is used. * * * And the different problems are only distantly related at best, for the terms are in common use in connection with situations turning on such different considerations as those that are relevant to questions pertaining to *ex post facto* legislation, the impairment of the obligations of contract, the enforcement of federal rights in the State courts and the multitudinous phases of the conflict of laws. * * *

Here we are dealing with a right to recover derived not from the United States but from one of the States. When, because the plaintiff happens to be a non-resident, such a right is enforceable in a federal as well as in a State court, the forms and mode of enforcing the right may at times, naturally enough, vary because the two judicial systems are not identic. But since a federal court adjudicating a State-created right solely because of the diversity of citizenship of the parties is for that purpose, in effect, only another court of the State, it cannot afford recovery if the right to recover is made unavailable by the State nor can it substantially affect the enforcement of the right as given by the State.

And so the question is not whether a statute of limitations is deemed a matter of "procedure" in some sense. The question is whether such a statute concerns merely the manner and the means by which a right to recover, as recognized by the State, is enforced, or whether such statutory limitation is a matter of substance in the aspect that alone is relevant to our problem, namely, does it significantly affect the result of a litigation for a federal court to disregard a law of a State that would be controlling in an action upon the same claim by the same parties in a State court?

It is therefore immaterial whether statutes of limitation are characterized either as "substantive" or "procedural" in State court opinions in any use of those terms unrelated to the specific issue before us. Erie R. Co. v. Tompkins was not an endeavor to formulate scientific legal terminology. It expressed a policy that touches vitally the proper distribution of judicial power between State and federal courts. In essence, the intent of that decision was to insure that, in all cases where a federal court is exercising jurisdiction solely because of the diversity of citizenship of the parties, the outcome of the litigation in the federal court should be substantially the same, so far as legal rules determine the outcome of a litigation, as it would be if tried in a State court. The nub of the policy that underlies Erie R. Co. v. Tompkins is that for the same transaction the accident of a suit by a non-resident litigant in a federal court instead of in a State court a block away should not lead to a substantially different result. * * * A policy so important to our federalism must be kept free from entanglements with analytical or terminological niceties.

Plainly enough, a statute that would completely bar recovery in a suit if brought in a State court bears on a State-created right vitally and not merely formally or negligibly. As to consequences that so intimately affect recovery or non-recovery a federal court in a diversity case should follow State law. * * *

Diversity jurisdiction is founded on assurance to non-resident litigants of courts free from susceptibility to potential local bias. The Framers of the Constitution, according to Marshall, entertained "apprehensions" lest distant suitors be subjected to local bias in State courts, or, at least, viewed with "indulgence the possible fears and apprehensions" of such suitors. Bank of the United States v. Deveaux, 5 Cranch 61, 87, 3 L. Ed. 38. And so Congress afforded out-of-State litigants another tribunal, not another body of law. The operation of a double system of conflicting laws in the same State is plainly hostile to the reign of law. Certainly, the fortuitous circumstance of residence out of a State of one of the parties to a litigation ought not to give rise to a discrimination against others equally concerned but locally resident. The source of substantive rights enforced by a federal court under diversity jurisdiction, it cannot be said too often, is the law of the States. * * *

The judgment is reversed and the case is remanded for proceedings not inconsistent with this opinion.

So ordered.

JUSTICE ROBERTS and JUSTICE DOUGLAS took no part in the consideration or decision of this case.

JUSTICE RUTLEDGE dissented in an opinion in which JUSTICE MURPHY joined.

* * * [T]he decision of today does not in so many words rule that Congress could not authorize the federal courts to administer equitable relief in accordance with the substantive rights of the parties, notwithstanding state courts had been forbidden by local statutes of limitations to do so. Nevertheless the implication to that effect seems strong, in view of the reliance upon Erie R. Co. v. Tompkins. * * * In any event, the question looms more largely in the issues than the Court's opinion appears to make it. For if legislative acquiescence in long-established judicial construction can make it part of a statute, it has done so in this instance. More is at stake in the implications of the decision, if not in the words of the opinion, than simply bringing federal and local law into accord upon matters clearly and exclusively within the constitutional power of the state to determine. It is one thing to require that kind of an accord in diversity cases when the question is merely whether the federal court must follow the law of the state as to burden of proof, * * * contributory negligence, * * * or perhaps in application of the so-called parol evidence rule. These ordinarily involve matters of substantive law, though nominated in terms of procedure. But in some instances their application may lie along the border between procedure or remedy and substance, where the one may or may not be in fact but another name for the other. It is exactly in this borderland, where procedural or remedial rights may or may not have the effect of determining the substantive ones completely, that caution is required in extending the rule of the Erie case by the very rule itself.

The words "substantive" and "procedural" or "remedial" are not talismanic. Merely calling a legal question by one or the other does not resolve it otherwise than as a purely authoritarian performance. * * * But they have come to designate in a broad way large and distinctive legal domains within the greater one of the law and to mark, though often indistinctly or with overlapping limits, many divides between such regions.

* * *

This division, like others drawn by the broad allocation of adjective or remedial and substantive, has areas of admixture of these two aspects of the law. In these areas whether a particular situation or issue presents one aspect or the other depends upon how one looks at the matter. * * *

Whenever this integration or admixture prevails in a substantial measure, so that a clean break cannot be made, there is danger either of nullifying the power of Congress to control not only how the federal courts may act, but what they may do by way of affording remedies, or of usurping that function, if the Erie doctrine is to be expanded judicially to include such situations to the utmost extent.

It may be true that if the matter were wholly fresh the barring of rights in equity by statutes of limitation would seem to partake more of the substantive than of the remedial phase of law. But the matter is not fresh and it is not without room for debate. A long tradition, in the states and here, as well as in the common law which antedated both state and federal law, has emphasized the remedial character of statutes of limitations, more especially in application to equity causes, on many kinds of issues requiring differentiation of such matters from more clearly and exclusively substantive ones. * * * The tradition now in question is equally long and unvaried. I cannot say the tradition is clearly wrong in this case more than in that. Nor can I say, as was said in the Erie case, that the matter is beyond the power of Congress to control. If that be conceded, I think Congress should make the change if it is to be made. The Erie decision was rendered in 1938. Seven years have passed without action by Congress to extend the rule to these matters. That is long enough to justify the conclusion that Congress also regards them as not governed by Erie and as wishing to make no change. This should be reason enough for leaving the matter at rest until it decides to act. * * *

Applicable statutes of limitations in state tribunals are not always the ones which would apply if suit were instituted in the courts of the state which creates the substantive rights for which enforcement is sought. The state of the forum is free to apply its own period of limitations, regardless of whether the state originating the right has barred suit upon it. Whether or not the action will be held to be barred depends therefore not upon the law of the state which creates the substantive right, but upon the law of the state where suit may be brought. This in turn will depend upon where it may be possible to secure service of process, and thus jurisdiction of the person of the defendant. It may be therefore that because of the plaintiff's inability to find the defendant in the jurisdiction which creates his substantive right, he will be foreclosed of remedy by the sheer necessity of going to the haven of refuge within which the defendant confines its "presence" for jurisdictional purposes. The law of the latter may bar the suit even though suit still would be allowed under the law of the state creating the substantive right.

NOTE AND QUESTIONS

To what extent does *York* require the displacement of a Federal Rule of Civil Procedure in favor of a contrary state practice? Shortly after *York,* the Supreme Court considered a trio of cases all decided by the Court on the same day. RAGAN v. MERCHANTS TRANSFER & WAREHOUSE CO., 337 U.S. 530, 69 S.Ct. 1233, 93 L.Ed. 1520 (1949), grew out of a highway accident that occurred on October 1, 1943. On September 4, 1945, Ragan filed a diversity action in a federal court in Kansas. However, service was not made on defendant until December 28. Kansas had a two-year statute of limitations on tort claims. Ragan claimed that according to Rule 3 of the Federal Rules, the suit was commenced (and hence the statute was tolled) by the filing of the complaint. Defendant countered that Kansas law dictated that service had to have been made within the two-year period. The Supreme Court held that state law would determine in diversity when the statute was tolled.

In COHEN v. BENEFICIAL INDUSTRIAL LOAN CORP., 337 U.S. 541, 69 S.Ct. 1221, 93 L.Ed. 1528 (1949), the Court held that a federal court must apply a New Jersey statute requiring plaintiff in a shareholder derivative suit to post a security-for-expenses bond—even though what is now Federal Rule 23.1, which ostensibly governs such cases, did not require a bond. The Court found that whether the New Jersey statute was classified as procedural or substantive, it created substantive liabilities for expenses. In the Court's view, Rule 23.1 did not contradict the New Jersey statute, but was addressed to independent concerns.

Finally, in WOODS v. INTERSTATE REALTY CO., 337 U.S. 535, 69 S.Ct. 1235, 93 L.Ed. 1524 (1949), the Court held that a Tennessee corporation that had not qualified to do business in Mississippi could not maintain a diversity action in a federal court in that state if, by virtue of its failure to qualify, the Mississippi state courts were closed to it.

In light of these decisions, do you agree that "[t]he *York* case, of necessity, spelled death to the hope for a completely uniform federal procedure"? Merrigan, Erie *to* York *to* Ragan—*A Triple Play on the Federal Rules*, 3 Vand. L. Rev. 711, 717 (1950). Is this result compelled by *Erie*?

BYRD v. BLUE RIDGE RURAL ELECTRIC COOPERATIVE, INC.

Supreme Court of the United States, 1958.
356 U.S. 525, 78 S.Ct. 893, 2 L.Ed.2d 953.

Certiorari to the United States Court of Appeals for the Fourth Circuit.

MR. JUSTICE BRENNAN delivered the opinion of the Court.

This case was brought in the District Court for the Western District of South Carolina. Jurisdiction was based on diversity of citizenship. * * * The petitioner, a resident of North Carolina, sued respondent, a South

Carolina corporation, for damages for injuries allegedly caused by the respondent's negligence. He had judgment on a jury verdict. The Court of Appeals for the Fourth Circuit reversed and directed the entry of judgment for the respondent. * * *

The respondent is in the business of selling electric power to subscribers in rural sections of South Carolina. The petitioner was employed as a lineman in the construction crew of a construction contractor. The contractor, R.H. Bouligny, Inc., held a contract with the respondent * * * for the building of some * * * power lines, the reconversion to higher capacities of * * * existing lines, and the construction of 2 new substations and a breaker station. The petitioner was injured while connecting power lines to one of the new substations.

One of respondent's affirmative defenses was that under the South Carolina Workmen's Compensation Act, the petitioner—because the work contracted to be done by his employer was work of the kind also done by the respondent's own construction and maintenance crews—had the status of a statutory employee of the respondent and was therefore barred from suing the respondent at law because obliged to accept statutory compensation benefits as the exclusive remedy for his injuries. Two questions concerning this defense are before us: (1) whether the Court of Appeals erred in directing judgment for respondent without a remand to give petitioner an opportunity to introduce further evidence; and (2) whether petitioner, state practice notwithstanding, is entitled to a jury determination of the factual issues raised by this defense.

* * *

[The Supreme Court initially decided to remand the case to the trial court to provide the petitioner an opportunity to introduce evidence on the question of whether the respondent was a statutory employer.]

A question is also presented as to whether on remand the factual issue is to be decided by the judge or by the jury. The respondent argues on the basis of the decision of the Supreme Court of South Carolina in Adams v. Davison–Paxon Co., 230 S.C. 532, 96 S.E.2d 566, that the issue of immunity should be decided by the judge and not by the jury. * * *

The respondent argues that this state-court decision governs the present diversity case and "divests the jury of its normal function" to decide the disputed fact question of the respondent's immunity under § 72–111. This is to contend that the federal court is bound under Erie R. Co. v. Tompkins * * * to follow the state court's holding to secure uniform enforcement of the immunity created by the State.

First. It was decided in Erie R. Co. v. Tompkins that the federal courts in diversity cases must respect the definition of state-created rights and obligations by the state courts. We must, therefore, first examine the rule in Adams v. Davison–Paxon Co. to determine whether it is bound up with these rights and obligations in such a way that its application in the federal court is required. * * *

The Workmen's Compensation Act is administered in South Carolina by its Industrial Commission. The South Carolina courts hold that, on judicial review of actions of the Commission under § 72–111, the question whether the claim of an injured workman is within the Commission's jurisdiction is a matter of law for decision by the court, which makes its own findings of fact relating to that jurisdiction. The South Carolina Supreme Court states no reasons in Adams v. Davison–Paxon Co. why, although the jury decides all other factual issues raised by the cause of action and defenses, the jury is displaced as to the factual issue raised by the affirmative defense under § 72–111. * * * A State may, of course, distribute the functions of its judicial machinery as it sees fit. The decisions relied upon, however, furnish no reason for selecting the judge rather than the jury to decide this single affirmative defense in the negligence action. They simply reflect a policy * * * that administrative determination of "jurisdictional facts" should not be final but subject to judicial review. The conclusion is inescapable that the Adams holding is grounded in the practical consideration that the question had theretofore come before the South Carolina courts from the Industrial Commission and the courts had become accustomed to deciding the factual issue of immunity without the aid of juries. We find nothing to suggest that this rule was announced as an integral part of the special relationship created by the statute. Thus the requirement appears to be merely a form and mode of enforcing the immunity * * * and not a rule intended to be bound up with the definition of the rights and obligations of the parties. * * *

Second. But cases following *Erie* have evinced a broader policy to the effect that the federal courts should conform as near as may be—in the absence of other considerations—to state rules even of form and mode where the state rules may bear substantially on the question whether the litigation would come out one way in the federal court and another way in the state court if the federal court failed to apply a particular local rule. E.g., Guaranty Trust Co. of New York v. York, * * *; Bernhardt v. Polygraphic Co., [p. 248, infra] * * *. Concededly the nature of the tribunal which tries issues may be important in the enforcement of the parcel of rights making up a cause of action or defense, and bear significantly upon achievement of uniform enforcement of the right. It may well be that in the instant personal-injury case the outcome would be substantially affected by whether the issue of immunity is decided by a judge or a jury. Therefore, were "outcome" the only consideration, a strong case might appear for saying that the federal court should follow the state practice.

But there are affirmative countervailing considerations at work here. The federal system is an independent system for administering justice to litigants who properly invoke its jurisdiction. An essential characteristic of that system is the manner in which, in civil common-law actions, it distributes trial functions between judge and jury and, under the influence—if not the command—of the Seventh Amendment, assigns the decisions of disputed questions of fact to the jury. * * * The policy of uniform enforcement of state-created rights and obligations * * * cannot in every case exact compliance with a state rule—not bound up with rights and obligations—which disrupts the federal system of allocating functions between judge and jury. * * * Thus the inquiry here is whether the federal policy favoring jury decisions of disputed fact questions should yield to the state rule in the interest of furthering the objective that the litigation should not come out one way in the federal court and another way in the state court.

We think that in the circumstances of this case the federal court should not follow the state rule. It cannot be gainsaid that there is a strong federal policy against allowing state rules to disrupt the judge-jury relationship in the federal courts. In Herron v. Southern Pacific Co., [283 U.S. 91, 51 S.Ct. 383, 75 L.Ed. 857 (1931),] * * * the trial judge in a personal-injury negligence action brought in the District Court for Arizona on diversity grounds directed a verdict for the defendant when it appeared as a matter of law that the plaintiff was guilty of contributory negligence. The federal judge refused to be bound by a provision of the Arizona Constitution which made the jury the sole arbiter of the question of contributory negligence. This Court sustained the action of the trial judge, holding that "state laws cannot alter the essential character or function of a federal court" because that function "is not in any sense a local matter, and state statutes which would interfere with the appropriate performance of that function are not binding upon the federal court under either the Conformity Act or the 'Rules of Decision' Act." * * * Perhaps even more clearly in light of the influence of the Seventh Amendment, the function assigned to the jury "is an essential factor in the process for which the Federal Constitution provides." * * * Concededly the *Herron* case was decided before Erie R. Co. v. Tompkins, but even when Swift v. Tyson * * * was governing law and allowed federal courts sitting in diversity cases to disregard state decisional law, it was never thought that state statutes or constitutions were similarly to be disregarded. * * * Yet *Herron* held that state statutes and constitutional provisions could not disrupt or alter the essential character or function of a federal court. * * *

Third. We have discussed the problem upon the assumption that the outcome of the litigation may be substantially affected by whether the issue of immunity is decided by a judge or a jury. But clearly there is not present here the certainty that a different result would follow * * * or even the strong possibility that this would be the case * * *. There are factors present here which might reduce that possibility. The trial judge in the federal system has powers denied the judges of many States to comment on the weight of evidence and credibility of witnesses, and discretion to grant a new trial if the verdict appears to him to be against the weight of the evidence. We do not think the likelihood of a different result is so strong as to require the federal practice of jury determination of disputed factual issues to yield to the state rule in the interest of uniformity of outcome. * * *

* * *

Reversed and remanded.

* * *

[JUSTICE WHITTAKER concurred in Part I of the Court's opinion but dissented from Part II on the ground that the South Carolina rule requiring "its courts—not juries—to determine whether jurisdiction over the subject matter of cases like this is vested in its Industrial Commission" should be honored by a federal court. JUSTICE FRANKFURTER and JUSTICE HARLAN dissented on the ground that the evidence required the district court to direct a verdict for the respondent.]

NOTES AND QUESTIONS

1. Do you agree with Justice Brennan's assertion that the South Carolina rule at issue in *Byrd* is "merely a form and mode of enforcing the immunity * * * and not a rule intended to be bound up with the definition of the rights and obligations of the parties"? Most states have adopted their worker compensation schemes only after carefully balancing the equities involved in the typical workplace accident. These statutes are complex and detailed and often are the result of a political compromise. Does it seem likely, then, that South Carolina randomly would have appropriated to the judge the function of defining a statutory employee?

2. In *Byrd,* Justice Brennan proposed what appears to be a balancing test for determining when a federal court may apply federal, rather than state, law in a diversity action. Does the balancing test in *Byrd* replace the outcome-determinative test of *York*? Whether it replaces the outcome-determinative test or not, how does Justice Brennan's balancing test work? If a state rule is "bound up with the definition of the rights and obligations of the parties," does a federal court still engage in balancing? How does a court determine whether a state rule is "bound up with the definition of the rights and obligations of the parties"? Once it begins to engage in the balancing process dictated in *Byrd,* how does a federal court identify and then weigh the competing state and federal policies? What sources should it examine in pursuing this inquiry?

3. In BERNHARDT v. POLYGRAPHIC CO. OF AMERICA, INC., 350 U.S. 198, 203, 76 S.Ct. 273, 276, 100 L.Ed. 199, 205 (1956), plaintiff brought an action in a Vermont state court for damages resulting from his discharge by defendant. Defendant removed the action to a federal district court and moved for a stay pending arbitration in New York pursuant to the contract. The District Court denied the stay, ruling that under *Erie* the arbitration provision was governed by Vermont law, which permitted revocation of an agreement to arbitrate any time before an award was made. The Second Circuit reversed on the ground that arbitration merely relates to the form of the trial. The Supreme Court disagreed and reversed and remanded, stating:

* * * If the federal court allows arbitration where the state court would disallow it, the outcome of litigation might depend on the courthouse where suit is brought. For the remedy by arbitration, whatever its merits or shortcomings, substantially affects the cause of action created by the State. The nature of the tribunal where suits are tried is an important part of the parcel of rights behind a cause of action. The change from a court of law to an arbitration panel may make a radical difference in ultimate result. Arbitration carries no right to trial by jury that is guaranteed both by the Seventh Amendment and by Ch. 1, Art. 12th, of the Vermont Constitution. Arbitrators do not have the benefit of judicial instruction on the law; they need not give their reasons for their results; the record of their proceedings is not as complete as it is in a court trial; and judicial review of an award is more limited than judicial review of a trial * * *.

After *Byrd,* would *Bernhardt* be decided the same way? Is state law governing arbitration bound up with the definition of the parties' rights and obligations?

4.   Given the federal interest in "an independent system for administering justice to litigants who properly invoke its jurisdiction," should a federal court in a diversity action employ a federal or state standard to determine the existence or nonexistence of in personam jurisdiction over a foreign corporation? Arrowsmith v. United Press Int'l, 320 F.2d 219 (2d Cir. 1963) (en banc), opted for the state standard, apparently overruling a contrary two-to-one decision in Jaftex Corp. v. Randolph Mills, Inc., 282 F.2d 508 (2d Cir. 1960). See 4 Wright & Miller, Federal Practice and Procedure: Civil 3d § 1075; 19 Wright, Miller & Cooper, Federal Practice and Procedure: Jurisdiction and Related Matters 2d § 4510.

––––––

In 1934, Congress passed 28 U.S.C. § 2072, commonly known as the Rules Enabling Act. Read the current version of this Act in the Supplement.

––––––

HANNA v. PLUMER

Supreme Court of the United States, 1965.
380 U.S. 460, 85 S.Ct. 1136, 14 L.Ed.2d 8.

Certiorari to the United States Court of Appeals for the First Circuit.

Mr. Chief Justice Warren delivered the opinion of the Court.

The question to be decided is whether, in a civil action where the jurisdiction of the United States District Court is based upon diversity of citizenship between the parties, service of process shall be made in the manner prescribed by state law or that set forth in Rule 4(d)(1) of the Federal Rules of Civil Procedure. [Rule 4(d)(1), has been amended several times since 1965. Most recently, this provision was renumbered as Rule 4(e)(2).]

On February 6, 1963, petitioner, a citizen of Ohio, filed her complaint in the District Court for the District of Massachusetts, claiming damages in excess of $10,000 for personal injuries resulting from an automobile accident in South Carolina, allegedly caused by the negligence of one Louise Plumer Osgood, a Massachusetts citizen deceased at the time of the filing of the complaint. Respondent, Mrs. Osgood's executor and also a Massachusetts citizen, was named as defendant. On February 8, service was made by leaving copies of the summons and the complaint with respondent's wife at his residence, concededly in compliance with Rule 4(d)(1) * * *. Respondent filed his answer on February 26, alleging, *inter alia,* that the action could not be maintained because it had been brought "contrary to and in violation of the provisions of Massachusetts General Laws (Ter. Ed.) Chapter 197, Section 9." That section provides:

> Except as provided in this chapter, an executor or administrator shall not be held to answer to an action by a creditor of the deceased which is not commenced within one year from the time of his giving bond for the performance of his trust, or to such an action which is commenced within said year unless before the expiration thereof the writ in such action has been served by delivery in hand upon such executor or administrator or service thereof accepted by him or a notice stating the name of the estate, the name and address of the creditor, the amount of the claim and the court in which the action has been brought has been filed in the proper registry of probate. * * *

On October 17, 1963, the District Court granted respondent's motion for summary judgment * * * [on the ground] that the adequacy of the service was to be measured by § 9, with which, the court held, petitioner had not complied. On appeal, petitioner * * * argued that Rule 4(d)(1) defines the method by which service of process is to be effected in diversity actions. The Court of Appeals for the First Circuit * * * unanimously affirmed. * * *

We conclude that the adoption of Rule 4(d)(1), designed to control service of process in diversity actions, neither exceeded the congressional mandate embodied in the Rules Enabling Act nor transgressed constitutional bounds, and that the Rule is therefore the standard against which the District Court should have measured the adequacy of the service. Accordingly, we reverse the decision of the Court of Appeals.

* * * Under the cases construing the scope of the Enabling Act, Rule 4(d)(1) clearly passes muster. Prescribing the manner in which a defendant is to be notified that a suit has been instituted against him, it relates to the "practice and procedure of the district courts." * * *

> The test must be whether a rule really regulates procedure,—the judicial process for enforcing rights and duties recognized by substantive law and for justly administering remedy and redress for disregard or infraction of them. Sibbach v. Wilson & Co., [312 U.S. 1, 15, 61 S.Ct. 422, 427, 85 L.Ed. 479, 486 (1941)]* * *.

In Mississippi Pub. Corp. v. Murphree, 326 U.S. 438, 66 S.Ct. 242, 90 L.Ed. 185, this Court upheld Rule 4(f) [now Rule 4(e)], which permits service of a summons anywhere within the State (and not merely the district) in which a district court sits:

> We think that Rule 4(f) is in harmony with the Enabling Act * * *. Undoubtedly most alterations of the rules of practice and procedure may and often do affect the rights of litigants. Congress' prohibition of any alteration of substantive rights of litigants was obviously not addressed to such incidental effects as necessarily attend the adoption of the prescribed new rules of procedure upon the rights of litigants who, agreeably to rules of practice and procedure, have been brought before a court authorized to determine their rights. * * * The fact that the application of Rule 4(f) will operate to subject petitioner's rights to adjudication by the district court for northern Mississippi will undoubtedly affect those rights. But it does not operate to abridge, enlarge or modify the rules of decision by which that court will adjudicate its rights. Id., at 445–446, 66 S.Ct. at 246.

Thus were there no conflicting state procedure, Rule 4(d)(1) would clearly control. National Equipment Rental, Ltd. v. Szukhent, * * * [p. 140, supra]. However, respondent, focusing on the contrary Massachusetts rule, calls to the Court's attention another line of cases, a line which—like the Enabling Act—had its birth in 1938. Erie R. Co. v. Tompkins, * * * overruling Swift v. Tyson, * * * held that federal courts sitting in diversity cases, when deciding questions of "substantive" law, are bound by state court decisions as well as state statutes. The broad command of *Erie* was therefore identical to that of the Enabling Act: federal courts are to apply state substantive law and federal procedural law. However, as subsequent cases sharpened the distinction between substance and procedure, the line of cases following *Erie* diverged markedly from the line construing the Enabling Act. * * *

Respondent, by placing primary reliance on *York* * * *, suggests that the *Erie* doctrine acts as a check on the Federal Rules of Civil Procedure, that despite the clear command of Rule 4(d)(1), *Erie* and its progeny demand the application of the Massachusetts rule. Reduced to essentials, the argument is: (1) *Erie*, as refined in *York*, demands that federal courts apply state law whenever application of federal law in its stead will alter the outcome of the case. (2) In this case, a determination that the Massachusetts service requirements obtain will result in immediate victory for respondent. If, on the other hand, it should be held that Rule 4(d)(1) is applicable, the litigation will continue, with possible victory for petitioner. (3) Therefore, *Erie* demands application of the Massachusetts rule. The syllogism possesses an appealing simplicity, but is for several reasons invalid.

In the first place, it is doubtful that, even if there were no Federal Rule making it clear that in hand service is not required in diversity actions, the *Erie* rule would have obligated the District Court to follow the

Massachusetts procedure. "Outcome determination" analysis was never intended to serve as a talisman. Byrd v. Blue Ridge Rural Elec. Cooperative * * *. Indeed, the message of *York* itself is that choices between state and federal law are to be made not by application of any automatic, "litmus paper" criterion, but rather by reference to the policies underlying the *Erie* rule. Guaranty Trust Co. of New York v. York * * *.

The *Erie* rule is rooted in part in a realization that it would be unfair for the character or result of a litigation materially to differ because the suit had been brought in a federal court. * * * [N]onsubstantial, or trivial, variations [are] not likely to raise the sort of equal protection problems which troubled the Court in *Erie*; they are also unlikely to influence the choice of a forum. [The concern that application of a federal rule in place of a state rule will have outcome-determinative effect on the resolution of the dispute]* * * cannot be read without reference to the twin aims of the *Erie* rule: discouragement of forum-shopping and avoidance of inequitable administration of the laws. * * *

The difference between the conclusion that the Massachusetts rule is applicable, and the conclusion that it is not, is of course at this point "outcome-determinative" in the sense that if we hold the state rule to apply, respondent prevails, whereas if we hold that Rule 4(d)(1) governs, the litigation will continue. But in this sense *every* procedural variation is "outcome-determinative." For example, having brought suit in a federal court, a plaintiff cannot then insist on the right to file subsequent pleadings in accord with the time limits applicable in state courts, even though enforcement of the federal timetable will, if he continues to insist that he must meet only the state time limit, result in determination of the controversy against him. So it is here. Though choice of the federal or state rule will at this point have a marked effect upon the outcome of the litigation, the difference between the two rules would be of scant, if any, relevance to the choice of a forum. Petitioner, in choosing her forum, was not presented with a situation where application of the state rule would wholly bar recovery; rather, adherence to the state rule would have resulted only in altering the way in which process was served. * * * Moreover, it is difficult to argue that permitting service of defendant's wife to take the place of in hand service of defendant himself alters the mode of enforcement of state-created rights in a fashion sufficiently "substantial" to raise the sort of equal protection problems to which the *Erie* opinion alluded.

There is, however, a more fundamental flaw in respondent's syllogism: the incorrect assumption that the rule of Erie R. Co. v. Tompkins constitutes the appropriate test of the validity and therefore the applicability of a Federal Rule of Civil Procedure. The *Erie* rule has never been invoked to void a Federal Rule. It is true that there have been cases where this Court has held applicable a state rule in the face of an argument that the situation was governed by one of the Federal Rules. But the holding of each such case was not that *Erie* commanded displacement of a Federal Rule by an inconsistent state rule, but rather that the scope of the Federal

Rule was not as broad as the losing party urged, and therefore, there being no Federal Rule which covered the point in dispute, *Erie* commanded the enforcement of state law. * * * (Here, of course, the clash is unavoidable; Rule 4(d)(1) says—implicitly, but with unmistakable clarity—that in hand service is not required in federal courts.) At the same time, in cases adjudicating the validity of Federal Rules, we have not applied the *York* rule or other refinements of *Erie*, but have to this day continued to decide questions concerning the scope of the Enabling Act and the constitutionality of specific Federal Rules in light of the distinction set forth in *Sibbach*. * * *

Nor has the development of two separate lines of cases been inadvertent. The line between "substance" and "procedure" shifts as the legal context changes. * * * It is true that both the Enabling Act and the *Erie* rule say, roughly, that federal courts are to apply state "substantive" law and federal "procedural" law, but from that it need not follow that the tests are identical. For they were designed to control very different sorts of decisions. When a situation is covered by one of the Federal Rules, the question facing the court is a far cry from the typical, relatively unguided *Erie* choice: the court has been instructed to apply the Federal Rule, and can refuse to do so only if the Advisory Committee, this Court, and Congress erred in their prima facie judgment that the Rule in question transgresses neither the terms of the Enabling Act nor constitutional restrictions.

We are reminded by the *Erie* opinion that neither Congress nor the federal courts can, under the guise of formulating rules of decision for federal courts, fashion rules which are not supported by a grant of federal authority contained in Article I or some other section of the Constitution; in such areas state law must govern because there can be no other law. But the opinion in *Erie*, which involved no Federal Rule and dealt with a question which was "substantive" in every traditional sense * * *, surely neither said nor implied that measures like Rule 4(d)(1) are unconstitutional. For the constitutional provision for a federal court system (augmented by the Necessary and Proper Clause) carries with it congressional power to make rules governing the practice and pleading in those courts, which in turn includes a power to regulate matters which, though falling within the uncertain area between substance and procedure, are rationally capable of classification as either. * * *

Erie and its offspring cast no doubt on the long-recognized power of Congress to prescribe housekeeping rules for federal courts even though some of those rules will inevitably differ from comparable state rules. * * * Thus, though a court, in measuring a Federal Rule against the standards contained in the Enabling Act and the Constitution, need not wholly blind itself to the degree to which the Rule makes the character and result of the federal litigation stray from the course it would follow in state courts, * * * it cannot be forgotten that the *Erie* rule, and the guidelines suggested in *York*, were created to serve another purpose altogether. To hold that a Federal Rule of Civil Procedure must cease to function whenever it alters the mode of enforcing state-created rights would be to disembowel either the Constitution's grant of power over federal procedure or Congress' attempt to exercise that power in the Enabling Act. Rule 4(d)(1) is valid and controls the instant case.

Reversed.

MR. JUSTICE BLACK concurs in the result.

MR. JUSTICE HARLAN, concurring.

* * *

Erie was something more than an opinion which worried about "forum-shopping and avoidance of inequitable administration of the laws," * * * although to be sure these were important elements of the decision. I have always regarded that decision as one of the modern cornerstones of our federalism, expressing policies that profoundly touch the allocation of judicial power between the state and federal systems. *Erie* recognized that there should not be two conflicting systems of law controlling the primary activity of citizens, for such alternative governing authority must necessarily give rise to a debilitating uncertainty in the planning of everyday affairs. And it recognized that the scheme of our Constitution envisions an allocation of law-making functions between state and federal legislative processes which is undercut if the federal judiciary can make substantive law affecting state affairs beyond the bounds of congressional legislative powers in this regard. * * *

* * *

* * * To my mind the proper line of approach in determining whether to apply a state or a federal rule, whether "substantive" or "procedural," is to stay close to basic principles by inquiring if the choice of rule would substantially affect those primary decisions respecting human conduct which our constitutional system leaves to state regulation. If so, *Erie* and the Constitution require that the state rule prevail, even in the face of a conflicting federal rule.

The Court weakens, if indeed it does not submerge, this basic principle by finding, in effect, a grant of substantive legislative power in the constitutional provision for a federal court system * * *, and through it, setting up the Federal Rules as a body of law inviolate. * * * So long as a reasonable man could characterize any duly adopted federal rule as "procedural," the Court, unless I misapprehend what is said, would have it apply no matter how seriously it frustrated a State's substantive regulation of the primary conduct and affairs of its citizens. Since the members of the Advisory Committee, the Judicial Conference, and this Court who formulated the Federal Rules are presumably reasonable men, it follows that the integrity of the Federal Rules is absolute. Whereas the unadulterated outcome and forum-shopping tests may err too far toward honoring state rules, I submit that the Court's "arguably procedural, *ergo* constitutional" test moves too fast and far in the other direction.

* * *

It remains to apply what has been said to the present case. * * * The evident intent of [the Massachusetts] statute is to permit an executor to distribute the estate which he is administering without fear that further liabilities may be outstanding for which he could be held personally liable. If the Federal District Court in Massachusetts applies Rule 4(d)(1) of the Federal Rules of Civil Procedure instead of the Massachusetts service rule, what effect would that have on the speed and assurance with which estates are distributed? As I see it, the effect would not be substantial. It would mean simply that an executor would have to check at his own house or the federal courthouse as well as the registry of probate before he could distribute the estate with impunity. As this does not seem enough to give rise to any real impingement on the vitality of the state policy which the Massachusetts rule is intended to serve, I concur in the judgment of the Court.

NOTES AND QUESTIONS

1. In SIBBACH v. WILSON & CO., 312 U.S. 1, 61 S.Ct. 422, 85 L.Ed. 479 (1941), plaintiff sued defendant in an Illinois federal district court for damages inflicted in Indiana. The Supreme Court affirmed the District Court's order that plaintiff undergo a physical examination pursuant to Federal Rule 35, despite an Illinois policy forbidding compulsory physical examinations. The Court concluded that the promulgation of Rule 35 was within the ambit of congressional power, since Rule 35 does not "abridge, enlarge, [or] modify substantive rights, in the guise of regulating procedure." Moreover, the Court rejected plaintiff's argument that a rule regulating procedure still could so affect a substantial personal right as to violate the Rules Enabling Act. In an opinion written by Justice Roberts, the Court held:

> * * * If we were to adopt the suggested criterion of the importance of the alleged right we should invite endless litigation and confusion * * *. The test must be whether a rule really regulates procedure—the judicial process for enforcing rights and duties recognized by substantive law and for justly administering remedy and redress for disregard or infraction of them. That the rules in question are such is admitted.

Id. at 14, 61 S.Ct. at 426, 85 L.Ed. at 485. Justice Frankfurter dissented. He argued that Rule 35, providing for "the invasion of the person," differs significantly from devices that affect only commercial matters. Moreover, because the Federal Rules become automatically effective absent a veto by Congress, he thought it inappropriate to draw any inference of propriety from congressional "non-action." To the contrary, "to make the drastic change that Rule 35 sought to introduce would require explicit legislation." Id. at 18, 61 S.Ct. at 428, 85 L.Ed. at 487.

2. Since *Hanna*, commentators have been attempting to define precisely the test to be used to answer *Erie* questions. Consider the following:

* * * [T]he indiscriminate mixture of all questions respecting choices between federal and state law in diversity cases, under the single rubric of "the Erie doctrine" or "the Erie problem," has served to make a major mystery out of what are really three distinct and rather ordinary problems of statutory and constitutional interpretation. Of course there will be occasions with respect to all three on which reasonable persons will differ, but that does not make the problems mysterious or even very unusual. The United States Constitution, I shall argue, constitutes the relevant text only where Congress has passed a statute creating law for diversity actions, and it is in this situation alone that *Hanna*'s "arguably procedural" test controls. Where a nonstatutory rule is involved, the Constitution necessarily remains in the background, but it is functionally irrelevant because the applicable statutes are significantly more protective of the prerogatives of state law. Thus, where there is no relevant Federal Rule of Civil Procedure or other Rule promulgated pursuant to the Enabling Act and the federal rule in issue is therefore wholly judge-made, whether state or federal law should be applied is controlled by the Rules of Decision Act, the statute construed in *Erie* and *York*. Where the matter in issue is covered by a Federal Rule, however, the Enabling Act— and not the Rules of Decision Act itself or the line of cases construing it— constitutes the relevant standard. To say that, however, and that is one of the things *Hanna* said, is by no means to concede the validity of all Federal Rules, for the Enabling Act contains significant limiting language of its own. The Court has correctly sensed that that language cannot be construed to protect state prerogatives as strenuously as the Rules of Decision Act protects them in the absence of a Federal Rule. However, the Court's recent appreciation that the Enabling Act constitutes the only check on the Rules—that "Erie" does not stand there as a backstop— should lead it in an appropriate case to take the Act's limiting language more seriously than it has in the past.

Ely, *The Irrepressible Myth of* Erie, 87 Harv. L. Rev. 693, 697–98 (1974).

Compare Professor Ely's analysis with the following:

If a valid and pertinent federal rule exists, then of course it applies, notwithstanding any state rule to the contrary. The supremacy clause says so. The real task under *Erie,* therefore, is not to choose between federal law and state law, but rather to decide if there really is a valid federal rule on the issue. * * * [T]he Rules of Decision Act is an explicit grant of authority: It directs the federal courts to apply state law with regard to any issue that is not governed by a pertinent and valid federal rule. It reminds the federal courts that if a valid federal rule exists— whether constitutional, statutory, or judge-made—the federal rule shall govern. * * *

To understand how *Erie* operates in diversity cases, it is important to distinguish between the *pertinence* of federal rules and their *validity*. To say a federal rule is "pertinent" means that it was intended or designed to govern the issue at hand—that the rule's purposes would be served by applying it. To say a rule is "valid" means that it has been adopted in conformity with the legal norms controlling the creation of federal law—

that it is consistent with the Constitution and other organic statutes regulating the formation of federal law. These combined qualities of pertinence and validity are necessary and sufficient for the proper application of a federal rule: If either quality is absent, a federal rule cannot be lawfully applied; if both are present, the federal rule must be applied.

* * *

Federal rules of civil procedure should be analyzed in the same way as federal statutes, except the rules must satisfy an additional standard of validity. The pertinence analysis is precisely the same for rules as it is for other laws. The court must determine whether the framers of a rule intended that it govern the issue at hand; if so (and if the rule is valid), the rule applies; if not, state law applies.

Westen & Lehman, *Is There Life for* Erie *After the Death of Diversity?,* 78 Mich. L. Rev. 311, 314–15, 342, 359 (1980).

GASPERINI v. CENTER FOR HUMANITIES, INC.

Supreme Court of the United States, 1996.
518 U.S. 415, 116 S.Ct. 2211, 135 L.Ed.2d 659.

Certiorari to the United States Court of Appeals for the Second Circuit.

Justice Ginsburg delivered the opinion of the Court.

Under the law of New York, appellate courts are empowered to review the size of jury verdicts and to order new trials when the jury's award "deviates materially from what would be reasonable compensation." N. Y. Civ. Prac. Law and Rules (CPLR) § 5501(c) * * *. Under the Seventh Amendment, which governs proceedings in federal court, but not in state court, "the right of trial by jury shall be preserved, and no fact tried by a jury, shall be otherwise re-examined in any Court of the United States, than according to the rules of the common law." The compatibility of these provisions, in an action based on New York law but tried in federal court by reason of the parties' diverse citizenship, is the issue we confront in this case. * * *

We hold that New York's law controlling compensation awards for excessiveness or inadequacy can be given effect, without detriment to the Seventh Amendment, if the review standard set out in CPLR § 5501(c) is applied by the federal trial court judge, with appellate control of the trial court's ruling limited to review for "abuse of discretion."

I

Petitioner William Gasperini, a journalist for CBS News and the Christian Science Monitor, began reporting on events in Central America in 1984. * * * During the course of his seven-year stint in Central America, Gasperini took over 5,000 slide transparencies, depicting active war zones, political leaders, and scenes from daily life. In 1990, Gasperini agreed to supply his original color transparencies to The Center for Humanities, Inc. (Center) for use in an educational videotape, Conflict in Central America. Gasperini selected 300 of his slides for the Center; its videotape included 110 of them. The Center agreed to return the original transparencies, but upon the completion of the project, it could not find them.

Gasperini commenced suit in the United States District Court for the Southern District of New York, invoking the court's diversity jurisdiction * * *. The Center conceded liability for the lost transparencies and the issue of damages was tried before a jury.

At trial, Gasperini's expert witness testified that the "industry standard" within the photographic publishing community valued a lost transparency at $1,500. * * *

After a three-day trial, the jury awarded Gasperini $450,000 in compensatory damages. This sum, the jury foreperson announced, "is [$]1500 each, for 300 slides." Moving for a new trial under Federal Rule of Civil Procedure 59, the Center attacked the verdict on various grounds, including excessiveness. Without comment, the District Court denied the motion. * * *

The Court of Appeals for the Second Circuit vacated the judgment entered on the jury's verdict. * * * Mindful that New York law governed the controversy, the Court of Appeals endeavored to apply CPLR § 5501(c), which instructs that, when a jury returns an itemized verdict, as the jury did in this case, the New York Appellate Division "shall determine that an award is excessive or inadequate if it deviates materially from what would be reasonable compensation." * * * Surveying Appellate Division decisions that reviewed damage awards for lost transparencies, the Second Circuit concluded that testimony on industry standard alone was insufficient to justify a verdict; prime among other factors warranting consideration were the uniqueness of the slides' subject matter and the photographer's earning level.

Guided by Appellate Division rulings, the Second Circuit held that the $450,000 verdict "materially deviates from what is reasonable compensation." * * * [T]he Second Circuit set aside the $450,000 verdict and ordered a new trial, unless Gasperini agreed to an award of $100,000.

This case presents an important question regarding the standard a federal court uses to measure the alleged excessiveness of a jury's verdict in an action for damages based on state law. We therefore granted certiorari. * * *

II

Before 1986, state and federal courts in New York generally invoked the same judge-made formulation in responding to excessiveness attacks on jury verdicts: courts would not disturb an award unless the amount was so exorbitant that it "shocked the conscience of the court." * * *

In both state and federal courts, trial judges made the excessiveness assessment in the first instance, and appellate judges ordinarily deferred to the trial court's judgment. * * *

In 1986, as part of a series of tort reform measures, New York codified a standard for judicial review of the size of jury awards. Placed in CPLR § 5501(c), the prescription reads:

> "In reviewing a money judgment . . . in which it is contended that the award is excessive or inadequate and that a new trial should have been granted unless a stipulation is entered to a different award, the appellate division shall determine that an award is excessive or inadequate if it deviates materially from what would be reasonable compensation." * * *

* * * New York state-court opinions confirm that § 5501(c)'s "deviates materially" standard calls for closer surveillance than "shock the conscience" oversight. * * *

Although phrased as a direction to New York's intermediate appellate courts, § 5501(c)'s "deviates materially" standard, as construed by New York's courts, instructs state trial judges as well. * * * Application of § 5501(c) at the trial level is key to this case.

To determine whether an award "deviates materially from what would be reasonable compensation," New York state courts look to awards approved in similar cases. * * *

III

In cases like Gasperini's, in which New York law governs the claims for relief, does New York law also supply the test for federal-court review of the size of the verdict? The Center answers yes. The "deviates materially" standard, it argues, is a substantive standard that must be applied by federal appellate courts in diversity cases. The Second Circuit agreed. * * * Gasperini, emphasizing that § 5501(c) trains on the New York Appellate Division, characterizes the provision as procedural, an allocation of decisionmaking authority regarding damages, not a hard cap on the amount recoverable. Correctly comprehended, Gasperini urges, § 5501(c)'s direction to the Appellate Division cannot be given effect by federal appellate courts without violating the Seventh Amendment's Reexamination Clause.

As the parties' arguments suggest, CPLR § 5501(c), appraised under *Erie R. Co. v. Tompkins* * * * and decisions in *Erie*'s path, is both "substantive" and "procedural": "substantive" in that § 5501(c)'s "deviates materially" standard controls how much a plaintiff can be awarded; "procedural" in that § 5501(c) assigns decisionmaking authority to New York's Appellate Division. Parallel application of § 5501(c) at the federal appellate level would be out of sync with the federal system's division of trial and appellate court functions, an allocation weighted by the Seventh Amendment. The dispositive question, therefore, is whether federal courts can give effect to the substantive thrust of § 5501(c) without untoward alteration of the federal scheme for the trial and decision of civil cases.

A

* * *

Classification of a law as "substantive" or "procedural" for *Erie* purposes is sometimes a challenging endeavor.[7] *Guaranty Trust Co. v. York,* [p. 239, supra,] * * * an early interpretation of *Erie*, propounded an "outcome-determination" test: "[D]oes it significantly affect the result of a litigation for a federal court to disregard a law of a State that would be controlling in an action upon the same claim by the same parties in a State court?" * * * A later pathmarking case, qualifying *Guaranty Trust*, explained that the "outcome-determination" test must not be applied mechanically to sweep in all manner of variations; instead, its application must be guided by "the twin aims of the *Erie* rule: discouragement of forum shopping and avoidance of inequitable administration of the laws." *Hanna v. Plumer* * * *.

Informed by these decisions, we address the question whether New York's "deviates materially" standard, codified in CPLR § 5501(c), is outcome affective in this sense: Would "application of the [standard] ... have so important an effect upon the fortunes of one or both of the litigants that failure to [apply] it would [unfairly discriminate against citizens of the forum State, or] be likely to cause a plaintiff to choose the federal court"? Id. * * *

* * *

It * * * appears that if federal courts ignore the change in the New York standard and persist in applying the "shock the conscience" test to damage awards on claims governed by New York law, " 'substantial' variations between state and federal [money judgments]" may be expected. * * * We therefore agree with the Second Circuit that New York's check on excessive damages implicates what we have called "twin aims." * * * Just as the *Erie* principle precludes a federal court from giving a state-created claim "longer life ... than [the claim] would have had in the state court," * * * so *Erie* precludes a recovery in federal court significantly larger than the recovery that would have been tolerated in state court.

B

CPLR § 5501(c) * * * is phrased as a direction to the New York Appellate Division. Acting essentially as a surrogate for a New York appellate forum, the Court of Appeals reviewed Gasperini's award to

---

7. Concerning matters covered by the Federal Rules of Civil Procedure, the characterization question is usually unproblematic: It is settled that if the Rule in point is consonant with the Rules Enabling Act, 28 U.S.C. § 2072, and the Constitution, the Federal Rule applies regardless of contrary state law. * * * Federal courts have interpreted the Federal Rules, however, with sensitivity to important state interests and regulatory policies. * * *

determine if it "deviate[d] materially" from damage awards the Appellate Division permitted in similar circumstances. The Court of Appeals performed this task without benefit of an opinion from the District Court, which had denied "without comment" the Center's Rule 59 motion. Concentrating on the authority § 5501(c) gives to the Appellate Division, Gasperini urges that the provision shifts fact finding responsibility from the jury and the trial judge to the appellate court. Assigning such responsibility to an appellate court, he maintains, is incompatible with the Seventh Amendment's Reexamination Clause, and therefore, Gasperini concludes, § 5501(c) cannot be given effect in federal court. Although we reach a different conclusion than Gasperini, we agree that the Second Circuit did not attend to "an essential characteristic of [the federal-court] system," * * * when it used § 5501(c) as "the standard for [federal] appellate review." * * *

* * *

The Seventh Amendment, which governs proceedings in federal court, but not in state court, bears not only on the allocation of trial functions between judge and jury, the issue in *Byrd*; it also controls the allocation of authority to review verdicts, the issue of concern here. * * *

Byrd [p. 244, supra,] involved the first Clause of the Amendment, the "trial by jury" Clause. This case involves the second, the "Reexamination" Clause. In keeping with the historic understanding, the Reexamination Clause does not inhibit the authority of trial judges to grant new trials "for any of the reasons for which new trials have heretofore been granted in actions at law in the courts of the United States." That authority is large. * * * This discretion includes overturning verdicts for excessiveness and ordering a new trial without qualification, or conditioned on the verdict winner's refusal to agree to a reduction (remittitur). * * *

In contrast, appellate review of a federal trial court's denial of a motion to set aside a jury's verdict as excessive is a relatively late, and less secure, development. * * *

* * *

* * * We now * * * make explicit what [was] * * * implicit in our [earlier decisions] * * *: "[N]othing in the Seventh Amendment ... precludes appellate review of the trial judge's denial of a motion to set aside [a jury verdict] as excessive." * * *

C

In *Byrd*, the Court faced a one-or-the-other choice: trial by judge as in state court, or trial by jury according to the federal practice. In the case before us, a choice of that order is not required, for the principal state and federal interests can be accommodated. The Second Circuit correctly recognized that when New York substantive law governs a claim for relief, New York law and decisions guide the allowable damages. * * *

New York's dominant interest can be respected, without disrupting the federal system, once it is recognized that the federal district court is capable of * * * apply[ing] the State's "deviates materially" standard in line with New York case law evolving under CPLR § 5501(c).[22] * * *

Within the federal system, practical reasons combine with Seventh Amendment constraints to lodge in the district court, not the court of appeals, primary responsibility for application of § 5501(c)'s "deviates materially" check. Trial judges have the "unique opportunity to consider the evidence in the living courtroom context," * * * while appellate judges see only the "cold paper record."

District court applications of the "deviates materially" standard would be subject to appellate review under the standard the Circuits now employ when inadequacy or excessiveness is asserted on appeal: abuse of discretion. * * * In light of *Erie*'s doctrine, the federal appeals court must be guided by the damage-control standard state law supplies, but as the Second Circuit itself has said: "If we reverse, it must be because of an abuse of discretion.... The very nature of the problem counsels restraint.... We must give the benefit of every doubt to the judgment of the trial judge."

IV

It does not appear that the District Court checked the jury's verdict against the relevant New York decisions demanding more than "industry standard" testimony to support an award of the size the jury returned in this case. As the Court of Appeals recognized, * * * the uniqueness of the photographs and the plaintiff's earnings as photographer—past and reasonably projected—are factors relevant to appraisal of the award. * * * Accordingly, we vacate the judgment of the Court of Appeals and instruct that court to remand the case to the District Court so that the trial judge, revisiting his ruling on the new trial motion, may test the jury's verdict against CPLR § 5501(c)'s "deviates materially" standard.

It is so ordered.

[The dissenting opinion of JUSTICE STEVENS is omitted.]

JUSTICE SCALIA, with whom the CHIEF JUSTICE and JUSTICE THOMAS join, dissenting.

I

Today the Court overrules a longstanding and well-reasoned line of precedent that has for years prohibited federal appellate courts from

---

22. Justice SCALIA finds in Federal Rule of Civil Procedure 59 a "federal standard" for new trial motions in " 'direct collision' " with, and " 'leaving no room for the operation of,' " a state law like CPLR § 5501(c). * * * The relevant prescription, Rule 59(a), has remained unchanged since the adoption of the Federal Rules by this Court in 1937. Rule 59(a) is as encompassing as it is uncontroversial. It is indeed "Hornbook" law that a most usual ground for a Rule 59 motion is that "the damages are excessive." See C. Wright, Law of Federal Courts 676–677 (5th ed. 1994). Whether damages are excessive for the claim-in-suit must be governed by some law. And there is no candidate for that governance other than the law that gives rise to the claim for relief—here, the law of New York. * * *

reviewing refusals by district courts to set aside civil jury awards as contrary to the weight of the evidence. * * *

The Court also holds today that a state practice that relates to the division of duties between state judges and juries must be followed by federal courts in diversity cases. On this issue, too, our prior cases are directly to the contrary.

* * *

II

The Court's holding that federal courts of appeals may review district court denials of motions for new trials for error of fact is not the only novel aspect of today's decision. The Court also directs that the case be remanded to the District Court, so that it may "test the jury's verdict against CPLR § 5501(c)'s 'deviates materially' standard." * * * This disposition contradicts the principle that "the proper role of the trial and appellate courts in the federal system in reviewing the size of jury verdicts is . . . a matter of federal law." * * *

* * * The Court approves the "accommodat[ion]" [in original] achieved by having district courts review jury verdicts under the "deviates materially" standard, because it regards that as a means of giving effect to the State's purposes "without disrupting the federal system." * * * But changing the standard by which trial judges review jury verdicts *does* disrupt the federal system, and is plainly inconsistent with the "strong federal policy against allowing state rules to disrupt the judge-jury relationship in the federal court." * * *

* * *

* * * It seems to me quite wrong to regard [Section 5501(c)] as a "substantive" rule for *Erie* purposes. The "analog[y]" to "a statutory cap on damages" * * * fails utterly. There is an absolutely fundamental distinction between a *rule of law* such as that, which would ordinarily be imposed upon the jury in the trial court's instructions, and a *rule of review*, which simply determines how closely the jury verdict will be scrutinized for compliance with the instructions. A tighter standard for reviewing jury determinations can no more plausibly be called a "substantive" disposition than can a tighter appellate standard for reviewing trial-court determinations. The one, like the other, provides additional assurance *that the law has been complied with*; but the other, like the one, *leaves the law unchanged*.

The Court commits the classic *Erie* mistake of regarding whatever changes the outcome as substantive * * *. * * * Outcome-determination "was never intended to serve as a talisman," and * * * does not have the power to convert the most classic elements of the process of assuring that the law is observed into the substantive law itself. The right to have a jury make the findings of fact, for example, is generally thought to favor plaintiffs, and that advantage is often thought significant enough to be the basis for forum selection. But no one would argue that *Erie* confers a right to a jury in federal court wherever state courts would provide it; or that, were it not for the Seventh Amendment, *Erie* would require federal courts to dispense with the jury whenever state courts do so.

In any event, the Court exaggerates the difference that the state standard will make. It concludes that different outcomes are likely to ensue depending on whether the law being applied is the state "deviates materially" standard of § 5501(c) or the "shocks the conscience" standard. * * * Of course, it is not the federal *appellate* standard but the federal *district-court* standard for granting new trials that must be compared with the New York standard to determine whether substantially different results will obtain—and it is far from clear that the district-court standard *ought* to be "shocks the conscience." * * * What seems to me far more likely to produce forum shopping is the consistent difference between the state and federal *appellate* standards, which the Court leaves untouched. * * * The only result that would produce the conformity the Court erroneously believes *Erie* requires is the one adopted by the Second Circuit and rejected by the Court: *de novo* federal appellate review under the § 5501(c) standard.

To say that application of § 5501(c) in place of the federal standard will not consistently produce disparate results is not to suggest that the decision the Court has made today is not a momentous one. The *principle* that the state standard governs is of great importance, since it bears the potential to destroy the uniformity of federal practice and the integrity of the federal court system. Under the Court's view, a state rule that directed courts "to determine that an award is excessive or inadequate if it deviates *in any degree* from *the proper measure of compensation*" would have to be applied in federal courts, effectively requiring federal judges to determine the amount of damages de novo, and effectively taking the matter away from the jury entirely. * * * Or consider a state rule that allowed the defendant a second trial on damages, with judgment ultimately in the amount of the lesser of two jury awards. * * * Under the reasoning of the Court's opinion, even such a rule as that would have to be applied in the federal courts.

The foregoing describes why I think the Court's *Erie* analysis is flawed. But in my view, one does not even reach the *Erie* question in this case. The standard to be applied by a district court in ruling on a motion for a new trial is set forth in Rule 59 of the Federal Rules of Civil Procedure, which provides that "[a] new trial may be granted . . . for any of the reasons for which new trials have heretofore been granted in actions at law *in the courts of the United States*" (emphasis added). [The language of Rule 59(a) was altered nonsubstantively in 2007.] That is undeniably a federal standard. * * * Federal district courts in the Second Circuit have interpreted that standard to permit the granting of new trials where " 'it is quite clear that the jury has reached a seriously erroneous result' " and letting the verdict stand would result in a " 'miscarriage of justice.' " * * * Assuming (as we have no reason to question) that this is a correct interpretation of what Rule 59 requires, it is undeniable that the Federal Rule is " 'sufficiently broad' to cause a 'direct collision' with the state law or, implicitly, to 'control the issue' before the court, thereby leaving no room for the operation of that law." * * * It is simply not possible to give controlling effect both to the federal standard and the state standard in reviewing the jury's award. That being so, the court has no choice but to apply the Federal Rule, which is an exercise of what we have called Congress's "power to regulate matters which, though falling within the uncertain area between substance and procedure, are rationally capable of classification as either * * *."

* * * I respectfully dissent.

NOTES AND QUESTIONS

1.   The first part of the Court's decision in *Gasperini* revived a *York*-style approach to determining the applicable law. Although *York* had not been overruled, its influence had waned after *Byrd* and *Hanna*, and the Court surprised many observers by using an outcome-determinative approach in *Gasperini*. What role do the "twin aims" of *Erie* continue to play in determining the applicable law?

2.   *Gasperini* did not discuss *Byrd* until it already had determined the applicable law. Why not? Like *Byrd*, *Gasperini* involves the division of trial functions between judge and jury. Does *Gasperini* provide a new approach that replaces *Byrd,* or can the two decisions be reconciled? See Freer, *Some Thoughts on the State of* Erie *After* Gasperini, 76 Texas L. Rev. 1637 (1998).

SECTION B.   THE PROBLEM OF ASCERTAINING STATE LAW

1.   DETERMINING WHICH STATE'S LAW GOVERNS

In *Erie,* the parties and the courts appear to have assumed that if state law applied, Pennsylvania tort law would govern, even though the action was being tried in a federal court in New York. Why did they make this assumption? Was the federal court free to choose the most appropriate state law to govern the dispute? Or was it that New York's choice-of-law rules pointed to an application of Pennsylvania law?

In KLAXON CO. v. STENTOR ELECTRIC MFG. CO., 313 U.S. 487, 61 S.Ct. 1020, 85 L.Ed. 1477 (1941), the Supreme Court held that in order to promote the desired uniform application of substantive law within a state, a federal court must apply the choice-of-law rules of the state in which it sits. The Court explained:

> * * * Whatever lack of uniformity this may produce between federal courts in different states is attributable to our federal system, which leaves to a state, within the limits permitted by the Constitution, the

right to pursue local policies diverging from those of its neighbors. It is not for the federal courts to thwart such local policies by enforcing an independent "general law" of conflict of laws. * * * [T]he proper function of [a] federal court is to ascertain what the state law is, not what it ought to be.

Id. at 496–97, 61 S.Ct. at 1022, 85 L.Ed. at 1480–81.

NOTES AND QUESTIONS

1. The Supreme Court reaffirmed the *Klaxon* rule in Day & Zimmermann, Inc. v. Challoner, 423 U.S. 3, 96 S.Ct. 167, 46 L.Ed.2d 3 (1975). Plaintiff filed a diversity action in Texas federal court seeking damages for death and personal injury resulting from the premature explosion of a 105 mm. howitzer round in Cambodia. The Court of Appeals declined to apply Texas choice-of-law rules, which it believed required application of the law of Cambodia. The Supreme Court vacated and remanded the judgment, emphasizing that "the conflict-of-law rules to be applied by a federal court in Texas must conform to those prevailing in the Texas state court" and that a diversity court "is not free to engraft onto those state rules exceptions or modifications which * * * have not commended themselves to the State in which the federal court sits." Id. at 5, 96 S.Ct. at 168, 46 L.Ed.2d at 5.

2. Could Congress enact a statute specifying choice-of-law rules for federal courts in diversity cases? In answering this question, remember that, although it is true today that every state contains at least one federal judicial district, there is no constitutional provision that compels this. What if Congress had established only regional courts? Under such a scheme, would Congress or the courts have been forced to establish their own choice-of-law rules?

3. The states have been allowed great leeway in establishing choice-of-law rules. In ALLSTATE INSURANCE CO. v. HAGUE, Note 4, p. 60, supra, the Supreme Court held that a state could apply its substantive law in a case, so long as the state had significant contacts or a significant aggregation of contacts with the parties and the transaction. Doesn't *Hague* encourage plaintiffs to forum shop and *Klaxon* seal defendant's fate?

4. If a diversity case is transferred under 28 U.S.C. § 1404(a), what law should the transferee court apply? Does it matter whether the plaintiff or the defendant moved to transfer? In VAN DUSEN v. BARRACK, Note 4, p. 219, supra, defendants sought to transfer the action from federal court in Pennsylvania to federal court in Massachusetts, where the state law was more favorable to their case. The Supreme Court rejected a wooden reading of *Erie*, which would require the transferee court to apply the law of the state in which it sits—that is, Massachusetts law. Rather, the Court determined that the "critical identity" is between the federal court that decides the case and the courts of the state in which the action was filed. According to the Court: "A change of venue under § 1404(a) generally should be, with respect to state law, but a change of courtrooms." It appears that *Van Dusen* makes it possible for a suit to be filed in federal court in one state and then transferred to a different state with the result that the law applied will differ from the law that would have applied if the suit had been filed initially in the transferee

court. See Maloy, *Forum Shopping? What's Wrong with That?*, 24 Quinnipiac L. Rev. 25 (2005).

5. How does the Class Action Fairness Act of 2005 ("CAFA") affect choice-of-law considerations? CAFA extends a federal forum to large-stakes class actions on a theory of minimal diversity, see p. 169, supra. Professor Woolley has argued that CAFA does not authorize federal courts to adopt their own choice-of-law rules; to the contrary, "federal courts remain rigidly bound by state choice-of-law rules in diversity actions." Woolley, Erie *and Choice of Law After the Class Action Fairness Act*, 80 Tul. L. Rev. 1723 (2006). Nevertheless, Professor Nagareda foresees a "coming clash" between CAFA and the *Klaxon* rule. Nagareda, *Aggregation and Its Discontents: Class Settlement Pressure, Class-Wide Arbitration, and CAFA*, 106 Colum. L. Rev. 1872, 1876–78 (2006). He observes that it "would be quite peculiar if the federal courts after CAFA were to refrain from application of a distinctively federal methodology for choice of law." Nagareda, *Bootstrapping in Choice of Law After the Class Action Fairness Act*, 74 UMKC L. Rev. 661, 684 (2006). Professor Sherry goes even further, and insists that "CAFA should be read as overruling *Erie* * * *, at least for the national-market cases that it places within federal court jurisdiction." Sherry, *Overruling* Erie: *Nationwide Class Actions and National Common Law*, 156 U. Pa. L. Rev. 2135, 2136 (2008). But see Burbank, *Aggregation on the Couch: The Strategic Uses of Ambiguity and Hypocrisy*, 106 Colum. L. Rev. 1924, 1943 (2006) ("[T]here is evidence that in enacting CAFA, Congress did not intend to alter the ordering of federal and state lawmaking authority established by *Erie* * * *."). Is the *Klaxon* rule constitutionally compelled? Is it required by the Rules of Decision Act?

2. ASCERTAINING THE STATE LAW

How difficult is it for a diversity court to ascertain the content of state law? Consider the following:

> Identification of state law is easy only in the presence of an on-point statute or law "declared ... by its highest court in a decision." In all other circumstances, federal courts must act as "another court of the State" and choose from a variety of sources, including high court dicta and lower court rulings. The situation is further complicated when these sources are in conflict, or when the vitality of older precedents is questioned by more recent pronouncements, creating uncertainty as to which should be followed. Worse yet, there may be no relevant precedent at all, requiring the federal court to make an "informed prophecy" of how the state high court would rule.

Kaye & Weissman, *Interactive Judicial Federalism: Certified Questions in New York*, 69 Fordham L. Rev. 373, 376–77 (2000) (citations omitted).

NOTES AND QUESTIONS

1. How should a diversity court ascertain the content of state law when the state's highest court has not addressed the question at issue? In McKEN-

NA v. ORTHO PHARMACEUTICAL CORP., 622 F.2d 657 (3d Cir.), certiorari denied 449 U.S. 976, 101 S.Ct. 387, 66 L.Ed.2d 237 (1980), the Court of Appeals, trying to avoid "speculative crystal-ball gazing," posited that the process of ascertaining the content of state law

> requires an examination of all relevant sources of that state's law in order to isolate those factors that would inform its decision. * * * In the absence of authority directly on point, decisions by that court in analogous cases provide useful indications of the court's probable disposition of a particular question of law. * * * Considered dicta by the state's highest court may also provide a federal court with reliable indicia of how the state tribunal might rule on a particular question.

Id. at 660–62.

2.   Certification provides another method of ascertaining state law. Certification is a procedure that allows the court of one system to petition the court of another for the answer to an unresolved legal question. In 1945, Florida became the first state to adopt such a procedure, which now is available in 45 states, the District of Columbia, and Puerto Rico. In all states that permit certification, the state's highest court accepts questions from the United States Supreme Court and from federal courts of appeal. Thirty-six states also accept questions from federal district courts. See Kaye & Weissman, Note 1, p. 267, supra, at 422–23 & App. A (collecting statutory provisions). In ARIZONANS FOR OFFICIAL ENGLISH v. ARIZONA, 520 U.S. 43, 76, 117 S.Ct. 1055, 1073, 137 L.Ed.2d 170, 199 (1997), involving a challenge to a state law making English the state's official language, the Supreme Court explained the importance of certification in allowing "a federal court faced with a novel state-law question to put the question directly to the State's highest court, reducing the cost, and increasing the assurance of gaining an authoritative response."

3.   In TUNICK v. SAFIR, 228 F.3d 135 (2d Cir. 2000), a photographer challenged the locality's refusal to grant him a permit to conduct a photo shoot of 75 to 100 nude models configured "in an abstract formation" on a residential street in New York City. Tunick claimed that his planned event was exempt from a New York statute that bans public nudity except for "any person entertaining or performing in a play, exhibition, show or entertainment." The Second Circuit petitioned New York's highest court to resolve the scope of the public nudity ban, emphasizing the need for expedition given the important First Amendment rights at stake. 209 F.3d 67 (2d Cir. 2000). But, the New York court declined to answer the certified questions, emphasizing that "even with an expedited schedule for new briefing, argument and deliberation, this Court's necessary decisional process would add some months to the life of this case." 94 N.Y.2d 709, 709 N.Y.S.2d 881, 731 N.E.2d 597 (2000).

4.   Does the difficulty of having to ascertain unsettled state law create new opportunities for forum shopping? Judge Calabresi of the Second Circuit Court of Appeals has warned:

> * * * [F]ederal courts often get state law wrong because federal judges don't know state law and are not the ultimate decisionmakers on it. Inevitably, this leads to considerable forum shopping of just the sort that

Erie sought to avoid. One party or the other tries to get into federal courts because it hopes that the federal courts will get the law wrong. I could give you any number of examples. For instance, the concept of duty in the tort law of New York is virtually unique to New York and is very complicated. As a result, federal judges who deal with the concept of duty in a New York tort case frequently get it wrong. They may be right in thinking that what they hold is what New York law ought to be, but it ain't New York law!

Calabresi, *Federal and State Courts: Restoring a Workable Balance*, 78 N.Y.U. L. Rev. 1293, 1300 (2003). He suggests that a federal appellate court, when faced with uncertain state law, should write an opinion stating what it thinks "that law ought to be," and then certify the question to the state's highest court. The state court would be free to decline the certification, but the federal court could then claim "authority to impose" its view "provisionally, until the highest court of the state decides to resolve the question." Id. at 1302. Does this approach solve the problem of delay?

SECTION C. FEDERAL "COMMON LAW"

Although *Erie* held that "[t]here is no federal general common law," p. 234, supra, the federal courts retain power to create federal common law, typically defined as "federal judge-made law—that is, rules of decision adopted and applied by federal courts that have the force and effect of positive federal law, but whose content cannot be traced by traditional methods of interpretation to federal or constitutional command." Clark, *Federal Common Law: A Structural Interpretation*, 144 U. Pa. L. Rev. 1245, 1247 (1996) (internal citations omitted). Commentators diverge on the source and scope of this power.

————

MELTZER, STATE COURT FORFEITURES OF FEDERAL RIGHTS, 99 Harv. L. Rev. 1128, 1167–71 (1986):

Despite *Erie*'s declaration that "[t]here is no federal general common law," courts have fashioned what Judge Friendly has termed "specialized federal common law" to govern a broad range of areas. Unlike the "spurious" federal common law of the era of Swift v. Tyson, [p. 232, supra,] this new federal common law is binding under the supremacy clause in the state courts.

The proper scope of federal common lawmaking is a matter of considerable uncertainty. If *Erie* held that federal court jurisdiction does not in itself provide the power to fashion common law, then some more specialized source must be found for each example of judicial lawmaking. The lawmaking power of federal courts has been viewed as far more limited than that of Congress, for two reasons extrapolated from the constitutional structure. The first is the idea of separation of powers and the supremacy (in matters not governed by the Constitution) of Congress.

But perhaps more important is the view that federal law is and should be interstitial, operating against a background of existing bodies of state law. Restricted federal common lawmaking reduces the number of agencies broadly fashioning federal rules of decision, and preserves the primary role for Congress, in which the interests of the states are more strongly represented—and in which inertia is more powerful. Hence, state law is presumptively operative, and if it is to be displaced, ordinarily it must be Congress that does so.

But these structural concerns do not indicate whether federal common law should be considered altogether illegitimate or simply restricted in scope. And important countervailing arguments support the existence of some common law power in the federal courts. Numerous cases raise issues implicating important federal interests that are not specifically governed by a statutory or constitutional rule. Congress could have enacted a rule governing the issue, but may not have done so, because it lacked time, foresight, or a political consensus. The Court has, accordingly, recognized that federal common law may be a " 'necessary expedient.' " Nor does Congress's failure to specify a view on a particular subject indicate that Congress preferred that state rules be followed. Here, as elsewhere, congressional inaction is hardly a clear-cut guide for determining congressional intent, and a failure by a court to make law is itself an important and controversial decision.

Thus, legislative inertia and the political safeguards of federalism are ultimately a double-edged sword. They help explain why the authority to make federal common law is nowhere near so broad as congressional authority to legislate, but also argue that federal common lawmaking may be necessary to fill in the interstices of congressional and constitutional mandates or otherwise to deal with matters of important national concern. Despite extensive discussion in the cases and commentary, no clear standard for judging the appropriateness of federal common law has emerged. [Nonetheless, some general points are] * * * accepted by most cases and commentators.

To begin with, there must be a strong need for the formulation of federal common law in order to justify displacing otherwise operative state rules. Moreover, federal common law, perhaps even more than federal law generally, should be interstitial, building upon the total "corpus juris" of the states. Federal common law fits most easily when it supplements federal constitutional or statutory provisions, providing rules of decision that implement or safeguard the norms embodied in such provisions.

Even where federal interests are implicated, it is often possible, and desirable, to rely upon extant state law for the rule of decision. Such reliance eliminates the need for (and possible difficulties in) fashioning a new rule from scratch, and also promotes intrastate uniformity, which may be of great value. Thus, the decision to formulate federal common law is one of judicial policy, in which a court must find that the advantages of borrowing state law are outweighed by either the need for national uniformity or the inconsistency of state law (either of states generally or of the particular state involved) with federal interests.

————

FIELD, SOURCES OF LAW: THE SCOPE OF FEDERAL COMMON LAW, 99 Harv. L. Rev. 881, 883–92 (1986):

* * *

The received academic tradition on federal common law assumes that there are particular enclaves in which federal common law is in fact appropriate, but that after Erie, federal common law power is the exception, not the rule. * * *

* * *

I suggest that judicial power to act is not limited to particular enclaves and that it is much broader than the usual references to judicial power would suggest. As I shall develop, the only limitation on courts' power to create federal common law is that the court must point to a federal enactment, constitutional or statutory, that it interprets as authorizing the federal common law rule. * * *

* * * I will use "federal common law" to refer to any rule of federal law created by a court (usually but not invariably a federal court) when the substance of that rule is not clearly suggested by federal enactments—constitutional or congressional.

————

KRAMER, THE LAWMAKING POWER OF THE FEDERAL COURTS, 12 Pace L. Rev. 263, 267–71 (1992):

* * * [L]awmaking in a democracy is supposed to be done by politically accountable, representative institutions, whereas courts operate on principles other than political accountability. That being so, why let courts make law? Why isn't the whole notion of common law undemocratic and hence improper?

Before proceeding further, let me clarify what I mean by "common law." Following other writers, my definition is a broad one: the common law includes any rule articulated by a court that is not easily found on the face of an applicable statute. This definition is designed to include exercises of judicial creativity and is made deliberately broad to minimize the unavoidable line-drawing problems that arise as interpretation shades imperceptibly into judicial lawmaking.

* * *

With these points in mind, return to the question deferred above: why let courts make common law in a representative democracy? In part, the answer must be that judge-made law is unavoidable. That is, courts must make a certain amount of common law simply because there is no clear line between "making" and "applying" law, between commands that are clear on the face of a statute and those made through an exercise of judgment and creativity. Deciding individual cases thus generates some common law because the process of adjudication necessarily entails articulating rules to elaborate and clarify the meaning and operation of statutory texts.

Nor would we want it otherwise. After all, if one function of independent adjudication is to relieve legislators of having to anticipate and deal with every possible contingency, it hardly makes sense to require courts to return every uncertainty to the legislature. The power to clarify legislation through interstitial lawmaking is thus an implicit but important part of the judicial function.

———

Federal common law has developed in several broad situations and is used to resolve cases involving important federal interests. Some commentators use the term "enclave" to refer to the special contexts in which a federal court will devise federal common law to resolve a dispute. An area in which federal common law typically may be used concerns the financial activities of the United States, involving such matters as the federal government's contract rights, tort liabilities, rights to college loans and proceeds due it, and the management of United States bonds and securities. E.g., Clearfield Trust Co. v. United States, 318 U.S. 363, 63 S.Ct. 573, 87 L.Ed. 838 (1943). When interstate disputes have erupted, federal common law has been adopted where it would be unfair to apply the statutes or decisional law from either state. See, e.g., Hinderlider v. La Plata River & Cherry Creek Ditch Co., 304 U.S. 92, 58 S.Ct. 803, 82 L.Ed. 1202 (1938) (dispute over the apportionment of the water of an interstate stream). Similarly, federal common law has become firmly established in the admiralty and maritime contexts because the desire for a uniform body of substantive law has long been considered of primary importance. See, e.g., Kossick v. United Fruit Co., 365 U.S. 731, 81 S.Ct. 886, 6 L.Ed.2d 56 (1961). Cases implicating the international relations of the United States have provided another occasion for resort to federal common law, including cases involving commercial disputes between United States citizens and foreign parties. See, e.g., Banco Nacional de Cuba v. Sabbatino, 376 U.S. 398, 84 S.Ct. 923, 11 L.Ed.2d 804 (1964). One of the most challenging contexts of federal common law lawmaking involves statutes that express national policy in a particular area but leave one or more of the specifics to be developed by the federal courts. Two questions typically arise in these cases. First, is the particular statutory gap at issue one that the federal courts should fill? If the answer is yes, on what sources should a federal court rely in order to derive the law? The answers to these questions can be crucial in shaping the overall national policy involved in the statute.

BOYLE v. UNITED TECHNOLOGIES CORP.

Supreme Court of the United States, 1988.
487 U.S. 500, 108 S.Ct. 2510, 101 L.Ed.2d 442.

Certiorari to the United States Court of Appeals for the Fourth Circuit.

JUSTICE SCALIA delivered the opinion of the Court.

This case requires us to decide when a contractor providing military equipment to the Federal Government can be held liable under state tort law for injury caused by a design defect.

I

On April 27, 1983, David A. Boyle, a United States Marine helicopter copilot, was killed when the CH–53D helicopter in which he was flying crashed off the coast of Virginia Beach, Virginia, during a training exercise. Although Boyle survived the impact of the crash, he was unable to escape from the helicopter and drowned. Boyle's father, petitioner here, brought this diversity action in Federal District Court against the Sikorsky Division of United Technologies Corporation (Sikorsky), which built the helicopter for the United States.

At trial, petitioner presented two theories of liability under Virginia tort law that were submitted to the jury. First, petitioner alleged that Sikorsky had defectively repaired a device called the servo in the helicopter's automatic flight control system, which allegedly malfunctioned and caused the crash. Second, petitioner alleged that Sikorsky had defectively designed the copilot's emergency escape system: the escape hatch opened out instead of in (and was therefore ineffective in a submerged craft because of water pressure), and access to the escape hatch handle was obstructed by other equipment. The jury returned a general verdict in favor of petitioner and awarded him $725,000. The District Court denied Sikorsky's motion for judgment notwithstanding the verdict.

The Court of Appeals reversed and remanded with directions that judgment be entered for Sikorsky. 792 F.2d 413 (CA4 1986). It found, as a matter of Virginia law, that Boyle had failed to meet his burden of demonstrating that the repair work performed by Sikorsky, as opposed to work that had been done by the Navy, was responsible for the alleged malfunction of the flight control system. Id., at 415–416. It also found, as a matter of federal law, that Sikorsky could not be held liable for the allegedly defective design of the escape hatch because, on the evidence presented, it satisfied the requirements of the "military contractor defense," which the court had recognized the same day in Tozer v. LTV Corp., * * * [792 F.2d 403, 414–15 (4th Cir. 1986)].

Petitioner sought review here, challenging the Court of Appeals' decision on three levels: First, petitioner contends that there is no justification in federal law for shielding Government contractors from liability for design defects in military equipment. Second, he argues in the alternative that even if such a defense should exist, the Court of Appeals' formulation of the conditions for its application is inappropriate. Finally, petitioner contends that the Court of Appeals erred in not remanding for a jury determination of whether the elements of the defense were met in this case. We granted certiorari * * *.

II

Petitioner's broadest contention is that, in the absence of legislation specifically immunizing Government contractors from liability for design defects, there is no basis for judicial recognition of such a defense. We disagree. * * * [W]e have held that a few areas, involving "uniquely federal interests," * * * are so committed by the Constitution and laws of the United States to federal control that state law is pre-empted and replaced, where necessary, by federal law of a content prescribed (absent explicit statutory directive) by the courts—so-called "federal common law." * * *

The dispute in the present case borders upon two areas that we have found to involve such "uniquely federal interests." We have held that obligations to and rights of the United States under its contracts are governed exclusively by federal law. * * * The present case does not involve an obligation to the United States under its contract, but rather liability to third persons. That liability may be styled one in tort, but it arises out of performance of the contract—and traditionally has been regarded as sufficiently related to the contract that until 1962 Virginia would generally allow design defect suits only by the purchaser and those in privity with the seller. * * *

Another area that we have found to be of peculiarly federal concern, warranting the displacement of state law, is the civil liability of federal officials for actions taken in the course of their duty. We have held in many contexts that the scope of that liability is controlled by federal law. * * * The present case involves an independent contractor performing its obligation under a procurement contract, rather than an official performing his duty as a federal employee, but there is obviously implicated the same interest in getting the Government's work done.

We think the reasons for considering these closely related areas to be of "uniquely federal" interest apply as well to the civil liabilities arising out of the performance of federal procurement contracts. * * *

Moreover, it is plain that the Federal Government's interest in the procurement of equipment is implicated by suits such as the present one—even though the dispute is one between private parties. * * * The imposition of liability on Government contractors will directly affect the terms of Government contracts: either the contractor will decline to manufacture the design specified by the Government, or it will raise its price. Either way, the interests of the United States will be directly affected.

That the procurement of equipment by the United States is an area of uniquely federal interest does not, however, end the inquiry. That merely establishes a necessary, not a sufficient, condition for the displacement of state law. * * * Displacement will occur only where, as we have variously described, a "significant conflict" exists between an identifiable "federal policy or interest and the [operation] of state law," * * * or the application of state law would "frustrate specific objectives" of federal legislation * * *.

* * *

* * * Here the state-imposed duty of care that is the asserted basis of the contractor's liability (specifically, the duty to equip helicopters with the sort of escape-hatch mechanism petitioner claims was necessary) is precisely contrary to the duty imposed by the Government contract (the duty to manufacture and deliver helicopters with the sort of escape-hatch mechanism shown by the specifications). Even in this sort of situation, it would be unreasonable to say that there is always a "significant conflict" between the state law and a federal policy or interest. If, for example, a federal procurement officer orders, by model number, a quantity of stock helicopters that happen to be equipped with escape hatches opening outward, it is impossible to say that the Government has a significant interest in that particular feature. That would be scarcely more reasonable than saying that a private individual who orders such a craft by model number cannot sue for the manufacturer's negligence because he got precisely what he ordered.

* * *

There is * * * a statutory provision that demonstrates the potential for, and suggests the outlines of, "significant conflict" between federal interests and state law in the context of Government procurement. In the [Federal Tort Claim Act], Congress authorized damages to be recovered against the United States for harm caused by the negligent or wrongful conduct of Government employees, to the extent that a private person would be liable under the law of the place where the conduct occurred. 28 U.S.C. § 1346(b). It excepted from this consent to suit, however,

> "[a]ny claim ... based upon the exercise or performance or the failure to exercise or perform a discretionary function or duty on the part of a federal agency or an employee of the Government, whether or not the discretion involved be abused." 28 U.S.C. § 2680(a).

We think that the selection of the appropriate design for military equipment to be used by our Armed Forces is assuredly a discretionary function within the meaning of this provision. It often involves not merely engineering analysis but judgment as to the balancing of many technical, military, and even social considerations, including specifically the trade-off between greater safety and greater combat effectiveness. And we are further of the view that permitting "second-guessing" of these judgments * * * through state tort suits against contractors would produce the same effect sought to be avoided by the FTCA exemption. The financial burden of judgments against the contractors would ultimately be passed through, substantially if not totally, to the United States itself, since defense contractors will predictably raise their prices to cover, or to insure against, contingent liability for the Government-ordered designs. To put the point differently: It makes little sense to insulate the Government against financial liability for the judgment that a particular feature of military equipment is necessary when the Government produces the equipment itself, but not when it contracts for the production. In sum, we are of the view that state law which holds Government contractors liable for design defects in military equipment does in some circumstances present a "significant conflict" with federal policy and must be displaced. * * *

* * *

Accordingly the judgment is vacated and the case is remanded.

So ordered.

JUSTICE BRENNAN, with whom JUSTICE MARSHALL and JUSTICE BLACKMUN join, dissenting.

* * * We may assume, for purposes of this case, that Lt. Boyle was trapped under water and drowned because respondent United Technologies negligently designed the helicopter's escape hatch. We may further assume that any competent engineer would have discovered and cured the defects, but that they inexplicably escaped respondent's notice. Had respondent designed such a death trap for a commercial firm, Lt. Boyle's family could sue under Virginia tort law and be compensated for his tragic and unnecessary death. But respondent designed the helicopter for the Federal Government, and that, the Court tells us today, makes all the difference: Respondent is immune from liability so long as it obtained approval of "reasonably precise specifications"—perhaps no more than a rubber stamp from a federal procurement officer who might or might not have noticed or cared about the defects, or even had the expertise to discover them.

If respondent's immunity "bore the legitimacy of having been prescribed by the people's elected representatives," we would be duty bound to implement their will, whether or not we approved. * * * Congress, however, has remained silent—and conspicuously so, having resisted a sustained campaign by Government contractors to legislate for them some defense. * * * The Court—unelected and unaccountable to the people—has unabashedly stepped into the breach to legislate a rule denying Lt. Boyle's family the compensation that state law assures them. This time the injustice is of this Court's own making.

Worse yet, the injustice will extend far beyond the facts of this case, for the Court's newly discovered Government contractor defense is breathtakingly sweeping. It applies not only to military equipment like the CH–53D helicopter, but (so far as I can tell) to any made-to-order gadget that the Federal Government might purchase after previewing plans—from NASA's Challenger space shuttle to the Postal Service's old mail cars. The contractor may invoke the defense in suits brought not only by military personnel like Lt. Boyle, or Government employees, but by anyone injured by a Government contractor's negligent design, including, for example, the children who might have died had respondent's helicopter crashed on the beach. It applies even if the Government has not intentionally sacrificed safety for other interests like speed or efficiency, and, indeed, even if the equipment is not of a type that is typically considered dangerous; thus, the contractor who designs a Government building can invoke the defense when the elevator cable snaps or the walls collapse. And the defense is invocable regardless of how blatant or easily remedied the defect, so long as the contractor missed it and the specifications approved by the Government, however unreasonably dangerous, were "reasonably precise." * * *

In my view, this Court lacks both authority and expertise to fashion such a rule, whether to protect the Treasury of the United States or the coffers of industry. Because I would leave that exercise of legislative power to Congress, where our Constitution places it, I would reverse the Court of Appeals and reinstate petitioner's jury award.

* * *

IV

At bottom, the Court's analysis is premised on the proposition that any tort liability indirectly absorbed by the Government so burdens governmental functions as to compel us to act when Congress has not. That proposition is by no means uncontroversial. The tort system is premised on the assumption that the imposition of liability encourages actors to prevent any injury whose expected cost exceeds the cost of prevention. If the system is working as it should, Government contractors will design equipment to avoid certain injuries (like the deaths of soldiers or Government employees), which would be certain to burden the Government. The Court therefore has no basis for its assumption that tort liability will result in a net burden on the Government (let alone a clearly excessive net burden) rather than a net gain.

Perhaps tort liability is an inefficient means of ensuring the quality of design efforts, but "[w]hatever the merits of the policy" the Court wishes to implement, "its conversion into law is a proper subject for congressional action, not for any creative power of ours." [United States v.] Standard Oil [Co. of Calif.], 332 U.S. [301], at 314–315, 67 S. Ct. [1604], at 1611[, 91 L. Ed. 2067, 2075 (1947)]. * * * If Congress shared the Court's assumptions and conclusion it could readily enact "A BILL [t]o place limitations on the civil liability of government contractors to ensure that such liability does not impede the ability of the United States to procure necessary goods and services," H.R. 4765, 99th Cong., 2d Sess. (1986); see also S. 2441, 99th Cong., 2d Sess. (1986). It has not.

Were I a legislator, I would probably vote against any law absolving multibillion dollar private enterprises from answering for their tragic mistakes, at least if that law were justified by no more than the unsupported speculation that their liability might ultimately burden the United States Treasury. Some of my colleagues here would evidently vote otherwise (as they have here), but that should not matter here. We are judges not legislators, and the vote is not ours to cast.

I respectfully dissent.

Justice Stevens, dissenting.

When judges are asked to embark on a lawmaking venture, I believe they should carefully consider whether they, or a legislative body, are better equipped to perform the task at hand. There are instances of so-called interstitial lawmaking that inevitably become part of the judicial process. * * * But when we are asked to create an entirely new doctrine—to answer "questions of policy on which Congress has not spoken," United States v. Gilman, 347 U.S. 507, 511, 74 S.Ct. 695, 697, 98 L.Ed. 898 (1954)—we have a special duty to identify the proper decisionmaker before trying to make the proper decision.

When the novel question of policy involves a balancing of the conflicting interests in the efficient operation of a massive governmental program and the protection of the rights of the individual—whether in the social welfare context, the civil service context, or the military procurement context—I feel very deeply that we should defer to the expertise of the Congress. * * *

NOTES AND QUESTIONS

1. What is the "uniquely federal interest" at stake in *Boyle*? Is it protecting the federal fisc? According respect to the policy choices of the elected branches? Should it matter that the United States was not named as a party in the action? Professors Green and Matasar argue that the *Boyle* majority should have based the federal common law defense "entirely on the sole federal interest implicated—protection of government decisionmaking. The Court then could have crafted a rule narrowly tailored to further that interest." Green & Matasar, *The Supreme Court and the Products Liability Crisis: Lessons from* Boyle's *Government Contractor Defense*, 63 S. Cal. L. Rev. 637, 642 (1989–1990). Would this approach have affected the result in *Boyle*? Is it more respectful of state interests?

2. How broad is the *Boyle* defense? Does it apply only to military contractors? To any contractor that provides goods and services to the United States? Compare *In re Hawaii Federal Asbestos Cases*, 960 F.2d 806 (9th Cir. 1992) (declining to apply *Boyle* defense in products liability suit brought on behalf of individuals exposed to asbestos dust while serving in United States

Navy), with *Silverstein v. Northrop Grunman Corp.*, 367 N.J.Super. 361, 842 A.2d 881 (2004) (holding that manufacturer of postal vehicle could raise *Boyle* defense in products liability suit filed by postal worker injured when vehicle rolled over in accident). In confining the *Boyle* defense only to military equipment manufactured for the United States, the Ninth Circuit explained:

> That *Boyle* speaks of the military contractor defense as immunizing contractors only with respect to the military equipment they produce for the United States is consistent with the purposes the Court ascribes to that defense. The Boyle Court noted that the military makes highly complex and sensitive decisions regarding the development of new equipment for military usage. Allowing the contractors who are hired to manufacture that equipment to be sued for the injuries caused by it would impinge unduly on the military's decisionmaking process. The contractors would either refuse to produce the military equipment for the Government or would raise their prices to insure against the potential liability for the Government's design. * * *

> These same concerns do not exist in respect to products readily available on the commercial market. The fact that the military may order such products does not make them "military equipment." The products have not been developed on the basis of involved judgments made by the military but in response to the broader needs and desires of end-users in the private sector. The contractors, furthermore, already will have factored the costs of ordinary tort liability into the price of their goods. That they will not enjoy immunity from tort liability with respect to the goods sold to one of their customers, the Government is unlikely to affect their marketing behavior or their pricing.

In re Hawaii Federal Asbestos Cases, 960 F.2d at 811. See Bellia, Jr., *State Courts and the Making of Federal Common Law*, 133 U. Pa. L. Rev. 825, 846–49 (2005).

3. In 1979, Vietnam veterans, their spouses, and their children filed a federal lawsuit in the Eastern District of New York alleging injury from the veterans' exposure to Agent Orange, a phenoxy herbicide that the military used in South East Asia. Defendants were private companies alleged to have designed, manufactured, or marketed the chemical. The lawsuit was consolidated for pretrial purposes with six hundred similar cases filed nationwide. See *Procedural History of the Agent Orange Product Liability Litigation*, 52 Brooklyn L. Rev. 335 (1986). The trial court denied a motion to dismiss for lack of subject-matter jurisdiction, finding that plaintiffs' claims arose under federal common law and so federal question jurisdiction was available. The Second Circuit reversed, finding no "identifiable" federal policy, and so no basis for fashioning a federal common law rule of decision. In re Agent Orange Prod. Liab. Litig., 506 F.Supp. 737, 741–42 (E.D.N.Y.), reversed 635 F.2d 987, 995 (2d Cir. 1980), certiorari denied 454 U.S. 1128, 102 S.Ct. 980, 71 L.Ed.2d 116 (1981). The case went forward on the basis of diversity jurisdiction, and the court later considered which state's law to apply to the dispute. In IN RE "AGENT ORANGE" PRODUCT LIABILITY LITIGATION, 580 F.Supp. 690 (E.D.N.Y. 1984), the District Court explained that any state presented with the question of what law to apply to plaintiffs' claims would seek to determine

"federal or national consensus substantive law," rather than simply apply the law of its own forum:

> * * * [A] state court passing on the claims of an individual or a group of veterans might well recognize the unfairness in treating differently legally identical claims involving servicemen who fought a difficult foreign war shoulder-to-shoulder and were exposed to virtually identical risks. As the Supreme Court stated in a related context, because "the Armed Services perform a unique, nationwide function in protecting the security of the United States," it makes "little sense for the Government's liability to members of the Armed Services [to be] dependent on the fortuity of where the soldier happened to be stationed at the time of his injury." * * *
>
> It quickly becomes apparent that it is impossible through sensible application of Restatement (Second) choice of law doctrine or analysis to identify the interest of any one state as being sufficiently greater than that of any others to a degree sufficient to justify the application of that state's law in resolving the issues in this litigation. * * * A state court * * *, because of its inability to identify and select any other state's law to be applied as the rule of decision and because of the need for uniformity across the country, would seek to divine what the national rule of decision with regard to product liability law would be so that such law would appropriately reflect the national and international characteristics of this case. * * *

Id. at 703. Was the District Court's approach faithful to *Klaxon*, p. 265, supra? How would *Boyle*, p. 273, supra, alter the District Court's analysis? See In re Agent Orange Product Liability Litigation, 517 F.3d 76 (2d Cir. 2008) (affirming district court's dismissal of plaintiffs' claim as barred under government contractor defense).

4. Does the availability of federal common law influence your view on whether disputes under the Class Action Fairness Act ("CAFA"), p. 169, supra, are to be decided by state law?

NOTE ON FEDERAL COMMON LAW AND FEDERAL RULES OF PRECLUSION

Federal common law plays an important role in determining the preclusive effect of a federal judgment, a topic that will be studied in Chapter 15, infra. Although the question in the past has been in doubt, it is now settled that the preclusive effect of a federal judgment "is not directly governed by the text of either the Constitution or the provisions of [28 U.S.C.] § 1738." Shapiro, Civil Procedure: Preclusion in Civil Actions 144–45 (2001). See generally 18B Wright, Miller & Cooper, Federal Practice and Procedure: Federal Jurisdiction and Related Matters § 4468. Instead, as the Supreme Court made clear in Semtek International Inc. v. Lockheed Martin Corp., 531 U.S. 497, 121 S.Ct. 1021, 149 L.Ed.2d 32 (2001), the preclusive effect of a federal judgment, even where the federal court sits in diversity, is governed by federal common law. See *Leading Cases*, 115 Harv. L. Rev. 467 (2001). However, in determining the content of the federal rule of preclusion, the federal court may choose to borrow a state rule. See Burbank, Semtek, *Forum*

Shopping, and Federal Common Law, 77 Notre Dame L. Rev. 1027 (2002). Why is the creation of a federal common law rule of preclusion consistent with the Rules of Decision Act? See Degnan, *Federalized Res Judicata*, 85 Yale L.J. 741 (1976).

SECTION D.   FEDERAL LAW IN THE STATE COURTS

State courts often are called upon to construe and apply federal law. Indeed, Congress has created a number of statutory causes of action, such as actions under the Federal Employers' Liability Act, that can be asserted by plaintiff in either a state or federal court but which defendant cannot remove from a state court. When a state attempts to adjudicate such a right, the Supremacy Clause, U.S. Const. Art. VI, requires the application of federal law. See Ward v. Bd. of County Com'rs of Love County, 253 U.S. 17, 40 S.Ct. 419, 64 L.Ed. 751 (1920). A federally created right also may become germane to a state-court action when it is interposed as a defense to a claim based on state law. For example, in an action for royalties due under a contract licensing the use of a copyright or patent, defendant commonly will assert that the copyright or patent is invalid under the substantive tests established by the Copyright or Patent Act or that the copyright or patent has been used in violation of the federal antitrust laws. See, e.g., Sola Elec. Co. v. Jefferson Elec. Co., 317 U.S. 173, 63 S.Ct. 172, 87 L.Ed. 165 (1942). By way of further example, federal law may become relevant to a state lawsuit because of the presence of some federal interest or policy or because one of the parties asserts a right protected by the United States Constitution. Finally, federal decisional law may come into play because it provides precedents bearing on issues being litigated before the state court in a nonfederal action.

DICE v. AKRON, CANTON & YOUNGSTOWN R. CO.

Supreme Court of the United States, 1952.
342 U.S. 359, 72 S.Ct. 312, 96 L.Ed. 398.

Certiorari to the Supreme Court of Ohio.

Opinion of the Court by MR. JUSTICE BLACK, announced by MR. JUSTICE DOUGLAS.

Petitioner, a railroad fireman, was seriously injured when an engine in which he was riding jumped the track. Alleging that his injuries were due to respondent's negligence, he brought this action for damages under the Federal Employers' Liability Act, 35 Stat. 65, 45 U.S.C. § 51 et seq., in an Ohio court of common pleas. Respondent's defenses were (1) a denial of negligence and (2) a written document signed by petitioner purporting to release respondent in full for $924.63. Petitioner admitted that he had signed several receipts for payments made him in connection with his injuries but denied that he had made a full and complete settlement of all his claims. He alleged that the purported release was void because he had signed it relying on respondent's deliberately false statement that the document was nothing more than a mere receipt for back wages.

After both parties had introduced considerable evidence the jury found in favor of petitioner and awarded him a $25,000 verdict. The trial judge later entered judgment notwithstanding the verdict. In doing so he reappraised the evidence as to fraud, found that petitioner had been "guilty of supine negligence" in failing to read the release, and accordingly held that the facts did not "sustain either in law or equity the allegations of fraud by clear, unequivocal and convincing evidence." This judgment notwithstanding the verdict was reversed by the Court of Appeals of Summit County, Ohio, on the ground that under federal law, which controlled, the jury's verdict must stand because there was ample evidence to support its finding of fraud. The Ohio Supreme Court, one judge dissenting, reversed the Court of Appeals' judgment and sustained the trial court's action, holding that: (1) Ohio, not federal, law governed; (2) under that law petitioner, a man of ordinary intelligence who could read, was bound by the release even though he had been induced to sign it by the deliberately false statement that it was only a receipt for back wages; and (3) under controlling Ohio law factual issues as to fraud in the execution of this release were properly decided by the judge rather than by the jury. * * *

First. We agree with the Court of Appeals of Summit County, Ohio, and the dissenting judge in the Ohio Supreme Court and hold that validity of releases under the Federal Employers' Liability Act raises a federal question to be determined by federal rather than state law. Congress in § 1 of the Act granted petitioner a right to recover against his employer for damages negligently inflicted. State laws are not controlling in determining what the incidents of this federal right shall be. * * * Manifestly the federal rights affording relief to injured railroad employees under a federally declared standard could be defeated if states were permitted to have the final say as to what defenses could and could not be properly interposed to suits under the Act. Moreover, only if federal law controls can the federal Act be given that uniform application throughout the country essential to effectuate its purposes. * * * Releases and other devices designed to liquidate or defeat injured employees' claims play an important part in the federal Act's administration. * * * Their validity is but one of the many interrelated questions that must constantly be determined in these cases according to a uniform federal law.

Second. In effect the Supreme Court of Ohio held that * * * the negligence of an innocent worker is sufficient to enable his employer to benefit by its deliberate fraud. Application of so harsh a rule to defeat a railroad employee's claim is wholly incongruous with the general policy of the Act to give railroad employees a right to recover just compensation for injuries negligently inflicted by their employers. And this Ohio rule is out of harmony with modern judicial and legislative practice to relieve injured persons from the effect of releases fraudulently obtained. * * * We hold that the correct federal rule is that * * * a release of rights under the Act is void when the employee is induced to sign it by the deliberately false and material statements of the railroad's authorized representatives made to deceive the employee as to the contents of the release. The trial court's charge to the jury correctly stated this rule of law.

Third. Ohio provides and has here accorded petitioner the usual jury trial of factual issues relating to negligence. But Ohio treats factual questions of fraudulent releases differently. It permits the judge trying a negligence case to resolve all factual questions of fraud "other than fraud in the factum." The factual issue of fraud is thus split into fragments, some to be determined by the judge, others by the jury.

It is contended that since a state may consistently with the Federal Constitution provide for trial of cases under the Act by a nonunanimous verdict, Minneapolis & St. Louis R. Co. v. Bombolis, 241 U.S. 211, Ohio may lawfully eliminate trial by jury as to one phase of fraud while allowing jury trial as to all other issues raised. The *Bombolis* case might be more in point had Ohio abolished trial by jury in all negligence cases including those arising under the federal Act. But Ohio has not done this. It has provided jury trials for cases arising under the federal Act but seeks to single out one phase of the question of fraudulent releases for determination by a judge rather than by a jury. * * *

We have previously held that "The right to trial by jury is 'a basic and fundamental feature of our system of federal jurisprudence'" and that it is "part and parcel of the remedy afforded railroad workers under the Employers' Liability Act." Bailey v. Central Vermont R. Co., 319 U.S. 350, 354. We also recognized in that case that to deprive railroad workers of the benefit of a jury trial where there is evidence to support negligence "is to take away a goodly portion of the relief which Congress has afforded them." It follows that the right to trial by jury is too substantial a part of the rights accorded by the Act to permit it to be classified as a mere "local rule of procedure" for denial in the manner that Ohio has here used. * * *

Reversed and remanded with directions.

MR. JUSTICE FRANKFURTER, whom MR. JUSTICE REED, MR. JUSTICE JACKSON and MR. JUSTICE BURTON join, concurring for reversal but dissenting from the Court's opinion.

Ohio, as do many other States, maintains the old division between law and equity as to the mode of trying issues, even though the same judge administers both. * * * [I]n all cases in Ohio, the judge is the trier of fact on this issue of fraud, rather than the jury. It is contended that the Federal Employers' Liability Act requires that Ohio courts send the fraud issue to a jury in the cases founded on that Act. To require Ohio to try a particular issue before a different fact-finder in negligence actions brought under the Employers' Liability Act from the fact-finder on the identical issue in every other negligence case disregards the settled distribution of judicial power between Federal and State courts where Congress authorizes concurrent enforcement of federally-created rights.

* * *

In 1916 the Court decided without dissent that States in entertaining actions under the Federal Employers' Liability Act need not provide a jury system other than that established for local negligence actions. States are not compelled to provide the jury required of Federal courts by the Seventh Amendment. Minneapolis & St. L.R. Co. v. Bombolis * * *. In the thirty-six years since this early decision after the enactment of the Federal Employers' Liability Act * * *, the *Bombolis* case has often been cited by this Court but never questioned. Until today its significance has been to leave to States the choice of the fact-finding tribunal in all negligence actions, including those arising under the Federal Act. * * *

Although a State must entertain negligence suits brought under the Federal Employers' Liability Act if it entertains ordinary actions for negligence, it need conduct them only in the way in which it conducts the run of negligence litigation. The *Bombolis* case directly establishes that the Employers' Liability Act does not impose the jury requirements of the Seventh Amendment on the States *pro tanto* for Employers' Liability litigation. If its reasoning means anything, the *Bombolis* decision means that, if a State chooses not to have a jury at all, but to leave questions of fact in all negligence actions to a court, certainly the Employers' Liability Act does not require a State to have juries for negligence actions brought under the Federal Act in its courts. Or, if a State chooses to retain the old double system of courts, common law and equity * * *, surely there is nothing in the Employers' Liability Act that requires traditional distribution of authority for disposing of legal issues as between common law and chancery courts to go by the board. * * * So long as all negligence suits in a State are treated in the same way, by the same mode of disposing equitable, non-jury, and common law, jury issues, the State does not discriminate against Employers' Liability suits nor does it make any inroad upon substance.

Ohio and her sister States with a similar division of functions between law and equity are not trying to evade their duty under the Federal Employers' Liability Act * * *. The States merely exercise a preference in adhering to historic ways of dealing with a claim of fraud; they prefer the traditional way of making unavailable through equity an otherwise valid defense. The State judges and local lawyers who must administer the Federal Employers' Liability Act in State courts are trained in the ways of local practice; it multiplies the difficulties and confuses the administration of justice to require, on purely theoretical grounds, a hybrid of State and Federal practice in the State courts as to a single class of cases. Nothing in the Employers' Liability Act or in the judicial enforcement of the Act for over forty years forces such judicial hybridization upon the States. The fact that Congress authorized actions under the Federal Employers' Liability Act to be brought in State as well as in Federal courts seems a strange basis for the inference that Congress overrode State procedural arrangements controlling all other negligence suits in a State * * *. Such an inference is admissible, so it seems to me, only on the theory that Congress included as part of the right created by the Employers' Liability Act an assumed likelihood that trying all issues to juries is more favorable to plaintiffs. * * *

Even though the method of trying the equitable issue of fraud which the State applies in all other negligence cases governs Employers' Liability cases, two questions remain for decision: Should the validity of the release be tested by a Federal or a State standard? And if by a Federal one, did the Ohio courts in the present case correctly administer the standard? If the States afford courts for enforcing the Federal Act, they must enforce the substance of the right given by Congress. They cannot depreciate the legislative currency issued by Congress—either expressly or by local methods of enforcement that accomplish the same result. * * * In order to prevent diminution of railroad workers' nationally-uniform right to recover, the standard for the validity of a release of contested liability must be Federal. * * *

NOTES AND QUESTIONS

1. Is the process of applying federal law in a state court identical to the process of applying state law in a federal court under the *Erie* doctrine? How does a state court ascertain federal law? Suppose, for example, that there is a conflict between the federal courts of appeals over what a statute means, or over an issue of federal common law. Is the state court free to adopt any position it wishes? What if the federal courts never have ruled on the issue? Should the state court try to figure out how the federal courts might rule? Which federal court? How does a state court determine which aspects of federal law it must apply? See Clermont, *Reverse*-Erie, 82 Notre Dame L. Rev. 1 (2006).

2. Why might a state court or legislature voluntarily incorporate or apply federal law to a state-created right? Would such an incorporation or application present a federal question for purposes of original jurisdiction in the federal district courts or appellate jurisdiction in the United States Supreme Court? See generally Hart, *The Relations Between State and Federal Law,* 54 Colum. L. Rev. 489, 536–38 (1954); Note, *Supreme Court Review of State Interpretations of Federal Law Incorporated by Reference,* 66 Harv. L. Rev. 1498 (1953). Are the federal courts bound by the state construction of the incorporated federal law?

CHAPTER 7

MODERN PLEADING

■ ■ ■

In this Chapter, we explore modern pleading rules and their relation to other procedural devices. Traditionally, pleading rules served four functions: (1) providing notice of the nature of a claim or defense; (2) identifying baseless claims; (3) setting out each party's view of the facts; and (4) narrowing the issues. Modern pleading rules generally are not calculated to perform the last three of these functions. Instead, the framers of the Federal Rules of Civil Procedure were satisfied that the need to deter baseless claims that may clog a court's calendar could be achieved by requiring a short and plain statement of the claim showing that the plaintiff is entitled to relief, together with a certification that the pleadings are not frivolous (Federal Rule 11), and by establishing post-pleading but pre-trial devices designed to screen claims for procedural and merit defects (most notably, the motion to dismiss under Federal Rule 12(b)(6) and the motion for summary judgment under Federal Rule 56). The Federal Rules also create a wide array of discovery devices that obviate the need for the parties to provide a detailed statement of the facts at the pleading stage. An important question about modern pleading is whether it generates excessive costs by allowing the filing of baseless suits that require discovery and court time. As you read the materials in this Chapter, consider the implications of revising the pleading rules to make it more difficult to bring suit generally and whether possible amendments should be applicable only to particular issues or claims.

SECTION A. THE COMPLAINT

1. PLEADING AT COMMON LAW

Pleading rules in the United State trace their origins to the writ system and forms of action that developed during the reign of Henry II in twelfth-century England. As Sir Henry Maine famously stated, the common law developed "in the interstices of Procedure," as courts adapted the writs and recognized new forms of action such as case, indebitatus assumpsit, and trover. Maine, Early Law and Custom 389 (1886). Even after eight centuries of common law development, it remains true, as

Oliver Wendell Holmes observed, that "whenever we trace a leading doctrine of substantive law far enough back, we are very likely to find some forgotten circumstance of procedure at its source." Koffler & Reppy, Handbook of Common Law Pleading xi (1969).

NOTES AND QUESTIONS

1. Pleading rules owe their origins to the manner of allegation that developed in the English royal courts during the medieval period. A person with a grievance against another sought justice from the king, and the king issued a writ, ordering the sheriff to bring the other person before the king's judges to answer the complaint. In the course of the twelfth century, this pattern became standardized. When it became established that the king's courts would hear a particular kind of case, the complainant in such a case could obtain a writ from the king's chief minister, the chancellor, as a matter of course. The writ was simply the document that commenced the action, similar in function to the modern summons. But each writ came to embody a form of action, a concept that governed the method of commencing the suit, the substantive requirements of the case, the manner of trial, and the type of sanction that would attend the eventual judgment. There was a writ for each type of dispute that the royal courts would hear; thus, for example, there was a writ of trespass, a writ of debt, and a writ of nuisance. If plaintiff selected a writ that did not fit the dispute, the action would fail.

2. Plaintiff's claim was set forth in the *declaration*. Stripped of much verbiage, and stated in modern English, it might have said: "Defendant promised to deliver a horse to plaintiff and plaintiff promised to pay 100 dollars for it, but defendant has refused to deliver the horse."

3. A substantive response to a claim, other than an expression of total agreement, would require defendant to demur or to plead. A *demurrer* would challenge the legal sufficiency of the plaintiff's declaration. If defendant did not demur, he responded to the declaration in a plea. Pleas were of two types, dilatory and peremptory. A *dilatory plea* did not deny the merits of plaintiff's claim, but rather challenged plaintiff's right to have the court hear the case and included pleas to the jurisdiction of the court. A *peremptory plea*, or plea in bar, was on the merits.

4. If defendant entered a plea, plaintiff had three choices. First, he could demur on the ground that the plea did not state a valid defense. For example, if plaintiff had alleged a breach of contract and defendant had pleaded that he was a minor at the time the contract was entered into, the demurrer would raise the question whether defendant's minority was a defense. Second, plaintiff could plead in a *replication* that defendant had not been a minor. Or, finally, plaintiff might have admitted that defendant had been a minor and pleaded, in a *confession and avoidance,* that defendant had lied about his age.

2. DETAIL REQUIRED UNDER THE CODES

The first significant reform in procedure occurred in England in the period between 1825 and 1834, when one form of writ was adopted for all three common law courts and all but three real actions were abolished, debt and detinue were reshaped, and the wager of law was ended. The capstone of the reform was a body of new rules of pleading, called the Hilary Rules—which led to disastrous results. "Under the common-law system the matter was bad enough with a pleading question decided in every sixth case. But under the Hilary Rules it was worse. Every fourth case decided a question on the pleadings. Pleading ran riot." Whittier, *Notice Pleading,* 31 Harv. L. Rev. 501, 507 (1918). Fortunately, corrective action was not long in coming. The Common Law Procedure Acts of 1852, 1854, and 1860 weakened the forms of action, expanded joinder, and liberalized pleading. Finally, the Judicature Acts of 1873 and 1875 combined Chancery and the common law courts into one Supreme Court of Judicature, fused law and equity, and abolished the forms of action.

Meanwhile in the United States, New York took the lead in reforming common law pleading. In 1848, the New York legislature enacted a Code of Civil Procedure, commonly called the Field Code. This Code proved to be the prototype for numerous state codes—at one time more than half the states had codes patterned to some degree after the Field Code—and the precursor of the Federal Rules. Code pleading differed from the writ system by requiring plaintiffs "to state factual support for all elements of each cause of action. Compliance with these requirements was intended not only to flesh out the extent of the pleader's knowledge of the facts underlying the claim, but also to determine the legitimacy of the claim itself." Main, *Procedural Uniformity and the Exaggerated Role of Rules: A Survey of Intra–State Uniformity in Three States That Have Not Adopted the Federal Rules of Civil Procedure,* 46 Vill. L. Rev. 311, 327 (2001). Even today, some states persist in retaining code pleading and continue to require a "statement of facts" constituting a "cause of action"; others call for a "statement of facts" demonstrating a "right to relief." Is there an important difference between these formulations? Some state provisions specifically call for a statement of "ultimate facts." A number of these code states soften any harsh results of technical enforcement by stating that a pleading is satisfactory if it gives "fair notice" to the opposing party.

––––––

GILLISPIE v. GOODYEAR SERVICE STORES, 258 N.C. 487, 128 S.E.2d 762 (1963). Plaintiff alleged:

[T]he defendants, without cause or just excuse and maliciously came upon and trespassed upon the premises occupied by the plaintiff as a residence, and by the use of harsh and threatening language and physical force directed against the plaintiff assaulted the plaintiff and placed her in great fear, and humiliated and embarrassed her by subjecting her to public scorn and ridicule, and caused her to be seized and exhibited to the public as a prisoner, and to be confined in a public jail, all to her great humiliation, embarrassment and harm.

Under the North Carolina code then in force, plaintiff was required to make a "plain and concise statement of the facts constituting a cause of action." North Carolina cases interpreting the pleading standard had stated that the complaint must "disclose the issuable facts" and allege "the material, essential and ultimate facts upon which plaintiff's right of action is based." The court held that the allegations were insufficient, noting that the pleading was necessary not only to enable the opposing party to respond but also to enable the court to declare the law upon the facts stated. The court could not do so if "a mere legal conclusion" such as "assault" or "trespass" is stated. The court concluded:

> The complaint states no facts upon which * * * legal conclusions may be predicated. Plaintiff's allegations do not disclose *what* occurred, *when* it occurred, *where* it occurred, *who* did *what*, the relationships between defendants and plaintiff or of defendants *inter se*, or any other factual data that might identify the occasion or describe the circumstances of the alleged wrongful conduct of defendants.

Id. at 490, 128 S.E.2d at 766.

The court also discussed the sufficiency of pleadings in other types of cases:

> When a complaint alleges defendant is indebted to plaintiff in a certain amount and such debt is due, but does not allege in what manner or for what cause defendant became indebted to plaintiff, it is demurrable for failure to state facts sufficient to constitute a cause of action. * * *

> "In an action or defense based upon negligence, it is not sufficient to allege the mere happening of an event of an injurious nature and call it negligence on the part of the party sought to be charged. This is necessarily so because negligence is not a fact in itself, but is the legal result of certain facts. Therefore, the facts which constitute the negligence charged and also the facts which establish such negligence as the proximate cause, or as one of the proximate causes, of the injury must be alleged." Shives v. Sample, 238 N.C. 724, 79 S.E.2d 193.

Id. at 489–90, 128 S.E.2d at 765.

Notes and Questions

1. Is the court in *Gillispie* legitimately concerned with the inability of defendants to ascertain the claims against them in order that they might answer and prepare their defenses? Can it be said that the pleading in *Gillispie* is unsatisfactory because the trial judge will not know what evidence is or is not relevant?

2. To what extent might the court in *Gillispie* have been motivated by the notion that a detailed account of the facts might well show that plaintiff did not have a valid claim for relief? Is it significant that at the time of the

Gillispie decision North Carolina did not have a provision for summary judgment that allowed a party to challenge an opponent's pleadings which had no basis in fact? Has the North Carolina court simply followed a hard and fast line concerning the "fact" pleading requirement, thereby undermining its basic purpose as a device for pretrial communication?

3.   Plaintiff was given leave to amend the complaint after the *Gillispie* decision. Suppose that plaintiff's amended complaint also is deficient. Will she be given leave to amend again? How should the right to amend affect the question of whether or not a pleading is or is not satisfactory?

————

COOK, STATEMENTS OF FACT IN PLEADING UNDER THE CODES, 21 Colum. L. Rev. 416, 416–19, 423 (1921):

In * * * [California Packing Corp. v. Kelly Storage & Distributing Co., 228 N.Y. 49, 126 N.E. 269 (1920)] the plaintiff alleged in his complaint that the promise for the breach of which he was suing was made in exchange for "a valuable consideration." The case went to the Court of Appeals upon the question whether this allegation is a "statement of fact" or a "conclusion of law." [The court held it was the former.] * * * An examination of the authorities in [New York and] other code jurisdictions reveals a conflict of authority. * * *

* * *

[Upon careful analysis] * * * it will appear at once that there is no logical distinction between statements which are grouped by the courts under the phrases "statements of fact" and "conclusions of law." It will also be found that many, although by no means all, pleadings held bad because they are said to plead "evidence" rather than "the facts constituting the cause of action" or defense really do nevertheless "state" the operative facts which the pleader will have to prove at the trial, but in a form different from that to which courts and lawyers are accustomed to recognize as a proper method of pleading.

* * *

The facts of life which compose the group of "operative facts" to which the law attaches legal consequences are always *specific* and not *generic.* * * * [I]n an action on the case for, let us say, negligently injuring the plaintiff by the operation of an automobile, the "operative" or "ultimate" facts proved at the trial will always be specific. It will appear that the defendant was driving a particular kind of automobile at some particular rate of speed, *etc., etc.* If now a plaintiff were to state the facts thus specifically in his complaint he would doubtless be told by the average court that he had "pleaded his evidence" and not the "facts constituting the cause of action." This would of course be erroneous. What is according to accepted notions the proper way to plead is merely a mode of stating the facts generically rather than specifically.

It must of course be recognized that at times a pleader really does err by "pleading evidence," i.e., by stating, generically or specifically, facts which do not form part of the group of operative facts, but are merely facts from which by some process of logical inference the existence of the operative facts can be inferred. More often, however, the "error" consists merely in pleading the operative facts more specifically than is usual.

* * * Let us now examine "conclusions of law." The first thing noticed upon analysis is that a so-called "conclusion of law" is a generic statement which can be made only after some legal rule has been applied to some specific group of operative facts. Consider, for example, a statement in a pleading that "defendant owes plaintiff $500." Standing by itself in a pleading this is usually treated as a mere "conclusion of law." It can, however, be made only when one knows certain facts and also the applicable legal rule. It is, in fact, the conclusion of a logical argument: Whenever certain facts, a, b, c, *etc.*, exist, B (defendant) owes A (plaintiff) $500; facts a, b, c, *etc.*, exist; therefore B owes A $500. This being so, when the bare statement is made that "B owes A $500" we may, if we wish, regard it as a statement in generic form that all the facts necessary to create the legal duty to pay money described by the word "owe" are true as between A and B. In dealing, for example, with misrepresentation, such statements are more often than otherwise regarded in exactly this way. The same statement may, however, under proper circumstances be merely a statement as to the law applicable to facts given or known, and so be purely a statement of a "conclusion of law." * * *

* * * How specific or how generic statements in a pleading may and must be can obviously not be settled by mere logic, but according to notions of fairness and convenience. The pleading should give the adversary and the court reasonable notice of the real nature of the claim or defense; nothing more should be required.

NOTE AND QUESTIONS

"Quite commonly an allegation has been held bad as a statement of law only. The stating of evidence, while subject to criticism, is not so often held to render the pleading bad, since the court itself will draw the ultimate conclusion where it is the one necessarily following from the allegations made." Clark, Code Pleading § 38, at 228 (2d ed. 1947). When does the ultimate conclusion "necessarily follow"? Compare Robinson v. Meyer, 135 Conn. 691, 693–94, 68 A.2d 142, 143 (1949), in which the court inferred title by adverse possession on the basis of allegations of "all the facts necessary to establish ouster," with O'Regan v. Schermerhorn, 25 N.J.Misc. 1, 50 A.2d 10 (Sup. Ct. 1946), in which the court refused to infer the defense of truth in a defamation suit where defendant alleged he believed the statement to be true and further alleged the facts on which that belief was based.

3.   DETAIL REQUIRED UNDER THE FEDERAL RULES OF CIVIL PROCEDURE

―――――

Read Federal Rules of Civil Procedure 8(a) and 12(b) in the Supplement.

―――――

NOTE ON NOTICE PLEADING

Modern pleading arrived in 1938 when the Federal Rules of Civil Procedure came into effect. In 1934, Congress passed the Rules Enabling Act, 28 U.S.C. § 2072, authorizing the United States Supreme Court to promulgate rules of procedure for the district courts. The next year, the United States Supreme Court appointed an Advisory Committee of distinguished lawyers, judges, and law professors to prepare and submit a draft of unified rules. The Supreme Court carefully reviewed and made a number of changes in the rules recommended by the Committee. The rules, as adopted by the Court on December 20, 1937, were transmitted to the Attorney General and were submitted by him to the 75th Congress on January 3, 1938. Pursuant to the terms of the Rules Enabling Act, the rules came into effect when the Congress adjourned without taking action to postpone their effective date. Examples of the simplicity of pleading under Rule 8(a) are found in the Appendix of Forms, which are set out in the Supplement following the Federal Rules of Civil Procedure; in particular see Forms 11 and 15. Note that in 1946, Rule 84 was amended to state that the Forms were not mere guides but were themselves "sufficient under the rules."

―――――

In CONLEY v. GIBSON, 355 U.S. 41, 78 S.Ct. 99, 2 L.Ed.2d 80 (1957), the Supreme Court expressed its views on the degree of detail required by Federal Rule 8(a):

> * * * In appraising the sufficiency of the complaint we follow, of course, the accepted rule that a complaint should not be dismissed for failure to state a claim unless it appears beyond doubt that the plaintiff can prove no set of facts in support of his claim which would entitle him to relief. * * *

> * * * [T]he Federal Rules of Civil Procedure do not require a claimant to set out in detail the facts upon which he bases his claim. To the contrary, all the Rules require is "a short and plain statement of the claim" that will give the defendant fair notice of what the plaintiff's claim is and the grounds upon which it rests. The illustrative forms appended to the Rules plainly demonstrate this. Such simplified

"notice pleading" is made possible by the liberal opportunity for discovery and the other pretrial procedures established by the Rules to disclose more precisely the basis of both claim and defense and to define more narrowly the disputed facts and issues. Following the simple guide of Rule 8(f) that "all pleadings shall be so construed as to do substantial justice," we have no doubt that petitioner's complaint adequately set forth a claim and gave the respondents fair notice of its basis. The Federal Rules reject the approach that pleading is a game of skill in which one misstep by counsel may be decisive to the outcome and accept the principle that the purpose of pleading is to facilitate a proper decision on the merits. * * *

Id. at 45–48, 78 S.Ct. 102–03, 2 L.Ed.2d at 84–86.

NOTES AND QUESTIONS

1. Consider which, if any, of the following pleadings would be sufficient to state a claim under Federal Rule 8(a)(2). Does Form 11 in the Supplement provide a benchmark for judging any of these?

(a) D is legally liable to P for damages.

(b) D negligently caused P's injury.

(c) D negligently caused P's injuries on July 4, 2010, at Dreamworld Amusement Park.

(d) D negligently operated a roller coaster ride on which P was a passenger on July 4, 2010 at Dreamworld Amusement Park. As a result of this negligence, P suffered a broken arm and was otherwise injured, and P incurred hospital and other medical expenses and was prevented from transacting business, resulting in damages of $500,000.

(e) D negligently operated a roller coaster ride on which P was a passenger on July 4, 2010 at Dreamworld Amusement Park. D was negligent because it was operating the roller coaster at excessive speed and the ride was improperly maintained. As a result of this negligence, P suffered a broken arm and was otherwise injured, and P incurred hospital and other medical expenses and was prevented from transacting business, resulting in damages of $500,000.

(f) D negligently operated a roller coaster ride on which P was a passenger on July 4, 2010 at Dreamworld Amusement Park. D was negligent because it was operating the roller coaster at excessive speed (the roller coaster was traveling at a speed of 32 mph, exceeding the safe speed by 5 mph), and the ride was improperly maintained. As a result of this negligence, P suffered a broken arm and was otherwise injured and P incurred hospital and other medical expenses and was prevented from transacting business, resulting in damages of $500,000.

(g) D negligently operated a roller coaster ride on which P was a passenger on July 4, 2010 at Dreamworld Amusement Park. D was negligent because it was operating the roller coaster at excessive speed (the roller coaster was traveling at a speed of 32 mph, exceeding the safe speed by 5 mph), and the ride was improperly maintained. P was not contributorily negligent. As a result of this negligence, P suffered a broken arm and was otherwise injured, and P incurred hospital and other medical expenses and was prevented from transacting business, resulting in damages of $500,000.

2. With the exception of actions based on fraud or mistake, which are dealt with in Rule 9(b), and actions for securities fraud, which are governed by a special federal statute, there are no provisions, aside from Rule 8(a) regarding pleading requirements in the federal courts. That did not deter defendants from seeking to impose heightened pleading requirements in a variety of actions, including civil rights and antitrust lawsuits and other complex litigation. See Marcus, *The Puzzling Persistence of Pleading Practice*, 76 Texas L. Rev. 1749 (1998); Fairman, *The Myth of Notice Pleading*, 45 Ariz. L. Rev. 987, 1002 (2003) ("Frequently, courts use the language of Rule 8 and notice pleading yet still impose higher pleading requirements.").

3. In LEATHERMAN v. TARRANT COUNTY NARCOTICS INTELLI-GENCE & COORDINATION UNIT, 507 U.S. 163, 113 S.Ct. 1160, 122 L.Ed.2d 517 (1993), a unanimous Supreme Court held that a federal court may not apply a more stringent pleading standard in civil rights cases alleging municipal liability under 42 U.S.C. § 1983:

> The phenomenon of litigation against municipal corporations based on claimed constitutional violations by their employees dates from our decision in [Monell v. City Dep't of Soc. Servs. of City of New York, 436 U.S. 658, 98 S.Ct. 2018, 56 L.Ed.2d 611 (1978)], where we for the first time construed § 1983 to allow such municipal liability. Perhaps if Rules 8 and 9 were rewritten today, claims against municipalities under § 1983 might be subjected to the added specificity requirement of Rule 9(b). But that is a result which must be obtained by the process of amending the Federal Rules, and not by judicial interpretation. In the absence of such an amendment, federal courts and litigants must rely on summary judgment and control of discovery to weed out unmeritorious claims sooner rather than later.

Id. at 168–69, 113 S.Ct. at 1163, 122 L.Ed.2d at 524. *Leatherman* left open whether lower courts may impose heightened pleading requirements on plaintiffs bringing civil rights claims against government officials who claim qualified immunity.

4. In BAUTISTA v. LOS ANGELES COUNTY, 216 F.3d 837 (9th Cir. 2000), a federal civil rights action, the trial court dismissed plaintiffs' second amended complaint with prejudice. On appeal, three distinguished Court of Appeals judges wrote separate opinions. Judge Schwarzer, writing for the court, summarized the complaint as follows:

> The first claim, on behalf of twenty of the named plaintiffs, alleges that they were over the age of forty [which brings them within the scope of the federal statute prohibiting discrimination on the basis of age] and were denied employment by defendant in favor of younger employees. The second claim, on behalf of fifty-one named plaintiffs, alleges that defendant discriminated against them on account of their race, national origin and ancestry by denying them employment while employing less qualified

Anglo employees. The third claim, on behalf of three named plaintiffs, alleges that plaintiff discriminated against them on the basis of their physical disabilities while employing less qualified employees.

Id. at 840. Judge Schwarzer found the complaint to be insufficient because each individual plaintiff had failed to allege that "he or she is a member of a particular protected class, was qualified and applied for the position he or she sought, and was rejected on a prohibited ground." Id. However, he voted to reverse the trial judge, finding it an abuse of discretion that the court had failed to give plaintiffs guidance on how to cure the pleading defects and a chance to do so. Judge Reinhardt concurred, arguing that the complaint was sufficient under Rule 8:

> True, the complaint states the relevant facts at a high level of generality. But that is the point of notice pleadings[.] * * * [T]o the extent that a complaint lacks detail that the defendants believe they need * * * they can obtain such detail readily through interrogatories or early depositions. Surely Judge Schwarzer does not intend to say that each plaintiff in a multi-plaintiff action must plead separately each element of his or her claim in repetitious separate paragraphs.

Id. at 843. Judge O'Scannlain dissented. He agreed that the complaint was deficient, but found no abuse of discretion in the trial court's failing to give plaintiffs and their "experienced counsel" guidance on how to plead their case. Id. at 844.

Which of these positions makes the most sense? Compare Sparrow v. United Air Lines, Inc., 216 F.3d 1111, 1115 (D.C. Cir. 2000) (holding complaint is sufficient if it alleges "I was turned down for a job because of my race").

5. In SWIERKIEWICZ v. SOREMA N.A., 534 U.S. 506, 122 S.Ct. 992, 152 L.Ed.2d 1 (2002), the Supreme Court rebuffed yet another opportunity to impose a heightened pleading requirement on civil rights claims, this time in a case alleging employment discrimination in violation of federal law. Justice Thomas delivered the opinion for a unanimous Court:

> This case presents the question whether a complaint in an employment discrimination lawsuit must contain specific facts establishing a prima facie case of discrimination * * *. We hold that an employment discrimination complaint need not include such facts and instead must contain only "a short and plain statement of the claim showing that the pleader is entitled to relief." Fed. Rule Civ. Proc. 8(a)(2).

> Petitioner Akos Swierkiewicz is a native of Hungary, who at the time of his complaint was 53 years old. * * * In April 1989, petitioner began working for respondent Sorema N.A., a reinsurance company headquartered in New York and principally owned and controlled by a French parent corporation. Petitioner was initially employed in the position of senior vice president and chief underwriting officer (CUO). Nearly six years later, Francois M. Chavel, respondent's Chief Executive Officer, demoted petitioner to a marketing and services position and transferred the bulk of his underwriting responsibilities to Nicholas Papadopoulo, a 32–year-old who, like Mr. Chavel, is a French national. About a year later,

Mr. Chavel stated that he wanted to "energize" the underwriting department and appointed Mr. Papadopoulo as CUO. Petitioner claims that Mr. Papadopoulo had only one year of underwriting experience at the time he was promoted, and therefore was less experienced and less qualified to be CUO than he, since at that point he had 26 years of experience in the insurance industry.

Following his demotion, petitioner contends that he "was isolated by Mr. Chavel ... [and] excluded from business decisions and meetings and denied the opportunity to reach his true potential at SOREMA." * * * Petitioner unsuccessfully attempted to meet with Mr. Chavel to discuss his discontent. Finally, in April 1997, petitioner sent a memo to Mr. Chavel outlining his grievances and requesting a severance package. Two weeks later, respondent's general counsel presented petitioner with two options: He could either resign without a severance package or be dismissed. Mr. Chavel fired petitioner after he refused to resign.

Petitioner filed a lawsuit alleging that he had been terminated on account of his national origin in violation of Title VII of the Civil Rights Act of 1964, 78 Stat. 253, as amended, 42 U.S.C. § 2000e et seq. (1994 ed. and Supp. V), and on account of his age in violation of the Age Discrimination in Employment Act of 1967 (ADEA), 81 Stat. 602, as amended, 29 U.S.C. § 621 et seq. (1994 ed. and Supp. V). * * * The United States District Court for the Southern District of New York dismissed petitioner's complaint because it found that he "ha[d] not adequately alleged a prima facie case, in that he ha[d] not adequately alleged circumstances that support an inference of discrimination." * * * The * * * Second Circuit affirmed * * *. We granted certiorari, * * * and now reverse.

Applying Circuit precedent, the Court of Appeals required petitioner to plead a prima facie case of discrimination in order to survive respondent's motion to dismiss. * * * In the Court of Appeals' view, petitioner was thus required to allege in his complaint: (1) membership in a protected group; (2) qualification for the job in question; (3) an adverse employment action; and (4) circumstances that support an inference of discrimination. * * *

The prima facie case * * *, however, is an evidentiary standard, not a pleading requirement. * * * [T]his Court has reiterated that the prima facie case relates to the employee's burden of presenting evidence that raises an inference of discrimination. * * *

This Court has never indicated that the requirements for establishing a prima facie case * * * also apply to the pleading standard that plaintiffs must satisfy in order to survive a motion to dismiss. * * *

* * * [U]nder a notice pleading system, it is not appropriate to require a plaintiff to plead facts establishing a prima facie case because * * * [this] framework does not apply in every employment discrimination case. For instance, if a plaintiff is able to produce direct evidence of discrimination, he may prevail without proving all the elements of a prima facie case. * * * Under the Second Circuit's heightened pleading standard, a plaintiff without direct evidence of discrimination at the time of his complaint must plead a prima facie case of discrimination, even though discovery

might uncover such direct evidence. It thus seems incongruous to require a plaintiff, in order to survive a motion to dismiss, to plead more facts than he may ultimately need to prove to succeed on the merits if direct evidence of discrimination is discovered.

* * * Given that the prima facie case operates as a flexible evidentiary standard, it should not be transposed into a rigid pleading standard for discrimination cases.

Furthermore, imposing the Court of Appeals' heightened pleading standard in employment discrimination cases conflicts with Federal Rule of Civil Procedure 8(a)(2), which provides that a complaint must include only "a short and plain statement of the claim showing that the pleader is entitled to relief." * * * Such a statement must simply "give the defendant fair notice of what the plaintiff's claim is and the grounds upon which it rests." [Conley v. Gibson, p. 292, supra.] This simplified notice pleading standard relies on liberal discovery rules and summary judgment motions to define disputed facts and issues and to dispose of unmeritorious claims. * * *

[The Court then explained that "Rule 8(a)'s simplified pleading standard applies to all civil actions, with limited exceptions," and that "[o]ther provisions of the Federal Rules * * * are inextricably linked" to this simplified pleading standard.]

Applying the relevant standard, petitioner's complaint easily satisfies the requirements of Rule 8(a) because it gives respondent fair notice of the basis for petitioner's claims. Petitioner alleged that he had been terminated on account of his national origin in violation of Title VII and on account of his age in violation of the ADEA. * * * His complaint detailed the events leading to his termination, provided relevant dates, and included the ages and nationalities of at least some of the relevant persons involved with his termination. * * * These allegations give respondent fair notice of what petitioner's claims are and the grounds upon which they rest. * * * In addition, they state claims upon which relief could be granted under Title VII and the ADEA.

Respondent argues that allowing lawsuits based on conclusory allegations of discrimination to go forward will burden the courts and encourage disgruntled employees to bring unsubstantiated suits. * * * Whatever the practical merits of this argument, the Federal Rules do not contain a heightened pleading standard for employment discrimination suits. * * * Furthermore, Rule 8(a) establishes a pleading standard without regard to whether a claim will succeed on the merits. "Indeed it may appear on the face of the pleadings that a recovery is very remote and unlikely but that is not the test." Scheuer [v. Rhodes], 416 U.S. [232], at 236, 94 S.Ct. 1683, 1686, 40 L.Ed.2d 90, 96 (1974).

* * *

NOTE ON THE SHIFT TO PLAUSIBLE PLEADING

Complex litigation, such as antitrust disputes, is an area in which some federal courts considered imposing heightened pleading requirements on plaintiffs. The heavy costs of litigating such cases raised concerns where the pleadings did not indicate that plaintiff had a strong case. The Supreme Court weighed in on this question in the case that follows and modified the *Conley* standard.

BELL ATLANTIC CORP. v. TWOMBLY

Supreme Court of the United States, 2007.
550 U.S. 544, 127 S.Ct. 1955, 167 L.Ed.2d 929.

Certiorari to the United States Court of Appeals for the Second Circuit.

JUSTICE SOUTER delivered the opinion of the Court.

* * *

I

* * *

[Plaintiffs, subscribers to local telephone services, filed a class action against the major U.S. telephone companies [hereinafter ILCs], alleging that they had violated § 1 of the Sherman Antitrust Act through efforts (1) to inhibit the growth of local phone companies [hereinafter CLEC's] and (2) to eliminate competition among themselves in territories where any one was dominant.]

* * *

The United States District Court for the Southern District of New York dismissed the complaint for failure to state a claim upon which relief can be granted. The District Court acknowledged that "plaintiffs may allege a conspiracy by citing instances of parallel business behavior that suggest an agreement," but emphasized that "while '[c]ircumstantial evidence of consciously parallel behavior may have made heavy inroads into the traditional judicial attitude toward conspiracy[, . . .] "conscious parallelism" has not yet read conspiracy out of the Sherman Act entirely.'" 313 F.Supp.2d 174, 179 (2003) * * *. Thus, the District Court understood that allegations of parallel business conduct, taken alone, do not state a claim under § 1; plaintiffs must allege additional facts that "ten[d] to exclude independent self-interested conduct as an explanation for defendants' parallel behavior." * * * The District Court found plaintiffs' allegations of parallel ILEC actions to discourage competition inadequate because "the behavior of each ILEC in resisting the incursion of CLECs is fully explained by the ILEC's own interests in defending its individual territory." * * * As to the ILECs' supposed agreement against competing with each other, the District Court found that the complaint does not "alleg[e] facts ... suggesting that refraining from competing in other territories as CLECs was contrary to [the ILECs'] apparent economic interests, and consequently [does] not rais[e] an inference that [the ILECs'] actions were the result of a conspiracy." * * *

The Court of Appeals for the Second Circuit reversed, holding that the District Court tested the complaint by the wrong standard. It held that "plus factors are not *required* to be pleaded to permit an antitrust claim based on parallel conduct to survive dismissal." 425 F.3d 99, 114 (2005) (emphasis in original). Although the Court of Appeals took the view that plaintiffs must plead facts that "include conspiracy among the realm of 'plausible' possibilities in order to survive a motion to dismiss," it then said that "to rule that allegations of parallel anticompetitive conduct fail to support a plausible conspiracy claim, a court would have to conclude that there is no set of facts that would permit a plaintiff to demonstrate that the particular parallelism asserted was the product of collusion rather than coincidence." *Ibid*.

We granted certiorari to address the proper standard for pleading an antitrust conspiracy through allegations of parallel conduct, * * * and now reverse.

II

A

Because § 1 of the Sherman Act "does not prohibit [all] unreasonable restraints of trade ... but only restraints effected by a contract, combination, or conspiracy, * * * [t]he crucial question" is whether the challenged anticompetitive conduct "stem[s] from independent decision or from an agreement, tacit or express," * * *. While a showing of parallel "business behavior is admissible circumstantial evidence from which the fact finder may infer agreement," it falls short of "conclusively establish[ing] agreement or ... itself constitut[ing] a Sherman Act offense." * * * Even "conscious parallelism," a common reaction of "firms in a concentrated market [that] recogniz[e] their shared economic interests and their interdependence with respect to price and output decisions" is "not in itself unlawful." * * *

* * *

B

This case presents the antecedent question of what a plaintiff must plead in order to state a claim under § 1 of the Sherman Act. Federal Rule of Civil Procedure 8(a)(2) requires only "a short and plain statement of the claim showing that the pleader is entitled to relief," in order to "give the defendant fair notice of what the ... claim is and the grounds upon which it rests," *Conley v. Gibson,* * * *. While a complaint attacked by a Rule 12(b)(6) motion to dismiss does not need detailed factual allegations

* * *, a plaintiff's obligation to provide the "grounds" of his "enti-tle[ment] to relief" requires more than labels and conclusions, and a formulaic recitation of the elements of a cause of action will not do, see *Papasan v. Allain,* 478 U.S. 265, 286, 106 S. Ct. 2932, 92 L. Ed. 2d 209 (1986) (on a motion to dismiss, courts "are not bound to accept as true a legal conclusion couched as a factual allegation"). Factual allegations must be enough to raise a right to relief above the speculative level, see 5 C. Wright & A. Miller, Federal Practice and Procedure § 1216, pp. 235–236 (3d ed. 2004) (hereinafter Wright & Miller) ("[T]he pleading must contain something more ... than ... a statement of facts that merely creates a suspicion [of] a legally cognizable right of action") * * * on the assump-tion that all the allegations in the complaint are true (even if doubtful in fact) * * *.

In applying these general standards to a § 1 claim, we hold that stating such a claim requires a complaint with enough factual matter (taken as true) to suggest that an agreement was made. Asking for plausible grounds to infer an agreement does not impose a probability requirement at the pleading stage; it simply calls for enough fact to raise a reasonable expectation that discovery will reveal evidence of illegal agree-ment. And, of course, a well-pleaded complaint may proceed even if it strikes a savvy judge that actual proof of those facts is improbable, and "that a recovery is very remote and unlikely." * * * In identifying facts that are suggestive enough to render a § 1 conspiracy plausible, we have the benefit of the prior rulings and considered views of leading commenta-tors * * * that lawful parallel conduct fails to bespeak unlawful agree-ment. It makes sense to say, therefore, that an allegation of parallel conduct and a bare assertion of conspiracy will not suffice. Without more, parallel conduct does not suggest conspiracy, and a conclusory allegation of agreement at some unidentified point does not supply facts adequate to show illegality. Hence, when allegations of parallel conduct are set out in order to make a § 1 claim, they must be placed in a context that raises a suggestion of a preceding agreement, not merely parallel conduct that could just as well be independent action.

* * *

We alluded to the practical significance of the Rule 8 entitlement requirement in *Dura Pharmaceuticals, Inc. v. Broudo,* 544 U.S. 336, 125 S.Ct. 1627, 161 L.Ed.2d 577 (2005), when we explained that something beyond the mere possibility of loss causation must be alleged, lest a plaintiff with " 'a largely groundless claim' " be allowed to " 'take up the time of a number of other people, with the right to do so representing an *in terrorem* increment of the settlement value.' " *Id.,* at 347, 125 S.Ct. 1627 * * *.

Thus, it is one thing to be cautious before dismissing an antitrust complaint in advance of discovery * * * but quite another to forget that proceeding to antitrust discovery can be expensive. As we indicated over 20 years ago * * *, "a district court must retain the power to insist upon some specificity in pleading before allowing a potentially massive factual controversy to proceed." * * * That potential expense is obvious enough in the present case: plaintiffs represent a putative class of at least 90 percent of all subscribers to local telephone or high-speed Internet service in the continental United States, in an action against America's largest telecommunications firms (with many thousands of employees generating reams and gigabytes of business records) for unspecified (if any) instances of antitrust violations that allegedly occurred over a period of seven years.

It is no answer to say that a claim just shy of a plausible entitlement to relief can, if groundless, be weeded out early in the discovery process through "careful case management," * * * given the common lament that the success of judicial supervision in checking discovery abuse has been on the modest side. See, *e.g.*, Easterbrook, Discovery as Abuse, 69 B.U. L. Rev. 635, 638 (1989) ("Judges can do little about impositional discovery when parties control the legal claims to be presented and conduct the discovery themselves"). And it is self-evident that the problem of discovery abuse cannot be solved by "careful scrutiny of evidence at the summary judgment stage," much less "lucid instructions to juries"; * * * the threat of discovery expense will push cost-conscious defendants to settle even anemic cases before reaching those proceedings. Probably, then, it is only by taking care to require allegations that reach the level suggesting conspiracy that we can hope to avoid the potentially enormous expense of discovery in cases with no " 'reasonably founded hope that the [discovery] process will reveal relevant evidence' " to support a § 1 claim * * *.[6]

Plaintiffs do not, of course, dispute the requirement of plausibility and the need for something more than merely parallel behavior * * *, and their main argument against the plausibility standard at the pleading stage is its ostensible conflict with an early statement of ours construing Rule 8. Justice Black's opinion for the Court in *Conley v. Gibson* spoke not

---

6. The dissent takes heart in the reassurances of plaintiffs' counsel that discovery would be " ' "phased" ' " and "limited to the existence of the alleged conspiracy and class certification." * * * But determining whether some illegal agreement may have taken place between unspecified persons at different ILECs (each a multibillion dollar corporation with legions of management level employees) at some point over seven years is a sprawling, costly, and hugely time-consuming undertaking not easily susceptible to the kind of line drawing and case management that the dissent envisions. Perhaps the best answer to the dissent's optimism that antitrust discovery is open to effective judicial control is a more extensive quotation of the authority just cited, a judge with a background in antitrust law. Given the system that we have, the hope of effective judicial supervision is slim: "The timing is all wrong. The plaintiff files a sketchy complaint (the Rules of Civil Procedure discourage fulsome documents), and discovery is launched. A judicial officer does not know the details of the case the parties will present and in theory *cannot* know the details. Discovery is used to find the details. The judicial officer always knows less than the parties, and the parties themselves may not know very well where they are going or what they expect to find. A magistrate supervising discovery does not—cannot—know the expected productivity of a given request, because the nature of the requester's claim and the contents of the files (or head) of the adverse party are unknown. Judicial officers cannot measure the costs and benefits to the requester and so cannot isolate impositional requests. Requesters have no reason to disclose their own estimates because they gain from imposing costs on rivals (and may lose from an improvement in accuracy). The portions of the Rules of Civil Procedure calling on judges to trim back excessive demands, therefore, have been, and are doomed to be, hollow. We cannot prevent what we cannot detect; we cannot detect what we cannot define; we cannot define 'abusive' discovery except in theory, because in practice we lack essential information." Easterbrook, Discovery as Abuse, 69 B.U. L. Rev. 635, 638–639 (1989).

only of the need for fair notice of the grounds for entitlement to relief but of "the accepted rule that a complaint should not be dismissed for failure to state a claim unless it appears beyond doubt that the plaintiff can prove no set of facts in support of his claim which would entitle him to relief." * * * This "no set of facts" language can be read in isolation as saying that any statement revealing the theory of the claim will suffice unless its factual impossibility may be shown from the face of the pleadings; and the Court of Appeals appears to have read *Conley* in some such way when formulating its understanding of the proper pleading standard * * *.

On such a focused and literal reading of *Conley's* "no set of facts," a wholly conclusory statement of claim would survive a motion to dismiss whenever the pleadings left open the possibility that a plaintiff might later establish some "set of [undisclosed] facts" to support recovery. So here, the Court of Appeals specifically found the prospect of unearthing direct evidence of conspiracy sufficient to preclude dismissal, even though the complaint does not set forth a single fact in a context that suggests an agreement. * * * It seems fair to say that this approach to pleading would dispense with any showing of a " 'reasonably founded hope' " that a plaintiff would be able to make a case * * *. Mr. Micawber's optimism would be enough.

* * *

* * * [A]fter puzzling the profession for 50 years, this famous observation has earned its retirement. The phrase is best forgotten as an incomplete, negative gloss on an accepted pleading standard: once a claim has been stated adequately, it may be supported by showing any set of facts consistent with the allegations in the complaint. * * * *Conley,* then, described the breadth of opportunity to prove what an adequate complaint claims, not the minimum standard of adequate pleading to govern a complaint's survival.

III

When we look for plausibility in this complaint, we agree with the District Court that plaintiffs' claim of conspiracy in restraint of trade comes up short. To begin with, the complaint leaves no doubt that plaintiffs rest their § 1 claim on descriptions of parallel conduct and not on any independent allegation of actual agreement among the ILECs. * * * Although in form a few stray statements speak directly of agreement, on fair reading these are merely legal conclusions resting on the prior allegations. * * * The nub of the complaint, then, is the ILECs' parallel behavior, consisting of steps to keep the CLECs out and manifest disinterest in becoming CLECs themselves, and its sufficiency turns on the suggestions raised by this conduct when viewed in light of common economic experience.

* * * [T]here is no reason to infer that the companies had agreed among themselves to do what was only natural anyway; so natural, in fact, that if alleging parallel decisions to resist competition were enough to

imply an antitrust conspiracy, pleading a § 1 violation against almost any group of competing businesses would be a sure thing.

Plaintiffs' second conspiracy theory rests on the competitive reticence among the ILECs themselves * * *.

But * * * [such a lack of competition is] not suggestive of conspiracy, not if history teaches anything. In a traditionally unregulated industry with low barriers to entry, sparse competition among large firms dominating separate geographical segments of the market could very well signify illegal agreement, but here we have an obvious alternative explanation. * * * [Historically] monopoly was the norm in telecommunications, not the exception. * * * The ILECs were born in that world, doubtless liked the world the way it was, and surely knew the adage about him who lives by the sword. Hence, a natural explanation for the noncompetition alleged is that the former Government-sanctioned monopolists were sitting tight, expecting their neighbors to do the same thing.

* * *

The judgment of the Court of Appeals for the Second Circuit is reversed, and the cause is remanded for further proceedings consistent with this opinion.

It is so ordered.

JUSTICE STEVENS, with whom JUSTICE GINSBURG joins except as to Part IV, dissenting.

* * * [T]his is a case in which there is no dispute about the substantive law. If the defendants acted independently, their conduct was perfectly lawful. If, however, that conduct is the product of a horizontal agreement among potential competitors, it was unlawful. Plaintiffs have alleged such an agreement and, because the complaint was dismissed in advance of answer, the allegation has not even been denied. Why, then, does the case not proceed? Does a judicial opinion that the charge is not "plausible" provide a legally acceptable reason for dismissing the complaint? I think not.

Respondents' amended complaint describes a variety of circumstantial evidence and [¶ 51 of the complaint] * * * allege[s] that petitioners entered into an agreement that has long been recognized as a classic *per se* violation of the Sherman Act. * * *

* * *

The Court and petitioners' legal team are no doubt correct that the parallel conduct alleged is consistent with the absence of any contract, combination, or conspiracy. But that conduct is also entirely consistent with the *presence* of the illegal agreement alleged in the complaint. And the charge that petitioners "agreed not to compete with one another" is not just one of "a few stray statements," * * * it is an allegation describing unlawful conduct. As such, the Federal Rules of Civil Procedure, our longstanding precedent, and sound practice mandate that the District

Court at least require some sort of response from petitioners before dismissing the case.

Two practical concerns presumably explain the Court's dramatic departure from settled procedural law. Private antitrust litigation can be enormously expensive, and there is a risk that jurors may mistakenly conclude that evidence of parallel conduct has proved that the parties acted pursuant to an agreement when they in fact merely made similar independent decisions. Those concerns merit careful case management, including strict control of discovery, careful scrutiny of evidence at the summary judgment stage, and lucid instructions to juries; they do not, however, justify the dismissal of an adequately pleaded complaint without even requiring the defendants to file answers denying a charge that they in fact engaged in collective decision making. More importantly, they do not justify an interpretation of Federal Rule of Civil Procedure 12(b)(6) that seems to be driven by the majority's appraisal of the plausibility of the ultimate factual allegation rather than its legal sufficiency.

I

* * *

Under the relaxed pleading standards of the Federal Rules, the idea was not to keep litigants out of court but rather to keep them in. The merits of a claim would be sorted out during a flexible pretrial process and, as appropriate, through the crucible of trial. * * *

II

It is in the context of this history that *Conley v. Gibson* * * * must be understood. * * *

Consistent with the design of the Federal Rules, *Conley's* "no set of facts" formulation permits outright dismissal only when proceeding to discovery or beyond would be futile. Once it is clear that a plaintiff has stated a claim that, if true, would entitle him to relief, matters of proof are appropriately relegated to other stages of the trial process. Today, however, in its explanation of a decision to dismiss a complaint that it regards as a fishing expedition, the Court scraps *Conley's* "no set of facts" language. Concluding that the phrase has been "questioned, criticized, and explained away long enough" * * * the Court dismisses it as careless composition.

If *Conley's* "no set of facts" language is to be interred, let it not be without a eulogy. That exact language, which the majority says has "puzzl[ed] the profession for 50 years," * * * has been cited as authority in a dozen opinions of this Court and four separate writings. In not one of those 16 opinions was the language "questioned," "criticized," or "explained away." Indeed, today's opinion is the first by any Member of this Court to express *any* doubt as to the adequacy of the *Conley* formulation. Taking their cues from the federal courts, 26 States and the District of Columbia utilize as their standard for dismissal of a complaint the very language the majority repudiates: whether it appears "beyond doubt" that "no set of facts" in support of the claim would entitle the plaintiff to relief.

Petitioners have not requested that the *Conley* formulation be retired, nor have any of the six *amici* who filed briefs in support of petitioners. I would not rewrite the Nation's civil procedure textbooks and call into doubt the pleading rules of most of its States without far more informed deliberation as to the costs of doing so. Congress has established a process—a rulemaking process—for revisions of that order. * * *

* * *

* * * *Conley's* statement that a complaint is not to be dismissed unless "no set of facts" in support thereof would entitle the plaintiff to relief is hardly "puzzling." * * * It reflects a philosophy that, unlike in the days of code pleading, separating the wheat from the chaff is a task assigned to the pretrial and trial process. *Conley's* language, in short, captures the policy choice embodied in the Federal Rules and binding on the federal courts.

We have consistently reaffirmed that basic understanding of the Federal Rules in the half century since *Conley*. * * *

* * *

Everything today's majority says would * * * make perfect sense if it were ruling on a Rule 56 motion for summary judgment and the evidence included nothing more than the Court has described. But it should go without saying * * * that a heightened production burden at the summary judgment stage does not translate into a heightened pleading burden at the complaint stage. The majority rejects the complaint in this case because—in light of the fact that the parallel conduct alleged is consistent with ordinary market behavior—the claimed conspiracy is "conceivable" but not "plausible." * * * But even if the majority's speculation is correct, its "plausibility" standard is irreconcilable with Rule 8 and with our governing precedents. * * * [F]ear of the burdens of litigation does not justify factual conclusions supported only by lawyers' arguments rather than sworn denials or admissible evidence.

* * *

III

[T]he theory on which the Court permits dismissal is that, so far as the Federal Rules are concerned, no agreement has been alleged at all. This is a mind-boggling conclusion.

* * * I am * * * willing to entertain the majority's belief that any agreement among the companies was unlikely. But the plaintiffs allege in three places in their complaint * * * that the ILECs did in fact agree both to prevent competitors from entering into their local markets and to forgo competition with each other. And as the Court recognizes, at the motion to dismiss stage, a judge assumes "that all the allegations in the complaint are true (even if doubtful in fact)." * * *

The majority circumvents this obvious obstacle to dismissal by pretending that it does not exist. The Court admits that "in form a few stray statements in the complaint speak directly of agreement," but disregards those allegations by saying that "on fair reading these are merely legal conclusions resting on the prior allegations" of parallel conduct. * * * The Court's dichotomy between factual allegations and "legal conclusions" is the stuff of a bygone era * * *. That distinction was a defining feature of code pleading * * *, but was conspicuously abolished when the Federal Rules were enacted in 1938. * * *. "Defendants entered into a contract" is no more a legal conclusion than "defendant negligently drove," see [Federal Rules Form 11]. Indeed it is less of one.

To be clear, if I had been the trial judge in this case, I would not have permitted the plaintiffs to engage in massive discovery based solely on the allegations in this complaint. On the other hand, I surely would not have dismissed the complaint without requiring the defendants to answer the charge that they "have agreed not to compete with one another and otherwise allocated customers and markets to one another." Even a sworn denial of that charge would not justify a summary dismissal without giving the plaintiffs the opportunity to take depositions from * * * at least one responsible executive representing each of the * * * defendants.

* * *

IV

* * *

The transparent policy concern that drives the decision is the interest in protecting antitrust defendants—who in this case are some of the wealthiest corporations in our economy—from the burdens of pretrial discovery. * * * Even if it were not apparent that the legal fees petitioners have incurred in arguing the merits of their Rule 12(b) motion have far exceeded the cost of limited discovery, or that those discovery costs would burden respondents as well as petitioners, that concern would not provide an adequate justification for this law-changing decision. For in the final analysis it is only a lack of confidence in the ability of trial judges to control discovery, buttressed by appellate judges' independent appraisal of the plausibility of profoundly serious factual allegations, that could account for this stark break from precedent.

* * *

Accordingly, I respectfully dissent.

NOTE AND QUESTIONS

Does the *Twombly* case, with its harsh attack on Conley v. Gibson and the "no set of facts" standard, imply that there is a new heightened pleading requirement for all actions in the federal courts, in that any stated claim for relief must be "plausible"? In ERICKSON v. PARDUS, 551 U.S. 89, 127 S.Ct. 2197, 167 L.Ed.2d 1081 (2007), which was decided less than one month after *Twombly*, the Supreme Court again examined the Rule 8(a) pleading requirement. In that case plaintiff, a federal prisoner, filed a pro se lawsuit, alleging that he had been denied proper treatment for a case of hepatitis C, placing his life in jeopardy. The trial court dismissed the action under Rule 12(b)(6) on the ground that the complaint failed to allege that defendant's actions had caused substantial harm, and the Court of Appeals affirmed, finding petitioner had made "only conclusory allegations" of an "independent harm" resulting from the denial of treatment. Erickson v. Pardus, 198 Fed. Appx. 695, 698 (10th Cir. 2006). The Supreme Court reversed, per curiam, stating:

> Federal Rule of Civil Procedure 8(a)(2) requires only "a short and plain statement of the claim showing that the pleader is entitled to relief." Specific facts are not necessary; the statement need only " 'give the defendant fair notice of what the ... claim is and the grounds on which it rests.' " *Bell Atlantic v. Twombly* * * * (quoting *Conley v. Gibson*, 355 U.S. 41, 47 * * * *).

Id. at 93, 127 S.Ct. at 2200, 167 L.Ed.2d at 1085. In light of the *Erickson* decision, along with its quotation from *Conley*, questions remained about the general applicability of *Twombly*'s plausibility standard. See Ides, Bell Atlantic *and the Principle of Substantive Sufficiency Under Federal Rule of Civil Procedure 8(a)(2): Toward a Structured Approach to Federal Pleading Practice*, 243 F.R.D. 604 (2006). The Supreme Court answered some of these questions in the decision that follows.

ASHCROFT v. IQBAL

Supreme Court of the United States, 2009.
556 U.S. ____, 129 S.Ct. 1937, 173 L.Ed.2d 868.

Certiorari to the United States Court of Appeals for the Second Circuit.

JUSTICE KENNEDY delivered the opinion of the Court.

[Plaintiff, a Pakistani Muslim man, filed a discrimination suit challenging his detention in a maximum-security unit as a person of "high interest" during the federal government's investigation of the attacks of September 11, 2001.]

* * *

To survive a motion to dismiss, a complaint must contain sufficient factual matter, accepted as true, to "state a claim to relief that is plausible on its face." [*Twombly*, p. 298, supra.] A claim has facial plausibility when the plaintiff pleads factual content that allows the court to draw the reasonable inference that the defendant is liable for the misconduct alleged. * * * The plausibility standard is not akin to a "probability requirement," but it asks for more than a sheer possibility that a defendant has acted unlawfully. * * * Where a complaint pleads facts that are "merely consistent with" a defendant's liability, it "stops short of the line between possibility and plausibility of 'entitlement to relief.' " * * *

Two working principles underlie our decision in *Twombly*. First, the tenet that a court must accept as true all of the allegations contained in a complaint is inapplicable to legal conclusions. Threadbare recitals of the elements of a cause of action, supported by mere conclusory statements, do not suffice. * * * (Although for the purposes of a motion to dismiss we must take all of the factual allegations in the complaint as true, we "are not bound to accept as true a legal conclusion couched as a factual allegation" (internal quotation marks omitted)). Rule 8 marks a notable and generous departure from the hyper-technical, code-pleading regime of a prior era, but it does not unlock the doors of discovery for a plaintiff armed with nothing more than conclusions. Second, only a complaint that states a plausible claim for relief survives a motion to dismiss. *Id.*, at 556. Determining whether a complaint states a plausible claim for relief will, as the Court of Appeals observed, be a context-specific task that requires the reviewing court to draw on its judicial experience and common sense. 490 F.3d, at 157–158. But where the well-pleaded facts do not permit the court to infer more than the mere possibility of misconduct, the complaint has alleged—but it has not "show[n]"—"that the pleader is entitled to relief." Fed. Rule Civ. Proc. 8(a)(2).

In keeping with these principles a court considering a motion to dismiss can choose to begin by identifying pleadings that, because they are no more than conclusions, are not entitled to the assumption of truth. While legal conclusions can provide the framework of a complaint, they must be supported by factual allegations. When there are well-pleaded factual allegations, a court should assume their veracity and then determine whether they plausibly give rise to an entitlement to relief.

* * *

B

Under *Twombly*'s construction of Rule 8, we conclude that respondent's complaint has not "nudged [his] claims" of invidious discrimination "across the line from conceivable to plausible." * * *

We begin our analysis by identifying the allegations in the complaint that are not entitled to the assumption of truth. Respondent pleads that petitioners "knew of, condoned, and willfully and maliciously agreed to subject [him]" to harsh conditions of confinement "as a matter of policy, solely on account of [his] religion, race, and/or national origin and for no legitimate penological interest." Complaint ¶ 96, * * *. * * * These bare assertions, much like the pleading of conspiracy in Twombly, amount to nothing more than a "formulaic recitation of the elements" of a constitutional discrimination claim, * * * namely, that petitioners adopted a policy " 'because of,' not merely 'in spite of,' its adverse effects upon an identifiable group." * * * [Pers. Adm. of Mass. v.] Feeney, 442 U.S. [256,]

at 279. As such, the allegations are conclusory and not entitled to be assumed true. To be clear, we do not reject these bald allegations on the ground that they are unrealistic or nonsensical. We do not so characterize them any more than the Court in *Twombly* rejected the plaintiffs' express allegation of a " 'contract, combination or conspiracy to prevent competitive entry,' " because it thought that claim too chimerical to be maintained. It is the conclusory nature of respondent's allegations, rather than their extravagantly fanciful nature, that disentitles them to the presumption of truth.

We next consider the factual allegations in respondent's complaint to determine if they plausibly suggest an entitlement to relief. The complaint alleges that "the [FBI], under the direction of Defendant MUELLER, arrested and detained thousands of Arab Muslim men … as part of its investigation of the events of September 11." Complaint ¶ 47, * * *. It further claims that "[t]he policy of holding post-September-11th detainees in highly restrictive conditions of confinement until they were 'cleared' by the FBI was approved by Defendants ASHCROFT and MUELLER in discussions in the weeks after September 11, 2001." Id., ¶ 69, * * *. Taken as true, these allegations are consistent with petitioners' purposefully designating detainees "of high interest" because of their race, religion, or national origin. But given more likely explanations, they do not plausibly establish this purpose.

The September 11 attacks were perpetrated by 19 Arab Muslim hijackers who counted themselves members in good standing of al Qaeda, an Islamic fundamentalist group. Al Qaeda was headed by another Arab Muslim—Osama bin Laden—and composed in large part of his Arab Muslim disciples. It should come as no surprise that a legitimate policy directing law enforcement to arrest and detain individuals because of their suspected link to the attacks would produce a disparate, incidental impact on Arab Muslims, even though the purpose of the policy was to target neither Arabs nor Muslims. On the facts respondent alleges the arrests Mueller oversaw were likely lawful and justified by his nondiscriminatory intent to detain aliens who were illegally present in the United States and who had potential connections to those who committed terrorist acts. As between that "obvious alternative explanation" for the arrests, and the purposeful, invidious discrimination respondent asks us to infer, discrimination is not a plausible conclusion.

But even if the complaint's well-pleaded facts give rise to a plausible inference that respondent's arrest was the result of unconstitutional discrimination, that inference alone would not entitle respondent to relief. It is important to recall that respondent's complaint challenges neither the constitutionality of his arrest nor his initial detention * * *. Respondent's constitutional claims against petitioners rest solely on their ostensible "policy of holding post-September-11th detainees" in the [Administrative Maximum Special Housing Unit, known as "ADMAX SHU"] once they were categorized as "of high interest." Complaint ¶ 69, * * *. To prevail on that theory, the complaint must contain facts plausibly showing that petitioners purposefully adopted a policy of classifying post-September-11 detainees as "of high interest" because of their race, religion, or national origin.

This the complaint fails to do. Though respondent alleges that various other defendants, who are not before us, may have labeled him a person of "of high interest" for impermissible reasons, his only factual allegation against petitioners accuses them of adopting a policy approving "restrictive conditions of confinement" for post-September-11 detainees until they were " 'cleared' by the FBI." Ibid. Accepting the truth of that allegation, the complaint does not show, or even intimate, that petitioners purposefully housed detainees in the ADMAX SHU due to their race, religion, or national origin. All it plausibly suggests is that the Nation's top law enforcement officers, in the aftermath of a devastating terrorist attack, sought to keep suspected terrorists in the most secure conditions available until the suspects could be cleared of terrorist activity. Respondent does not argue, nor can he, that such a motive would violate petitioners' constitutional obligations. He would need to allege more by way of factual content to "nudg[e]" his claim of purposeful discrimination "across the line from conceivable to plausible."

* * *

C

Respondent offers three arguments that bear on our disposition of his case, but none is persuasive.

1

Respondent first says that our decision in *Twombly* should be limited to pleadings made in the context of an antitrust dispute. * * * This argument is not supported by *Twombly* and is incompatible with the Federal Rules of Civil Procedure. Though *Twombly* determined the sufficiency of a complaint sounding in antitrust, the decision was based on our interpretation and application of Rule 8. * * * That Rule in turn governs the pleading standard "in all civil actions and proceedings in the United States district courts." Fed. Rule Civ. Proc. 1. Our decision in *Twombly* expounded the pleading standard for "all civil actions," * * * and it applies to antitrust and discrimination suits alike. * * *

2

Respondent next implies that our construction of Rule 8 should be tempered where, as here, the Court of Appeals has "instructed the district court to cabin discovery in such a way as to preserve" petitioners' defense of qualified immunity "as much as possible in anticipation of a summary judgment motion." * * * We have held, however, that the question presented by a motion to dismiss a complaint for insufficient pleadings does not turn on the controls placed upon the discovery process. * * *

Our rejection of the careful-case-management approach is especially important in suits where Government-official defendants are entitled to assert the defense of qualified immunity. The basic thrust of the qualified-immunity doctrine is to free officials from the concerns of litigation, including "avoidance of disruptive discovery." Siegert v. Gilley, 500 U.S. 226, 236, 111 S.Ct. 1789, 114 L.Ed.2d 277 (1991) (KENNEDY, J., concurring in judgment). There are serious and legitimate reasons for this. If a government official is to devote time to his or her duties, and to the formulation of sound and responsible policies, it is counterproductive to require the substantial diversion that is attendant to participating in litigation and making informed decisions as to how it should proceed. Litigation, though necessary to ensure that officials comply with the law, exacts heavy costs in terms of efficiency and expenditure of valuable time and resources that might otherwise be directed to the proper execution of the work of the Government. The costs of diversion are only magnified when Government officials are charged with responding to * * * "a national and international security emergency unprecedented in the history of the American Republic." * * *

It is no answer to these concerns to say that discovery for petitioners can be deferred while pretrial proceedings continue for other defendants. It is quite likely that, when discovery as to the other parties proceeds, it would prove necessary for petitioners and their counsel to participate in the process to ensure the case does not develop in a misleading or slanted way that causes prejudice to their position. Even if petitioners are not yet themselves subject to discovery orders, then, they would not be free from the burdens of discovery.

We decline respondent's invitation to relax the pleading requirements on the ground that the Court of Appeals promises petitioners minimally intrusive discovery. That promise provides especially cold comfort in this pleading context, where we are impelled to give real content to the concept of qualified immunity for high-level officials who must be neither deterred nor detracted from the vigorous performance of their duties. Because respondent's complaint is deficient under Rule 8, he is not entitled to discovery, cabined or otherwise.

3

Respondent finally maintains that the Federal Rules expressly allow him to allege petitioners' discriminatory intent "generally," which he equates with a conclusory allegation. It follows, respondent says, that his complaint is sufficiently well pleaded because it claims that petitioners discriminated against him "on account of [his] religion, race, and/or national origin and for no legitimate penological interest." Complaint ¶ 96, * * *. Were we required to accept this allegation as true, respondent's complaint would survive petitioners' motion to dismiss. But the Federal Rules do not require courts to credit a complaint's conclusory statements without reference to its factual context.

It is true that Rule 9(b) requires particularity when pleading "fraud or mistake," while allowing "[m]alice, intent, knowledge, and other conditions of a person's mind [to] be alleged generally." But "generally" is a relative term. In the context of Rule 9, it is to be compared to the particularity requirement applicable to fraud or mistake. Rule 9 merely excuses a party from pleading discriminatory intent under an elevated pleading standard. It does not give him license to evade the less rigid-though still operative-strictures of Rule 8. See 5A C. Wright & A. Miller, Federal Practice and Procedure § 1301, p. 291 (3d ed. 2004) ("[A] rigid rule requiring the detailed pleading of a condition of mind would be undesirable because, absent overriding considerations pressing for a specificity requirement, as in the case of averments of fraud or mistake, the general 'short and plain statement of the claim' mandate in Rule 8(a) ... should control the second sentence of Rule 9(b)"). And Rule 8 does not empower respondent to plead the bare elements of his cause of action, affix the label "general allegation," and expect his complaint to survive a motion to dismiss.

V

We hold that respondent's complaint fails to plead sufficient facts to state a claim for purposeful and unlawful discrimination against petitioners. The Court of Appeals should decide in the first instance whether to remand to the District Court so that respondent can seek leave to amend his deficient complaint.

The judgment of the Court of Appeals is reversed, and the case is remanded for further proceedings consistent with this opinion.

[The dissenting opinion of Justice Souter, in which Justices Stevens, Ginsburg, and Breyer joined, is omitted.]

NOTES AND QUESTIONS

1. How important are uniform pleading rules? What problems might arise from having pleading rules depend on the category of the lawsuit? Should courts retain discretion to adapt pleading rules in specific cases? See Subrin, *Fudge Points and Thin Ice in Discovery Reform and the Case for Selective Substance–Specific Procedure*, 46 Fla. L. Rev. 27, 28 (1994).

2. How should the anticipated costs of discovery affect the pleading standard in a particular case? Professor Epstein has argued that "as the costs of discovery mount, the case for terminating litigation earlier in the cycle gets ever stronger," and that early termination is particularly appropriate "in those cases where the plaintiff relies on public information, easily assembled and widely available, that can be effectively rebutted by other public evidence." Epstein, Bell Atlantic v. Twombly: *How Motions To Dismiss Become (Disguised) Summary Judgments*, 25 Wash. U. J. L. & Pol'y 61, 66–67 (2007). For a critical comment, see *Leading Cases*, 121 Harv. L. Rev. 305, 309–15 (2007).

3. State courts, when deciding a motion to dismiss under state law, are not required to follow either the Federal Rules or federal judicial standards

governing the sufficiency of a complaint. Justice Stevens pointed out in his dissent that about half of the states did, in fact, follow the *Conley* "no set of facts" standard. State courts so far have not unanimously retreated from *Conley* and embraced the *Twombly* plausibility standard. Compare Sisney v. Best Inc., 754 N.W.2d 804 (S.D. 2008) (adopting *Twombly* pleading standard for state court pleadings), with Colby v. Umbrella, Inc., 184 Vt. 1, 955 A.2d 1082 (2008) (rejecting *Twombly* and retaining *Conley* standard for state court pleadings) and Cullen v. Auto–Owners Insurance Co., 218 Ariz. 417, 189 P.3d 344 (2008) (rejecting both *Twombly* and *Conley* standards and retaining unique Arizona state pleading requirements).

4. *Twombly* and *Iqbal* provide a window into a fascinating debate about judicial case management as an alternative to stricter pleading standards. See Chapter 11, infra. The *Twombly* majority commented that "the success of judicial supervision in checking discovery abuse has been on the modest side," citing a 1989 law review article that contended the trial courts are impotent in this area. Since 1983, the Federal Rules have been amended in important ways to curb litigation expense and to increase the court's managerial authority. See Cavanagh, Twombly, *the Federal Rules of Civil Procedure and the Courts*, 82 St. John's L. Rev. 877 (2008). Justice Stevens, in his *Twombly* dissent, underscored that "[t]he Court vastly underestimates a district court's case-management arsenal," 550 U.S. at 595 n. 13, 127 S.Ct. at 1988 n.13, 167 L.Ed.2d at 964 n.13, and a respected district court judge has sharply questioned this aspect of the majority's decision. See McMahon, *The Law of Unintended Consequences: Shockwaves in the Lower Courts After* Bell Atlantic Corp. v. Twombly, 41 Suffolk U. L. Rev. 851, 869–70 (2008). In *Iqbal*, the Court likewise criticized case management. See p. 311, supra. Keep an open mind on these issues as we study such topics as sanctions, discovery case plans, case management, and summary judgment.

4. THE BURDEN OF PLEADING AND THE BURDEN OF PRODUCTION

The burden of pleading an issue usually is assigned to the party who has the burden of producing evidence on that issue at trial, although "the burden of pleading need not coincide with the burden of producing evidence." Hamabe, *Functions of Rule 12(b)(6) in the Federal Rules of Civil Procedure: A Categorization Approach*, 15 Campbell L. Rev. 119, 172 (1993). Typically, plaintiff must put forth evidence on certain matters basic to the claim for relief, or he cannot prevail. In a slander action, for example, plaintiff must introduce evidence that the remarks were made, that they were published, and that he was injured thereby. If plaintiff rests his case without producing evidence on any one of these issues, the court will dismiss the action and enter judgment for defendant. Therefore, plaintiff must plead those matters he must prove. The rationale for the rule is simple. If plaintiff cannot legitimately allege the existence of each of the basic elements of his claim, it may be assumed that he would not be able to introduce evidence on them at trial.

On the other hand, plaintiff normally does not have to plead matters on which defendant must introduce proof. If plaintiff were required to plead the nonexistence of every defense, not only would the pleading be long, complex, and fraught with danger for a plaintiff who omitted a remote possibility, but also the pleadings would not reveal, in any direct way, the defenses upon which defendant actually intended to rely. By placing the burden of pleading defenses on defendant, the court and parties know exactly on which of the many possible defenses he intends to introduce evidence, thus making preparation for trial and the actual work at trial more manageable. Once defendant has established a defense at trial, plaintiff will then have a second burden of production, this time to introduce evidence as to facts that will avoid defendant's defense. For example, if defendant proves that allegedly slanderous statements were made to plaintiff's prospective employer under conditions that rendered the statements privileged, plaintiff then must carry the burden of producing evidence showing that the statements were made maliciously and solely with intent to injure plaintiff, thereby vitiating the defense. Obviously, plaintiff is not required to plead, in the original complaint, matters to avoid defenses, since he cannot tell which defenses will be raised until the answer is filed. In some jurisdictions plaintiff is required to set forth matters that avoid defendant's defenses in a second pleading, which serves as a reply to the answer; in other jurisdictions the decision whether to require a reply is left to the trial court's discretion. Matters of avoidance are limited and well recognized so that a reply is most often unnecessary.

Other Considerations in Allocating the Burden of Pleading

Sometimes plaintiff is required to plead in the complaint the nonexistence of certain defenses upon which defendant has the burden of proof, although as we have seen, such a requirement is technically illogical. The reason for these special rules is a combination of the historical and practical. Consider, for example, a case in which plaintiff sues defendant on an overdue note. Payment of a note traditionally has been considered a defense to be proved by defendant, who by virtue of having a receipt usually is in a better position to put in evidence on the issue. Nevertheless, plaintiff, as part of the claim, must allege nonpayment. Without such an allegation the complaint would really say nothing justifying legal action; it simply would set forth the existence of the note without mentioning the nature of the breach of its terms. To inform the court and defendant as to the basis of the complaint, an allegation of nonpayment is essential. It is only when a defense, such as payment, goes to the very heart of the action, so that plaintiff should, in order to state a claim, be required to face the issue and allege in good faith that such defense does not exist, that the burden of pleading and the burden of producing evidence need not coincide. Another example occurs in the slander context in which some courts consider the truth of the remarks an absolute defense. In some of these jurisdictions, although not all, falsity is thought to be so much a part of the basic action, that plaintiff must plead it, even though defendant has the burden of introducing evidence of truth. The rule that plaintiff must plead an issue that is "essential" has been criticized as "meaningless" and "circular." Lee, *Pleading and Proof: The Economics of Legal Burdens*, 1997 B.Y.U. L. Rev. 1, 1.

Because of the technical imbalance in cases in which plaintiff must plead the nonexistence of a defense in order to state a claim, some courts require defendant, if he really intends to pursue the defense, to raise it specially in the answer, rather than by simply denying plaintiff's allegation; otherwise the defense will be waived. Thus, before such an issue actually is tried, it will be pleaded both in the complaint and in the answer.

Allocation of the pleading burden sometimes is specified by rules or statutes that set forth matters that are to be considered defenses and contained in the answer. See, e.g., Federal Rule 8(c), in which the enumerated matters usually are those that traditionally have been treated as defenses both as to the burden of pleading and the burden of proof. Not all jurisdictions adhere to these traditional views, however. For example, contributory negligence historically was treated as a defense, but today, in a number of jurisdictions, plaintiff, in order to prevail in a negligence case, must prove his own due care. If the pleading rule in these jurisdictions deems the issue of plaintiff's negligence to be a defense, it creates a serious anomaly, since defendant must raise the issue even though plaintiff is required to prove it. Furthermore, since a defense is waived if defendant does not plead it, the failure of defendant to raise the matter in the answer seems to obviate any need for plaintiff to prove the matter, thus thwarting the express policy of the jurisdiction requiring plaintiff to prove his own due care.

5. PLEADING SPECIAL MATTERS

Read Federal Rule of Civil Procedure 9 and the related materials in the Supplement.

NOTES AND QUESTIONS

1. Why should Rule 9(b) single out fraud and mistake for heightened pleading? See Richman, Lively & Mell, *The Pleading of Fraud: Rhymes Without Reason*, 60 S. Cal. L. Rev. 959 (1987). Commentators typically point to four policies favoring the pleading of fraud with particularity: "protection of reputation, deterrence of frivolous or strike suits, defense of completed transactions, and providing adequate notice." Fairman, *Heightened Pleading*, 81 Texas L. Rev. 551, 563 (2002). What are the costs of imposing a heightened pleading requirement?

2. Fraud involves some aspect of concealment by defendant. Yet some courts in construing the particularity requirement demand that plaintiff

specify "the who, what, when, where and how" of defendant's acts. Fairman, Note 1, supra, at 565–66. But see Jairett v. First Montauk Corp., 203 F.R.D. 181, 186 (E.D.Pa. 2001) (stating that "[i]n assessing fraud claims under Rule 9(b), the Court of Appeals for the Third Circuit has held that plaintiffs need not plead the 'date, place or time' of the fraud, so long as they use an 'alternative means of injecting precision and some measure of substantiation into their allegations of fraud' ") (citation omitted). Without discovery, how likely is a plaintiff to have access to information setting out the details of the alleged fraud? Is the particularity requirement of Rule 9(b) justified as a way to shield defendants from the expense of burdensome discovery requests in lawsuits that appear to be marginal? Would a better solution be to shift the expense of discovery in fraud cases? See Sovern, *Reconsidering Federal Civil Rule 9(b): Do We Need Particularized Pleading Requirements in Fraud Cases?*, 104 F.R.D. 143 (1985).

3. Congress became particularly dissatisfied with the application of Rule 9(b) in securities fraud cases and responded by enacting the Private Securities Litigation Reform Act (PSLRA) of 1995, Pub. L. No. 104–67, 109 Stat. 737 (1995). The PSLRA imposes a "super-heightened pleading standard" on such lawsuits. Miller, *The Pretrial Rush to Judgment: Are the "Litigation Explosion," "Liability Crisis," and Efficiency Clichés Eroding Our Day in Court and Jury Trial Commitments?*, 78 N.Y.U. L. Rev. 982, 1012 (2003). Professor Miller has explained:

> The statute requires that the complaint specify each statement alleged to have been misleading and give the reason or reasons why each is misleading. In addition, if an allegation is made on information and belief, all facts on which that belief is formed must be stated with particularity. * * * Finally, facts giving rise to a "strong inference" that the defendant acted with scienter must be stated with particularity.

Id. The Act also stays discovery until after the motion to dismiss has been decided.

Unfortunately, the PSLRA left ambiguous just what a plaintiff must allege to survive a motion to dismiss, and pleading standards have diverged from circuit to circuit. In 2007, the Supreme Court attempted to clarify one of the most controversial of those pleading requirements.

TELLABS, INC. v. MAKOR ISSUES AND RIGHTS, LTD.

Supreme Court of the United States.
551 U.S. 308, 127 S.Ct. 2499, 168 L.Ed.2d 179 (2007).

Certiorari to the United States Court of Appeals for the Seventh Circuit.

JUSTICE GINSBURG delivered the opinion of the Court.

* * *

Exacting pleading requirements are among the control measures Congress included in the PLSRA. The Act requires plaintiffs to state with particularity both the facts constituting the alleged violation, and the facts evidencing scienter, *i.e.*, the defendant's intention "to deceive, manipulate, or defraud." *Ernst & Ernst v. Hochfelder*, 425 U.S. 185, 194, and n. 12 (1976) * * *. This case concerns the latter requirement * * *. [The Act requires that] plaintiffs must "state with particularity facts giving rise to a strong inference that the defendant acted with the required state of mind." * * *

Congress left the key term "strong inference" undefined, and Courts of Appeals have divided on its meaning. In the case before us, the Court of Appeals for the Seventh Circuit held that the "strong inference" standard would be met if the complaint "allege[d] facts from which, if true, a reasonable person could infer that the defendant acted with the required intent." 437 F.3d 588, 602 (2006). That formulation, we conclude, does not capture the stricter demand Congress sought to convey * * *. Rather, to determine whether a complaint's scienter allegations can survive threshold inspection for sufficiency, a court * * * must engage in a comparative evaluation; it must consider, not only inferences urged by the plaintiff, as the Seventh Circuit did, but also competing inferences rationally drawn from the facts alleged. An inference of fraudulent intent may be plausible, yet less cogent than other, nonculpable explanations for the defendant's conduct. To qualify as "strong" we hold an inference of scienter must be more than merely plausible or reasonable—it must be cogent and at least as compelling as any opposing inference of nonfraudulent intent.

* * *

* * * Prior to the enactment of the PSLRA, the sufficiency of a complaint for securities fraud was governed not by Rule 8, but by the heightened pleading standard set forth in Rule 9(b). * * *

* * *

Setting a uniform pleading standard for * * * [such] actions was among Congress' objectives when it enacted the PSLRA. * * * With no clear guide from Congress other than its "inten[tion] to strengthen the pleading requirements," H.R. Conf. Rep., p.41, Courts of Appeals have diverged again, this time in construing the term "strong inference." * * * Our task is to prescribe a workable construction of the "strong inference" standard, a reading geared to the PSLRA's twin goals: to curb frivolous, lawyer-driven litigation, while preserving investors' ability to recover on meritorious claims.

* * *

We establish the following prescriptions: *First*, faced with a Rule 12(b)(6) motion to dismiss * * * courts must * * * accept all factual allegations in the complaint as true. * * *

Second, courts must consider the complaint in its entirety, as well as other sources courts ordinarily examine when ruling on Rule 12(b)(6) motions to dismiss, in particular, documents incorporated into the complaint by reference, and matters of which a court may take judicial notice. * * * The inquiry * * * is whether *all* of the facts alleged, taken collectively, give rise to a strong inference of scienter, not whether any individual allegation, scrutinized in isolation, meets that standard. * * *

Third, in determining whether pleaded facts give rise to a "strong" inference of scienter, the court must take into account plausible opposing inferences. The Seventh Circuit expressly declined to engage in such a comparative inquiry. * * *

The strength of an inference cannot be decided in a vacuum. The inquiry is inherently comparative: How likely is it that one conclusion, as compared to others, follows from the underlying facts? * * * A complaint will survive, we hold, only if a reasonable person would deem the inference of scienter cogent and at least as compelling as any opposing inference one could draw from the facts alleged.

* * *

While we reject the Seventh Circuit's approach * * *, we do not decide whether, under the standard we have described, * * * [plaintiff's] allegations warrant "a strong inference that * * * [defendants] acted with the required state of mind." * * * Neither the District Court nor the Court of Appeals had the opportunity to consider the matter in light of the prescriptions we announce today. We therefore vacate the Seventh Circuit's judgment so that the case can be reexamined in accord with our construction * * *.

* * *

[Justice Scalia and Justice Alito, in separate concurring opinions, each argued that the majority's test is flawed. To establish the "strong inference" required by the PSLRA, they expressed the belief that the inference of scienter must be "more plausible" than any opposing inference, not just equal to it.]

NOTES AND QUESTIONS

1. In DURA PHARMACEUTICALS, INC. v. BROUDO, 544 U.S. 336, 125 S.Ct. 1627, 161 L.Ed.2d 577 (2005), the Supreme Court, reversing a decision of the Ninth Circuit, addressed the question of what a complaint must allege to plead an economic loss caused by defendant's misrepresentation. Justice Breyer wrote the opinion for a unanimous Court.

> A private plaintiff who claims securities fraud must prove that the defendant's fraud caused an economic loss. * * * We consider a Ninth Circuit holding that a plaintiff can satisfy this requirement—a requirement that courts call "loss causation"—simply by alleging in the complaint and subsequently establishing that "the price" of the security "*on the date of purchase* was inflated because of the misrepresentation." * * * In our view the Ninth Circuit is wrong * * *.

* * *

[The Private Securities Litigation Reform Act] makes clear Congress' intent to permit private securities fraud actions for recovery where, but only where, plaintiffs adequately allege and prove the traditional elements of causation and loss. By way of contrast, the Ninth Circuit's approach would allow recovery where a misrepresentation leads to an inflated purchase price but nonetheless does not proximately cause any economic loss. That is to say, it would permit recovery where these two traditional elements in fact are missing.

* * *

Our holding about plaintiffs' need to *prove* proximate causation and economic loss leads us also to conclude that the plaintiffs' complaint here failed adequately to *allege* these requirements. We concede that the Federal Rules of Civil Procedure require only "a short and plain statement of the claim showing that the pleader is entitled to relief." Fed. Rule Civ. Proc. 8(a)(2). And we assume, at least for argument's sake, that neither the Rules nor the securities statutes impose any special further requirement in respect to the pleading of proximate causation or economic loss. * * *

* * * [P]laintiffs' lengthy complaint contains only one statement that we can fairly read as describing the loss caused by the defendants' * * * misrepresentations. That statement says that the plaintiffs "paid artificially inflated prices for Dura's securities" and suffered "damage[s]." * * * The statement implies that the plaintiffs' loss consisted of the "artificially inflated" purchase "prices." The complaint's failure to claim that Dura's share price fell significantly after the truth became known suggests that the plaintiffs considered the allegation of purchase price inflation alone sufficient. The complaint contains nothing that suggests otherwise.

* * * [T]he "artificially inflated purchase price" is not itself a relevant economic loss. And the complaint nowhere else provides the defendants with notice of what the relevant economic loss might be or of what the causal connection might be between that loss and the misrepresentation * * *.

We concede that ordinary pleading rules are not meant to impose a great burden upon a plaintiff. * * * But it should not prove burdensome for a plaintiff who has suffered an economic loss to provide a defendant with some indication of the loss and the causal connection that the plaintiff has in mind. * * *

Id. at 338–47, 125 S.Ct. at 1633–34, 161 L.Ed.2d at 586–88.

2. Congress changed the pleading standard for securities fraud claims in order to deter the filing of frivolous cases. See Perino, *Did the Private Securities Litigation Reform Act Work?*, 2003 U. Ill. L. Rev. 913, 913 (2003). However, some commentators have warned that the Act "may also work to chill meritorious litigation" by making it too expensive "to pursue even claims that may turn out to be meritorious." Choi, *The Evidence on Securities Class Actions*, 57 Vand. L. Rev. 1465, 1472–73 (2004). See also Spindler, *Why Shareholders Want Their CEOs To Lie More After* Dura Pharmaceuticals, 95

Geo. L.J. 653, 657, 691 (2007) (arguing that *Dura* encourages corporate fraud by effectively immunizing it from judicial review).

6. PLEADING DAMAGES

Read Federal Rule of Civil Procedure 9(g) in the Supplement.

NOTES AND QUESTIONS

1. Federal Rule 9(g) "maintains the traditional distinction between general damages, which can be alleged without particularity, and special damages, which require the pleading of considerable detail." 5A Wright & Miller, Federal Practice and Procedure: Civil 3d § 1310.

2. Should medical bills incurred as a result of personal injuries be considered special damages requiring special pleading or should they be provable as a logical and necessary result of the injuries themselves? See Sossamon v. Nationwide Mut. Ins. Co., 243 S.C. 552, 135 S.E.2d 87 (1964), which held a general allegation of damages sufficient to permit proof of doctor and hospital bills. In Estate of Coggins v. Wagner Hopkins, Inc., 183 F.Supp.2d 1126 (W.D. Wis. 2001), plaintiff sought to recover unpaid health insurance benefits. The District Court found it was sufficient for plaintiff to have alleged a "list of denied benefits" without indicating a "monetary value for each of the allegedly denied benefits." However, in Hogan v. Wal–Mart Stores, Inc., 167 F.3d 781, 783 (2d Cir. 1999), the court held that under New York law, "aggravation of a pre-existing condition is an element of special damages which must be specially pleaded and proved before recovery therefore can be allowed [internal citations omitted]."

3. In contract actions, special damages are those that normally would not be foreseen as the consequence of defendant's breach. Bibeault v. Advanced Health Corp., 2002 WL 24305 (S.D.N.Y. 2002). Special damages can be recovered from a defaulting party who was informed that they might result from a breach. See Bumann v. Maurer, 203 N.W.2d 434, 440–41 (N.D. 1972).

4. Although the normal consequence of failing to plead special damages is being barred from proving them at trial, it is important to note that with regard to a few types of cases the existence of special damages is an integral part of the claim, and the failure to plead them renders the complaint subject to a demurrer or motion to dismiss. See, e.g., Paine–Erie Hosp. Supply, Inc. v. Lincoln First Bank, 82 Misc.2d 432, 370 N.Y.S.2d 370 (Sup. Ct. 1975). Should the degree of specificity required in pleading special damages be the same in all cases or should it depend on whether the special damages simply are added elements of injury or are an integral part of the claim? Does the fact that a distinction along these lines is drawn by the courts of the state in which the federal court is sitting have any relevance to a federal court's construction of Federal Rule 9(g)?

7. PRAYER FOR RELIEF

———

Read Federal Rules of Civil Procedure 8(a)(3) and 54(c) in the Supplement.

———

BAIL v. CUNNINGHAM BROTHERS, INC.

United States Court of Appeals, Seventh Circuit, 1971.
452 F.2d 182.

PELL, CIRCUIT JUDGE. * * * The final contention raised by defendant on this appeal is that the judgment against defendant should be remitted from $135,000 to $85,000.

Plaintiff's original complaint sought damages in the amount of $100,000. On the morning the trial was to begin, plaintiff presented a motion to amend the complaint requesting that the ad damnum clause in the complaint against defendant be increased from $100,000 to $250,000. The district judge denied this motion " * * * for the reason that the case is at issue, it is set for trial this date, and the defendant was not given notice of the filing of the motion."

The jury notwithstanding the complaint-contained limitation of $100,000 returned a verdict for the higher figure of $150,000. In a post-trial motion Bail sought and was granted leave to amend the complaint by increasing the ad damnum clause to $150,000. Bail had received $15,000 from another defendant originally named in the complaint in return for "a covenant not to pursue." This payment had been set off, leaving the final judgment of $135,000. It has been said that the office of the ad damnum in a pleading is to fix the amount beyond which a party may not recover on the trial of his action. Gable v. Pathfinder Irrigation District, 159 Neb. 778, 68 N.W.2d 500, 506 (1955). However, an examination of the cases reveals that the rule thus enunciated, if indeed it still be a rule, has flexibility to the virtual point of nonexistence. Thus, in *Gable* the court pointed out that there was also a general rule that amendment may be made to a pleading which did not change the issues or affect the quantum of proof as to a material fact and that no good reason was apparent for not applying this privilege of amendment to the ad damnum clause. Id. at 506.

In the case before us, even though it is a diversity case, a matter of procedure is involved and governed, therefore, entirely by the federal rules. Riggs, Ferris & Geer v. Lillibridge, 316 F.2d 60, 62 (2d Cir. 1963).

* * *

There is substantial authority for the proposition that pursuant to Rule 54(c) a claimant may be awarded damages in excess of those demanded in his pleadings. * * *

Cunningham, however, contends that the authority is not all one way * * * [citing, inter alia,] the case of Wyman v. Morone, 33 A.D.2d 168, 306 N.Y.S.2d 115 (1969), to the effect that under New York law the granting of the motion to increase the amount sued for, after a jury has rendered its verdict, is an abuse of discretion. We, of course, in view of Rule 54(c) are not in any way bound by the interpretation of this lower court of New York as to the law of that state but do observe that there apparently was some significance attached to the extended delay in moving to amend and in any event feel that the dissenting opinion in *Wyman* swims with the main current of judicial thinking in this particular area as opposed to the contrary movement of the majority opinion.

The difficulty, if any there be, posed here, however, lies in the fact that Bail attempted to amend the ad damnum clause in advance of trial and the right of amendment was denied by the court. In this respect the case would seem to be one of first impression as no case involving this exact factual situation has been brought to our attention. It appears to us that the motion to amend, even though on the morning of the trial, should have been granted. It not having been granted, our inquiry must be as to whether the normal rule prevailing under 54(c) should be varied. In our opinion, it should not be.

On oral argument, inquiry was directed to counsel for Cunningham as to how the conduct of the trial would have differed if the pretrial motion to amend had been granted. The thought was ventured that the attorneys might have tried the case differently, that they might have argued damages to the jury (which subject they conspicuously avoided in final argument) or they might have cross-examined more extensively. With hindsight, they may well think that they should have argued damages even if no post-trial amendment were to be permitted and the limitation on recovery were left at $100,000. In essence, however, we cannot see that the quantum of proof as to any material fact varied or that any change of issues resulted, or would have resulted, from an amendment of the ad damnum clause. Counsel competently and vigorously defended on the theory of no liability whatsoever, and we can find no basis for an assumption that $100,000 is such an insignificant amount that counsel somehow would try harder if they knew that the exposure might be $250,000.

No doubt if the ad damnum had sought some insignificant amount such as $1,000, the case would not have received the attention from trial counsel that it did. In the case before us, however, defense counsel were never confronted with an insignificant amount. It perhaps is unfortunate that the district court did not permit the amendment as requested in advance of trial so as to eliminate the claim that the defendant somehow was prejudiced in relying on this. Finding, however, no real prejudice we will follow the rule generally prevailing to the effect that even though the party was not successful in demanding such relief in his pleadings, he was entitled thereto under the evidence. At least the jury thought that he was so entitled, and we find no basis for upsetting their determination irrespective of whether we would have reached this exact amount in assessing damages. Further, the district court who heard the evidence on a front line basis was satisfied that the amendment should be allowed on a post-trial motion.

Although Bail's counsel under the constraint of the court's ruling did confine his final argument to an amount within the unamended ad damnum clause, it is not entirely unreasonable to assume that he and his client would have been well satisfied with a verdict of $100,000 and, indeed, it does not stretch the imagination too far to conceive that a settlement could have been arrived at for less than that figure if the general practical pattern of settlements in personal injury cases had had any application here. Nevertheless, the case was not settled and inasmuch as the damages cannot be shown to be excessive, nor to have been dictated by passion and prejudice, the verdict will stand. While Cunningham finds some source of complaint in the fact that plaintiff's counsel himself argued less than $100,000 and while it may not now be much solace to Cunningham, nevertheless there was the trial advantage to the defense that plaintiff was precluded from arguing a larger sum.

What we have had to say with regard to the ad damnum clause is indicative of the anachronistic character of the clause. Indeed, there is a well publicized school of thought that it should be done away with altogether. * * * It is true that in some suits it is necessary to allege a jurisdictional amount, but ordinarily this is far less than the ad damnum prayer and can be gleaned in most instances from the pleadings and discovery procedures.

As a matter of fact in the case before us it appears from the record that the jury was in no way aware of the amount of the ad damnum in the complaint and, therefore, clearly their verdict did not reflect a conscious arrival at a figure in excess of the ad damnum.

* * *

Affirmed.

NOTES AND QUESTIONS

1. Is the damage prayer anachronistic as the court in *Bail* suggests? Should it be abolished? What problems would that create? Would elimination of the ad damnum clause have avoided the uncertainty upon which defendant in *Bail* based the claim of prejudice?

2. Federal Rule 54(c) limits relief in default cases to the ad damnum clause. Why should a defendant who defaults be protected by a cap on damages, but a defendant who participates be exposed to damages greater than those pleaded by the plaintiff? See 10 Wright, Miller & Kane, Federal Practice and Procedure: Civil 3d § 2663.

3. In ANHEUSER–BUSCH, INC. v. JOHN LABATT LTD., 89 F.3d 1339, 1349 (8th Cir. 1996), certiorari denied 519 U.S. 1109, 117 S.Ct. 944, 136

L.Ed.2d 833 (1997), plaintiff failed to mention punitive damages in its pleadings or answers to interrogatories. Plaintiff did plead a valid claim for injurious falsehood under state law and requested instructions on punitive damages a week prior to the trial. Over defendant's objections, the matter was presented to the jury, which awarded punitive damages in the amount of $5 million. The trial court struck the punitive damage award on the ground that plaintiff had not given sufficient notice of its intent to seek punitive damages. The appellate court affirmed. It did not cite Federal Rules 8(a)(3), 9(g), or 54(c). Should it have been unnecessary for plaintiff to specify punitive damages in its demand for relief so long as the alleged facts would justify such an award?

SECTION B. RESPONDING TO THE COMPLAINT

1. THE TIME PERMITTED FOR A RESPONSE

———

Read Federal Rule of Civil Procedure 12(a) and the accompanying materials in the Supplement.

———

Rule 12(a) gives most defendants twenty-one days from the service of the complaint to respond either by a motion pursuant to Rule 12 or by answering the complaint. In reality, defense counsel routinely requests, and plaintiff's counsel routinely consents to, an extension of defendant's time to answer. These agreements generally are considered a matter of courtesy among counsel, and Rule 6(b) authorizes the court to grant these extensions. Although practices vary, most judges will order an extension based upon a written stipulation of the attorneys.

2. THE MOTION TO DISMISS FOR FAILURE TO STATE A CLAIM

———

Read Federal Rules of Civil Procedure 12(b), 12(c), 12(d), and 12(f) and the accompanying materials in the Supplement.

———

NOTES AND QUESTIONS

1. Rule 12(b)(6), the federal system's counterpart to the common law demurrer, is one of a number of procedural devices, together with summary judgment, partial summary judgment, directed verdict, and judgment notwith-

standing the verdict, all of which are discussed later, that are designed to screen out frivolous and nonmeritorious cases.

2.   Under *Conley*, p. 292, supra, federal courts hesitated before dismissing a complaint on a Rule 12(b)(6) motion, taking as the standard " * * * whether the claimant is entitled to offer evidence to support the claims." However, even before *Twombly*, courts had shown an increasing willingness to dismiss an action at the threshold stage. Compare these two statements by Professor Miller, the first made in 1984, and the second in 2003:

> [R]ule 12(b)(6), the vaunted motion to dismiss for failure to state a claim upon which relief can be granted * * *, is a wonderful tool on paper, but * * * it was last effectively used during the McKinley Administration.

Miller, The August 1983 Amendments to the Federal Rules of Civil Procedure: Promoting Effective Case Management and Lawyer Responsibility 7–8 (Fed. Jud. Center 1984).

> * * * [I]n In re MCI Worldcom, Inc. Securities Litigation, * * * [191 F.Supp.2d 778 (S.D. Miss. 2002),] the plaintiff class complaint alleged in great detail material misrepresentations and omissions in violation of the Securities Exchange Act. The district court granted the defendants' motion to dismiss, which almost seems whimsical given more recent public revelations about the company apparently burying billions of dollars of costs with accounting machinations to create a false picture of the company's profits and sales. * * * At one point in the opinion the plaintiffs are faulted for not presenting any "direct evidence," which is not required on a motion challenging the sufficiency of a pleading; elsewhere the court draws inferences against the plaintiffs, again contrary to the well-established rules of pleading construction on a Rule 12(b)(6) motion. * * * Also striking is that the dismissal was with prejudice, the judge denying a request for leave to replead. In practical effect, the court seems to have demanded that the plaintiffs establish their case at the pleading stage.

Miller, *The Pretrial Rush to Judgment: Are the "Litigation Explosion," "Liability Crisis," and Efficiency Clichés Eroding Our Day in Court and Jury Trial Commitments?*, 78 N.Y.U. L. Rev. 982, 1073 (2003).

3.   How does *Twombly* affect the standard that a court should use to resolve mixed questions of fact and law when deciding a Rule 12(b)(6) motion? In HARTFORD ACCIDENT & INDEMNITY CO. v. MERRILL LYNCH, PIERCE, FENNER & SMITH, INC., 74 F.R.D. 357 (W.D. Okl. 1976), plaintiff sued defendant for negligently failing to inform a bank that its employee was investing with defendant in margin accounts. The employee had forged signatures on certain certificates of deposit drawn from that bank that he had used as collateral to procure personal loans from other banks. When the employee defaulted, the lending banks recovered their losses from plaintiff under plaintiff's blanket fidelity bond. Plaintiff alleged that defendant's failure to inform was the proximate cause of its loss. The court dismissed plaintiff's claim, treating the question of proximate cause as a question of law for the Court:

* * * In considering the allegations of the Complaint, the Court finds that the facts contained therein are insufficient to show any causal connection between the alleged negligent acts of Merrill Lynch in failing to advise Conine's employer and obtaining said employer's permission for him to engage in trading on margin accounts and the loss sustained by Plaintiff on its banker's fidelity bond. The Complaint fails to show the required proximate cause between the negligence alleged and the injuries complained of as a matter of law.

Id. at 358. Does the *Erie* doctrine require a federal court sitting in diversity to follow the Oklahoma courts' declaration that under proper circumstances the existence of proximate cause is a question of law?

3. ANSWERING THE COMPLAINT

———

Read Federal Rule of Civil Procedure 8 in the Supplement.

———

a. Denials

Rule 8 requires defendant to make one of three responses to the contents of plaintiff's complaint. Defendant may admit, deny, or plead insufficient information in response to each allegation. In answering, it is not sufficient for defendant to claim that "the documents 'speak for themselves.'" Kortum v. Raffles Holdings, Ltd. 2002 WL 31455994, at *4 (N.D. Ill. 2002). Rule 8(b)(6) provides that all averments to which defendant does not specifically respond are deemed admitted. To avoid an unintended admission, defendants often add an all-inclusive paragraph in their answers denying each and every averment of the complaint unless otherwise admitted.

A defendant under Rule 8 and most state rules also may deny generally the entire complaint, but general denials tend to defeat the purpose of pleading as a means of narrowing and focusing the issues in controversy. For this reason, the Federal Rules discourage the use of the general denial, which must be made in good faith and only in situations in which everything in the complaint can be denied legitimately. Using a general denial can be risky. If a court decides that a general denial does not "fairly respond to the substance of the allegation," it may deem defendant to have admitted plaintiff's specific averments.

NOTE AND QUESTION

Does a general denial put in issue such matters as capacity or conditions precedent? How does Federal Rule 9 affect your answers? See 5 Wright & Miller, Federal Practice and Procedure: Civil 3d § 1265.

b. Affirmative Defenses

Rule 8(c) lists nineteen affirmative defenses that must be raised specifically. An affirmative defense is defined as encompassing "two types of pleadings: ones that admit the allegations of the complaint but suggest some other reason why there is no right of recovery, and ones that concern allegations outside of the plaintiff's prima facie case that the defendant therefore cannot raise by a simple denial in the answer." 5 Wright & Miller, Federal Practice & Procedure: Civil 3d § 1271. The function of Rule 8(c) is to provide notice to plaintiff of the possible existence of the defenses and defendant's intention to advance them. In determining whether a defense not listed in Rule 8(c) must be raised affirmatively, courts look to federal statutes in federal question cases and to state practice in diversity cases.

NOTE AND QUESTION

Does the plausibility standard announced by the Court in *Twombly*, p. 298, supra, apply to Federal Rule 8(c)? Is it significant that Federal Rule 8(a)(2) requires a "showing that the pleader is entitled to relief," but Federal Rule 8(c) makes no reference to a "showing"?

SECTION C.   THE REPLY

Read Federal Rule of Civil Procedure 7(a) and the accompanying materials in the Supplement.

NOTES AND QUESTIONS

1.   Is Federal Rule 7(a), when read in conjunction with Rule 8(b)(6), consistent with Federal Rule 8(b)(1)-(5), which requires defendant to answer plaintiff's allegations specifically?

2.   A plaintiff must reply to an answer that contains counterclaims; otherwise, a reply is within the discretion of the court. See Federal Rule 7(a). Why, given liberal discovery rules, should it ever be necessary to order a reply? Might a reply be helpful in laying the foundation for a motion to dismiss? See 5 Wright & Miller, Federal Practice and Procedure: Civil 3d § 1185.

3.   Allegations to which a reply is not required are considered avoided or denied and plaintiff may controvert them at trial. See Federal Rule 8(b)(6). Conversely, matters requiring a responsive pleading are taken as admitted if not denied in the reply or if a reply is not filed. See Federal Rule 8(b)(6).

SECTION D.   AMENDMENTS

Read Federal Rule of Civil Procedure 15 and the accompanying materials in the Supplement.

BEECK v. AQUASLIDE 'N' DIVE CORP.

United States Court of Appeals, Eighth Circuit, 1977.
562 F.2d 537.

BENSON, DISTRICT JUDGE.

* * *

This case is an appeal from the trial court's exercise of discretion on procedural matters in a diversity personal injury action.

Jerry A. Beeck was severely injured on July 15, 1972, while using a water slide. He and his wife, Judy A. Beeck, sued Aquaslide 'N' Dive Corporation (Aquaslide), a Texas corporation, alleging it manufactured the slide involved in the accident, and sought to recover substantial damages on theories of negligence, strict liability and breach of implied warranty.

Aquaslide initially admitted manufacture of the slide, but later moved to amend its answer to deny manufacture; the motion was resisted. The district court granted leave to amend. On motion of the defendant, a separate trial was held on the issue of "whether the defendant designed, manufactured or sold the slide in question." This motion was also resisted by the plaintiffs. The issue was tried to a jury, which returned a verdict for the defendant, after which the trial court entered summary judgment of dismissal of the case. Plaintiffs took this appeal, and stated the issues presented for review to be:

1. Where the manufacturer of the product, a water slide, admitted in its Answer and later in its Answer to Interrogatories both filed prior to the running of the statute of limitations that it designed, manufactured and sold the water slide in question, was it an abuse of the trial court's discretion to grant leave to amend to the manufacturer in order to deny these admissions after the running of the statute of limitations?

* * *

I.   Facts

* * *

In 1971 Kimberly Village Home Association of Davenport, Iowa, ordered an Aquaslide product from one George Boldt, who was a local distributor handling defendant's products. The order was forwarded by Boldt to Sentry Pool and Chemical Supply Co. in Rock Island, Illinois, and Sentry forwarded the order to Purity Swimming Pool Supply in Hammond, Indiana. A slide was delivered from a Purity warehouse to Kimberly Village, and was installed by Kimberly employees. On July 15, 1972, Jerry A. Beeck was injured while using the slide at a social gathering sponsored at Kimberly Village by his employer, Harker Wholesale Meats, Inc. Soon after the accident investigations were undertaken by representatives of the separate insurers of Harker and Kimberly Village. On October 31, 1972, Aquaslide first learned of the accident through a letter sent by a representative of Kimberly's insurer to Aquaslide * * *. Aquaslide forwarded this notification to its insurer. Aquaslide's insurance adjuster made an on-site investigation of the slide in May, 1973, and also interviewed persons connected with the ordering and assembly of the slide. An inter-office letter dated September 23, 1973, indicates that Aquaslide's insurer was of the opinion the "Aquaslide in question was definitely manufactured by our insured." The complaint was filed October 15, 1973. Investigators for three different insurance companies, representing Harker, Kimberly and the defendant, had concluded that the slide had been manufactured by Aquaslide, and the defendant, with no information to the contrary, answered the complaint on December 12, 1973, and admitted that it "designed, manufactured, assembled and sold" the slide in question.

The statute of limitations on plaintiff's personal injury claim expired on July 15, 1974. About six and one-half months later Carl Meyer, president and owner of Aquaslide, visited the site of the accident prior to the taking of his deposition by the plaintiff. From his on-site inspection of the slide, he determined it was not a product of the defendant. Thereafter, Aquaslide moved the court for leave to amend its answer to deny manufacture of the slide.

II. Leave to Amend

* * *

In Foman v. Davis, 371 U.S. 178, 83 S.Ct. 227, 9 L.Ed.2d 222 (1962), the Supreme Court had occasion to construe * * * Rule 15(a) * * *:

> Rule 15(a) declares that leave to amend "shall be freely given when justice so requires," this mandate is to be heeded. * * * [This provision was renumbered as Rule 15(a)(2), and the language was altered by the 2007 restyling of the Federal Rules. These changes are not substantive.] If the underlying facts or circumstances relied upon by a plaintiff may be a proper subject of relief, he ought to be afforded an opportunity to test his claim on the merits. In the absence of any apparent or declared reason—such as undue delay, bad faith or dilatory motive on the part of the movant, repeated failure to cure deficiencies by amendments previously allowed, undue prejudice to the opposing party by virtue of allowance of the amendment, futility

of amendment, etc.—the leave sought should, as the rules require, be "freely given." Of course, the grant or denial of an opportunity to amend is within the discretion of the District Court * * *.

371 U.S. at 182, 83 S.Ct. at 230. * * *

This Court in Hanson v. Hunt Oil Co., 398 F.2d 578, 582 (8th Cir. 1968), held that "[p]rejudice *must be shown.*" (Emphasis added). The burden is on the party opposing the amendment to show such prejudice. In ruling on a motion for leave to amend, the trial court must inquire into the issue of prejudice to the opposing party, in light of the particular facts of the case. * * *

Certain principles apply to appellate review of a trial court's grant or denial of a motion to amend pleadings. First, as noted in Foman v. Davis, allowance or denial of leave to amend lies within the sound discretion of the trial court * * * and is reviewable only for an abuse of discretion. * * * The appellate court must view the case in the posture in which the trial court acted in ruling on the motion to amend. * * *

It is evident from the order of the district court that in the exercise of its discretion in ruling on defendant's motion for leave to amend, it searched the record for evidence of bad faith, prejudice and undue delay which might be sufficient to overbalance the mandate of Rule 15(a) * * * and Foman v. Davis, that leave to amend should be "freely given." Plaintiffs had not at any time conceded that the slide in question had not been manufactured by the defendant, and at the time the motion for leave to amend was at issue, the court had to decide whether the defendant should be permitted to litigate a material factual issue on its merits.

In inquiring into the issue of bad faith, the court noted the fact that the defendant, in initially concluding that it had manufactured the slide, relied upon the conclusions of three different insurance companies, each of which had conducted an investigation into the circumstances surrounding the accident. This reliance upon investigations of three insurance companies, and the fact that "no contention has been made by anyone that the defendant influenced this possibly erroneous conclusion," persuaded the court that "defendant has not acted in such bad faith as to be precluded from contesting the issue of manufacture at trial." The court further found "[t]o the extent that 'blame' is to be spread regarding the original identification, the record indicates that it should be shared equally."

In considering the issue of prejudice that might result to the plaintiffs from the granting of the motion for leave to amend, the trial court held that the facts presented to it did not support plaintiffs' assertion that, because of the running of the two year Iowa statute of limitations on personal injury claims, the allowance of the amendment would sound the "death knell" of the litigation. In order to accept plaintiffs' argument, the court would have had to assume that the defendant would prevail at trial on the factual issue of manufacture of the slide, and further that plaintiffs would be foreclosed, should the amendment be allowed, from proceeding against other parties if they were unsuccessful in pressing their claim against Aquaslide. On the state of the record before it, the trial court was unwilling to make such assumptions, and concluded "[u]nder these circumstances, the Court deems that the possible prejudice to the plaintiffs is an insufficient basis on which to deny the proposed amendment." The court reasoned that the amendment would merely allow the defendant to contest a disputed factual issue at trial, and further that it would be prejudicial to the defendant to deny the amendment.

The court also held that defendant and its insurance carrier, in investigating the circumstances surrounding the accident, had not been so lacking in diligence as to dictate a denial of the right to litigate the factual issue of manufacture of the slide.

On this record we hold that the trial court did not abuse its discretion in allowing the defendant to amend its answer.

NOTES AND QUESTIONS

1. Consider the following explanation of Rule 15's purpose and scope:

Rule 15 reflects two of the most important policies of the federal rules. First, the rule's purpose is to provide maximum opportunity for each claim to be decided on its merits rather than on procedural technicalities. This is demonstrated by the emphasis Rule 15 places on the permissive approach that the district courts are to take to amendment requests, no matter what their character may be; the rule is in sharp contrast to the common law and code restriction that amendments could not change the original cause of action. * * *

Second, Rule 15 reflects the fact that the federal rules assign the pleadings the limited role of providing the parties with notice of the nature of the pleader's claim or defense and the transaction, event, or occurrence that has been called into question; they no longer carry the burden of fact revelation and issue formulation, which now is discharged by the discovery process, or control the trial phase of the action. * * *

6 Wright, Miller & Kane, Federal Practice and Procedure: Civil 2d § 1471. How might the shift from notice pleading to plausible pleading affect a court's interpretation of Rule 15?

2. Parties may amend their pleadings before trial and during trial. How should the timing of the motion affect the court's willingness to permit a party to amend a pleading?

3. Rule 15(a) allows for the automatic amendment of a pleading before a response has been served, or within twenty-one days of the service of the original pleading if no response is required. After that, an amending party must obtain the leave of the court or the consent of the opposing party.

4. Parties also may amend their pleadings during the trial to conform to issues raised by unexpected evidence, but must get leave of the court to do so. See Rule 15(b). They also may add supplemental pleadings to their original pleadings to cover events that occur after the original pleading. See Rule 15(d).

WORTHINGTON v. WILSON

United States Court of Appeals, Seventh Circuit, 1993.
8 F.3d 1253.

MANION, CIRCUIT JUDGE:

In his 42 U.S.C. § 1983 complaint, Richard Worthington claimed that while being arrested the arresting officers purposely injured him. When he filed suit on the day the statute of limitations expired, he named "three unknown named police officers" as defendants. Worthington later sought to amend the complaint to substitute police officers Dave Wilson and Jeff Wall for the unknown officers. The district court concluded that the relation back doctrine of Fed. R. Civ. P. 15(c) did not apply, and dismissed the amended complaint. Worthington v. Wilson, 790 F.Supp. 829 (C.D. Ill. 1992). We affirm.

I.

On February 25, 1989, Richard Worthington was arrested by a police officer in the Peoria Heights Police Department. At the time of his arrest, Worthington had an injured left hand, and he advised the arresting officer of his injury. According to Worthington's complaint, the arresting officer responded by grabbing Worthington's injured hand and twisting it, prompting Worthington to push the officer away and tell him to "take it easy." A second police officer arrived at the scene, and Worthington was wrestled to the ground and handcuffed. The police officers then hoisted Worthington from the ground by the handcuffs, which caused him to suffer broken bones in his left hand.

Exactly two years later, on February 25, 1991, Worthington filed a five-count complaint in the Circuit Court of Peoria County, Illinois, against the Village of Peoria Heights and "three unknown named police officers," stating the above facts and alleging that he was deprived of his constitutional rights in violation of 42 U.S.C. § 1983. Counts one through three of the complaint named the police officers in their personal and official capacities, and alleged a variety of damages. * * *

* * *

[The action was removed to federal court, and plaintiff obtained leave to file an amended complaint.]

On June 17, 1991, Worthington filed an amended complaint in which he substituted as the defendants Dave Wilson and Jeff Wall, two of the twelve or so members of the Peoria Heights Police Department, for the "unknown named police officers" who arrested him on February 25, 1989. Wilson and Wall moved to dismiss the amended complaint primarily on grounds that Illinois' two-year statute of limitations expired, Ill. Ann. Stat. ch. 735, ¶ 5/13–202 (Smith–Hurd 1993), and that the amendment did not relate back to the filing of the original complaint under Rule 15(c).

Worthington responded to this motion, and a hearing was conducted before a magistrate judge on October 31, 1991.

* * *

On March 17, 1992, the district judge held a hearing on the objections to the magistrate judge's recommendations. Prior to the hearing, the district judge notified the parties that Rule 15(c), on which Wilson and Wall based their argument, had been amended effective December 1, 1991, and asked them to address the effect of this amendment on the motion to dismiss.

On April 27, 1992, the district judge granted Wilson's and Wall's motion to dismiss the amended complaint under revised Rule 15(c) * * *. Worthington appeals this dismissal. * * *

II.

Rule 15(c) was amended to provide broader "relation back" of pleadings when a plaintiff seeks to amend his complaint to change defendants. * * *

Prior to this amendment, the standard for relation back under Rule 15(c) was set out in Schiavone v. Fortune, 477 U.S. 21, 106 S.Ct. 2379, 91 L.Ed.2d 18 (1986):

> * * * (1) the basic claim must have arisen out of the conduct set forth in the original pleading; (2) the party to be brought in must have received such notice that it will not be prejudiced in maintaining its defense; (3) that party must or should have known that, but for a mistake concerning identity, the action would have been brought against it; and (4) the second and third requirements must have been fulfilled within the proscribed limitations period.

Id. at 29, 106 S.Ct. at 2384, 91 L.Ed.2d at 27.

The Advisory Committee Notes to amended Rule 15(c) indicate that the amendment repudiates the holding in *Schiavone* that notice of a lawsuit's pendency must be given within the applicable statute of limitations period. The Advisory Committee stated:

> An intended defendant who is notified of an action within the period allowed by [Rule 4(m)] for service of a summons and complaint may not under the revised rule defeat the action on account of a defect in the pleading with respect to the defendant's name, provided that the requirements of clauses (A) and (B) have been met. If the notice requirement is met within the [Rule 4(m)] period, a complaint may be amended at any time to correct a formal defect such as a misnomer or misidentification.

* * *

In this case, Wilson and Wall did not know of Worthington's action before the limitations period expired, as was required by *Schiavone*, but they were aware of its pendency within the extra 120 days provided by new Rule 15(c). *Worthington*, 790 F.Supp. at 833. Since the amendment was decisive to the issue of "notice," the district judge retroactively applied new Rule 15(c), finding it "just and practicable" to do so. *Id.* at 833–34. We have no need to consider the retroactivity of amended Rule 15(c) as it might apply in this case because Worthington's amended complaint did not relate back under either the old or new version of Rule 15(c).

Both versions of Rule 15(c) require that the new defendants "knew or should have known that, but for a mistake concerning the identity of the proper party, the action would have been brought against the party." In *Wood v. Worachek*, 618 F.2d 1225 (7th Cir. 1980), we construed the "mistake" requirement of Rule 15(c):

> A plaintiff may usually amend his complaint under Rule 15(c) to change the theory or statute under which recovery is sought; or to correct a misnomer of plaintiff where the proper party plaintiff is in court; or to change the capacity in which the plaintiff sues; or to substitute or add as plaintiff the real party interest; or to add additional plaintiffs where the action, as originally brought, was a class action. Thus, amendment with relation back is generally permitted in order to correct a misnomer of a defendant where the proper defendant is already before the court and the effect is merely to correct the name under which he is sued. But a new defendant cannot normally be substituted or added by amendment after the statute of limitations has run.

> * * *

> Rule 15(c)(2) [current Rule 15(c)(3)] permits an amendment to relate back only where there has been an error made concerning the identity of the proper party and where that party is chargeable with knowledge of the mistake, but it does not permit relation back where, as here, there is a lack of knowledge of the proper party. Thus, in the absence of a mistake in the identification of the proper party, it is irrelevant for the purposes of Rule 15(c)(2) [current Rule 15(c)(3)] whether or not the purported substitute party knew or should have known that the action would have been brought against him.

Id. at 1229 & 1230 (citation omitted). * * * The record shows that there was no mistake concerning the identity of the police officers. At oral argument, counsel for Worthington indicated that he did not decide to file suit until one or two days before the statute of limitations had expired. At that point, neither Worthington nor his counsel knew the names of the two police officers who allegedly committed the offense. Thus, the complaint was filed against "unknown police officers." Because Worthington's failure to name Wilson and Wall was due to a lack of knowledge as to their identity, and not a mistake in their names, Worthington was prevented from availing himself of the relation back doctrine of Rule 15(c).

Worthington argues that the amended complaint should relate back based on the district judge's proposed reading of Rule 15(c) as not having a separate "mistake" requirement. The district judge construed the word "mistake" to mean "change the party or the naming of the party." *Worthington*, 790 F.Supp. at 835. This construction, however, ignores the continuing vitality of *Wood*'s holding which interprets the "mistake" requirement under the old version of Rule 15(c). That holding remains unaffected by the 1991 amendment to Rule 15(c).

Worthington argues alternatively that equitable tolling should bar Wilson and Wall from asserting a statute of limitations defense because the officers fraudulently concealed their identity from him. * * * Worthington concedes that he only mentioned the tolling argument obliquely in his pleadings. The district judge raised the tolling argument sua sponte at the hearing on the motion to dismiss. This appeal is the first time that the parties have had an opportunity to fully brief the tolling argument, so it is not waived. * * *

Under Illinois law, a plaintiff who alleges fraudulent concealment to toll the statute of limitations must set forth affirmative acts or words by the defendants which prevented him from discovering their identity. * * * Worthington states that he "was in too much pain to think clearly and seek the names of the officers immediately"; that "law enforcement avoided revealing the names of the arresting officers by offering [him] a very generous plea bargain before the discovery process even began"; that he accepted the plea bargain, "[c]onfident that the names could be learned by other means"; and, that the " 'other means' turned out to be completely fruitless" because the police department "completely stonewalled" his attempts to uncover Wilson's and Wall's names. These statements negate any claim of fraudulent concealment. They do not establish that either Wilson or Wall concealed his identity from Worthington. Nor do they establish that the Peoria Heights Police Department engaged in any conduct designed to deceive Worthington. The statements suggest that the failure to name Wilson and Wall was due to Worthington's own lack of diligence in learning their identity.

* * *

III.

We conclude that the amendment adding Wilson and Wall failed to satisfy the "mistake" requirement of Rule 15(c). As a result, relation back was precluded, and Worthington's complaint was time-barred under Illinois law. * * *

Affirmed.

NOTES AND QUESTIONS

1. Rule 15(c), as amended in 1991, mandates that, when an original pleading is amended, the new pleading "relates back to the date of the

original pleading.'' They are considered by the court as if they had been pleaded in the initial pleading. If the statute of limitations expired between the original pleading and the amendment, the party still may be allowed to raise the claim.

2. Before Rule 15(c) was amended there was disagreement among the circuits about whether relation back is ''substantive'' or ''procedural.'' In SCHIAVONE v. FORTUNE, described at p. 333, supra, a diversity case, plaintiffs mistakenly failed to name the correct defendant in the original complaint. Plaintiffs meant to sue the owners of *Fortune* magazine; however, instead of naming ''Time, Incorporated,'' they named ''Fortune,'' which is not a legal entity. Plaintiffs were unable to serve ''Fortune,'' so they amended their complaint to name ''Time, Incorporated.'' Both the amendment and service of process on ''Time, Incorporated'' took place after the statute of limitations had run. The Supreme Court applied Rule 15(c) instead of New Jersey's more liberal relation back rule because the plaintiff had conceded in the District Court that the New Jersey rule governing relation back was procedural and not substantive. Does the subsequent revision of Rule 15 obviate having to determine whether state or federal law governs the amendment? Does Rule 15(c)(1)(A) incorporate state relation back law into the Federal Rules?

3. Should a federal court apply Rule 15(c)(1)(A) or Rule 15(c)(1)(C) when it confronts a state relation back rule that is more restrictive than Rule 15(c)(1)(C)? Would this present an *Erie* problem? Note that subdivisions (c)(1)(A), (c)(1)(B), and (c)(1)(C) are alternative methods of relation back. Whose rights are impaired if Rule 15(c)(1)(A) is applied? If Rule 15(c)(1)(C) is applied?

4. Do you agree that Rule 15(c)'s use of the term ''mistake'' does not include plaintiff's lack of knowledge of defendant's actual name or identity? Are there any circumstances in which a ''John Doe'' designation ought to satisfy the Rule 15 requirement? See Wasserman, *Civil Rights Plaintiffs and John Doe Defendants: A Study in Section 1983 Procedure*, 25 Cardozo L. Rev. 793, 843 (2003). How does Federal Rule 11, see pp. 337–44, infra, affect your answer?

SECTION E.　SUPPLEMENTAL PLEADINGS

———

Read Federal Rules of Civil Procedure 7(a) and 15(d) in the Supplement.

———

NOTES AND QUESTIONS

1. Federal Rule 15(d) provides that the court may allow the filing of a supplemental pleading ''setting out any transaction, occurrence, or event that happened after the date of the pleading to be supplemented.'' A supplemental

pleading can be used to cure defects in the original pleading, to add new claims, or to provide additional facts that update the complaint. See 6A Wright, Miller & Kane, Federal Practice and Procedure: Civil 2d § 1504.

2. Are supplemental pleadings governed by the same relation back analysis as amended pleadings? In DAVIS v. PIPER AIRCRAFT CORP., 615 F.2d 606, 609 n.3 (4th Cir. 1980), plaintiff moved to amend his complaint pursuant to Rule 15(a)(1) to allege his capacity as ancillary administrator of an estate, by appointment made after the statute of limitations had run. The Court of Appeals noted that:

> Technically this was more properly an attempt to file a supplemental pleading under Fed. R. Civ. P. 15(d) than an amended pleading under Fed. R. Civ. P. 15(a) [now Rule 15(a)(1)] because the new matter occurred after rather than before the original complaint was filed. For relation back purposes, the technical distinction between the two is not of critical importance, and is frequently simply disregarded by courts * * *. So long as the test of Fed. R. Civ. P. 15(c) is met, a supplemental pleading should ordinarily be given the same relation back effect as an amended pleading. * * * On that basis, our analysis will treat Fed. R. 15(c) as applying to the supplemental pleading actually attempted here. * * *

SECTION F.   PROVISIONS TO DETER FRIVOLOUS PLEADINGS

———

Read Federal Rules of Civil Procedure 11 and 23.1 and related materials in the Supplement.

———

SUROWITZ v. HILTON HOTELS CORP.

Supreme Court of the United States, 1966.
383 U.S. 363, 86 S.Ct. 845, 15 L.Ed.2d 807.

Certiorari to the United States Court of Appeals for the Seventh Circuit.

MR. JUSTICE BLACK delivered the opinion of the Court.

[Petitioner, Dora Surowitz, a stockholder in Hilton Hotels Corporation, filed a derivative action on behalf of herself and other stockholders charging that the officers and directors of the corporation had defrauded it of several million dollars in violation of the Securities Act of 1933, the Securities Exchange Act of 1934, and the Delaware General Corporation Law. The complaint was 60 printed pages and signed by petitioner's counsel in compliance with Rule 11 of the Federal Rules which, at the time, provided that "The signature of an attorney constitutes a certificate by him that he has read the pleading; that to the best of his knowledge, information, and belief there is good ground to support it; and that it is not interposed for delay." Petitioner also verified the complaint pursuant to Rule 23(b) [now Rule 23.1], stating that some of the allegations in the complaint were true and that she "on information and belief" thought that all the other allegations were true. (The language of both Federal Rule 11 and Federal Rule 23 has been altered since publication of this opinion.) The district court, before requiring defendants to answer, granted their motion to depose petitioner.]

* * * In this examination Mrs. Surowitz showed in her answers to questions that she did not understand the complaint at all, that she could not explain the statements made in the complaint, that she had a very small degree of knowledge as to what the lawsuit was about, that she did not know any of the defendants by name, that she did not know the nature of their alleged misconduct, and in fact that in signing the verification she had merely relied on what her son-in-law had explained to her about the facts in the case. On the basis of this examination, defendants moved to dismiss the complaint, alleging that "1. It is a sham pleading, and 2. Plaintiff, Dora Surowitz, is not a proper party plaintiff. . . . " In response, Mrs. Surowitz's lawyer, in an effort to cure whatever infirmity the court might possibly find in Mrs. Surowitz's verification in light of her deposition, filed two affidavits which shed much additional light on an extensive investigation which had preceded the filing of the complaint. Despite these affidavits the District Judge dismissed the case holding that Mrs. Surowitz's affidavit was "false," that being wholly false it was a nullity, that being a nullity it was as though no affidavit had been made in compliance with Rule 23, that being false the affidavit was a "sham" and Rule 23(b) required that he dismiss her case, and he did so, "with prejudice."

The Court of Appeals affirmed the District Court's dismissal * * * despite the fact that the charges made against the defendants were viewed as very serious and grave charges of fraud and that "many of the material allegations of the complaint are obviously true and cannot be refuted." 342 F.2d, at 607. We cannot agree with either of the courts below and reverse their judgments. * * *

Mrs. Surowitz, the plaintiff and petitioner here, is a Polish immigrant with a very limited English vocabulary and practically no formal education. For many years she has worked as a seamstress in New York where by reason of frugality she saved enough money to buy some thousands of dollars worth of stocks. She was of course not able to select stocks for herself with any degree of assurance of their value. Under these circumstances she had to receive advice and counsel and quite naturally she went to her son-in-law, Irving Brilliant. Mr. Brilliant had graduated from the Harvard Law School, possessed a master's degree in economics from Columbia University, was a professional investment advisor, and in addition to his degrees and his financial acumen, he wore a Phi Beta Kappa key. In 1957, six years before this litigation began, he bought some stock for his mother-in-law in the Hilton Hotels Corporation, paying a little more than $2,000 of her own money for it. * * *

About December 1962, Mrs. Surowitz received through the mails a notice from the Hilton Hotels Corporation announcing its plan to purchase a large amount of its own stock. Because she wanted it explained to her, she took the notice to Mr. Brilliant. Apparently disturbed by it, he straightway set out to make an investigation. Shortly thereafter he went to Chicago, Illinois, where Hilton Hotels has its home office and talked the matter over with Mr. Rockler. Mr. Brilliant and Mr. Rockler had been friends for many years. * * * The two decided to investigate further, and for a number of months both pursued whatever avenues of information that were open to them. By August of 1963 on the basis of their investigation, both of them had reached the conclusion [that defendants were engaged in a fraudulent scheme, and Mr. Brilliant explained this to Mrs. Surowitz]. * * *

* * * When, on the basis of this conversation, Mrs. Surowitz stated that she agreed that suit be filed in her name, Mr. Rockler prepared a formal complaint which he mailed to Mr. Brilliant. Mr. Brilliant then, according to both his affidavit and Mrs. Surowitz's testimony, read and explained the complaint to his mother-in-law before she verified it. Her limited education and her small knowledge about any of the English language, except the most ordinarily used words, probably is sufficient guarantee that the courts below were right in finding that she did not understand any of the legal relationships or comprehend any of the business transactions described in the complaint. She did know, however, that she had put over $2,000 of her hard-earned money into Hilton Hotels stock, that she was not getting her dividends, and that her son-in-law who had looked into the matter thought that something was wrong. She also knew that her son-in-law was qualified to help her and she trusted him. It is difficult to believe that anyone could be shocked or harmed in any way when, in the light of all these circumstances, Mrs. Surowitz verified the complaint, not on the basis of her own knowledge and understanding, but in the faith that her son-in-law had correctly advised her either that the statements in the complaint were true or to the best of his knowledge he believed them to be true.

* * * Rule 23(b) was not written in order to bar derivative suits. Unquestionably it was originally adopted and has served since in part as a means to discourage "strike suits" by people who might be interested in getting quick dollars by making charges without regard to their truth so as to coerce corporate managers to settle worthless claims in order to get rid of them. * * *

When the record of this case is reviewed in the light of the purpose of Rule 23(b)'s verification requirement, there emerges the plain, inescapable fact that this is not a strike suit or anything akin to it. Mrs. Surowitz was not interested in anything but her own investment made with her own money. Moreover, there is not one iota of evidence that Mr. Brilliant, her son-in-law and counselor, sought to do the corporation any injury in this litigation. In fact his purchases for the benefit of his family of more than $50,000 of securities in the corporation, including a $10,000 debenture, all made years before this suit was brought, manifest confidence in the corporation, not a desire to harm it in any way. The Court of Appeals in affirming the District Court's dismissal, however, indicated that whether Mrs. Surowitz and her counselors acted in good faith and whether the charges they made were truthful were irrelevant once Mrs. Surowitz demonstrated in her oral testimony that she knew nothing about the content of the suit. * * *

We cannot construe Rule 23 or any other one of the Federal Rules as compelling courts to summarily dismiss, without any answer or argument at all, cases like this where grave charges of fraud are shown by the record to be based on reasonable beliefs growing out of careful investigation. The basic purpose of the Federal Rules is to administer justice through fair trials, not through summary dismissals as necessary as they may be on occasion. These rules were designed in large part to get away from some of the old procedural booby traps which common-law pleaders could set to prevent unsophisticated litigants from ever having their day in court. If rules of procedure work as they should in an honest and fair judicial system, they not only permit, but should as nearly as possible guarantee that bona fide complaints be carried to an adjudication on the merits. Rule 23(b), like the other civil rules, was written to further, not defeat the ends of justice. The serious fraud charged here, which of course has not been proven, is clearly in that class of deceitful conduct which the federal securities laws were largely passed to prohibit and protect against. There is, moreover, not one word or one line of actual evidence in this record indicating that there has been any collusive conduct or trickery by those who filed this suit except through intimations and insinuations without any support from anything any witness has said. The dismissal of this case was error. It has now been practically three years since the complaint was filed and as yet none of the defendants have even been compelled to admit or deny the wrongdoings charged. They should be. The cause is reversed and remanded to the District Court for trial on the merits.

Reversed and remanded.

MR. JUSTICE HARLAN, concurring.

Rule 23(b) directs that in a derivative suit "the complaint shall be verified by oath" but nothing dictates that the verification be that of the plaintiff shareholder. * * * In the present circumstances, it seems to me the affidavit of Walter J. Rockler, counsel for Mrs. Surowitz, amounts to an adequate verification by counsel, which I think is permitted by a reasonable interpretation of the Rule at least in cases such as this. On this premise, I agree with the decision of the Court.

NOTES AND QUESTIONS

1. Why does Rule 23.1 require verification? Why doesn't the Rule 11 procedure suffice? Should the verification requirement be limited to particular allegations? See Comment, *Verification of Complaint in Stockholders' Derivative Suits under Rule 23(b)*, 114 U. Pa. L. Rev. 614 (1966).

2. In those state courts in which fact pleadings generally do not have to be verified, there are certain exceptions. Some of the typical ones found in state practice are: petitions for divorce; petitions brought by the state to enjoin a nuisance; and complaints to obtain support of an illegitimate child. E.g., Iowa Code Ann. § 600B.13. What makes these actions sufficiently distinctive to require verification?

3. In Roussel v. Tidelands Capital Corp., 438 F.Supp. 684, 688 (N.D. Ala. 1977), the court reaffirmed the dismissal of an action under Rule 23.1, because, among other things, plaintiff admitted he verified the pleading without reading it, and thus he had demonstrated he was not likely to represent the shareholders fairly and adequately. Why is a dismissal ever an appropriate way of enforcing the verification provision of Rule 23.1? Shouldn't plaintiff be prosecuted for the crime of perjury instead? Of what significance is it that any recovery in a suit under Rule 23.1 goes directly to the corporation, not to plaintiff? Suppose the statute of limitations on the claim runs just before the dismissal. What additional problems would this raise?

NOTE ON FEDERAL RULE OF CIVIL PROCEDURE 11

Pleading rules serve important public functions. In particular, they allow private individuals to enforce regulatory norms, and so create incentives to deter wrongful conduct. However, pleading rules also provide an opportunity for abuse. For example, is it appropriate for a party to institute a colorable claim with the sole intention of pressuring another party into settling? Or would it be right for a party who has been sued on a legitimate claim to interpose a counterclaim on a questionable legal theory simply to induce plaintiff to drop the suit? A sound pleading system must strike an appropriate balance between rules that are too permissive, and allow for the filing of lawsuits that lack any merit, and rules that are too demanding, and block the filing of lawsuits that would have merit.

Federal Rule 11 attempts to curb abuse of the federal pleading rules by imposing affirmative duties on attorneys and by raising the possibility of sanctions for failure to discharge those duties. As is clear from *Surowitz*, the pre–1983 incarnation of Rule 11 employed a subjective standard to assess attorney conduct—so long as attorneys acted in good faith, they were not subject to sanctions even if it later became clear that their legal theory was faulty or that the facts did not support their claims.

> Rule 11, as originally adopted in 1937, * * * provided that an attorney's signature on a pleading certified that there was good ground to support the pleading and that it was not interposed for delay. The rule also stated that a pleading signed "with intent to defeat the purpose of the rule ... may be stricken [and that] [f]or a willful violation of this rule an attorney may be subjected to appropriate disciplinary action." * * * During the succeeding forty-five years, the Rule proved to be ineffective and little used.

Schwarzer, *Rule 11: Entering a New Era*, 28 Loy. L.A. L. Rev. 7, 7–8 (1994). Between 1938 and 1976, there were only twenty-three reported cases in which a party invoked Rule 11 to strike a pleading and only nine cases in which violations were found. Risinger, *Honesty in Pleading and its Enforcement: Some "Striking" Problems with Federal Rule of Civil Procedure 11*, 61 Minn. L. Rev. 1 (1976).

The 1983 amendment to Rule 11 made several important changes to overcome the reluctance of courts to impose sanctions and to ensure that attorneys would "stop and think" before filing papers. One commentary explains, "[t]he 1983 amendment required lawyers and litigants to conduct reasonable prefiling factual and legal inquiries, while certifying that their papers were factually well grounded and legally warranted. The 1983 revision to Rule 11 also mandated that judges levy sanctions on counsel and parties who did not discharge these responsibilities." Sanner & Tobias, *Rule 11 and Rule Revision*, 37 Loy. L.A. L. Rev. 573, 575 (2004).

The number of Rule 11 motions increased dramatically after the 1983 amendment. By 1991, over 3,000 proceedings dealing with Rule 11 had been reported. See Vairo, *Rule 11: Where We Are and Where We Are Going,* 60 Fordham L. Rev. 475, 480 (1991). And, as one court recognized, "[t]he large number of reported opinions can only be a fraction of the large number of instances in which sanctions have been imposed under" Rule 11. Zaldivar v. City of Los Angeles, 780 F.2d 823, 829 (9th Cir. 1986). Between 1989 and 1992, Rule 11 was the subject of five Supreme Court decisions.

One study of the 1983 version of Rule 11 revealed that it had a significant impact on the behavior of attorneys even when no sanctions were awarded. Kritzer, Marshall & Zemans, *Rule 11: Moving Beyond the Cosmic Anecdote*, 75 Judicature 269 (1992). In the twelve months preceding the study, 24.5 percent of lawyers had experienced an in-court reference to Rule 11, and 30.3 percent had experienced an out-of-court reference to Rule 11. More than one-third of the lawyers surveyed said that a fear of sanctions resulted in "extra pre-filing review of pleadings, motions, or other documents subject to Rule 11," lending credence to the notion that it was encouraging lawyers to "stop and think" before acting.

An irony of practice under the 1983 amendment was that Rule 11 itself became a source of tactical litigation. According to some, it was used as a "hardball" technique to intimidate and harass opponents by many of the very attorneys whose abusive behavior Rule 11 was meant to control. See Gaiardo v. Ethyl Corp., 835 F.2d 479, 484–85 (3d Cir. 1987); Cole, *Rule 11 Now*, 17 Litigation 10 (1991).

In addition, commentators expressed concern that Rule 11 was having a chilling effect on legitimate, but disfavored, categories of lawsuits such as civil rights claims. One commentary notes that under the 1983 version, "Rule 11 motions were filed and granted against civil rights plaintiffs more frequently than any other class of litigant, and numerous judges vigorously enforced the provision against the plaintiffs, levying large sanctions on them." Tobias, *The 1993 Revision to Federal Rule 11*, 70 Ind. L.J. 171, 171 (1994).

In 1989, the Advisory Committee on the Federal Rules of Civil Procedure began to review the 1983 version of Rule 11. It gathered comments and proposed another set of amendments, which the Supreme Court adopted and which became effective in 1993. See Willging, *Past and Potential Uses of Empirical Research in Civil Rulemaking*, 77 Notre Dame L. Rev. 1121, 1147–

53 (2002). The 1993 amendment preserved the "stop and think" objective of the 1983 version of the Rule, but tried to avoid any "chilling effect" on counsel's advancing novel legal theories. The amendment also eliminated the compensatory character that Rule 11 had acquired as a result of courts' almost routinely imposing monetary sanctions for violations of the Rule. See Nelken, *Has the Chancellor Shot Himself in the Foot? Looking for Middle Ground on Rule 11 Sanctions*, 41 Hastings L.J. 383 (1990).

The current version of Rule 11 is simpler, allows more court discretion in the imposition of monetary sanctions, and has added a twenty-one day "safe harbor" during which the filing party may withdraw the challenged paper without censure. Furthermore, the 1993 amendment changes the requirement that an attorney have a "good faith" motive for an argument for a change in law to a requirement that the argument be nonfrivolous, and adds a clause for the establishment of new law. The current version of the Rule also applies to all representations to the court, including the later advocacy of a previously presented position. Finally, the current version of Rule 11 also allows sanctions against the law firms or parties responsible for violations, as well as against the signer of the document.

In dissenting from the adoption of the 1993 amendment, Justice Scalia wrote:

> The proposed revision would render the Rule toothless, by allowing judges to dispense with sanction, by disfavoring compensation for litigation expenses, and by providing a 21–day "safe harbor". * * * The Rules should be solicitous of the abused (the courts and the opposing party), and not of the abuser. Under the revised Rule, parties will be able to file thoughtless, reckless, and harassing pleadings, secure in the knowledge that they have nothing to lose: If objection is raised, they can retreat without penalty. The proposed revision contradicts what this court said only three years ago: "Baseless filing puts the machinery of justice in motion, burdening courts and individuals alike with needless expense and delay." Cooter & Gell v. Hartmarx Corp., 496 U.S. 384, 398, 110 S.Ct. 2447, 110 L.Ed.2d 359 (1990).

Order of the Supreme Court Amending the Federal Rules of Civil Procedure (April 22, 1993), reprinted in 146 F.R.D. 404, 507 (1993) (Scalia, J., dissenting). For an analysis of the impact of the 1993 version of Rule 11, see Yablon, *Hindsight, Regret, and Safe Harbors in Rule 11 Litigation*, 37 Loy. L.A. L. Rev. 599, 605 (2004).

The 1993 amendment has marked a shift away from the compensatory focus of the 1983 version to an emphasis, instead, on deterrence. "In ordering sanctions the courts are encouraged to consider a sliding scale, ordering only those sanctions necessary to achieve deterrence, thereby protecting the courts with the least adverse possible consequence of the litigants." Armour, *Practice Makes Perfect: Judicial Discretion and the 1993 Amendments to Rule 11*, 24 Hofstra L. Rev. 677, 771 (1996). Sanctions that have been imposed include requiring the errant attorney to circulate the court's opinion finding him in violation of Rule 11 to every member of his firm; suspending or disbarring the attorney; judicially reprimanding the attorney in open court or through publication of a critical opinion; or requiring the attorney to take continuing legal education courses.

NOTES AND QUESTIONS

1. How extensive an inquiry must an attorney undertake to satisfy the Rule's requirement that a claim is "warranted by existing law"? In GOLDEN EAGLE DISTRIBUTING CORP. v. BURROUGHS CORP., 103 F.R.D. 124 (N.D. Cal. 1984), reversed 801 F.2d 1531 (9th Cir. 1986), rehearing denied with a dissenting opinion 809 F.2d 584 (9th Cir. 1987), plaintiff's counsel cited a 1965 California Supreme Court case supporting its argument, but did not refer to a 1979 California Supreme Court opinion that was inconsistent with the 1965 case. Counsel distinguished the later case in its reply brief after it had been cited by the opposition, arguing that the 1965 case had not been overruled. Counsel also did not address two intermediate court opinions that discussed the effect of the 1979 opinion on the 1965 opinion. The District Court held that Rule 11 sanctions were appropriate for counsel's failing to cite adverse authority. On appeal, the Ninth Circuit unanimously reversed. The court conceded that Rule 11 was designed to create an affirmative duty of investigation, both as to law and as to fact, before motions are filed. But the court went on to say that, in order to avoid chilling creativity in advocacy, courts should be careful not to hold lawyers to a standard measured by what the judge later decides. Would the 1993 amendment alter the analysis?

2. Rule 11 is not the only sanctioning provision available to the federal courts. The most notable other provision is 28 U.S.C. § 1927, which gives courts authority to impose excess costs against attorneys who have "unreasonably and vexatiously" increased the costs of litigation by "multipl[ying] the proceedings." The statute requires a determination of bad faith. Courts also have an "inherent power" to sanction parties. In CHAMBERS v. NASCO, INC., 501 U.S. 32, 111 S.Ct. 2123, 115 L.Ed.2d 27 (1991), the Supreme Court held, five-to-four, in an opinion by Justice White, that the District Court properly used its "inherent power" to sanction a party's bad-faith conduct. Justice White explained that federal courts have an "inherent power" to punish conduct that abuses the judicial process and have discretion to fashion an appropriate sanction. He reasoned that neither Section 1927, Rule 11, nor other Federal Rules displace a court's inherent power to impose attorney's fees as a sanction for bad-faith conduct. Justice Kennedy dissented and severely criticized the ruling: "By inviting district courts to rely on inherent authority as a substitute for attention to the careful distinctions contained in the rules and statutes, today's decision will render these sources of authority superfluous in many instances." Id. at 67, 111 S.Ct. at 2144, 115 L.Ed.2d at 59. See Hart, *And the Chill Goes On—Federal Civil Rights Plaintiffs Beware: Rule 11 vis-à-vis 28 U.S.C. § 1927 and the Court's Inherent Power*, 37 Loy. L.A. L. Rev. 645 (2004).

CHAPTER 8

JOINDER OF CLAIMS AND PARTIES: EXPANDING THE SCOPE OF THE CIVIL ACTION

■ ■ ■

In this Chapter, we examine procedures that allow litigants to combine claims and parties in one lawsuit. The simplest form of lawsuit is bilateral: one plaintiff asserts one claim against one defendant. Although the equity courts were more flexible, the common-law courts, with their emphasis on the unitary civil action, rarely deviated from this model, and joinder was permitted only along strict and formalistic lines. See Sunderland, *Joinder of Actions,* 18 Mich. L. Rev. 571 (1920). As the complexity of society increased and more intricate disputes were generated, the need for avoiding piecemeal litigation became widely recognized. The most obvious method of accomplishing this objective was to permit expansion of the action by allowing the addition of parties and claims to the suit. Broadly speaking, joinder rules today fall into one of two categories: permissive rules, which give a litigant the option of joining parties and claims in a single lawsuit; and mandatory rules, which require a litigant to do so. It is important to remember that the question of joinder is separate from whether the court may exercise jurisdiction over the party or claim to be joined. See Federal Rule 82. The materials in this Chapter, together with Chapter 9 on class actions, focus on some of the most innovative and controversial features of civil procedure today.

SECTION A. JOINDER OF CLAIMS

1. HISTORICAL LIMITATIONS ON THE PERMISSIVE JOINDER OF CLAIMS

At common law, a plaintiff could join claims in a single lawsuit only if they were a part of the same writ and so belonged to the same form of action. Although the codes were somewhat more liberal, the typical code provision authorized joinder of claims only where they fell within one of several statutory classes, which generally included the following:

(a) Contracts express or implied;

(b) Injuries to the person;

(c) Injuries to character;

(d) Injuries to property;

(e) Actions to recover real property, with or without damages;

(f) Actions to recover chattels, with or without damages; and

(g) Actions arising out of the same transaction or transactions connected with the same subject of the action.

NOTE AND QUESTIONS

In what ways do these categories differ from the use of the common-law forms of action as guidelines for the joinder of claims? What is the logic of each of these classes? Is the code approach to joinder of claims any less formalistic than the common-law theory? Joinder at common law and under the codes is discussed in Blume, *A Rational Theory for Joinder of Causes of Action and Defences, and for the Use of Counterclaims,* 26 Mich. L. Rev. 1 (1927).

2. PERMISSIVE JOINDER OF CLAIMS BY PLAINTIFFS UNDER FEDERAL RULE 18

———

Read Federal Rule of Civil Procedure 18 in the Supplement.

———

M. K. v. TENET

United States District Court, District of Columbia, 2002.
216 F.R.D. 133.

URBINA, DISTRICT JUDGE:

[The action was filed by six former employees of the Central Intelligence Agency (CIA), alleging that the CIA, its Director, and other defendants obstructed plaintiffs' access to counsel in violation of federal law. In a proposed second amended complaint, plaintiffs added nine named plaintiffs and provided information about existing claims to cure deficiencies in the original complaint. Defendants moved to sever the claims of the initial six plaintiffs under Federal Rule of Civil Procedure 21.]

* * *

The court now addresses the defendants' instant motion to sever. In the defendants' view, the plaintiffs' obstruction-of-counsel claim consists of "a series of unrelated, isolated grievances, unique to each plaintiff, each of which would have to be decided on its own set of law and facts, and each potentially presenting a 'novel' constitutional claim." * * * Thus, the defendants ask this court to sever the claims of the six existing plaintiffs * * * under Federal Rule of Civil Procedure 21. * * * By the same token, the defendants ask the court to deny the plaintiffs' proposed Rule 20 joinder of the nine new plaintiffs and the 30 new "Doe" defendants. * * *

The plaintiffs, however, argue that the court should not sever the six existing plaintiffs because both prongs of the Rule 20(a) [now Rule 20(a)(1)] joinder requirement are satisfied. The court need not extensively address the joinder of the six existing plaintiffs' new claims because the court is convinced that under the unrestricted joinder provision of Federal Rule of Civil Procedure 18, such joinder of new claims is possible. * * *

NOTES AND QUESTIONS

1. Federal Rule 18 removes all obstacles to joinder of claims and permits the joinder of both legal and equitable actions; the only restriction on the claims that may be joined is imposed by subject-matter jurisdiction requirements. What are the advantages of permitting the liberal joinder of claims? Are there any disadvantages? How much credence should we give to the efficiency rationale? If each claim is different, are there material efficiency gains?

2. In SPORN v. HUDSON TRANSIT LINES, 265 A.D. 360, 38 N.Y.S.2d 512 (1st Dep't 1942), the court had before it an attempt to join five causes of action for negligence resulting in personal injuries with one cause of action for malicious prosecution. It stated:

> The causes of action for negligence and for malicious prosecution are essentially different in nature; each type involves different rules of law; each requires different testimony to establish a case and each carries a different measure of damages. If a single jury were to try both types of action at the one time, there is a strong likelihood that confusion would exist in the minds of the jurors as to the rules of law to be applied to the respective actions and they would undoubtedly entertain much difficulty in applying the various parts of testimony introduced to the appropriate cause of action.

Id. at 361–62, 38 N.Y.S.2d at 514. Would the result in *Sporn* have been different if the action had been brought in a federal court? Read Federal Rule 42. Does the availability of severance of claims eliminate all of the objections to permitting unrestricted joinder of claims as an initial matter? To what extent does the court's power to sever claims prevent the system from achieving the objectives of a liberal joinder rule?

3. Federal Rule 18 describes the claims that plaintiff may assert against defendant; it does not require plaintiff to join all such claims in a single action. Should there be compulsory joinder of all related claims existing between plaintiff and defendant? See Friedenthal, *Joinder of Claims, Counterclaims and Cross–Complaints: Suggested Revision of the California Provisions*, 23 Stan. L. Rev. 1, 11–17 (1970); Greenbaum, *Jacks or Better to Open: Procedural Limitations on Co-Party and Third-Party Claims*, 74 Minn. L. Rev.

507, 535–37 (1990). Michigan's joinder provision, Michigan Court Rule 2.203, which is in the Supplement following Federal Rule 18, is unusual in that it provides for the compulsory joinder of certain claims. See 6A Wright, Miller & Kane, Federal Practice and Procedure: Civil 2d § 1582.

4. Even though the joinder of claims by plaintiffs in the federal courts is permissive, the principles of res judicata, which prohibit the splitting of a cause of action into two or more lawsuits, often have the effect of compelling plaintiff to join all related claims. See generally Blume, *Required Joinder of Claims,* 45 Mich. L. Rev. 797 (1947). Thus, for example, if A and B are involved in an automobile accident in which A suffers both bodily injury and damage to her automobile, the risk of res judicata typically will lead A to join both claims in one action, even though Federal Rule 18 does not require her to do so.

SECTION B. ADDITION OF CLAIMS BY DEFENDANT

1. COUNTERCLAIMS

a. A Short History of Counterclaims

The counterclaim in its present form did not exist at common law, although it has well-recognized precursors in set-off and recoupment and in equity practice. The philosophy underlying set-off and recoupment was the common sense view that someone should not be compelled to pay one moment what he will be entitled to recover back the next. Judge Clark outlined the development and theory of set-off and recoupment as follows:

> * * * At first * * * [recoupment] was limited to a showing of payment, or of former recovery. Later, recoupment was developed so as to allow a defendant to show for the purpose of reducing the plaintiff's recovery any facts arising out of the transaction sued upon or connected with the subject thereof, which facts might have founded an independent action in favor of the defendant against the plaintiff. * * * It was not necessary that the opposing claims be liquidated, or that they be of the same character; i.e., a claim in "tort" could be set off against one in "contract." It was essential, however, that the claims of both plaintiff and defendant involve the same "subject-matter," or arise out of the "same transaction" * * *.

> But where the defendant's claims arose out of a transaction different from that sued upon, the common-law recoupment was unavailable. The defendant, therefore, was compelled to bring a separate suit in order to satisfy his claim against the plaintiff. Equity, at an early date, relieved the defendant of this hardship by allowing a set-off of claims [arising out of a transaction different from the plaintiff's claim] * * *.

> Under the set-off * * *, it was necessary that the demands either be liquidated, or arise out of contract or judgment. It was necessary, also,

that the demands be due the defendant in his own right against the plaintiff, or his assignor, and be not already barred by the statute of limitations * * *.

Clark, Code Pleading § 100, at 634–36 (2d ed. 1947). The utility of the common law recoupment and set-off practice was limited because in the former situation defendant was not permitted to recover affirmative relief; the claim could be used only to reduce or "net out" plaintiff's recovery. In the case of set-off, the claim had to be for a liquidated amount.

The movement for procedural reform in the mid-nineteenth century gave passing attention to the problem of defendant's claims against plaintiff; the original New York Field Code of 1848 made no provision for counterclaims. Amendments in 1852 corrected this omission and permitted as a counterclaim:

1. A cause of action arising out of the contract or transaction set forth in the complaint, as the foundation of the plaintiff's claim, or connected with the subject of the action; and

2. In an action arising on contract, any other cause of action arising on contract, and existing at the commencement of the action.

See Blume, *A Rational Theory for Joinder of Causes of Action and Defences, and for the Use of Counterclaims*, 26 Mich. L. Rev. 1, 48 (1927). The English Judicature Act of 1873 eliminated the historic limitations on defendant's ability to assert claims against plaintiff. Then, at the beginning of this century, a number of states amended their codes to adopt the English practice.

b. Federal Rule of Civil Procedure 13

Read Federal Rules of Civil Procedure 13(a)–(f) and the accompanying material in the Supplement.

Federal Rules 13(a) and (b) draw a distinction between counterclaims that are compulsory and those that are permissive. The distinction turns on the definition of a transaction or occurrence. See McFarland, *In Search of the Transaction or Occurrence: Counterclaims*, 40 Creighton L. Rev. 699, 699 (2007). The classic definition of transaction is found in MOORE v. NEW YORK COTTON EXCHANGE, 270 U.S. 593, 46 S.Ct. 367, 70 L.Ed. 750 (1926). Plaintiff sought to compel defendant to install a price quotation ticker in plaintiff's place of business. Defendant counterclaimed for damages, alleging that although plaintiff had been denied permission to use quotations from defendant's exchange, plaintiff "was purloining them and giving them out." In the course of holding defendant's counterclaim compulsory under former Equity Rule 30, the Court said:

* * * "Transaction" is a word of flexible meaning. It may comprehend a series of many occurrences, depending not so much upon the immediateness of their connection as upon their logical relationship. The refusal to furnish the quotations is one of the links in the chain which constitutes the transaction upon which appellant here bases its cause of action. It is an important part of the transaction constituting the subject-matter of the counterclaim. It is the one circumstance without which neither party would have found it necessary to seek relief. Essential facts alleged by appellant enter into and constitute in part the cause of action set forth in the counterclaim. That they are not precisely identical, or that the counterclaim embraces additional allegations, as, for example, that appellant is unlawfully getting the quotations, does not matter. To hold otherwise would be to rob this branch of the rule of all serviceable meaning, since the facts relied upon by the plaintiff rarely, if ever, are in all particulars, the same as those constituting the defendant's counterclaim. * * *

Id. at 610, 46 S.Ct. at 371, 70 L.Ed. at 757.

Courts use at least four different tests in determining whether claims arise out of the same transaction or occurrence for purposes of characterizing a counterclaim as compulsory or permissive:

(a) Are the issues of fact and law raised by the claim and counterclaim largely the same?

(b) Would res judicata bar a subsequent suit on defendant's claim absent the compulsory counterclaim rule?

(c) Will substantially the same evidence support or refute plaintiff's claim as well as defendant's counterclaim?

(d) Is there any logical relation between the claim and the counterclaim?

See Kane, *Original Sin and the Transaction in Federal Civil Procedure*, 76 Texas L. Rev. 1723 (1998). What are the strengths and weaknesses of each of these tests? See 6 Wright, Miller & Kane, Federal Practice and Procedure: Civil 2d § 1410.

Before the enactment of 28 U.S.C. § 1367, a compulsory counterclaim fell within the ancillary jurisdiction of the federal court and so did not require an independent basis of subject-matter jurisdiction. See 6 Wright, Miller & Kane, Federal Practice and Procedure: Civil 2d § 1414. As the Third Circuit explained in GREAT LAKES RUBBER CORP. v. HERBERT COOPER CO., 286 F.2d 631, 633–34 (3d Cir. 1961):

[T]he issue of the existence of ancillary jurisdiction and the issue as to whether a counterclaim is compulsory are to be answered by the same test. * * * The tests are the same because Rule 13(a) [now Rule 13(a)(1)(A)] and the doctrine of ancillary jurisdiction are designed to abolish the same evil, viz., piecemeal litigation in the federal courts.

Currently, 28 U.S.C. § 1367(a) provides for supplemental jurisdiction over claims "so related to claims in the action" that are within the court's "original jurisdiction that they form part of the same case or controversy" under Article III of the federal Constitution. Is this test the same or different than the requirement of Rule 13 that claims arise out of the same "transaction and occurrence" for purposes of distinguishing compulsory from permissive counterclaims? If it is broader, does Section 1367(a) allow for the exercise of supplemental jurisdiction over some permissive counterclaims or exclude some compulsory counterclaims?

The states do not have identical rules for compulsory counterclaims. The Minnesota compulsory-counterclaim rule, for example, is virtually identical to Federal Rule 13(a)(1)(A), except that the reference to "occurrence" is omitted, which has led that state's courts to read the Rule restrictively. In HOUSE v. HANSON, 245 Minn. 466, 72 N.W.2d 874 (1955), the Minnesota Supreme Court held that "Rule 13.01 was approved by this court with the express understanding and intent that the omission therefrom of the word 'occurrence' would insure that tort counterclaims would not be compulsory."

NOTE ON CONSEQUENCES OF FAILING TO PLEAD A COUNTERCLAIM

Rule 13(a) is silent as to the consequences of failing to plead a compulsory counterclaim. It seems clear that an unasserted compulsory counterclaim cannot be raised in a subsequent suit in a federal court, although courts differ as to the proper theory for reaching this conclusion. Some apply a res judicata principle; others use waiver; and yet another group relies on estoppel. Compare Scott, *Collateral Estoppel by Judgment*, 56 Harv. L. Rev. 1 (1942) (res judicata theory), with Wright, *Estoppel by Rule: The Compulsory Counterclaim Under Modern Pleading*, 38 Minn. L. Rev. 423 (1954) (estoppel). Does it make any difference which theory is used? Do you agree that a defendant who defaults and fails to file an answer to a complaint ought to be barred from later filing a transactionally related claim as a separate action? For a critical view, see Peterson, *The Misguided Law of Compulsory Counterclaims in Default Cases*, 50 Ariz. L. Rev. 1107 (2008).

Several exceptions to the compulsory counterclaim rule are set out in the text of Rule 13(a) itself. In UNION PAVING CO. v. DOWNER CORP., 276 F.2d 468 (9th Cir. 1960), the court discussed the passage in Rule 13(a)(2)(A) providing that waiver will not result from the failure to assert a counterclaim that already is the subject of litigation pending in another court:

> * * * The purpose of this exception is seemingly to prevent one party from compelling another to try his cause of action in a court not of the latter's choosing when the same cause of action is already the subject of pending litigation in another forum, one which was probably chosen by the owner of the cause of action concerned. * * *

Id. at 470–71.

2. CROSS–CLAIMS

Read Federal Rules of Civil Procedure 13(g) and (h) and the accompanying material in the Supplement.

NOTE AND QUESTIONS

What standard does Federal Rule 13(g) set for the joinder of claims between coplaintiffs and codefendants?

SECTION C. IDENTIFYING PARTIES WHO MAY SUE AND BE SUED

Read Federal Rule of Civil Procedure 17 in the Supplement.

NOTE AND QUESTIONS

"The purpose of requiring the real party in interest to prosecute a lawsuit is to avoid prejudice and the possibility of duplicate lawsuits. * * * [Rule 17(a)] also exists to allow a defendant to set out all of its defenses in one action." Verizon New Jersey, Inc. v. Ntegrity Telecontent Servs., Inc., 219 F.Supp.2d 616, 635 (D.N.J. 2002). Another court identifies the rule's "preeminent concern * * * [as] whether the suing party has sufficient legal rights to ensure that the outcome of the case will be *res judicata* * * *. The Ezra Charitable Trust v. Rent–Way, Inc., 136 F.Supp.2d 435, 443 (W.D. Pa. 2001). Is Rule 17 necessary?

NOTE ON CAPACITY, STANDING, AND REAL PARTY IN INTEREST

In addition to the requirement that the party suing or being sued be the real party in interest, two other concepts are relevant to determining who may sue or be sued—"capacity" and "standing."

Capacity refers to the ability of an individual or corporation to enforce rights or to be sued by others. Many states, for example, have special rules to deal with suits by or against minors and mental incompetents. See Federal Rules 17(b) and 17(c). Capacity rules are designed to protect a party by ensuring that she is represented adequately. Thus, a representative will be appointed to advance the interests of a minor or a mental incompetent, who might not be able to understand fully the nature of the issues involved in the lawsuit. Real-party-in-interest rules serve to protect the opposing party's interests by ensuring that only the litigant who has a true stake in the outcome can sue or be sued. This prevents situations in which a potential defendant might first be sued by the person who holds the nominal title to a claim, and after successfully defending that claim, be subjected to a second action by the real party in interest. See Commonwealth of Puerto Rico v. Cordeco Dev. Corp., 534 F.Supp. 612, 614 (D.P.R. 1982).

Standing focuses on who may seek a remedy for an alleged violation of law. It requires that plaintiff demonstrate a concrete injury in order to ensure both development of the facts and law, and respect for separation of powers. See Hershkoff, *State Courts and the "Passive Virtues": Rethinking the Judicial Function*, 114 Harv. L. Rev. 1833, 1843 (2001). In the federal system, standing rules derive from Article III of the United States Constitution. Current doctrine requires plaintiff to "allege personal injury fairly traceable to the defendant's allegedly unlawful conduct and likely to be redressed by the requested relief." Allen v. Wright, 468 U.S. 737, 751, 104 S.Ct. 3315, 3324, 82 L.Ed.2d 556, 569 (1984). Standing rules are justified partly by the need to conserve judicial resources by ensuring that the courts decide only bona fide disputes between adverse parties. How do standing rules effectuate adversarial values?

It is possible to have a case in which a real party in interest (the beneficiary of a will, for example) lacks capacity to sue (perhaps because the party is a minor). Moreover, even if this hypothetical beneficiary had capacity to sue, standing to raise particular claims might be lacking. So, for example, the beneficiary of the will might not be able to bring an action against the government on the ground that the estate tax is used for illegal purposes by the government since the injury suffered is of a general nature, not particular to the litigant, and hence the beneficiary lacks standing to sue.

SECTION D. CLAIMS INVOLVING MULTIPLE PARTIES

1. PERMISSIVE JOINDER OF PARTIES

Read Federal Rules of Civil Procedure 20, 21, and 42(a) in the Supplement.

a. Historical Limitations on Permissive Joinder of Parties

Joinder of parties at common law was controlled by the substantive rules of law, often as reflected in the forms of action, rather than by notions of judicial economy and trial convenience. Plaintiffs who were asserting joint rights were compelled by these principles to join their respective claims in a single action; permissive joinder of plaintiffs, in the sense of plaintiffs having an option to join their claims when they were not joint, did not exist. The common-law rules governing joinder of defendants were slightly more flexible: joint tortfeasors and defendants whose contract obligations were both joint and several could be joined at plaintiff's option.

The equity courts adopted a more flexible approach to permissive joinder of parties than prevailed in the common-law courts. They allowed all persons having an interest in the subject matter of the action or in the relief demanded to join in a single proceeding. The early codes adopted the equity rule as a general provision governing joinder of parties. See Bone, *Mapping the Boundaries of the Dispute: Conceptions of Ideal Lawsuit Structure from the Field Code to the Federal Rules*, 89 Colum. L. Rev. 1 (1989). In many states, joinder of plaintiffs was restricted to those cases in which all plaintiffs were interested in both the subject matter of the action and all the relief demanded. Joinder of defendants was even more restricted by code provisions relating to joinder of causes of action, which typically required all parties to be interested in each of the joined causes.

b. Permissive Joinder Under Federal Rule 20

———

Read Federal Rule of Civil Procedure 20 in the Supplement.

———

M. K. v. TENET

United States District Court, District of Columbia, 2002.
216 F.R.D. 133.

URBINA, DISTRICT JUDGE:

[The court's discussion of Federal Rule 18 is omitted, see p. 346, supra.]

* * *

The plaintiffs cite to the first prong of Rule 20(a) [now Rule 20(a)(1)(A)], also known as the "transactional test," and argue that the defendants' acts and omissions pertaining to the plaintiffs' obstruction-of-counsel claims are "logically related" events that the court can regard as "arising out of the same transaction, occurrence or series of transactions or occurrences." * * * The court agrees with the plaintiffs' assertion that "logically related" events may consist of an alleged "consistent pattern of ... obstruction of security-cleared counsel by [the] [d]efendants." * * * Specifically, each of the existing plaintiffs allege that they were injured by the defendants through employment-related matters, such as retaliation, discrimination, and the denial of promotions and overseas assignments.

* * * After each employment dispute began, each of the plaintiffs or the plaintiffs' counsel sought access to employee and agency records. * * * The defendants, however, denied and continue to deny the plaintiffs and/or their counsel access to the plaintiffs' requested information. * * * As such, without this relevant information, the plaintiffs cannot effectively prepare or submit administrative complaints to the defendants or attempt to seek legal recourse through the applicable Title VII discrimination, Privacy Act, or First, Fifth, and Seventh Amendment claims.* * * The court concludes that the alleged repeated pattern of obstruction of counsel by the defendants against the plaintiffs is "logically related" as "a series of transactions or occurrences" that establishes an overall pattern of policies and practices aimed at denying effective assistance of counsel to the plaintiffs. * * * In this case, each plaintiff alleges that the defendants' policy and practice of obstruction of counsel has damaged the plaintiffs. * * * Further, each plaintiff requests declaratory and injunctive relief. * * * Thus, the court determines that each plaintiff in this case has satisfied the first prong of Rule 20(a). * * *

Turning to the second prong of Rule 20(a) [now Rule 20(a)(1)(B)], the plaintiffs aver that each of their claims are related by a common question of law or fact. * * * Specifically, one question of law or fact that is common to each of the six existing plaintiffs is whether the defendants' September 4, 1998 notice restricting the plaintiffs' counsel from accessing records intruded on the plaintiffs' substantial interest in freely discussing their legal rights with their attorneys. * * * Indeed, the question of law or fact that is common to all may be whether the "defendants have engaged in a common scheme or pattern of behavior" that effectively denies the plaintiffs' legal right to discuss their claims with their counsel. * * * The plaintiffs also allege that the defendants' policy or practice of obstruction of counsel "is implemented through [a] concert of action among CIA management and the Doe Defendants," who are now named in the second amended complaint. * * * In light of the aforementioned common questions of law and fact, the court concludes that the plaintiffs meet the second prong of Rule 20(a). * * *

The court need not stop here in its Rule 20(a) analysis. Indeed, it appears that there exists a further basis supporting the plaintiffs' position challenging severance * * *[.] Each plaintiff alleges common claims under the Privacy Act. * * * Specifically, the plaintiffs' second amended complaint alleges that the defendants "maintained records about the plaintiffs in unauthorized systems of records in violation of § 552a(e)(4) of the Privacy Act" and that the defendants "failed to employ proper physical safeguards for records in violation of § 552a(e)(10) of the Privacy Act." * * * The plaintiffs also allege that the defendants wrongfully denied the plaintiffs and plaintiffs' counsel access to records in violation of § 552a(d)(1) of the Privacy Act and "illegally maintained specific records describing their First Amendment activities in violation of § 552a(e)(7) of the Privacy Act." * * * Furthermore, the plaintiffs' first amended complaint contains similar allegations. Through their alleged Privacy Act violations, the plaintiffs are united by yet another "question of law or fact" that is common to each of them. * * * Accordingly, the court concludes that the plaintiffs satisfy the second prong of Rule 20(a) and, thus, the court denies the defendants' motion to sever.

On a final note, in denying the defendants' motion to sever, the court defers to the policy underlying Rule 20, which is to promote trial convenience, expedite the final determination of disputes, and prevent multiple lawsuits. * * * Indeed, the Supreme Court addressed this important policy in United Mine Workers of America v. Gibbs, * * * [p. 195, supra,] stating that "[u]nder the rules, the impulse is toward entertaining the broadest possible scope of action consistent with fairness to the parties; joinder of claims, parties, and remedies is strongly encouraged." *Id.* at 724, 86 S.Ct. 1130. In accordance with *Gibbs*, the court believes that the joinder or non-severance of the six existing plaintiffs and their new claims under Rule 20(a) will promote trial convenience, expedite the final resolution of disputes, and act to prevent multiple lawsuits, extra expense to the parties, and loss of time to the court and the litigants in this case. * * * For this added reason, the court denies the defendants' motion to sever.

IV. Conclusion

For all of the foregoing reasons, the court grants the plaintiffs' motion to amend and denies the defendants' motion to sever. * * *

NOTE AND QUESTIONS

Federal Rule 20 sets out a different standard for the joinder of parties than that of Federal Rule 18 for joinder of claims. How do you explain the difference between the rules? One commentator says that "Rule 20 is only slightly more demanding than Rule 18." Oakley, *Joinder and Jurisdiction in the Federal District Courts: The State of the Union of Rules and Statutes*, 69 Tenn. L. Rev. 35, 35–36 (2001). Do you agree with that analysis?

2. MANDATORY JOINDER OF PERSONS

———

Read Federal Rule of Civil Procedure 19 in the Supplement.

———

a. The Traditional Concept of "Indispensable" Parties

Before the adoption of Federal Rule 19, the principle of mandatory joinder was a judicially created doctrine. SHIELDS v. BARROW, 58 U.S. (17 How.) 130, 15 L.Ed. 158 (1854), established the notion that parties could be classified as necessary or indispensable depending on the nature of their substantive rights ("joint" or "severable"). The consequences of this classification were extremely important. If an absent party who was not subject to the jurisdiction of the court or whose joinder would destroy the pre-existing diversity of citizenship was labeled indispensable, the entire action had to be dismissed. On the other hand, if the absentee merely was necessary, the court might exercise its discretion in determining whether or not to continue without that person. Because plaintiff might have been deprived of any remedy if a party was found to be indispensable, courts often strained to avoid that conclusion. As might be suspected, this method had a debilitating effect on the standard for classification. (Until 2007, Federal Rule 19 used the common law term "indispensable" to refer to parties who are required to be joined.)

b. Required Joinder of Persons Under Federal Rule 19

PROVIDENT TRADESMENS BANK & TRUST CO. v. PATTERSON

Supreme Court of the United States, 1968.
390 U.S. 102, 88 S.Ct. 733, 19 L.Ed.2d 936.

Certiorari to the Circuit Court of Appeals for the Third Circuit.

MR. JUSTICE HARLAN delivered the opinion of the Court.

This controversy, involving in its present posture the dismissal of a declaratory judgment action for nonjoinder of an "indispensable" party, began nearly 10 years ago with a traffic accident. An automobile owned by Edward Dutcher, who was not present when the accident occurred, was being driven by Donald Cionci, to whom Dutcher had given the keys. John Lynch and John Harris were passengers. The automobile crossed the median strip of the highway and collided with a truck being driven by Thomas Smith. Cionci, Lynch, and Smith were killed and Harris was severely injured.

Three tort actions were brought. Provident Tradesmens Bank, the administrator of the estate of passenger Lynch and petitioner here, sued the estate of the driver, Cionci, in a diversity action. Smith's administratrix, and Harris in person, each brought a state-court action against the estate of Cionci, Dutcher, the owner, and the estate of Lynch. These Smith and Harris actions, for unknown reasons, have never gone to trial and are still pending. The Lynch action against Cionci's estate was settled for $50,000, which the estate of Cionci, being penniless, has never paid.

Dutcher, the owner of the automobile and a defendant in the as yet untried tort actions, had an automobile liability insurance policy with Lumbermens Mutual Casualty Company, a respondent here. That policy had an upper limit of $100,000 for all claims arising out of a single accident. This fund was potentially subject to two different sorts of claims by the tort plaintiffs. First, Dutcher himself might be held vicariously liable as Cionci's "principal"; the likelihood of such a judgment against

Dutcher is a matter of considerable doubt and dispute. Second, the policy by its terms covered the direct liability of any person driving Dutcher's car with Dutcher's "permission."

The insurance company had declined, after notice, to defend in the tort action brought by Lynch's estate against the estate of Cionci, believing that Cionci had not had permission and hence was not covered by the policy. The facts allegedly were that Dutcher had entrusted his car to Cionci, but that Cionci had made a detour from the errand for which Dutcher allowed his car to be taken. The estate of Lynch, armed with its $50,000 liquidated claim against the estate of Cionci, brought the present diversity action for a declaration that Cionci's use of the car had been "with permission" of Dutcher. The only named defendants were the company and the estate of Cionci. The other two tort plaintiffs were joined as plaintiffs. Dutcher, a resident of the State of Pennsylvania as were all the plaintiffs, was not joined either as plaintiff or defendant. The failure to join him was not adverted to at the trial level.

The major question of law contested at trial was a state-law question. * * * The District Court * * * directed verdicts in favor of the two estates. * * * The jury * * * found that Cionci had had permission, and hence awarded a verdict to Harris also.

Lumbermens appealed the judgment to the Court of Appeals for the Third Circuit, raising various state-law questions.[1] The Court of Appeals did not reach any of these issues. Instead, after reargument *en banc,* it decided, 5–2, to reverse on two alternative grounds neither of which had been raised in the District Court or by the appellant.

The first of these grounds was that Dutcher was an indispensable party. The court held that the "adverse interests" that had rendered Dutcher incompetent to testify under the Pennsylvania Dead Man Rule also required him to be made a party. The court did not consider whether the fact that a verdict had already been rendered, without objection to the nonjoinder of Dutcher, affected the matter. Nor did it follow the provision of Rule 19 of the Federal Rules of Civil Procedure that findings of "indispensability" must be based on stated pragmatic considerations. It held, to the contrary, that the right of a person who "may be affected" by the judgment to be joined is a "substantive" right, unaffected by the federal rules; that a trial court "may not proceed" in the absence of such a person; and that since Dutcher could not be joined as a defendant without destroying diversity jurisdiction the action had to be dismissed.

* * * Concluding that the inflexible approach adopted by the Court of Appeals in this case exemplifies the kind of reasoning that the Rule was designed to avoid, we reverse.

---

1. Appellants challenged the District Court's ruling on the Dead Man issue that Dutcher was incompetent to testify under Pennsylvania law against an estate if he had an adverse interest to that of the estate, the fairness of submitting the question as to Harris to a jury that had been directed to find in favor of the two estates whose position was factually indistinguishable, and certain instructions.

I.

* * *

We may assume, at the outset, that Dutcher falls within the category of persons who, under [Rule 19] (a), should be "joined if feasible." The action was for an adjudication of the validity of certain claims against a fund. Dutcher, faced with the possibility of judgments against him, had an interest in having the fund preserved to cover that potential liability. Hence there existed, when this case went to trial, at least the possibility that a judgment might impede Dutcher's ability to protect his interest, or lead to later relitigation by him.

The optimum solution, an adjudication of the permission question that would be binding on all interested persons, was not "feasible," however, for Dutcher could not be made a defendant without destroying diversity. Hence the problem was the one to which Rule 19(b) appears to address itself: in the absence of a person who "should be joined if feasible," should the court dismiss the action or proceed without him? Since this problem emerged for the first time in the Court of Appeals, there were also two subsidiary questions. First, what was the effect, if any, of the failure of the defendants to raise the matter in the District Court? Second, what was the importance, if any, of the fact that a judgment, binding on the parties although not binding on Dutcher, had already been reached after extensive litigation? The three questions prove, on examination, to be interwoven.

We conclude, upon consideration of the record and applying the "equity and good conscience" test of Rule 19(b), that the Court of Appeals erred in not allowing the judgment to stand.

Rule 19(b) suggests four "interests" that must be examined in each case to determine whether, in equity and good conscience, the court should proceed without a party whose absence from the litigation is compelled. Each of these interests must, in this case, be viewed entirely from an appellate perspective since the matter of joinder was not considered in the trial court. First, the plaintiff has an interest in having a forum. Before the trial, the strength of this interest obviously depends upon whether a satisfactory alternative forum exists. On appeal, if the plaintiff has won, he has a strong additional interest in preserving his judgment. Second, the defendant may properly wish to avoid multiple litigation, or inconsistent relief, or sole responsibility for a liability he shares with another. After trial, however, if the defendant has failed to assert this interest, it is quite proper to consider it foreclosed.

Third, there is the interest of the outsider whom it would have been desirable to join. Of course, since the outsider is not before the court, he cannot be bound by the judgment rendered. This means, however, only that a judgment is not *res judicata* as to, or legally enforceable against, a nonparty. It obviously does not mean either (a) that a court may never issue a judgment that, in practice, affects a nonparty or (b) that (to the contrary) a court may always proceed without considering the potential effect on nonparties simply because they are not "bound" in the technical sense. Instead, as Rule 19(a) expresses it, the court must consider the extent to which the judgment may "as a practical matter impair or impede his ability to protect" his interest in the subject matter [this provision is now Rule 19(a)(1)(B)(i) and the language has been altered]. When a case has reached the appeal stage the matter is more complex. The judgment appealed from may not in fact affect the interest of any outsider even though there existed, before trial, a possibility that a judgment affecting his interest would be rendered. When necessary, however, a court of appeals should, on its own initiative, take steps to protect the absent party, who of course had no opportunity to plead and prove his interest below.

Fourth, there remains the interest of the courts and the public in complete, consistent, and efficient settlement of controversies. We read the Rule's third criterion, whether the judgment issued in the absence of the nonjoined person will be "adequate," to refer to this public stake in settling disputes by wholes, whenever possible, for clearly the plaintiff, who himself chose both the forum and the parties defendant, will not be heard to complain about the sufficiency of the relief obtainable against them. After trial, considerations of efficiency of course include the fact that the time and expense of a trial have already been spent.

Rule 19(b) also directs a district court to consider the possibility of shaping relief to accommodate these four interests. Commentators had argued that greater attention should be paid to this potential solution to a joinder stymie, and the Rule now makes it explicit that a court should consider modification of a judgment as an alternative to dismissal. Needless to say, a court of appeals may also properly require suitable modification as a condition of affirmance.

Had the Court of Appeals applied Rule 19's criteria to the facts of the present case, it could hardly have reached the conclusion it did. We begin with the plaintiffs' viewpoint. It is difficult to decide at this stage whether they would have had an "adequate" remedy had the action been dismissed before trial for nonjoinder: we cannot here determine whether the plaintiffs could have brought the same action, against the same parties plus Dutcher, in a state court. After trial, however, the "adequacy" of this hypothetical alternative, from the plaintiffs' point of view, was obviously greatly diminished. Their interest in preserving a fully litigated judgment should be overborne only by rather greater opposing considerations than would be required at an earlier stage when the plaintiffs' only concern was for a federal rather than a state forum.

Opposing considerations in this case are hard to find. The defendants had no stake, either asserted or real, in the joinder of Dutcher. They showed no interest in joinder until the Court of Appeals took the matter into its own hands. This properly forecloses any interest of theirs, but for purposes of clarity we note that the insurance company, whose liability was limited to $100,000, had or will have full opportunity to litigate each claim on that fund against the claimant involved. Its only concern with the absence of Dutcher was and is to obtain a windfall escape from its defeat at trial.

The interest of the outsider, Dutcher, is more difficult to reckon. The Court of Appeals, concluding that it should not follow Rule 19's command to determine whether, as a practical matter, the judgment impaired the nonparty's ability to protect his rights, simply quoted the District Court's reasoning on the Dead Man issue as proof that Dutcher had a "right" to be joined:

> The subject matter of this suit is the coverage of Lumbermens' policy issued to Dutcher. Depending upon the outcome of this trial, Dutcher may have the policy all to himself or he may have to share its coverage with the Cionci Estate, thereby extending the availability of the proceeds of the policy to satisfy verdicts and judgments in favor of the two Estate plaintiffs. Sharing the coverage of a policy of insurance with finite limits with another, and thereby making that policy available to claimants against that other person is immediately worth less than having the coverage of such policy available to Dutcher alone. By the outcome in the instant case, to the extent that the two Estate plaintiffs will have the proceeds of the policy available to them in their claims against Cionci's estate, Dutcher will lose a measure of protection. Conversely, to the extent that the proceeds of this policy are not available to the two Estate plaintiffs Dutcher will gain. * * * It is sufficient for the purpose of determining adversity [of interest] that it appears clearly that the measure of Dutcher's protection under this policy of insurance is dependent upon the outcome of this suit. That being so, Dutcher's interest in these proceedings is adverse to the interest of the two Estate plaintiffs, the parties who represent, on this record, the interests of the deceased persons in the matter in controversy.[11]

There is a logical error in the Court of Appeals' appropriation of this reasoning for its own quite different purposes: Dutcher had an "adverse" interest (sufficient to invoke the Dead Man Rule) because he would have been *benefited* by a ruling *in favor of* the insurance company; the question before the Court of Appeals, however, was whether Dutcher was *harmed* by the judgment *against* the insurance company.

The two questions are not the same. If the three plaintiffs had lost to the insurance company on the permission issue, that loss would have ended the matter favorably to Dutcher. If, as has happened, the three plaintiffs obtain a judgment against the insurance company on the permission issue, Dutcher may still claim that as a nonparty he is not estopped by that judgment from relitigating the issue. At that point it might be argued that Dutcher should be bound by the previous decision because, although technically a nonparty, he had purposely bypassed an adequate

---

11. 218 F.Supp. 802, 805–806, quoted at 365 F.2d, at 805.

opportunity to intervene. We do not now decide whether such an argument would be correct under the circumstances of this case. If, however, Dutcher is properly foreclosed by his failure to intervene in the present litigation, then the joinder issue considered in the Court of Appeals vanishes, for any rights of Dutcher's have been lost by his own inaction.

If Dutcher is not foreclosed by his failure to intervene below, then he is not "bound" by the judgment in favor of the insurance company and, in theory, he has not been harmed. There remains, however, the practical question whether Dutcher is likely to have any need, and if so will have any opportunity, to relitigate. The only possible threat to him is that if the fund is used to pay judgments against Cionci the money may in fact have disappeared before Dutcher has an opportunity to assert his interest. Upon examination, we find this supposed threat neither large nor unavoidable.

The state-court actions against Dutcher had lain dormant for years at the pleading stage by the time the Court of Appeals acted. Petitioner asserts here that under the applicable Pennsylvania vicarious liability law there is virtually no chance of recovery against Dutcher. We do not accept this assertion as fact, but the matter could have been explored below. Furthermore, even in the event of tort judgments against Dutcher, it is unlikely that he will be prejudiced by the outcome here. The potential claimants against Dutcher himself are identical with the potential claimants against Cionci's estate. Should the claimants seek to collect from Dutcher personally, he may be able to raise the permission issue defensively, making it irrelevant that the actual monies paid from the fund may have disappeared: Dutcher can assert that Cionci did not have his permission and that therefore the payments made on Cionci's behalf out of Dutcher's insurance policy should properly be credited against Dutcher's own liability. Of course, when Dutcher raises this defense he may lose, either on the merits of the permission issue or on the ground that the issue is foreclosed by Dutcher's failure to intervene in the present case, but Dutcher will not have been prejudiced by the failure of the District Court here to order him joined.

If the Court of Appeals was unconvinced that the threat to Dutcher was trivial, it could nevertheless have avoided all difficulties by proper phrasing of the decree. The District Court, for unspecified reasons, had refused to order immediate payment on the Cionci judgment. Payment could have been withheld pending the suits against Dutcher and relitigation (if that became necessary) by him. In this Court, furthermore, counsel for petitioners represented orally that they, the tort plaintiffs, would accept a limitation of all claims to the amount of the insurance policy. Obviously such a compromise could have been reached below had the Court of Appeals been willing to abandon its rigid approach and seek ways to preserve what was, as to the parties, subject to the appellants' other contentions, a perfectly valid judgment.

The suggestion of potential relitigation of the question of "permission" raises the fourth "interest" at stake in joinder cases—efficiency. It might have been preferable, at the trial level, if there were a forum available in which both the company and Dutcher could have been made defendants, to dismiss the action and force the plaintiffs to go elsewhere. Even this preference would have been highly problematical, however, for the actual threat of relitigation by Dutcher depended on there being judgments against him and on the amount of the fund, which was not revealed to the District Court. By the time the case reached the Court of Appeals, however, the problematical preference on efficiency grounds had entirely disappeared: there was no reason then to throw away a valid judgment just because it did not theoretically settle the whole controversy.

II.

Application of Rule 19(b)'s "equity and good conscience" test for determining whether to proceed or dismiss would doubtless have led to a contrary result below. The Court of Appeals' reasons for disregarding the Rule remain to be examined. The majority of the court concluded that the Rule was inapplicable because "substantive" rights are involved, and substantive rights are not affected by the Federal Rules. Although the court did not articulate exactly what the substantive rights are, or what law determines them, we take it to have been making the following argument: (1) there is a category of persons called "indispensable parties"; (2) that category is defined by substantive law and the definition cannot be modified by rule; (3) the right of a person falling within that category to participate in the lawsuit in question is also a substantive matter, and is absolute.

With this we may contrast the position that is reflected in Rule 19. Whether a person is "indispensable," that is, whether a particular lawsuit must be dismissed in the absence of that person, can only be determined in the context of particular litigation. There is a large category, whose limits are not presently in question, of persons who, in the Rule's terminology, should be "joined if feasible," and who, in the older terminology, were called either necessary or indispensable parties. Assuming the existence of a person who should be joined if feasible, the only further question arises when joinder is not possible and the court must decide whether to dismiss or to proceed without him. To use the familiar but confusing terminology, the decision to proceed is a decision that the absent person is merely "necessary" while the decision to dismiss is a decision that he is "indispensable." The decision whether to dismiss (i.e., the decision whether the person missing is "indispensable") must be based on factors varying with the different cases, some such factors being substantive, some procedural, some compelling by themselves, and some subject to balancing against opposing interests. Rule 19 does not prevent the assertion of compelling substantive interests; it merely commands the courts to examine each controversy to make certain that the interests really exist. To say that a court "must" dismiss in the absence of an indispensable party and that it "cannot proceed" without him puts the matter the wrong way around: a court does not know whether a particular person is "indispensable" until it has examined the situation to determine whether it can proceed without him.

The Court of Appeals concluded, although it was the first court to hold, that the 19th century joinder cases in this Court created a federal, common-law, substantive right in a certain class of persons to be joined in the corresponding lawsuits. At the least, that was not the way the matter started. The joinder problem first arose in equity and in the earliest case giving rise to extended discussion the problem was the relatively simple one of the inefficiency of litigation involving only some of the interested persons. [Elmendorf v. Taylor, 23 U.S. (10 Wheat.) 152, 6 L.Ed. 289 (1825).] * * *

Following this case there arose three cases, also in equity, that the Court of Appeals here held to have declared a "substantive" right to be joined. It is true that these cases involved what would now be called "substantive" rights. This substantive involvement of the absent person with the controversy before the Court was, however, in each case simply an inescapable fact of the situation presented to the Court for adjudication. The Court in each case left the outsider with no more "rights" than it had already found belonged to him. The question in each case was simply whether, given the substantive involvement of the outsider, it was proper to proceed to adjudicate as between the parties.

* * *

The most influential of the cases in which this Court considered the question whether to proceed or dismiss in the absence of an interested but not joinable outsider is Shields v. Barrow, 17 How. 130, referred to in the opinion below. There the Court attempted, perhaps unfortunately, to stage general definitions of those persons without whom litigation could or could not proceed. In the former category were placed

> Persons having an interest in the controversy, and who ought to be made parties, in order that the court may act on that rule which requires it to decide on, and finally determine the entire controversy, and do complete justice, by adjusting all the rights involved in it. These persons are commonly termed necessary parties; but if their interests are separable from those of the parties before the court, so that the court can proceed to a decree, and do complete and final justice, without affecting other persons not before the court, the latter are not indispensable parties.

The persons in the latter category were

> Persons who not only have an interest in the controversy, but an interest of such a nature that a final decree cannot be made without either affecting that interest, or leaving the controversy in such a condition that its final termination may be wholly inconsistent with equity and good conscience.

These generalizations are still valid today, and they are consistent with the requirements of Rule 19, but they are not a substitute for the analysis required by that Rule. Indeed, the second *Shields* definition states, in rather different fashion, the criteria for decision announced in Rule 19(b). One basis for dismissal is prejudice to the rights of an absent party that *"cannot"* be avoided in issuance of a final decree. Alternatively, if the decree can be so written that it protects the interests of the absent persons, but as so written it leaves the controversy so situated that the outcome may be inconsistent with "equity and good conscience," the suit should be dismissed.

The majority of the Court of Appeals read Shields v. Barrow to say that a person whose interests "may be affected" by the decree of the court is an indispensable party, and that all indispensable parties have a "substantive right" to have suits dismissed in their absence. We are unable to read *Shields* as saying either. It dealt only with persons whose interests must, unavoidably, be affected by a decree and it said nothing about substantive rights. Rule 19(b), which the Court of Appeals dismissed as an ineffective attempt to change the substantive rights stated in *Shields,* is, on the contrary, a valid statement of the criteria for determining whether to proceed or dismiss in the forced absence of an interested person. It takes, for aught that now appears, adequate account of the very real, very substantive claims to fairness on the part of outsiders that may arise in some cases. This, however, simply is not such a case.

* * *

The judgment is vacated and the case is remanded to the Court of Appeals * * *.

NOTES AND QUESTIONS

1. *Provident Tradesmens* interpreted the amended version of Federal Rule 19, which was promulgated in 1966. Examine the Advisory Committee's Note to Rule 19, which is set out in the Supplement. What impact does the amendment have on the distinction between "persons required to be joined if feasible," of Rule 19(a), and "a person who is required to be joined if feasible cannot be joined," of Rule 19(b)? Given the amendment, what is the purpose of Rule 12(b)(7)? Of Rule 12(h)? For a negative appraisal of the amended text, see Fink, *Indispensable Parties and the Proposed Amendment to Federal Rule 19,* 74 Yale L.J. 403 (1965). For a discussion urging further reform of Federal Rule 19, see Freer, *Rethinking Compulsory Joinder: A Proposal to Restructure Federal Rule 19,* 60 N.Y.U. L. Rev. 1061 (1985).

2. What was the basis of the Court's finding in *Provident Tradesmens* with regard to prejudice for purposes of Rule 19(b) if Dutcher was not joined? Consider the following comments in an article written shortly after the Third Circuit decision dismissing the action and before the Supreme Court's decision:

> * * * How has Dutcher been affected? The judgment declaring that Cionci was driving with permission does not bind Dutcher legally, since

he was not a party. Dutcher is free to contest the point with all, including the insurer. Be it noted that although he testified in the action, Dutcher made no attempt to intervene; as the minority suggests, he might have reasonably preferred to stay out of the action. Whereas a judgment declaring Cionci to be an insured did not bind Dutcher, a judgment the other way would very likely have inured to Dutcher's benefit * * *.

Kaplan, *Continuing Work of the Civil Committee: 1966 Amendments of the Federal Rules of Civil Procedure (I)*, 81 Harv. L. Rev. 356, 373 (1967).

3. In what ways might the court shape relief in order to lessen any prejudice? Is the court free simply to grant a remedy other than the one originally requested—for example, by awarding money damages when specific performance might have a detrimental impact on the absentee? Of what importance is the availability of another forum in determining whether the action must be dismissed in the absence of someone whose joinder is not feasible? For a case in which the court determined that it was impossible to shape the relief so as to avoid prejudice to absent parties, see Wichita & Affiliated Tribes of Oklahoma v. Hodel, 788 F.2d 765, 776 (D.C. Cir. 1986).

4. What weight should be given to the various factors listed in Federal Rule 19? Because there is no precise formula for determining whether a particular nonparty must be joined under Rule 19(a), the decision has to be made in light of the general policies of the Rule. Can you articulate what those policies are? For example, what is the difference between the Rule 19(a)(1)(A) standard that in the absence of the nonparty "the court cannot accord complete relief among existing parties," and the factor listed in Rule 19(b)(3), "whether a judgment rendered in the person's absence would be adequate"? The test set out in Rule 19(a)(1)(B) focuses on the prejudicial effect of not joining the absentee. What type of prejudice must be shown to meet this requirement? See generally Tobias, *Rule 19 and the Public Rights Exception to Party Joinder*, 65 N.C. L. Rev. 745 (1987).

5. Should a court dismiss an action because of plaintiff's failure to join a required party plaintiff, even though defendant can join the missing party as a Rule 13(h) party to a compulsory counterclaim? In ASSOCIATED DRY GOODS CORP. v. TOWERS FINANCIAL CORP., 920 F.2d 1121, 1124 (2d Cir. 1990), defendant, a commercial subtenant, sought to dismiss plaintiff tenant's action for payment of rent because the tenant had failed to join the building's owner as an indispensable party plaintiff. Plaintiff did not join the building's owner because he was nondiverse, which would strip the court of subject-matter jurisdiction. The District Court dismissed the action pursuant to Rule 19(b). The Second Circuit reversed:

> The drafters of Rule 19(b) did not assign relative weight to each of the factors enumerated in the Rule. Instead, the Rule allows courts themselves to determine the emphasis to be placed on each consideration according to "the facts of [the] given case and in light of the governing equity-and-good-conscience test." * * * In this case, we view as dispositive Towers' ability to avoid all prejudice to itself by asserting a compulsory counterclaim against Associated pursuant to Rule 13(a) and adding * * * [the building's owner] as a party to the counterclaim under Rule 13(h). * * *

6. What should the result be when plaintiff, a citizen of state A, sues defendant, a citizen of state B, in a federal district court in state B, and, on defendant's motion, the court requires that X, a citizen of state A, be joined as a defendant in the action? See 7 Wright, Miller & Kane, Federal Practice and Procedure: Civil 3d § 1611; Steinman, *Postremoval Changes in the Party Structure of Diversity Cases: The Old Law, the New Law, and Rule 19*, 38 U. Kan. L. Rev. 863 (1990).

7. REPUBLIC OF THE PHILIPPINES v. PIMENTEL, 553 U.S. ___, 128 S.Ct. 2180, 171 L.Ed.2d 131 (2008), concerned the application of Rule 19 to a foreign government that claimed sovereign immunity from suit. The case involved competing claims to $35 million that had been deposited illegally into a New York bank on behalf of Ferdinand Marcos while he was President of the Republic of the Philippines. The New York bank holding the assets filed a federal interpleader action [interpleader is described on p. 369, infra,] in the District of Hawaii to resolve rival claims by the Republic of the Philippines, a special Philippine Commission investigating the former President's alleged misuse of office, and victims of human rights abuses. On a parallel track, the Republic and the Commission filed an action in a special Philippines court to recover the assets; they moved to dismiss the federal interpleader action on the ground that they were entitled to sovereign immunity and that in their absence the interpleader action could not go forward under Federal Rule 19. The Ninth Circuit held that the interpleader action could go forward even if the foreign entities were absent, finding that their claims were time barred, and it affirmed the District Court's award of the contested assets to the human rights victims (known as the "Pimental class"). The United States Supreme Court granted certiorari, and ordered dismissal of the interpleader action on the ground that the federal appellate court erred in giving insufficient weight to the assertion of sovereign immunity and to the prejudice that the foreign parties [collectively, the "Republic"] would suffer if the interpleader action were to go forward in their absence.

In applying Rule 19(b), the majority emphasized that joinder decisions "can be complex, and determinations are case specific." Looking to the first Rule 19(b) factor, the Court held that the decision to proceed in the absence of the Republic ignored the substantial prejudice that the absent party would suffer, given the Republic's "unique interest in resolving the ownership" issues "and in determining if, and how, the assets should be used to compensate those persons who suffered grievous injury," explaining there "is a comity interest in allowing a foreign state to use its own courts for a dispute if it has a right to do so." Id. at ___, 128 S.Ct. at 2190, 171 L.Ed.2d at 145–46. Turning to Rule 19(b)(2), the Court concluded that prejudice could not be lessened through the design of alternative remedies. As to Rule 19(b)(3), the appeals court "understood 'adequacy' to refer to satisfaction of the Pimentel class' claims. But adequacy refers to the 'public stake in settling disputes by wholes, whenever possible.' [citing *Provident Tradesmens*, p. 357, supra] * * *." Id. at ___, 128 S.Ct. at 2193, 171 L.Ed.2d at 148. Allowing the federal interpleader action to go forward without the Republic would not, in the Court's view, "further the public interest in settling the dispute as a whole" because the Republic "would not be bound by the judgment * * *." Id. Finally, the Court clarified that under Rule 19(b)(4), the question of plaintiff's adequacy of remedy refers in this case to the bank as stakeholder, and not to the tort victims. Dismissing the interpleader action would protect the New York bank by providing "an effective defense against piecemeal litigation and inconsistent, conflicting judgments," and, in any event, any prejudice to the stakeholder "is outweighed by prejudice to the absent entities invoking sovereign immunity." Id. at ___, 128 S.Ct. at 2193, 171 L.Ed.2d at 149. The Court concluded:

> The Court of Appeals' failure to give sufficient weight to the likely prejudice to the Republic and the Commission should the interpleader proceed in their absence would, in the usual course, warrant reversal and remand for further proceedings. In this case, however, that error and our further analysis under the additional provisions of Rule 19(b) lead us to conclude the action must be dismissed. This leaves the Pimentel class, which has waited for years now to be compensated for grievous wrongs, with no immediate way to recover on its judgment against Marcos. And it leaves * * * [the stakeholder] without a judgment.
>
> The balance of equities may change in due course. One relevant change may occur if it appears that the Sandiganbayan [the special court hearing the Republic's claim] cannot or will not issue its ruling within a reasonable period of time. Other changes could result when and if there is a ruling. * * * We do note that if [the stakeholder] * * *, or other parties, elect to commence further litigation in light of changed circumstances, it would not be necessary to file the new action in the District Court where this action arose, provided venue and jurisdictional requirements are satisfied elsewhere. The present action, however, may not proceed."

Id. at ___, 128 S.Ct. at 2193, 171 L.Ed.2d at 149–50. Justice Stevens dissented in part. He criticized the Court for taking "a more 'inflexible approach' " to the question of mandatory parties than required by Rule 19, citing *Provident Tradesmens*, p. 357, supra, and for ignoring the parties' interest "in a prompt resolution" of their claims. Id. at ___, 128 S.Ct. at 2197, 171 L.Ed.2d at 153.

SECTION E. IMPLEADER

———

Read Federal Rule of Civil Procedure 14 and the accompanying material in the Supplement.

———

1. THE HISTORICAL USE OF IMPLEADER

Consider the following:

When *A* sues *B*, there is often a third party, *C*, who may ultimately be liable to *B* for all or some part of the damages which *A* might recover. This liability * * * may be based on such legal relationships as those which arise from a contract of indemnity for loss or liability or a right to contribution from a joint tortfeasor. If it were necessary for *B* to institute a separate action to recover reimbursement from *C*, the issue of *B*'s liability to *A* would often have to be relitigated between *B* and *C*, since *C*, not a party to the original litigation, would generally not be bound by the prior determination. * * * Even if *B* could obtain a wholly consistent result against *C*, the courts would have been burdened by two trials and *B* might have been seriously handicapped by having to satisfy *A*'s judgment long before his recovery over from *C*. * * *

* * * [Federal Rule 14(a)] has its roots in the common-law procedure of "vouching to warranty," whereby a person whose title to land had been attacked could notify his vendor of the attack if the latter had warranted the title. The vendor, whether or not he chose to participate, would then be bound by the prior determination in a subsequent suit by his vendee. * * *

Developments in the Law—Multiparty Litigation in the Federal Courts, 71 Harv. L. Rev. 877, 907 (1958). See also Neiderman & Reed, *Vouching In Under the U.C.C.: Its History, Modern Use, and Questions About Its Continued Viability*, 23 J.L. & Com. 1, 1 (2003). How did the historic practice of "vouching to warranty" differ from third-party practice under Federal Rule 14?

2. THIRD–PARTY PRACTICE UNDER FEDERAL RULE OF CIVIL PROCEDURE 14

"In exercising its discretion the court should endeavor to effectuate the purpose of Rule 14, which means that impleader is to be allowed if it will avoid circuity of action and eliminate duplication of suits based on closely related matters." 6 Wright, Miller & Kane, Federal Practice and Procedure: Civil 2d § 1443. Would it be appropriate to order separate trials under Federal Rule 42 if the litigation became too complex?

SECTION F. INTERPLEADER IN THE FEDERAL COURTS

———

Read Federal Rule of Civil Procedure 22, 28 U.S.C. §§ 1335, 1397, and 2361, and the accompanying material in the Supplement.

———

STATE FARM FIRE & CASUALTY CO. v. TASHIRE
Supreme Court of the United States, 1967.
386 U.S. 523, 87 S.Ct. 1199, 18 L.Ed.2d 270.

[This case arose out of a collision between a Greyhound bus and a pickup truck in Shasta County, California in September, 1964. Two of the bus passengers were killed and 33 others were injured, as were the bus driver, the driver of the truck, and its passenger. One of the dead and 10 of the injured passengers were Canadians; the rest of the individuals were citizens of five American states.

Four of the injured passengers filed suit in California state courts seeking damages in excess of $1,000,000 and naming as defendants: Greyhound Lines, Inc.; Nauta, the bus driver; Clark, the driver of the truck; and Glasgow, the truck passenger who apparently was its owner. Each of the individual defendants was a citizen of Oregon; Greyhound was a California corporation. Before the California cases came to trial and before any other suits were filed, petitioner, State Farm Fire & Casualty Company, an Illinois corporation, brought this interpleader action in the United States District Court for the District of Oregon.

State Farm asserted that at the time of the collision it had in force an insurance policy covering Clark, the driver of the truck, for bodily injury liability up to $10,000 per person and $20,000 per occurrence. State Farm further asserted that the aggregate damages sought in actions already filed in California and other anticipated actions far exceeded the amount of its maximum liability under the policy. Accordingly, it paid into court the sum of $20,000 and asked the court (1) to require all claimants to establish their claims against Clark and his insurer in the Oregon proceeding and in no other action, and (2) to discharge State Farm from all further obligations under its policy. Alternatively, State Farm requested a decree that the insurer owed no duty to Clark and was not liable on the policy, and asked the court to refund the $20,000 deposit. State Farm joined as defendants Clark, Glasgow, Nauta, Greyhound, and each of the prospective claimants. Jurisdiction was predicated both upon the Federal Interpleader Act and general diversity of citizenship. Personal service was effected on each of the American defendants and registered mail was employed to give notice to the 11 Canadian claimants.

The Oregon District Court issued an order requiring each of the defendants to show cause why he should not be restrained from filing or prosecuting any proceeding affecting the property or obligation involved in the interpleader action. In response, several of the defendants contended that the policy did cover the accident and advanced various arguments for the position that interpleader was inappropriate.

When a temporary injunction along the lines sought by State Farm issued, the respondents moved to dismiss and, in the alternative, sought a change of venue to the district in which the collision had occurred. After a hearing, the District Court declined to dissolve the temporary injunction but continued the motion for a change of venue. Later, the temporary injunction was broadened so that all suits against Clark, State Farm, Greyhound, and Nauta had to be prosecuted in the interpleader proceeding.

On interlocutory appeal, the Ninth Circuit reversed on the ground that in states, such as Oregon, that do not permit a "direct action" against an insurance company until a judgment is obtained against the insured, State Farm could not invoke federal interpleader until the claims against the insured had been reduced to judgment. The Court of Appeals held that prior to that time claimants with unliquidated tort claims are not "claimants" within the meaning of Section 1335 of Title 28 and are not "persons having claims against the plaintiff" within the meaning of Federal Rule 22. (The language of Rule 22 has since been altered without any substantive change.) The Ninth Circuit directed that the temporary injunction be dissolved and the action be dismissed. The Supreme Court granted certiorari.]

Certiorari to the United States Court of Appeals for the Ninth Circuit.

MR. JUSTICE FORTAS delivered the opinion of the Court.

* * *

I.

Before considering the issues presented by the petition for certiorari, we find it necessary to dispose of a question neither raised by the parties nor passed upon by the courts below. Since the matter concerns our jurisdiction, we raise it on our own motion. * * * The interpleader statute * * * has been uniformly construed to require only "minimal diversity," that is, diversity of citizenship between two or more claimants, without regard to the circumstance that other rival claimants may be co-citizens. The language of the statute, the legislative purpose broadly to remedy the problems posed by multiple claimants to a single fund, and the consistent judicial interpretation tacitly accepted by Congress, persuade us that the statute requires no more. There remains, however, the question whether such a statutory construction is consistent with Article III of our Constitution * * *. In Strawbridge v. Curtiss, * * * [p. 165, supra], this Court held that the diversity of citizenship statute required "complete diversity": where co-citizens appeared on both sides of a dispute, jurisdiction was lost. But Chief Justice Marshall there purported to construe only "The words of the act of Congress," not the Constitution itself. And in a variety of contexts this Court and the lower courts have concluded that Article III poses no obstacle to the legislative extension of federal jurisdiction, founded on diversity, so long as any two adverse parties are not co-citizens. Accordingly, we conclude that the present case is properly in the federal courts.

II.

We do not agree with the Court of Appeals that, in the absence of a state law or contractual provision for "direct action" suits against the insurance company, the company must wait until persons asserting claims against its insured have reduced those claims to judgment before seeking to invoke the benefits of federal interpleader. * * *

Considerations of judicial administration demonstrate the soundness of this view which, in any event, seems compelled by the language of the present statute, which is remedial and to be liberally construed. Were an insurance company required to await reduction of claims to judgment, the first claimant to obtain such a judgment or to negotiate a settlement might appropriate all or a disproportionate slice of the fund before his fellow claimants were able to establish their claims. The difficulties such a race to judgment pose for the insurer, and the unfairness which may result to some claimants, were among the principal evils the interpleader device was intended to remedy.

III.

The fact that State Farm had properly invoked the interpleader jurisdiction under § 1335 did not, however, entitle it to an order both enjoining prosecution of suits against it outside the confines of the interpleader proceeding and also extending such protection to its insured, the alleged tortfeasor. Still less was Greyhound Lines entitled to have that order expanded so as to protect itself and its driver, also alleged to be tortfeasors, from suits brought by its passengers in various state or federal courts. Here, the scope of the litigation, in terms of parties and claims, was vastly more extensive than the confines of the "fund," the deposited proceeds of the insurance policy. In these circumstances, the mere existence of such a fund cannot, by use of interpleader, be employed to accomplish purposes that exceed the needs of orderly contest with respect to the fund.

There are situations, of a type not present here, where the effect of interpleader is to confine the total litigation to a single forum and proceeding. One such case is where a stakeholder, faced with rival claims to the fund itself, acknowledges—or denies—his liability to one or the other of the claimants. In this situation, the fund itself is the target of the claimants. It marks the outer limits of the controversy. It is, therefore, reasonable and sensible that interpleader, in discharge of its office to protect the fund, should also protect the stakeholder from vexatious and multiple litigation. In this context, the suits sought to be enjoined are squarely within the language of 28 U.S.C. § 2361 * * *.

But the present case is another matter. Here, an accident has happened. Thirty-five passengers or their representatives have claims which they wish to press against a variety of defendants: the bus company, its driver, the owner of the truck, and the truck driver. The circumstance that one of the prospective defendants happens to have an insurance policy is a fortuitous event which should not of itself shape the nature of the ensuing litigation. * * * [A]n insurance company whose maximum interest in the case cannot exceed $20,000 and who in fact asserts that it has no interest at all, should not be allowed to determine that dozens of tort plaintiffs must be compelled to press their claims—even those claims which are not against the insured and which in no event could be satisfied out of the meager insurance fund—in a single forum of the insurance company's choosing. There is nothing in the statutory scheme, and very little in the judicial and academic commentary upon that scheme, which requires that the tail be allowed to wag the dog in this fashion.

State Farm's interest in this case * * * receives full vindication when the court restrains claimants from seeking to enforce against the insurance company any judgment obtained against its insured, except in the interpleader proceeding itself. To the extent that the District Court sought to control claimants' lawsuits against the insured and other alleged tortfeasors, it exceeded the powers granted to it by the statutory scheme.

We recognize, of course, that our view of interpleader means that it cannot be used to solve all the vexing problems of multiparty litigation arising out of a mass tort. But interpleader was never intended to perform such a function, to be an all-purpose "bill of peace." Had it been so intended, careful provision would necessarily have been made to insure that a party with little or no interest in the outcome of a complex controversy should not strip truly interested parties of substantial rights—such as the right to choose the forum in which to establish their claims, subject to generally applicable rules of jurisdiction, venue, service of process, removal, and change of venue. None of the legislative and academic sponsors of a modern federal interpleader device viewed their accomplishment as a "bill of peace," capable of sweeping dozens of lawsuits out of the various state and federal courts in which they were brought and into a single interpleader proceeding. * * *

In light of the evidence that federal interpleader was not intended to serve the function of a "bill of peace" in the context of multiparty litigation arising out of a mass tort, of the anomalous power which such a construction of the statute would give the stakeholder, and of the thrust of the statute and the purpose it was intended to serve, we hold that the interpleader statute did not authorize the injunction entered in the present case. Upon remand, the injunction is to be modified consistently with this opinion.

IV.

The judgment of the Court of Appeals is reversed * * *.

[JUSTICE DOUGLAS dissented on the ground that the litigants were not "claimants" to the fund as required by the Federal Interpleader Act. He pointed out that the insurance policy specifically provided that no action could be brought against the company until the insured's obligation was determined. Furthermore, he argued, both California and Oregon law did not permit a direct action against the insurer until after final judgment against the insured. The Justice also took issue with the majority's construction of the words "may claim" in the Federal Interpleader Act.]

NOTES AND QUESTIONS

1. Interpleader is a device designed to enable a party who might be exposed to multiple claims to money or property under her control to settle

the controversy in a single proceeding. For example, if two people claim that each is the sole beneficiary of a life insurance policy, the insurance company, in the absence of a joinder device such as interpleader, would be required to defend against both in two actions. Not only would the company be forced to incur the expense of additional litigation, but it would be faced with the possibility that, in separate lawsuits, *both* claimants might win. See 7 Wright, Miller & Kane, Federal Practice and Procedure: Civil 3d § 1702.

2.   The historic territorial approach to jurisdiction over the person raised a number of peculiar problems in the interpleader context. Occasionally, the stakeholder was not able to obtain in personam jurisdiction over all of the claimants in any one state because of the limitations imposed by the Due Process Clause of the Fourteenth Amendment. To overcome this difficulty, courts often characterized interpleader as an in rem or quasi in rem proceeding and predicated jurisdiction on the presence of the stake within the territorial reach of the court.

3.   Congress passed the Federal Interpleader Act in 1917. The statute was successively broadened in 1926 and 1936 and was reconstituted in 1948 as part of the United States Judicial Code. It now appears as 28 U.S.C. §§ 1335, 1397, 2361.

4.   Section 1397 permits venue to be laid in any judicial district in which one or more of the claimants reside, and Section 2361 permits nationwide service of process in order to reach all of the claimants. Further recognition of the interstate quality of interpleader and the need for the exercise of federal judicial power in this context is the provision in Section 1335 permitting the federal courts to assert jurisdiction when the stake is worth as little as $500, and where there is diversity of citizenship between or among "[t]wo or more adverse claimants."

5.   Interpleader under the Federal Interpleader Act is referred to as "statutory interpleader." Interpleader under Federal Rule 22, known as "rule interpleader," is somewhat different. Although the fourfold requirements of the old equitable remedy are not necessary, the usual jurisdictional, venue, and process limitations still apply.

6.   Consider the statement in *Tashire* that "our view of interpleader means that it cannot be used to solve all the vexing problems of multiparty litigation arising out of a mass tort." 386 U.S. at 535, 87 S.Ct. at 1206, 18 L.Ed.2d at 278. Does this view prohibit cross-claims between interpleader claimants, the assertion of an unrelated claim by a disinterested stakeholder against a claimant, or a counterclaim by a claimant against the stakeholder? See generally 7 Wright, Miller & Kane, Federal Practice and Procedure: Civil 3d § 1715.

SECTION G.   INTERVENTION

––––––

Read Federal Rule of Civil Procedure 24 in the Supplement.

––––––

Assume that a person learns that a lawsuit is pending, and that a judgment in that action might indirectly affect her interests. Should she be allowed to enter it as an additional party? Rule 24, which governs intervention, allows a third person to interject him or herself into a lawsuit, cutting against the grain of the traditional notion that a plaintiff is allowed to control his suit. See 7C Wright, Miller & Kane, Federal Practice and Procedure: Civil 3d § 1901. A noted commentator explains:

> A civil action, in the Anglo–American tradition, has usually been thought of as a private controversy between plaintiff and defendant. Although outsiders were sometimes permitted to take part in order to protect their interests, they were more often regarded by the court and the parties as undesired intermeddlers who would be required to protect themselves—if they could—by bringing a lawsuit of their own. Indeed after courts of admiralty, and later of equity, recognized intervention as a proper means of asserting an interest in property in the custody of the court, there remained considerable uncertainty for many years about whether, and to what extent, intervention could be permitted in a routine action at law.

> But in recent decades the increased complexity of litigation and the growing number of cases involving the public interest or a wide variety of private interests have been accompanied by a steady change in the attitude toward intervention. Both intervention of right and permissive intervention were given new vitality in the federal system by adoption of [R]ule 24 of the Federal Rules of Civil Procedure in 1938, and subsequent amendments have broadened their scope.

Shapiro, *Some Thoughts on Intervention before Courts, Agencies, and Arbitrators*, 81 Harv. L. Rev. 721, 721–22 (1968) (footnotes omitted).

SMUCK v. HOBSON

United States Court of Appeals, District of Columbia Circuit, 1969.
132 U.S. App. D.C. 372, 408 F.2d 175.

[In Hobson v. Hansen, 269 F. Supp. 401 (D.D.C. 1967), a class action brought on behalf of black and poor children, the court found that plaintiffs were being denied their constitutional rights to equal educational opportunities because the District of Columbia schools were being operated on a basis that was racially and economically discriminatory. The Board of Education voted not to appeal and ordered Dr. Carl Hansen, the Superintendent of Schools, not to appeal. Nonetheless, Dr. Hansen and Carl Smuck, one of the dissenting Board members, filed notices of appeal. In addition, motions to intervene were made in the District Court and in the Court of Appeals by Dr. Hansen and twenty parents who said they "dissent from" the court's decision. The Court of Appeals decided to hold the direct appeals in abeyance and remanded the intervention motions for a hearing. The District Court granted the motions to intervene, even though neither Hansen nor the parents had shown a substantial interest that could be protected only through intervention, "in order to give the Court of Appeals an opportunity to pass on the intervention questions raised here, and the questions to be raised by the appeal on the merits * * *." Hobson v. Hansen, 44 F.R.D. 18, 33 (D.D.C. 1968). The Court of Appeals then considered the matter *en banc.*]

BAZELON, CHIEF JUDGE.

* * * These appeals challenge the findings of the trial court that the Board of Education has in a variety of ways violated the Constitution in administering the District of Columbia schools. Among the facts that distinguish this case from the normal grist of appellate courts is the absence of the Board of Education as an appellant. Instead, the would-be appellants are Dr. Carl F. Hansen, the resigned superintendent of District schools, who appeals in his former official capacity and as an individual; Carl C. Smuck, a member of the Board of Education, who appeals in that capacity; and the parents of certain school children who have attempted to intervene in order to register on appeal their "dissent" from the order below.

* * * Whatever standing he might have possessed to appeal as a named defendant in the original suit * * * disappeared when Dr. Hansen left his official position. Presumably because he was aware of this, he subsequently moved to intervene under Rule 24(a) [now Rule 24(a)(2)] of the Rules of Civil Procedure in order to appeal as an individual. * * * He does not claim that a reversal or modification of the order by this Court would make his return to office likely. Consequently, the supposed impact of the decision upon his tenure is irrelevant insofar as an appeal is concerned, since a reversal would have no effect. Dr. Hansen thus has no "interest relating to the property or transaction which is the subject of the action" sufficient for Rule 24(a), and intervention is therefore unwarranted.

We also find that Mr. Smuck has no appealable interest as a member of the Board of Education. While he was in that capacity a named defendant, the Board of Education was undeniably the principal figure and could have been sued alone as a collective entity. Appellant Smuck had a fair opportunity to participate in its defense, and in the decision not to appeal. Having done so, he has no separate interest as an individual in the litigation. The order directs the board to take certain actions. But since its decisions are made by vote as a collective whole, there is no apparent way in which Smuck as an individual could violate the decree and thereby become subject to enforcement proceedings.

The motion to intervene by the parents presents a more difficult problem requiring a correspondingly more detailed examination of the requirements for intervention of right.

* * *

The phrasing of Rule 24(a)(2) as amended parallels that of Rule 19(a)(2) [now Rule 19(a)(1)(B)] concerning joinder. But the fact that the two rules are entwined does not imply that an "interest" for the purpose of one is precisely the same as for the other. The occasions upon which a petitioner should be allowed to intervene under Rule 24 are not necessarily limited to those situations when the trial court should compel him to become a party under Rule 19. And while the division of Rule 24(a) and (b) into "Intervention of Right" and "Permissible Intervention" might superficially suggest that only the latter involves an exercise of discretion by the court, the contrary is clearly the case.

The effort to extract substance from the conclusory phrase "interest" or "legally protectable interest" is of limited promise. Parents unquestionably have a sufficient "interest" in the education of their children to justify the initiation of a lawsuit in appropriate circumstances, as indeed was the case for the plaintiff-appellee parents here. But in the context of intervention the question is not whether a lawsuit should be begun, but whether already initiated litigation should be extended to include additional parties. The 1966 amendments to Rule 24(a) have facilitated this, the true inquiry, by eliminating the temptation or need for tangential expeditions in search of "property" or someone "bound by a judgment." It would be unfortunate to allow the inquiry to be led once again astray by a myopic fixation upon "interest." Rather, as Judge Leventhal recently concluded for this Court, "[A] more instructive approach is to let our construction be guided by the policies behind the 'interest' requirement. * * * [T]he 'interest' test is primarily a practical guide to disposing of lawsuits by involving as many apparently concerned persons as is compatible with efficiency and due process."[12]

The decision whether intervention of right is warranted thus involves an accommodation between two potentially conflicting goals: to achieve judicial economies of scale by resolving related issues in a single lawsuit, and to prevent the single lawsuit from becoming fruitlessly complex or unending. Since this task will depend upon the contours of the particular controversy, general rules and past decisions cannot provide uniformly dependable guides. The Supreme Court, in its only full-dress examination of Rule 24(a) since the 1966 amendments, found that a gas distributor was entitled to intervention of right although its only "interest" was the economic harm it claimed would follow from an allegedly inadequate plan for divestiture approved by the Government in an antitrust proceeding.[14] While conceding that the Court's opinion granting intervention in Cascade Natural Gas Corp. v. El Paso Natural Gas Co. "is certainly susceptible of a very broad reading," the trial judge here would distinguish the decision on the ground that the petitioner "did show a strong direct economic interest, for the new company [to be created by divestiture] would be its sole supplier." Yet while it is undoubtedly true that "*Cascade* should not be

---

12.   Nuesse v. Camp, 128 U.S. App. D.C. 172, 385 F.2d 694, 700 (1967).

14.   Cascade Natural Gas Corp. v. El Paso Natural Gas Co., 386 U.S. 129, 132–136, 87 S.Ct. 932, 17 L.Ed.2d 814 (1967).

read as a carte blanche for intervention by anyone at any time," there is no apparent reason why an "economic interest" should always be necessary to justify intervention. The goal of "disposing of lawsuits by involving as many apparently concerned persons as is compatible with efficiency and due process" may in certain circumstances be met by allowing parents whose only "interest" is the education of their children to intervene. In determining whether such circumstances are present, the first requirement of Rule 24(a)(2), that of an "interest" in the transaction, may be a less useful point of departure than the second and third requirements, that the applicant may be impeded in protecting his interest by the action and that his interest is not adequately represented by others.

This does not imply that the need for an "interest" in the controversy should or can be read out of the rule. But the requirement should be viewed as a prerequisite rather than relied upon as a determinative criterion for intervention. If barriers are needed to limit extension of the right to intervene, the criteria of practical harm to the applicant and the adequacy of representation by others are better suited to the task. If those requirements are met, the nature of his "interest" may play a role in determining the sort of intervention which should be allowed—whether, for example, he should be permitted to contest all issues, and whether he should enjoy all the prerogatives of a party litigant.

Both courts and legislatures have recognized as appropriate the concern for their children's welfare which the parents here seek to protect by intervention. While the artificiality of an appeal without the Board of Education cannot be ignored, neither can the importance of the constitutional issues decided below. The relevance of substantial and unsettled questions of law has been recognized in allowing intervention to perfect an appeal. And this Court has noted repeatedly, "obviously tailored to fit ordinary civil litigation, [the provisions of Rule 24] require other than literal application in atypical cases."[20] We conclude that the interests asserted by the intervenors are sufficient to justify an examination of whether the two remaining requirements for intervention are met.

* * *

[The court then determined that the disposition of the action might impair the applicants' ability to protect their interests if they were not allowed to intervene.]

The remaining requirement for intervention is that the applicant not be adequately represented by others. No question is raised here but that the Board of Education adequately represented the intervenors at the trial below; the issue rather is whether the parents were adequately represented by the school board's decision not to appeal. The presumed good faith of the board in reaching this decision is not conclusive. * * * As the conditional wording of Rule 24(a)(2) suggests in permitting intervention

---

20. Textile Workers Union, etc. v. Allendale Co., 226 F.2d 765, 767 (D.C. Cir. 1955) (en banc), cert. denied, Allendale Co. v. Mitchell, 351 U.S. 909, 76 S.Ct. 699, 100 L.Ed. 1444 (1956), cited in Nuesse v. Camp, 128 U.S. App. D.C. 172, 385 F.2d 694, 700 (1967).

"unless the applicant's interest is adequately represented by existing parties," "the burden [is] on those opposing intervention to show the adequacy of the existing representation." In this case, the interests of the parents who wish to intervene in order to appeal do not coincide with those of the Board of Education. The school board represents all parents within the District. The intervening appellants may have more parochial interests centering upon the education of their own children. While they cannot of course ask the Board to favor their children unconstitutionally at the expense of others, they like other parents can seek the adoption of policies beneficial to their own children. Moreover, considerations of publicity, cost, and delay may not have the same weight for the parents as for the school board in the context of a decision to appeal. And the Board of Education, buffeted as it like other school boards is by conflicting public demands, may possibly have less interest in preserving its own untrammeled discretion than do the parents. It is not necessary to accuse the board of bad faith in deciding not to appeal or of a lack of vigor in defending the suit below in order to recognize that a restrictive court order may be a not wholly unwelcome haven.

* * *

Our holding that the appellants would be practically disadvantaged by a decision without appeal in this case and that they are not otherwise adequately represented necessitates a closer scrutiny of the precise nature of their interest and the scope of intervention that should accordingly be granted. The parents who seek to appeal do not come before this court to protect the good name of the Board of Education. Their interest is not to protect the board, or Dr. Hansen, from an unfair finding. Their asserted interest is rather the freedom of the school board—and particularly the new school board recently elected—to exercise the broadest discretion constitutionally permissible in deciding upon educational policies. Since this is so, their interest extends only to those parts of the order which can fairly be said to impose restraints upon the Board of Education. And because the school board is not a party to this appeal, review should be limited to those features of the order which limit the discretion of the old or new board.

* * *

[A partial concurring opinion by JUDGE McGOWAN and dissenting opinions by JUDGES DANAHER and BURGER are omitted.]

NOTES AND QUESTIONS

1. In addition to the reasons offered in *Smuck,* typical grounds for the assertion of inadequacy of representation for purposes of intervening as of right under Rule 24(a)(2) are: the applicant's interests are not represented at all, Purnell v. City of Akron, 925 F.2d 941 (6th Cir. 1991); the applicant and the attorney who supposedly represents his interest are antagonistic, United States v. C.M. Lane Lifeboat Co., 25 F.Supp. 410 (E.D.N.Y. 1938), but see

Stadin v. Union Elec. Co., 309 F.2d 912 (8th Cir. 1962), certiorari denied 373 U.S. 915, 83 S.Ct. 1298, 10 L.Ed.2d 415 (1963); and there is collusion between the representative and the adverse parties, Commonwealth of Virginia v. Westinghouse Elec. Corp., 542 F.2d 214 (4th Cir. 1976). It often is held that the United States adequately represents the public interest in antitrust suits, so intervention in those cases is denied absent a clear showing to the contrary. Is this approach justifiable? How does the Department of Justice determine what the public interest is?

2. What factors affect the standard for adequate representation? In NATURAL RESOURCES DEFENSE COUNCIL, INC. v. NEW YORK STATE DEPARTMENT OF ENVIRONMENTAL CONSERVATION, 834 F.2d 60 (2d Cir. 1987), the American Petroleum Institute (API) appealed a District Court order denying its motion to intervene in a "citizen suit" brought by the Natural Resources Defense Council, Inc. and other groups concerned with air pollution against the New York State Department of Environmental Conservation, the United States Environmental Protection Agency, and the administrators of both agencies. The Court of Appeals affirmed:

> * * * API contends that in this suit it too has an interest different from that of New York. API's interest, it urges, is economic, whereas the State's interest is governmental.
>
> We think API misperceives the concept of an interest "adequately represented" within the meaning of Rule 24. A putative intervenor does not have an interest not adequately represented by a party to a lawsuit simply because it has a motive to litigate that is different from the motive of an existing party. So long as the party has demonstrated sufficient motivation to litigate vigorously and to present all colorable contentions, a district judge does not exceed the bounds of discretion by concluding that the interests of the intervenor are adequately represented. * * *

Id. Is this case consistent with *Smuck*? Why do you think the two come out differently? See Vreeland, *Public Interest Groups, Public Law Litigation, and Federal Rule 24(a)*, 57 U. Chi. L. Rev. 279 (1990).

3. Rule 24 treats intervention as a permissive joinder device, so that the "outsider" to the litigation has the option of joining the lawsuit or not. Should a court ever require a potential party to intervene in a lawsuit? The Supreme Court considered and rejected this position in MARTIN v. WILKS, 490 U.S. 755, 109 S.Ct. 2180, 104 L.Ed.2d 835 (1989). The case involved a challenge by white firefighters to hiring decisions taken by the City of Birmingham pursuant to consent decrees that had been entered in federal civil rights suits on behalf of black individuals who allegedly had been denied employment or promotion on the basis of their race. The District Court dismissed the white firefighters' lawsuit on the ground, among others, that the plaintiffs had not intervened in the prior cases and therefore could not collaterally challenge the consent decrees. The Supreme Court, five–to–four, held that "[k]nowledge of a lawsuit" does not obligate a party to intervene in a lawsuit: "a party seeking a judgment binding on another cannot obligate that person to intervene; he must be joined." Id. at 763–65, 109 S.Ct. 2185–86, 104 L.Ed.2d at 846–47. Justice Stevens, in a dissent, underscored that "in complex litigation this Court has squarely held that a sideline-sitter may be

bound as firmly as an actual party if he had adequate notice and a fair opportunity to intervene and if the judicial interest in finality is sufficiently strong." Id. at 793, 109 S.Ct. at 2200–01, 104 L.Ed.2d at 863. Why did Federal Rule 19 not require the joinder of the white firefighters in the earlier discrimination suits? Are you persuaded that permissive party-initiated joinder is a better approach than a rule of mandatory intervention? See Brunet, *The Triumph of Efficiency and Discretion Over Competing Complex Litigation Policies*, 10 Rev. Litig. 273 (1991).

CHAPTER 9

CLASS ACTIONS

■ ■ ■

This Chapter explores class action practice under Federal Rule 23. A noted commentator has said: "Perhaps the most dramatic development in civil procedure in recent decades has been the growth of interest in the class action as an actual and potential means of resolving a wide range of disputes." Shapiro, *Class Actions: The Class as Party and Client*, 73 Notre Dame L. Rev. 913, 913 (1998). Probably no procedural device more often finds itself at the center of political controversy, or is as frequently featured in a newspaper headline, as that of the class action. The materials are designed to introduce you to this complex yet fascinating topic through an examination of the history of the class action device, the operation of Federal Rule 23, the problems that have developed with different kinds of class actions, and the policy questions that this practice raises. The class action, like all of the Federal Rules, continues to be a work in progress. The Advisory Committee on Civil Rules of the United States Judicial Conference, with the aid of numerous lawyers and academics, frequently considers whether Rule 23 is in need of revision and, if so, what shape any changes should take. As you progress through this Chapter, put yourself in the role of a member of the Committee and ask what amendments, if any, you would make.

———

Read Federal Rule of Civil Procedure 23 in the Supplement.

———

SECTION A. OVERVIEW AND THEMES

Class action practice developed to address situations in which it is not feasible for a plaintiff to sue individually or for all of those relevant to a dispute to be joined in a single action. The procedure allows a single plaintiff to represent similarly situated persons and to advance their claims. By its very structure, the class action device presents concerns about the due process rights of absent class members and the proper application of the rules of finality. See generally Issacharoff, *Governance and Legitimacy in the Law of Class Actions*, 1999 Sup. Ct. Rev. 337 (1999). Each decision about whether to proceed on a class basis obliges a judge to balance the advantages of a single adjudication with notions of fairness to absent people whose claims may be extinguished by the action.

The class action device can be viewed simply as another joinder device, or it can be viewed as something different—a representational device that empowers the named class representative to act on behalf of others similarly situated whether they could have sued independently, or even wanted to do so. See Hutchinson, *Class Actions: Joinder or Representational Device?*, 1984 Sup. Ct. Rev. 459. Although the 1966 amendments to Rule 23 moved in the direction of the representational model, courts (including the Supreme Court) have vacillated between these two views of the procedure. Is the class action only a procedural convenience that goes slightly beyond Rule 20, or is the device completely different from other approaches to aggregate litigation? For discussions of this issue, see Silver, *Comparing Class Actions and Consolidations*, 10 Rev. Litig. 495 (1991); Cabraser, *The Class Action Counterreformation*, 57 Stan. L. Rev. 1475 (2005).

One other general issue should engage your attention. The rules governing class actions depart from the traditional adversarial notion that individuals can be bound by a court judgment only when they themselves have had a day in court. See Bone, *Rethinking the "Day in Court" Ideal and Nonparty Preclusion*, 67 N.Y.U. L. Rev. 193 (1992). What justifies this departure? What is there about the procedures that have been developed around the class action device that makes it possible and fair to bind a party who has not made an appearance in court?

SECTION B. A SHORT HISTORY OF THE CLASS ACTION

The class action procedure traces back to the seventeenth-century "bill of peace," a procedural device utilized in England by the Courts of Chancery. The "bill" allowed an action to be brought by or against representative parties when (1) the number of persons involved was too large to permit joinder, (2) all the members of the group possessed a joint interest in the question being adjudicated, and (3) the named parties adequately represented the interests of those who were not present. If these three conditions were met, the judgment that ultimately was entered was binding on all the members of the represented group. An excellent summary of the history of class actions can be found in Yeazell, *From Medieval Group Litigation to the Modern Class Action* (1987).

Since then, the class action procedure has undergone substantial development. The evolution of the rules governing class actions in part parallels an evolution in society and in society's understanding of the role of courts and of individual rights. As two early commentators on the Federal Rules put it:

> Modern society seems increasingly to expose men to * * * group injuries for which individually they are in a poor position to seek legal redress, either because they do not know enough or because such redress is disproportionately expensive. If each is left to assert his rights alone if and when he can, there will at best be a random and fragmentary enforcement, if there is any at all. This result is not only unfortunate in the particular case, but it will operate seriously to impair the deterrent effect of the sanctions which underlie much contemporary law. The problem of fashioning an effective and inclusive group remedy is thus a major one.

Kalven & Rosenfield, *The Contemporary Function of a Class Suit,* 8 U. Chi. L. Rev. 684, 686 (1941).

Provisions for class actions based upon the English procedure existed in various state codes and the Federal Equity Rules. Federal Rule 23, as originally adopted in 1938, marked "a bold * * * attempt to encourage more frequent use of class actions," making the device available in both legal and equitable actions in the federal courts. 7A Wright, Miller & Kane, Federal Practice and Procedure: Civil 3d § 1752. The original rule, however, proved very confusing to apply, and in 1966 the Advisory Committee rewrote Rule 23 to provide a functional test for class certification and to provide some procedural guidance for the courts with regard to handling class actions. The amendments also made clear that a judgment in a class action is binding on all class members, except in those cases in which the right to opt-out applies and has been exercised.

———

Class action practice greatly expanded after the 1966 amendments to Federal Rule 23. However, at the time of their adoption, the mass tort phenomenon—"in those days often called 'mass accidents' "—had not yet developed. Resnik, *Aggregation, Settlement, and Dismay*, 80 Cornell L. Rev. 918, 922 (1995). Indeed, the Advisory Committee that drafted the 1966 amendments sounded a note of caution that one accident would affect different parties in different ways raising different factual and legal issues—a feature it saw as incompatible with unitary adjudication. Since then, attitudes have changed, and in recent years mass tort class actions have become relatively common, although fraught with controversy. Some commentators view mass tort class actions as efficient vehicles for resolving disputes by multiple litigants who have similar claims against the same defendant, particularly when practical considerations make individual lawsuits unlikely or impossible. However, as will be seen below, the use of class actions in this context has posed numerous and complex procedural questions. Some commentators have criticized these suits for generating unwarranted legal fees, for causing inflated product prices, for contributing to corporate bankruptcies, and for raising due process concerns because of the lack of plaintiff autonomy. On the other hand, commentators have emphasized that mass tort class actions are critical for securing judicial access, for promoting efficiency, and for creating incentives that deter institutional wrongdoing. See generally Coffee, Jr., *Class Wars: The Dilemma of the Mass Tort Class Action*, 95 Colum. L. Rev. 1343 (1995).

The 1966 amendments also expanded the use of class actions in public law cases involving civil rights and such issues as desegregation, affirmative action, and voter registration. Some commentators regard class actions as an essential form of First Amendment expression that provides a critical bulwark against executive and legislative abuse. However, questions also have been raised whether it is appropriate to use class action litigation to overturn legislative decisions that have been reached by democratic majorities. See Redish, *Class Actions and the Democratic Difficulty: Rethinking the Intersection of Private Litigation and Public Goals*, 2003 U. Chi. Legal F. 71 (2003).

———

MILLER, OF FRANKENSTEIN MONSTERS AND SHINING KNIGHTS: MYTH, REALITY, AND THE "CLASS ACTION PROBLEM," 92 Harv. L. Rev. 664, 665–66 (1979):

* * * Opinions regarding the effect of the [1966] revision [to Federal Rule 23] range over an amazing gamut. Class action adherents would have us believe it is a panacea for a myriad of social ills, which deters unlawful conduct and compensates those injured by it. Catch phrases such as "therapeutic" or "prophylactic" and "[taking] care of the smaller guy" are frequently trumpeted. Its opponents have rallied around characterizations of the procedure as a form of "legalized blackmail" or a "Frankenstein Monster." They also have charged widespread abuse of the rule by lawyers and litigants on both sides of the "v.," including unprofessional practices relating to attorneys' fees, "sweetheart" settlement deals, dilatory motion practice, harassing discovery, and misrepresentations to judges. Finally, some have questioned the wisdom of imposing the burdens of class actions on an already overtaxed federal judiciary. They assert that many Rule 23 cases are unmanageable and inordinately protracted by opposing counsel, creating a certain millstone or dinosaur character that diverts federal judges from matters more worthy of their energies.

* * *

———

Eight years after Professor Miller wrote his *Harvard Law Review* article, he served as the Reporter for a study of complex litigation for the American Law Institute. In it, he wrote:

Class actions have proven to be the most effective legal technique for avoiding piecemeal litigation and preserving legal resources. Nevertheless, the class action suit continues to be eyed with suspicion by many courts. In complex cases, the goals of the class action device have been frustrated by strict adherence to the requirements of Rule 23. Often, complex multiparty, multiforum cases are denied class action treatment. Certification of large scale tort action classes is rare. Courts deny certification based on decisions that the commonality of interest requirement is not satisfied and based on fear that the size of the class would make the litigation unwieldy and inefficient.

Generally, present treatment of class action suits begins with an initial skepticism towards the class. Cases that involve incidents of personal injury occurring in a series of related events that may be separated by time or geography are usually denied certification. In the case of property damage, the class may receive certification but courts are wary that the litigation may degenerate into individual suits over specific pieces of property. Courts are split as to whether mass tort cases should be certified as * * * cases [in which litigants are not permitted to opt-out of the class]. Proponents argue that certification is more beneficial when total damages requested exceeds defendant's net worth. Detractors are concerned that such certification is merely a shortcut around notice and opt-out requirements. * * *

The usefulness of the class action device for future complex litigation raises two issues concerning the suitability of class actions to modern litigation needs. The first issue is whether the scope of the class action should be broadened to include more types of litigation. The second is whether courts should increase the frequency with which they certify mandatory classes. Presently, class actions are used relatively infrequently in many multiparty, multiforum litigation contexts. With some adjustments the class action device could be made a valuable litigation tool.

American Law Institute, Preliminary Study of Complex Litigation, Report, 61–70 (1987). The Preliminary Study was followed by a comprehensive exploration of the subject, which led to the American Law Institute's formal approval of Complex Litigation: Statutory Recommendations and Analysis (1994). In 2003, the American Law Institute began a major reexamination of the class action in the context of an assessment of aggregate litigation. See American Law Institute, Principles of the Law of Aggregate Litigation, Council Draft No. 2, Nov. 18, 2008. (Prelim. Draft No. 5, Sept. 12, 2008).

———

Questions about the use and abuse of class action procedure have generated a great deal of discussion and research. In 1996, the Research Division of the Federal Judicial Center conducted an empirical study of the use of Rule 23 in four federal districts. Willging, Hooper & Niemic, *An*

Empirical Analysis of Rule 23 to Address the Rulemaking Challenges, 71 N.Y.U. L. Rev. 74 (1996). It was a surprise to some that the study found that not all applications of Rule 23 are difficult; indeed, there are significant numbers of "routine" class actions, particularly in the securities and civil rights contexts. The study also seemed to demonstrate that attorney's fees were not disproportionate to class recoveries. As with most civil litigation, class actions follow the general pattern of settlement in lieu of trial. Although anecdotes abound that the mere instigation of a class action suit or at least its certification coerces settlements even in frivolous cases, the study seemed to belie that notion because the certified cases that settled had survived motions to dismiss or motions for summary judgment. See also Silver, *"We're Scared to Death": Class Certification and Blackmail*, 78 N.Y.U. L. Rev. 1357 (2003).

Although Rule 23 retains "the basic architecture" of the 1966 version, it also has undergone some important changes. See Bronsteen & Fiss, *The Class Action Rule*, 78 Notre Dame L. Rev. 1419, 1420 (2003). First, amendments to Rule 23 have brought more demanding requirements for notice, the availability of interlocutory appeals, and opportunities for greater judicial supervision of class counsel and their fees in an effort to afford better protection to absent class members. Second, Congress has made a federal forum available for most large stakes, interstate, state-law class actions on the basis of minimal diversity jurisdiction. See Class Action Fairness Act of 2005, amending 28 U.S.C. §§ 1332, 1453. Finally, Congress has changed the rules of class action practice for particular areas of law.

Securities Fraud: Congress has enacted specific additional requirements for securities fraud class actions filed under federal law. See The Private Securities Litigation Reform Act of 1995 (PSLRA), codified in scattered sections of 15 U.S.C. In 1998, Congress passed the Securities Litigation Uniform Standards Act of 1998 which preempts certain state law securities class action claims. See 15 U.S.C. § 78bb(f)(1).

Immigration: Congress has restricted classwide relief in certain immigration cases. See The Omnibus Consolidated Appropriations Act of 1997, Pub. L. No. 104–208 § 306(a)(2), 110 Stat. 3009–610 (1996).

Legal Services: Congress has barred indigent litigants, represented by lawyers in organizations that receive any money from the federally funded Legal Services Corporation, from participating in class action lawsuits, unless the organizations establish privately financed physically and legally separate affiliate organizations through which to do this work. See The Legal Services Corporation Act, 88 Stat. 378, 42 U.S.C. § 2996e(d)(5); Omnibus Consolidated Rescissions and Appropriations Act of 1996, Pub. L. No. 104–134, § 504(a)(7), 110 Stat. 1321–53.

As you read the materials that follow, consider the different goals that class actions are expected to serve and how effective the practice has been in different legal contexts.

NOTE ON CLASS ACTIONS FROM AN INTERNATIONAL PERSPECTIVE

Commentators frequently point to the class action as "a uniquely American procedural device." Sherman, *Group Litigation Under Foreign Legal Systems: Variations and Alternatives to American Class Actions*, 52 DePaul L. Rev. 401, 401 (2002). English group litigation orders are far more limited than representative actions in the United States, and it has long been assumed that civil law systems are resistant to the class action. See Andrews, *Multi-Party Proceedings in England: Representative and Group Actions*, 11 Duke J. Comp. & Int'l L. 249 (2001); Rowe, *Debates over Group Litigation in Comparative Perspective: What Can We Learn from Each Other?*, 11 Duke J. Comp. & Int'l L. 157, 158 (2001). However, international interest in the class action, or at least in aggregative mechanisms that allow for group or representative litigation, seems to be on the upsurge. Professor Gidi writes: "Despite initial skepticism and strong academic opposition, good sense has suggested and experience proven, that class actions are compatible with civil law systems." Gidi, *Class Actions in Brazil—A Model for Civil Law Countries*, 51 Am. J. Comp. L. 311, 313 (2003). Professor Nagareda likewise has pointed to "greater receptiveness" among foreign countries toward aggregate litigation, although he emphasizes that these trends so far have stopped short of adopting American-style class actions. See Nagareda, *Aggregate Litigation Across the Atlantic and the Future of American Exceptionalism*, 62 Vand. L. Rev. 1 (2009). For an overview of current developments, see Chase, Hershkoff, Silberman, Taniguchi, Varano & Zuckerman, Civil Litigation in Comparative Context 390–423 (Chase & Hershkoff eds., 2007).

SECTION C. OPERATION OF THE CLASS ACTION DEVICE

Federal Rule 23, which has had a significant impact on state class action procedures, provides a paradigm that can be used to study the operation of class action provisions generally. Although there are defendant class actions, the plaintiff class action (which is far more common) will be the model used in this discussion.

1. INITIATION OF CLASS ACTIONS

Class action lawsuits are commenced in the same way as other lawsuits, namely by the filing of a complaint and the service of a summons. The difference, however, is that a class action lawsuit is filed in a representative capacity on behalf of persons who are similarly situated to the named plaintiff. These represented parties are said to be "absent" and probably do not even know that a lawsuit is being filed. See Fiss, *The Political Theory of the Class Action*, 53 Wash. & Lee L. Rev. 21, 25 (1996). The complaint caption will specify the name of the representative plaintiff and also will indicate that the lawsuit is being filed in a representative capacity. The class action complaint typically will allege the claims of the named plaintiff and also sets forth classwide allegations of the unnamed putative class members.

In practice, attorneys often play a critical role in causing class suits to be brought. Sometimes, attorneys simply persuade individuals who have a legal problem that the best way to obtain a remedy is by filing a class action embracing the claims of others who are similarly situated. Other times, attorneys actually solicit clients for class suits. In what some think is a modern version of ambulance chasing, a lawyer, upon hearing of a disaster, may contact one of the victims and offer to serve as counsel in a class action. The Supreme Court has held that this form of solicitation—for the lawyer's personal gain—is prohibited by legal ethics rules. See Ohralik v. Ohio State Bar Ass'n, 436 U.S. 447, 98 S.Ct. 1912, 56 L.Ed.2d 444 (1978). But there are other examples in which the solicitation of clients for class suits is permissible and indeed an important part of democratic life. For instance, during the 1960's and 1970's NAACP lawyers went to the South to inform minorities of their legal rights and to offer themselves as counsel to those who decided to bring suit. The Supreme Court has held that offers of legal services in this context are a form of political expression, and that prohibitions against solicitation are invalid on First Amendment grounds. See In re Primus, 436 U.S. 412, 98 S.Ct. 1893, 56 L.Ed.2d 417 (1978).

2. CERTIFICATION

a. Federal Rule 23(a): "Prerequisites"

A plaintiff seeking to file a class action complaint in federal court does not need permission from the court. However, the court will not certify the lawsuit as a class action unless various prerequisites are satisfied. The plaintiff bringing the action has the burden to meet each of these requirements. Rule 23(c)(1)(A) obliges the court to "determine by order" whether to certify the class "[a]t an early practicable time."

1. *The Requirement of a Class.* Conceptually, the first requirement plaintiff must meet is that there be a class. This may sound self-evident, but the 1966 amendment to Rule 23 did not specify this requirement and the condition was only judicially-created. Rule 23 has been amended to require the court that issues the certification order "to define the class and the class claims, issues, or defenses." Federal Rule 23(c)(1)(B). Because a classwide judgment will have profound effects on unnamed class members, definition of the class is important in order to specify which individuals will be affected by the lawsuit and which will not.

Although there is no hard-and-fast rule governing definition of the class, courts generally require that a proposed class definition "be precise, objective, and presently ascertainable," and also that it "not depend on subjective criteria or the merits of the case or require extensive factual inquiry to determine who is a class member." In re Copper Antitrust Litigation, 196 F.R.D. 348 (W.D. Wis. 2000) (citations omitted); see generally 7A Wright, Miller & Kane, Federal Practice and Procedure: Civil 3d § 1760. Class definitions may fail if they are too broad (e.g., "all learning disabled children in the state of Texas"); too specific (e.g., "all people with Spanish surnames having Spanish, Mexican, or Indian ancestry who spoke Spanish as a primary or secondary language"); too vague (e.g., "all users of drug X who suffered medical problems"); or too amorphous (e.g., "all recipients of unsolicited SPAM messages"). In Rink v. Cheminova, Inc., 203 F.R.D. 648 (M.D. Fla. 2001), the court rejected, as lacking "sufficient precision or specificity," a proposed subclass consisting of all persons living or employed in certain Florida counties from June 1997 through October 1998 and who were exposed to malathion-based insecticide during the class period. What was the problem with this class definition?

2. *The Class Representative Must Be a Member of the Class.* The second requirement is that the class representative must be a member of the class. This requirement, grounded in the language of Rule 23(a) that "[o]ne or more members of a class may sue or be sued as representative parties," is sometimes analogized to that of a standing requirement. See Lee v. Washington, 390 U.S. 333, 88 S.Ct. 994, 19 L.Ed.2d 1212 (1968). Gratz v. Bollinger, 539 U.S. 244, 123 S.Ct. 2411, 156 L.Ed.2d 257 (2003), involved a challenge to a public university's use of racial criteria in the selection of its students for admission. The Supreme Court held that plaintiff, a transfer student, had standing to represent absent class members challenging the university's freshman admission policy because the university used the same criteria in selecting freshmen and transfer students.

A problem may arise if a named plaintiff's claim is resolved before the class is certified. In that event, the action may be dismissed as moot even though a live controversy remains as to other class members. However, if the matter at issue is such that the class representative's individual interest, in the normal course of events, will expire before a ruling can be made on class certification (such as pretrial detention without a probable cause hearing), the class may be certified despite the mootness of the named plaintiff's claim. See Gerstein v. Pugh, 420 U.S. 103, 110–11 n.11, 95 S.Ct. 854, 861 n.11, 43 L.Ed.2d 54, 63 n.11 (1975). Moreover, a class action generally is not rendered moot if the named plaintiff's claim becomes moot after class certification. See Sosna v. Iowa, 419 U.S. 393, 95 S.Ct. 553, 42 L.Ed.2d 532 (1975).

3. *Joinder of All Members Is "Impracticable":* Rule 23(a)(1) requires that the class be so numerous that joinder of all members is "impracticable." In most instances this requirement is mechanical. In Dukes v. Wal–Mart Stores, Inc., 222 F.R.D. 137 (N.D. Cal. 2004), affirmed 474 F.3d 1214 (9th Cir. 2007), opinion withdrawn and superseded on denial of rehearing, 509 F.3d 1168 (9th Cir. 2007), and rehearing en banc granted, 556 F.3d

919 (9th Cir. 2009), an employment-discrimination case under Title VII of the Civil Rights Act of 1964, the court found it "beyond dispute that joinder would be impracticable" when the class was alleged to include "at least 1.5 million women who have been employed over the past five years at roughly 3,400 stores." However, classes with far fewer members satisfy the Rule 23(a)(1) prerequisite. If a class has more than forty members, numerosity usually is met; if the class numbers less than twenty-five, numerosity usually is lacking. When the class is between twenty-five and forty members, variables such as the geographic dispersion of class members and the size of their individual claims become important. Why might joinder be considered impracticable if the monetary value of the individual claims is small?

4. *"Questions of Law or Fact Common to the Class"*: Rule 23(a)(2), the "commonality" requirement, mandates that the action raise questions of law or fact common to the class. Courts tend to give this requirement a "permissive application so that common questions have been found to exist in a wide range of contexts" and even a single but significant common question is sometimes sufficient. 7A Wright, Miller & Kane, Federal Practice and Procedure: Civil 3d § 1763. The critical question is whether "differences in the factual background of each claim will affect the outcome of the legal issue." Califano v. Yamasaki, 442 U.S. 682, 99 S.Ct. 2545, 61 L.Ed.2d 176 (1979). In some cases the existence of discrete, individualized injuries has been held to defeat a finding of commonality. In Donaldson v. Microsoft Corp., 205 F.R.D. 558, 565 (W.D. Wash. 2001), an employment discrimination case, plaintiff alleged "individualized discrimination on the basis of race, coupled with proof that other people of color work in the same environment." The court declined to find commonality. How would you amend the complaint to satisfy the commonality requirement? Is the defect a matter of law or of fact? Would it be sufficient to allege discrimination on the basis of a "system-wide practice or policy that affects all of the putative class members"? Armstrong v. Davis, 275 F.3d 849 (9th Cir. 2001).

5. *The Representative Claims or Defenses "Are Typical" of the Class*: Rule 23(a)(3), the "typicality" prerequisite, requires that the claims or defenses of the representative party be typical of those of the class. Some commentators question whether this requirement serves any independent purpose since any objective it might serve already will be achieved by the commonality requirement of Rule 23(a)(2) and the adequacy requirement of Rule 23(a)(4). Typicality usually is found "when each class member's claim arises from the same course of events, and each class member makes similar legal arguments to provide the defendant's liability." Marisol v. Giuliani, 126 F.3d 372, 376 (2d Cir. 1997). The goal is to ensure that "the named plaintiff's claim and the class claims are so interrelated that the interests of the class members will be fairly and adequately protected in their absence." Id.

6. *"Fairly and Adequately Protect the Interests of the Class"*: Rule 23(a)(4), that the representative party "will fairly and adequately protect

the interests of the class," derives its importance from two factors. First, Rule 23(a)(4) reflects the due process concern that a class action judgment ought not to bind parties who have not *literally* had their "day in court" unless, as members of a defined group with similar claims and proper representation, they have had a *figurative* day in court. Rule 23(a)(4) ensures the quality of the representation that due process requires. In AMCHEM PRODUCTS, INC. v. WINDSOR, 521 U.S. 591, 626, 117 S.Ct. 2231, 2251, 138 L.Ed.2d 689, 714 (1997), a settlement class involving current and future asbestos-related claims, the Supreme Court explained the purpose of the adequacy requirement as serving "to uncover conflicts of interest between named parties and the class they seek to represent."

Second, a defect in the adequacy of representation in an action might leave the judgment vulnerable to collateral attack. See Stephenson v. Dow Chemical Co., 273 F.3d 249 (2d Cir. 2001), affirmed in part by an equally divided court and vacated in part 539 U.S. 111, 123 S.Ct. 2161, 156 L.Ed.2d 106 (2003). It would be an extremely wasteful expenditure of time and effort to go through the certification process, complete extensive discovery, negotiate and approve a settlement or actually adjudicate the merits of the case, and draft and enter a judgment, only to have every-thing unraveled years later by someone who does not want to be bound by the result and claims that the adequacy requirement was not met.

Rule 23(a)(4) focuses on the adequacy of the representative plaintiff; an amendment to Rule 23 adopted in 2003 establishes a separate inquiry into the adequacy of class counsel. See Federal Rule 23(g). Some commen-tators have questioned the significance of having an adequate representa-tive plaintiff, arguing that class counsel in reality takes the laboring oar to represent the interests of the class. See Burns, *Decorative Figureheads: Eliminating Class Representatives in Class Actions*, 42 Hastings L.J. 165 (1990). Concerns also have been raised that courts are not sufficiently vigorous in their assessing of adequacy. One empirical study concluded that the courts under review failed to consider "legitimate grounds for attacking unqualified representatives" and that they ignored basic factors such as honesty and knowledge about the case. See Klonoff, *The Judicia-ry's Flawed Application of Rule 23's "Adequacy of Representation" Re-quirement*, 2004 Mich. St. L. Rev. 671, 673 (2004). What factors should a court consider in assessing adequacy of representation? For different perspectives on this question, see Woolley, *The Availability of Collateral Attack for Inadequate Representation in Class Suits*, 79 Texas L. Rev. 383, 387 (2000); Bassett, *When Reform Is Not Enough: Assuring More than Merely "Adequate" Representation in Class Actions*, 38 Ga. L. Rev. 927 (2004); Dana, *Adequacy of Representation After* Stephenson*: A Rawl-sian/Behavioral Economics Approach to Class Action Settlements*, 55 Emo-ry L.J. 279 (2006).

NOTE ON THE "LEAD PLAINTIFF" IN SECURITIES CLASS ACTIONS

In 1995, Congress passed the Private Securities Litigation Reform Act (PSLRA) which, among other things, requires the court to appoint a "lead plaintiff" in securities class actions. The PSLRA establishes "a presumption that the individual so selected should be the one with the largest financial interest in the relief sought by the class." 7A Wright, Miller & Kane, Federal Practice and Procedure: Civil 3d § 1767. The requirement responds to concerns that class actions are "lawyer driven" and subject to collusion and unfairness. By creating incentives for shareholders with large financial stakes to assume a leadership position in the litigation, the PSLRA strives to create incentives for monitoring attorney performance. See Seligman, *Rethinking Private Securities Litigation*, 73 U. Cin. L. Rev. 95, 105 (2004); Fisch, *Class Action Reform: Lessons from Securities Litigation*, 39 Ariz. L. Rev. 533 (1997).

b.   Federal Rule 23(b): The Types of Class Actions

After the district judge has determined that the suit satisfies the six prerequisites already discussed, she must decide into which of the three categories of class actions enumerated in Rule 23(b) it falls.

1.   *"Prejudice Class Actions" Under Rule 23(b)(1)*: Both clauses of this provision ask whether individual actions might cause prejudice that can be avoided by using the class action device. Certification under this provision is said to create a "mandatory" class action: the absent class member cannot opt out of the class.

Subdivision (A) looks for prejudice to the nonclass party; subdivision (B) inquires into prejudice to members of the class. Subdivision (A) deals with the risk that individual actions would create "incompatible standards of conduct" for the party opposing the class. It is important to note that the Rule does *not* refer to the situation in which the defendant in a series of actions would have to pay damages to some claimants but not to others. Rather, the Rule applies when different results in individual actions would place the opposing party (usually the defendant) in a position of total uncertainty, not knowing how to treat the class as a whole. For example, consider a voting rights dispute involving a question of eligibility for registration. If applicants sue individually, some may win and others may lose. The election board then would be in the position of not knowing whether to register all the individuals similarly situated who have not brought suit. If a class action is brought, the judgment will bind all of the class members, and the board can take appropriate action. A similar logic applies in cases involving rate-making proceedings or riparian rights.

Subdivision (B) of Rule (23)(b)(1) contemplates that individual actions "would be dispositive of the interests" or "substantially impair or impede" the ability of nonparties to protect their interests. The classic example is a case in which there are multiple claimants to a limited fund, such as the proceeds of an insurance policy. If litigants are allowed to proceed individually, there is a risk that those who sue first will deplete the fund and leave nothing for the latecomers; thus, the latter group would "as a practical matter" be prejudiced by individual actions. See generally 7AA Wright, Miller & Kane, Federal Practice and Procedure: Civil 3d § 1772.

2. *Injunctive and Declaratory Relief Under Rule 23(b)(2)*: More class action cases have been brought under this provision than under Rules 23(b)(1) and 23(b)(3). Its primary application is in injunction suits such as civil rights, employment discrimination, consumer, or environmental cases in which the goal is to change defendant's behavior or policy prospectively and not to provide individual compensation to class members for injuries they suffered in the past. On the theory that an injunctive class is cohesive, notice is not deemed essential in such cases. See Wetzel v. Liberty Mutual Ins. Co., 508 F.2d 239, certiorari denied 421 U.S. 1011, 95 S.Ct. 2415, 44 L.Ed.2d 679 (1975). Note that for an action to fall within Rule 23(b)(2), the defendant's conduct need only be "generally applicable" to the class; there is no requirement that the conduct be damaging or offensive to every class member. Thus, a suit to enjoin the enforcement of a school dress code can be instituted under Rule 23(b)(2) even though a majority of the students are not offended by the code and are willing to comply with it, since the school, by trying to enforce the code, acts in a manner generally applicable to the entire student body.

3. *Damage Class Actions Under Rule 23(b)(3)*: This provision, the category most often used in adjudicating a wide range of damage actions, including mass torts, allows the certification of a class when the tie among the members is that they claim to have been injured in the same way by defendant. Two special prerequisites govern the application of this provision. First, questions of law or fact common to the class members must "predominate" over any questions affecting only individual class members. Second, the court must find that a "class action is superior to other available methods for fairly and efficiently adjudicating the controversy." These special requirements are designed to ensure that the efficiency and economy objectives of Rule 23(b)(3) are met. Given the non-natural character of the group that comprises a class under subdivision (b)(3), Rule 23 requires additional procedural protections for the absent class members in the form of mandatory notice and the right to opt-out of the class. See Eisenberg & Miller, *The Role of Opt-Outs and Objectors in Class Action Litigation: Theoretical and Empirical Issues*, 57 Vand. L. Rev. 1529 (2004).

Rule 23(b)(3) outlines four factors that the court should consider in deciding the superiority and predominance questions. The fourth one mentioned, difficulties likely to be encountered in the management of a class action, generally is viewed as key. Matters such as the size or contentiousness of the class, the number of class members who seek to intervene and participate in the action, and the onerousness of the Rule 23(c)(2) notice requirement are to be considered when deciding if the class action is manageable. Although it is easy to state the Rule 23(b)(3) tests, the district courts have not applied them with a great deal of uniformity.

Questions of predominance and superiority have become highly individualistic and fact dependent. In determining "predominance," it remains unclear whether the district judge is to count the issues and see whether a majority are common, or to evaluate the issues and see if the most important are common. Furthermore, in some cases common and individual issues seem to be in equilibrium no matter which method of determining predominance is followed. The key to resolving this difficulty lies in ascertaining whether the efficiency and economy of common adjudication outweigh the interest each class member may have in an individual adjudication. The "superiority" prerequisite thus obliges the court to compare the class action with other adjudicative possibilities. The most obvious include leaving the disputants to individual actions, administrative proceedings, or an agreement to be bound by the result in a single "test" case. Another option is the availability for consolidation of multidistrict cases under 28 U.S.C. § 1407. Consider the questions associated with the "superiority" prerequisite as you read the following case.

CASTANO v. AMERICAN TOBACCO CO.

United States Court of Appeals, Fifth Circuit, 1996.
84 F.3d 734.

SMITH, CIRCUIT JUDGE.

In what may be the largest class action ever attempted in federal court, the district court in this case embarked "on a road certainly less traveled, if ever taken at all," * * * and entered a class certification order. The court defined the class as:

(a) All nicotine-dependent persons in the United States ... who have purchased and smoked cigarettes manufactured by the defendants;

(b) the estates, representatives, and administrators of these nicotine-dependent cigarette smokers; and

(c) the spouses, children, relatives and "significant others" of these nicotine-dependent cigarette smokers as their heirs or survivors.

Concluding that the district court abused its discretion in certifying the class, we reverse.

I.

A. The Class Complaint

The plaintiffs filed this class complaint against the defendant tobacco companies and the Tobacco Institute, Inc., seeking compensation solely for the injury of nicotine addiction. The gravamen of their complaint is the novel and wholly untested theory that the defendants fraudulently failed to inform consumers that nicotine is addictive and manipulated the level of nicotine in cigarettes to sustain their addictive nature. * * *

* * *

B. The Class Certification Order

* * * [T]he district court granted, in part, plaintiffs' motion for class certification, concluding that the prerequisites of FED. R. CIV. P. 23(a) had been met. * * *

The court * * * grant[ed] the plaintiffs' motion to certify the class under FED. R. CIV. P. 23(b)(3), organizing the class action issues into four categories: (1) core liability; (2) injury-in-fact, proximate cause, reliance and affirmative defenses; (3) compensatory damages; and (4) punitive damages. * * * It then analyzed each category to determine whether it met the predominance and superiority requirements of rule 23(b)(3). Using its power to sever issues for certification under FED. R. CIV. P. 23(c)(4), the court certified the class on core liability and punitive damages, and certified the class conditionally pursuant to FED. R. CIV. P. 23(c)(1).

* * *

The district court erred in its analysis in two distinct ways. First, it failed to consider how variations in state law affect predominance and superiority. Second, its predominance inquiry did not include consideration of how a trial on the merits would be conducted.

Each of these defects mandates reversal. Moreover, at this time, while the tort is immature, the class complaint must be dismissed as class certification cannot be found to be a superior method of adjudication.

A. Variations in State Law

* * *

A district court's duty to determine whether the plaintiff has borne its burden on class certification requires that a court consider variations in state law when a class action involves multiple jurisdictions. * * *

* * *

A thorough review of the record demonstrates that, in this case, the district court did not properly consider how variations in state law affect predominance. * * *

The district court's review of state law variances can hardly be considered extensive; it conducted a cursory review of state law variations and gave short shrift to the defendants' arguments concerning variations. * * *

* * *

The court also failed to perform its duty to determine whether the class action would be manageable in light of state law variations. The court's only discussion of manageability is a citation and the claim that "[w]hile manageability of the liability issues in this case may well prove to be difficult, the Court finds that any such difficulties pale in comparison to the specter of thousands, if not millions, of similar trials of liability proceeding in thousands of courtrooms around the nation." * * *

* * *

* * * [W]hether the specter of millions of cases outweighs any manageability problems in this class is uncertain when the scope of any manageability problems is unknown. Absent considered judgment on the manageability of the class, a comparison to millions of individual trials is meaningless.

B. Predominance

The district court's second error was that it failed to consider how the plaintiffs' addiction claims would be tried, individually or on a class basis. * * * The district court * * * believed that it could not go past the pleadings for the certification decision. The result was an incomplete and inadequate predominance inquiry.

* * *

A district court certainly may look past the pleadings to determine whether the requirements of rule 23 have been met. Going beyond the pleadings is necessary, as a court must understand the claims, defenses, relevant facts, and applicable substantive law in order to make a meaningful determination of the certification issues. * * *

The district court * * * just assumed that because the common issues would play a part in every trial, they must be significant. The court's [approach] * * * would write the predominance requirement out of the rule, and any common issue would predominate if it were common to all the individual trials. * * *

The court's treatment of the fraud claim also demonstrates the error inherent in its approach. * * * [A] fraud class action cannot be certified when individual reliance will be an issue. * * *

The problem with the district court's approach is that after the class trial, it might have decided that reliance must be proven in individual trials. The court then would have been faced with the difficult choice of decertifying the class * * * and wasting judicial resources, or continuing with a class action that would have failed the predominance requirement of rule 23(b)(3). * * *

III.

In addition to the reasons given above, regarding the district court's procedural errors, this class must be decertified because it independently fails the superiority requirement of rule 23(b)(3). In the context of mass tort class actions, certification dramatically affects the stakes for defendants. Class certification magnifies and strengthens the number of unmeritorious claims. * * * Aggregation of claims also makes it more likely that a defendant will be found liable and results in significantly higher damage awards. * * *

In addition to skewing trial outcomes, class certification creates insurmountable pressure on defendants to settle, whereas individual trials would not. * * * The risk of facing an all-or-nothing verdict presents too high a risk, even when the probability of an adverse judgment is low. * * * These settlements have been referred to as judicial blackmail.

It is no surprise then, that historically, certification of mass tort litigation classes has been disfavored. The traditional concern over the rights of defendants in mass tort class actions is magnified in the instant case. Our specific concern is that a mass tort cannot be properly certified without a prior track record of trials from which the district court can draw the information necessary to make the predominance and superiority analysis required by rule 23. This is because certification of an immature tort results in a higher than normal risk that the class action may not be superior to individual adjudication.

* * * The court acknowledged the extensive manageability problems with this class. Such problems include difficult choice of law determinations, subclassing of eight claims with variations in state law, *Erie* guesses, notice to millions of class members, further subclassing to take account of transient plaintiffs, and the difficult procedure for determining who is nicotine-dependent. Cases with far fewer manageability problems have given courts pause. * * *

The district court's rationale for certification in spite of such problems—i.e., that a class trial would preserve judicial resources in the millions of inevitable individual trials—is based on pure speculation. * * *

What the district court failed to consider, and what no court can determine at this time, is the very real possibility that the judicial crisis may fail to materialize. The plaintiffs' claims are based on a new theory of liability and the existence of new evidence. Until plaintiffs decide to file individual claims, a court cannot, from the existence of injury, presume that all or even any plaintiffs will pursue legal remedies. * * *

As he stated in the record, plaintiffs' counsel in this case has promised to inundate the courts with individual claims if class certification is denied. Independently of the reliability of this self-serving promise, there is reason to believe that individual suits are feasible. First, individual damage claims are high, and punitive damages are available in most states. The expense of litigation does not necessarily turn this case into a negative value suit, in part because the prevailing party may recover attorneys' fees under many consumer protection statutes. * * *

* * *

The remaining rationale for superiority—judicial efficiency—is also lacking. In the context of an immature tort, any savings in judicial resources is speculative, and any imagined savings would be overwhelmed by the procedural problems that certification of a *sui generis* cause of action brings with it.

* * *

The district court's predominance inquiry, or lack of it, squarely presents the problems associated with certification of immature torts. Determining whether the common issues are a "significant" part of each individual case has an abstract quality to it when no court in this country has ever tried an injury-as-addiction claim. * * *

Yet, an accurate finding on predominance is necessary before the court can certify a class. * * * Premature certification deprives the defendant of the opportunity to present that argument to any court and risks decertification after considerable resources have been expended.

* * *

The plaintiffs' final retort is that individual trials are inadequate because time is running out for many of the plaintiffs. They point out that prior litigation against the tobacco companies has taken up to ten years to wind through the legal system. * * *

* * * [T]he plaintiffs' claim that time is running out ignores the reality of the class action device. In a complicated case involving multiple jurisdictions, the conflict of law question itself could take decades to work its way through the courts. Once that issue has been resolved, discovery, subclassing, and ultimately the class trial would take place. Next would come the appellate process. After the class trial, the individual trials and appeals on comparative negligence and damages would have to take place. The net result could be that the class action device would lengthen, not shorten, the time it takes for the plaintiffs to reach final judgment.

* * *

* * * For the forgoing reasons, we REVERSE and REMAND with instructions that the district court dismiss the class complaint.

NOTES AND QUESTIONS

1. The Fifth Circuit decertified a class that was estimated to include fifty million nicotine-dependent tobacco users. 84 F.3d at 737; see Castano v. American Tobacco Co., 160 F.R.D. 544, at 548–50 (E.D. La. 1995). In reaching its decision, the court emphasized that the class action complaint alleged an "immature tort" in the sense that no tobacco suit ever had been filed based on the *Castano* plaintiff's theory. See 84 F.3d at 749. Plaintiffs claimed that defendants had failed to inform consumers of the addictive nature of nicotine and had manipulated cigarette nicotine levels to sustain smokers' addiction. The court asserted that these theories had not been litigated sufficiently in the context of individual tobacco cases to assess whether a class action would be a superior way to adjudicate such claims. Is the court's point valid? What is "immature" about a tort that alleges a company's failure to warn of a product's defects or of its injurious character, especially when defendant allegedly manufactured the product knowing it would have the injurious effect? Other courts of appeal also have looked to the maturity of the tort in determining whether class certification or other aggregative techniques are appropriate. See In re Chevron U.S.A., 109 F.3d 1016 (5th Cir. 1997); In re

Rhone–Poulenc, Inc., 51 F.3d 1293 (7th Cir. 1995). How long must the class action be held in abeyance before the plaintiff's theory is thought "mature" enough? See Walker v. Liggett Group, Inc., 175 F.R.D. 226 (S.D. W.Va. 1997) (not certifying class of tobacco smokers in lawsuit against Liggett Group, smallest of big five tobacco companies, following the *Castano* rationale).

2. After the *Castano* class failed and legislative reform of the tobacco industry proved unlikely, over forty states filed lawsuits against tobacco companies to recover expenditures made for tobacco-related illnesses. See Player, Note—*After the Fall: The Cigarette Papers, the Global Settlement, and the Future of Tobacco Litigation*, 49 S.C. L. Rev. 311 (1998). The companies negotiated a settlement with the Attorneys General of these states, and in November 1998, the settlement was accepted by forty-six states, the District of Columbia, and five territories. This settlement included payments to the states totaling $206 billion to be paid over the next twenty-five years. Additional settlement provisions included prohibiting tobacco companies from targeting minors in their advertising, using cartoon characters to sell cigarettes, and giving out free samples of tobacco products except in adult establishments. The tobacco companies also were directed to make available to the public all of their research on tobacco. See Dagan & White, *Governments, Citizens, and Injurious Industries*, 75 N.Y.U. L. Rev. 354 (2000).

Considering the terms of this settlement, do you agree that the state governments adequately represented the interests of individual smokers? In what ways might the government's collective interest have diverged from those of individual smokers? See Bianchini, *The Tobacco Agreement that Went Up in Smoke: Defining the Limits of Congressional Intervention into Ongoing Mass Tort Litigation*, 87 Cal. L. Rev. 703, 728–34 (1999). Is it significant that the state governments' settlement did not extinguish the claims of individual smokers against the tobacco companies? The failure of *Castano*, a federal court class action, led some plaintiffs to seek relief in state court, with mixed results. See Ieyoub & Eisenberg, *Class Actions in the Gulf South Symposium: State Attorney General Actions, the Tobacco Litigation, and the Doctrine of Parens Patriae*, 74 Tul. L. Rev. 1859 (2000).

In Florida, a jury verdict for $145 billion in punitive damages to the class was reversed on appeal to the District Court of Appeal with instructions to decertify the class. See Liggett Group Inc. v. Engle, 853 So.2d 434 (Fla. App. 2003). The Supreme Court of Florida approved in part, quashed in part, and remanded. See Engle v. Liggettt Group, Inc., 945 So.2d 1246 (Fla. 2006), certiorari denied R.J. Reynolds Tobacco Co. v. Engle, 552 U.S. 941, 128 S.Ct. 96, 169 L.Ed.2d 244, rehearing denied 552 U.S. 1056, 128 S.Ct. 694, 169 L.Ed.2d 541 (2007).

In Louisiana, a class action judgment held that defendants had concealed negative information about smoking from the public and also breached an assumed duty to disclose such information. The court ordered the establishment of a ten-year smoking cessation program funded by a $600 million jury award, and the judgment was affirmed in part on appeal. See Scott v. American Tobacco Co., Inc., 949 So.2d 1266 (La. App. 2007), certiorari denied Philip Morris USA Inc. v. Jackson, ___ U.S. ___, 128 S.Ct. 2908, 171 L.Ed.2d 842 (2008).

Smokers also filed individual state law actions. In Florida, a jury entered a verdict of more than $500,000, and the verdict was affirmed on a theory of strict liability design defect. See Liggett Group, Inc. v. Davis, 973 So.2d 467 (Fla. App. 2007). In Oregon, a jury entered a verdict of $821,485 in compensatory and $79.5 million in punitive damages for the smoking-related death of plaintiff's husband. See Williams v. Philip Morris Inc., 182 Ore.App. 44, 48 P.3d 824 (2002). The Supreme Court vacated and remanded, holding that a punitive damage award based in part on the jury's desire to punish the tobacco company for harm to nonparties violated the Due Process Clause. 549 U.S. 346, 127 S.Ct. 1057, 166 L.Ed.2d 940 (2007). On remand, the Oregon appeals court adhered to its prior decision, 344 Or. 45, 176 P.3d 1255, and the Supreme Court granted certiorari in part ___ U.S. ___, 128 S.Ct. 2904, 171 L.Ed.2d 840 (2008), and dismissed the writ as improvidently granted. 556 U.S. ___, 129 S.Ct. 1436, 173 L.Ed.2d 346 (2009). How do you think *Philip Morris* will affect future mass tort class actions? See Stier, *Now It's Personal: Punishment and Mass Tort Litigation after Philip Morris v. Williams*, 2 Charleston L. Rev. 433 (2008); Cabraser & Nelson, *Class Action Treatment of Punitive Damages Issues After* Philip Morris v. Williams: *We Can Get There From Here,* 2 Charleston L. Rev. 407 (2008).

NOTE ON "HYBRID" CLASS ACTIONS

How hermetic are the three categories of class actions created by Rule 23(b)? Is it appropriate to certify an action as a (b)(2) class if plaintiffs seek damages in addition to injunctive and declaratory relief? The Advisory Committee Note to Rule 23(b)(2) states that it "does not extend to cases in which the appropriate final relief relates exclusively or predominantly to money damages." In JOHNSON v. GENERAL MOTORS CORP., 598 F.2d 432 (5th Cir. 1979), plaintiffs alleged claims of racial discrimination. In an earlier racial discrimination class suit involving the same factory, plaintiffs had sought both injunctive and compensatory relief. The injunction was granted, and damages were awarded to the class representatives, but not to the absent class members. Plaintiff in the subsequent suit, Johnson, claimed that he had not received notice of the first suit, and attempted to prosecute his own suit for damages. The Fifth Circuit panel said:

> In light of these developments, we have previously suggested that when both monetary and injunctive relief are sought in an action certified under Rule 23(b)(2), notice may be mandatory if absent class members are to be bound. * * * [But w]hen only equitable relief is sought in an action involving a cohesive plaintiff group such as a class of black employees at an assembly plant, the due process interests of absent members will usually be safeguarded by adequate representation alone. As the Advisory Committee on Rule 23 stated, "[i]n the degree that there is cohesiveness or unity in the class and the representation is effective, the need for notice to the class will tend toward a minimum." * * * Where, however, individual monetary claims are at stake, the balance swings in favor of the provision of some form of notice. It will not always be necessary for the notice in such cases to be equivalent to that required

in (b)(3) actions. * * * In some cases it may be proper to delay notice until a more advanced stage of the litigation; for example, until after class-wide liability is proven. * * * Before an absent class member may be forever barred from pursuing an individual damage claim, however, due process requires that he receive some form of notice that the class action is pending and that his damage claims may be adjudicated as part of it.

Id. at 437–38. Do you agree with this reasoning?

The courts of appeal differ in their approach to hybrid cases. The Sixth Circuit has held that individual compensatory claims never can be brought in a class action certified under Rule 23(b)(2) because damage claims always predominate over injunctive or declaratory relief. See Coleman v. General Motors Acceptance Corp., 296 F.3d 443 (6th Cir. 2002). The Second Circuit will certify hybrid classes under Rule 23(b)(2), see Robinson v. Metro–North Commuter R.R. Co., 267 F.3d 147 (2d Cir. 2001), certiorari denied 535 U.S. 951, 122 S.Ct. 1349, 152 L.Ed.2d 251 (2002), but district courts have required notice and opt-out procedures as a condition of doing so. See Matyasovszky v. Housing Authority of the City of Bridgeport, 226 F.R.D. 35 (D. Conn. 2005). In Ticor Title Insurance Co. v. Brown, 511 U.S. 117, 114 S.Ct. 1359, 128 L.Ed.2d 33 (1994), the Supreme Court suggested that there is "at least a substantial possibility" that in actions seeking monetary damages, classes can be certified only under Rule 23(b)(3), which permits opt-out, and not under Rule 23(b)(1) and (b)(2), which do not. Id. at 121, 114 S.Ct. at 1361, 128 L.Ed.2d at 38.

c.   Rule 23(c) Certification Decisions

The district court must issue its certification order "[a]t an early practicable time" and retains authority to change the order any time "before final judgment." Rule 23(c)(1)(A), (C). The court's ongoing authority is regarded as "critical, because the scope and contour of a class may change radically as discovery progresses and more information is gathered about the nature of the putative class members' claims." Prado–Steiman v. Bush, 221 F.3d 1266, 1273 (11th Cir. 2000). See 7AA Wright, Miller & Kane, Federal Practice and Procedure: Civil 3d § 1785.4.

The Rule 23(c) certification order defines the substantive claims, issues, or defenses the suit will consider. See Fed. R. Civ. P. 23(c)(1)(B). For instance, a class suit might entertain a broad range of issues (such as allegations of company-wide gender discrimination in hiring, promotion, and pay, as well as allegations of sexual harassment by foremen in all of the company's factories), or it might take a more narrow approach (limiting the class issues to allegations of gender discrimination in a single plant's promotion decisions). A judge even may decide to certify a "partial class action"—that is, considering on a class basis only a limited number of factual issues relevant to a larger cause of action. For example, although controversial, a judge in a products liability suit could create a "partial class action" by certifying only the issue of whether a pharmaceutical manufacturer knew of a drug's potentially lethal side effects before introducing it on the market. In such a case, individual suits, litigated simultaneously or subsequently, would be pursued on the other issues. Finally, the certification process addresses the notice that is to be given to the absent class members and appoints class counsel under Rule 23(g). These requirements are discussed in the sections that follow.

3. RULE 23(c) AND THE REQUIREMENT OF NOTICE

a. The Court's Role

The question of notice to absent class members has tremendous theoretical and practical importance to class actions. Until this point in the action, the absent class members, whose rights stand to be adjudicated and precluded by the court, have not yet been formally told that a lawsuit is going forward on their behalf. As a matter of due process, a party must receive notice and be afforded an opportunity to be heard before rights are extinguished. Provision of adequate notice thus is an essential prerequisite to the binding effect of a class action judgment. Commentators see the notice requirement as serving two related purposes: "One is to check on the adequacy of representation being provided to the class, and the other is to render viable the right of unnamed class members to take certain protective measures, specifically to intervene or to opt out of the lawsuit." Bronsteen & Fiss, *The Class Action Rule*, 78 Notre Dame L. Rev. 1419, 1435 (2003).

Whether the court directs that notice be given to the absent class members depends on the kind of class action that has been certified. Notice to class members is not expressly required by the Rule in so-called mandatory class actions (those certified as a "prejudice" class under Rule 23(b)(1) or as an "injunctive" class under Rule 23(b)(2)). See Rule 23(c)(2)(A). Do you agree that a presumption of class coherence in these cases is sufficient to avoid the need for notice? See Rule 23 Advisory Committee Note to the 1963 Amendment. A leading commentary recommends that provision of some notice "probably is the best practice in most cases." 7B Wright, Miller & Kane, Federal Practice and Procedure: Civil 3d § 1793. Notice to class members expressly is required in a damages class action under subdivision (b)(3).

b. The Content of Notice and Who Should Receive Notice

The content of the notice provided likewise depends on the category of class that has been certified. Courts have tremendous discretion on this score in mandatory class actions. However, Rule 23(c)(2)(B) is prescriptive and requires provision of "the best notice that is practicable under the circumstances, including individual notice to all members who can be identified through reasonable effort." What is the reason for this approach? Under Rule 23(c)(2)(B), if the class member does nothing, he or she is automatically deemed a part of the lawsuit; any judgment that is entered will bar the absentee's future relitigation of claims. If the class member does not want to be a part of the class action, he or she can opt out and file an independent lawsuit. What information must the notice include? See Federal Rule 23(c)(2)(B)(i)–(vii).

If notice is to serve its function, it must be intelligible to the person who receives it. See Federal Rule 23(c)(2)(B) (requiring "plain easily understood language"). Only then can a potential class member make an informed decision about opting out of the class. Is it likely that non-lawyers will understand the notice they receive? Is the possibility that the notice will not be understood likely to be greatest in those cases in which class members are most in need of protection?

c. Costs

The Supreme Court has held that the costs of providing notice must be borne by the party seeking class treatment. See EISEN v. CARLISLE & JACQUELIN, 417 U.S. 156, 94 S.Ct. 2140, 40 L.Ed.2d 732 (1974). If the class suit is successful, the costs of sending notice may be subtracted from the class recovery, thus making each class member share the costs on a pro-rata basis. The costs of producing a mailing list often constitute a large part of the overall expense of providing notice. In some class actions, defendant's records will be the best, if not the only, source of information from which a list can be constructed. In the past, some litigants sought to use the discovery process to obtain a plaintiff-class mailing list. This shifted to defendant a major portion of the expenses of providing notice, because in federal discovery practice the party that must comply with a discovery request must bear the costs of production. The Supreme Court disapproved this practice in OPPENHEIMER FUND, INC. v. SANDERS, 437 U.S. 340, 98 S.Ct. 2380, 57 L.Ed.2d 253 (1978), but did not prohibit the representative from requesting certain business records of defendant that might aid in preparing the class mailing list. However, allocation of the costs of notice also is affected by the timing of its provision. If notice is provided after defendant's liability has been determined, which party ought to bear the cost of its provision? Compare Macarz v. Transworld Systems, Inc., 201 F.R.D. 54, 58 (D. Conn. 2001) and Hartman v. Wick, 678 F.Supp. 312, 328–29 (D.D.C. 1988), with Larsen v. JBC Legal Group, 235 F.R.D. 191 (E.D.N.Y. 2006).

4. RULE 23(g) ORDERS APPOINTING CLASS COUNSEL

The traditional conception of the attorney-client relation assumes that (1) the attorney gives advice to the client and the client makes final decisions about litigation strategy, and (2) the attorney acts with virtually unmitigated loyalty to the client's best interest. Class action litigation strains both of these notions. Class action attorneys exercise unusually significant control over decisions made on behalf of the class, but it is difficult to define "loyalty to the client" when it is not clear who the "client" is. Should the attorney give complete loyalty to the interests and wishes of the class representative? To those of each member of the class?

To the attorney's conception of the best interests of the class as a whole? See Shapiro, *Class Actions: The Class as Party and Client*, 73 Notre Dame L. Rev. 913 (1998). These questions are difficult ones, and current ethical rules offer attorneys little help in resolving them. Another complication is that class actions may involve a large number of independent lawyers or legal teams representing interests that might be in tension even if not in conflict. See Kane, *Of Carrots and Sticks: Evaluating the Role of the Class Action Lawyer,* 66 Texas L. Rev. 385, 390 (1987). Class members may not be in a strong position to monitor the performance of class counsel, even though the lawyers' interests are not inevitably aligned with those of the clients. Compare Coffee, Jr., *Class Action Accountability: Reconciling Exit, Voice, and Loyalty in Representative Litigation*, 100 Colum. L. Rev. 370 (2000), with Gilles & Friedman, *Exploding the Class Action Agency Costs Myth: The Social Utility of Entrepreneurial Lawyers*, 155 U. Pa. L. Rev. 103 (2006). Rule 23, which originally did not address questions about class counsel, was amended in 2003 to deal with these and other perceived problems. What requirements does Rule 23(g) impose on the district court as a condition of the certification order? Are these the only factors that you think relevant to a decision appointing class counsel? Why is it important for the court to have authority to appoint interim counsel before issuing its certification order? See 7B Wright, Miller & Kane, Federal Practice and Procedure: Civil 3d § 1802.3. What is the relationship between the court's determination of adequacy of representation under Rule 23(a)(4) and the duty to appoint class counsel under Rule 23(g)?

5. INTERLOCUTORY APPEALS FROM CERTIFICATION ORDERS

Certification is among the most critical stages in the life of a class action. The papers, hearings, and discovery that inevitably are generated force the court to analyze the nature of the parties and the issues involved in the case. The certification process is even more critical from the parties' point of view. Most importantly, the certification decision dictates the relative leverage that the parties can bring to settlement negotiations. The value of settlement leverage cannot be underestimated, because most class suits are settled before trial. Moreover, for the party opposing the class, a certification order means more than a loss of leverage; the threat that a class may be certified may be a danger in itself, because the certification of a class may create unfavorable publicity.

Given the tactical importance of the certification stage, Rule 23 was amended in 1998 to add a provision allowing interlocutory appeal from an order granting or denying class certification. The Advisory Committee Note accompanying Rule 23(f) explains:

> * * * [M]any suits with class action allegations present familiar and almost routine issues that are not more worthy of immediate appeal than many other interlocutory rulings. Yet several concerns justify

expansion of present opportunities to appeal. An order denying certification may confront the plaintiff with a situation in which the only sure path to appellate review is by proceeding to final judgment on the merits of an individual claim that, standing alone, is far smaller than the costs of litigation. An order granting certification, on the other hand, may force a defendant to settle rather than incur the costs of defending a class action and run the risk of potentially ruinous liability.

The circuit courts have taken different approaches to appeals under Rule 23(f). The First Circuit suggests:

> * * * First, an appeal ordinarily should be permitted when a denial of class status effectively ends the case (because, say, the named plaintiff's claim is not of a sufficient magnitude to warrant the costs of stand-alone litigation). Second, an appeal ordinarily should be permitted when the grant of class status raises the stakes of the litigation so substantially that the defendant likely will feel irresistible pressure to settle. Third, an appeal ordinarily should be permitted when it will lead to clarification of a fundamental issue of law.

Waste Management Holdings, Inc. v. Mowbray, 208 F.3d 288, 293 (1st Cir. 2000). However, the Eleventh Circuit has expressed "caution against routinely granting appellate review" under Rule 23(f), out of concern that the district court "may feel constrained from revisiting the issue and thereby potentially triggering a new round of appellate proceedings with the inevitable delay and effort of such proceedings." Prado–Steiman v. Bush, 221 F.3d 1266, 1272–73 (11th Cir. 2000).

6. RULE 23(d) ORDERS REGULATING THE CONDUCT OF PRETRIAL AND TRIAL PROCEEDINGS

Rule 23(d) authorizes the district court to issue other orders regulating the conduct of class action proceedings. For example, the court may create a timetable for discovery and for the presentation of issues at trial; set time limits on oral presentations made by counsel; establish a committee of counsel (consisting of the attorneys representing various members of the class) to make decisions about the prosecution of the class case; and, regulate the substantive aspects of discovery (for example, by determining the parties from whom discovery may be sought and the items which may be requested). Frequently, courts will issue the management orders after they have held a pretrial conference. Because the class representative, in practice, may be only an incomplete proxy for the absentees' interests, the court sometimes must supplement treatment of the class representative's claims with proceedings designed to evaluate some aspect of each class member's individual claims.

The necessity of these supplementary proceedings to "individualize" aspects of a class suit may vary with the relief sought. Some classwide injunctions may resemble individual suits for injunctive relief closely in the sense that the problems involved in proving the defendant's liability, of determining the proper relief, and of administering relief are all quite difficult, but are not increased materially by class treatment. Classwide requests for mandatory injunctions, however, for example to desegregate a school system or to secure reapportionment of an electoral district, may present more formidable questions that require additional judicial management. See Garth, *Conflict and Dissent in Class Actions: A Suggested Perspective*, 77 Nw. U. L. Rev. 492, 518–20 (1982). Classwide suits for damages inevitably create problems that are not present in traditional binary litigation. The court in these damage class actions must complete three analytically separate tasks: it must determine if defendant is liable; it must calculate the amount of damages to the class; and, it must distribute the proper share of the award to individual class members. Often, one or more of these tasks demands fragmentation or "individualization" of the class. See Rosenberg, *Individual Justice and Collectivizing Risk–Based Claims in Mass–Exposure Cases*, 71 N.Y.U. L. Rev. 210 (1996); Edelman, Nagareda & Silver, *The Allocation Problem in Multiple–Claimant Representations*, 14 Sup. Ct. Econ. Rev. 95 (2006).

7. SETTLEMENT

Rule 23(e) imposes a virtually unique obligation on the district court to approve any decision to settle, dismiss, or compromise a class action. Rule 23(e) reflects the same philosophical concerns that already have been discussed in connection with adequacy of representation. First, due process demands that the absent class members be protected from an unfair settlement made because the representative parties have lost their enthusiasm for the litigation or are themselves receiving a substantial benefit at the expense of the absentees. In addition, the efficiency and economy objectives of Rule 23 would be subverted if the judgment produced by the settlement proves to be vulnerable to collateral attack, a situation that might arise if the settlement does not take proper account of the rights of the absent class members. What requirements does Rule 23(e) impose in terms of notice and an opportunity to be heard? What is the significance of providing class members a second chance at opting out of any proposed settlement? See Federal Rule 23(e)(4); Rutherglen, *Better Late Than Never: Notice and Opt Out at the Settlement Stage of Class Actions*, 71 N.Y.U. L. Rev. 258 (1996); Rubenstein, *The Fairness Hearing: Adversarial and Regulatory Approaches*, 53 UCLA L. Rev. 1435 (2006).

What factors ought to guide a court in deciding that a settlement proposal is fair, reasonable, and in the best interests of the individuals who will be affected by it? Proponents of a settlement have the burden of satisfying Rule 23(e)(2). Whether the class as a whole favors the proposed settlement is an extremely important consideration in the court's assessment. The preference of any particular class member, however, is not dispositive. Settlements can be approved over the objections of the class representatives, as well as those of absent class members who have received and responded to the settlement notice. However, objecting class members are free to appeal the court's decision approving the settlement when a judgment based on it is entered. Concerns about the class action settlement process remain one of the most controversial features of Rule 23 practice.

The Class Action Fairness Act, 28 U.S.C. § 1712, imposes special requirements on the district court to assess the fairness, reasonableness, and adequacy of settlements that rely on "coupons." Coupons typically permit the class members to purchase goods at a discount from defendant. See, for example, In re Domestic Air Transportation Antitrust Litigation, 148 F.R.D. 297 (N.D. Ga. 1993), an antitrust suit against the airline industry, where the settlement resulted in the distribution of discount flight coupons to be used for future travel by class members. SYNFUEL TECHNOLOGIES, INC. v. DHL EXPRESS (USA), 463 F.3d 646 (7th Cir. 2006), involved a suit against a package delivery company for allegedly overcharging customers. The District Court approved a settlement that provided class members with the choice of accepting a number of prepaid shipping envelopes or thirty dollars cash, in addition to injunctive relief that prospectively changed defendant's billing practices. The Court of Appeals vacated the judgment, finding that the District Court had not assessed the fairness of the settlement adequately. Although CAFA did not govern the lawsuit, the Seventh Circuit pointed to Congress's requirement under that statute of heightened judicial scrutiny of coupon settlements; moreover, although pre-paid envelopes are not coupons, the appeals court drew the analogy that "they are a form of in-kind compensation that shares some characteristics of coupons, including forced future business with the defendant * * *." Id. at 654. See generally Leslie, *The Need To Study Coupon Settlements in Class Action Litigation*, 18 Geo. J. Legal Ethics 1395 (2005). Why should a settlement's reliance on coupons raise special concerns for the judiciary's fairness inquiry?

NOTE ON SETTLEMENT CLASS ACTIONS

A mass tort class action suit may involve millions of individual claims and expose the parties to large and unpredictable transaction costs. These actions thus create significant economic incentives for settlement. Would it be appropriate to certify an action that is filed only for the purposes of settlement, if plaintiff has no intention of ever litigating the claims? Why might defendant agree to such a result? Why might the class representatives also want to accept an early negotiated deal? The possibility of settlement class actions brings to the foreground questions about the adequacy of representation, as well as the role of class actions as an instrument of social policy. In ORTIZ v. FIBREBOARD CORP., 527 U.S. 815, 119 S.Ct. 2295, 144 L.Ed.2d 715 (1999), the Supreme Court faced the propriety of a settlement class in a major products liability action involving asbestos exposure. The Court decertified the class.

Chief Justice Rehnquist concurred in *Ortiz*, stating that the problem requires a legislative solution. However, although Congress since at least 1977 has considered legislation to compensate those injured by exposure to asbestos, the problem has continued to be unremedied. See Stengel, *The Asbestos End–Game*, 62 N.Y.U. Ann. Surv. Am. L. 223 (2006). Professor Carrington observes:

> America's experience with asbestos litigation should teach us to appreciate both the merits and the limits of our system of ex post regulation of business. The civil trial is an important social and political institution on which the public depends for the protection of consumers, workers, and the environment. Even Corporate America cannot long do without it. But civil courts are not a system and cannot be made into a system fit to deal with individual matters as monstrously complex as the scientific issues to be resolved in asbestos cases. Nor can courts usefully try cases before they arise; premature resolution invites the filing of dubious claims. If legislatures insist on leaving such proliferations of complex disputes for the courts, they should be expected to provide enough judges, courtrooms, and juries to timely resolve disputes on their merits for the parties involved. Finally, it is long past the time to reconsider a health care system that is heavily dependent on litigation as the path to medical treatment of sickness and injury.

Carrington, *Asbestos Lessons: The Consequences of Asbestos Litigation*, 26 Rev. Litig. 583, 611–12 (2007).

8. ATTORNEYS' FEES

Federal Rule 23(h), adopted in 2003, authorizes the court to award a reasonable attorney's fee in any action certified as a class action. However, long before the amendment made this power explicit, courts routinely awarded such fees to the attorney for the successful representative party. The rationale for this practice was that since counsel's representation on behalf of the named plaintiffs has conferred a benefit on all the class members, fairness demanded that compensation be awarded out of any fund ordered for the class. In other contexts, courts awarded attorneys' fees out of the common fund created by the recovery from defendant. The Supreme Court has rejected the argument that fee awards are prohibited by the traditional American rule that the losing party shall not be forced to bear the winning parties' legal expenses. Boeing Co. v. Van Gemert, 444 U.S. 472, 100 S.Ct. 745, 62 L.Ed.2d 676 (1980). Courts use different approaches in setting the amount of class action attorneys' fees. See generally Resnik, Curtis & Hensler, *Individuals within the Aggregate: Relationships, Representation, and Fees*, 71 N.Y.U. L. Rev. 296 (1996).

SECTION D. DUE PROCESS CONSIDERATIONS

HANSBERRY v. LEE

Supreme Court of the United States, 1940.
311 U.S. 32, 61 S.Ct. 115, 85 L.Ed. 22.

[This suit was brought in an Illinois state court on behalf of a class of landowners to enforce a racially restrictive covenant involving land in the City of Chicago. The covenant provided that it was not effective unless signed by the "owners of 95 per centum of the frontage." Plaintiff alleged that Hansberry, a black man, had purchased some of the restricted land from an owner who had signed the agreement and that suit was being brought to enjoin the sale as a breach of the covenant. He further alleged that the binding effect of the covenant had been established in an earlier Illinois state court action holding that 95 percent of all the landowners involved had signed the agreement. In response, defendants pleaded that they were not bound by the earlier judgment since they had not been parties to that suit and were not successors in interest or in privity with any of the parties to that action. Thus, they argued it would be a denial of due process to hold them to the first decree.

The Illinois Circuit Court held that the issue whether the covenant was valid was res judicata, even though it found that only about 54 percent of the owners actually had signed the agreement and that the previous judgment rested on a "false and fraudulent" stipulation of the parties. The Supreme Court of Illinois affirmed. It found that although the stipulation was untrue it was not fraudulent or collusive. The Illinois court then went on to conclude that the first action had been a "class" or "representative" suit, and as such it was binding on all the class members unless reversed or set aside on direct proceedings. The court then held that Hansberry and the persons who had sold the land to him were members of the class represented in the first action and consequently were bound by the decree in that suit.]

Certiorari to the Supreme Court of the State of Illinois.

Mr. Justice Stone delivered the opinion of the Court.

* * *

* * * [W]hen the judgment of a state court, ascribing to the judgment of another court the binding force and effect of *res judicata*, is challenged for want of due process it becomes the duty of this Court to examine the course of procedure in both litigations to ascertain whether the litigant whose rights have thus been adjudicated has been afforded such notice and opportunity to be heard as are requisite to the due process which the Constitution prescribes. * * *

It is a principle of general application in Anglo–American jurisprudence that one is not bound by a judgment *in personam* in a litigation in which he is not designated as a party or to which he has not been made a party by service of process. Pennoyer v. Neff, [p. 33, supra,] * * *. A judgment rendered in such circumstances is not entitled to the full faith and credit which the Constitution and statutes of the United States * * * prescribe * * * and judicial action enforcing it against the person or property of the absent party is not that due process which the Fifth and Fourteenth Amendments requires. * * *

To these general rules there is a recognized exception that, to an extent not precisely defined by judicial opinion, the judgment in a "class" or "representative" suit, to which some members of the class are parties, may bind members of the class or those represented who were not made parties to it. * * *

The class suit was an invention of equity to enable it to proceed to a decree in suits where the number of those interested in the subject of the litigation is so great that their joinder as parties in conformity to the usual rules of procedure is impracticable. Courts are not infrequently called upon to proceed with causes in which the number of those interested in the litigation is so great as to make difficult or impossible the joinder of all because some are not within the jurisdiction or because their whereabouts is unknown or where if all were made parties to the suit its continued abatement by the death of some would prevent or unduly delay a decree. In such cases where the interests of those not joined are of the same class as the interests of those who are, and where it is considered that the latter fairly represent the former in the prosecution of the litigation of the issues in which all have a common interest, the court will proceed to a decree. * * *

It is evident that the considerations which may induce a court thus to proceed, despite a technical defect of parties, may differ from those which must be taken into account in determining whether the absent parties are bound by the decree or, if it is adjudged that they are, in ascertaining whether such an adjudication satisfies the requirements of due process and of full faith and credit. Nevertheless there is scope within the framework of the Constitution for holding in appropriate cases that a judgment rendered in a class suit is *res judicata* as to members of the class who are not formal parties to the suit. * * * With a proper regard for divergent local institutions and interests * * *, this Court is justified in saying that there has been a failure of due process only in those cases where it cannot be said that the procedure adopted, fairly insures the protection of the interests of absent parties who are to be bound by it. * * *

It is familiar doctrine of the federal courts that members of a class not present as parties to the litigation may be bound by the judgment where they are in fact adequately represented by parties who are present, or where they actually participate in the conduct of the litigation in which members of the class are present as parties * * * or where the interest of the members of the class, some of whom are present as parties, is joint, or where for any other reason the relationship between the parties present and those who are absent is such as legally to entitle the former to stand in judgment for the latter. * * *

In all such cases, * * * we may assume for present purposes that such procedure affords a protection to the parties who are represented though absent, which would satisfy the requirements of due process and full faith and credit. * * * Nor do we find it necessary for the decision of this case to say that, when the only circumstance defining the class is that the determination of the rights of its members turns upon a single issue of fact or law, a state could not constitutionally adopt a procedure whereby some of the members of the class could stand in judgment for all, provided that the procedure were so devised and applied as to insure that those present are of the same class as those absent and that the litigation is so conducted as to insure the full and fair consideration of the common issue. * * * We decide only that the procedure and the course of litigation sustained here by the plea of res judicata do not satisfy these requirements.

The restrictive agreement did not purport to create a joint obligation or liability. If valid and effective its promises were the several obligations of the signers and those claiming under them. The promises ran severally to every other signer. It is plain that in such circumstances all those alleged to be bound by the agreement would not constitute a single class in any litigation brought to enforce it. Those who sought to secure its benefits by enforcing it could not be said to be in the same class with or represent those whose interest was in resisting performance, for the agreement by its terms imposes obligations and confers rights on the owner of each plot of land who signs it. If those who thus seek to secure the benefits of the agreement were rightly regarded by the state Supreme Court as constituting a class, it is evident that those signers or their successors who are interested in challenging the validity of the agreement and resisting its performance are not of the same class in the sense that their interests are identical so that any group who had elected to enforce rights conferred by the agreement could be said to be acting in the interest of any others who were free to deny its obligation.

Because of the dual and potentially conflicting interests of those who are putative parties to the agreement in compelling or resisting its performance, it is impossible to say, solely because they are parties to it, that any two of them are of the same class. Nor without more, and with the due regard for the protection of the rights of absent parties which due process exacts, can some be permitted to stand in judgment for all.

It is one thing to say that some members of a class may represent other members in a litigation where the sole and common interest of the class in the litigation, is either to assert a common right or to challenge an asserted obligation. * * * It is quite another to hold that all those who are free alternatively either to assert rights or to challenge them are of a single class, so that any group, merely because it is of the class so constituted, may be deemed adequately to represent any others of the class in litigating their interests in either alternative. Such a selection of representatives for purposes of litigation, whose substantial interests are not necessarily or even probably the same as those whom they are deemed to represent, does not afford that protection to absent parties which due process requires. The doctrine of representation of absent parties in a class suit has not hitherto been thought to go so far. * * * Apart from the opportunities it would afford for the fraudulent and collusive sacrifice of the rights of absent parties, we think that the representation in this case no more satisfies the requirements of due process than a trial by a judicial officer who is in such situation that he may have an interest in the outcome of the litigation in conflict with that of the litigants. * * *

The plaintiffs in the [first] case sought to compel performance of the agreement in behalf of themselves and all others similarly situated. They did not designate the defendants in the suit as a class or seek any injunction or other relief against others than the named defendants, and the decree which was entered did not purport to bind others. In seeking to enforce the agreement the plaintiffs in that suit were not representing the petitioners here whose substantial interest is in resisting performance. The defendants in the first suit were not treated by the pleadings or decree as representing others or as foreclosing by their defense the rights of others, and even though nominal defendants, it does not appear that their interest in defeating the contract outweighed their interest in establishing its validity. For a court in this situation to ascribe to either the plaintiffs or defendants the performance of such functions on behalf of petitioners here, is to attribute to them a power that it cannot be said that they had assumed to exercise, and a responsibility which, in view of their dual interests it does not appear that they could rightly discharge.

Reversed.

NOTES AND QUESTIONS

1. The events leading up to Hansberry v. Lee involve important efforts to desegregate residential housing in Chicago. See Kamp, *The History Behind* Hansberry v. Lee, 20 U.C. Davis L. Rev. 481 (1987). See also Tidmarsh, *The Story of* Hansberry: *The Rise of Modern Class Actions*, in Civil Procedure Stories 233–94 (Clermont ed., 2d ed. 2008).

2. In what ways does the Due Process Clause affect the legitimacy of a class action? In earlier cases that you have studied, due process has required the provision of notice and an opportunity to be heard to a defendant in a lawsuit. See, Chapter 3, supra. In *Hansberry,* the Supreme Court shifted its attention to the protection of plaintiffs and focused on the adequacy of representation. See 7A Wright, Miller & Kane, Federal Practice and Procedure: Civil 3d § 1765.

3. At what point in a proceeding does a court evaluate the adequacy of class action representation? GONZALES v. CASSIDY, 474 F.2d 67 (5th Cir. 1973), concerned the effect of a class action that successfully challenged the constitutionality of a Texas statute requiring uninsured motorists to post security when sued for a car accident or else have their drivers' licenses suspended. Class action relief was applied retroactively to the representative plaintiff and prospectively to all other class members. Plaintiff alleged that

the class representative was inadequate for having failed to appeal on the issue of retroactivity. The Fifth Circuit outlined a two-part test for reviewing whether the named plaintiff has represented the class adequately as to make the judgment in the suit binding on the absent class members:

> * * * (1) Did the trial court in the first suit correctly determine, initially, that the representative would adequately represent the class? and (2) Does it appear, after the termination of the suit, that the class representative adequately protected the interest of the class? * * *

Id. at 72. The court held that the original plaintiff's failure to appeal the initial judgment rendered him an inadequate representative of the class, since "he was representing approximately 150,000 persons, who, although having had their licenses and registration receipts suspended without due process, were denied any relief by the * * * [trial] court's prospective * * * application of its decision." Id. at 76. The court remanded the case to the District Court for reconsideration of the retroactivity question. Implicit in the two prongs of *Gonzales* is the notion that adequacy of representation may be examined more than once and by different courts: first, by the court certifying the class; second, by an appellate court; and third, by a court called upon to evaluate the binding effect of the class action on a class member who seeks to litigate in a later action.

4. If the adequacy of representation provided by the class representative is important to safeguarding the due process rights of class members, courts must be vigilant in examining potential conflicts of interest among class members. The conflict of interest in *Hansberry* unquestionably was enough to preclude a finding of adequate representation. In other cases, however, the conflict of interest may be less sharply defined.

Consider whether, as a trial court judge, you would certify the following proposed classes:

(a) The complaint alleges discrimination in hiring, promotion, and conditions of employment; the proposed class includes current minority employees, minorities whose employment applications were denied, and future minority applicants and employees; the sole class representative is a current employee of the company.

(b) Would your answer to (a) be any different if there were a second class representative whom the defendant arguably had failed to hire because of discrimination?

(c) An airline has a practice of discharging flight attendants who become pregnant. A suit for injunctive relief is brought on behalf of female airline cabin attendants, including those stewardesses who still are employed. Reinstatement of the former stewardesses, with no loss of seniority, would leapfrog them over the less senior stewardesses who still are actively employed.

(d) Members of the proposed class in a products-liability suit reside in all parts of the nation, and there are significant differences in the products-liability laws of the various states. Should the class be certified as a single class? Suppose the injured parties can be divided into two groups for whom the applicable laws are substantially the same? What if four groupings are needed? Sixteen? At what point would this subclassing create intolerable management problems?

5. In RICHARDS v. JEFFERSON COUNTY, ALABAMA, 517 U.S. 793, 116 S.Ct. 1761, 135 L.Ed.2d 76 (1996), the Court further elaborated the due-process requirements recognized in *Hansberry*. Petitioners brought a class action on behalf of all nonfederal employees challenging a state employment tax. Their claims were dismissed as barred under a court's earlier judgment that the tax was constitutional. The earlier case had been litigated by the acting director of finance for a city and by the city itself, and it had been consolidated with a separate suit brought by three state taxpayers. The United States Supreme Court reversed. In its decision, the Court relied on a number of grounds to explain why the petitioners in *Richards* were not adequately represented in the prior litigation and so could not be barred from pressing their constitutional claims in a separate action: first, plaintiffs in the first action had not given petitioners notice of their lawsuit; second, the taxpayer-plaintiffs in the first action had not sued on behalf of a class, and the judgment did not purport to bind nonparties; third, the government-plaintiffs had not purported to represent the pecuniary interests of petitioners, who were county and not city taxpayers; and fourth, the first action was not a special proceeding designed to be brought on behalf of the public. The Court stated:

> Even assuming that our opinion in *Hansberry* may be read to leave open the possibility that in some class suits adequate representation might cure a lack of notice * * *, it may not be read to permit the application of res judicata here. Our opinion explained that a prior proceeding, to have binding effect on absent parties, would at least have to be "so devised and applied as to insure that those present are of the same class as those absent and that the litigation is so conducted as to insure the full and fair consideration of the common issue." * * * It is plain that the * * * prior action * * * does not fit such a description.

Id. at 801, 116 S.Ct. at 1767, 135 L.Ed.2d at 86.

6. Professor Coffee has argued that a court's inquiry into adequacy of representation should be guided by principles of exit, loyalty, and voice. See Coffee, *Class Action Accountability: Reconciling Exit, Voice, and Loyalty in Representative Litigation*, 100 Colum. L. Rev. 370 (2000). What do these terms mean in the class action context? The Supreme Court has focused on loyalty as a way to ensure class cohesion. Might there be a danger that this approach will generate internecine division of warring subclasses, and ultimately may weaken the claim that the class action is superior to adjudication of individual claims? On the other hand, increasing voice may not be appropriate for class actions, either, because class representatives actually play a very small role in the development of a large class action. Is the best solution the enhancement of class members' exit opportunities at all stages of the litigation? Is this suggestion feasible?

SECTION E. CLASS ACTIONS AND JURISDICTION

1. SUBJECT–MATTER JURISDICTION

A class action based upon a federal question usually does not raise any special problems of subject-matter jurisdiction. A class action based upon diversity, however, does raise two special questions: first, to which class members should the court look in determining whether there is diversity of citizenship and, second, to which class members should the court look in evaluating the amount-in-controversy requirement? In addition, the Class Action Fairness Act has established special jurisdictional rules for class actions that come within its provisions.

In SUPREME TRIBE OF BEN-HUR v. CAUBLE, 255 U.S. 356, 41 S.Ct. 338, 65 L.Ed. 673 (1921), the Supreme Court held that determinations of diversity of citizenship in class actions should be based on the citizenship of the named parties only. See generally 7A Wright, Miller & Kane, Federal Practice and Procedure: Civil 3d § 1755. How does this rule apply to a class action brought by an unincorporated association? A court usually looks to the citizenship of each member of the association to determine whether there is diversity of citizenship. Examine 28 U.S.C. § 1332 (c)(1). How does CAFA change this rule for class actions that come within its terms?

In ZAHN v. INTERNATIONAL PAPER CO., 414 U.S. 291, 94 S.Ct. 505, 38 L.Ed.2d 511 (1973), petitioners, owners of property fronting on Lake Champlain in Orwell, Vermont, brought a diversity action seeking damages from International Paper Co., a New York corporation, for allegedly polluting the waters of the lake and damaging the value and utility of the surrounding properties. The claims of each of the named plaintiffs were found to satisfy the $10,000 jurisdictional amount, but the District Court was convinced "to a legal certainty" that not every individual owner in the class had suffered pollution damages in excess of $10,000. The Supreme Court held that each plaintiff in a Rule 23(b)(3) class action must satisfy the amount-in-controversy requirement for there to be diversity jurisdiction over the suit. Again, the majority opinion rested on the traditional rules that courts had used for aggregating claims.

In EXXON MOBIL CORP. v. ALLAPATTAH SERVICES, INC., 545 U.S. 546, 125 S.Ct. 2611, 162 L.Ed.2d 502 (2005), the Supreme Court held, five-to-four, that the 1990 enactment of the supplemental jurisdiction statute, 28 U.S.C. § 1367, overruled *Zahn*. See p. 203, supra. The Court explained that when the complaint includes "at least one claim that satisfies the amount-in-controversy requirement, and there are no other relevant jurisdictional defects, the district court, beyond all question, has original jurisdiction over that claim," and that the court then "can turn to the question whether it has a constitutional and statutory basis for exercising supplemental jurisdiction over the other claims in the action."

The Court found "[n]othing in the text of § 1367(b)" that could be read to withhold "supplemental jurisdiction over the claims of plaintiffs certified as class action members pursuant to Rule 23." Id. at 559–60, 125 S.Ct. at 2620–21, 162 L.Ed.2d at 521–22.

NOTE ON THE CLASS ACTION FAIRNESS ACT OF *2005*

The Class Action Fairness Act, adopted in 2005, authorizes federal jurisdiction on the basis of minimal diversity for any interstate class action that comes within its terms. See Chapter 4, p. 169, supra. Examine the language of Section 1332(d). What is the required amount in controversy for a class action under CAFA? Does the court look to the named plaintiff to determine whether the jurisdictional amount is satisfied? How is minimal diversity determined? Can class actions that meet the jurisdictional require-ments of CAFA be removed to federal court? See 28 U.S.C. § 1453. CAFA excludes various categories of class actions from the statute's scope. What are those exceptions? See 28 U.S.C. § 1332(d)(5)(A) (primary defendants are States, State officials, or other governmental entities); Section 1332 (d)(5)(B) (class contains "less than 100" members); and Section 1332(d)(9)(A)–(B) (action "solely involves a claim" involving certain securities and corporate governance issues). Finally, the district court has discretion to decline juris-diction under CAFA based on an assessment of six enumerated factors. See 28 U.S.C. § 1332(d)(3)(A)–(F). "No guidance is given as to how the court is to weigh or balance those factors." 7A Wright, Miller & Kane, Federal Practice and Procedure: Civil 3d § 1756.2.

One commentator calls CAFA "the most significant change in class action practice since the federal class action rule was amended in 1996." Sherman, *Class Actions after the Class Action Fairness Act of 2005*, 80 Tul. L. Rev. 1593 (2006). CAFA's impact on class action practice is not yet clear. See Marcus, *Modes of Procedural Reform*, 31 Hastings Int'l & Comp. L. Rev. 157, 184 (2008). In the short run, CAFA has increased the number of diversity class actions in the federal courts, and these cases largely involve contracts, torts, consumer protection, fraud, and property damage. See Lee & Willging, The Impact of the Class Action Fairness Act of 2005 on the Federal Courts: Fourth Interim Report to the Judicial Conference Advisory Committee on Civil Rules 1–2 (Federal Judicial Center, April 2008). How these cases are affecting the federal judicial workload remains to be seen. Professor Nagareda warns that channeling state law class actions to federal court will cause a "backdoor" revision of state-law substantive rights. See Nagareda, *Aggregation and Its Discontents: Class Settlement Pressure, Class–Wide Arbitration, and CAFA*, 106 Colum. L. Rev. 1872, 1876 (2006). Is that result consistent with *Erie*? See Note 5, p. 267, supra.

2. PERSONAL JURISDICTION

Class actions raise interesting problems related to personal jurisdic-tion. Must the requirements of *International Shoe*, p. 46, supra, be satisfied in order for the class action judgment to bind a particular member of a defendant class? Similarly, must the due process requirements of personal jurisdiction be met before a court can bind any individual member of a plaintiff class? Do the traditional doctrines of personal jurisdiction apply to absentee class members who are beyond the court's jurisdiction? The following case addresses that question.

———

PHILLIPS PETROLEUM CO. v. SHUTTS

Supreme Court of the United States, 1985.
472 U.S. 797, 105 S.Ct. 2965, 86 L.Ed.2d 628.

[During the 1970's, Phillips Petroleum produced or purchased natural gas from leased land located in 11 states. Shutts and several other royalty owners possessing rights to leases from which Phillips Petroleum produced gas brought a class action against the company in a Kansas state court, seeking to recover interest on royalty payments that had been delayed. The trial court certified a class consisting of 33,000 royalty owners. The class representative provided each class member with a notice by first-class mail describing the action and informing each member that he could appear in person or by counsel, that otherwise he would be represented by the named royalty owners, and that class members would be included in the class and bound by the judgment unless they "opted out" of the action by returning a "request for exclusion." The final class consisted of some 28,100 members, who resided in all 50 states, the District of Columbia, and several foreign countries. Notwithstanding that over 99% of the gas leases in question and some 97% of the plaintiff class members had no apparent connection to Kansas except for the lawsuit, the trial court applied Kansas contract and equity law to every claim and found Phillips Petroleum liable for interest on the suspended royalties to all class members. The Kansas Supreme Court affirmed over the company's contentions that the Due Process Clause of the Fourteenth Amendment prevented Kansas from adjudicating the claims of all the class members, and that the Due Process Clause and the Full Faith and Credit Clause prohibited application of Kansas law to all of the transactions between it and the class members.]

Certiorari to the Supreme Court of Kansas.

JUSTICE REHNQUIST delivered the opinion of the Court.

* * *

I

* * *

* * * As a class-action defendant petitioner is in a unique predicament. If Kansas does not possess jurisdiction over this plaintiff class, petitioner will be bound to 28,100 judgment holders scattered across the globe, but none of these will be bound by the Kansas decree. Petitioner could be subject to numerous later individual suits by these class members because a judgment issued without proper personal jurisdiction over an absent party is not entitled to full faith and credit elsewhere and thus has no res judicata effect as to that party. Whether it wins or loses on the merits, petitioner has a distinct and personal interest in seeing the entire plaintiff class bound by res judicata just as petitioner is bound. The only way a class action defendant like petitioner can assure itself of this binding effect of the judgment is to ascertain that the forum court has jurisdiction over every plaintiff whose claim it seeks to adjudicate, sufficient to support a defense of res judicata in a later suit for damages by class members.

While it is true that a court adjudicating a dispute may not be able to predetermine the res judicata effect of its own judgment, petitioner has alleged that it would be obviously and immediately injured if this class-action judgment against it became final without binding the plaintiff class. We think that such an injury is sufficient to give petitioner standing on its own right to raise the jurisdiction claim in this Court.

* * *

II

Reduced to its essentials, petitioner's argument is that unless out-of-state plaintiffs affirmatively consent, the Kansas courts may not exert jurisdiction over their claims. Petitioner claims that failure to execute and return the "request for exclusion" provided with the class notice cannot constitute consent of the out-of-state plaintiffs; thus Kansas courts may exercise jurisdiction over these plaintiffs only if the plaintiffs possess the sufficient "minimum contacts" with Kansas as that term is used in cases involving personal jurisdiction over out-of-state defendants. * * * Since Kansas had no prelitigation contact with many of the plaintiffs and leases involved, petitioner claims that Kansas has exceeded its jurisdictional reach and thereby violated the due process rights of the absent plaintiffs.

In *International Shoe* we were faced with an out-of-state corporation which sought to avoid the exercise of personal jurisdiction over it as a defendant by Washington state court. We held that the extent of the defendant's due process protection would depend "upon the quality and nature of the activity in relation to the fair and orderly administration of the laws * * *." We noted that the Due Process Clause did not permit a State to make a binding judgment against a person with whom the State had no contacts, ties, or relations. * * * If the defendant possessed certain minimum contacts with the State, so that it was "reasonable and just, according to our traditional conception of fair play and substantial justice" for a State to exercise personal jurisdiction, the State could force the defendant to defend himself in the forum, upon pain of default, and could bind him to a judgment. * * *

The purpose of this test, of course, is to protect a defendant from the travail of defending in a distant forum, unless the defendant's contacts with the forum make it just to force him to defend there. * * *

Although the cases like *Shaffer* [, p. 98, supra,] and *Woodson*, [p. 61, supra], which petitioner relies on for a minimum contacts requirement all dealt with out-of-state defendants or parties in the procedural posture of a defendant, * * * petitioner claims that the same analysis must apply to absent class action plaintiffs. In this regard petitioner correctly points out that a chose in action is a constitutionally recognized property interest possessed by each of the plaintiffs. * * * An adverse judgment by Kansas courts in this case may extinguish the chose in action forever through res judicata. Such an adverse judgment, petitioner claims, would be every bit as onerous to an absent plaintiff as an adverse judgment on the merits would be to a defendant. Thus, the same due process protections should apply to absent plaintiffs: Kansas should not be able to exert jurisdiction over the plaintiffs' claims unless the plaintiffs have sufficient minimum contacts with Kansas.

We think petitioner's premise is in error. The burdens placed by a State upon an absent class-action plaintiff are not of the same order or magnitude as those it places upon an absent defendant. An out-of-state defendant summoned by a plaintiff is faced with the full powers of the forum State to render judgment *against* it. The defendant must generally hire counsel and travel to the forum to defend itself from the plaintiff's claim, or suffer a default judgment. The defendant may be forced to participate in extended and often costly discovery, and will be forced to respond in damages or to comply with some other form of remedy imposed by the court should it lose the suit. The defendant may also face liability for court costs and attorney's fees. These burdens are substantial, and the minimum contacts requirement of the Due Process Clause prevents the forum State from unfairly imposing them upon the defendant.

A class-action plaintiff, however, is in quite a different posture. The Court noted this difference in Hansberry v. Lee * * * [p. 410, supra,] which explained that a "class" or "representative" suit was an exception to the rule that one could not be bound by judgment *in personam* unless one was made fully a party in the traditional sense. * * * As the Court pointed out in *Hansberry,* the class action was an invention of equity to enable it to proceed to a decree in suits where the number of those interested in the litigation was too great to permit joinder. The absent parties would be bound by the decree so long as the named parties adequately represented the absent class and the prosecution of the litigation was within the common interest. * * *

Modern plaintiff class actions follow the same goals, permitting litigation of a suit involving common questions when there are too many plaintiffs for proper joinder. Class actions also may permit the plaintiffs to pool claims which would be uneconomical to litigate individually. For example, this lawsuit involves claims averaging about $100 per plaintiff; most of the plaintiffs would have no realistic day in court if a class action were not available.

In sharp contrast to the predicament of a defendant haled into an out-of-state forum, the plaintiffs in this suit were not haled anywhere to defend themselves upon pain of a default judgment. As commentators have noted, from the plaintiffs' point of view a class action resembles a "quasi-administrative proceeding, conducted by the judge." * * *

A plaintiff class in Kansas and numerous other jurisdictions cannot first be certified unless the judge, with the aid of the named plaintiffs and defendant, conducts an inquiry into the common nature of the named plaintiffs' and the absent plaintiffs' claims, the adequacy of representation, the jurisdiction possessed over the class, and any other matters that will bear upon proper representation of the absent plaintiffs' interest. * * * Unlike a defendant in a civil suit, a class-action plaintiff is not required to fend for himself. * * * The court and named plaintiffs protect his interests. Indeed, the class-action defendant itself has a great interest in ensuring that the absent plaintiffs' claims are properly before the forum. In this case, for example, the defendant sought to avoid class certification by alleging that the absent plaintiffs would not be adequately represented and were not amenable to jurisdiction. * * *

The concern of the typical class-action rules for the absent plaintiffs is manifested in other ways. Most jurisdictions, including Kansas, require that a class action, once certified, may not be dismissed or compromised without the approval of the court. In many jurisdictions such as Kansas the court may amend the pleadings to ensure that all sections of the class are represented adequately. * * *

Besides this continuing solicitude for their rights, absent plaintiff class members are not subject to other burdens imposed upon defendants. They need not hire counsel or appear. They are almost never subject to counterclaims or cross-claims, or liability for fees or costs. Absent plaintiff class members are not subject to coercive or punitive remedies. Nor will an adverse judgment typically bind an absent plaintiff for any damages, although a valid adverse judgment may extinguish any of the plaintiff's claims which was litigated.

Unlike a defendant in a normal civil suit, an absent class-action plaintiff is not required to do anything. He may sit back and allow the litigation to run its course, content in knowing that there are safeguards provided for his protection. In most class actions an absent plaintiff is provided at least with an opportunity to "opt out" of the class, and if he takes advantage of that opportunity he is removed from the litigation entirely. This was true of the Kansas proceedings in this case. The Kansas procedure provided for the mailing of a notice to each class member by first-class mail. The notice, as we have previously indicated, described the action and informed the class member that he could appear in person or by counsel, in default of which he would be represented by the named plaintiffs and their attorneys. The notice further stated that class members would be included in the class and bound by the judgment unless they "opted out" by executing and returning a "request for exclusion" that was included in the notice.

Petitioner contends, however, that the "opt out" procedure provided by Kansas is not good enough, and that an "opt in" procedure is required to satisfy the Due Process Clause of the Fourteenth Amendment. Insofar as plaintiffs who have no minimum contacts with the forum State are concerned, an "opt in" provision would require that each class member affirmatively consent to his inclusion within the class.

Because States place fewer burdens upon absent class plaintiffs than they do upon absent defendants in nonclass suits, the Due Process Clause need not and does not afford the former as much protection from state-court jurisdiction as it does the latter. The Fourteenth Amendment does protect "persons," not "defendants," however, so absent plaintiffs as well as absent defendants are entitled to some protection from the jurisdiction of a forum State which seeks to adjudicate their claims. In this case we hold that a forum State may exercise jurisdiction over the claim of an absent class-action plaintiff, even though that plaintiff may not possess the minimum contacts with the forum which would support personal jurisdiction over a defendant. If the forum State wishes to bind an absent plaintiff concerning a claim for money damages or similar relief at law,[3] it must provide minimal procedural due process protection. The plaintiff must receive notice plus an opportunity to be heard and participate in the litigation, whether in person or through counsel. The notice must be the best practicable, "reasonably calculated, under all the circumstances, to apprise interested parties of the pendency of the action and afford them an opportunity to present their objections." * * * The notice should describe the action and the plaintiffs' rights in it. Additionally, we hold that due process requires at a minimum that an absent plaintiff be provided with an opportunity to remove himself from the class by executing and returning an "opt out" or "request for exclusion" form to the court. Finally, the Due Process Clause of course requires that the named plaintiff at all times adequately represent the interests of the absent class members. * * *

We reject petitioner's contention that the Due Process Clause of the Fourteenth Amendment requires that absent plaintiffs affirmatively "opt in" to the class, rather than be deemed members of the class if they do not "opt out." We think that such a contention is supported by little, if any precedent, and that it ignores the differences between class action plaintiffs, on the one hand, and defendants in non-class civil suits on the other. Any plaintiff may consent to jurisdiction. * * * The essential question, then, is how stringent the requirement for a showing of consent will be.

3. Our holding today is limited to those class actions which seek to bind known plaintiffs concerning claims wholly or predominately for money judgments. We intimate no view concerning other types of class action lawsuits, such as those seeking equitable relief. Nor, of course, does our discussion of personal jurisdiction address class actions where the jurisdiction is asserted against a *defendant* class.

We think that the procedure followed by Kansas, where a fully descriptive notice is sent first-class mail to each class member, with an explanation of the right to "opt out," satisfies due process. Requiring a plaintiff to affirmatively request inclusion would probably impede the prosecution of those class actions involving an aggregation of small individual claims, where a large number of claims are required to make it economical to bring suit. * * * The plaintiff's claim may be so small, or the plaintiff so unfamiliar with the law, that he would not file suit individually, nor would he affirmatively request inclusion in the class if such a request were required by the Constitution. If, on the other hand, the plaintiff's claim is sufficiently large or important that he wishes to litigate it on his own, he will likely have retained an attorney or have thought about filing suit, and should be fully capable of exercising his right to "opt out."

In this case over 3,400 members of the potential class did "opt out," which belies the contention that "opt out" procedures result in guaranteed jurisdiction by inertia. Another 1,500 were excluded because the notice and "opt out" form was undeliverable. We think that such results show that the "opt out" procedure provided by Kansas is by no means *pro forma,* and that the Constitution does not require more to protect what must be the somewhat rare species of class member who is unwilling to execute an "opt out" form, but whose claim is nonetheless so important that he cannot be presumed to consent to being a member of the class by his failure to do so. Petitioner's "opt in" requirement would require the invalidation of scores of state statutes and of the class-action provision of the Federal Rules of Civil Procedure, and for the reasons stated we do not think that the Constitution requires the State to sacrifice the obvious advantages in judicial efficiency resulting from the "opt out" approach for the protection of the *rara avis* portrayed by petitioner.

We therefore hold that the protection afforded the plaintiff class members by the Kansas statute satisfies the Due Process Clause. The interests of the absent plaintiffs are sufficiently protected by the forum State when those plaintiffs are provided with a request for exclusion that can be returned within a reasonable time to the court. * * * Both the Kansas trial court and the Supreme Court of Kansas held that the class received adequate representation, and no party disputes that conclusion here. We conclude that the Kansas court properly asserted personal jurisdiction over the absent plaintiffs and their claims against petitioner.

III

The Kansas courts applied Kansas contract and Kansas equity law to every claim in this case, notwithstanding that over 99% of the gas leases and some 97% of the plaintiffs in the case had no apparent connection to the State of Kansas except for this lawsuit. Petitioner protested that the Kansas courts should apply the laws of the States where the leases were located, or at least apply Texas and Oklahoma law because so many of the leases came from those States. The Kansas courts disregarded this contention and found petitioner liable for interest on the suspended royalties as a matter of Kansas law, and set the interest rates under Kansas equity principles.

Petitioner contends that total application of Kansas substantive law violated the constitutional limitations on choice of law mandated by the Due Process Clause of the Fourteenth Amendment and the Full Faith and Credit Clause of Article IV, § 1. We must first determine whether Kansas law conflicts in any material way with any other law which could apply. There can be no injury in applying Kansas law if it is not in conflict with that of any other jurisdiction connected to this suit.

Petitioner claims that Kansas law conflicts with that of a number of States connected to this litigation, especially Texas and Oklahoma. These putative conflicts range from the direct to the tangential, and may be addressed by the Supreme Court of Kansas on remand under the correct constitutional standard. * * *

* * *

The conflicts on the applicable interest rates, alone—which we do not think can be labeled "false conflicts" without a more thorough-going treatment than was accorded them by the Supreme Court of Kansas— certainly amounted to millions of dollars in liability. We think that the Supreme Court of Kansas erred in deciding on the basis that it did that the application of its laws to all claims would be constitutional.

Four Terms ago we addressed a similar situation in Allstate Ins. Co. v. Hague [, Note 4, p. 60, supra] * * *. In that case we were confronted with two conflicting rules of state insurance law. Minnesota permitted the "stacking" of separate uninsured motorist policies while Wisconsin did not. Although the decedent lived in Wisconsin, took out insurance policies and was killed there, he was employed in Minnesota and after his death his widow moved to Minnesota for reasons unrelated to the litigation, and was appointed personal representative of his estate. She filed suit in Minnesota courts, which applied the Minnesota stacking rule.

The plurality in *Allstate* noted that a particular set of facts giving rise to litigation could justify, constitutionally, the application of more than one jurisdiction's laws. The plurality recognized, however, that the Due Process Clause and the Full Faith and Credit Clause provided modest restrictions on the application of forum law. These restrictions required "that for a State's substantive law to be selected in a constitutionally permissible manner, that State must have a significant contact or significant aggregation of contacts, creating state interests, such that choice of its law is neither arbitrary nor fundamentally unfair." * * * The dissenting Justices were in substantial agreement with this principle. * * *

The plurality in *Allstate* affirmed the application of Minnesota law because of the forum's significant contacts to the litigation which supported the State's interest in applying its law. * * * Kansas' contacts to this litigation, as explained by the Kansas Supreme Court, can be gleaned from the opinion below.

Petitioner owns property and conducts substantial business in the State, so Kansas certainly has an interest in regulating petitioner's conduct in Kansas. * * * Moreover, oil and gas extraction is an important business to Kansas, and although only a few leases in issue are located in Kansas, hundreds of Kansas plaintiffs were affected by petitioner's suspension of royalties; thus the court held that the State has a real interest in protecting "the rights of these royalty owners both as individual residents of [Kansas] and as members of this particular class of plaintiffs." * * *

* * *

Kansas must have a "significant contact or aggregation of contacts" to the claims asserted by each member of the plaintiff class, contacts "creating state interests" in order to ensure that the choice of Kansas law is not arbitrary or unfair. * * * Given Kansas' lack of "interest" in claims unrelated to that State, and the substantive conflict with jurisdictions such as Texas, we conclude that application of Kansas law to every claim in this case is sufficiently arbitrary and unfair as to exceed constitutional limits.

When considering fairness in this context, an important element is the expectation of the parties. There is no indication that when the leases involving land and royalty owners outside of Kansas were executed, the parties had any idea that Kansas law would control. Neither the Due Process Clause nor the Full Faith and Credit Clause requires Kansas "to substitute for its own [laws], applicable to persons and events within it, the conflicting statute of another state," * * * but Kansas "may not abrogate the rights of parties beyond its borders having no relation to anything done or to be done within them." * * *

Here the Supreme Court of Kansas took the view that in a nationwide class action where procedural due process guarantees of notice and adequate representation were met, "the laws of the forum should be applied unless compelling reasons exist for applying a different law." * * * Whatever practical reasons may have commended this rule to the Supreme Court of Kansas, for the reasons already stated we do not believe that it is consistent with the decisions of this Court. We make no effort to determine for ourselves which law must apply to the various transactions involved in this lawsuit, and we reaffirm our observation in *Allstate* that in many situations a state court may be free to apply one of several choices of law. But the constitutional limitations laid down in cases such as *Allstate* * * * must be respected even in a nationwide class action.

We therefore affirm the judgment of the Supreme Court of Kansas insofar as it upheld the jurisdiction of the Kansas courts over the plaintiff class members in this case, and reverse its judgment insofar as it held that Kansas law was applicable to all of the transactions which it sought to adjudicate. We remand the case to that court for further proceedings not inconsistent with this opinion.

JUSTICE POWELL took no part in the decision of this case.

[JUSTICE STEVENS wrote an opinion concurring in Parts I and II of the Court's opinion and dissenting from Part III.]

NOTES AND QUESTIONS

1. On remand to the Kansas courts after the Supreme Court's decision in *Shutts,* Phillips Petroleum continued to press the argument that the laws of five states (Louisiana, New Mexico, Oklahoma, Texas, and Wyoming) differed in important respects from the law of Kansas—in particular on the issue of liability for interest on suspended royalties and on the issue of the applicable interest rate where liability is found. These two issues constituted the heart of the legal controversy in the case, and the five identified states embraced 97 percent of the leases involved. In addressing this argument, the Kansas Supreme Court first analyzed the Supreme Court's decision in *Shutts:*

> * * * As to the choice of law question, however, it was ruled the application of Kansas law to all of the investors' claims for interest violated the due process and full faith and credit clauses. In its analysis, the Court first noted that if the law of Kansas was not in conflict with any of the other jurisdictions connected to the suit, then there would be no injury in applying the law of Kansas. * * * The Court then cited differences in the laws of Kansas, Texas, and Oklahoma which Phillips *contended* existed. It appears, however, no analysis was made by the Court to determine whether these differences existed in fact. * * *

Shutts v. Phillips Petroleum Co., 240 Kan. 764, 767, 732 P.2d 1286, 1291 (1987), certiorari denied 487 U.S. 1223, 108 S.Ct. 2883, 101 L.Ed.2d 918 (1988) (emphasis in original). The Kansas court then examined the laws of the five states—only to conclude that *none* of the five was in conflict with the law of Kansas. It therefore entered a new judgment reflecting no change in the original outcome of the case regarding liability and the applicable prejudgment interest rate. See generally Miller & Crump, *Jurisdiction and Choice of Law in Multistate Class Actions After* Phillips Petroleum Co. v. Shutts, 96 Yale L.J. 1 (1986).

2. In Shaffer v. Heitner, p. 98, supra, the Supreme Court stated that "all assertions of state-court jurisdiction must be evaluated according to the standards set forth in *International Shoe* and its progeny." Does *Shutts* mean that class plaintiffs are not entitled to this protection? Or is *Shutts* based upon the inference of consent from a class member's failure to opt-out of the class? Rule 23 imposes notice and opt-out requirements only in subdivision (b)(3) class actions. Does the concept, articulated in *Shutts,* that the right to opt out is a fundamental due process requirement mean that there is a constitutional right to opt out of class suits brought as Rule 23 (b)(1) or (b)(2) class actions? Footnote 3 in the *Shutts* opinion, p. 422, supra, implies that the ruling is limited to subdivision (b)(3) class actions but applies—at a minimum—to claims "wholly or predominately for monetary judgments." This has caused some confusion about what to do when there is a hybrid class action

for both equitable and monetary relief. See p. 401, supra. The Supreme Court has twice heard arguments on the applicability of *Shutts* to Rule 23(b)(1) and (b)(2) classes, but dismissed both cases on the ground that certiorari had been improperly granted. See Ticor Title Ins. Co. v. Brown, 511 U.S. 117, 114 S.Ct. 1359, 128 L.Ed.2d 33 (1994), and Adams v. Robertson, 520 U.S. 83, 117 S.Ct. 1028, 137 L.Ed.2d 203 (1997).

3. VENUE

Only the residences of the class representatives are important for purposes of venue; the residences of absent class members and intervenors are irrelevant. See 7A Wright, Miller & Kane, Federal Practice and Procedure: Civil 3d § 1757.

SECTION F. THE PRECLUSIVE EFFECT OF A CLASS ACTION JUDGMENT

In Hansberry v. Lee, p. 410, supra, the Court said that due process is satisfied and the judgment is binding on all class members when the interests of the class are represented adequately during the suit. Questions remain, however, as to when a class action judgment properly binds all class members.

In STEPHENSON v. DOW CHEMICAL CO., 273 F.3d 249 (2d Cir. 2001), affirmed by an equally divided Court, in part, and vacated on other grounds, in part 539 U.S. 111, 123 S.Ct. 2161, 156 L.Ed.2d 106 (2003), the Court considered whether to accord preclusive effect to a class action judgment involving veterans of the war in Vietnam. See p. 279, supra. In 1983, the Eastern District of New York certified a plaintiff class consisting of "all persons who were in the United States, New Zealand or Australian Armed Forces at any time from 1962 to 1971 who were injured in or near Vietnam by exposure to Agent Orange or other phenoxy herbicides, [and the] spouses, parents and children of veterans born before January 1, 1984, directly or derivatively injured as a result of the exposure." The class included 15,000 named plaintiffs and nearly 2.5 million potential class members. See In re "Agent Orange" Product Liability Litigation, 100 F.R.D. 718 (E.D.N.Y. 1983), affirmed 818 F.2d 145 (2d Cir. 1987), certiorari denied 484 U.S. 1004, 108 S.Ct. 695, 98 L.Ed.2d 648 (1988). The next year, the case settled and defendants agreed to establish a $180 million fund to make payments to individual class members and to agencies that serve Vietnam veterans. In approving the settlement, the district judge declined to appoint counsel for a subclass of veterans whose injuries might be latent and so who might need to file future claims, but the judge stated that he was taking their interests into account. For a discussion of the District Court proceedings, see Rubenstein, *Finality in Class Action Litigation: Lessons from Habeas*, 82 N.Y.U. L. Rev. 790, 801–04 (2007). Fifteen years later, Stephenson, a Vietnam veteran who had not opted out of the court-approved settlement, was diagnosed with cancer. He believed that his condition was caused by his exposure to Agent Orange during his years of military service. However, under the class settlement, Stephenson was not entitled to any money because he did not file his claim before 1994, the cut-off date for getting compensation. Stephenson filed an individual action, which was dismissed as precluded by the settlement. On appeal, the Second Circuit reversed, holding that the interests of future claimants had not been represented adequately and therefore could not be precluded by the settlement. The Supreme Court affirmed by an equally divided Court without opinion. On remand, the District Court dismissed the claim. See Isaacson v. Dow Chem. Co. (In re "Agent Orange" Product Liability Litigation), 304 F.Supp.2d 404 (E.D.N.Y. 2004), stay lifted 344 F.Supp.2d 873 (E.D.N.Y. 2004). *Stephenson* leaves open important questions about adequacy of representation and collateral challenges to class action settlements. See Nagareda, *Administering Adequacy in Class Representation*, 82 Texas L. Rev. 287 (2003); Wirt, *Missed Opportunity:* Stephenson v. Dow Chemical Co. *and the Finality of Class Action Settlements*, 109 Penn. St. L. Rev. 1297 (2005).

CHAPTER 10

PRETRIAL DEVICES FOR OBTAINING INFORMATION: DEPOSITIONS AND DISCOVERY

■ ■ ■

In this Chapter, we examine procedures that allow and in some situations require parties to exchange information during the pretrial stage of a litigation. American discovery practice, said by some commentators to be of "constitutional foundation," Hazard, *From Whom No Secrets Are Hid*, 76 Texas L. Rev. 1665, 1694 (1998), appears rather exceptional from the perspective of judicial systems in other nations. See Subrin, *Discovery in Global Perspective: Are We Nuts?*, 52 DePaul L. Rev. 299 (2002). Discovery did not exist at common law, and only limited discovery was available in early English equity practice. The introduction of broad discovery with the Federal Rules of Civil Procedure ushered in a "revolution" that has radically altered litigation practice. Subrin, *Fishing Expeditions Allowed: The Historical Background to the 1938 Federal Discovery Rules*, 39 B.C. L. Rev. 691, 738 (1998). Over the years, the federal discovery rules have been amended numerous times to deal with an array of issues such as delay, cost, and technological change. Although discovery is an intensely practical topic, it also is among "the most debated, and in some cases the most fractious and vexing, aspect of litigation today." Beckerman, *Confronting Civil Discovery's Fatal Flaws*, 84 Minn. L. Rev. 505, 505 (2000).

SECTION A. THE GENERAL SCOPE OF DISCOVERY

———

Read Federal Rule of Civil Procedure 26 in the Supplement.

———

1. THE ROLE OF DISCOVERY
IN CIVIL LITIGATION

Modern discovery serves a number of purposes that are important to individual litigants and to the civil justice system as a whole.

From the private perspective, the first, and least controversial, purpose of discovery is the preservation of relevant information that might not be available at trial. Basically, this objective relates to the testimony of witnesses who are aged or ill or who will be out of the jurisdiction at the time the trial commences. The earliest discovery procedures in the federal courts were designed primarily for this purpose. See *Developments in the Law—Discovery*, 74 Harv. L. Rev. 940, 949 (1961). The second purpose is to ascertain and isolate those issues that actually are in controversy between the parties. There is little dispute that it is appropriate for one party to ask whether another party contests the existence or nonexistence of a fact that the pleadings formally have put in issue. A third purpose of discovery is to find out what testimony and other evidence is available on each of the disputed factual issues. Prior to discovery, a party could ascertain these matters only through private investigation; if, for example, a witness refused to discuss a matter with a party, there was no way to learn the substance of that witness's testimony in advance of trial. As a result, cases often turned on the parties' relative access to the facts and their ability to keep certain matters secret until the trial. Views about discovery reflect a division between those who favor broad discovery to obviate all traces of surprise and those who allege the need for privacy of investigation and adversarial development of evidence.

From the public perspective, discovery helps to promote transparency by making information about government and corporate practice available to a broader set of individuals than just the parties to a lawsuit. Discovery also enables individual litigants to serve as private attorneys general on behalf of the public. Professor Carrington has explained:

> Private litigants do in America much of what is done in other industrial states by public officers working within an administrative bureaucracy. Every day, hundreds of American lawyers caution their clients that an unlawful course of conduct will be accompanied by serious risk of exposure at the hands of some hundreds of thousands of lawyers, each armed with a subpoena power by which misdeeds can be uncovered. Unless corresponding new powers are conferred on public officers, constricting discovery would diminish the disincentives for lawless behavior across a wide spectrum of forbidden conduct.

Carrington, *Renovating Discovery*, 49 Ala. L. Rev. 51, 54 (1997). See also Higginbotham, *Foreword*, 49 Ala. L. Rev. 1, 4–5 (1997) ("Congress has elected to use the private suit, private attorneys-general as an enforcing mechanism for the anti-trust laws, the securities laws, environmental laws, civil rights and more. In the main, the plaintiff in these suits must discover his evidence from the defendant. Calibration of discovery is calibration of the level of enforcement of the social policy set by Congress.'').

2. DISCOVERY PRIOR TO COMMENCING A LAWSUIT

Read Federal Rule of Civil Procedure 27 in the Supplement.

IN RE PETITION OF SHEILA ROBERTS FORD

United States District Court, Middle District of Alabama, 1997.
170 F.R.D. 504.

THOMPSON, CHIEF JUDGE.

* * *

On November 15, 1996, Ford filed, through counsel, her petition pursuant to [Federal] Rule [of Civil Procedure] 27. In the petition, Ford asks "for leave to proceed with the deposition of Elmore County Sheriff Bill Franklin." She alleges that she "expects to be a party to an action in the United States District Court for the Middle District of Alabama, Northern Division, but is presently unable to bring said action"; that the "anticipated action surrounds the shooting death of Fred William Roberts by law-enforcement officers of Elmore County on November 8, 1996"; that she "is the Administratrix of the Estate of Fred William Roberts"; that she "intends to establish who the appropriate party defendants to the anticipated action are through the testimony of Elmore County Sheriff Bill Franklin"; that she "is unable to determine the appropriate party defendants and the basic facts surrounding the death of Fred William Roberts without the testimony of Sheriff Franklin" and "needs to establish an accurate account of the events that took place ... before the memories of those involved fade or become dist[or]ted by publicity"; and that she is "requesting the deposition of ... Franklin" because he "was the commanding officer of the Elmore County deputies believed to be involved in the shooting of ... Roberts" and he "is expected to identify the facts involved in Mr. Roberts' shooting death as well as the identity of the law enforcement officers involved." Ford also gave the names, addresses, and descriptions of the persons she expected to be adverse parties.

* * *

A hearing was held on the petition on December 13. At the hearing, Sheriff Franklin appeared through counsel and stated that he opposed the petition because it was not authorized by Rule 27. Ford responded by reaffirming that she needed to take Sheriff Franklin's deposition in order "to determine ... the basic facts surrounding the death of Fred William Roberts." Without this information, she said, she could not determine whom to sue. She did not know whether Sheriff Franklin or one of his deputies shot Roberts and whether the shooting was justified.

II. Discussion

* * *

Admittedly, Ford * * * asserts in her petition a desire to preserve testimony; she states that she "needs to establish an accurate account of the events that took place before the memories of those involved fade or become dist[or]ted by publicity." This reason is not credible, however. Ford can do this by simply filing suit today. She presented no evidence that Sheriff Franklin's testimony is in imminent danger of being lost because he is gravely ill or about to leave the country. Ford therefore wishes only to discover or uncover what happened on November 8. The simple question for the court is whether Rule 27 authorizes such relief.

* * * [T]he first and obvious place to look to determine whether Rule 27 authorizes pre-complaint discovery is the language of the rule itself. If the language of the rule is unambiguous and dispositive and is reasonable within its context, then the court should go no further and simply should enforce the language. Here, Rule 27 meets this straightforward test.

Subsection (a)(1) of Rule 27 provides, as stated, that "A person who desires to *perpetuate* testimony regarding any matter that may be cognizable in any court of the United States may file a verified petition." (Emphasis added.) Subsection (a)(3) then provides that an order allowing examination may be entered only "If the court is satisfied that the *perpetuation* of the testimony may prevent a failure or delay of justice." (Emphasis added.) [The language of these provisions has been altered by the 2007 restyling of the Federal Rules. These changes are not substantive.] Rule 27's coverage therefore extends only to the "perpetuation" of testimony. The term "perpetuate" is defined as "to make perpetual," "preserve from extinction," or "cause to last indefinitely." Webster's Third International Dictionary, unabridged 1685 (1976); see also Black's Law Dictionary 1027 (5th ed. 1979) ("perpetuating testimony" is a "means ... for *preserving* the testimony of witness, which might otherwise be lost before the trial in which it is intended to be used") (emphasis added). Here, Ford seeks to discover or uncover testimony, not to perpetuate it. She seeks pre-complaint discovery of evidence, not pre-complaint perpetuation of it. There is nothing before the court to indicate that Sheriff Franklin's testimony is in imminent danger of being lost. Rather, Ford simply wants to know who shot Roberts and why. Rule 27 simply does not provide for such discovery.

* * *

Ford also argues that Rule 27 should be read in conjunction with Rule 11 * * *. The problem, however, is that Rule 27 is not a vehicle for compliance with Rule 11. As stated, the language in Rule 27 is clear that the rule authorizes the perpetuation of evidence, not the discovery or uncovering of it. * * *

To be sure, the court in In the Matter of Alpha Industries, 159 F.R.D. 456 (S.D.N.Y. 1995), reached a contrary understanding of the relationship between Rule 11 and Rule 27. There, as explained by the district court, * * * "[I]n the case at bar, *the fact that petitioner must delay bringing suit until receiving the information sought is a sufficient showing to allow the use of Rule 27 to perpetuate respondent's testimony.*" Alpha Industries, 159 F.R.D. at 457 * * * (emphasis added).

This court disagrees with Alpha Industries * * *.

The court is not without sympathy for Ford. She is understand[ably] deeply troubled by and concerned about the shooting death of her father. If a law enforcement officer was at fault she desires to have him or her held accountable in a court of law. But, under Rule 11, she cannot file suit against any one without first having uncovered some "evidentiary support" for holding the person liable or having obtained some preliminary evidence that there is likely to be some "evidentiary support after a reasonable opportunity for further investigation or discovery." [The language as changed now appears in Rule 11(b)(3).] Similarly, the defense of qualified immunity protects law enforcement officials from federal suit in the absence of detailed factual allegations of a violation of a clearly established federal right. * * * However, without the discovery incident to litigation, Ford is without the means to uncover whether her father was a victim of foul play in violation of a clearly established federal right. Her predicament is a "Catch 22." Indeed, she must feel that, under the rules established by our civil justice system, a law enforcement officer can get away with murder. This court has no answer for her, however, other than that Rule 27 does not offer an avenue of relief.

* * *

It is further ORDERED that costs are taxed against petitioner Ford, for which execution may issue.

<h3 style="text-align:center">NOTES AND QUESTIONS</h3>

1. What are the advantages and disadvantages of a provision permitting a prospective plaintiff to discover facts to aid in deciding whether or not a legal action is justified and in ascertaining against whom it should be brought? How should the costs of such a procedure be allocated between the prospective plaintiff and the prospective defendant? Does the Supreme Court's establishment of a "plausibility" standard for pleading, p. 297, supra, affect your view on this subject? For a discussion of Rule 27, arguing that courts should allow precomplaint discovery "both to preserve evidence and to help frame a complaint," see Kronfeld, Note—*The Preservation and Discovery of Evidence Under Federal Rule of Civil Procedure 27*, 78 Geo. L.J. 593 (1990).

2. Texas, among a small number of states, allows a private individual to take a presuit deposition in order to investigate a potential claim. Texas Rule 202 provides that a person "may petition the court for an order authorizing the taking of a deposition on oral examination or written questions either: (a) to perpetuate or obtain the person's own testimony or that of any other person for use in an anticipated suit; or (b) to investigate a potential claim or suit." Tex. R. Civ. P. 202.1(a)-(b). In order to prevent abuse of the rule, what should a court require petitioner to demonstrate? See Hoffman, *Access to Information, Access to Justice: The Role of Presuit Investigatory Discovery*, 40 U. Mich. J.L. Reform 217 (2007).

3. THE SCOPE OF DISCOVERY: RELEVANCE

———

Read Federal Rule of Civil Procedure 26 and the accompanying materials in the Supplement.

———

NOTES AND QUESTIONS

1. Rule 26(b) was amended in 2000 and now limits discovery requests to material "relevant to any party's claim or defense." However, "[f]or good cause," the court may order further discovery "of any matter relevant to the subject matter involved in the action," which returns discovery to its prior scope. The Advisory Committee Note to the changes in Rule 26(b)(1) explains:

> The Committee intends that the parties and the court focus on the actual claims and defenses involved in the action. The dividing line between information relevant to the claims and defenses and that relevant only to the subject matter of the action cannot be defined with precision. A variety of types of information not directly pertinent to the incident in suit could be relevant to the claims or defenses raised in a given action. For example, other incidents of the same type, or involving the same product could be properly discoverable under the revised standard. Information about organizational arrangements or filing systems of a party could be discoverable if likely to yield or lead to the discovery of admissible information. Similarly, information that could be used to impeach a likely witness, although not otherwise relevant to the claims or defenses, might be properly discoverable. * * *

2. In WORLD WRESTLING FEDERATION ENTERTAINMENT, INC. v. WILLIAM MORRIS AGENCY, INC., 204 F.R.D. 263 (S.D.N.Y. 2001), a breach of contract action, the court refused to allow plaintiff to discover defendant's contractual agreements with third parties, explaining that the "treatment of one contracting party in the entertainment field does not really illuminate or is not really relevant to how another party in the entertainment field is treated" (internal citation omitted). Is this ruling consistent with the Advisory Committee Note discussed above? For an analysis of decisions

interpreting the new claim-or-defense relevance standard, see Rowe, *A Square Peg in a Round Hole? The 2000 Limitation on the Scope of Federal Civil Discovery*, 69 Tenn. L. Rev. 13 (2001).

3. Courts are still developing how best to effectuate the new claim-and-defense approach to relevance. What do you think of a test that looks to the "logical relationship between the information sought and possible proof or refutation of the claim or defense at trial"? What are its advantages and disadvantages? See Stempel & Herr, *Applying Amended Rule 26(b)(1) in Litigation: The New Scope of Discovery*, 199 F.R.D. 396 (2001).

4. The concept of proportionality, introduced by amendment to the Federal Rules in 1983, further limits the concept of relevance and is currently set out in Rule 26(b)(2)(C). The goal of proportionality is "to promote judicial limitation of the amount of discovery on a case-by-case basis to avoid abuse or overuse of discovery * * *." 8 Wright, Miller & Marcus, Federal Practice and Procedure: Civil 2d § 2008.1. The reporter to the Advisory Committee that first adopted proportionality as a limitation on discovery called it a "180–degree shift" in discovery philosophy. See Miller, The August 1983 Amendments to the Federal Rules of Civil Procedure: Promoting Effective Case Management and Lawyer Responsibility 32–33 (Fed. Jud. Center 1984). However, in practice, the amendment "created only a ripple" in the caselaw, and in 2000 the rules were amended again to underscore this limitation. 8 Wright, Miller & Marcus, Federal Practice and Procedure: Civil 2d § 2008.1. In 2006, amendments to Rule 26(b)(2)(C) imposed specific limitations on the discovery of electronically stored information.

5. What weight should a court give to a party's individual resources in setting limits on discovery? Is a discovery request that otherwise would be barred or disproportionate to the needs of a case permissible simply because the party from whom the discovery is sought has a "deep pocket"? On the other hand, should a relatively wealthy litigant be able to buy additional discovery by offering to pay the expenses of a financially weak litigant? Should relatively wealthy antagonists be permitted to stipulate to unlimited discovery?

6. *Twombly* may be read as suggesting that the cost of discovery is a factor to be considered in deciding a motion to dismiss, p. 312, supra. To what extent should the court's assessment of the likelihood of a party's prevailing on the merits enter, if at all, into a decision about the scope of discovery? In a case that predates *Twombly*, CABLE ELECTRIC PRODUCTS, INC. v. GEN-MARK, INC., 586 F.Supp. 1505 (N.D. Cal. 1984), vacated on other grounds 770 F.2d 1015 (Fed. Cir. 1985), the court granted summary judgment to defendant in an unfair-competition action brought by the manufacturer of a light-sensitive "night light." It rejected plaintiff's request that the court not rule on the motion until it had the opportunity to complete discovery concerning actual confusion that may have been occurring in the marketplace as a result of alleged similarities in labeling and packaging the products, since the court thought that the probability was "vanishingly small" that plaintiff could uncover such evidence. If Rule 26(b)(2)(C)(iii) had been in effect when *Cable Electric Products* was decided, could the decision have been supported on the ground that "the burden or expense of the proposed discovery

outweighs its likely benefit"? See generally Note, *Summary Judgment Before the Completion of Discovery: A Proposed Revision of Federal Rule of Civil Procedure 56(f)*, 24 U. Mich. J.L. Reform 253 (1990).

4. THE CONCEPT OF PROPORTIONALITY AND DISCRETIONARY LIMITS ON DISCOVERY

————

Read Federal Rule of Civil Procedure 26(c) in the Supplement.

————

SEATTLE TIMES CO. v. RHINEHART

Supreme Court of the United States, 1984.
467 U.S. 20, 104 S.Ct. 2199, 81 L.Ed.2d 17.

[Rhinehart and the Aquarian Foundation, a religious group of which Rhinehart was spiritual leader, brought an action for defamation and invasion of privacy in a Washington state court against the publishers and authors of several critical articles. Pursuant to state discovery rules modeled on the Federal Rules, the trial court issued an order compelling plaintiffs to identify donors and the amounts each contributed and to produce a list of the foundation's members. However, the court also issued a protective order prohibiting defendants from publishing the information or otherwise using it except as necessary to prepare for and try the case. Plaintiffs had submitted affidavits showing that public release of donor and membership lists would adversely affect foundation membership and subject its members to harassment. Both sides appealed and the Washington Supreme Court affirmed both orders. The state Supreme Court held that the protective order served the interest of the judiciary in protecting the integrity of its discovery processes, an interest sufficient to sustain it against the claim that it infringed on First Amendment rights.]

Certiorari to the Supreme Court of Washington.

JUSTICE POWELL delivered the opinion of the Court.

* * *

* * * The Washington Civil Rules enable parties to litigation to obtain information "relevant to the subject matter involved" that they believe will be helpful in the preparation and trial of the case. Rule 26, however, must be viewed in its entirety. Liberal discovery is provided for the sole purpose of assisting in the preparation and trial, or the settlement, of litigated disputes. Because of the liberality of pretrial discovery permitted by Rule 26(b)(1), it is necessary for the trial court to have the authority to issue protective orders conferred by Rule 26(c). It is clear from experience that pretrial discovery by depositions and interrogatories has a significant potential for abuse. This abuse is not limited to matters of delay and expense; discovery also may seriously implicate privacy interests of litigants and third parties. The Rules do not distinguish between public and private information. Nor do they apply only to parties to the litigation, as relevant information in the hands of third parties may be subject to discovery.

There is an opportunity, therefore, for litigants to obtain—incidentally or purposefully—information that not only is irrelevant but if publicly released could be damaging to reputation and privacy. The government clearly has a substantial interest in preventing this sort of abuse of its processes. * * * The prevention of the abuse that can attend the coerced production of information under a State's discovery rule is sufficient justification for the authorization of protective orders.[22]

We also find that the provision for protective orders in the Washington Rules requires, in itself, no heightened First Amendment scrutiny. To be sure, Rule 26(c) confers broad discretion on the trial court to decide when a protective order is appropriate and what degree of protection is required. The Legislature of the State of Washington, following the example of the Congress in its approval of the Federal Rules of Civil Procedure, has determined that such discretion is necessary, and we find no reason to disagree. The trial court is in the best position to weigh fairly the competing needs and interests of parties affected by discovery.[23] The unique character of the discovery process requires that the trial court have substantial latitude to fashion protective orders.

The facts in this case illustrate the concerns that justifiably may prompt a court to issue a protective order. As we have noted, the trial court's order allowing discovery was extremely broad. It compelled respondents—among other things—to identify all persons who had made donations over a 5–year period to Rhinehart and the Aquarian Foundation, together with the amounts donated. In effect the order would compel disclosure of membership as well as sources of financial support. The Supreme Court of Washington found that dissemination of this information would "result in annoyance, embarrassment and even oppression." * * * It is sufficient for purposes of our decision that the highest court in the State found no abuse of discretion in the trial court's decision to issue a protective order pursuant to a constitutional state law. We therefore hold that where, as in this case, a protective order is entered on a showing of good cause as required by Rule 26(c), is limited to the context of pretrial civil discovery, and does not restrict the dissemination of the information if gained from other sources, it does not offend the First Amendment.

---

22. The Supreme Court of Washington properly emphasized the importance of ensuring that potential litigants have unimpeded access to the courts: "[A]s the trial court rightly observed, rather than expose themselves to unwanted publicity, individuals may well forego the pursuit of their just claims. The judicial system will thus have made the utilization of its remedies so onerous that the people will be reluctant or unwilling to use it, resulting in frustration of a right as valuable as that of speech itself." 654 P.2d, at 689. * * *

23. In addition, heightened First Amendment scrutiny of each request for a protective order would necessitate burdensome evidentiary findings and could lead to time-consuming interlocutory appeals, as this case illustrates. * * *

The judgment accordingly is

Affirmed.

[The concurring opinion of JUSTICE BRENNAN, with whom JUSTICE MARSHALL joined, is omitted.]

NOTES AND QUESTIONS

1. What is "good cause" for a protective order under Rule 26(c)? The courts generally have required the moving party to demonstrate that "disclosure will work a clearly defined and very serious injury." Publicker Indus., Inc. v. Cohen, 733 F.2d 1059, 1071 (3d Cir. 1984). The movant must make a showing "by specific examples or articulated reasoning," Cipollone v. Liggett Group, Inc., 785 F.2d 1108, 1121 (3d Cir. 1986), certiorari denied 484 U.S. 976, 108 S.Ct. 487, 98 L.Ed.2d 485 (1987), and cannot rely on "stereotyped and conclusory statements." General Dynamics Corp. v. Selb Mfg. Co., 481 F.2d 1204, 1212 (8th Cir. 1973). Courts then use a balancing test to determine whether the protective order should issue. Pansy v. Borough of Stroudsburg, 23 F.3d 772, 787 (3d Cir. 1994). What factors ought the court weigh? Does a balancing test of this character make application of the discovery rules unpredictable and uneven?

2. Do additional factors come into play when a party seeks discovery from a top government official? Federal appellate courts generally permit discovery of such officials only in "extraordinary circumstances." Arnold v. Pennsylvania Dept. of Transp., 477 F.3d 105, 423 (3d Cir. 2007). However, in rare cases, even presidents "have responded to written interrogatories, given depositions and provided videotaped trial testimony." Clinton v. Jones, 520 U.S. 681, 691 n.14, 117 S.Ct. 1636, 1643 n.14, 137 L.Ed.2d 945, 959 n.14 (1997). What factors ought to guide the District Court's approach to discovery in these circumstances? Of what significance are case management techniques that allow the court to cabin discovery in ways that minimize its potentially disruptive effect on executive function? See Ashcroft v. Iqbal, p. 307, supra.

3. To what extent is it relevant that a suit is chiefly brought for the purpose of obtaining private information about defendant to disclose it publicly? Suppose a third person, desirous of obtaining such private information, finances plaintiff's suit?

4. Should the court have issued an order denying or compelling discovery in each of these cases:

(a) MUTUAL OF OMAHA INSURANCE. CO. v. GARRIGAN, 31 Ohio Misc. 1, 4, 285 N.E.2d 395, 396–97 (1971). Plaintiff insurance company brought an action against the widow of its insured, asking for a declaration that the insured's death by carbon monoxide poisoning had not been accidental and hence was not covered by the policy. The company sought to discover the corpse, which would have required disinterment.

(b) WILLIAMS v. THOMAS JEFFERSON UNIVERSITY, 343 F.Supp. 1131, 1132 (E.D. Pa. 1972). Plaintiff, in a medical malpractice action involving abortion, sought to discover the names of women who previously had abortions at defendant hospital. The stated purpose was to gather evidence to impeach testimony expected to be given by defendant doctor.

(c) RASMUSSEN v. SOUTH FLORIDA BLOOD SERVICE, INC., 500 So.2d 533 (Fla. 1987), and SNYDER v. MEKHJIAN, 125 N.J. 328, 593 A.2d 318 (1991). In both of these cases, persons who claimed to have received an HIV-positive blood transfusion sought discovery from a blood bank as to the identity of the blood donor.

(d) BUCHER v. RICHARDSON HOSPITAL AUTHORITY, 160 F.R.D. 88 (D.C. Tex. 1994). Parents sued a hospital alleging that their daughter was abused sexually while she was a patient there receiving treatment. Defendant sought to depose the minor. In support of the motion to quash, a psychiatrist testified that the minor "has an impulse control disorder and is a suicide risk if deposed."

5. It has become commonplace in large cases for parties to stipulate to protective orders negotiated by opposing counsel. And judges generally assent to these agreements, in large part to move cases along and avoid controversy. The stipulations typically provide for "umbrella" protection for confidential information, which is defined as any information that is designated "confidential" by the producing party. The result of these orders is that virtually all nonpublic documents are designated confidential without any individualized review. See Moskowitz, *Discovering Discovery: Non-Party Access to Pretrial Information in the Federal Courts 1938–2006*, 78 U. Colo. L. Rev. 817 (2006). Why have these orders become so common? What is the strategic significance for a defendant of a confidentiality order? Does disclosure to third persons open the door to misuse of the court system for blackmail or extortion through the threat of suits involving sensitive issues? What does a plaintiff's attorney gain by agreeing to a broad protective order? Are these orders consistent with the Supreme Court's analysis in *Seattle Times*, p. 436, supra? Or is some degree of judicial review necessary? Should umbrella orders be enforced as written? What standard should a court apply if asked to modify an existing protective order to permit the disclosure of discovered material to non-parties? Is it relevant that the matter shielded from public view by the protective order is alleged to impact public health and safety? For a discussion of these issues, see Miller, *Confidentiality, Protective Orders, and Public Access to the Courts*, 105 Harv. L. Rev. 428 (1991). On protective orders generally, see Friedenthal, *Secrecy and Confidentiality in Civil Litigation: Discovery and Party Agreements*, 9 J. of L. & Pol'y 61 (2000). For a range of views on the subject, see *Symposium: Secrecy in Litigation*, 81 Chi.-Kent L. Rev. 305 (2006).

SECTION B. MANDATORY DISCLOSURE AND THE DISCOVERY PLAN

1. MANDATORY DISCLOSURE

———

Read Federal Rule of Civil Procedure 26(a) in the Supplement.

———

The Federal Rules were amended in 1993 to require the parties to transmit information "without awaiting a discovery request." Fed. R. Civ.

P. 26(a)(1)(A). The proposal to establish a duty of mandatory disclosure generated intense controversy among judges, practitioners, and legal scholars, and the Supreme Court divided, six to three, in its support of the provision. Arguments against mandatory disclosure focused on its inconsistency with adversarial principles, and concerns that it would increase expense and cause delay. Early commentators expressed concern that mandatory disclosure would decrease the likelihood of settlement, but more recent analysis suggests that mandatory disclosure, because it equalizes the availability of credible information, reduces the number of disputes that proceed to trial. Rule 26 was amended again in
2000 and Rule
26(a)(1) now requires a party, as part of its initial
disclosure, to produce
only information that will "support its claims and defenses." Previously, each party had to provide information "relevant to disputed facts alleged with particularity in the pleadings." The 2000 amendment also exempts from mandatory initial and pretrial disclosures information to be used "solely for impeachment."

What does mandatory disclosure require in terms of actual production of documents? In COMAS v. UNITED TELEPHONE CO. OF KANSAS, 1995 WL 476691 (D. Kan. 1995), the Magistrate Judge explained:

> Initial disclosures may be made by describing or categorizing potentially relevant materials so that the opposing party may "make an informed decision regarding which documents might need to be examined." Fed. R. Civ. P. 26(a)(1) advisory committee's notes (1993 Am.). The rule does not require that either party produce documents at this initial stage. If only a description or categorization is provided, "the other part[y] [is] expected to obtain the documents desired by proceeding under Rule 34 or through informal requests."

> Rule 26(a)(1) allows initial disclosures to be made by producing copies of the relevant documents. Parties, therefore, may agree to produce all relevant documents without discovery requests. Production at this stage speeds the discovery process.

As adopted in 1993, mandatory disclosure applied to every type of case. In 2000, the amendment added a new provision, Rule 26(a)(1)(B), excluding eight types of cases in which there is little need for discovery or in which a party is likely to be conducting his or her own case. Is it appropriate in this circumstance to depart from the rule of uniform rule making? Should the court have discretion to order mandatory disclosure? See Subrin, *Uniformity in Procedural Rules and the Attributes of a Sound Procedural System: The Case for Presumptive Limits*, 49 Ala. L. Rev. 79 (1997).

2. THE DISCOVERY PLAN

———

Read Federal Rule of Civil Procedure 26(f) in the Supplement.

———

An important part of the judicial response to concerns about discovery abuse is reflected in the series of amendments to Rules 16 and 26 to encourage active judicial supervision of the discovery process. In 1980, Rule 26(f) was adopted to provide for a discovery conference among the parties and the court, but it was not contemplated as a routine procedure. Then, in 1983, Rule 16 was amended to encourage district courts to schedule early pretrial conferences and required them, after consultation with the parties by pretrial conference or otherwise, to issue scheduling orders limiting the time for the parties, among other things, to complete discovery. In 1993, Rule 26(f) was altered and harmonized with Rule 16. Rule 26(f) was amended to require the parties to meet by themselves to arrange for mandatory disclosures under Rule 26(a)(1) and to develop a comprehensive proposed discovery plan that they then present to the court prior to the time the court's scheduling order is due under Rule 16(b). However, courts were free to issue standing orders that exempted all, or certain types of cases, from the Rule 26(f) requirements. In 2000, Rule 26(f) was amended once again. First, it eliminated the need of the parties to "meet," instead allowing them to "confer" to avoid logistical problems that sometimes sent litigants to court for relief. Second, it eliminated standing exemption orders but left intact the power of the court to exempt or alter the requirements for any particular case before it. (The amended rule does exempt those special cases that are exempted from mandatory disclosure under Rule 26(a)(1).) These Rules are designed to counter the procrastination and delay that is natural to busy lawyers and to give the courts ample control over the discovery process. Rule 26(f) also expects the parties, when conferring, to consider "the possibilities for promptly settling or resolving the case." How does the early exchange of information promote that goal?

SECTION C. THE MECHANICS OF REQUESTED DISCOVERY

1. DEPOSITIONS AND DEPOSITIONS UPON WRITTEN QUESTIONS

———

Read Federal Rules of Civil Procedure 26(d), 30, and 31 in the Supplement.

———

An oral deposition allows a party to question any person (the "deponent"), whether a party or not, under oath. The Federal Rules spell out in detail when, how, before whom, and on what notice as to time and place a deposition may be taken (see Federal Rules 28, 29, 30, 31, and 32(d)). Invariably, the parties designate as officer the reporter who records the questions, the answers, and any objections made by the parties or by the witness. Under Federal Rule 30(d)(1), "a deposition is limited to 1 day of 7 hours," but the court may authorize additional time "if needed to fairly examine the deponent or if the deponent, another person, or any other circumstance impedes or delays the examination." When the deposition is concluded, the reporter prepares a transcript, which the deponent then is called upon to sign. Federal Rule 30(a)(2)(A)(i) sets a presumptive limit of ten depositions for each party.

An attorney schedules a deposition merely by serving a notice on the opposing attorney. The notice must include the name and address of the deponent, if known, and the date, time, and place of the deposition. If the deponent is a party, the notice is sufficient to require the party's appearance, and a subpoena is unnecessary. The notice may include a demand that the party produce documents and other items of evidence at the deposition, in which case the procedure of Rule 34 applies.

Under Federal Rule 30(b)(6) an attorney may notice the deposition of a corporation or association, requiring the latter to produce the person or persons having knowledge of the subject matter upon which the deposition is to be taken. Of course, the party seeking the information must detail the issues that are to be explored in order that the organization can ascertain which of its personnel has the relevant knowledge. This form of corporate deposition is useful particularly when the party taking the deposition is unaware of which individual or individuals within a large organization have the information that is needed.

If the deponent is not a party, the notice of deposition will not be sufficient to compel the nonparty's appearance. There is no requirement that a nonparty be subpoenaed to a deposition. However, a nonparty is not subject to any sanction if he is not subpoenaed and does not appear, or if he appears but fails to bring requested documents or other items. A person who fails to respond to a subpoena will be subject to a citation for contempt of court. In addition, if a party notices a deposition, but does not subpoena the witness, and, if the witness fails to appear, that party may be ordered to pay the reasonable expenses, including attorneys' fees, of any other party for wasting time appearing at the place where the deposition was to be taken. Thus, unless full cooperation of the nonparty witness is certain, the use of a subpoena is advisable. Finally, the presumptive seven-hour limit on a deposition may be ineffective to protect a nonparty from a long, intense session because the parties can agree among themselves to a longer deposition for a nonparty.

The usual expectation is that a deposition will proceed without court involvement. The deponent usually will answer even those questions to which counsel object, unless the deponent's counsel instructs him not to answer. Counsel interpose objections at depositions to preserve their right to object to another party's use of the deposition's transcript at trial. Counsel must object at the deposition if the ground for the objection is one that might be corrected at the time. Under Rule 30(c)(2), a deponent may be instructed not to answer only when necessary "to preserve a privilege, to enforce a limitation ordered by the court, or to present a motion under Rule 30(d)(3)" to terminate or limit an examination that is oppressive or conducted in bad faith. Moreover, Rule 30(d)(2) authorizes the imposition of costs and attorney's fees to sanction any culpable individual who "impedes, delays, or frustrates the fair examination of the deponent."

NOTES AND QUESTIONS

1. The oral deposition has been called "[t]he most important of the discovery devices":

> It is the only significant discovery device that may be directed against any person, and is not confined to parties to the action. It is the only discovery device that permits examination and cross-examination of a live witness by counsel, where there is no opportunity to reflect and carefully shape the information given. Thus, despite its expense, it is the most valuable device if the deponent has important information.

Wright & Kane, Federal Courts § 84 (6th ed. 2002). Under the 1938 version of Federal Rule 30, the parties competed to take the first deposition, in an attempt to pin down an opponent before submitting himself or his own witnesses to the discovery process. How does the 1938 version differ from present deposition practice? Have amendments, including mandatory disclosure and the discovery conference, altered the parties' strategic approach to priority?

2. Review the rules governing the deposition of a corporate party. What if a corporate party whose deposition is noted under Rule 30(b)(6) deliberately selects a person to testify who appears for the deposition but who lacks information sufficient to respond to the questions asked? Can the court order sanctions under Rule 37(d) without first issuing an order to compel discovery and giving the deponent an opportunity to comply? For a rejection of the literal reading of the Rule, see Black Horse Lane Assoc., L.P. v. Dow Chemical Corp., 228 F.3d 275 (3d Cir. 2000) (lack of knowledge by selected deponent is tantamount to failure to appear under Rule 37(d)).

3. Federal Rule 31 authorizes the taking of depositions upon written questions from parties and nonparties. The answers are given orally after the "officer" puts the questions to the deponent. In practice, written depositions are rarely used. 8A Wright, Miller & Marcus, Federal Practice and Procedure: Civil 2d § 2131. Why? When might they be useful?

2. INTERROGATORIES TO PARTIES

———

Read Federal Rule of Civil Procedure 33 in the Supplement.

———

Written interrogatories allow one party to send to another a series of questions to be answered under oath within a specific time. The procedure is extremely simple. No court order is required and no officers need be appointed; the entire exchange is accomplished by mail. If a question is thought to be improper, the responding party may say so rather than answering. The interrogating party then has the option of seeking a court order requiring an answer. An important advantage of interrogatories exists to the extent that a party has a duty to respond to interrogatories not only on the basis of her own knowledge but also with regard to the knowledge of other persons, including her lawyers, employees, and other agents, that reasonably can be obtained through investigation. Under Rule 33(b)(1)(B) such an obligation clearly exists for a party who is a public or private corporation, an association, or a government entity. Unfortunately, however, the language of Rule 33(b)(1)(A), as restyled in 2007, is unclear as to an individual party, even one who operates a large solo proprietorship. On its face, and contrasted with Rule 33(b)(1)(B), it appears to require such a party to respond only on the basis of her personal knowledge. Prior to the amendment, which was intended to be stylistic only, the Rule could have been read to require all parties to respond on the basis of their investigations and it seems likely that that will be the way in which the courts will interpret the restyled rule.

Interrogatories had been cited as the most abused of the available discovery devices and the Federal Rules have been amended a number of times to police the process. In 1980, then Rule 33(c) (now Rule 33(d)) was amended to require a party exercising the option to produce its business records to specify the records from which the answer can be found in sufficient detail to permit the interrogating party to locate and to identify them as readily as can the party served. The clarification sought to prevent the party served with interrogatories from directing the party who propounded them to a mass of business records or by offering to make all their records available.

NOTES AND QUESTIONS

1. How extensive should the duty of investigation be under Rule 33? Should a corporate party be charged with the responsibility of finding out what is known by each of its employees regardless of the size and nature of the business? Should the duty extend to information known to employees of subsidiary corporations that are not parties? To what extent should the duty include former employees?

2. In 1993, Rule 33(a) was amended to impose a presumptive limit of 25 interrogatories, including all discrete parts, that a party may serve. The Notes of the Advisory Committee indicate that although parties cannot evade the

limitation "through the device of joining as 'subparts' questions that seek information about discrete separate subjects," nevertheless "a question asking about communications of a particular type should be treated as a single interrogatory" even though it asks for a number of specific details regarding the particular communication. See WILLIAMS v. BOARD OF COUNTY COMMISSIONERS, 192 F.R.D. 698, 701–02 (D. Kan. 2000) (finding that seven interrogatories containing 117 subparts "exceeded the maximum number of interrogatories allowed"). How else might a court define a single interrogatory for purposes of the Rule?

3.   May a party use an interrogatory to probe an adversary's legal theories or a question of law? See Johnston & Johnston, *Contention Interrogatories in Federal Court*, 148 F.R.D. 441 (1993). Rule 33(a)(2) provides that an interrogatory " * * * is not objectionable merely because it asks for an opinion or contention that relates to fact or the application of law to fact * * *." The following case explores the appropriate boundaries to this Rule.

IN RE CONVERGENT TECHNOLOGIES SECURITIES LITIGATION

United States District Court, Northern District of California, 1985.
108 F.R.D. 328.

BRAZIL, MAGISTRATE JUDGE.

The principal issue in this discovery dispute can be simply framed: *when* (at which juncture in the pretrial period) should plaintiffs answer "contention" interrogatories served by defendants. The parties do *not* disagree about *whether* the questions should be answered. The sole question is when. * * *

* * *

I.   General Principles

* * *

At the outset I point out that the phrase "contention interrogatory" is used imprecisely to refer to many different kinds of questions. Some people would classify as a contention interrogatory any question that asks another party to indicate *what* it contends. Some people would define contention interrogatories as embracing only questions that ask another party *whether* it makes some specified contention. Interrogatories of this kind typically would begin with the phrase "Do you contend that...." Another kind of question that some people put in the category "contention interrogatory" asks an opposing party to state all the *facts* on which it *bases* some specified contention. Yet another form of this category of interrogatory asks an opponent to state all the *evidence* on which it *bases* some specified contention. Some contention interrogatories ask the responding party to take a position, and then to explain or defend that position, with respect to *how the law applies to facts*. A variation on this theme involves interrogatories that ask parties to spell out the *legal basis* for, or theory behind, some specified contention.

It is not uncommon for a set of "contention interrogatories" to include *all* of these kinds of questions. * * *

* * *

Despite assertions to the contrary by defendants, no party has an absolute right to have answers to contention interrogatories, or to any kind of interrogatory. * * * After 1983, a court can determine whether any given interrogatory is "otherwise proper" only after considering, among other things, whether it is interposed for any improper purpose, and whether it is "unreasonable or unduly burdensome or expensive, given the needs of the case, the discovery already had in the case, the amount in controversy, and the importance of the issues at stake in the litigation." If it were clear, for example, that by using some other discovery tool a party could acquire information of comparable quality while imposing less of a burden on an opponent, a court would be constrained to rule that a contention interrogatory need not be answered, regardless of when in the pretrial period it was served. * * *

* * *

* * * [T]here is considerable recent authority for the view that the wisest general policy is to defer propounding and answering contention interrogatories until near the end of the discovery period. On the other hand, * * * there may be situations in which this general policy should give way to showings, in specific factual settings, that important interests would be advanced if answers were provided early to at least some contention interrogatories. * * *

Because the benefits that can flow from clarifying and narrowing the issues in litigation *early* in the pretrial period are potentially significant * * *, it would be unwise to create a rigid rule, even if applicable to only certain categories of cases, that would always protect parties from having to answer contention interrogatories until some predetermined juncture in the pretrial period.

On the other hand, there is substantial reason to believe that the *early* knee jerk filing of sets of contention interrogatories that systematically track all the allegations in an opposing party's pleadings is a serious form of discovery abuse. * * *

This follows in part from the court's skepticism about the *quality* of the information that *early* responses to contention interrogatories are likely to contain. Counsel drafting responses to these kinds of interrogatories early in the pretrial period may fear being boxed into a position * * * that might be used to try to limit the subject areas of their subsequent discovery. Lawyers generally attempt to maximize and preserve their

options while providing as little tactical help to their opponents as possible
* * *.

* * *

The court concludes that the following procedure is appropriate with respect to contention interrogatories filed before most other discovery has been completed. The propounding party must craft specific, limited (in number) questions. The responding party must examine such questions in good faith and, where it appears that answering them would materially contribute to any of the goals discussed in this opinion, must answer the interrogatories. If answering some, but not all, of the questions would materially contribute to any of the goals described above, the responding party must answer those questions. Where the responding party feels, in good faith, that providing early answers would not contribute enough to justify the effort involved, that party should telephone or write opposing counsel to explain the basis for his position. If opposing counsel continues to press for early answers, the responding party should enter objections * * * or seek permission from the Court to file an objection to the interrogatories as a group. Thereafter, the burden would fall on the propounding party to seek an order compelling answers. In seeking such an order, the propounding party would bear the burden of justification described above. To the extent, if any, that this procedure modifies the way burdens might be allocated with respect to other kinds of discovery disputes, this court believes that the problems associated with the early filing of contention interrogatories, discussed above, justify the different treatment.

The sections that follow help clarify how this court will apply these general principles.

II.   Application of Principles to Motions as Presented

* * *

D.   *Defendant Burroughs Contention Interrogatories*

Defendant Burroughs Corporation has filed a set of 15 interrogatories which, counting subparts, add up to at least 52 questions, many of which are compound and expansive, in part because the allegations against Burroughs in plaintiffs' Complaint are more than occasionally compound and expansive. * * *

* * *

* * * The court fails to see how substantial interests of Burroughs will be harmed it if is forced to wait until no more than 60 days after completion of [certain relevant] * * * document production for answers to its interrogatories. If, prior to the time plaintiffs are required by this order to respond to Burroughs' contention interrogatories, plaintiffs seek to obtain additional discovery from Burroughs, and thus to impose costs on

Burroughs that it feels it cannot be fairly asked to incur, Burroughs may approach the court for a protective order.

* * *

3. DISCOVERY AND PRODUCTION OF PROPERTY

Read Federal Rules of Civil Procedure 34 and 45 in the Supplement.

Rule 34 and its state counterparts allow a party to request other parties to produce documents, electronically stored information, and tangible things in their possession or control. How does Rule 34 define electronically stored information? The Rule also allows a party entry to the other party's land or property for such activities as inspection, survey, or measurement. What are the first steps a party must take in order to make a document request? See Federal Rules 26(d)(1) and (f). What kind of notice must then be served on the opponent? See Federal Rule 34(b).

A request for information must describe the items to be discovered "with reasonable particularity," a standard that varies with circumstances. Most courts allow discovery of general categories of items if the description is easily understood (e.g., all written communications between plaintiff and defendant between July 1 and September 1, 2005). Many attorneys combine Rule 33 interrogatories that ask the opposing party to identify documents with a Rule 34 request that the party produce "all documents identified" in the opposing party's answers to the interrogatories. Although the standard for requesting documents is a flexible one, the writing of a request calls for a great deal of precision.

A request must specify a reasonable time, place, and manner for the inspection. The time usually is set at least thirty days after service of the request because the opposing party generally has at least thirty days to respond. The place typically designated for production of documents is the office of the requesting party's attorney, unless it is more convenient to examine the documents where they are kept or to have them copied at some other place. The manner depends on the kind of items requested. In practice, attorneys negotiate these matters.

The party that receives a request serves a written response on the requesting party, as well as any other parties to the lawsuit, within the time specified by the Rule. The response states the responding party's objections, if any, to part or all of the requested production or inspection. Absent objection, the responding party must produce the documents as requested, or admit counsel to its premises for the scheduled inspection.

In 1980, Rule 34(b) was amended to deal with the problem of a litigant who responds to a request by producing a large number of unsorted documents, some of which are unrelated to the case. A leading commentary explains:

> * * * [T]he problem addressed in the 1980 amendment was the shifting of materials from the sequence in which they were ordinarily kept to somewhere else, perhaps intended to make them hard to find. For instance, a critical internal memorandum might be taken from the memoranda file and buried among mounds of invoices. The amendment forbids the producing party from thus making it harder to find such items. Similarly, the producing party does have a burden to select and produce the items requested rather than simply dumping large quantities of unrequested materials onto the discovering party along with the items actually sought under Rule 34.

8A Wright, Miller & Marcus, Federal Practice and Procedure: Civil 2d § 2213.

Although Rule 34 is limited to parties, amendments to Rule 45 (adopted in 1991) allow a "virtually identical procedure to obtain material from nonparties." 8A Wright, Miller & Marcus, Federal Practice and Procedure: Civil 2d § 2204. If the request for production of documents or inspection of premises is addressed to a nonparty, the litigant must serve a subpoena pursuant to Rule 45. Under former Rule 45, it was not possible to make use of a subpoena to obtain documents or inspect property. Rather, the litigant had to take the nonparty's deposition and in connection with the deposition serve a subpoena ordering the nonparty to bring the designated items to the deposition. In the alternative, the litigant could bring a separate action against the nonparty to obtain discovery. The necessity of using these cumbersome procedures was eliminated when Rule 45 was amended in 1991. The amended Rule now provides that an attorney may issue a subpoena commanding any person to give testimony, to produce and permit inspection and copying of designated records or other tangible objects, or to permit inspection of premises. Rule 45 provides procedures by which a nonparty can obtain protection from unjust invasions of privacy or other important demands.

NOTE ON DISCOVERY OF ELECTRONIC DATA

The Federal Rules were adopted before the fax machine or laptop computer came into existence. They have, however, been adapted periodically to meet changes in technology that have affected litigation practice. In 1970, for example, Federal Rule 34 was amended to include "data compilations from which information can be obtained" as among the documents that can be requested under the rule. Since then, computers have increased dramatically the volume of electronically stored information that lawyers and their clients generate in the course of business and other activity:

> In 2000, fewer than 10 billion e-mail messages were sent per day worldwide. By 2005, the number of e-mails sent per day [was] projected to surpass 35 billion * * *. According to a 2003 survey by the Meta Group,

80 percent of business people say e-mail is more valuable than the telephone. More than 7 billion office documents are produced each year, and a recent study from the University of California, Berkeley, concluded that as much as 93% of it is in digital format. Office workers are estimated to be involved in at least 30 e-mail communications per work day and to create about 300 megabytes of electronic documents per year.

Shapiro & Kilpatrick, *E-Mail Discovery and Privilege*, 23 Corp. Counsel Rev. 203, 203 (2004).

Electronically stored information ("ESI") presents challenges that are not raised by the discovery of paper documents. A number of factors deserve mention. The sheer volume of ESI and the ease with which it can be duplicated has increased exponentially the amount of information that may be discovered. In addition, ESI possesses the quality of "persistence," in the sense that it cannot simply be shredded and discarded. ESI likewise has a "dynamic, changeable content" that may transform without any targeted or intentional activity by the user (for example, booting up a computer may change the content of data). Moreover, ESI, unlike paper documents, contains metadata, defined as "information about the document or file that is recorded by the computer to assist the computer and often the user in storing and retrieving the document or file at a later date." The challenges of discovering ESI are compounded by its "environment-dependence," in the sense that ESI "may be incomprehensible when separated from its environment," and by the periodic obsolescence of computer systems. Finally, ESI may be dispersed in different archival media, making it difficult to determine the origin of ESI, yet ESI can often be searched with relative ease. See The Sedona Principles: Best Practices Recommendations & Principles for Addressing Electronic Document Production, SK071 ALI–ABA 363, 373 (2004).

In 2006—following a decade of study by the Advisory Committee on Civil Rules, Discovery Subcommittee—amendments to the Federal Rules on electronic discovery took effect. The amendments in part adapted existing language to include electronic discovery. Federal Rule 34 was amended to change the term documents and data compilations from the 1970 version to "documents and electronically stored information." The hope is that this broader term will allow the rule to adapt alongside constantly changing information technology. Rule 34 also now provides a procedure for producing electronically stored information: unless otherwise requested pursuant to Rule 34, the responding party must produce electronically stored information in the form in which it is ordinarily maintained or in a form that is reasonably useful. Further, Rule 34 allows a party to avoid production of information in separate forms; a party need not provide duplicate physical and electronic copies of a document. The 2006 amendments also make clear that Rule 16 (pretrial conferences), Rule 26 (mandatory disclosure, relevance, and proportionality), Rule 33 (interrogatories), Rule 37 (sanctions), and Rule 45 (subpoenas), encompass the discovery of electronically stored information.

Issues concerning the limits and costs of discovering electronic information have generated complicated questions for courts. The amended rules seek to limit the burden of electronic discovery by identifying a category of information that is "not reasonably accessible." Federal Rule

26(b)(2)(c). Courts currently must resolve how to determine if an electronic discovery request is reasonable; how the costs of electronic discovery should be allocated between the parties; and the appropriate scope and content of sanctions.

4. PHYSICAL AND MENTAL EXAMINATIONS

———

Read Federal Rule of Civil Procedure 35 in the Supplement.

———

In many lawsuits, a party will need to have its own medical professionals physically examine an adverse party whose condition is in controversy. However, a compelled medical examination involves an intrusion on a person's privacy, and some medical tests can entail discomfort and pain. Rule 35 requires a court order for an examination and imposes strict standards. A court can force a party to submit to examination or to make persons under their legal custody or control available for examination. But the person's physical or mental condition must be in controversy, and the movant must show "good cause" to compel the examination. The determination of good cause involves weighing the pain, danger, or intrusiveness of the examination against the need for, or usefulness of, the information to be gained.

In practice, most physical and mental examinations occur as a result of agreements between attorneys. The primary effect of Rule 35 is to encourage parties to stipulate to examinations. Examinations are routine in personal injury actions, as well as in litigation involving issues of paternity, incompetence, and undue influence. Of course, the Rule is available in those cases in which the parties cannot agree. Stipulations typically address questions concerning the time and place of the examination, and the procedures to be used. Rule 35 gives the examined party the right to a copy of the examiner's report, even if he or she submitted to an examination without the compulsion of a court order. What is the effect of the examined party's requesting a copy of the report?

———

SCHLAGENHAUF v. HOLDER

Supreme Court of the United States, 1964.
379 U.S. 104, 85 S.Ct. 234, 13 L.Ed.2d 152.

Certiorari to the United States Court of Appeals for the Seventh Circuit.

MR. JUSTICE GOLDBERG delivered the opinion of the Court.

This case involves the validity and construction of Rule 35(a) of the Federal Rules of Civil Procedure as applied to the examination of a defendant in a negligence action. * * *

An action based on diversity of citizenship was brought in the District Court seeking damages arising from personal injuries suffered by passengers of a bus which collided with the rear of a tractor-trailer. The named defendants were The Greyhound Corporation, owner of the bus; petitioner, Robert L. Schlagenhauf, the bus driver; Contract Carriers, Inc., owner of the tractor; Joseph L. McCorkhill, driver of the tractor; and National Lead Company, owner of the trailer. Answers were filed by each of the defendants denying negligence.

Greyhound then cross-claimed against Contract Carriers and National Lead for damage to Greyhound's bus, alleging that the collision was due solely to their negligence in that the tractor-trailer was driven at an unreasonably low speed, had not remained in its lane, and was not equipped with proper rear lights. Contract Carriers filed an answer to this cross-claim denying its negligence and asserting "[t]hat the negligence of the driver of the * * * bus [petitioner Schlagenhauf] proximately caused and contributed to * * * Greyhound's damages."

* * *

Contract Carriers and National Lead then petitioned the District Court for an order directing petitioner Schlagenhauf to submit to both mental and physical examinations by one specialist in each of the following fields:

(1) Internal medicine;

(2) Ophthalmology;

(3) Neurology; and

(4) Psychiatry.

For the purpose of offering a choice to the District Court of one specialist in each field, the petition recommended two specialists in internal medicine, ophthalmology, and psychiatry, respectively, and three specialists in neurology—a total of nine physicians. The petition alleged that the mental and physical condition of Schlagenhauf was "in controversy" as it had been raised by Contract Carriers' answer to Greyhound's cross-claim. This was supported by a brief of legal authorities and an affidavit of Contract Carriers' attorney stating that Schlagenhauf had seen red lights 10 to 15 seconds before the accident, that another witness had seen the rear lights of the trailer from a distance of three-quarters to one-half mile, and that Schlagenhauf had been involved in a prior accident.

* * *

While disposition of this petition was pending, National Lead filed its answer to Greyhound's cross-claim and itself "cross-claimed" against Greyhound and Schlagenhauf for damage to its trailer. * * *

The District Court, on the basis of the petition filed by Contract Carriers, and without any hearing, ordered Schlagenhauf to submit to nine examinations—one by each of the recommended specialists—despite the fact that the petition clearly requested a total of only four examinations.

Petitioner applied for a writ of mandamus in the Court of Appeals against the respondent, the District Court Judge, seeking to have set aside the order requiring his mental and physical examinations. The Court of Appeals denied mandamus, one judge dissenting * * *.

We granted certiorari to review undecided questions concerning the validity and construction of Rule 35. * * *

Rule 35 on its face applies to all "parties," which under any normal reading would include a defendant. Petitioner contends, however, that the application of the Rule to a defendant would be an unconstitutional invasion of his privacy, or, at the least, be a modification of substantive rights existing prior to the adoption of the Federal Rules of Civil Procedure and thus beyond the congressional mandate of the Rules Enabling Act.

These same contentions were raised [and rejected] in Sibbach v. Wilson & Co., [Note 1, p. 255, supra,] * * * by a plaintiff in a negligence action who asserted a physical injury as a basis for recovery. * * * Petitioner does not challenge the holding in *Sibbach* as applied to plaintiffs. He contends, however, that it should not be extended to defendants. We can see no basis * * * for such a distinction. * * * Issues cannot be resolved by a doctrine of favoring one class of litigants over another.

We recognize that, insofar as reported cases show, this type of discovery in federal courts has been applied solely to plaintiffs, and that some early state cases seem to have proceeded on a theory that a plaintiff who seeks redress for injuries in a court of law thereby "waives" his right to claim the inviolability of his person.

* * * [The Court then rejected the "waiver" theory on the basis of language in the *Sibbach* case.] The chain of events leading to an ultimate determination on the merits begins with the injury of the plaintiff, an involuntary act on his part. Seeking court redress is just one step in this chain. If the plaintiff is prevented or deterred from this redress, the loss is thereby forced on him to the same extent as if the defendant were prevented or deterred from defending against the action.

* * *

Petitioner contends that even if Rule 35 is to be applied to defendants, which we have determined it must, nevertheless it should not be applied to him as he was not a party in relation to Contract Carriers and National Lead—the movants for the mental and physical examinations—at the time the examinations were sought. * * * While it is clear that the person to be examined must be a party to the case,[12] we are of the view that * * * Rule 35 only requires that the person to be examined be a party to the "action," not that he be an opposing party *vis-à-vis* the movant. There is no doubt that Schlagenhauf was a "party" to this "action" by virtue of the original complaint. * * * Insistence that the movant have filed a pleading against the person to be examined would have the undesirable result of an unnecessary proliferation of cross-claims and counterclaims and would not be in keeping with the aims of a liberal, nontechnical application of the Federal Rules. * * *

While the Court of Appeals held that petitioner was not a party *vis-à-vis* National Lead or Contract Carriers at the time the examinations were first sought, it went on to hold that he had become a party *vis-à-vis* National Lead by the time of a second order entered by the District Court and thus was a party within its rule. This second order, identical in all material respects with the first, was entered on the basis of supplementary petitions filed by National Lead and Contract Carriers. These petitions gave no new basis for the examinations, except for the allegation that petitioner's mental and physical condition had been additionally put in controversy by the National Lead answer and cross-claim, which had been filed subsequent to the first petition for examinations. Although the filing of the petition for mandamus intervened between these two orders, we accept, for purposes of this opinion, the determination of the Court of Appeals that this second order was the one before it and agree that petitioner was clearly a party at this juncture under any test.

Petitioner next contends that his mental or physical condition was not "in controversy" and "good cause" was not shown for the examinations, both as required by the express terms of Rule 35.

* * *

It is notable * * * that in none of the other discovery provisions is there a restriction that the matter be "in controversy," and only in Rule 34 is there Rule 35's requirement that the movant affirmatively demonstrate "good cause."[a]

This additional requirement of "good cause" was reviewed by Chief Judge Sobeloff in Guilford National Bank of Greensboro v. Southern Ry. Co., 297 F.2d 921, 924 (C.A. 4th Cir.), in the following words:

> * * * The specific requirement of good cause would be meaningless if good cause could be sufficiently established by merely showing that the desired materials are relevant, for the relevancy standard has already been imposed by Rule 26(b). Thus, by adding the words " * * * good cause * * *," the Rules indicate that there must be greater showing of need under Rules 34 and 35 than under the other discovery rules.

---

12. Although petitioner was an agent of Greyhound, he was himself a party to the action. He is to be distinguished from one who is not a party but is, for example, merely the agent of a party. * * *

a. The "good cause" requirement was eliminated from Rule 34 in 1970.

The courts of appeals in other cases have also recognized that Rule 34's good-cause requirement is not a mere formality, but is a plainly expressed limitation on the use of that Rule. This is obviously true as to the "in controversy" and "good cause" requirements of Rule 35. They are not met by mere conclusory allegations of the pleadings—nor by mere relevance to the case—but require an affirmative showing by the movant that each condition as to which the examination is sought is really and genuinely in controversy and that good cause exists for ordering each particular examination. Obviously, what may be good cause for one type of examination may not be so for another. The ability of the movant to obtain the desired information by other means is also relevant.

Rule 35, therefore, requires discriminating application by the trial judge, who must decide, as an initial matter in every case, whether the party requesting a mental or physical examination or examinations has adequately demonstrated the existence of the Rule's requirements of "in controversy" and "good cause," which requirements, as the Court of Appeals in this case itself recognized, are necessarily related. 321 F.2d, at 51. * * *

Of course, there are situations where the pleadings alone are sufficient to meet these requirements. A plaintiff in a negligence action who asserts mental or physical injury * * * places that mental or physical injury clearly in controversy and provides the defendant with good cause for an examination to determine the existence and extent of such asserted injury. This * * * applies equally to a defendant who asserts his mental or physical condition as a defense to a claim, such as, for example, where insanity is asserted as a defense to a divorce action. * * *

Here, however, Schlagenhauf did not assert his mental or physical condition either in support of or in defense of a claim. His condition was sought to be placed in issue by other parties. Thus, under the principles discussed above, Rule 35 required that these parties make an affirmative showing that petitioner's mental or physical condition was in controversy and that there was good cause for the examinations requested. This, the record plainly shows, they failed to do.

The only allegations in the pleadings relating to this subject were the general conclusory statement in Contract Carriers' answer to the cross-claim that "Schlagenhauf was not mentally or physically capable of operating" the bus at the time of the accident and the limited allegation in National Lead's cross-claim that, at the time of the accident, "the eyes and vision of * * * Schlagenhauf was [sic] impaired and deficient."

The attorney's affidavit attached to the petition for the examinations provided:

> That * * * Schlagenhauf, in his deposition * * * admitted that he saw red lights for 10 to 15 seconds prior to a collision with a semi-tractor trailer unit and yet drove his vehicle on without reducing speed and without altering the course thereof.

The only eye-witness to this accident known to this affiant * * * testified that immediately prior to the impact between the bus and truck that he had also been approaching the truck from the rear and that he had clearly seen the lights of the truck for a distance of three-quarters to one-half mile to the rear thereof.

* * * Schlagenhauf has admitted in his deposition * * * that he was involved in a [prior] similar type rear end collision. * * *

This record cannot support even the corrected order which required one examination in each of the four specialties of internal medicine, ophthalmology, neurology, and psychiatry. Nothing in the pleadings or affidavit would afford a basis for a belief that Schlagenhauf was suffering from a mental or neurological illness warranting wide-ranging psychiatric or neurological examinations. Nor is there anything stated justifying the broad internal medicine examination.

The only specific allegation made in support of the four examinations ordered was that the "eyes and vision" of Schlagenhauf were impaired. Considering this in conjunction with the affidavit, we would be hesitant to set aside a visual examination if it had been the only one ordered. However, as the case must be remanded to the District Court because of the other examinations ordered, it would be appropriate for the District Judge to reconsider also this order in light of the guidelines set forth in this opinion.

* * *

Accordingly, the judgment of the Court of Appeals is vacated and the case remanded to the District Court to reconsider the examination order in light of the guidelines herein formulated and for further proceedings in conformity with this opinion.

Vacated and remanded.

Mr. Justice Black, with whom Mr. Justice Clark joins, concurring in part and dissenting in part.

* * *

In a collision case like this one, evidence concerning very bad eyesight or impaired mental or physical health which may affect the ability to drive is obviously of the highest relevance. It is equally obvious, I think, that when a vehicle continues down an open road and smashes into a truck in front of it although the truck is in plain sight and there is ample time and room to avoid collision, the chances are good that the driver has some physical, mental or moral defect. When such a thing happens twice, one is even more likely to ask, "What is the matter with that driver? Is he blind or crazy?" Plainly the allegations of the other parties were relevant and put the question of Schlagenhauf's health and vision "in controversy." * * *

Mr. Justice Douglas, dissenting in part.

* * * When the defendant's doctors examine plaintiff, they are normally interested only in answering a single question: did plaintiff in fact sustain the specific injuries claimed? But plaintiff's doctors will naturally be inclined to go on a fishing expedition in search of *anything* which will tend to prove that the defendant was unfit to perform the acts which resulted in the plaintiff's injury. And a doctor for a fee can easily discover something wrong with any patient—a condition that in prejudiced medical eyes might have caused the accident. Once defendants are turned over to medical or psychiatric clinics for an analysis of their physical well-being and the condition of their psyche, the effective trial will be held there and not before the jury. There are no lawyers in those clinics to stop the doctor from probing this organ or that one, to halt a further inquiry, to object to a line of questioning. And there is no judge to sit as arbiter. The doctor or the psychiatrist has a holiday in the privacy of his office. The defendant is at the doctor's (or psychiatrist's) mercy; and his report may either overawe or confuse the jury and prevent a fair trial.

* * *

Neither the Court nor Congress up to today has determined that any person whose physical or mental condition is brought into question during some lawsuit must surrender his right to keep his person inviolate. Congress did, according to *Sibbach*, require a plaintiff to choose between his privacy and his purse; but before today it has not been thought that any other "party" had lost this historic immunity. Congress and this Court can authorize such a rule. But a rule suited to purposes of discovery against defendants must be carefully drawn in light of the great potential of blackmail.

* * *

[JUSTICE HARLAN'S dissenting opinion is omitted.]

NOTES AND QUESTIONS

1. What kinds of diagnostic tests may be ordered under Rule 35? In STORMS v. LOWE'S HOME CENTERS, INC., 211 F.R.D. 296 (W.D. Va. 2002), the District Court declined to order "a mere vocational assessment not connected with any physical or mental examination * * *." The court explained that although the 1991 amendment to Rule 35 "explicitly expanded the scope of *examiners* to be covered, it did not expand the scope of *examinations* available under the Rule." Id. at 298. Do you agree with this interpretation of the Rule?

2. In WINTERS v. TRAVIA, 495 F.2d 839 (2d Cir. 1974), the court refused to order plaintiff to submit to a physical or mental examination. Plaintiff was a Christian Scientist seeking damages on the ground that forced medication administered to her during involuntary hospitalization violated her right to freedom of religion. The court ruled that her present condition was not in controversy since plaintiff was willing to abandon any claim that any present or anticipated physical or mental disability or condition was

caused by the medical treatment on which the case was based. To what extent should a party's religious beliefs affect the scope of the discovery in a civil lawsuit?

3. In ABDULWALI v. WASHINGTON METRO AREA TRANSIT AUTHORITY, 193 F.R.D. 10 (D.D.C. 2000), plaintiff sued for negligent infliction of emotional distress resulting from the witnessing of her child being killed in a subway train accident. Defendant sought a psychiatric examination of plaintiff, who requested the court to permit her attorney to attend the examination and to have the examination recorded. She also requested that she receive any notes made by the psychiatrist during the examination and that the examination be limited to three hours duration. The court rejected all of plaintiff's requests, noting that the greater weight of federal authority favors the exclusion of a party's attorney. How might the presence of counsel affect the examination?

What arguments could the parties make to support their positions? Would it make a difference if plaintiff sought damages for physical injuries and the examination was not psychiatric? Suppose plaintiff wanted to have her own physician present, rather than her lawyer? Should she be able to have her husband or her mother attend? Are there special times when attendance by another person or a recording of the examination should be permitted or not permitted? See Wyatt & Bales, *The Presence of Third Parties at Rule 35 Examinations*, 71 Temp. L. Rev. 103 (1998).

5. REQUESTS TO ADMIT

Read Federal Rule of Civil Procedure 36 in the Supplement.

Rule 36 authorizes a party to serve on another party written requests to admit the truth of certain matters of fact or of the application of law to fact, or the genuineness of a document or other evidence that may be used at trial. Rule 36 is not a true discovery device since it does not require the responding party to disclose information. Requests for admissions are used to shape information already known into statements that expedite the trial by limiting the issues in dispute and by obviating some of the formalities that control the introduction of evidence at trial. Although responses to other discovery devices are not conclusive proof and may be contradicted at trial, responses to Rule 36 requests constitute conclusive evidence, unless withdrawn, and cannot be contradicted at trial. However, requests for admissions may function as a discovery device if a party uses them early enough in the litigation to help identify the issues not in dispute and to target the remaining issues for discovery.

A request for admission may be served without the necessity of a court order at any time after the parties have conferred in accordance with Rule 26(d), although usually not later than thirty days before a fixed trial date. Rule 36 provides that each matter of admission must be set forth separately, but says nothing else about the format for requests. However, Form 51, appended to the Federal Rules of Civil Procedure in the Supplement, provides an illustration of a request for admissions.

The party who receives a request to admit must respond under oath and in timely fashion, admitting or denying each matter for which an admission is requested, or providing a detailed explanation why it cannot admit or deny the matter. The responding party also may object to a request because improperly phrased (as "vague," "ambiguous," "a compound sentence," or otherwise defectively drafted), or because it seeks privileged or protected information. The responding party may request a court to extend its time to respond. (Rule 29 provides that counsel may stipulate to extend the time limits set forth in Rule 36 unless the stipulation would "interfere with the time set for completing discovery, for hearing a motion, or for trial.")

If the party who receives a request to admit does nothing, the matter in the request is deemed admitted. The effects of Rule 36, unlike other discovery rules, are self-executing. Once the time to respond has passed, the requesting party can rely on the matters admitted and take no further discovery on those issues. If a party serves a late response, and the opponent refuses to accept it, a court may excuse the party's failure to respond in a timely manner. Likewise, a court may permit a party to withdraw or modify an admission in a timely response. In either situation, the court's decision turns on the degree of prejudice the requesting party will suffer because of its reliance on the admission. Because courts so frequently granted a responding party's request for relief from its failure to respond, leaving requesting parties uncertain about the validity of the admission, and, hence, the necessity of developing evidence for trial, Rule 36(a) was amended in 1970 to permit a requesting party to move for an order deeming the matter to be admitted. Thus, a litigant takes a serious risk by failing to respond to requests for admissions. The court may well find that the failure was not justified, that the admissions have been made, and that, as a result, summary judgment is appropriate. See, e.g., Jones v. Sweeney, 2000 WL 1611129 (N.D. Ind. 2000).

Although Rule 36 and its state counterparts can be enormously useful, in practice requests for admissions are the least used of the discovery devices. See Connolly, Holleman & Kuhlman, Judicial Controls and the Civil Litigation Process: Discovery 28 (Fed. Jud. Center 1978). Attorneys tend to think of requests to admit as part of trial preparation, not discovery. They postpone their use to the very end, and frequently fail to file requests before the time fixed by the court to complete discovery runs out. See Dombroff, Discovery 260 (1986).

6. THE DUTY TO SUPPLEMENT RESPONSES

———

Read Federal Rule of Civil Procedure 26(e) and the accompanying Advisory Committee's Notes in the Supplement.

———

Rule 26(e), adopted in 1970, amended in 1993, and restyled in 2007, was designed to eliminate inconsistent decisions regarding the existence and scope of the duty to update discovery answers. The 1993 amendments to Rule 26(e) broadened the obligation to supplement discovery responses, requiring that disclosures and responses to interrogatories, requests for production, and requests for admissions be supplemented "if the party learns that in some material respect the disclosure or response is incomplete or incorrect" and if the updated information has not otherwise been made known to the other parties. Note that the Rule is not all-encompassing. What information obtained subsequent to the original responses is not covered by it?

SECTION D. SPECIAL PROBLEMS REGARDING THE SCOPE OF DISCOVERY

1. MATERIALS PREPARED IN ANTICIPATION OF TRIAL

———

Read Federal Rule of Civil Procedure 26(b)(3) and the accompanying materials in the Supplement.

———

HICKMAN v. TAYLOR

Supreme Court of the United States, 1947.
329 U.S. 495, 67 S.Ct. 385, 91 L.Ed. 451.

Certiorari to the Circuit Court of Appeals for the Third Circuit.

MR. JUSTICE MURPHY delivered the opinion of the Court.

This case presents an important problem under the Federal Rules * * * as to the extent to which a party may inquire into oral and written statements of witnesses, or other information, secured by an adverse party's counsel in the course of preparation for possible litigation after a claim has arisen. Examination into a person's files and records, including those resulting from the professional activities of an attorney, must be judged with care. It is not without reason that various safeguards have been established to preclude unwarranted excursions into the privacy of a man's work. At the same time, public policy supports reasonable and necessary inquiries. Properly to balance these competing interests is a delicate and difficult task.

On February 7, 1943, the tug "J.M. Taylor" sank while engaged in helping to tow a car float of the Baltimore & Ohio Railroad across the Delaware River at Philadelphia. The accident was apparently unusual in nature, the cause of it still being unknown. Five of the nine crew members were drowned. Three days later the tug owners and the underwriters employed a law firm, of which respondent Fortenbaugh is a member, to defend them against potential suits by representatives of the deceased crew members and to sue the railroad for damages to the tug.

A public hearing was held on March 4, 1943, before the United States Steamboat Inspectors, at which the four survivors were examined. This testimony was recorded and made available to all interested parties. Shortly thereafter, Fortenbaugh privately interviewed the survivors and took statements from them with an eye toward the anticipated litigation; the survivors signed these statements on March 29. Fortenbaugh also interviewed other persons believed to have some information relating to the accident and in some cases he made memoranda of what they told him. At the time when Fortenbaugh secured the statements of the survivors, representatives of two of the deceased crew members had been in communication with him. Ultimately claims were presented by representatives of all five of the deceased; four of the claims, however, were settled without litigation. The fifth claimant, petitioner herein, brought suit in a federal court under the Jones Act on November 26, 1943, naming as defendants the two tug owners, individually and as partners, and the railroad.

One year later, petitioner filed 39 interrogatories directed to the tug owners. The 38th interrogatory read: "State whether any statements of the members of the crews of the Tugs 'J.M. Taylor' and 'Philadelphia' or of any other vessel were taken in connection with the towing of the car float and the sinking of the Tug 'John M. Taylor'. Attach hereto exact copies of all such statements if in writing, and if oral, set forth in detail the exact provisions of any such oral statements or reports."

Supplemental interrogatories asked whether any oral or written statements, records, reports or other memoranda had been made concerning any matter relative to the towing operation, the sinking of the tug, the salvaging and repair of the tug, and the death of the deceased. If the answer was in the affirmative, the tug owners were then requested to set forth the nature of all such records, reports, statements or other memoranda.

The tug owners, through Fortenbaugh, answered all of the interrogatories except No. 38 and the supplemental ones just described. While admitting that statements of the survivors had been taken, they declined to summarize or set forth the contents. They did so on the ground that such requests called "for privileged matter obtained in preparation for litigation" and constituted "an attempt to obtain indirectly counsel's private files." It was claimed that answering these requests "would involve practically turning over not only the complete files, but also the telephone records and, almost, the thoughts of counsel."

In connection with the hearing on these objections, Fortenbaugh made a written statement and gave an informal oral deposition explaining the circumstances under which he had taken the statements. But he was not expressly asked in the deposition to produce the statements. The District Court for the Eastern District of Pennsylvania, sitting en banc, held that the requested matters were not privileged. 4 F.R.D. 479. The court then decreed that the tug owners and Fortenbaugh, as counsel and agent for the tug owners forthwith "Answer Plaintiff's 38th interrogatory and supplemental interrogatories; produce all written statements of witnesses obtained by Mr. Fortenbaugh, as counsel and agent for Defendants; state in substance any fact concerning this case which Defendants learned through oral statements made by witnesses to Mr. Fortenbaugh whether or not included in his private memoranda and produce Mr. Fortenbaugh's memoranda containing statements of fact by witnesses or to submit these memoranda to the Court for determination of those portions which should be revealed to Plaintiff." Upon their refusal, the court adjudged them in contempt and ordered them imprisoned until they complied.

The Third Circuit Court of Appeals, also sitting en banc, reversed the judgment of the District Court. 153 F.2d 212. It held that the information here sought was part of the "work product of the lawyer" and hence privileged from discovery under the Federal Rules of Civil Procedure. The importance of the problem, which has engendered a great divergence of views among district courts, led us to grant certiorari. * * *

There is an initial question as to which of the deposition-discovery rules is involved in this case. Petitioner, in filing his interrogatories, thought that he was proceeding under Rule 33.

* * * [I]t does not appear from the record that petitioner filed a motion under Rule 34 for a court order directing the production of the documents in question. Indeed, such an order could not have been entered as to Fortenbaugh since Rule 34, like Rule 33, is limited to parties to the proceeding, thereby excluding their counsel or agents.

Thus to the extent that petitioner was seeking the production of the memoranda and statements gathered by Fortenbaugh in the course of his activities as counsel, petitioner misconceived his remedy. Rule 33 did not permit him to obtain such memoranda and statements as adjuncts to the interrogatories addressed to the individual tug owners. A party clearly cannot refuse to answer interrogatories on the ground that the information sought is solely within the knowledge of his attorney. But that is not this case. Here production was sought of documents prepared by a party's attorney after the claim has arisen. Rule 33 does not make provision for such production, even when sought in connection with permissible interrogatories. Moreover, since petitioner was also foreclosed from securing them through an order under Rule 34, his only recourse was to take Fortenbaugh's deposition under Rule 26 and to attempt to force Fortenbaugh to produce the materials by use of a subpoena *duces tecum* in accordance with Rule 45. * * * But despite petitioner's faulty choice of action, the District Court entered an order, apparently under Rule 34, commanding the tug owners and Fortenbaugh, as their agent and counsel, to produce the materials in question. Their refusal led to the anomalous result of holding the tug owners in contempt for failure to produce that which was in the possession of their counsel and of holding Fortenbaugh in contempt for failure to produce that which he could not be compelled to produce under either Rule 33 or Rule 34.

But under the circumstances we deem it unnecessary and unwise to rest our decision upon this procedural irregularity, an irregularity which is not strongly urged upon us and which was disregarded in the two courts below. * * * [T]he basic question at stake is whether any of those devices may be used to inquire into materials collected by an adverse party's counsel in the course of preparation for possible litigation. The fact that the petitioner may have used the wrong method does not destroy the main thrust of his attempt. * * * [I]n the present circumstances, for the purposes of this decision, the procedural irregularity is not material. * * *

In urging that he has a right to inquire into the materials secured and prepared by Fortenbaugh, petitioner emphasizes that the deposition-discovery portions of the Federal Rules of Civil Procedure are designed to enable the parties to discover the true facts and to compel their disclosure wherever they may be found. It is said that inquiry may be made under these rules, epitomized by Rule 26, as to any relevant matter which is not privileged; and since the discovery provisions are to be applied as broadly and liberally as possible, the privilege limitation must be restricted to its narrowest bounds. On the premise that the attorney-client privilege is the one involved in this case, petitioner argues that it must be strictly confined to confidential communications made by a client to his attorney. And since the materials here in issue were secured by Fortenbaugh from third persons rather than from his clients, the tug owners, the conclusion is reached that these materials are proper subjects for discovery under Rule 26.

As additional support for this result, petitioner claims that to prohibit discovery under these circumstances would give a corporate defendant a tremendous advantage in a suit by an individual plaintiff. Thus in a suit by an injured employee against a railroad or in a suit by an insured person against an insurance company the corporate defendant could pull a dark veil of secrecy over all the pertinent facts it can collect after the claim arises merely on the assertion that such facts were gathered by its large staff of attorneys and claim agents. At the same time, the individual plaintiff, who often has direct knowledge of the matter in issue and has no counsel until some time after his claim arises could be compelled to disclose all the intimate details of his case. By endowing with immunity from disclosure all that a lawyer discovers in the course of his duties, it is said, the rights of individual litigants in such cases are drained of vitality and the lawsuit becomes more of a battle of deception than a search for truth.

But framing the problem in terms of assisting individual plaintiffs in their suits against corporate defendants is unsatisfactory. Discovery concededly may work to the disadvantage as well as to the advantage of individual plaintiffs. Discovery, in other words, is not a one-way proposition. It is available in all types of cases at the behest of any party, individual or corporate, plaintiff or defendant. The problem thus far transcends the situation confronting this petitioner. And we must view that problem in light of the limitless situations where the particular kind of discovery sought by petitioner might be used.

We agree, of course, that the deposition-discovery rules are to be accorded a broad and liberal treatment. No longer can the time-honored cry of "fishing expedition" serve to preclude a party from inquiring into the facts underlying his opponent's case. Mutual knowledge of all the relevant facts gathered by both parties is essential to proper litigation. To that end, either party may compel the other to disgorge whatever facts he has in his possession. The deposition-discovery procedure simply advances the stage at which the disclosure can be compelled from the time of trial to the period preceding it, thus reducing the possibility of surprise. But discovery, like all matters of procedure, has ultimate and necessary boundaries. As indicated by Rules 30(b) and (d) and 31(d), limitations inevitably arise when it can be shown that the examination is being conducted in bad faith or in such a manner as to annoy, embarrass or oppress the person subject to the inquiry. [These matters are now covered by Rule 26(c).] And as Rule 26(b) provides, further limitations come into existence when the inquiry touches upon the irrelevant or encroaches upon the recognized domains of privilege.

We also agree that the memoranda, statements and mental impressions in issue in this case fall outside the scope of the attorney-client privilege and hence are not protected from discovery on that basis. * * *

But the impropriety of invoking that privilege does not provide an answer to the problem before us. Petitioner has made more than an ordinary request for relevant, non-privileged facts in the possession of his adversaries or their counsel. He has sought discovery as of right of oral and written statements of witnesses whose identity is well known and whose availability to petitioner appears unimpaired. He has sought production of these matters after making the most searching inquiries of his opponents as to the circumstances surrounding the fatal accident, which inquiries were sworn to have been answered to the best of their information and belief. Interrogatories were directed toward all the events prior to, during and subsequent to the sinking of the tug. Full and honest answers to such broad inquiries would necessarily have included all pertinent information gleaned by Fortenbaugh through his interviews with the witnesses. Petitioner makes no suggestion, and we cannot assume, that the tug owners or Fortenbaugh were incomplete or dishonest in the framing of their answers. In addition, petitioner was free to examine the public testimony of the witnesses taken before the United States Steamboat Inspectors. We are thus dealing with an attempt to secure the production of written statements and mental impressions contained in the files and the mind of the attorney Fortenbaugh without any showing of necessity or any indication or claim that denial of such production would unduly prejudice the preparation of petitioner's case or cause him any hardship or injustice. For aught that appears, the essence of what petitioner seeks either has been revealed to him already through the interrogatories or is readily available to him direct from the witnesses for the asking.

* * *

In our opinion, neither Rule 26 nor any other rule dealing with discovery contemplates production under such circumstances. That is not because the subject matter is privileged or irrelevant, as those concepts are used in these rules. Here is simply an attempt, without purported necessity or justification, to secure written statements, private memoranda and personal recollection prepared or formed by an adverse party's counsel in the course of his legal duties. As such, it falls outside the arena of discovery and contravenes the public policy underlying the orderly prosecution and defense of legal claims. Not even the most liberal of discovery theories can justify unwarranted inquiries into the files and the mental impressions of an attorney.

Historically, a lawyer is an officer of the court and is bound to work for the advancement of justice while faithfully protecting the rightful interests of his clients. In performing his various duties, however, it is essential that a lawyer work with a certain degree of privacy, free from unnecessary intrusion by opposing parties and their counsel. Proper preparation of a client's case demands that he assemble information, sift what he considers to be the relevant from the irrelevant facts, prepare his legal theories and plan his strategy without undue and needless interference. That is the historical and the necessary way in which lawyers act within the framework of our system of jurisprudence to promote justice and to protect their clients' interests. This work is reflected, of course, in interviews, statements, memoranda, correspondence, briefs, mental impressions, personal beliefs, and countless other tangible and intangible ways—aptly though roughly termed by the Circuit Court of Appeals in this case (153 F.2d 212, 223) as the "work product of the lawyer." Were such materials open to opposing counsel on mere demand, much of what is now put down in writing would remain unwritten. An attorney's thoughts, heretofore inviolate, would not be his own. Inefficiency, unfairness and sharp practices would inevitably develop in the giving of legal advice and in the preparation of cases for trial. The effect on the legal profession would be demoralizing. And the interests of the clients and the cause of justice would be poorly served.

We do not mean to say that all written materials obtained or prepared by an adversary's counsel with an eye toward litigation are necessarily free from discovery in all cases. Where relevant and non-privileged facts remain hidden in an attorney's file and where production of those facts is essential to the preparation of one's case, discovery may properly be had. Such written statements and documents might, under certain circumstances, be admissible in evidence or give clues as to the existence or location of relevant facts. Or they might be useful for purposes of impeachment or corroboration. And production might be justified where the witnesses are no longer available or can be reached only with difficulty. Were production of written statements and documents to be precluded under such circumstances, the liberal ideals of the deposition-discovery portions of the Federal Rules * * * would be stripped of much of their meaning. But the general policy against invading the privacy of an attorney's course of preparation is so well recognized and so essential to an orderly working of our system of legal procedure that a burden rests on the one who would invade that privacy to establish adequate reasons to justify production through a subpoena or court order. That burden, we believe, is necessarily implicit in the rules as now constituted.

Rule 30(b), as presently written, gives the trial judge the requisite discretion to make a judgment as to whether discovery should be allowed as to written statements secured from witnesses. But in the instant case there was no room for that discretion to operate in favor of the petitioner. No attempt was made to establish any reason why Fortenbaugh should be forced to produce the written statements. There was only a naked, general demand for these materials as of right and a finding by the District Court that no recognizable privilege was involved. That was insufficient to justify discovery under these circumstances and the court should have sustained the refusal of the tug owners and Fortenbaugh to produce.

But as to oral statements made by witnesses to Fortenbaugh, whether presently in the form of his mental impressions or memoranda, we do not believe that any showing of necessity can be made under the circumstances of this case so as to justify production. Under ordinary conditions, forcing an attorney to repeat or write out all that witnesses have told him and to deliver the account to his adversary gives rise to grave dangers of inaccuracy and untrustworthiness. No legitimate purpose is served by such production. The practice forces the attorney to testify as to what he remembers or what he saw fit to write down regarding witnesses' remarks. Such testimony could not qualify as evidence; and to use it for impeachment or corroborative purposes would make the attorney much less an officer of the court and much more an ordinary witness. The standards of the profession would thereby suffer.

Denial of production of this nature does not mean that any material, nonprivileged facts can be hidden from the petitioner in this case. He need not be unduly hindered in the preparation of his case, in the discovery of facts or in his anticipation of his opponents' position. Searching interrogatories directed to Fortenbaugh and the tug owners, production of written documents and statements upon a proper showing and direct interviews with the witnesses themselves all serve to reveal the facts in Fortenbaugh's possession to the fullest possible extent consistent with public policy. Petitioner's counsel frankly admits that he wants the oral statements only to help prepare himself to examine witnesses and to make sure that he has overlooked nothing. That is insufficient under the circumstances to permit him an exception to the policy underlying the privacy of Fortenbaugh's professional activities. If there should be a rare situation justifying production of these matters, petitioner's case is not of that type.

We fully appreciate the wide-spread controversy among the members of the legal profession over the problem raised by this case. It is a problem that rests on what has been one of the most hazy frontiers of the discovery process. But until some rule or statute definitely prescribes otherwise, we are not justified in permitting discovery in a situation of this nature as a matter of unqualified right. When Rule 26 and the other discovery rules were adopted, this Court and the members of the bar in general certainly did not believe or contemplate that all the files and mental processes of lawyers were thereby opened to the free scrutiny of their adversaries. And we refuse to interpret the rules at this time so as to reach so harsh and unwarranted a result.

We therefore affirm the judgment of the Circuit Court of Appeals.

Affirmed.

MR. JUSTICE JACKSON, concurring.

* * *

To consider first the most extreme aspect of the requirement in litigation here, we find it calls upon counsel, if he has had any conversations with any of the crews of the vessels in question or of any other, to "set forth in detail the exact provision of any such oral statements or reports." Thus the demand is not for the production of a transcript in existence but calls for the creation of a written statement not in being. But the statement by counsel of what a witness told him is not evidence when written. Plaintiff could not introduce it to prove his case. What, then, is the purpose sought to be served by demanding this of adverse counsel?

Counsel for the petitioner candidly said on argument that he wanted this information to help prepare himself to examine witnesses, to make sure he overlooked nothing. He bases his claim to it in his brief on the view that the Rules were to do away with the old situation where a law suit developed into "a battle of wits between counsel." But a common law trial is and always should be an adversary proceeding. Discovery was hardly intended to enable a learned profession to perform its functions either without wits or on wits borrowed from the adversary.

The real purpose and the probable effect of the practice ordered by the district court would be to put trials on a level even lower than a "battle of wits." I can conceive of no practice more demoralizing to the Bar than to require a lawyer to write out and deliver to his adversary an account of what witnesses have told him. Even if his recollection were perfect, the statement would be his language permeated with his inferences. Every one who has tried it knows that it is almost impossible so fairly to record the expressions and emphasis of a witness that when he testifies in the environment of the court and under the influence of the leading question there will not be departures in some respects. Whenever the testimony of the witness would differ from the "exact" statement the lawyer had delivered, the lawyer's statement would be whipped out to impeach the witness. Counsel producing his adversary's "inexact" statement could lose nothing by saying, "Here is a contradiction, gentlemen of the jury. I do not know whether it is my adversary or his witness who is not telling the truth, but one is not." Of course, if this practice were adopted, that scene would be repeated over and over again. The lawyer who delivers such statements often would find himself branded a deceiver afraid to take the stand to support his own version of the witness's conversation with him, or else he will have to go on the stand to defend his own credibility—perhaps against that of his chief witness, or possibly even his client.

Every lawyer dislikes to take the witness stand and will do so only for grave reasons. This is partly because it is not his role; he is almost invariably a poor witness. But he steps out of professional character to do it. He regrets it; the profession discourages it. But the practice advocated here is one which would force him to be a witness, not as to what he has seen or done but as to other witnesses' stories, and not because he wants to do so but in self-defense.

And what is the lawyer to do who has interviewed one whom he believes to be a biased, lying or hostile witness to get his unfavorable statements and know what to meet? He must record and deliver such statements even though he would not vouch for the credibility of the witness by calling him. Perhaps the other side would not want to call him either, but the attorney is open to the charge of suppressing evidence at the trial if he fails to call such a hostile witness even though he never regarded him as reliable or truthful.

Having been supplied the names of the witnesses, petitioner's lawyer gives no reason why he cannot interview them himself. If an employee-witness refuses to tell his story, he, too, may be examined under the Rules. He may be compelled on discovery as fully as on the trial to disclose his version of the facts. But that is his own disclosure—it can be used to impeach him if he contradicts it and such a deposition is not useful to promote an unseemly disagreement between the witness and the counsel in the case.

It is true that the literal language of the Rules would admit of an interpretation that would sustain the district court's order. * * * But all such procedural measures have a background of custom and practice which was assumed by those who wrote and should be by those who apply them. * * * Certainly nothing in the tradition or practice of discovery up to the time of these Rules would have suggested that they would authorize such a practice as here proposed.

The question remains as to signed statements or those written by witnesses. Such statements are not evidence for the defendant. * * * Nor should I think they ordinarily could be evidence for the plaintiff. But such a statement might be useful for impeachment of the witness who signed it, if he is called and if he departs from the statement. There might be circumstances, too, where impossibility or difficulty of access to the witness or his refusal to respond to requests for information or other facts would show that the interests of justice require that such statements be made available. Production of such statements are governed by Rule 34 and on "Showing good cause therefore" the court may order their inspection, copying or photographing. No such application has here been made; the demand is made on the basis of right, not on showing of cause. [The requirement of "good cause" was removed by the 1970 amendment to Rule 34.]

I agree to the affirmance of the judgment of the Circuit Court of Appeals which reversed the district court.

Mr. Justice Frankfurter joins in this opinion.

Notes and Questions

1. In 1970, Federal Rule 26(b)(3) was added to deal with the discovery of work product. In what ways does the work-product doctrine in the Rule differ from that stated in *Hickman*? Does *Hickman* survive the codification of the work-product doctrine in the Rule in any way? See Clermont, *Surveying Work Product*, 68 Cornell L. Rev. 755 (1983).

2. Does Rule 26(b)(3) protect documents containing the results of a party's investigations made prior to hiring an attorney or the initiation of litigation? Does it protect material prepared as part of an organization's normal course of business even if the probability of litigation is overwhelming? Should protection cover the following circumstances?

a) A company prepares a memorandum about a contemplated transaction recognizing that the transaction may result in litigation;

b) A company is engaged in merger discussions with another company, which requests a candid assessment of the likelihood of success in pending litigations; or

c) A company prepares financial statements for its executives, including reserves for projected litigation.

See United States v. Adlman, 134 F.3d 1194 (2d Cir. 1998) (providing comprehensive discussion of different positions). Would the electronic storage of these communications affect your analysis?

3.   What circumstances constitute a sufficient showing of necessity to overcome work-product protection under Rule 26(b)(3)? In SNEAD v. AMERI-CAN EXPORT–ISBRANDTSEN LINES, INC., 59 F.R.D. 148, 151 (E.D. Pa. 1973), plaintiff, who had brought suit to recover for personal injuries, moved for a court order requiring defendant to answer interrogatories as to whether defendant had possession of any secret motion pictures taken of plaintiff that would tend to bear on the scope of plaintiff's injuries. The court held as follows:

> * * * The only time there will be a substantial need to know about surveillance pictures will be in those instances where there would be a major discrepancy between the testimony the plaintiff will give and that which the films would seem to portray. By the same token this would be the only instance where there is a substantial need to withhold that information from plaintiff's counsel. If the discrepancy would be the result of the plaintiff's untruthfulness, the substantial need for his counsel to know of the variance can hardly justify making the information available to him. On the other hand, if the discrepancy would result from misleading photography, the necessary background information should be made available to the plaintiff's attorney so the fraud can be exposed. It goes without saying that the means to impeach should not be the exclusive property of the defense. * * *

> I conclude these purposes can best be achieved by requiring the defense to disclose the existence of surveillance films or be barred from showing them at trial. If the defense has films and decides it wants to use them, they should be exhibited to the plaintiff and his counsel. * * *

> Before any of these disclosures, however, the defense must be given an opportunity to depose the plaintiff fully as to his injuries, their effects, and his present disabilities. Once his testimony is memorialized in deposition, any variation he may make at trial to conform to the surveillance films can be used to impeach his credibility, and his knowledge at deposition that the films may exist should have a salutary effect on any tendency to be expansive. * * *

Isn't it true that whenever a document or other item is to be introduced into evidence by one party, there will be a need for discovery, at least for the purpose of determining whether such an item has been forged, distorted, or altered in some way?

Is the *Snead* court's view as to the relevance of surveillance films too narrow? Impeachment is solely for the purpose of casting doubt on the veracity of a witness. But films of a party's physical condition also may be direct evidence of the condition itself. Certainly evidence that bears directly on the facts at issue in the case cannot be kept hidden until trial and then held to be admissible. The vast majority of courts thus permit discovery of such evidence if it is to be used at trial, regardless of its intended purpose. See Gutshall v. New Prime, Inc., 196 F.R.D. 43 (W.D. Va. 2000). Suppose in *Snead* the motion pictures strongly supported plaintiff's case and would not have been introduced at trial by defendant. Should they be protected from discovery by plaintiff? See Fisher v. National R.R. Passenger Corp., 152 F.R.D. 145 (S.D. Ind. 1993).

4. How can Rule 26(b)(3)(B), which provides protection "against disclosure of the mental impressions, conclusions, opinions or legal theories of a party's attorney or other representative concerning litigation," be harmonized with Rules 33(c) and 36(a), which allow interrogatories and requests for admissions involving opinions or contentions that relate to fact or the application of law to fact? Consider these problems:

(a) Should a party have to disclose the selection of documents made by counsel to prepare a witness for deposition?

(b) Can a party depose the opposing party's attorney to determine whether discovery production has been complete?

For a discussion of these and other problems, see Waits, *Opinion Work Product: A Critical Analysis of Current Law and a New Analytical Framework*, 73 Ore. L. Rev. 385 (1994).

2. PRIVILEGES AND WORK PRODUCT— THE EXTENT OF PROTECTION

Rule 26(b)(1) limits discovery to "any nonprivileged matter," and the usual view has been that the same rules of privilege apply to discovery as apply at the trial. A privilege rule gives a person a right to refuse to disclose information that he otherwise would be required to provide. It also may give a person the right to prevent someone else from disclosing information, or it may give its possessor a right to refuse to become a witness. A rule of privilege is a counterweight to the general power of courts to compel testimony. Modern pretrial discovery involves an extension of the judicial power to compel disclosure and has been met by the expansion of old privileges and the creation of new ones that will check this power.

One rule of privilege that all American courts recognize is the attorney-client privilege. They also agree on its basic contours. For the privilege to attach to a communication, four elements must be present:

(1) [T]he asserted holder of the privilege is or sought to be a client; (2) the person to whom the communication was made (a) is a member of the bar of a court, or his subordinate and (b) in connection with this communication is acting as a lawyer; (3) the communication relates to a fact of which the attorney was informed (a) by his client (b) without the presence of strangers (c) for the purpose of securing primarily either (i) an opinion on law or (ii) legal services or (iii) assistance in some legal proceeding, and not (d) for the purpose of committing a crime or tort; and (4) the privilege has been (a) claimed and (b) not waived by the client.

United States v. United Shoe Machinery Corp., 89 F.Supp. 357, 358–59 (D. Mass. 1950).

Because the attorney-client privilege results in the suppression of relevant facts, courts tend to construe it narrowly and to resolve doubtful cases against a finding of privilege. One observer has said that "[w]hile often unexpressed, the crucial factor limiting the privilege's availability is not the past law of the privilege but the developing rules of liberal discovery. * * * At least when precedent is not absolutely clear, whether a party can assert the privilege will often depend less on the jurisdiction's law of privilege than on the particular judge's attitude toward liberal discovery." Bartell, The Attorney-Client Privilege and the Work-Product Doctrine, in ALI–ABA Civil Procedure and Litigation in Federal and State Courts (Vol. I), at 507 (1987).

In UPJOHN CO. v. UNITED STATES, 449 U.S. 383, 101 S.Ct. 677, 66 L.Ed.2d 584 (1981), the Court considered the applicability of the attorney-client privilege in the corporate context. At issue were communications made by corporate employees to the company's General Counsel at the direction of corporate superiors in order to secure legal advice from counsel in connection with tax summonses from the Internal Revenue Service. The communications consisted of responses to a questionnaire designed by General Counsel to determine whether the company had made illegal payments. The Court declined to limit the scope of the privilege to officers and agents who control corporate policy.

> The control group test adopted by the court below thus frustrates the very purpose of the privilege by discouraging the communication of relevant information by employees of the client to attorneys seeking to render legal advice to the client corporation. The attorney's advice will also frequently be more significant to noncontrol group members than to those who officially sanction the advice, and the control group test makes it more difficult to convey full and frank legal advice to the employees who will put into effect the client corporation's policy. * * *

> The narrow scope given the attorney-client privilege by the court below not only makes it difficult for corporate attorneys to formulate sound advice when their client is faced with a specific legal problem but also threatens to limit the valuable efforts of corporate counsel to ensure their client's compliance with the law. In light of the vast and complicated array of regulatory legislation confronting the modern corporation, corporations, unlike most individuals, "constantly go to lawyers to find out how to obey the law[.]" * * * [I]f the purpose of the attorney-client privilege is to be served, the attorney and client must be able to predict with some degree of certainty whether particular discussions will be protected. An uncertain privilege, or one which purports to be certain but results in widely varying applications by the courts, is little better than no privilege at all. The very terms of the test adopted by the court below suggest the unpredictability of its application. The test restricts the availability of the privilege to those officers who play a "substantial role" in deciding and directing a corporation's legal response. * * *

The communications at issue were made by Upjohn employees to counsel for Upjohn acting as such, at the direction of corporate superiors in order to secure legal advice from counsel. * * * Information, not available from upper-echelon management, was needed to supply a basis for legal advice concerning compliance with securities and tax laws, foreign laws, currency regulations, duties to shareholders, and potential litigation in each of these areas. The communications concerned matters within the scope of the employees' corporate duties, and the employees themselves were sufficiently aware that they were being questioned in order that the corporation could obtain legal advice. The questionnaire identified Thomas as "the company's General Counsel" and referred in its opening sentence to the possible illegality of payments such as the ones on which information was sought. * * * A statement of policy accompanying the questionnaire clearly indicated the legal implications of the investigation. The policy statement was issued "in order that there be no uncertainty in the future as to the policy with respect to the practices which are the subject of this investigation." It began "Upjohn will comply with all laws and regulations," and stated that commissions or payments "will not be used as a subterfuge for bribes or illegal payments" and that all payments must be "proper and legal." Any future agreements with foreign distributors or agents were to be approved "by a company attorney" and any questions concerning the policy were to be referred "to the company's General Counsel." * * * This statement was issued to Upjohn employees worldwide, so that even those interviewees not receiving a questionnaire were aware of the legal implications of the interviews. Pursuant to explicit instructions from the Chairman of the Board, the communications were considered "highly confidential" when made, * * * and have been kept confidential by the company. Consistent with the underlying purposes of the attorney-client privilege, these communications must be protected against compelled disclosure.

The Court of Appeals declined to extend the attorney-client privilege beyond the limits of the control group test for fear that doing so would entail severe burdens on discovery and create a broad "zone of silence" over corporate affairs. Application of the attorney-client privilege to communications such as those involved here, however, puts the adversary in no worse position than if the communications had never taken place. The privilege only protects disclosure of communications; it does not protect disclosure of the underlying facts by those who communicated with the attorney * * *. Here the Government was free to question the employees who communicated with Thomas and outside counsel. Upjohn has provided the IRS with a list of such employees, and the IRS has already interviewed some 25 of them. While it would probably be more convenient for the Government to secure the results of petitioner's internal investigation by simply subpoenaing the questionnaires and notes taken by petitioner's attorneys, such considerations of convenience do not overcome the policies served by the attorney-client privilege. * * *

Id. at 392–97, 101 S.Ct. 684–86, 66 L.Ed.2d at 592–96.

NOTES AND QUESTIONS

1.   In state courts, the attorney-client privilege is a creation of state law (state common law or statute), not of federal law. For state courts, therefore, the *Upjohn* decision is not binding authority, and several have not found its reasoning to be persuasive. See, e.g., Consolidation Coal Co. v. Bucyrus–Erie Co., 89 Ill.2d 103, 59 Ill.Dec. 666, 432 N.E.2d 250 (1982) (rejecting *Upjohn* and adopting "control group" test).

In federal courts, the privilege is solely a matter of federal law, except that Federal Rule of Evidence 501 directs a federal district court sitting in a diversity case to apply the privilege law that would be applied by the courts of the state in which the federal court sits. When federal and state law claims are joined, federal law may govern the attorney-client privilege, Valente v. Pepsico, Inc., 68 F.R.D. 361, 366 n.10 (D. Del. 1975), unless the allegedly privileged communication relates solely to the state law claims.

2.   Historically, the attorney-client privilege and the work-product protection were waived if the protected communication was disclosed voluntarily. Once waived the party could be forced to disclose not only the specific communication but all communications involving the same subject matter. See Duplan Corp. v. Deering Milliken, Inc., 379 F.Supp. 388 (D. S.C. 1974). Given the breadth of modern discovery of documents and electronically stored information, the danger of an inadvertent disclosure of protected materials resulting in a waiver has become significant. The costs of discovery have escalated in a number of cases in which individuals are hired to scan every document or piece of information before turning it over to an opposing party. Concern over the injustice that this can cause has been addressed in Rule 26(b)(5)(B) and by enactment of Federal Rule of Evidence 502 that provides relief in federal courts from waiver in cases of inadvertent disclosure or when disclosure occurred despite reasonable efforts to prevent it. It is important to note, however, that the protection afforded by these rules applies only when materials are turned over in the course of a formal proceeding or to a governmental agency. Revealing the contents to a prospective witness or to an expert or to a nonparty is likely to result in a waiver. When protected information is formally sought, the responding party must assert the grounds of the privilege or protection; it cannot selectively reveal a portion of a communication and maintain the privilege for the remainder. See, e.g., Nguyen v. Excel Corp., 197 F.3d 200, 206 (5th Cir. 1999).

3.   The attorney-client privilege is an example of an "absolute" privilege. If the privilege attaches to a communication, a court cannot compel its disclosure no matter how compelling the adversary's need for the information. Some privileges are "qualified." How might this difference affect the courts' handling of the two types of privileges?

4.   The attorney-client privilege is just one of the privileges that affect the scope of discovery. The Constitution is the source of several privileges—

for example, the Fifth Amendment privilege against self-incrimination. Other privileges are founded on common law and statutes. Among the widely recognized privileges are the privileges for communications between husband and wife, priest and penitent, and physician and patient. Other privileges struggle for recognition—for example, a privilege for communications between accountants and their clients. See generally *Developments in the Law— Privileged Communications*, 98 Harv. L. Rev. 1450 (1985).

5. The 1993 amendments to the Federal Rules added a new Rule 26(b)(5), which requires that a claim of privilege or work product be made expressly and that the nature of the items withheld be described in a manner that enables other parties to assess the applicability of the privilege. Failure to comply will result in a loss of protection. In MOLONEY v. UNITED STATES, 204 F.R.D. 16 (D. Mass. 2001), a medical malpractice action, plaintiff deposed the attending physician and asked questions about the doctor's conversations about plaintiff's treatment. During the deposition, the following colloquy occurred:

> [Plaintiff's counsel] * * *: Tell me how you came to speak to Dr. Barrett * * * about * * * [plaintiff]?
>
> [Defendant's counsel] * * *: I'm going to object at this point. I think that this conversation may be privileged and so I'm going to assert the objection with respect to privilege. I think you can ascertain the chronology of the conversation, but with respect to the subject, at this point in time I'm going to object and instruct her not to answer as to substance. We may change the position but at this point in time, I believe that this conversation is privileged.
>
> [Plaintiff's counsel]* * *: Privileged on what grounds?
>
> [Defendant's counsel] * * *: Attorney/client and work product privilege in anticipation of litigation. * * *

Id. at 18. Later in the deposition, the colloquy resumed:

> [Plaintiff's counsel] * * *: I just [want] to be clear for the record, Mary, that your position is that these are privileged under the attorney/client privilege and the work product privilege?
>
> [Defendant's counsel] * * *: At this time that's my position.
>
> * * *
>
> [Plaintiff's counsel] * * *: Again, your position on those is they're privileged by virtue of the attorney/client privilege or the attorney work product privilege?
>
> [Defendant's counsel] * * *: At this time, yes, that's my assertion.
>
> [Plaintiff's counsel] * * *: Just so you'll know, I'm going to move to compel these. Obviously if you don't agree that they're not privileged— well, I'm going to expect more than a telephone deposition. I mean, I really don't think that's an acceptable way, at least from my point of view. I want a witness to talk about these things. I think this could be absolutely critical in my preparation of this case.
>
> [Defendant's counsel] * * *: We'll talk about that. * * *

Id. at 19. Plaintiff later moved to compel production, and defendant resisted, claiming protection under the federal self-critical analysis privilege, federal medical peer review privilege, and state statutory privilege, but not work-product protection or attorney-client privilege. The District Court ordered production, explaining: "[I]t defies logic to permit counsel to assert one privilege so as to preclude testimony at a deposition, but thereafter research and claim an entirely different privilege in response to a motion to compel. Such conduct most assuredly circumvents both the letter and the spirit of Rules 26(b)(5) and 30(d)(1) [now Rule 30(c)(2)]." Did defendant's counsel provide sufficient information? What more could she have done?

3. EXPERT INFORMATION

————

Read Federal Rule of Civil Procedure 26(a)(2) and 26(b)(4) in the Supplement.

————

KRISA v. EQUITABLE LIFE ASSURANCE SOCIETY

United States District Court, Middle District of Pennsylvania, 2000.
196 F.R.D. 254.

VANASKIE, CHIEF JUDGE.

This case concerns Equitable's decision to deny Krisa's application for disability benefits under insurance policies issued to Krisa by Equitable. * * *

A. The Production of Draft Expert Reports and Written Analyses Pre-pared by Testifying Experts

Krisa seeks production of preliminary reports and other documents created by Equitable's experts in connection with this litigation. Equitable responds that it need not produce the draft reports and written analyses generated by its experts because such documents are protected by the work product doctrine codified in Rule 26(b)(3) * * *. Equitable's argu-ment disregards the fact that the protection afforded by Rule 26(b)(3) is subject to Rule 26(b)(4), which generally authorizes discovery of testifying expert witnesses. * * * [T]he structure of Rule 26 and the Advisory Committee Notes that accompanied the authorization of expert witness discovery in 1970 suggest the conclusion that documents prepared by expert witnesses are not within the ambit of the work product doctrine. * * * [T]he Rules plainly contemplate discovery of not only the opinions the testifying experts intend to advance at trial, but also preliminary or tentative opinions expressed by the testifying experts that may be in conflict with their final opinions. * * *

The conclusion that draft reports and other documents prepared by Equitable's witnesses in this case are not covered by the work product privilege is consistent with the policy considerations underlying the privilege. The work product privilege is based upon "the general policy against invading the privacy of an attorney's course of preparation." Bogosian v. Gulf Oil Corp., 738 F.2d 587, 592 (3d Cir. 1984) * * *. * * * Equitable's representations indicate that counsel's mental processes and opinions are not contained in the expert's draft reports. Thus, requesting production of these documents will not invade the privacy to be accorded Equitable's trial counsel in developing litigation strategies and theories. Moreover, Krisa could be deprived of information that would be material to effective cross-examination of Equitable's experts if deprived of the expression of the evolution of the experts' opinions.

B.   Communications From Equitable's Counsel to Testifying Expert Witnesses

There has been a significant split among courts that have addressed whether core attorney work product shared with a party's expert is discoverable. * * *

* * *

* * * Our Court of Appeals addressed this issue in *Bogosian*, 738 F.2d at 595, and held that core work product generated by an attorney was shielded from discovery even if disclosed to an expert. * * *

Although courts have noted that "the reasoning of those cases interpreting the Rule prior to 1993 [when the Rule was amended] * * * is probably obsolete," they have remained divided on whether attorney work product is discoverable when given to an expert.

Several courts have held that the 1993 Amendments to Rule 26(a)(2) were "designed to mandate full disclosure of those materials reviewed by an expert witness, regardless of whether they constitute opinion work product." Karn [v. Ingersoll–Rand Co., 168 F.R.D. 633, 637 (N.D. Ind. 1996)]. * * * Those courts that have favored the disclosure of attorney work product argue that their "bright-line" interpretation "makes good sense on several policy grounds: effective cross-examination of expert witnesses will be enhanced; the policies underlying the work product doctrine will not be violated; and, finally, litigation certainty will be achieved—counsel will know exactly what documents will be subject to disclosure and can react accordingly." Karn, 168 F.R.D. at 639.

However, other courts have rejected the reasoning of Karn [and other cases]. * * * In Haworth, [Inc. v. Herman Miller, Inc., 162 F.R.D. 289 (W.D. Mich. 1995),] the court stated that "for the high privilege accorded attorney opinion work product not to apply would require clear and unambiguous language...." Id. at 295. * * *

The policy reason apparently given the most weight by courts in favor of the "bright-line" rule for production of materials disclosed to an expert is that an expert cannot be properly impeached without knowledge of all the relevant materials that shaped the expert's opinion. *E.g.*, Karn, 168 F.R.D. at 639. In Begosian, however, our Court of Appeals noted that "the marginal value on cross-examination that the expert's view may have originated with an attorney's opinion or theory does not warrant over-riding the strong policy against disclosure of documents consisting of core attorney's work product." 738 F.2d at 595. The Third Circuit recognized that even where an expert's opinion originated with the attorney, the most effective way to discredit an opposing expert is the presentation of one's own credible expert. * * *

Adoption of a "bright-line" rule in favor of mandating production of attorney work product, while increasing the potential for a party to effectively cross-examine an opponent's expert, abridges the attorney work product privilege without specific authority to do so. * * *

Only one document sent by Equitable's counsel to an expert contains attorney work product, and only one document prepared by an expert witness * * * embodies core work product. * * * Equitable will not be compelled to produce those documents.

NOTES AND QUESTIONS

1.   Until 1993, discovery regarding the information of experts who were called to testify was limited to interrogatories unless the District Court otherwise provided. That year, the Federal Rules were amended to include a requirement of mandatory disclosure, which affects the exchange of information about expert witnesses. See Fed. R. Civ. P. 26(a)(2)(A)-(C). In addition, Rule 26(e)(1) imposes a duty to supplement the mandatory disclosures, and this obligation extends to an expert's responses during a deposition. The Advisory Committee note to the 1993 amendment of Rule 26(a)(2)(A), referred to in *Krisa*, provides:

> The report is to disclose the data and other information considered by the expert and any other exhibits or charts that summarize or support the expert's opinions. Given this obligation of disclosure, litigants should no longer be able to argue that materials furnished to their experts to be used in forming their opinions—whether or not ultimately relied upon by the expert—are privileged or otherwise protected from disclosure when such persons are testifying or being deposed.

Do you agree with the District Court's decision in *Krisa*? In *Krisa*, the documents were not cited by the expert in his report, and arguably were not relied on by the expert in forming his opinion. What if the expert not only relied on the documents, but also specifically cited them in his report? See Doe v. Luzerne County, 2008 WL 2518131 (N.D. Pa. 2008).

2.   Rule 26(b)(4)(B) permits discovery of facts and opinions from an expert employed in anticipation of trial and who will not be called to testify, but only upon a showing of special circumstances. What circumstances justify discovery under this provision? See Disidore v. Mail Contractors of America, Inc., 196 F.R.D. 410, 415–19 (D. Kan. 2000). What if an expert who will not testify at trial develops materials that are then provided to another expert for the party who will testify? Should work-product protection apply to those materials that the expert states did not form a basis for his conclusions? See

Mickum, *Guise, Contrivance, or Artful Dodging? The Discovery Rules Governing Testifying Employee Experts*, 24 Rev. Litig. 301 (2005).

SECTION E.   SANCTIONS AND JUDICIAL SUPERVISION OF DISCOVERY

————

Read Federal Rule of Civil Procedure 37 in the Supplement.

————

Although the Federal Rules went into effect in 1938, until relatively recently judges showed extreme reluctance to apply available sanctions when faced with violations of the discovery rules. One commentary explains:

> The typical pattern of sanctioning that emerges from the reported cases is one in which the delay, obfuscation, contumacy, and lame excuses on the part of litigants and their attorneys are tolerated without any measured remedial action until the court is provoked beyond endurance. At that point the court punishes one side or the other with a swift and final termination of the lawsuit by dismissal or default. This "all or nothing" approach to sanctions results in considerable laxity in the day-to-day application of the rules. Attorneys are well aware that sanctions will be imposed only in the most flagrant situations.

Rodes, Ripple & Mooney, Sanctions Imposable for Violations of the Federal Rules of Civil Procedure 85 (Fed. Jud. Center 1981). Spurred in part by the Supreme Court's opinions in NATIONAL HOCKEY LEAGUE v. METROPOLITAN HOCKEY CLUB, INC., 427 U.S. 639, 96 S.Ct. 2778, 49 L.Ed.2d 747 (1976), and ROADWAY EXPRESS, INC. v. PIPER, 447 U.S. 752, 100 S.Ct. 2455, 65 L.Ed.2d 488 (1980), which strongly supported the use of sanctions, judges increasingly have applied and upheld sanctions in a much wider variety of situations. See American Bar Association, Sanctions: Rule 11 and Other Powers 34–36, 46–48, 61–70, 79–82, 97–101, 115–16, 128–29, 138–42, 158–60, 170, 175–77, 182, 186–87 (2d ed. 1988) (surveying recent decisions); see also American Law Institute–American Bar Association, Sanctions in Civil Litigation: A Review of Sanctions by Rule, Statute, and Inherent Power (2007). A survey of decisions involving the discovery of electronic information before the 2006 amendments found that courts granted sanctions in about two-thirds of the cases, most often where a party had willfully destroyed documents in violation of a court order or caused prejudice to the opposing party. See Scheindlin & Wangkeo, *Electronic Discovery Sanctions in the Twenty-First Century*, 11 Mich. Telecomm. & Tech. L. Rev. 71, 73 (2004).

NOTES AND QUESTIONS

1. How do discovery disputes get to court? How does the Rule 26(c) route differ from that of Rule 37(a)? Under both, the parties must first confer to try to resolve their differences. What other potential sanction does Rule 26(g) add? How do these three provisions differ from Rule 11?

2. Rule 37 was revised in 1993 to reflect the addition of the mandatory disclosure provision in Rule 26(a), by providing a means to compel that disclosure. What happens if a party fails to disclose information in accordance with Rule 26(a) then seeks to introduce the information as evidence at trial? In this circumstance, must the opposing party move to block introduction of the evidence?

3. The district courts have broad discretion to impose sanctions to remedy discovery abuse. See In re Phenylpropanolamine (PPA) Prods. Liab. Litig., 460 F.3d 1217, 1226–32 (9th Cir. 2006). The most severe sanction that a court can impose is dismissal of plaintiff's complaint or ordering the entry of judgment against defendant. See Chrysler Corp. v. Carey, 186 F.3d 1016, 1020–22 (8th Cir. 1999) (affirming entry of judgment of liability against defendants). This extreme sanction is disfavored because the courts are reluctant to deny a litigant her day in court. An appellate court will scrutinize the decision closely to ensure that the determination is within the proper bounds of the trial court's discretion, but can affirm even if a more modest sanction is available. See Everyday Learning Corp. v. Larson, 242 F.3d 815 (8th Cir. 2001). Other possible sanctions include the imposition of costs, attorneys' fees, and expenses, see, e.g., Legault v. Zambarano, 105 F.3d 24, 28 (1st Cir. 1997) (imposing on client and lawyer monetary sanction equal to cost of fees reasonably expended by opposing party), as well as reprimands and censure. See Slawotsky, *Rule 37 Discovery Sanctions—The Need for Supreme Court Ordered National Uniformity*, 104 Dick. L. Rev. 471, 479–80 (2000). What factors ought to guide a court's choice of sanctions for discovery abuse?

CHAPTER 11

CASE MANAGEMENT

■ ■ ■

This Chapter examines the history, theory, and practice of judicial case management techniques. One of the hallmark features of the adversary system is its reliance on the parties to initiate the action and to move the proceeding forward toward resolution. However, rising caseloads, increased expense, liberal discovery practice, and shifting attitudes toward civil litigation have caused courts and commentators to rethink this basic adversarial assumption. Professor Miller, for example, has asked whether "the adversary system as we know it has become too costly and inefficient a device for resolving civil disputes." Miller, *The Adversary System: Dinosaur or Phoenix*, 69 Minn. L. Rev. 1, 19 (1984). Judicial case management techniques reflect one significant response to this perceived problem.

SECTION A.   RULE 16 AND THE DEVELOPMENT OF CASE MANAGEMENT TECHNIQUES

———

Read Federal Rule of Civil Procedure 16 and the accompanying materials in the Supplement.

———

MILLER, THE PRETRIAL RUSH TO JUDGMENT: ARE THE "LITIGATION EXPLOSION," "LIABILITY CRISIS," AND EFFICIENCY CLICHÉS ERODING OUR DAY IN COURT AND JURY TRIAL COMMITMENTS?, 78 N.Y.U. L. Rev. 982, 1003 (2004) (footnotes omitted):

Federal district judges began utilizing management techniques on an ad hoc basis in the years following the Second World War. These experimental procedures were organized under the aegis of the Handbook of Recommended Procedure for the Trial of Protracted Cases and then the Manual on Complex Litigation, which first appeared in the 1960s. Their principles were given greater prominence and officially sanctioned in 1983, and then embellished further in 1993 by amendments to Rule 16; prior to these amendments the Rule described a discretionary and rather simple eve-of-trial conference. Given that by the early 1980s only an estimated six percent of cases actually reached trial and the lion's share of resource expenditures occurred pretrial, the Rule was of little help in reducing the institution-to-termination litigation timeframe, let alone achieving any systemic economy. Recognizing that judicial intervention should occur shortly after commencement, Rule 16 was transformed into a provision that encouraged—and in time effectively mandated—judicial management throughout the pretrial proceedings.

———

SHAPIRO, FEDERAL RULE 16: A LOOK AT THE THEORY AND PRACTICE OF RULEMAKING, 137 U. Pa. L. Rev. 1969, 1977, 1980–84 (1989) (footnotes omitted):

* * * Rule [16 was] designed to substitute for formal pleadings the less formal processes of discussion and exchange as ways of narrowing issues for trial and of expediting proof. But because flexibility and discretion were the watchwords, judges were not instructed to do anything; they would only be encouraged to act. At the same time, they were not given express power to act coercively in any way not authorized by other, more formal procedures, and the comments of several important figures in the drafting of the rules left little doubt of their resistance to the coercive use of the conference.

* * *

* * * [A]n extraordinary range of practices * * * developed within the framework of the Rule [as promulgated in 1938]. While in some districts judges made relatively little use of the Rule, and seldom required pretrial conferences, other districts promulgated elaborate local rules that required pretrial conferences in most or all cases and/or imposed heavy burdens on counsel to confer in advance and to prepare detailed pretrial orders for the judge's consideration. Some judges held pretrial conferences early and often, and were encouraged to do so in complex cases by the Manual for Complex Litigation. Some judges saw the pretrial conference as the chance to compel the parties to produce information that had not been (and perhaps could not be) sought in routine pretrial discovery; others saw the occasion as an opportunity to rid the case of frivolous or insubstantial issues of fact or law, whether or not requested to do so by one of the parties in an appropriate motion; still others saw the conference as a device to facilitate settlement, and saw the judge as a major player in that process.

* * *

At a more general level, the major development during this period was a sea-change in the attitude of many, perhaps most, judges toward their role in the pretrial period—a change that occurred with surprisingly little concern for the purposes and limitations of Rule 16. Judges began to see themselves less as neutral adjudicators—deciding what the parties brought to them for decision and proceeding at a pace to be determined by the parties—and more as managers of a costly and complicated process. Many district courts began to assign judges to a case from the beginning, and many judges, encouraged by this system and by the increased availability of magistrates and other support staff, began to manage their cases with a firm hand. Crowded dockets, costly discovery, and delay were seen as problems not just for the litigants but for the system, and even the litigants were thought of as frequent victims of their lawyers' self-interest. The role of the judge, then, was to keep cases moving at a reasonable pace, and to see that cases not be needlessly tried. Indeed, the concept of disposition without trial began to embrace a variety of inventive techniques other than simple mediation and settlement.

* * *

The purposes of the [1983] amended Rule has been described in the Advisory Committee's Note and in comments by its Reporter, Arthur Miller. A major purpose was to recognize, and indeed to embrace, the strong trend toward increased judicial management of litigation from an early stage of the lawsuit. Among the means of expressing this purpose were the authorization of an early scheduling conference at which various deadlines would be established and further conferences agreed upon, and the inclusion among the subjects to be discussed of a number of matters relating not to the trial itself but to the pretrial period.

* * *

SECTION B.   THE OPERATION OF RULE 16

Rule 16 was amended in 1993 to strengthen the trial judge's authority to manage the litigation and facilitate disposition of the case. The Rule provides deadlines for specific litigation activities, makes explicit and expands the topics to be discussed at the pretrial conference, provides for greater supervision of discovery, allows for earlier consideration of Rule 56 motions, and confirms the judge's authority to encourage settlement by ordering the parties to be present at pretrial conferences. Rule 16 also clarifies the scope of trial court discretion to impose sanctions on the parties for such dereliction as failing to comply with a scheduling order or absence from, or lack of preparation for, a pretrial conference. The 2006 amendment to Rule 16(b) makes clear that the scheduling order can address the discovery or disclosure of electronically stored information.

NOTES AND QUESTIONS

1. What standard applies when a party seeks to amend its pleadings after the deadline in the scheduling order has expired? In KASSNER v. 2ND

AVENUE DELICATESSEN INC., 496 F.3d 229 (2d Cir. 2007), an employment discrimination action, plaintiffs moved to amend the complaint before defendants had filed an answer, but one month after the date specified in the Rule 16(b) scheduling order as the final date for amending the pleadings. Although Rule 15 allows for amendment of the pleading as a matter or course, the Second Circuit held that this provision of Rule 15(a) "is subject to the district court's discretion to limit the time for amendment of the pleadings in a scheduled order issued under Rule 16(b)." Id. at 244. In this case, however, the court of appeals reversed and remanded, finding that the trial court had abused its discretion by failing to consider whether plaintiff could demonstrate good cause to amend the complaint after the deadline in the scheduling order had passed. The Second Circuit explained:

> On remand, the district court must exercise its discretion under Rule 16(b) to determine whether the scheduling order should be modified so as to allow an amended complaint. * * * [T]he primary consideration is whether the moving party can demonstrate diligence. It is not, however, the only consideration. The district court * * * also may consider other relevant factors including, in particular, whether allowing the amendment of the pleading at this stage of the litigation will prejudice defendants. * * *

Id. at 245.

2. What counts as "good cause" to modify a pretrial scheduling order? In FAHIM v. MARRIOTT HOTEL SERVICES, INC., 551 F.3d 344, 348 (5th Cir. 2008), the Court of Appeals relied on a four-factor test in affirming denial of a belated motion to amend a pleading: "(1) the explanation for the failure to timely move for leave to amend; (2) the importance of the amendment; (3) potential prejudice in allowing the amendment; and (4) the availability of a continuance to cure such prejudice." How does the Rule 16 inquiry differ from that of Rule 15?

SECTION C. THE FINAL PRETRIAL ORDER

PAYNE v. S.S. NABOB

United States Court of Appeals, Third Circuit, 1962.
302 F.2d 803.

McLAUGHLIN, CIRCUIT JUDGE.

In this personal injury admiralty action libellant filed a pretrial memorandum stating that he was relying upon the condition of a winch to prove his cause of action. The judge's pretrial report noted that. Sometime later the suit went to trial. Libellant's attorney included in his opening the fact that the loading had been handled improperly as an important element of his proof of unseaworthiness. The impleaded stevedore employer objected as it was outside the scope of the pretrial memorandum and report. The trial court sustained the objection. Two witnesses on behalf of the libellant, not listed in his pretrial memorandum, were not allowed to testify. Libellant's attorney moved for a continuance and this was denied.

* * *

Appellant * * * would have it that the Standing Order [local rule adopting Rule 16] did not furnish any ground for the court's barring of the unseaworthy allegation and of the witnesses not mentioned in the appellant's pretrial memorandum or the court's pretrial report. This seems to be founded on the thought that a pretrial memorandum is merely preparatory to the conference and that the court's pretrial order is the sole proof of the results of the pretrial procedure. In this instance, goes the contention, the function of appellant's memorandum was exhausted at the conference and since no pretrial "order" was made there were no binding results of the pretrial steps. [Padovani v. Bruchhausen, 293 F.2d 546 (2d Cir. 1961)] * * * is cited for this, where it states:

"Nothing in the rule [16] affords basis for clubbing the parties into admissions they do not willingly make; but it is a way of advancing the trial ultimately to be had by setting forth points on which the parties are agreed after a conference directed by a trained judge."

Appellant was not clubbed into admissions he did not willingly make. It was his own voluntary statement of the basis of his claim that was included in the pretrial report of the judge. The report was never objected to as incorrectly outlining appellant's pretrial statement.

The position now taken that the pretrial report of the trial judge because it is not titled as an "order" does not comply with Rule 16 is without merit. Appellant's pretrial memorandum was filed. In accordance with the Standing Order it contained a "brief summary statement of both the facts of this case and counsel's contention as to the liability of defendant." It also contained "The names and addresses of all witnesses (except rebuttal) whom the plaintiff expects to call to testify at the time of trial." The pretrial conference was held in due course and attended by the attorneys for the parties. Based on the pretrial memoranda and the conference, the district judge drew and filed his report. There was no complaint concerning it or any part of it down to and including the trial until libellant's attorney was stopped in his opening as he went beyond his pretrial outline of alleged liability. The pretrial "report"[2] drawn, signed

---

2.   "Pre–Trial Report of Judge Van Dusen

Date Pre–Trial Held: 9/21/59 No. on Consolidated List: 2109 303 of 1958 in Admiralty

Case Title: Hosea Payne v. S.S. Nabob & North German Lloyd v. Lavino Shipping Co.

1.   Trial Counsel: LC Philip Dorfman, Esq. & Saul C. Waldbaum, Esq.

R—Robert A. Hauslohner, Esq. (T. Mount will try)

IR—F. Hastings Griffin, Jr., Esq. (P. Price will try)

2.   Amendments: If IR wishes to amend pre-trial memo, notice to be given to undersigned.

3.   Discovery: Respondent will answer impleaded respondent's interrogatories (unexecuted copies to be furnished counsel by September 23).

4.   L's Claim: Ship unseaworthy due to improper port winch on after side at #2 hatch. Brakes would not hold when set in neutral. Port winch on house-fall did not work from early hours of morning. See pre-trial memo.

5.   R's Claim: Sole cause of injuries was L's negligence and that of his fellow workmen. Two men pushed draft into L and 2 other men said nothing was defective in winches. See pre-trial memo. IR's position—see pre-trial memo.

6.   Stipulations:

and filed by the pretrial judge properly and fully (having the particular litigation and its requirements in mind) complies with the requirements of Rule 16. It, including its references to the pretrial memoranda, succinctly fulfilled the letter and spirit of pretrial. It reduced the action to essentials, eliminated surplusage, enabled the parties and the court to prepare for a trial of stated issues, named witnesses and contained no hidden charms. The argument to the contrary, depending as it does on a quibble over the word "report", is rootless.

It is asserted on behalf of the appellant that the Standing Order can only be construed as a request to stipulate, that counsel had no intention of stipulating and that no warning or notice was given by the Standing Order that failure to list the requirements ordered would constitute a stipulation or a waiver of all other theories. Rule 16 gives as the first purpose of pretrial "The simplification of issues". [This language has been altered without any substantive change.] Under the Standing Order counsel were asked to furnish "A brief summary of both the facts of the case and counsel's contentions as to the liability of the defendant." That was done. Libellant's contentions as to the liability of the defendant were inserted into the Court's Report with the note "See pre-trial memo". The Report was filed September 28, 1959. The trial did not commence until March 14, 1960, a five and a half months interval during which no effort was made to change the signed and filed contentions of the libellant regarding the liability of the defendant or to add names of witnesses. The facts that the situation was plain on its face and that the practice was well settled by then, (the Standing Order having been in effect since October 23, 1958), set the tone for this contention on behalf of appellant. Krieger v. Ownership Corporation, 270 F.2d 265 (3 Cir. 1959), relied upon by appellant is inapposite. We there held that disputed issues of fact *actually raised* at the pretrial stage could not be resolved by the trial court on motion for summary judgment. It has long been the law that attorneys at the pretrial stage "owe a duty to the court and opposing counsel to make a full and fair disclosure of their views as to what the real issues at the trial will be." Cherney v. Holmes, 185 F.2d 718, 721 (7th Cir. 1950) * * *. It is through such disclosure at pretrial that trial prejudice can be avoided. The awareness of appellant's attorney to the trial situation is apparent in his request for a continuance when he told the court "I think under the circumstances I would move for a continuance of the case to give *the other side* ample time, because actually this is a question of surprise." * * * [Emphasis supplied in original.]

It is argued also that the court abused its discretion by refusing to permit amendment of the pretrial memorandum. This was not an easy decision for the trial judge. His inclination clearly, as is habitual with judges, was to help. And help he would have if, in his opinion, he could

---

7. Issues:

8. Legal Issues:

9. Trial Time: 6 days

Francis L. Van Dusen, J."

have done so fairly. But he was confronted with the realization that if he granted the request or allowed a continuance of the trial he was repudiating the whole pretrial theory and system as understood and followed in the Eastern District at a crucial period of its existence. Pretrial was finally on a firm foundation there. The judges had all given it generous and complete attention. This, with the gradual realization of the bar that pretrial was here to stay as a vital element of litigation practice and its resultant full cooperation, had made pretrial procedure routine in the Eastern District. One consequence was that directly and indirectly enormous relief was given the badly clogged trial list. It was admittedly vitally important to make sure that pretrial procedure would continue to function properly. One necessary phase of attaining that objective was, as expressed by the trial judge, "We have come to the point of enforcing it very strictly." In the circumstances he considered himself obliged to deny the motions to amend the pretrial memorandum with respect to liability allegations and witnesses. The refusal of appellant's motion for a continuance is in the same category.

Beyond all doubt the judge acted entirely within his discretion. It was difficult for him, it took courage but it was what this sound, experienced judge had to do as he saw it, in accordance with his judicial obligation.

The decree of the district court will be affirmed.

NOTES AND QUESTIONS

1. Courts generally treat the final pretrial order, including the stipulations, agreements, and statements of counsel made at the final pretrial conference, as binding for purposes of trial. Many of the benefits associated with the use of the pretrial order depend upon its binding effect. But given the exigencies that are an inevitable part of litigation, particularly at the trial level, is strict finality reasonable?

2. What happens if a claim is included in a complaint but omitted from a pretrial order? Conversely, if a claim is included in a pretrial order that does not appear in the complaint, is it necessary to amend the pleading? Does Rule 16(d) provide an answer?

SECTION D. CASE MANAGEMENT SANCTIONS

NICK v. MORGAN'S FOODS, INC.

United States Court of Appeals, Eighth Circuit, 2001.
270 F.3d 590.

McMILLIAN, CIRCUIT JUDGE.

[The District Court imposed a monetary sanction on a defendant and its counsel for failing to participate in good faith in court-ordered alternative dispute resolution ("ADR") in an effort to settle the lawsuit.]

* * *

* * * Nick filed suit against appellant on June 15, 1998, alleging sexual harassment and retaliation in violation of Title VII of the Civil Rights Act of 1964, as amended, 42 U.S.C. § 2000e et seq. At that time, appellant was represented by outside counsel Robert Seibel, but all business decisions were made by appellant's in-house counsel Barton Craig. Pursuant to Fed. R. Civ. P. 16(f) [now, Rule 16(b)(1)(B)], a pretrial scheduling conference was held on May 20, 1999. The parties consented to ADR with a court-appointed mediator pursuant to E.D. Mo. L.R. 6.01–6.05 ("the local rules"), and agreed to report back to the district court with the results of the ADR by September 30, 1999. On August 2, 1999, the district court issued an Order * * * mandating that the ADR process be conducted in compliance with the local rules and listing other specific requirements. * * * These requirements included, inter alia, that, at least seven days before the first ADR conference, each party shall supply the mediator with a memorandum presenting a summary of the disputed facts and its position on liability and damages; that all parties, counsel, corporate representatives and claims professionals with settlement authority shall attend all mediation conferences and participate in good faith; and that noncompliance with any court deadline could result in the imposition of sanctions against the appropriate party or parties.

On appellant's request, the district court agreed to postpone the first ADR conference until October 18, 1999. Appellant did not file the memorandum that was required to be filed at least seven days before the first ADR conference. In attendance at the conference on October 18, 1999 was the court-appointed mediator; Nick; Nick's counsel; appellant's outside counsel, Seibel; and a corporate representative of appellant who had no independent knowledge of the facts of the case and had permission to settle only up to $500. Any settlement offer over $500 had to be relayed by telephone to Craig, who chose not to attend the ADR conference on the advice of outside counsel Seibel. During the ADR conference, Nick twice made offers of settlement that were rejected without a counteroffer by appellant. The ADR conference ended shortly thereafter without a settlement having been reached.

After the ADR conference, the mediator informed the district court of appellant's minimal level of participation, and the district court issued an order directing appellant to show cause why it should not be sanctioned for its failure to participate in good faith in the court-ordered ADR process. In an October 29, 1999 response, appellant asserted that the Referral Order was only a set of nonbinding guidelines and admitted that it decided not to comply with the guidelines because doing otherwise would be a waste of time and money. On the same day, Nick moved to sanction appellant for failing to participate in good faith in the ADR process and requested attorneys' fees and costs arising out of her participation in the mediation.

The district court held a hearing on its show cause order and Nick's motion for sanctions on December 1, 1999, at which time Seibel confirmed that appellant's corporate representative at the ADR conference had only $500 settlement authority; that any change in appellant's position could only be made by Craig, who was not present but available by telephone; and that counsel had indeed failed to file the pre-ADR conference memorandum. After hearing argument by both parties, the district court concluded that appellant failed to participate in good faith in the court-ordered ADR process and sanctioned appellant $1,390.63 and appellant's outside counsel $1,390.62. These sanctions were calculated to cover the cost of the ADR conference fees ($506.25) and Nick's attorneys' fees ($2,275.00). The court also ordered appellant to pay a $1,500.00 fine to the Clerk of the District Court as a sanction for failing to prepare the required memorandum and for its decision to send a corporate representative with limited authority to settle to the ADR conference. The district court ordered appellant and appellant's outside counsel each to pay $30.00 to Nick for the costs she incurred attending the ADR conference.

On December 20, 1999, appellant filed a Motion for Reconsideration and Vacation of the Court's Order Granting Plaintiff's Motion for Sanctions (motion for reconsideration). The district court denied the motion for reconsideration and imposed additional sanctions against appellant and appellant's counsel in the amount of $1,250.00 each to be paid to the Clerk of the District Court for vexatiously increasing the costs of litigation by filing a frivolous motion. This appeal followed. Appellant appeals the sanctions levied against it that are to be paid to the Clerk of the District Court; Appellant does not contest the sanctions levied against it that are to be paid to Nick and her counsel.

* * *

Appellant argues that, whereas Rule 11 * * * authorizes monetary fines payable to the court, Rule 16 does not. * * * Rule 16(f) expressly permits a judge to impose any other sanction the judge deems appropriate in addition to, or in lieu of, reasonable expenses. * * * Here, the district court judge acted well within his discretion by imposing a monetary fine payable to the Clerk of the District Court as a sanction for failing to prepare the required memorandum, deciding to send a corporate representative with limited authority to the ADR conference, and for vexatiously increasing the costs of litigation by filing a frivolous motion for reconsideration.

* * *

Appellant urges that the "uncontroverted facts on the record conclusively establish that all of the conduct which irritated the Trial Court was the exclusive product of Appellant's trial lawyer and unknown to Appellant." * * * Appellant argues that the affidavits of Craig and Seibel establish that it had no knowledge that its conduct was sanctionable and that its outside counsel was solely responsible for the noncompliance. * * * Appellant claims that Seibel did not pass along to Craig the necessity for a memorandum, and that, although Seibel advised Craig of the district court's Referral Order and the relevant local rules, Craig read neither and relied instead on the advice of Seibel. * * * Appellant further claims that Seibel advised Craig that his attendance at the ADR conference was not necessary. * * * For this reason, appellant argues that the district court abused its discretion in imposing the sanctions against it and not solely against its outside counsel.

It is undisputed that appellant did not provide the court-ordered memorandum to the mediator because appellant's outside counsel considered it unnecessary and duplicative, and thus too costly. * * * It is further undisputed that appellant's corporate representative at the ADR conference had settlement authority limited to $500 * * *, and that any settlement offer over $500 could only be considered by Craig, who was not present and only available by telephone. * * * Appellant argues that its counsel, Seibel, failed to inform appellant that Craig was required to attend the mediation and instead erroneously assured appellant that sending its highest ranking manager in Missouri was sufficient. * * * This argument incorrectly frames the issue because the problem was not the rank of the corporate representative but the corporate representative's ability to meaningfully participate in the ADR conference and to reconsider the company's position on settlement at that conference.

It is a well-established principle in this Circuit that a party may be held responsible for the actions of its counsel. * * * While forcing parties to answer for their attorneys' behavior may seem harsh * * * litigants who are truly misled and victimized by their attorneys have recourse in malpractice actions. * * * [T]he sanction imposed by the district court need only be proportionate to the litigant's transgression. * * *

* * *

In sum, we hold that the district court did not abuse its discretion in imposing monetary sanctions against appellant for its lack of good faith participation in the ADR process, for its failure to comply with the district court's August 2, 1999, Referral Order, and for vexatiously increasing the costs of litigation by filing a frivolous motion for reconsideration. The order of the district court is affirmed.

NOTES AND QUESTIONS

1. Should the failure to abide by a pretrial order ever result in dismissal of the suit? Is the remedy of monetary penalties preferable to the relatively drastic remedy of dismissal? Is Rule 16 intended as a compensatory remedy (designed to deter and to reimburse the opposing party and the court for the cost of any deviations from a pretrial order made by a party) or as a punitive remedy designed to encourage compliance with the court order? See Brazil,

Improving Judicial Controls over the Pretrial Development of Civil Actions: Model Rules for Case Management and Sanctions, 1981 Am. B. Found. Research J. 873, 921–55.

2. How do Rule 16 sanctions differ from those that may be imposed under Rule 11?

3. In TORRES v. COMMONWEALTH OF PUERTO RICO, 485 F.3d 5 (1st Cir. 2007), the First Circuit affirmed the District Court's denial of a potentially dispositive but belated pretrial motion asserting sovereign and qualified immunity. The court emphasized, "Whatever the merits of the excuse, trial courts are not required to accept at face value litigants' reasons for their failure to meet deadlines." Id. at 10–11. Should the result be the same if defendant files a belated motion to dismiss for lack of subject-matter jurisdiction?

4. Is it an abuse of discretion to impose Rule 16 monetary sanctions on a corporate defendant that accidentally fails to produce documents until after the deadline has expired? In TRACINDA CORP. v. DAIMLERCHRYSLER AG, 502 F.3d 212 (3d Cir. 2007), the appeals court affirmed a discovery sanction of $556,061 for defendant's failing to produce 61 pages of documents until a year after discovery had closed and on the eve of the last day of trial, in a case in which defendant already had produced 250,000 documents. A Special Master found no evidence of bad faith or intentional misconduct, and instead attributed the failure to the negligence of a third-party vendor that had copied the documents. Nevertheless, the appeals court upheld the sanction against charges that it was "unjust," underscoring the prejudicial effect of the discovery failure and the substantial costs that the error imposed on the opposing party. The court rejected out of hand defendant's suggestion that the sanction would create perverse incentives for parties to correct litigation mistakes made in good faith:

> Production errors discovered at the pre-trial stage of litigation will result in little, if any, expense or prejudice to the opposing party and therefore are not likely to warrant the imposition of sanctions under Rule 16(f). On the other hand, if a litigant knows that even inadvertent failure to produce relevant documents may result in a sanction when the existence of the documents is discovered during trial, the litigant may exercise more care in ensuring that all relevant documents are produced.

> DaimlerChrysler * * * argues that our holding will have the effect of deterring future litigants from admitting and rectifying discovery errors. However, * * * the obligation on parties and counsel to come forward with relevant documents not produced during discovery is "absolute." Indeed, the failure to do so can result in penalties more severe than monetary sanctions including dismissal of the case. We are not concerned about chilling conduct that is compulsory and required by law.

Id. at 243. Is it appropriate for an appellate court to review a Rule 16 monetary sanction as an abuse of discretion?

CHAPTER 12

ADJUDICATION WITHOUT TRIAL OR BY SPECIAL PROCEEDINGS

■ ■ ■

In this Chapter, we examine summary procedures that allow a court to dispose of an action without a full-blown trial. The main focus is Federal Rule 56, which permits a court to enter judgment if a material issue of fact is not in dispute and the movant is entitled to judgment as a matter of law. See 10A Wright, Miller & Kane, Federal Practice and Procedure: Civil 3d § 2712. When the rule was first promulgated, courts used Rule 56 sparingly, "to weed out frivolous and sham cases, and cases for which the law had a quick and definitive answer." Wald, *Summary Judgment at Sixty*, 76 Texas L. Rev. 1897 (1997). However, the percentage of cases disposed of by Rule 56 motions doubled between 1975 and 2000, see Coleman, *The* Celotex *Initial Burden Standard and an Opportunity to "Revivify" Rule 56*, 32 S. Ill. U. L.J. 295, 295 (2008), and some commentators now warn that the "hyperactive" use of summary judgment and other pretrial motions "threatens longstanding constitutional values." Miller, *The Pretrial Rush to Judgment: Are the "Litigation Explosion," "Liability Crisis," and Efficiency Clichés Eroding Our Day in Court and Jury Trial Commitments?*, 78 N.Y.U. L. Rev. 982, 2093 (2003). The materials in this Chapter raise important questions about the current nature of civil litigation and the values that ought to inform procedural reform.

SECTION A. FEDERAL RULE OF CIVIL PROCEDURE 56 AND THE MOTION FOR SUMMARY JUDGMENT

———

Read Federal Rule of Civil Procedure 56 and the accompanying materials in the Supplement.

———

1. SUMMARY JUDGMENT: A SHORT HISTORY

FRIEDENTHAL & GARDNER, JUDICIAL DISCRETION TO DENY
SUMMARY JUDGMENT IN THE ERA OF MANAGERIAL JUDGING, 31
Hofstra L. Rev. 91, 96 (2002) (footnotes omitted):

Modern summary judgment has its root in nineteenth century English law. Both the 1855 Summary Procedure on Bills of Exchange Act,
more commonly known as Keating's Act, and the Judicature Act of 1873
allowed plaintiffs summary adjudication in their collection of liquidated
claims when they demonstrated no dispute as to the terms of an agreement to provide goods or services, the actual provision of those goods or
services, and nonpayment. The purpose of these acts was to "reduce delay
and expense resulting from frivolous defenses." Although forms of summary proceedings existed in the United States as early as 1769, several
states enacted summary judgment statutes based on the English model in
the late 1800s. These American statutes were similar to the English Acts
in that they were limited to use by plaintiffs and could only be used for
claims appropriately resolved by documentary proof. Initially, judges expressed reluctance in granting summary judgment motions, viewing summary judgment as a drastic remedy. Yet by the mid–1920s, judges granted
more than half of such motions before them.

NOTES AND QUESTIONS

1. Summary proceedings and other "shortcuts" to judgment often are
characterized as devices to reduce cost and to avoid delay. Not all commentators agree, however, that summary judgment practice is efficient. To the
contrary, a recent study concludes: "In some courts and types of cases, it may
be a useful tool for avoiding costly trials, but in others, it may be wasting
resources and imposing delay." Rave, Note—*Questioning the Efficiency of
Summary Judgment*, 81 N.Y.U. L. Rev. 875, 909 (2006). Can summary
procedure be justified by any value other than efficiency?

2. Does a district court's dismissal of a case on summary judgment
undermine the constitutional commitment to trial by jury, at least in those
cases in which the Seventh Amendment would afford such a right? Given the
constitutional dimension of the issue, is it ever appropriate for a court to use
Federal Rule 56 as a docket-clearing device? Compare Thomas, *Why Summary
Judgment Is Unconstitutional*, 93 Va. L. Rev. 139 (2007), with Nelson,
Summary Judgment and the Progressive Constitution, 93 Iowa L. Rev. 1653
(2008), and Brunet, *Summary Judgment Is Constitutional*, 93 Iowa L. Rev.
1625 (2008).

2. THE MOVANT'S BURDEN

———

Read the material on the Burden of Production on pp. 542–44, infra.

———

ADICKES v. S.H. KRESS & CO., 398 U.S. 144, 90 S.Ct. 1598, 26 L.Ed.2d 142 (1970), involved a civil rights claim filed by a white New York City school teacher who had volunteered to teach at a "Freedom School" in Hattiesburg, Mississippi during the summer of 1964. The District Court found the following undisputed facts:

> On August 14, 1964, plaintiff and six Negro students sought to integrate the Hattiesburg Public Library, but were refused the use of its facilities and shortly thereafter the library was closed by the Chief of Police of Hattiesburg. On leaving the library, plaintiff and the six students proceeded to a Woolworth store for the purposes of eating lunch and, on the way, plaintiff observed policemen following them. Since the Woolworth store was crowded, the plaintiff and her group went to defendant's store and sat down in two lunch booths and ordered lunch. The waitress took the orders of the six Negroes, but refused to take plaintiff's order. The six Negroes refused to eat unless plaintiff was served. They left the store and had proceeded only a short distance when a police officer, previously observed by plaintiff, arrested her for vagrancy.

Adickes v. S.H. Kress & Co., 252 F.Supp. 140, 142 (S.D.N.Y. 1966). Plaintiff's complaint raised two counts: first, that the denial of restaurant service violated her civil rights; and second, that the refusal to serve and her subsequent arrest were the result of a conspiracy between defendant and the town police.

Defendant Kress moved for summary judgment, and supported its motion with affidavits from the store manager, the chief of police, and the arresting officers denying the existence of a pre-arranged scheme to arrest Adickes after she was denied service. The store manager's affidavit also stated that he had arranged for Adickes not to be served because he believed a riot would otherwise take place. In opposing the motion, Adickes responded by pressing her circumstantial case. She noted the allegation in the complaint that the policeman who arrested her had earlier been in the store, and pointed out that defendant had failed to dispute this allegation. She adduced her sworn deposition testimony that "one of [her] students saw a policeman come in," and she offered an unsworn statement by a Kress employee (given by Kress to Adickes in discovery) stating that the officer who arrested Adickes once she was outside the restaurant had been in the store before she was refused service. Adickes also submitted an affidavit disputing the store manager's statement that serving her would have created a riot.

The District Court denied the motion with respect to the first count, but granted summary judgment on the second, finding that there was "no evidence in the complaint or in the affidavits and other papers from which a 'reasonably-minded person' might draw an inference of conspiracy." Id. at 144, and the court of appeals affirmed 409 F.2d 121, 126–27 (2d Cir. 1968). The Supreme Court reversed, finding that the movant had not met its procedural burden "of showing the absence of any disputed material fact." 398 U.S. at 148, 90 S.Ct. at 1603, 26 L.Ed. at 149.

> * * * [Kress] did not carry its burden because of its failure to foreclose the possibility that there was a policeman in the Kress store while petitioner was awaiting service, and that this policeman reached an understanding with some Kress employee that petitioner not be served.
>
> It is true that * * * [the store manager] claimed in his deposition that he had not seen or communicated with a policeman prior to his tacit signal to * * * the supervisor of the food counter [not to serve Adickes]. But respondent did not submit any affidavits from * * * [the supervisor of the food counter], or from * * * the waitress who actually refused petitioner service, either of whom might well have seen and communicated with a policeman in the store. Finally, we find it particularly noteworthy that the two officers involved in the arrest each failed in his affidavit to foreclose the possibility (1) that he was in the store while petitioner was there; and (2) that, upon seeing petitioner with Negroes, he communicated his disapproval to a Kress employee, thereby influencing the decision not to serve petitioner.
>
> Given these unexplained gaps in the materials submitted by respondent, we conclude that respondent failed to fulfill its initial burden of demonstrating what is a critical element in this aspect of the case—that there was no policeman in the store. If a policeman were present, we think it would be open to a jury, in light of the sequence that followed, to infer from the circumstances that the policeman and a Kress employee had a "meeting of the minds" and thus reached an understanding that petitioner should be refused service. Because "[o]n summary judgment the inferences to be drawn from the underlying facts contained in [the moving party's] materials must be viewed in the light most favorable to the party opposing the motion," * * * we think respondent's failure to show there was no policeman in the store requires reversal.

Id. at 158, 90 S.Ct. at 1609, 26 L.Ed.2d at 159.

The Court rejected Kress's argument that because the form of plaintiff's evidence did not satisfy Rule 56(e)—for example, the deposition was hearsay and the waitress's statement was unsworn—plaintiff could not avoid summary judgment.

> If respondent had met its initial burden by, for example, submitting affidavits from the policemen denying their presence in the store at the time in question, Rule 56(e) would then have required petitioner to have done more than simply rely on the contrary allegation in her complaint. To have avoided conceding this fact for purposes of summary judgment, petitioner would have had to come forward with either (1) the affidavit of someone who saw the policeman in the store or (2) an affidavit under Rule 56(f) explaining why at that time it was impractical to do so. Even though not essential here to defeat respon-

dent's motion, the submission of such an affidavit would have been the preferable course for petitioner's counsel to have followed. * * *

Id. at 159–60, 90 S.Ct. at 1609–10, 26 L.Ed.2d at 155–56.

NOTE AND QUESTIONS

Under *Adickes*, can a defendant who moves for summary judgment meet its initial burden only by disproving the existence of all material facts? Does this mean that the movant must "negate the nonmovant's allegations," or is the burden less than that? Professors Issacharoff and Loewenstein point out that the Court in *Adickes* "did not address what evidence, short of Kress's satisfying its complete burden of proof of negating the existence of issues in dispute, might suffice to shift the burden of production to the plaintiff to establish the viability of her case." Issacharoff & Loewenstein, *Second Thoughts About Summary Judgment*, 100 Yale L.J. 73, 80 (1990). Would reading *Adickes* to impose a "foreclose the possibility" standard on a defendant who moves for summary judgment impermissibly shift plaintiff's burden of proof at trial to the defendant at the Rule 56 stage of the proceeding? See Louis, *Federal Summary Judgment: A Critical Analysis*, 83 Yale L.J. 745, 751–53 (1974).

CELOTEX CORP. v. CATRETT

Supreme Court of the United States, 1986.
477 U.S. 317, 106 S.Ct. 2548, 91 L.Ed.2d 265.

Certiorari to the United States Court of Appeals for the District of Columbia Circuit.

JUSTICE REHNQUIST delivered the opinion of the Court.

* * *

Respondent commenced this lawsuit in September 1980, alleging that the death in 1979 of her husband, Louis H. Catrett, resulted from his exposure to products containing asbestos manufactured or distributed by 15 named corporations. Respondent's complaint sounded in negligence, breach of warranty, and strict liability.

* * *

Petitioner's summary judgment motion, which was first filed in September 1981, argued that summary judgment was proper because respondent had "failed to produce evidence that any [Celotex] product . . . was the proximate cause of the injuries alleged within the jurisdictional limits of [the District] Court." In particular, petitioner noted that respondent had failed to identify, in answering interrogatories specifically requesting such information, any witnesses who could testify about the decedent's exposure to petitioner's asbestos products. In response to petitioner's summary judgment motion, respondent then produced three documents which she claimed "demonstrate that there is a genuine material factual dispute" as to whether the decedent had ever been exposed to petitioner's asbestos products. The three documents included a transcript of a deposition of the decedent, a letter from an official of one of the decedent's former employers whom petitioner planned to call as a trial witness, and a letter from an insurance company to respondent's attorney, all tending to establish that the decedent had been exposed to petitioner's asbestos products in Chicago during 1970–1971. Petitioner, in turn, argued that the three documents were inadmissible hearsay and thus could not be considered in opposition to the summary judgment motion.

In July 1982, almost two years after the commencement of the lawsuit, the District Court granted [the motion] * * * because "there [was] no showing that the plaintiff was exposed to the defendant Celotex's product in the District of Columbia or elsewhere within the statutory period." * * * Respondent appealed * * *. The majority of the Court of Appeals held that petitioner's summary judgment motion was rendered "fatally defective" by the fact that petitioner "made no effort to adduce *any* evidence, in the form of affidavits or otherwise, to support its motion." * * * According to the majority, Rule 56(e) * * *, and this Court's decision in Adickes v. S.H. Kress & Co., * * * establish that "the party opposing the motion for summary judgment bears the burden of responding *only after* the moving party has met its burden of coming forward with proof of the absence of any genuine issues of material fact." * * * [The Rule's language has been altered without any changes in substance.] The majority therefore declined to consider petitioner's argument that none of the evidence produced by respondent in opposition to the motion for summary judgment would have been admissible at trial. * * *

We think that the position taken by the majority of the Court of Appeals is inconsistent with the standard for summary judgment set forth in Rule 56(c) * * *. In our view, the plain language of Rule 56(c) mandates the entry of summary judgment, after adequate time for discovery and upon motion, against a party who fails to make a showing sufficient to establish the existence of an element essential to that party's case, and on which that party will bear the burden of proof at trial. * * *

Of course, a party seeking summary judgment always bears the initial responsibility of informing the district court of the basis for its motion, and identifying those portions of "the pleadings, depositions, answers to interrogatories, and admissions on file, together with the affidavits, if any," which it believes demonstrate the absence of a genuine issue of material fact. But unlike the Court of Appeals, we find no express or implied requirement in Rule 56 that the moving party support its motion with affidavits or other similar materials *negating* the opponent's claim. On the contrary, Rule 56(c), which refers to "the affidavits, *if any*" (emphasis added), suggests the absence of such a requirement. And if there were any doubt about the meaning of Rule 56(c) in this regard, such doubt is clearly removed by Rules 56(a) and (b), which provide that claimants and defendants, respectively, may move for summary judgment *"with or without supporting affidavits"* (emphasis added). The import of these subsections is that, regardless of whether the moving party accompanies its summary judgment motion with affidavits, the motion may, and should, be granted so long as whatever is before the district court demonstrates that the standard for the entry of summary judgment, as set forth in Rule 56(c), is satisfied. One of the principal purposes of the summary judgment rule is to isolate and dispose of factually unsupported claims or defenses, and we think it should be interpreted in a way that allows it to accomplish this purpose.

Respondent argues, however, that Rule 56(e), by its terms, places on the nonmoving party the burden of coming forward with rebuttal affidavits, or other specified kinds of materials, only in response to a motion for summary judgment "made and supported as provided in this rule." According to respondent's argument, since petitioner did not "support" its motion with affidavits, summary judgment was improper in this case. But as we have already explained, a motion for summary judgment may be made pursuant to Rule 56 "with or without supporting affidavits." In cases like the instant one, where the nonmoving party will bear the burden of proof at trial on a dispositive issue, a summary judgment motion may properly be made in reliance solely on the "pleadings, depositions, answers to interrogatories, and admissions on file." Such a motion, whether or not accompanied by affidavits, will be "made and supported as provided in this rule," and Rule 56(e) therefore requires the nonmoving party to go beyond the pleadings and by her own affidavits, or by the "depositions, answers to interrogatories, and admissions on file," designate "specific facts showing that there is a genuine issue for trial."

* * *

The Court of Appeals in this case felt itself constrained, however, by language in our decision in Adickes v. S.H. Kress & Co., [p. 494, supra,] * * *. In the course of its opinion, the *Adickes* Court said that "both the commentary on and the background of the 1963 Amendment conclusively show that it was not intended to modify the burden of the moving party . . . to show initially the absence of a genuine issue concerning any material fact." * * * We think that this statement is accurate in a literal sense, since we fully agree with the *Adickes* Court that the 1963 Amendment to Rule 56(e) was not designed to modify the burden of making the showing generally required by Rule 56(c). It also appears to us that, on the basis of the showing before the Court in *Adickes,* the motion for summary judgment in that case should have been denied. But we do not think the *Adickes* language quoted above should be construed to mean that the burden is on the party moving for summary judgment to produce evidence showing the absence of a genuine issue of material fact, even with respect to an issue on which the nonmoving party bears the burden of proof. Instead, as we have explained, the burden on the moving party may be discharged by "showing"—that is, pointing out to the District Court—that there is an absence of evidence to support the nonmoving party's case.

The last two sentences of Rule 56(e) were added, as this Court indicated in *Adickes,* to disapprove a line of cases allowing a party opposing summary judgment to resist a properly made motion by reference only to its pleadings. While the *Adickes* Court was undoubtedly correct in concluding that these two sentences were not intended to *reduce* the burden of the moving party, it is also obvious that they were not adopted to *add to* that burden. Yet that is exactly the result which the reasoning of the Court of Appeals would produce; in effect, an amendment to Rule 56(e) designed to *facilitate* the granting of motions for summary judgment would be interpreted to make it *more difficult* to grant such motions. Nothing in the two sentences themselves requires this result, for the reasons we have previously indicated, and we now put to rest any inference that they do so.

* * *

Respondent commenced this action in September 1980, and petitioner's motion was filed in September 1981. The parties had conducted discovery, and no serious claim can be made that respondent was in any sense "railroaded" by a premature motion for summary judgment. Any potential problem with such premature motions can be adequately dealt with under Rule 56(f), which allows a summary judgment motion to be denied, or the hearing on the motion to be continued, if the nonmoving party has not had an opportunity to make full discovery.

In this Court, respondent's brief and oral argument have been devoted as much to the proposition that an adequate showing of exposure to petitioner's asbestos products was made as to the proposition that no such showing should have been required. But the Court of Appeals declined to address either the adequacy of the showing made by respondent in opposition to petitioner's motion for summary judgment, or the question whether such a showing, if reduced to admissible evidence, would be sufficient to carry respondent's burden of proof at trial. We think the Court of Appeals with its superior knowledge of local law is better suited than we are to make these determinations in the first instance.

The Federal Rules of Civil Procedure have for more than 50 years authorized motions for summary judgment upon proper showings of the lack of a genuine, triable issue of material fact. Summary judgment procedure is properly regarded not as a disfavored procedural shortcut, but rather as an integral part of the Federal Rules as a whole, which are designed "to secure the just, speedy and inexpensive determination of every action." * * * Before the shift to "notice pleading" accomplished by the Federal Rules, motions to dismiss a complaint or to strike a defense were the principal tools by which factually insufficient claims or defenses could be isolated and prevented from going to trial with the attendant unwarranted consumption of public and private resources. But with the advent of "notice pleading," the motion to dismiss seldom fulfills this function any more, and its place has been taken by the motion for summary judgment. Rule 56 must be construed with due regard not only for the rights of persons asserting claims and defenses that are adequately based in fact to have those claims and defenses tried to a jury, but also for the rights of persons opposing such claims and defenses to demonstrate in the manner provided by the Rule, prior to trial, that the claims and defenses have no factual basis.

The judgment of the Court of Appeals is accordingly reversed, and the case is remanded for further proceedings consistent with this opinion.

It is so ordered.

JUSTICE WHITE, concurring.

I agree that the Court of Appeals was wrong in holding that the moving defendant must always support his motion with evidence or affidavits showing the absence of a genuine dispute about a material fact. I also agree that the movant may rely on depositions, answers to interrogatories and the like to demonstrate that the plaintiff has no evidence to prove his case and hence that there can be no factual dispute. But the movant must discharge the burden the rules place upon him: It is not enough to move for summary judgment without supporting the motion in any way or with a conclusory assertion that the plaintiff has no evidence to prove his case.

* * *

Petitioner Celotex does not dispute that if respondent has named a witness to support her claim, summary judgment should not be granted without Celotex somehow showing that the named witness' possible testimony raises no genuine issue of material fact. * * * It asserts, however, that respondent has failed on request to produce any basis for her case. Respondent, on the other hand, does not contend that she was not obligated to reveal her witnesses and evidence but insists that she has revealed enough to defeat the motion for summary judgment. Because the Court of Appeals found it unnecessary to address this aspect of the case, I agree that the case should be remanded for further proceedings.

JUSTICE BRENNAN, with whom THE CHIEF JUSTICE and JUSTICE BLACKMUN join, dissenting.

This case requires the Court to determine whether Celotex satisfied its initial burden of production in moving for summary judgment on the ground that the plaintiff lacked evidence to establish an essential element of her case at trial. I do not disagree with the Court's legal analysis. The Court clearly rejects the ruling of the Court of Appeals that the defendant must provide affirmative evidence disproving the plaintiff's case. Beyond this, however, the Court has not clearly explained what is required of a moving party seeking summary judgment on the ground that the non-moving party cannot prove its case. This lack of clarity is unfortunate: district courts must routinely decide summary judgment motions, and the Court's opinion will very likely create confusion. For this reason, even if I agreed with the Court's result, I would have written separately to explain more clearly the law in this area. However, because I believe that Celotex did not meet its burden of production under Federal Rule * * * 56, I respectfully dissent from the Court's judgment.

I

* * * The burden of establishing the nonexistence of a "genuine issue" is on the party moving for summary judgment. * * * This burden has two distinct components: an initial burden of production, which shifts to the nonmoving party if satisfied by the moving party; and an ultimate burden of persuasion, which always remains on the moving party. * * * The court need not decide whether the moving party has satisfied its ultimate burden of persuasion unless and until the court finds that the moving party has discharged its initial burden of production.

* * *

The manner in which this showing can be made depends upon which party will bear the burden of persuasion on the challenged claim at trial. If the *moving* party will bear the burden of persuasion at trial that party must support its motion with credible evidence—using any of the material specified in Rule 56(c)—that would entitle it to a directed verdict if not controverted at trial. * * * Such an affirmative showing shifts the burden of production to the party opposing the motion and requires that party either to produce evidentiary materials that demonstrate the existence of a "genuine issue" for trial or to submit an affidavit requesting additional time for discovery. * * *

If the burden of persuasion at trial would be on the *non-moving* party, the party moving for summary judgment may satisfy Rule 56's burden of production in either of two ways. First, the moving party may submit affirmative evidence that negates an essential element of the nonmoving party's claim. Second, the moving party may demonstrate to the Court that the nonmoving party's evidence is insufficient to establish an essential element of the nonmoving party's claim. * * * If the nonmoving party cannot muster sufficient evidence to make out its claim, a trial would be useless and the moving party is entitled to summary judgment as a matter of law. * * *

Where the moving party adopts this second option and seeks summary judgment on the ground that the nonmoving party—who will bear the burden of persuasion at trial—has no evidence, the mechanics of discharging Rule 56's burden of production are somewhat trickier. Plainly, a conclusory assertion that the nonmoving party has no evidence is insufficient. * * * Such a "burden" of production is no burden at all and would simply permit summary judgment procedure to be converted into a tool for harassment. * * * Rather, as the Court confirms, a party who moves for summary judgment on the ground that the nonmoving party has no evidence must affirmatively show the absence of evidence in the record. * * * This may require the moving party to depose the nonmoving party's witnesses or to establish the inadequacy of documentary evidence. If there is literally no evidence in the record, the moving party may demonstrate this by reviewing for the court the admissions, interrogatories and other exchanges between the parties that are in the record. Either way, however, the moving party must affirmatively demonstrate that there is no evidence in the record to support a judgment for the nonmoving party.

If the moving party has not fully discharged this initial burden of production, its motion for summary judgment must be denied, and the Court need not consider whether the moving party has met its ultimate burden of persuasion. Accordingly, the nonmoving party may defeat a motion for summary judgment that asserts that the nonmoving party has no evidence by calling the Court's attention to supporting evidence already in the record that was overlooked or ignored by the moving party.

* * *

II

I do not read the Court's opinion to say anything inconsistent with or different than the preceding discussion. My disagreement with the Court concerns the application of these principles to the facts of this case.

* * *

On these facts, there is simply no question that Celotex failed to discharge its initial burden of production. Having chosen to base its motion on the argument that there was no evidence in the record to support plaintiff's claim, Celotex was not free to ignore supporting evidence that the record clearly contained. Rather, Celotex was required, as an initial matter, to attack the adequacy of this evidence. Celotex' failure to fulfill this simple requirement constituted a failure to discharge its initial burden of production under Rule 56, and thereby rendered summary judgment improper.

* * *

[A dissenting opinion by JUSTICE STEVENS is omitted.]

NOTE AND QUESTIONS

Is the decision in *Celotex* consistent with *Adickes*? Consider the following:

* * * [A] party may satisfy the standard for summary judgment by one or both of two methods. First, the movant may, by submitting affirmative evidence, negate an element essential to the opposing party's claim or defense. Second, the movant may show that the opposing party lacks sufficient evidence to establish an essential element of its claim or defense. *Celotex* involved the second method exclusively; *Adickes*, arguably, involved a combination of the two methods. The defendant in *Adickes* offered affirmative evidence in the form of the deposition of the store manager and affidavits from the involved officers. In addition, the defendant pointed to statements in the plaintiff's deposition that the plaintiff lacked any knowledge of communications between the police and Kress employees. The inadequacy of Kress's motion was not its failure to offer affirmative evidence, but rather that the affirmative evidence it offered was insufficient to establish the absence of a genuine issue of a material fact. *Adickes*, therefore, should not be read as requiring the moving party to negate an essential element of the opposing party's case by affirmative evidence in every instance. Rather, the decision may be viewed as stating the proposition that the moving party is required to sustain its burden of proving the absence of a genuine issue of a material fact by affirmative evidence only if it must utilize the first method, or a combination of the two methods, of obtaining summary judgment. If the moving party is able to use the second method exclusively, it is only required to show that the opposing party has failed to establish sufficient evidence of an essential element of its claim or defense. Celotex, viewed in this light, is therefore consistent with the *Adickes* decision. By failing to fully explain this distinction, however, Justice Rehnquist's statements, while correct in the context of the *Celotex* decision, appear to eviscerate *Adickes* and may promote rather than resolve doctrinal confusion.

Foremaster, *The Movant's Burden in a Motion for Summary Judgment*, 1987 Utah L. Rev. 731, 748–49.

———

    SCOTT v. HARRIS, 550 U.S. 372, 127 S.Ct. 1769, 167 L.Ed.2d 686 (2007). This case raises the issue, as a follow-up to Justice Brennan's dictum in *Celotex*, as to when a party with the burden of proof on an issue nevertheless might argue successfully for a summary judgment in its favor. In the action, plaintiff Harris suffered severe personal injuries when his vehicle, engaged in a police chase, was forced off of the road by defendant Scott, a deputy police officer. Plaintiff sued Scott, alleging that the latter had used excessive force in violation of Harris's Fourth Amendment rights. Defendant Scott moved for summary judgment on the basis of qualified immunity. The District Court denied the motion and the Court of Appeals for the Eleventh Circuit affirmed. The Supreme Court reversed as follows:

> [Harris's] * * * version of events (unsurprisingly) differs substantially from Scott's version. When things are in such a posture courts are required to view the facts and draw reasonable inferences "in the light most favorable to the party opposing the [summary judgment] motion." *United States* v. *Diebold, Inc.,* 369 U.S. 654, 655, 82 S.Ct. 993, 8 L.Ed.2d 176 (1962). * * * In qualified immunity cases, this usually means adopting (as the Court of Appeals did here) the plaintiff's version of the facts.

> There is, however, an added wrinkle in this case: the existence in the record of a videotape capturing the events in question. There are no allegations or indications that this videotape was doctored or altered in any way, nor any contention that what it depicts differs from what

actually happened. The videotape quite clearly contradicts the version of the story told by * * * [Harris] and adopted by the Court of Appeals. * * * Indeed, reading the lower court's opinion, one gets the impression that * * * [Harris], rather than fleeing from police, was attempting to pass his driving test * * *.

The videotape tells quite a different story. * * * Far from [Harris] being the cautious and controlled driver the lower court depicts, what we see on the video more closely resembles a Hollywood-style car chase of the most frightening sort, placing police officers and innocent bystanders alike at great risk of serious injury.

At the summary judgment stage, facts must be viewed in the light most favorable to the nonmoving party only if there is a "genuine" dispute as to those facts. Fed. Rule Civ. Proc. 56(c). As we have emphasized, "[w]hen the moving party has carried its burden under Rule 56(c) its opponent must do more than show that there is some metaphysical doubt as to the material facts.... Where the record taken as a whole could not lead a rational trier of fact to find for the nonmoving party, there is no 'genuine issue for trial.' " *Matsushita Elec. Industrial Co.* v. *Zenith Radio Corp.*, 475 U.S. 574, 586–587, 106 S.Ct. 1348, 89 L.Ed.2d 538 (1986) [alteration in original]. * * * When opposing parties tell two different stories, one of which is blatantly contradicted by the record, so that no reasonable jury could believe it, a court should not adopt that version of the facts for purposes of ruling on a motion for summary judgment. * * * The Court of Appeals should not have relied on such visible fiction; it should have viewed the facts in the light depicted by the videotape.

* * *

The car chase that * * * [Harris] initiated in this case posed a substantial and immediate risk of serious physical injury to others; no reasonable jury could conclude otherwise. Scott's attempt to terminate the chase by forcing respondent off the road was reasonable, and Scott is entitled to summary judgment.

Id. at 378–81, 127 S.Ct. at 1774–76, 1779, 167 L.Ed.2d at 692–95, 697.

NOTES AND QUESTIONS

1.   What if there had been no videotape available in *Scott*? Could Scott have presented affidavits or other evidence in order to secure a summary judgment? Suppose Scott presented affidavits of witnesses which, if true, would have established his defense of immunity. Could Harris decline to introduce contrary affidavits and yet avoid summary judgment merely by arguing that a jury would be entitled to disbelieve Scott's witnesses when they testified at trial?

2.   The Supreme Court uploaded to its website the video at issue in *Scott*, see http://www.supremecourtus.gov/opinions/video/scott_v_harris.rmvb. After

viewing the video, do you agree with the Court's conclusion that "no reasonable juror" could find that the driver's flight did not pose a danger to the public? A study based on a sample of 1350 viewers of the video found that although a "fairly substantial majority did interpret the facts the way the Court did, * * * members of various subcommunities did not. African Americans, low-income workers, and residents of the Northeast * * * tended to form more pro-plaintiff views of the facts than did the Court. So did individuals who characterized themselves as liberals and Democrats." Based on these findings, the authors criticized the Court's approach in *Scott* for its characterizing as "unreasonable" the views of those who drew different inferences from the videotaped evidence:

> * * * Although an admitted minority of American society, citizens disposed to see the facts differently from the *Scott* majority share a perspective founded on common experiences and values. By insisting that a case like *Scott* be decided summarily, the Court not only denied those citizens an opportunity, in the context of jury deliberations, to inform and possibly change the view of citizens endowed with a different perspective. It also needlessly bound the result in the case to a process of decisionmaking that deprived the decision of any prospect of legitimacy in the eyes of that subcommunity whose members saw the facts differently.

Kahan, Hoffman & Braman, *Whose Eyes Are You Going To Believe?* Scott v. Harris *and the Perils of Cognitive Illiberalism*, 122 Harv. L. Rev. 837, 841–42 (2009). Is this concern unique to summary judgment cases that involve videotaped evidence? See Schneider, *The Dangers of Summary Judgment: Gender and Federal Litigation*, 59 Rutgers L. Rev. 705 (2007).

————

ANDERSON v. LIBERTY LOBBY, INC., 477 U.S. 242, 106 S.Ct. 2505, 91 L.Ed.2d 202 (1986). Willis Carto, a right-wing publisher, and Liberty Lobby, the organization he headed, filed a libel suit against *The Investigator* magazine, its president, and its publisher, columnist Jack Anderson, for articles that portrayed plaintiffs as neo-Nazi, anti-Semitic, racist, and fascist. Following discovery, defendants moved for summary judgment on the ground that plaintiffs could not prove by clear and convincing evidence that defendants had acted with actual malice—with knowledge that the statements were false or with reckless disregard of whether they were true or false—the standard required by New York Times Co. v. Sullivan, 376 U.S. 254, 84 S.Ct. 710, 11 L.Ed.2d 686 (1964), and its progeny for libel suits brought by public figures. In support of the motion, defendants submitted an affidavit from Charles Bermant, the employee who had written the allegedly libelous articles, stating that he had spent a substantial amount of time researching and writing the articles. His affidavit also detailed the sources for each of the statements in the article, and affirmed that he believed the facts he reported to be true. Plaintiffs responded to the motion by pointing to numerous claimed inaccuracies in the articles. On the issue of malice, plaintiffs showed that one of Bermant's sources was a twelve-year-old article published in *Time* magazine that had been the subject of an earlier libel suit by plaintiff, which resulted in a settlement under which *Time* paid Carto a sum of money and published a favorable article about Liberty Lobby, and that one of the co-authors of the *Time* article was an editor of *The Investigator*. Plaintiffs also showed that another source was a freelance journalist whom Bermant had never met and who was not asked to, and never did, identify his sources. Finally, they showed that another editor of *The Investigator* had told the magazine's president that the articles were "terrible" and "ridiculous."

The District Court granted the motion for summary judgment. The Court of Appeals reversed, ruling that it was irrelevant on a motion for summary judgment that the standard for proving actual malice was clear and convincing evidence, rather than a preponderance of evidence. In an opinion written by Justice White, the Court reversed:

> * * * [I]n ruling on a motion for summary judgment, the judge must view the evidence presented through the prism of the substantive evidentiary burden. This conclusion is mandated by the nature of this determination. The question here is whether a jury could reasonably find *either* that the plaintiff proved his case by the quality and quantity of evidence required by the governing law *or* that he did not. Whether a jury could reasonably find for either party, however, cannot be defined except by the criteria governing what evidence would enable the jury to find for either the plaintiff or the defendant: It makes no sense to say that a jury could reasonably find for either party without some benchmark as to what standards govern its deliberations and within what boundaries its ultimate decision must fall, and these standards and boundaries are in fact provided by the applicable evidentiary standards.

> Our holding that the clear-and-convincing standard of proof should be taken into account does not denigrate the role of the jury. It by no means authorizes trial on affidavits. Credibility determinations, the weighing of the evidence, and the drawing of legitimate inferences from the facts are jury functions, not those of a judge, whether he is ruling on a motion for summary judgment or for a directed verdict. The evidence of the non-movant is to be believed, and all justifiable inferences are to be drawn in his favor. * * * Neither do we suggest that the trial courts should act other than with caution in granting summary judgment or that the trial court may not deny summary judgment in a case where there is reason to believe that the better course would be to proceed to a full trial. * * *

Id. at 254–56, 106 S.Ct. at 2513–14, 91 L.Ed.2d 215–16.

NOTES AND QUESTIONS

1. Is it ever appropriate to define the burden of production in terms of the burden of persuasion? See pp. 542–44, infra. In answering this question,

should any weight be given to the " * * * difference between prejudging whether an item of evidence will be admissible in trial and on the other hand ruling contemporaneously at trial on the same question"? Kennedy, *Federal Summary Judgment: Reconciling* Celotex v. Catrett *with* Adickes v. Kress *and the Evidentiary Problem Under Rule 56*, 6 Rev. Litig. 227, 232–33 (1987).

2. The law distinguishes between two types of evidence: direct and indirect. A witness's statement that "I saw the light and it was green" is direct evidence that the light was green. The inferences required to credit the testimony are that the witness is speaking honestly and accurately recalls the incident. A witness's statement that "I saw the car in the next lane go through the intersection without slowing down" is indirect or circumstantial evidence that the light was green, but is also consistent with the conclusion that "the car in the next lane also ran the red light." The inferences required to believe that the light was green depend not only on the assumption that the witness is worthy of belief, but also on some implicit generalizations about how well drivers obey the law and the probability of two drivers simultaneously running a red light. These examples are taken from Collins, Note— *Summary Judgment and Circumstantial Evidence*, 40 Stan. L. Rev. 491, 493 (1988). In *Anderson*, the parties presented indirect evidence that was in conflict. By requiring the Rule 56 decision to take account of plaintiff's trial burden, did the Court impermissibly authorize the trial court to weigh the evidence? If not, how does *Anderson* affect the standard a judge must use in deciding a motion for summary judgment?

———

MATSUSHITA ELECTRIC INDUSTRIAL CO. v. ZENITH RADIO CORP., 475 U.S. 574, 106 S.Ct. 1348, 89 L.Ed.2d 538 (1986). Plaintiffs, a group of American television manufacturers, alleged that a group of twenty-one Japanese manufacturers and distributors conspired to fix prices in an effort to monopolize the American market. The trial court granted defendant's motion for summary judgment, but the Third Circuit reversed, arguing that a genuine issue for trial existed because "there is both direct evidence of certain kinds of concert of action and circumstantial evidence having some tendency to suggest that other kinds of concert of action may have occurred," such that "a reasonable factfinder could find a conspiracy to depress prices in the American market in order to drive out American competitors, which conspiracy was funded by excess profits obtained in the Japanese market." Id. at 581, 106 S.Ct. at 1352–53, 89 L.Ed.2d at 548–49. The Supreme Court reversed, finding that the Court of Appeals had made two errors. First, "the 'direct evidence' on which the court relied had little, if any, relevance to the alleged predatory pricing conspiracy"; and second, "the court failed to consider the absence of a plausible motive to engage in predatory pricing." Id. at 595, 106 S.Ct. at 1360, 89 L.Ed.2d at 558. The Supreme Court underscored that an absence of plausible motive for the conspiracy "is highly relevant to whether a 'genuine issue for trial' exists within the meaning of Rule 56(e)":

Lack of motive bears on the range of permissible conclusions that might be drawn from ambiguous evidence: if petitioners had no rational economic motive to conspire, and if their conduct is consistent with other, equally plausible explanations, the conduct does not give rise to an inference of conspiracy. * * * In sum, in light of the absence of any rational motive to conspire, neither petitioner's pricing practices, nor their conduct in the Japanese market, nor their agreements respecting prices and distribution in the American market, suffice to create a "genuine issue for trial." * * *

Id. at 595–96, 106 S.Ct. at 1360–61, 89 L.Ed.2d at 558–59.

Notes and Questions

1. The Supreme Court in *Matsushita* stated that on remand the Court of Appeals could find predatory pricing only if the evidence would tend " 'to exclude the possibility' that petitioners underpriced respondents to compete for business rather than to implement an economically senseless conspiracy." Id. at 597–98, 106 S.Ct. at 1362, 89 L.Ed.2d at 559. Under this standard, is the trier of fact permitted to select between competing inferences from the undisputed evidence if the inferences seem equally plausible? What is the relation between the Rule 56 standard and the requirement of plausibility at the pleading stage? See p. 297, supra. Consider whether different notions of plausibility might affect the granting of summary judgment in the following cases:

(a) Two cars enter an intersection at right angles and strike one another killing both drivers and all passengers. There are no eyewitnesses to the accident. The only evidence available is that there was a working traffic light; thus one of the drivers, but only one, had to go through a red light.

(b) X must take a certain pill once a day to remain alive. The pill is highly toxic. To take two within 24 hours is fatal. X is found dead in his bedroom and the evidence is clear that he took two pills that day. If X died by accident, his estate will receive a large sum of insurance money; if he committed suicide, the amount will be substantially reduced. Several hours before his death, X made out a new will, substantially different from the one previously in force. It also shows that at about the same time, X made plans to accompany several friends on a fishing trip on the following day.

Problems adapted from: Friedenthal, *Cases on Summary Judgment: Has There Been a Material Change in Standards?*, 63 Notre Dame L. Rev. 770, 784–86 (1988).

2. For a comprehensive discussion of the Court's changing approach to summary judgment, see Miller, *The Pretrial Rush to Judgment: Are the "Litigation Explosion," "Liability Crisis," and Efficiency Clichés Eroding Our Day in Court and Jury Trial Commitments?*, 78 N.Y.U. L. Rev. 982 (2003).

NOTE ON PARTIAL SUMMARY JUDGMENT

Rules and statutes permitting summary judgment normally provide that in circumstances in which judgment cannot be granted on the entire action, the court at least may withdraw from trial those aspects of the case that are established in the summary-judgment proceeding. See, e.g., Federal Rule 56(d). Furthermore, in a substantial number of jurisdictions the trial court may enter judgment with regard to any single claim that has been fully determined. See, e.g., Federal Rule 54(b). A major question remains, however, whether a party may secure the entry of summary judgment as to part of a claim that has not been fully adjudicated. For example, if plaintiff salesperson alleges that defendant employer owes him five items of back salary, and plaintiff conclusively establishes a right to two of those items, should plaintiff be entitled to a judgment on the amount of the two items in order to collect immediately from defendant? Do Federal Rules 56(a) and 56(b) answer the problem? A number of federal courts have denied relief by reading Rule 56(a) in light of Rule 54(b) or Rule 56(d). What justification, if any, exists for these decisions? See 10B Wright, Miller & Kane, Federal Practice and Procedure: Civil 3d § 2737.

SECTION B.   DISMISSAL OF ACTIONS

————

Read Federal Rule of Civil Procedure 41 and the materials accompanying it in the Supplement.

————

1.   VOLUNTARY DISMISSAL

The voluntary dismissal allows the moving party to extricate himself from the lawsuit without affecting his legal rights before significant judicial and litigant resources are expended. Generally, a voluntary dismissal places the parties in the position they occupied before the lawsuit began; it does not, in general, have the effect of an adjudication on the merits. Because voluntary dismissal might be used to harass defendants, if a party attempts to dismiss after previously doing so with respect to the same cause of action, the dismissal is granted, but is viewed as being an adjudication on the merits. See 9 Wright & Miller, Federal Practice and Procedure: Civil 3d §§ 2361–68. What effect does a voluntary dismissal have on the statute of limitations? Is the statute tolled while the initial complaint is active? Or does the notion that the dismissal returns the parties to the position they occupied before the action require the court to refuse to consider the previous action for purposes of applying the statute of limitations?

————

McCANTS v. FORD MOTOR CO., 781 F.2d 855 (11th Cir. 1986). McCants, a member of the United States Army Reserve on a two-week active duty training mission, was killed while riding in a military jeep built by Ford. His administratrix commenced a wrongful death suit in federal district court in Alabama. After discovery had proceeded for about a year, interrogatories were served and answered, and defendant had moved for summary judgment based on Alabama's one-year general statute of limitations, plaintiff moved for voluntary dismissal of the action without prejudice under Rule 41(a)(2), in order to file a new suit in Mississippi, where the controlling statute of limitations had not expired. The District Court granted the motion to dismiss, and simultaneously denied Ford's motion for summary judgment.

WOJTAS v. CAPITAL GUARDIAN TRUST CO., 477 F.3d 924 (7th Cir. 2007). Plaintiff, the owner of an Individual Retirement Account, instructed the custodian to roll over the investment into a new IRA managed by a successor custodian. An employee at the successor custodian converted the funds and later was convicted of mail fraud. Plaintiff sued the original custodian for breach of fiduciary duty and negligence, alleging that defendant had failed to verify that the successor custodian was legally qualified. Defendant answered and moved for judgment on the pleadings, arguing that both claims were time-barred under Wisconsin's two-year statute of limitations, and, in the alternative, that plaintiff failed to state a claim upon which relief could be granted. Plaintiff responded to the latter argument but also moved for a voluntary dismissal without prejudice, in order to refile the action in Illinois, where the controlling statute of limitations was longer. The District Court denied the motion for voluntary dismissal and granted the motion for judgment on the pleadings. The Court of Appeals affirmed, finding that plaintiff's failure to respond to the statute of limitations argument constituted a waiver, and further, that it would be an abuse of the District Court's discretion to permit voluntary dismissal "where the defendant would suffer 'plain legal prejudice' as a result." Id. at 927.

NOTES AND QUESTIONS

1. At common law, plaintiff was permitted, at any time prior to judgment, to dismiss a case voluntarily and without prejudice to refiling the action. Today the right to dismiss voluntarily generally is governed by a rule or statute that permits a dismissal before "trial" or "commencement" of trial. These provisions have raised many problems of interpretation regarding the meaning of the words "trial" and "commencement." A few courts have held that "before trial" means at any time prior to submission of the case to the jury or court for decision. See generally Annot., 1 A.L.R.3d 711 (1965). What justification is there for this construction?

2. In *McCants,* plaintiff moved to dismiss after defendant had made a motion for summary judgment. Could a plaintiff move to dismiss before losing

such a motion and refile in another, possibly more sympathetic, court? Could plaintiff do this repeatedly? One commentator sees a party's unilateral right to seek dismissal under Rule 41(a) as "an anachronism in an age of managerial judging." Solimine & Lippert, *Deregulating Voluntary Dismissals*, 36 U. Mich. J.L. Reform 367, 367 (2003) (suggesting reform of the rule). Is that view correct?

2. DISMISSAL FOR FAILURE TO PROSECUTE

Courts long have been regarded as possessing inherent discretionary power to dismiss an action if plaintiff does not proceed to trial with "due diligence." Exactly when this power should be invoked has been a matter about which judges have disagreed. Should simple delay by plaintiff be sufficient to justify dismissal, or should prejudice to defendant also be required? In MESSENGER v. UNITED STATES, 231 F.2d 328, 331 (2d Cir. 1956), the court said: "The operative condition of the Rule is lack of due diligence on the part of the plaintiff—not a showing by the defendant that it will be prejudiced by denial of its motion. * * * It may well be that the latter factor may be considered by the court, especially in cases of moderate or excusable neglect, in the formulation of its discretionary ruling." Does this standard make sense? Does it have any practical utility as a guide for the trial judge? What is its effect on appellate-court review of the trial court's exercise of discretion?

Some jurisdictions control dismissals for want of prosecution by statute. In the federal system, Rule 41(b) "allows dismissal for the plaintiff's failure to prosecute, [and] is intended as a safeguard against delay in litigation and harassment of a defendant." 9 Wright & Miller, Federal Practice and Procedure: Civil 3d § 2370. In view of the fact that, by definition, cases in which there is a failure to prosecute are not consuming judicial time or energy, why is a formal dismissal procedure necessary?

SECTION C.   DEFAULT JUDGMENT

———

Read Federal Rule of Civil Procedure 55 and the accompanying materials in the Supplement.

———

COULAS v. SMITH

Supreme Court of Arizona, 1964.
96 Ariz. 325, 395 P.2d 527.

UDALL, CHIEF JUSTICE. This is an appeal from an order of the Superior Court of Pima County, denying a motion to set aside a judgment entered against the appellant.

* * *

The plaintiff filed a complaint against the defendant and cross-claimant on two counts. The first count was for $669.32 on an open account. The second count was on a promissory note upon which $3,666.67 was alleged to be due. The cross-claimant answered individually by his attorney and denied any liability to the plaintiff on either count and thereafter filed a cross-claim against the defendant in which he sought judgment against the defendant for any sums or amounts which the plaintiff may obtain against him by virtue of the judgment; for the sum of $4,000 on a debt alleged to be owed by the defendant to him, and $500 attorney's fees. The defendant appeared individually by his attorneys and answered the complaint of the plaintiff, answered the cross-claim of the cross-claimant, and counterclaimed against the plaintiff, seeking damages in the sum of $18,000. The plaintiff replied to the defendant's counter-claim.

On July 11, 1958, the lower court made an order setting the case for trial on October 10, 1958. All counsel were notified by the clerk of the court. On October 6, 1958, counsel for the plaintiff and counsel for the cross-claimant stipulated that the trial be set for December 10, 1958. The lower court ordered that the prior trial date be vacated and the case be reset for trial on December 10, 1958. All counsel were regularly notified by the clerk of the new trial setting. The defendant's counsel was not present before the court on October 6, 1958, and did not participate in the stipulation vacating the original trial setting and resetting the case for trial on December 10, 1958. The defendant and defendant's counsel deny ever receiving any notice from the clerk concerning the new trial date.

On December 10, 1958, the new trial date, the case came on regularly to be heard. The defendant did not appear either in person or by counsel. The court made the following minute entry during the course of the trial:

* * *

The plaintiff Smith and the defendant Bray announce ready for trial.

William J. Bray is sworn, cross-examined, and examined.

Plaintiff's Exhibit 1, being a promissory note in the sum of $4,000.00 dated February 14, 1955, is marked for identification and admitted in evidence.

Nicholas Coulas having failed to appear at this time either in person or by counsel, and it further appearing that this case was previously set for trial both as to the issues framed by the complaint and answer thereto of the defendant Nicholas Coulas and as to the cross-claim filed by the defendant William J. Bray, Jr., against the defendant Nicholas Coulas,

IT IS HEREBY ORDERED that the default of the said defendant Nicholas Coulas be entered as to said complaint and as to said cross-claim and the court proceeding to hear evidence pertaining to said complaint and cross-claim and being fully advised in the premises,

IT IS THEREFORE ORDERED that judgment is hereby rendered * * * against the defendant Nicholas Coulas * * *.

The plaintiff obtained judgment against the defendant on both counts and against the cross-claimant as to count two (the promissory note). The cross-claimant obtained judgment against the defendant on the promissory note. The judgment was entered on December 11, 1958.

On October 29, 1960, nearly two years later, the defendant filed a motion to set aside and vacate the judgment. The trial court denied this motion. * * *

The defendant subsequently filed this appeal.

The defendant contends that the "default" judgment entered against him was void, since he did not receive 3 days' notice of the application for judgment by default pursuant to Rule 55(b) of the Arizona Rules of Civil Procedure * * *. The defendant's contention would be valid if the judgment below was a judgment by default. A default judgment obtains when a defendant fails to plead or otherwise defend. Rule 55. If he has made an appearance in the case, he must be given 3 days' notice of application for judgment by default. * * *

However, the defendant's contention is invalid here since the judgment below was not a default judgment. It should be noted that the defendant did plead to the merits. He answered the complaint and filed a counterclaim. He then failed to appear at the trial in person or by counsel. The trial proceeded, evidence was heard, and a judgment on the merits of the plaintiff's and counter-claimant's claims was entered. The judgment was not by default within the meaning of Rule 55. Therefore Rule 55(b) with its 3–day notice requirement is not applicable. In fact, the trial court would have erred if a default was entered, since the case was at issue. Bass v. Hoagland, 172 F.2d 205 (5th Cir. 1949), cert. denied, 338 U.S. 816, 70 S. Ct. 57, 94 L. Ed. 494 (1949) * * *.

The following language is from Bass v. Hoagland * * * concerning the applicability of Rule 55:

"Rule 55(a) authorizes the clerk to enter a default * * *. This does not require that to escape default the defendant must not only file a sufficient answer to the merits, but must also have a lawyer or be present in court when the case is called for a trial. The words 'otherwise defend' refer to attacks on the service, or motions to dismiss, or for better particulars, and the like, which may prevent default without presently pleading to the merits. *When Bass by his attorney filed a denial of the plaintiff's case neither the clerk nor the judge could enter a default against him. The burden of proof was put on the plaintiff in any trial. When neither Bass nor his attorney appeared at the trial, no default was generated;* the case was not confessed. The plaintiff might proceed, but he would have to prove his case." 172 F.2d p. 210 (emphasis added).

* * *

* * * It should * * * be stated that once an answer on the merits is filed and the case is at issue, a default judgment is not proper, and if the defendant fails to appear at the trial a judgment on the merits may be entered against him upon proper proof.

* * *

The contention of the defendant that he did not receive notice of the new trial date is not substantiated by the minutes. The record indicates that the clerk of the superior court notified all counsel of all of the orders and judgment pursuant to Rule 77(h) * * *. It is well settled that in the absence of a showing to the contrary a public officer, such as the clerk of the court in this case, is presumed to have performed the duty imposed upon him by law. * * * In addition, if the defendant's counsel did not receive the notice of the change of the trial date to December 10, 1958, he certainly would have learned of the change in the trial date when he appeared for trial on the earlier date, October 10, 1958.

Since the judgment of the lower court is merely voidable, at most, Rule 60(c) * * * prevents the defendant from attacking the judgment more than six months after it was entered. The defendant attempted to attack the judgment nearly two years after it was entered. * * * The lower court properly denied defendant's motion to set aside and vacate the judgment.

Judgment affirmed.

NOTES AND QUESTIONS

1. In BASS v. HOAGLAND, p. 513, supra, which is relied upon in *Coulas,* a default judgment was rendered in favor of plaintiff after defendant's counsel, who had filed an answer, had withdrawn from the case. The judgment recited that defendant had been informed of the withdrawal. Defendant did not appeal but collaterally attacked the judgment when enforcement was sought against him in another jurisdiction. Defendant claimed that he did not know of the counsel's withdrawal from the case and was not aware that the adverse judgment had been rendered. A majority of the Fifth Circuit held that, since an answer had been filed, defendant was not in default under Rule 55, that the entry of judgment without trial by jury, which had been demanded, was a violation of the Due Process Clause of the Fifth Amendment, and that the judgment was void. The court indicated that even if the case fell

within Rule 55, the failure to give notice under Rule 55(b)(2) might render the judgment void, although in that event no jury trial would be required. The dissenting judge took the position that defendant, by not attending trial, was in default, no jury trial was required and therefore the decision was not void and not subject to collateral attack. See Note, *Extending Collateral Attack: An Invitation to Repetitious Litigation*, 59 Yale L.J. 345 (1950). Compare Sheepscot Land Corp. v. Gregory, 383 A.2d 16, 22 (Me. 1978) (failure of defendant to appear for trial justifies default even though answer was filed).

2. Federal Rule 54(c) provides that plaintiff may recover all the relief to which he is entitled except that plaintiff is limited to the amount prayed for in the case of a default judgment. Suppose at trial in Coulas v. Smith plaintiff's evidence showed that defendant was liable for $10,000, although only $4,000 had been claimed. Would the court have been justified in awarding plaintiff the full amount?

CHAPTER 13

THE RIGHT TO A JURY AND OTHER ELEMENTS OF TRIAL

■ ■ ■

In prior Chapters we have explored the ways in which litigants initiate actions, prepare for trial, and avoid trial when possible. But trials do take place, and it is important to discuss and analyze how they proceed, how decisions ultimately are reached, and whether the process is a fair one. We focus in this Chapter on the jury trial, both when a right to a jury exists and the way in which it is implemented. Primarily we discuss matters in the context of federal courts. There are several reasons. First, each state has its own rules and procedures and it would be impossible to deal with each of them in any meaningful detail. Second, the federal system is a sound prototype for study since most states, generally speaking, employ procedures that follow those of the federal courts. In studying these matters, consider how the current drive to eliminate trials through summary procedure, settlement, and methods of alternative dispute resolution are affecting the nature and quality of civil justice in the United States. Is the right to a jury simply an antiquated trial procedure or does it help realize important democratic values?

SECTION A. TRIAL BY JURY

1. THE INSTITUTION OF TRIAL BY JURY

During its formative period the jury was an activist group that not only judged the evidence but also acquired much of it through its own investigation. An example of this drawn from twelfth-century English history is the "jury" used to compile the famous Domesday Book, which contained an inventory of William the Conqueror's realm. The Domesday "jury" viewed the land and formed its own judgments without using witnesses. Today, the jury is a passive, disinterested body that renders its decisions on the basis of the information placed before it.

The revered status of jury trial at common law is evidenced by Blackstone's statement that the right "has been, and I trust ever will be, looked upon as the glory of the English law * * * and * * * that it is the most transcendent privilege which any subject can enjoy or wish for, that he not be affected either in his property, his liberty, or his person, but by unanimous consent of twelve of his neighbors and equals." 3 Blackstone, *Commentaries* *378. Yet, in modern English practice, trial by jury in civil actions has been abandoned except in rare cases.

2. THE RIGHT TO A JURY TRIAL

a. The Nature of the Right Under the United States Constitution

Examine the Seventh Amendment to the United States Constitution and the state jury-trial guarantees in the Supplement. In what ways are the guarantees substantively different from one another? What reasons underlie these differences?

The federal Constitution and most state constitutions do not "create" a right to jury trial. Rather, they "preserve" the right as it existed at common law, either in 1791, the date of the Seventh Amendment's ratification, or, in the case of some states, as of the time the state constitution was adopted. Because the Seventh Amendment was assumed to incorporate the jury-trial practice as of 1791, federal judges frequently have been called upon to determine the actual availability of jury trial as of that date.

* * * The Amendment frequently is said to articulate a "historical test" for determining when the jury right attaches to a cause of action. If the issue in the context in which it arises would have been heard at common law in 1791, when the Seventh Amendment was adopted, or, "according to some judge," in 1938 when law and equity were merged, it is now triable of right to a jury * * *. There is no right to jury trial if viewed historically the issue would have been tried in the courts of equity or if otherwise it would have been tried without a jury.

* * *

[The historical test] * * * proved difficult to apply, particularly for a generation to which the distinctions between law and equity are ancient, and largely unlearned, history. Even if the history were known, it often could shed but dim light as novel kinds of actions were developed and as modern procedure permitted a hybrid form of lawsuit that could never have existed in the ancient days. A vast and controversial literature developed as scholars sought to solve what were essentially insoluble problems. * * * Courts also have complained of being held in "historical bondage" and have apologized for an analysis that "may seem to reek unduly of the study."

9 Wright & Miller, Federal Practice and Procedure: Civil 3d § 2302.

b. The Effect of Federal Rule 2 (The Single Form of Action) and Other Modern–Day Procedural Developments on the Right to Trial by Jury in Federal Courts

The formal elimination under Federal Rule 2 of separate actions in law and equity and other procedural innovations have raised a number of challenging issues regarding the historic right to a trial by jury.

(i) Maintenance of the Law–Equity Distinction

It is important to recognize that cases at law—those that were brought in the courts of law in 1791—continue to carry the right to trial by jury in cases in federal courts whereas suits in equity, historically decided by the chancellor, continue to be decided by judges, although they can, in their discretion, employ an advisory jury. See Federal Rule 39(c).

The distinction is based primarily on the nature of the relief sought. Relief at law is limited in general to compensatory damages along with the ejectment of a defendant who wrongfully is in occupation of plaintiff's land. Equity provides remedies when the law does not, and thus covers a "waterfront" of potential redress, from injunctions, to restitution, rescission, and reformation of contracts. In simple cases, therefore, a plaintiff, by designating the right to relief sought, is able to control whether or not a jury trial is required.

(ii) Cases Involving Both Equitable and Legal Relief

BEACON THEATRES, INC. v. WESTOVER

Supreme Court of the United States, 1959.
359 U.S. 500, 79 S.Ct. 948, 3 L.Ed.2d 988.

Certiorari to the United States Court of Appeals for the Ninth Circuit.

MR. JUSTICE BLACK delivered the opinion of the Court.

Petitioner, Beacon Theatres, Inc., sought by mandamus to require a district judge in the Southern District of California to vacate certain orders alleged to deprive it of a jury trial of issues arising in a suit brought against it by Fox West Coast Theatres, Inc. The Court of Appeals for the Ninth Circuit refused the writ, holding that the trial judge had acted within his proper discretion in denying petitioner's request for a jury. * * *

Fox had asked for declaratory relief against Beacon alleging a controversy arising under the Sherman Antitrust Act, 26 Stat. 209, as amended, 15 U.S.C. §§ 1, 2, and under the Clayton Act, 38 Stat. 731, 15 U.S.C. § 15, which authorizes suits for treble damages against Sherman Act violators. According to the complaint Fox operates a movie theatre in San Bernardino, California, and has long been exhibiting films under contracts with movie distributors. These contracts grant it the exclusive right to show "first run" pictures in the "San Bernardino competitive area" and provide for "clearance"—a period of time during which no other theatre can exhibit the same pictures. After building a drive-in theatre about 11 miles from San Bernardino, Beacon notified Fox that it considered contracts barring simultaneous exhibitions of first-run films in the two theatres to be overt acts in violation of the antitrust laws. Fox's complaint alleged that this notification, together with threats of treble damage suits against Fox and its distributors, gave rise to "duress and coercion" which deprived Fox of a valuable property right, the right to negotiate for exclusive first-run contracts. Unless Beacon was restrained, the complaint continued, irreparable harm would result. Accordingly, while its pleading was styled a "Complaint for Declaratory Relief," Fox prayed both for a declaration that a grant of clearance between the Fox and Beacon theatres is reasonable and not in violation of the antitrust laws, and for an injunction, pending final resolution of the litigation, to prevent Beacon from instituting any action under the antitrust laws against Fox and its distributors arising out of the controversy alleged in the complaint. Beacon filed an answer, a counterclaim against Fox, and a cross-claim against an exhibitor who had intervened. These denied the threats and asserted that there was no substantial competition between the two theatres, that the clearances granted were therefore unreasonable, and that a conspiracy existed between Fox and its distributors to manipulate contracts and clearances so as to restrain trade and monopolize first-run pictures in violation of the antitrust laws. Treble damages were asked.

Beacon demanded a jury trial of the factual issues in the case as provided by Federal Rule * * * 38(b). The District Court, however, viewed the issues raised by the "Complaint for Declaratory Relief," including the question of competition between the two theatres, as essentially equitable. Acting under the purported authority of Rules 42(b) and 57, it directed that these issues be tried to the court before jury determination of the validity of the charges of antitrust violations made in the counterclaim and cross-claim. A common issue of the "Complaint for Declaratory Relief," the counterclaim, and the cross-claim was the reasonableness of the clearances granted to Fox, which depended, in part, on the existence of competition between the two theatres. Thus the effect of the action of the District Court could be, as the Court of Appeals believed, "to limit the petitioner's opportunity fully to try to a jury every issue which has a bearing upon its treble damage suit," for determination of the issue of clearances by the judge might "operate either by way of res judicata or collateral estoppel so as to conclude both parties with respect thereto at the subsequent trial of the treble damage claim." * * *

The District Court's finding that the Complaint for Declaratory Relief presented basically equitable issues draws no support from the Declaratory Judgment Act, 28 U.S.C. §§ 2201, 2202; Fed. Rules Civ. Proc. 57. * * * That statute, while allowing prospective defendants to sue to establish their nonliability, specifically preserves the right to jury trial for both parties. It follows that if Beacon would have been entitled to a jury trial in a treble damage suit against Fox it cannot be deprived of that right merely because Fox took advantage of the availability of declaratory relief to sue Beacon first. Since the right to trial by jury applies to treble damage suits under the antitrust laws, and is, in fact, an essential part of the congressional plan for making competition rather than monopoly the rule of trade * * *, the Sherman and Clayton Act issues * * * were essentially jury questions.

Nevertheless the Court of Appeals * * * held that the question of whether a right to jury trial existed was to be judged by Fox's complaint read as a whole. In addition to seeking a declaratory judgment, the court said, Fox's complaint can be read as making out a valid plea for injunctive relief, thus stating a claim traditionally cognizable in equity. A party who is entitled to maintain a suit in equity for an injunction, said the court, may have all the issues in his suit determined by the judge without a jury regardless of whether legal rights are involved. The court then rejected the argument that equitable relief, traditionally available only when legal remedies are inadequate, was rendered unnecessary in this case by the filing of the counterclaim and cross-claim which presented all the issues necessary to a determination of the right to injunctive relief. Relying on American Life Ins. Co. v. Stewart, 300 U.S. 203, 215, 57 S. Ct. 377, 380, 81 L. Ed. 605, decided before the enactment of the Federal Rules * * *, it invoked the principle that a court sitting in equity could retain jurisdiction even though later a legal remedy became available. In such instances the equity court had discretion to enjoin the later lawsuit in order to allow the whole dispute to be determined in one case in one court. Reasoning by analogy, the Court of Appeals held it was not an abuse of discretion for the district judge, acting under Federal Rule * * * 42(b), to try the equitable cause first even though this might, through collateral estoppel, prevent a full jury trial of the counterclaim and cross-claim which were as effectively stopped as by an equity injunction. * * *

Beacon takes issue with the holding of the Court of Appeals that the complaint stated a claim upon which equitable relief could be granted. As initially filed the complaint alleged that threats of lawsuits by petitioner against Fox and its distributors were causing irreparable harm to Fox's business relationships. The prayer for relief, however, made no mention of the threats but asked only that pending litigation of the claim for declaratory judgment, Beacon be enjoined from beginning any lawsuits under the antitrust laws against Fox and its distributors arising out of the controversy alleged in the complaint. Evidently of the opinion that this prayer did not state a good claim for equitable relief, the Court of Appeals construed it to include a request for an injunction against threats of lawsuits. * * * But this fact does not solve our problem. Assuming that the pleadings can be construed to support such a request and assuming additionally that the complaint can be read as alleging the kind of harassment by a multiplicity of lawsuits which would *traditionally* have justified equity to take jurisdiction and settle the case in one suit, we are nevertheless of the opinion that, under the Declaratory Judgment Act and the Federal Rules * * *, neither claim can justify denying Beacon a trial by jury of all the issues in the antitrust controversy.

The basis of injunctive relief in the federal courts has always been irreparable harm and inadequacy of legal remedies. At least as much is required to justify a trial court in using its discretion under the Federal Rules to allow claims of equitable origins to be tried ahead of legal ones, since this has the same effect as an equitable injunction of the legal claims. And it is immaterial, in judging if that discretion is properly employed, that before the Federal Rules and the Declaratory Judgment Act were passed, courts of equity, exercising a jurisdiction separate from courts of law, were, in some cases, allowed to enjoin subsequent legal actions between the same parties involving the same controversy. This was because the subsequent legal action, though providing an opportunity to try the case to a jury, might not protect the right of the equity plaintiff to a fair and orderly adjudication of the controversy. * * * Under such circumstances the legal remedy could quite naturally be deemed inadequate. Inadequacy of remedy and irreparable harm * * * today must be determined, not by precedents decided under discarded procedures, but in the light of the remedies now made available by the Declaratory Judgment Act and the Federal Rules.

Viewed in this manner, the use of discretion by the trial court under Rule 42(b) to deprive Beacon of a full jury trial on its counterclaim and cross-claim, as well as on Fox's plea for declaratory relief, cannot be justified. Under the Federal Rules the same court may try both legal and equitable causes in the same action. * * *

Thus any defenses, equitable or legal, Fox may have to charges of antitrust violations can be raised either in its suit for declaratory relief or in answer to Beacon's counterclaim. On proper showing, harassment by threats of other suits, or other suits actually brought, involving the issues being tried in this case, could be temporarily enjoined pending the outcome of this litigation. Whatever permanent injunctive relief Fox might be entitled to on the basis of the decision in this case could, of course, be given by the court after the jury renders its verdict. In this way the issues between these parties could be settled in one suit giving Beacon a full jury trial of every antitrust issue. * * * By contrast, the holding of the court below while granting Fox no additional protection unless the avoidance of jury trial be considered as such, would compel Beacon to split his antitrust case, trying part to a judge and part to a jury. Such a result, which involves the postponement and subordination of Fox's own legal claim for declaratory relief as well as of the counterclaim which Beacon was compelled by the Federal Rules to bring, is not permissible.

Our decision is consistent with the plan of the Federal Rules and the Declaratory Judgment Act to effect substantial procedural reform while retaining a distinction between jury and nonjury issues and leaving substantive rights unchanged. Since in the federal courts equity has always acted only when legal remedies were inadequate, the expansion of adequate legal remedies provided by the Declaratory Judgment Act and the Federal Rules necessarily affects the scope of equity. Thus, the justification for equity's deciding legal issues once it obtains jurisdiction, and refusing to dismiss a case, merely because subsequently a legal remedy becomes available, must be re-evaluated in the light of the liberal joinder provisions of the Federal Rules which allow legal and equitable causes to be brought and resolved in one civil action. Similarly the need for, and therefore, the availability of such equitable remedies as Bills of Peace, *Quia Timet* and Injunction must be reconsidered in view of the existence of the Declaratory Judgment Act as well as the liberal joinder provision of the Rules. * * *

If there should be cases where the availability of declaratory judgment or joinder in one suit of legal and equitable causes would not in all respects protect the plaintiff seeking equitable relief from irreparable harm while affording a jury trial in the legal cause, the trial court will necessarily have to use its discretion in deciding whether the legal or equitable cause should be tried first. Since the right to jury trial is a constitutional one, however, while no similar requirement protects trials by the court, that discretion is very narrowly limited and must, wherever possible, be exercised to preserve jury trial. * * * [O]nly under the most imperative circumstances, circumstances which in view of the flexible procedures of the Federal Rules we cannot now anticipate, can the right to a jury trial of legal issues be lost through prior determination of equitable claims. * * *

As we have shown, this is far from being such a case.

* * *

The judgment of the Court of Appeals is reversed.

Reversed.

MR. JUSTICE FRANKFURTER took no part in the consideration or decision of this case.

MR. JUSTICE STEWART, with whom MR. JUSTICE HARLAN and MR. JUSTICE WHITTAKER concur, dissenting.

* * *

The Court today sweeps away * * * basic principles as "precedents decided under discarded procedures" * * *. It suggests that the Federal Rules * * * have somehow worked an "expansion of adequate legal remedies" so as to oust the District Courts of equitable jurisdiction, as well as to deprive them of their traditional power to control their own dockets. But obviously the Federal Rules could not and did not "expand" the substantive law one whit.

Like the Declaratory Judgment Act, the Federal Rules preserve inviolate the right to trial by jury in actions historically cognizable at common law, as under the Constitution they must. They do not create a right of trial by jury where that right "does not exist under the Constitution or statutes of the United States." Rule 39(a) [comparable language now found in Rule 38(a)]. Since Beacon's counterclaim was compulsory under the Rules, see Rule 13(a), it is apparent that by filing it Beacon could not be held to have waived its jury rights. * * * But neither can the counterclaim be held to have transformed Fox's original complaint into an action at law. * * *

The Rules make possible the trial of legal and equitable claims in the same proceeding, but they expressly affirm the power of a trial judge to determine the order in which claims shall be heard. Rule 42(b). Certainly the Federal Rules were not intended to undermine the basic structure of equity jurisprudence, developed over the centuries and explicitly recognized in the United States Constitution.

For these reasons I think the petition for a writ of mandamus should have been dismissed.

DAIRY QUEEN, INC. v. WOOD, 369 U.S. 469, 82 S.Ct. 894, 8 L.Ed.2d 44 (1962), arose out of a licensing agreement entered into by respondents, owners of the trademark "DAIRY QUEEN," under which petitioner agreed to pay $150,000 for the exclusive right to use that trademark in certain parts of Pennsylvania. The contract provided for a small initial payment, with the remaining payments to be made at the rate of 50 percent of all amounts received by petitioner on sales and franchises to deal with the trademark; minimum annual payments were to be made regardless of petitioner's receipts. In August, 1960, respondents wrote petitioner a letter in which they claimed that the latter had committed "a material breach of that contract" by defaulting on the contract's payment provisions and notified petitioner that the contract would be terminated unless the claimed default was remedied immediately. When petitioner continued to deal with the trademark, respondents brought an action for breach of contract praying for: (1) temporary and permanent injunctions to restrain petitioner from any future use of or dealing in the franchise and the trademark; (2) an accounting to determine the exact amount of money owed by petitioner and a judgment for that amount; and (3) an injunction pending an accounting to prevent petitioner from collecting any money from "Dairy Queen" stores in the territory.

The Eastern District of Pennsylvania granted a motion to strike petitioner's demand for a jury trial on the alternative grounds that either the action was "purely equitable" or, if not purely equitable, the legal issues were "incidental" to equitable issues, and, in either case, no right to trial by jury existed. The Third Circuit refused to mandamus the district judge to vacate this order. The Supreme Court reversed.

The Court first disposed of the District Court's conclusion that there is no right to jury trial on legal issues that are "incidental" to equitable issues.

* * * The holding in *Beacon Theatres* * * * applies whether the trial judge chooses to characterize the legal issues presented as "incidental" to equitable issues or not. Consequently, * * * *Beacon Theatres* requires that any legal issues for which a trial by jury is timely and properly demanded be submitted to a jury. * * *

Id. at 472–73, 82 S.Ct. at 897, 8 L.Ed.2d at 48.

As to the lower court's conclusion that the action was "purely equitable," the Court said:

* * * The most natural construction of the respondents' claim for a money judgment would seem to be that it is a claim that they are entitled to recover whatever was owed them under the contract as of the date of its purported termination plus damages for infringement of their trademark since that date. * * * As an action on a debt allegedly due under a contract, it would be difficult to conceive of an action of a more traditionally legal character. And as an action for damages based upon a charge of trademark infringement, it would be no less subject to cognizance by a court of law.

The respondents' contention that this money claim is "purely equitable" is based primarily upon the fact that their complaint is cast in terms of an "accounting," rather than in terms of an action for "debt" or "damages." But the constitutional right to trial by jury cannot be made to depend upon the choice of words used in the pleadings. The necessary prerequisite to the right to maintain a suit for an equitable accounting, like all other equitable remedies, is, as we pointed out in *Beacon Theatres*, the absence of an adequate remedy at law. Consequently, in order to maintain such a suit on a cause of action cognizable at law, as this one is, the plaintiff must be able to show that the "accounts between the parties" are of such a "complicated nature" that only a court of equity can satisfactorily unravel them. In view of the powers given to District Courts by Federal Rule * * * 53(b) to appoint masters to assist the jury in those exceptional cases where the legal issues are too complicated for the jury adequately to handle alone, the burden of such a showing is considerably increased and it will indeed be a rare case in which it can be met. * * * A jury, under proper instructions from the court, could readily determine the recovery, if any, to be had here, whether the theory finally settled upon is that of breach of contract, that of trademark infringement, or any combination of the two. * * *

Id. at 476–79, 82 S.Ct. at 899–900, 8 L.Ed.2d at 50–52.

———

ROSS v. BERNHARD, 396 U.S. 531, 90 S.Ct. 733, 24 L.Ed.2d 729 (1970). Plaintiffs brought a derivative suit in federal court against the directors of a closed-end investment company of which they were shareholders and joined the company's brokers, alleging that the company had been charged excessive brokerage fees. Plaintiffs' demand for jury trial, granted by the trial court but set aside by the Second Circuit, was upheld by the Supreme Court in a five-to-three decision:

> Derivative suits posed no Seventh Amendment problems where the action against the directors and third parties would have been by a bill in equity had the corporation brought the suit. Our concern is with cases based upon a legal claim of the corporation against directors or third parties. Does the trial of such claims at the suit of a stockholder and without a jury violate the Seventh Amendment?
>
> * * * The heart of the action is the corporate claim. If it presents a legal issue, one entitling the corporation to a jury trial under the Seventh Amendment, the right to a jury is not forfeited merely because the stockholder's right to sue must first be adjudicated as an equitable issue triable to the court. *Beacon* and *Dairy Queen* require no less.

Id. at 538–39, 90 S.Ct. at 739, 24 L.Ed.2d at 736.

NOTES AND QUESTIONS

1. A footnote in the majority opinion in *Ross* provides some guidance regarding the categorization of issues as legal or equitable for Seventh Amendment purposes:

> As our cases indicate, the "legal" nature of an issue is determined by considering, first, the pre-merger custom with reference to such questions; second, the remedy sought; and, third, the practical abilities and limitations of juries. * * *

396 U.S. at 538 n.10, 90 S.Ct. at 738 n.10, 24 L.Ed.2d at 736 n.10. The significance of the third factor mentioned by the Court—the practical abilities and limitations of juries—is unclear.

2. Some lower federal courts have read the third "consideration" mentioned in the *Ross* footnote, Note 1, above, as a basis for denying a jury trial in cases in which the number of parties, complexity of the issues, or conceptual sophistication of the evidence and applicable substantive law support a finding that a jury would not be a rational and capable fact-finder. See, e.g., In re Japanese Electronic Prods. Antitrust Litigation, 631 F.2d 1069 (3d Cir. 1980), affirmed in part and reversed in part on other grounds following summary judgment 723 F.2d 238, 319 (3d Cir. 1983), reversed on other grounds Matsushita Elec. Indus. Co. v. Zenith Radio Corp., 475 U.S. 574, 106 S.Ct. 1348, 89 L.Ed.2d 538 (1986). Other federal courts have rejected this approach as too great an incursion on the Seventh Amendment. See, e.g., In re United States Financial Secs. Litigation, 609 F.2d 411 (9th Cir. 1979), certiorari denied 446 U.S. 929, 100 S.Ct. 1866, 64 L.Ed.2d 281 (1980), overruling 75 F.R.D. 702 (S.D. Cal. 1977). This issue has arisen in major securities and antitrust suits, which present questions of a technical and esoteric nature arguably outstripping the capacity of even the most well-educated jurors.

The argument for the "complexity exception" is threefold. First, because this exception was recognized at common law at the time of the drafting and adoption of the Seventh Amendment, it is said to be consistent with the Constitution. Second, because there are practical limitations on jurors' knowledge, experience, and ability, it is argued that complex and esoteric cases, such as *Japanese Electronic* or *U.S. Financial Securities*, are best entrusted to the fact-finding capacity of an experienced trial judge. Third, it is contended that to submit to a jury issues exceeding its capacity for rational and sound decisionmaking constitutes a denial of the litigants' due process rights.

3. Do you see a relation between the complexity exception to the jury trial right and the Supreme Court's increasing tendency to dispose of discovery-rich cases on motions to dismiss or on summary judgment? These developments coincide with a drop in the number of jury trials overall. See Ellis, *Saving the Jury Trial*, 34 Brief 15 (Summer 2005). Professor Miller has offered the following analysis of these trends:

> The less confident a court is in a jury's ability to comprehend, retain, and apply quantities of technical, scientific, and economic information, or to distinguish intertwined legal and factual issues, the more disposed it may be to use the occasion of a summary judgment motion to decide mixed law and fact questions and those it labels "beyond dispute." Thus the court may tend to believe that its own determination will be more rational than that of a jury. However, jurors should not be assumed incompetent or unable to comprehend issues posed by difficult cases. In fact, the ability to employ court-appointed experts or masters under Rule 53 to assist a jury when issues are complex exhibits the Rules' presumption of juror competence.

Miller, *The Pretrial Rush to Judgment: Are the "Litigation Explosion," "Liability Crisis," and Efficiency Clichés Eroding Our Day in Court and Jury Trial Commitments?*, 78 N.Y.U. L. Rev. 982, 1108–09 (2003). Reconsider this issue when you read the *Markman* decision, p. 534, infra.

(iii) The Modern Effect of Historical Equity Jurisdiction Based on a Party's Legal Status

---

CHAUFFEURS, TEAMSTERS AND HELPERS LOCAL 391 v. TERRY

Supreme Court of the United States, 1990.
494 U.S. 558, 110 S.Ct. 1339, 108 L.Ed.2d 519.

Certiorari to the United States Court of Appeals for the Fourth Circuit.

JUSTICE MARSHALL delivered the opinion of the Court except as to Part III–A.

This case presents the question whether an employee who seeks relief in the form of backpay for a union's alleged breach of its duty of fair representation has a right to trial by jury. We hold that the Seventh Amendment entitles such a plaintiff to a jury trial.

I

McLean Trucking Company and the Chauffeurs, Teamsters, and Helpers Local Union No. 391 were parties to a collective-bargaining agreement that governed the terms and conditions of employment at McLean's terminals. The 27 respondents were employed by McLean as truckdrivers in bargaining units covered by the agreement, and all were members of the Union.

* * * Claiming a violation of their seniority rights, respondents filed a * * * grievance with the Union, but the Union declined to refer the charges to a grievance committee on the ground that the relevant issues had been determined in * * * prior proceedings.

In July 1983, respondents filed an action in District Court, alleging * * * that the Union had violated its duty of fair representation * * * [and] sought, *inter alia,* compensatory damages for lost wages and health benefits. * * *

Respondents had requested a jury trial in their pleadings. The Union moved to strike the jury demand on the ground that no right to a jury trial exists in a duty of fair representation suit. The District Court denied the motion to strike. After an interlocutory appeal, the Fourth Circuit affirmed the trial court, holding that the Seventh Amendment entitled respondents to a jury trial of their claim for monetary relief. 863 F.2d 334 (1988). We granted the petition for certiorari to resolve a circuit conflict on this issue * * * and now affirm the judgment of the Fourth Circuit.

II

The duty of fair representation is inferred from unions' exclusive authority under the National Labor Relations Act, 49 Stat. 449, 29 U.S.C. § 159(a) (1982 ed.), to represent all employees in a bargaining unit. * * * The duty requires a union "to serve the interests of all members without hostility or discrimination toward any, to exercise its discretion with complete good faith and honesty, and to avoid arbitrary conduct." * * *

III

* * *

To determine whether a particular action will resolve legal rights, we examine both the nature of the issues involved and the remedy sought. "First, we compare the statutory action to 18th-century actions brought in the courts of England prior to the merger of the courts of law and equity. Second, we examine the remedy sought and determine whether it is legal or equitable in nature." * * * The second inquiry is the more important in our analysis. * * *

A

An action for breach of a union's duty of fair representation was unknown in 18th-century England; in fact, collective bargaining was unlawful. * * * We must therefore look for an analogous cause of action that existed in the 18th century to determine whether the nature of this duty of fair representation suit is legal or equitable.

The Union contends that this duty of fair representation action resembles a suit brought to vacate an arbitration award because respondents seek to set aside the result of the grievance process. In the 18th century, an action to set aside an arbitration award was considered equitable. * * *

The arbitration analogy is inapposite, however, to the Seventh Amendment question posed in this case. No grievance committee has considered respondents' claim that the Union violated its duty of fair representation; the grievance process was concerned only with the employer's alleged breach of the collective-bargaining agreement. Thus, respondents' claim against the Union cannot be characterized as an action to vacate an arbitration award * * *.

The Union next argues that respondents' duty of fair representation action is comparable to an action by a trust beneficiary against a trustee for breach of fiduciary duty. Such actions were within the exclusive jurisdiction of courts of equity. * * * This analogy is far more persuasive than the arbitration analogy. Just as a trustee must act in the best interests of the beneficiaries, * * * a union, as the exclusive representative of the workers, must exercise its power to act on behalf of the employees in good faith * * *. Moreover, just as a beneficiary does not directly control the actions of a trustee, * * * an individual employee lacks direct control over a union's actions taken on his behalf * * *.

The trust analogy extends to a union's handling of grievances. In most cases, a trustee has the exclusive authority to sue third parties who injure the beneficiaries' interest in the trust, * * * including any legal claim the trustee holds in trust for the beneficiaries * * *. The trustee then has the sole responsibility for determining whether to settle, arbitrate, or otherwise dispose of the claim. * * * Similarly, the union typically has broad discretion in its decision whether and how to pursue an employee's grievance against an employer. * * * Just as a trust beneficiary can sue to enforce a contract entered into on his behalf by the trustee only if the trustee "improperly refuses or neglects to bring an action against the third person," * * * so an employee can sue his employer for a breach of the collective-bargaining agreement only if he shows that the union breached its duty of fair representation in its handling of the grievance * * *.

Respondents contend that their duty of fair representation suit is less like a trust action than an attorney malpractice action, which was historically an action at law * * *.

The attorney malpractice analogy is inadequate in several respects. Although an attorney malpractice suit is in some ways similar to a suit alleging a union's breach of its fiduciary duty, the two actions are fundamentally different. The nature of an action is in large part controlled by the nature of the underlying relationship between the parties. Unlike employees represented by a union, a client controls the significant decisions concerning his representation. Moreover, a client can fire his attorney if he is dissatisfied with his attorney's performance. This option is not available to an individual employee who is unhappy with a union's representation, unless a majority of the members of the bargaining unit share his dissatisfaction. * * * Thus, we find the malpractice analogy less convincing than the trust analogy.

Nevertheless, the trust analogy does not persuade us to characterize respondents' claim as wholly equitable. * * * "The Seventh Amendment question depends on the nature of the *issue* to be tried rather than the character of the overall action." * * * [T]o recover from the Union here, respondents must prove both that McLean violated § 301 by breaching the collective-bargaining agreement and that the Union breached its duty of fair representation. When viewed in isolation, the duty of fair representation issue is analogous to a claim against a trustee for breach of fiduciary duty. The § 301 issue, however, is comparable to a breach of contract claim—a legal issue.

Respondents' action against the Union thus encompasses both equitable and legal issues. The first part of our Seventh Amendment inquiry, then, leaves us in equipoise as to whether respondents are entitled to a jury trial.

B

Our determination under the first part of the Seventh Amendment analysis is only preliminary. * * * In this case, the only remedy sought is a request for compensatory damages representing backpay and benefits. Generally, an action for money damages was "the traditional form of relief offered in the courts of law." * * * This Court has not, however, held that "any award of monetary relief must *necessarily* be 'legal' relief." * * * Nonetheless, because we conclude that the remedy respondents seek has none of the attributes that must be present before we will find an exception to the general rule and characterize damages as equitable, we find that the remedy sought by respondents is legal.

First, we have characterized damages as equitable where they are restitutionary, such as in "action[s] for disgorgement of improper profits," * * *. * * * The backpay sought by respondents is not money wrongfully held by the Union, but wages and benefits they would have received from McLean had the Union processed the employees' grievances properly. Such relief is not restitutionary.

Second, a monetary award "incidental to or intertwined with injunctive relief" may be equitable. * * * Because respondents seek only money damages, this characteristic is clearly absent from the case.[8]

* * *

The Court has never held that a plaintiff seeking backpay under Title VII has a right to a jury trial. * * * Congress specifically characterized backpay under Title VII as a form of "equitable relief." * * * Congress made no similar pronouncement regarding the duty of fair representation. Furthermore, the Court has noted that backpay sought from an employer under Title VII would generally be restitutionary in nature * * *, in contrast to the damages sought here from the union. * * *

* * *

We hold, then, that the remedy of backpay sought in this duty of fair representation action is legal in nature. Considering both parts of the Seventh Amendment inquiry, we find that respondents are entitled to a jury trial on all issues presented in their suit.

* * *

It is so ordered.

JUSTICE BRENNAN, concurring in part and concurring in the judgment.

I agree with the Court that respondents seek a remedy that is legal in nature and that the Seventh Amendment entitles respondents to a jury trial on their duty of fair representation claims. * * * I do not join that part of the opinion which reprises the particular historical analysis this Court has employed to determine whether a claim is a "Sui[t] at common law" under the Seventh Amendment, * * * because I believe the historical test can and should be simplified.

* * *

To rest the historical test required by the Seventh Amendment solely on the nature of the relief sought would not, of course, offer the federal courts a rule that is in all cases self-executing. Courts will still be required to ask which remedies were traditionally available at law and which only in equity. But this inquiry involves fewer variables and simpler choices, on the whole, and is far more manageable than the scholasticist debates in

---

8. Both the Union and the dissent argue that the backpay award sought here is equitable because it is closely analogous to damages awarded to beneficiaries for a trustee's breach of trust. * * *. Such damages were available only in courts of equity because those courts had exclusive jurisdiction over actions involving a trustee's breach of his fiduciary duties. * * *

The Union's argument, however, conflates the two parts of our Seventh Amendment inquiry. Under the dissent's approach, if the action at issue were analogous to an 18th-century action within the exclusive jurisdiction of the courts of equity, we would necessarily conclude that the remedy sought was also equitable because it would have been unavailable in a court of law. This view would, in effect, make the first part of our inquiry dispositive. We have clearly held, however, that the second part of the inquiry—the nature of the relief—is more important to the Seventh Amendment determination. * * * The second part of the analysis, therefore, should not replicate the "abstruse historical" inquiry of the first part, * * * but requires consideration of the general types of relief provided by courts of law and equity.

which we have been engaged. Moreover, the rule I propose would remain true to the Seventh Amendment, as it is undisputed that, historically, "[j]urisdictional lines [between law and equity] were primarily a matter of remedy." McCoid, Procedural Reform and the Right to Jury Trial: A Study of *Beacon Theaters, Inc. v. Westover*, 116 U. Pa. L. Rev. 1 (1967). * * *

This is not to say that the resulting division between claims entitled to jury trials and claims not so entitled would exactly mirror the division between law and equity in England in 1791. But it is too late in the day for this Court to profess that the Seventh Amendment preserves the right to jury trial only in cases that would have been heard in the British law courts of the 18th century. * * *

We can guard * * * [the jury trial] right and save our courts from needless and intractable excursions into increasingly unfamiliar territory simply by retiring that prong of our Seventh Amendment test which we have already cast into a certain doubt. If we are not prepared to accord the nature of the historical analog sufficient weight for this factor to affect the outcome of our inquiry, except in the rarest of hypothetical cases, what reason do we have for insisting that federal judges proceed with this arduous inquiry? It is time we read the writing on the wall, especially as we ourselves put it there.

JUSTICE STEVENS, concurring in part and concurring in the judgment.

Because I believe the Court has made this case unnecessarily difficult by exaggerating the importance of finding a precise common-law analogue to the duty of fair representation, I do not join Part III–A of its opinion. * * *

* * * Duty of fair representation suits are for the most part ordinary civil actions involving the stuff of contract and malpractice disputes. There is accordingly no ground for excluding these actions from the jury right.

In my view, the evolution of this doctrine through suits tried to juries, the useful analogy to common-law malpractice cases, and the well-recognized duty to scrutinize any proposed curtailment of the right to a jury trial "with the utmost care," * * * provide a plainly sufficient basis for the Court's holding today. * * *

JUSTICE KENNEDY, with whom JUSTICE O'CONNOR and JUSTICE SCALIA join, dissenting.

* * *

I disagree with the analytic innovation of the Court that identification of the trust action as a model for modern duty of fair representation actions is insufficient to decide the case. The Seventh Amendment requires us to determine whether the duty of fair representation action "is more similar to cases that were tried in courts of law than to suits tried in courts of equity." * * * Having made this decision in favor of an equitable action, our inquiry should end. Because the Court disagrees with this proposition, I dissent.

* * *

* * * Although monetary damages might cause some statutory actions to resemble tort suits, the presence of monetary damages in this duty of fair representation action does not make it more analogous to a legal action than to an equitable action. Indeed, as shown above, the injunctive and monetary remedies available make the duty of fair representation suit less analogous to a malpractice action than to a suit against a trustee.

* * *

The Court must adhere to the historical test in determining the right to a jury because the language of the Constitution requires it. The Seventh Amendment "preserves" the right to jury trial in civil cases. We cannot preserve a right existing in 1791 unless we look to history to identify it. * * *

I would hesitate to abandon or curtail the historical test out of concern for the competence of the Court to understand legal history. We do look to history for the answers to constitutional questions. * * * Although opinions will differ on what this history shows, the approach has no less validity in the Seventh Amendment context than elsewhere.

If Congress has not provided for a jury trial, we are confined to the Seventh Amendment to determine whether one is required. Our own views respecting the wisdom of using a jury should be put aside. Like Justice Brennan, I admire the jury process. Other judges have taken the opposite view. * * * But the judgment of our own times is not always preferable to the lessons of history. Our whole constitutional experience teaches that history must inform the judicial inquiry. Our obligation to the Constitution and its Bill of Rights, no less than the compact we have with the generation that wrote them for us, do not permit us to disregard provisions that some may think to be mere matters of historical form.

NOTES AND QUESTIONS

1. In footnote 8 of his opinion in *Terry,* p. 530, supra, does Justice Marshall provide an adequate explanation for continuing to employ a two-prong test that values the second prong more than the first? Or does the historical analysis "needlessly convolute our Seventh Amendment jurisprudence," as Justice Brennan argues? Justices Marshall and Stevens and the dissenters all disagree on the appropriate historical model for a "duty of fair representation" action. Is this disagreement evidence in favor of severing the historical analysis from the Seventh Amendment test, or is it evidence in favor of keeping the analysis as it is?

2. The Supreme Court's analysis of the scope of the right to jury trial under the Seventh Amendment remains ongoing. In CITY OF MONTEREY v. DEL MONTE DUNES, 526 U.S. 687, 119 S.Ct. 1624, 143 L.Ed.2d 882 (1999), damages were sought under the Civil Rights Acts, 42 U.S.C. § 1983, on the

ground that the city had taken defendant's property without just compensation. The Court rendered three opinions, holding by a 5 to 4 majority, that a jury trial was proper. The four dissenting Justices argued that the case was at heart a condemnation action under the Fifth Amendment to the Constitution for which there is no right to trial by jury. Four Justices disagreed, noting that a condemnation action historically is one brought by the government conceding that it owes compensation to the owner of the property and seeking a fair evaluation of its worth. In *Del Monte Dunes*, the property owner initiated the suit, arguing that the actions of the county with regard to zoning deprived the owner of the value of the property. The four Justices held that such a case is akin historically to a tort action for damages, and thus carries the right to a jury trial under the Seventh Amendment. Justice Scalia concurred with them on the ground that Section 1983 itself, when an action is brought to recover damages, provides for a jury trial, regardless of the nature of the underlying cause.

3. In some states there is a right to jury trial in equity cases, which eliminates the problem presented by *Beacon Theatres* and *Dairy Queen*. In most states that have merged law and equity, however, issues similar to those in the federal courts have arisen since the adoption of the codes.

The Commissioners who prepared the original New York Code of Procedure (1848) were aware of the problem presented by abolishing the distinction between law and equity at a time when that state's constitution continued to guarantee "trial by jury in all cases in which it has been heretofore used." This language appeared in the New York Constitutions of 1777, 1821, 1846, and 1894. Because it was interpreted to mean that each successive constitution guaranteed jury trial in any case to which it had been extended by the legislature since the adoption of the preceding constitution, it was changed in the constitution of 1938 to guarantee jury trial only "in all cases in which it has heretofore been guaranteed by constitutional provision." N.Y. Const. Art. I, § 2. But they may have underestimated the difficulty. Not content to leave the issue solely one of constitutional interpretation as it has been in the federal courts, they attempted to solve it by specific provisions, N.Y. Code of Proc. §§ 208–09 (1848):

> § 208. Whenever, in an action for the recovery of money only, or of specific real or personal property, there shall be an issue of fact, it must be tried by a jury, unless a jury trial be waived * * *.

> § 209. Every other issue is triable by the court, which, however, may order the whole issue, or any specific question of fact involved therein, to be tried by a jury * * *.

These provisions were copied in a great many states. But "in most jurisdictions * * * the courts, while occasionally giving the statute some weight, have regarded it generally as merely restating the law-equity dichotomy, and have proceeded to make their determination on historical grounds." Note, *The Right to Jury Trial Under Merged Procedures,* 65 Harv. L. Rev. 453, 454 (1952). In civil actions in which damages alone are sought, there has been little difficulty in finding that a jury is required, and of course in traditional equity cases, such as those involving trusts or injunctions, no jury has been allowed. In most states, there has been a reluctance to allow a mixed form of trial, with some issues being tried by the court and some by a jury. When there have been "legal" and "equitable" issues in the same case, the tendency has been to find one or the other the "predominant" concern and try the case accordingly. Perhaps most frequently the decision has been to find the case "predominantly" equitable, with jury trial denied on the "legal" issues on the grounds that they are "incidental," or that a jury trial is waived by joining a legal claim in an equitable action. Id. at 454–55. For a classic example, see Hiatt v. Yergin, 152 Ind.App. 497, 284 N.E.2d 834 (1972).

The Supreme Court's decisions, from *Beacon Theatres* through *Del Monte Dunes,* have not had a broad impact on the state courts and, in the state opinions in which these cases have been discussed, the reception has been mixed. For state court opinions that have looked at the *Beacon Theatres*-line approvingly, see, e.g., Onvoy, Inc. v. Allete, Inc., 736 N.W.2d 611 (Minn. 2007); Perilli v. Board of Educ. Monongalia County, 182 W.Va. 261, 387 S.E.2d 315 (1989).

3. THE PROVINCE OF JUDGE AND JURY

WEINER, THE CIVIL JURY AND THE LAW–FACT DISTINCTION, 54 Calif. L. Rev. 1867, 1867–68 (1966):

The categories of "questions of law" and "questions of fact" have been the traditional touchstones by which courts have purported to allocate decision-making between judge and jury. * * * Many statutes in effect today echo * * * [the] dichotomy, utilizing the law and fact terminology to identify the respective provinces of the judge and the jurors in a civil case. None of these statutes, however, attempts to define what is meant by a question of law or a question of fact. Nor have the courts shown any inclination to fashion definitions which can serve as useful guidelines. Indeed, when faced with a dispute as to whether a specific issue should be resolved by the judge or the jury, the typical appellate opinion today does no more than label the question as one of law or of fact, perhaps citing some authorities which are equally devoid of any more detailed consideration of the point. * * * A question of law or a question of fact is a mere synonym for a judge question or a jury question.

MARKMAN v. WESTVIEW INSTRUMENTS, INC.

Supreme Court of the United States, 1996.
517 U.S. 370, 116 S.Ct. 1384, 134 L.Ed.2d 577.

Certiorari to the United States Court of Appeals for the Federal Circuit.

JUSTICE SOUTER delivered the opinion of the Court.

The question here is whether the interpretation of a so-called patent claim, the portion of the patent document that defines the scope of the patentee's rights, is a matter of law reserved entirely for the court, or subject to a Seventh Amendment guarantee that a jury will determine the meaning of any disputed term of art about which expert testimony is offered. We hold that the construction of a patent, including terms of art within its claim, is exclusively within the province of the court.

[The dispute involved competing claims to a patent used to monitor clothing in a dry-cleaning establishment. Both systems used a keyboard and data processor and generated records including bar codes. Respondent argued that petitioner's patent was not infringed by Westview's because the latter only records an inventory of receivables by tracking invoices, rather than an inventory of articles of clothing.]

* * * Part of the dispute hinges upon the meaning of the word "inventory," a term found in Markman's independent claim 1, which states that Markman's product can "maintain an inventory total" and "detect and localize spurious additions to inventory." The case was tried before a jury, which heard, among others, a witness produced by Markman who testified about the meaning of the claim language.

After the jury compared the patent to Westview's device, it found an infringement of Markman's claim 1 * * *. The District Court nevertheless granted Westview's deferred motion for judgment as a matter of law, one of its reasons being that the term "inventory" in Markman's patent encompasses "both cash inventory and the actual physical inventory of articles of clothing." * * * Under the trial court's construction of the patent, the production, sale, or use of a tracking system for dry cleaners would not infringe Markman's patent unless the product was capable of tracking articles of clothing throughout the cleaning process and generating reports about their status and location. Since Westview's system cannot do these things, the District Court directed a verdict. * * *

Markman appealed, arguing it was error for the District Court to substitute its construction of the disputed claim term "inventory" for the construction the jury had presumably given it. The United States Court of Appeals for the Federal Circuit affirmed, holding the interpretation of claim terms to be the exclusive province of the court and the Seventh Amendment to be consistent with that conclusion. * * * Markman sought our review on each point, and we granted certiorari. * * *

* * *

III

Since evidence of common-law practice at the time of the Framing does not entail application of the Seventh Amendment's jury guarantee to the construction of the claim document, we must look elsewhere to characterize this determination of meaning in order to allocate it as between court or jury. We accordingly consult existing precedent and consider both the relative interpretive skills of judges and juries and the statutory policies that ought to be furthered by the allocation.

A.

* * * [The Court examined the few cases that were alleged to be relevant and found them to be inconclusive. The Court indicated that, if anything, they supported the view that a jury determination of the issue was not required.]

B.

Where history and precedent provide no clear answers, functional considerations also play their part in the choice between judge and jury to define terms of art. We said in *Miller v. Fenton*, 474 U.S. 104, 114, 106 S. Ct. 445, 451, 88 L. Ed. 2d 405 (1985), that when an issue "falls somewhere between a pristine legal standard and a simple historical fact, the fact/law distinction at times has turned on a determination that, as a matter of sound administration of justice, one judicial actor is better positioned than another to decide the issue in question." So it turns out here, for judges, not juries, are the better suited to find the acquired meaning of patent terms.

The construction of written instruments is one of those things that judges often do and are likely to do better than jurors unburdened by training in exegesis. Patent construction in particular "is a special occupation, requiring, like all others, special training and practice. The judge, from his training and discipline, is more likely to give a proper interpretation to such instruments than a jury, and he is, therefore, more likely to be right, in performing such a duty, than a jury can be expected to be." *Parker v. Hulme*, 18 F. Cas., at 1140. Such was the understanding nearly a century and a half ago, and there is no reason to weigh the respective strengths of judge and jury differently in relation to the modern claim; quite the contrary, for "the claims of patents have become highly technical in many respects as the result of special doctrines relating to the proper form and scope of claims that have been developed in the courts and the Patent Office" Woodward, Definiteness and Particularity in Patent Claims, 46 Mich. L. Rev. 755, 765 (1948).

Markman would trump these considerations with his argument that a jury should decide a question of meaning peculiar to a trade or profession simply because the question is a subject of testimony requiring credibility determinations, which are the jury's forte. It is, of course, true that credibility judgments have to be made about the experts who testify in patent cases, and in theory there could be a case in which a simple credibility judgment would suffice to choose between experts whose testimony was equally consistent with a patent's internal logic. But our own experience with document construction leaves us doubtful that trial courts will run into many cases like that. In the main, we expect, any credibility determinations will be subsumed within the necessarily sophisticated analysis of the whole document, required by the standard construction rule that a term can be defined only in a way that comports with the instrument as a whole. * * * Thus, in these cases a jury's capabilities to evaluate demeanor, * * * to sense the "mainsprings of human conduct,"

* * * or to reflect community standards, * * * are much less significant than a trained ability to evaluate the testimony in relation to the overall structure of the patent. The decisionmaker vested with the task of construing the patent is in the better position to ascertain whether an expert's proposed definition fully comports with the specification and claims and so will preserve the patent's internal coherence. We accordingly think there is sufficient reason to treat construction of terms of art like many other responsibilities that we cede to a judge in the normal course of trial, notwithstanding its evidentiary underpinnings.

C.

Finally, we see the importance of uniformity in the treatment of a given patent as an independent reason to allocate all issues of construction to the court. As we noted in *General Elec. Co. v. Wabash Appliance Corp.*, 304 U.S. 364, 369, 58 S. Ct. 899, 902, 82 L. Ed. 1402 (1938), "[t]he limits of a patent must be known for the protection of the patentee, the encouragement of the inventive genius of others and the assurance that the subject of the patent will be dedicated ultimately to the public." Otherwise, a "zone of uncertainty which enterprise and experimentation may enter only at the risk of infringement claims would discourage invention only a little less than unequivocal foreclosure of the field," *United Carbon Co. v. Binney & Smith Co.*, 317 U.S. 228, 236, 63 S. Ct. 165, 170, 87 L. Ed. 232 (1942), and "[t]he public [would] be deprived of rights supposed to belong to it, without being clearly told what it is that limits these rights." *Merrill v. Yeomans*, 94 U.S. 568, 573, 24 L. Ed. 235 (1876). * * *

Uniformity would, however, be ill served by submitting issues of document construction to juries. Making them jury issues would not, to be sure, necessarily leave evidentiary questions of meaning wide open in every new court in which a patent might be litigated, for principles of issue preclusion would ordinarily foster uniformity. * * * But whereas issue preclusion could not be asserted against new and independent infringement defendants even within a given jurisdiction, treating interpretive issues as purely legal will promote (though it will not guarantee) intrajurisdictional certainty through the application of stare decisis on those questions not yet subject to interjurisdictional uniformity under the authority of the single appeals court.

* * *

Accordingly, we hold that the interpretation of the word "inventory" in this case is an issue for the judge, not the jury, and affirm the decision of the Court of Appeals for the Federal Circuit.

It is so ordered.

NOTE AND QUESTIONS

To what extent should the categorization of a particular issue as one of fact or law depend, as it did in part in *Markman*, on whether the question should be decided with reference to a fixed standard that applies to all members of the community impartially or as an ad hoc matter in particular cases? When an issue is classified as one of law, the rule binds litigants in subsequent cases. Of course, the crucial question is: when is the need for a precise legal standard sufficient to justify withdrawing the matter from the jury? In many contexts the answer depends on whether the system has accumulated enough experience on the issue to justify announcing a standard that will be binding in future cases. Another basis for differentiation is whether the issue involves a sensitive area that warrants a "popular" or "communal" judgment. Consider, for example, the case of a prosecution of a publisher for distributing an allegedly obscene book. Shouldn't the decision to give the question of obscenity to a judge or a jury depend on whether the need for certainty on that issue outweighs the desirability of a judgment by the community as reflected by several juries passing on the question in different locales? For a discussion of the issues raised by *Markman*, see Miller, *The Pretrial Rush to Judgment: Are the "Litigation Explosion," "Liability Crises," and Efficiency Clichés Eroding Our Day in Court and Jury Trial Commitments?*, 78 N.Y.U. L. Rev. 982, 1094–1126 (2003).

4. DEMAND AND WAIVER OF TRIAL BY JURY

———

Read Federal Rules of Civil Procedure 38 and 39 in the Supplement.

———

A party may waive the jury right after the filing of the complaint in an action. A party also may waive the jury right before litigation begins and, indeed, before a dispute even arises. A waiver of this sort can take the form of a contract clause that explicitly waives the jury right. Should an agreement to arbitrate a dispute, assented to before the dispute has arisen, be interpreted as an implicit waiver of the jury trial right?

Waiver of a constitutional right usually requires a voluntary, intentional, and knowing decision. Can a jury waiver that is made before a dispute arises meet this standard? Compare National Equip. Rental, Ltd. v. Hendrix, 565 F.2d 255 (2d Cir. 1977), with Bank South, N.W. v. Howard, 264 Ga. 339, 444 S.E.2d 799 (1994). What about an arbitration clause that does not mention the jury right? The Federal Arbitration Act, 9 U.S.C. § 1, enacted in 1925, authorizes federal courts to uphold pre-dispute arbitration agreements that do not violate law or public policy. Is it relevant that the clause appears in a form contract, rather than as the result of an arms-length negotiation between evenly matched business entities? See Sternlight, *Mandatory Binding Arbitration and the Demise of the Seventh Amendment Right to a Jury Trial*, 16 Ohio St. J. Disp. Resol. 669 (2001). The topic has generated considerable debate. Compare Ware, *Arbitration Clauses, Jury-Waiver Clauses, and Other Contractual Waivers of Constitutional Rights*, 67 Law & Contemp. Probs. 167 (2004), with Kepper, *Contractual Waiver of Seventh Amendment Rights: Using the Public Rights Doctrine to Justify a Higher Standard of Waiver for Jury Waiver Clauses than for Arbitration Clauses*, 91 Iowa L. Rev. 1345 (2006).

5. SELECTION AND COMPOSITION OF THE JURY

Jury selection is a two-stage process. First, a list of potential jurors, the venire, is compiled and they are assembled. A number of them, equal to the number who will serve, usually twelve or six, are then selected at random to sit as a tentative jury. Second, these tentative jurors are questioned by the judge and/or by the attorneys to determine whether each of them can decide the case fairly and appropriately. This questioning is called *"voir dire."* If one of them is dismissed, his or her place is taken by another member of the venire, selected at random, who is in turn subject to questioning. This process continues until the final panel is in place. For a summary of the empirical literature about *voir dire*, see Zalman & Tsoudis, *Plucking Weeds from the Garden: Lawyers Speak About Voir Dire*, 51 Wayne L. Rev. 163 (2005).

a. Empaneling the Jury

THIEL v. SOUTHERN PACIFIC CO., 328 U.S. 217, 66 S.Ct. 984, 90 L.Ed. 1181 (1946). Plaintiff, in an action for negligence, moved to strike the jury panel on the ground that it had been unfairly selected. The clerk of the court and the jury commissioner testified that they deliberately and intentionally had excluded from the jury lists all persons who work for a daily wage. They noted that in the past, because of the financial hardship imposed by jury service, those workers inevitably were excused by the judge. Workers who were paid by the week or the month, as well as the wives of daily wage earners were included on the jury lists. The Court held that such an exclusion cannot be justified "without doing violence to the democratic nature of the jury system. Were we to sanction an exclusion of this nature * * * we would breathe life into any latent tendencies to establish the jury as an instrument of the economically and socially privileged." Id. at 223–24, 66 S.Ct. at 987, 90 L.Ed. at 1186. Although the judge can excuse individuals for whom jury service would be a financial hardship, that cannot justify the exclusion of all daily wage earners regardless of whether an actual hardship is involved. The dissent noted that the matter was one of judicial administration, and that no constitutional issue was at stake. It took the position that selection of jurors from a jury pool that contained weekly wage earners and wives of daily workers was sufficient to avoid reversal of a judgment otherwise untainted by error.

NOTES AND QUESTIONS

1.   Read 28 U.S.C. §§ 1861–66 in the Supplement. The Report of the Committee on the Operation of the Jury System of the Judicial Conference of the United States, on which the present federal jury-selection statute is based, appears at 42 F.R.D. 353 (1967). How representative of the community is a federal jury in view of the substantial classes of people who are exempt or may be exempted under Section 1863(b)(6) or who may be excused under Section 1863(b)(5)? Qualifications for jury service vary from state to state and include such factors as citizenship, local residence, ownership of property, health, and payment of taxes. See Rottman, Flango, Cantrell, Hansen & LaFountain, State Court Organization 1998 tbls. 39–40 (2000) (stating jury qualifications, source lists, exemptions, excusals, and fees for all states).

2.   A guarantee of accessible jury service derives from both the Americans with Disabilities Act, 42 U.S.C. § 12101, enacted in 1990, and Section 504 of the Rehabilitation Act of 1973, 29 U.S.C. § 794. See Bleyer, McCarty & Wood, *Access to Jury Service for Persons with Disabilities*, 19 Mental & Physical Disability L. Rep. 249 (1995). In GALLOWAY v. SUPERIOR COURT, 816 F.Supp. 12 (D.D.C. 1993), the court held that blind persons cannot automatically be excluded. "[P]laintiff has offered uncontradicted evidence that blind individuals, like sighted jurors, weigh the content of the testimony given and examine speech patterns, intonation, and syntax in assessing credibility." Id. at 16. The court went on to note that with reasonable accommodation, a juror who otherwise might not be able to serve in a case may be qualified to do so. See Dickhute, *Jury Duty for the Blind in the Time of Reasonable Accommodations: The ADA's Interface with a Litigant's Right to a Fair Trial*, 32 Creighton L. Rev. 849 (1999); Blanck, Wilichowski & Schmeling, *Disability Civil Rights Law and Policy: Accessible Courtroom Technology*, 12 Wm. & Mary Bill Rts. J. 825 (2004).

3.   The most common method for creating jury lists is by relying on voter registration records. 28 U.S.C. § 1863(b)(2) requires federal jury lists to be based on these records, with the use of supplemental sources when that is necessary to promote the interests of fair representation, as described in 28 U.S.C. §§ 1861 and 1862. Supplemental sources can include driver's license or public utilities lists, state tax rolls, or telephone lists. Exclusive reliance on voter registration lists has been much criticized. Because of the under-representation of minority and low-income persons in voter registration records, as well as the low percentage of voters overall, many have argued that use of multiple lists should be constitutionally compelled. See generally King, *Racial Jurymandering: Cancer or Cure? A Contemporary Review of Affirmative Action in Jury Selection*, 68 N.Y.U. L. Rev. 707 (1993); Note, *Jury Source Lists: Does Supplementation Really Work?*, 82 Cornell L. Rev. 390 (1997); Note, *Jury Source Representativeness and the Use of Voter Registration Lists*, 65 N.Y.U. L. Rev. 590 (1990).

4.   The special or "blue ribbon" jury, which is composed of people who are specially selected because of their level of education, is an attempt to meet the contention that the ordinary juror is incompetent to deal with the complex problems of modern litigation. See Strier, *The Educated Jury: A Proposal for*

Complex Litigation, 47 DePaul L. Rev. 49 (1997). In FAY v. NEW YORK, 332 U.S. 261, 67 S.Ct. 1613, 91 L.Ed. 2043 (1947), the Supreme Court upheld the constitutionality of a New York statute that gave the trial court discretion to empanel a "blue ribbon" jury upon application of either party. Would the Supreme Court uphold a federal statute that provided for "blue ribbon" juries in federal courts? Are "blue ribbon" juries consistent with the Seventh Amendment or the idea that a person should be "judged by peers" or by a group that represents a cross-section of society? See Oldham, *Origins of the Special Jury*, 50 U. Chi. L. Rev. 137 (1983).

5. The use of questionnaires, personal interviews, and psychological tests has been suggested for ascertaining the competence of prospective jurors. See Note, *Psychological Tests and Standards of Competence for Selecting Jurors*, 65 Yale L.J. 531, 541 (1956). Wouldn't psychological testing of jurors result in the erosion of our traditional views of jury composition? Would they be permissible under *Thiel*? See generally Cecil, Hans & Wiggins, *Citizen Comprehension of Difficult Issues: Lesson from Civil Jury Trials*, 40 Am. U. L. Rev. 727 (1991).

6. Do large-scale national cases, such as inter-state class actions, require special juries? Should the jury in such cases be drawn from a national, rather than a state or local, pool? See Dooley, *National Juries for National Cases: Preserving Citizen Participation in Large-Scale Litigation*, 83 N.Y.U. L. Rev. 411 (2008). What problems do you foresee in assembling a jury pool on a national scale?

b. Challenging Individual Jurors

Challenges to individual jurors—sometimes called challenges to the polls—are of two kinds: for cause and peremptory. Challenges for cause permit a prospective juror to be rejected when partiality can be shown. Peremptory challenges permit rejection of jurors without any statement of reason and usually are based on an assumed partiality that may not be susceptible to proof.

Each party is permitted an unlimited number of challenges for cause. These challenges are determined by the trial judge, although some states have experimented with so-called "triers," independent officials who have the responsibility of determining challenges for cause. The number of peremptory challenges allowed each side varies among the states. The general range is from two to six. See Rottman, Flango, Cantrell, Hansen & LaFountain, State Court Organization 1998 tbl. 41 (2000) (stating number of peremptory challenges permitted in all states). In the federal courts each side is permitted three. See 28 U.S.C. § 1870. Should the number be increased if there are multiple parties on one or both sides? Since the number of peremptory challenges is limited, they usually are husbanded carefully. Can the use of the peremptory challenge be reconciled with the principle that a jury should be composed of a representative sampling of the community?

———

EDMONSON v. LEESVILLE CONCRETE COMPANY, INC.

Supreme Court of the United States, 1991.
500 U.S. 614, 111 S.Ct. 2077, 114 L.Ed.2d 660.

Certiorari to the United States Court of Appeals for the Fifth Circuit.

MR. JUSTICE KENNEDY delivered the opinion of the Court.

We must decide in the case before us whether a private litigant in a civil case may use peremptory challenges to exclude jurors on account of their race. * * * This civil case originated in a United States District Court, and we apply the equal protection component of the Fifth Amendment's Due Process Clause. * * *

I

Thaddeus Donald Edmonson, a construction worker, was injured in a job-site accident at Fort Polk, Louisiana, a federal enclave. Edmonson sued Leesville Concrete Company for negligence in the United States District Court for the Western District of Louisiana, claiming that a Leesville employee permitted one of the company's trucks to roll backward and pin him against some construction equipment. Edmonson invoked his Seventh Amendment right to a trial by jury.

During voir dire, Leesville used two of its three peremptory challenges authorized by statute to remove black persons from the prospective jury. Citing our decision in Batson v. Kentucky, 476 U.S. 79, 106 S. Ct. 1712, 90 L. Ed. 2d 69 (1986), Edmonson, who is himself black, requested that the District Court require Leesville to articulate a race-neutral explanation for striking the two jurors. The District Court denied the request on the ground that Batson does not apply in civil proceedings. As impaneled, the jury included 11 white persons and 1 black person. The jury rendered a verdict for Edmonson, assessing his total damages at $90,000. It also attributed 80% of the fault to Edmonson's contributory negligence, however, and awarded him the sum of $18,000.

Edmonson appealed, and a divided en banc panel affirmed * * *. We granted certiorari, and now reverse the Court of Appeals.

II

A

In Powers v. Ohio, 499 U.S. 400, 111 S. Ct. 1364, 113 L. Ed. 2d 411 (1991), we held that a criminal defendant, regardless of his or her race, may object to a prosecutor's race-based exclusion of persons from the petit jury. Our conclusion rested on a two-part analysis. First, following our opinions in Batson and in Carter v. Jury Commission of Greene County, 396 U.S. 320, 90 S. Ct. 518, 24 L. Ed. 2d 549 (1970), we made clear that a prosecutor's race-based peremptory challenge violates the equal protection rights of those excluded from jury service. * * * Second, we relied on well-established rules of third-party standing to hold that a defendant may raise the excluded jurors' equal protection rights. * * *

That an act violates the Constitution when committed by a government official, however, does not answer the question whether the same act offends constitutional guarantees if committed by a private litigant or his attorney. The Constitution's protections of individual liberty and equal protection apply in general only to action by the government. * * * Racial discrimination, though invidious in all contexts, violates the Constitution only when it may be attributed to state action. * * * Thus, the legality of the exclusion at issue here turns on the extent to which a litigant in a civil case may be subject to the Constitution's restrictions. * * *

The trial judge exercises substantial control over voir dire in the federal system. See Fed.Rule Civ.Proc. 47. The judge determines the range of information that may be discovered about a prospective juror, and so affects the exercise of both challenges for cause and peremptory challenges. In some cases, judges may even conduct the entire voir dire by themselves, a common practice in the District Court where the instant case was tried. See Louisiana Rules of Court, Local Rule W.D. La. 13.02 (1990). The judge oversees the exclusion of jurors for cause, in this way determining which jurors remain eligible for the exercise of peremptory strikes. In cases involving multiple parties, the trial judge decides how peremptory challenges shall be allocated among them. 28 U.S.C. § 1870. When a lawyer exercises a peremptory challenge, the judge advises the juror he or she has been excused. * * *

The principle that the selection of state officials, other than through election by all qualified voters, may constitute state action applies with even greater force in the context of jury selection through the use of peremptory challenges. Though the motive of a peremptory challenge may be to protect a private interest, the objective of jury selection proceedings is to determine representation on a governmental body. Were it not for peremptory challenges, there would be no question that the entire process of determining who will serve on the jury constitutes state action. The fact that the government delegates some portion of this power to private litigants does not change the governmental character of the power exercised. * * *

Here, as in most civil cases, the initial decision whether to sue at all, the selection of counsel, and any number of ensuing tactical choices in the course of discovery and trial may be without the requisite governmental character to be deemed state action. That cannot be said of the exercise of peremptory challenges, however; when private litigants participate in the selection of jurors, they serve an important function within the government and act with its substantial assistance. If peremptory challenges based on race were permitted, persons could be required by summons to be put at risk of open and public discrimination as a condition of their participation in the justice system. The injury to excluded jurors would be the direct result of governmental delegation and participation.

Finally, we note that the injury caused by the discrimination is made more severe because the government permits it to occur within the courthouse itself. Few places are a more real expression of the constitutional authority of the government than a courtroom, where the law itself unfolds. Within the courtroom, the government invokes its laws to determine the rights of those who stand before it. In full view of the public, litigants press their cases, witnesses give testimony, juries render verdicts, and judges act with the utmost care to ensure that justice is done.

Race discrimination within the courtroom raises serious questions as to the fairness of the proceedings conducted there. Racial bias mars the integrity of the judicial system and prevents the idea of democratic government from becoming a reality. * * * In the many times we have addressed the problem of racial bias in our system of justice, we have not "questioned the premise that racial discrimination in the qualification or selection of jurors offends the dignity of persons and the integrity of the courts." *Powers* * * *. To permit racial exclusion in this official forum compounds the racial insult inherent in judging a citizen by the color of his or her skin. * * *

III

It remains to consider whether a prima facie case of racial discrimination has been established in the case before us, requiring Leesville to offer race-neutral explanations for its peremptory challenges. In *Batson*, we held that determining whether a prima facie case has been established requires consideration of all relevant circumstances, including whether there has been a pattern of strikes against members of a particular race. * * * The same approach applies in the civil context, and we leave it to the trial courts in the first instance to develop evidentiary rules for implementing our decision.

The judgment is reversed, and the case is remanded for further proceedings consistent with our opinion.

It is so ordered.

JUSTICE O'CONNOR, with whom THE CHIEF JUSTICE and JUSTICE SCALIA join, dissenting.

* * * As an initial matter, the judge does not "encourage" the use of a peremptory challenge at all. The decision to strike a juror is entirely up to the litigant, and the reasons for doing so are of no consequence to the judge. It is the attorney who strikes. The judge does little more than acquiesce in this decision by excusing the juror. In point of fact, the government has virtually no role in the use of peremptory challenges. Indeed, there are jurisdictions in which, with the consent of the parties, voir dire and jury selection may take place in the absence of any court personnel. * * *

Whatever reason a private litigant may have for using a peremptory challenge, it is not the government's reason. The government otherwise establishes its requirements for jury service, leaving to the private litigant the unfettered discretion to use the strike for any reason. This is not part of the government's function in establishing the requirements for jury service. * * *

Racism is a terrible thing. It is irrational, destructive, and mean. Arbitrary discrimination based on race is particularly abhorrent when manifest in a courtroom, a forum established by the government for the resolution of disputes through "quiet rationality." * * * But not every opprobrious and inequitable act is a constitutional violation. The Fifth Amendment's Due Process Clause prohibits only actions for which the Government can be held responsible. The Government is not responsible for everything that occurs in a courtroom. The Government is not responsible for a peremptory challenge by a private litigant. I respectfully dissent.

————

In J.E.B. v. ALABAMA ex rel. T.B., 511 U.S. 127, 114 S.Ct. 1419, 128 L.Ed.2d 89 (1994), the State of Alabama, on behalf of the mother of a minor child, brought suit in a state court against the defendant for paternity and child support. The state used nine of its ten peremptory challenges to remove male jurors, with the result that the jury consisted solely of women. The Alabama courts rejected defendant's objection that the use of peremptory challenges solely to exclude persons on the basis of gender violated the Fourteenth Amendment's Equal Protection Clause. A divided Supreme Court, noting that both federal and state courts were in disagreement on the matter, reversed. Justice Blackmun, writing for himself and three others, stated:

> Discrimination in jury selection, whether based on race or on gender, causes harm to the litigants, the community and the individual jurors who are wrongfully excluded from participation in the judicial process. * * *

> * * * All persons, when granted the opportunity to serve on a jury, have the right not to be excluded summarily because of discriminatory and stereotypical presumptions that reflect and reinforce patterns of historical discrimination. Striking individual jurors on the assumption that they hold particular views simply because of their gender is "practically a brand upon them, affixed by the law, an assertion of their inferiority." *Strauder v. West Virginia*, 100 U.S. at 308, 25 L.Ed. 6664 (1880).

> Our conclusion that litigants may not strike potential jurors solely on the basis of gender does not imply the elimination of all peremptory challenges. * * * Parties still may remove jurors who they feel might be less acceptable than others on the panel; gender simply may not serve as a proxy for bias. * * * Even strikes based on characteristics that are disproportionately associated with one gender [e.g., employ-

ment in the military or as nurses] could be appropriate, absent a showing of pretext.

Id. at 140–43, 114 S.Ct. at 1427–29, 128 L.Ed.2d at 104–06.

Justice Kennedy concurred in a separate opinion strongly supporting the notion that sex discrimination in the courts could not be tolerated. Justice O'Connor also concurred in a separate opinion. She wrote:

> Today's decision severely limits a litigant's ability to act on * * * intuition, for the import of our holding is that any correlation between a juror's gender and attitudes is irrelevant as a matter of constitutional law. * * * [T]o say that gender makes no difference as a matter of law is not to say that gender makes no difference as a matter of fact. * * * In extending [our holdings on race] * * * to gender we have * * * taken a step closer to eliminating the peremptory challenge, and diminishing the ability of litigants to act on sometimes accurate gender-based assumptions about juror attitudes.

> * * *

> Accordingly, I adhere to my position that the Equal Protection Clause does not limit the exercise of peremptory challenges by private civil litigants * * *. This case itself presents no state action dilemma for here the State of Alabama itself filed the paternity suit. * * * But what of the next case? Will we, in the name of fighting gender discrimination, hold that the battered wife—on trial for wounding her abusive husband—is a state actor? Will we preclude her from using her peremptory challenges to ensure that the jury of her peers contains as many women members as possible? I assume we will, but I hope we will not.

Id. at 149–51, 114 S.Ct. at 1432–33, 128 L.Ed.2d at 109–10.

Justice Scalia, writing for himself and two other Justices, dissented. Essentially he agreed with Justice O'Connor's assessment of the importance of the peremptory challenge system and argued that it did not deny anyone the equal protection of the laws even in the case before the Court.

NOTES AND QUESTIONS

1. The Seventh Amendment does not apply to civil cases in state courts. On what basis did the Court in *J.E.B.* extend its reasoning in *Edmonson* to encompass state jury trials?

2. After *Batson*, *Edmonson*, and *J.E.B.*, should it be considered forbidden to exercise peremptory challenges on the basis of religion or political affiliation? In this regard, how do religion and politics differ from race and gender? See Gendleman, *The Equal Protection Clause, the Free Exercise Clause and Religion–Based Peremptory Challenges*, 63 U. Chi. L. Rev. 1639 (1996); Waggoner, *Peremptory Challenges and Religion: the Unanswered Prayer for a Supreme Court Opinion*, 36 Loy. U. Chi. L.J. 285 (2004). What about disability? Age? Sexual orientation?

SECTION B. THE SCOPE AND ORDER OF TRIAL

1. SETTING THE CASE FOR TRIAL

Trial will take place only after one of the parties or the court takes steps to have the case placed on the appropriate trial calendar and the court disposes of all the cases previously on that calendar. The technique for placing a case on a waiting list for trial will vary from jurisdiction to jurisdiction and from one judge to another. The Federal Rules contemplate that the trial judge, after consulting the parties, may schedule the date of trial. See, e.g., Federal Rule 16(b)(3)(B)(v) and (c)(2)(G). How is it possible to know when the previous cases assigned to a trial judge will be completed so that he and his courtroom will be available? Can one be certain that the lawyers will be free of other pressing obligations, or that crucial witnesses will not be indisposed? The answer, of course, is that there is no such certainty, but case management techniques and computers have helped to rationalize the flow of business through the courts and to increase predictability. See Nihan, *A Study in Contrasts: The Ability of the Federal Judiciary to Change Its Adjudicative and Administrative Structures*, 44 Am. U. L. Rev. 1693 (1995); Michels, *Case Management Techniques Work*, 18 Just. Sys. J. 75 (1995). For a description of a federal district judge's use of a running-calendar technique to manage his civil jury docket, see Young, *Vanishing Trials, Vanishing Juries, Vanishing Constitution*, 40 Suffolk U. L. Rev. 67, 90 (2006).

Delay nevertheless persists in the scheduling of civil jury trials, despite a decline in the number of trials overall. See Shuman, *When Time Does Not Heal: Understanding the Importance of Avoiding Unnecessary Delay in the Resolution of Tort Cases*, 7 Psychol. Pub. Pol'y & L. 880, 895 (2000). In the federal system, litigants may try to expedite the scheduling of a jury trial by consenting to have their case heard by a magistrate judge. See Murtha, *Why Do Lawyers Elect, or Not Elect, To Have Magistrate Judges Conduct Their Civil Trials*, 15–July Nev. Law. 32 (2007). Do you see problems with this approach?

What accounts for delay in the scheduling of civil jury trials? Some commentators emphasize that a lack of adequate funding may make it difficult for courts to pay jury fees or jury expenses. See Bunge, *Congressional Underappropriation for Civil Juries: Responding to the Attack on a Constitutional Guarantee*, 55 U. Chi. L. Rev. 237 (1988); DeBenedictis, *Tight Budget Squeezes Courts*, ABA Journal (Dec. 1992), at 22; *Even Jury Hiring is Frozen*, L.A. Times (Dec. 22, 2008), at 22. Others underscore the constitutional priority given to criminal trials. See generally Frase, *The Speedy Trial Act of 1974*, 43 U. Chi. L. Rev. 667 (1976). What other factors seem relevant?

2. ORDER OF TRIAL IN JURY CASES

Trial courts have the ability to split cases into discrete portions, trying claims or issues separately whenever that is convenient, economical, or avoids prejudice to a party or parties. See Federal Rules 42(b) and 16(c)(2)(M), and (O). When a particular case or aspect of a case comes before a jury, the court invariably has discretion to determine the order of trial, but a judge usually will not deviate from standard practice, which is as follows:

1.   Plaintiff's opening statement

2.   Defendant's opening statement

3.   Plaintiff's presentation of direct evidence

4.   Defendant's presentation of direct evidence

5.   Plaintiff's presentation of rebuttal evidence

6.   Defendant's presentation of rebuttal evidence

7.   Opening final argument by plaintiff

8.   Defendant's final argument

9.   Closing final argument by plaintiff

10.   Giving instructions to the jury

Although jury and nonjury cases generally are handled in the same way, there are a number of significant differences in scope. For example, the court often will dispense with the opening statement and the closing argument, and, of course, there is never a need to give instructions. Some jurisdictions provide that an attorney has an absolute right to argue, even in nonjury cases. Rarely will that right be exercised, however, if the judge, as is often the situation, makes clear that she believes an argument to be unnecessary.

3. THE BURDEN OF PROOF

a. The Burden of Production

The term "burden of proof" usually refers to two different burdens: the burden of production and the burden of persuasion. The burden of production, sometimes called the burden of going forward, usually is placed on plaintiff in civil actions. This means that plaintiff is responsible for "producing" a certain threshold amount of evidence to raise a claim. However, defendant must normally meet the burden of production with respect to affirmative defenses. The threshold is defined as the minimum amount of evidence needed to satisfy the standard of proof and, thus, win the case. Put another way, one has met the burden of production if he has produced enough evidence for a reasonable jury to decide in his favor. Therefore, one can meet the burden of production even if all the evidence produced is refuted by the opposing party.

Meeting the burden of production does not ensure victory—one must still "persuade" the fact finder—but failing to meet it will ensure defeat. If the party charged with the burden of production has failed to adduce enough evidence, a summary judgment motion (prior to trial) or a motion for judgment as a matter of law (at trial) will be granted. The burden of production must be met if the case is to be decided by the trier of fact.

b.   The Burden of Persuasion

If the burden of production is met, the case can move forward to the stage of persuasion. Once there is enough evidence for the plaintiff to win, defendant will try to cast doubt on the credibility or reliability of that evidence, in addition to bringing forth evidence of his own. Each party will try to persuade the trier of fact that its evidence is more weighty than the other's. If the plaintiff has the burden of persuasion, and does not convince the jury (or judge, in a bench trial) by the standard of proof required, the jury must rule for defendant. Even if plaintiff has satisfied the burden of production and the defendant brings forth no evidence of his own, if the jury is not persuaded that plaintiff's evidence is sufficiently reliable or credible, defendant must prevail.

c.   Standards for Meeting the Burden of Persuasion

The standard for meeting the burden of persuasion represents the quantity and quality of evidence a party must produce at trial to prevail. The three most common standards are (1) preponderance of the evidence, (2) clear and convincing evidence, and (3) beyond a reasonable doubt. These standards usually are not defined any more specifically than their plain meaning suggests, although a "preponderance" is considered to be "more than fifty percent," and the clear and convincing standard lies somewhere between a preponderance and "beyond a reasonable doubt."

In most civil cases, the party bearing the burden of persuasion must prove by a preponderance of the evidence that she is entitled to the relief requested. In some civil actions, such as libel and slander and child custody proceedings, the clear-and-convincing-evidence standard often is used. And in all criminal cases, the prosecution must prove its case beyond a reasonable doubt.

d.   Shifting Burdens

The burdens of production and persuasion usually fall on the same party at trial, either plaintiff or defendant. But there are times when the burden of production is placed on one party and the burden of persuasion on the other. In these cases, once the burden of production is satisfied, the burden of persuasion "shifts" to the other party.

One example of a type of action in which the burden shifts is an employment discrimination action alleging disparate impact or systemic disparate treatment under Title VII of the Civil Rights Act of 1964. In proceedings under this statute, the employee must make out a prima facie case (meet the burden of production) that there was discrimination. At that point, the burden of production shifts to the employer, who must produce a nondiscriminatory reason before the jury or lose for failing to meet its burden of production. The ultimate burden of persuasion stays with the employee. See Texas Dep't of Comm'y Affairs v. Burdine, 450 U.S. 248, 101 S.Ct. 1089, 67 L.Ed.2d 207 (1981)

———

SECTION C.   TAKING THE CASE FROM THE JURY—MOTIONS FOR JUDGMENT AS A MATTER OF LAW, FORMERLY DIRECTED VERDICTS AND JUDGMENTS NOTWITHSTANDING THE VERDICT

———

Read Federal Rule of Civil Procedure 50 in the Supplement.

———

Various procedural devices enable a judge to ensure that the jury carries out its functions. Rule 50(a) permits the judge, after the witnesses have testified and the evidence has been presented, to withhold the case from the jury and instead to enter judgment as a matter of law if the facts are sufficiently clear to require a particular result under the governing law (until 1991, this procedure was known as a "directed verdict"). Rule 50(b) authorizes a similar procedure for cases that have been submitted to the jury once the jurors have already reached a verdict. If the judge in this situation decides that judgment as a matter of law should have been granted, the court may set aside the verdict and enter judgment (until 1991, this procedure was known as a "judgment notwithstanding the verdict").

The Advisory Committee specifically noted that the 1991 language change did not alter the standards governing Rule 50(a) and Rule 50(b) motions. The Committee stated that the purpose of the amendment was to show that directed verdicts and judgments notwithstanding the verdict should be governed by identical standards, and that a motion under Rule 56 for summary judgment is to be governed by the same standard as well. Is the time when they are made the only significant difference among motions under Rule 50(a), Rule 50(b), and Rule 56?

———

DENMAN v. SPAIN

Supreme Court of Mississippi, 1961.
242 Miss. 431, 135 So.2d 195.

LEE, PRESIDING JUSTICE.

Betty Denman, a minor, * * * sued * * * [the] executrix of the estate of Joseph A. Ross, deceased, to recover damages for personal injuries sustained by her, allegedly resulting from the negligence of the decedent in the operation of an automobile. The issue was submitted to a jury on the evidence for the plaintiff—no evidence being offered for the defendant—and there was a verdict and judgment for the plaintiff in the sum of $5,000. However, on motion of the defendant, a judgment *non obstante veredicto* * * * was sustained and entered. From that action, the plaintiff has appealed.

* * *

The appellant contends that the evidence offered by her, together with the reasonable inferences therefrom, was sufficient to make an issue for the jury as to whether the alleged negligence of the deceased driver, Ross, proximately caused or contributed to the collision and the consequent damage * * *.

A careful scrutiny and analysis of the evidence is therefore necessary:

Sunday, March 23, 1958, was a rainy, foggy day. About six o'clock that afternoon, at dusk, Mrs. Eva B. Denman, accompanied by her granddaughter, Betty, the plaintiff, was driving her Ford car southward on U.S. Highway 49E. At that time, Joseph A. Ross, accompanied by Miss Euna Tanner and Mrs. J.L. Haining, was driving his Plymouth car northward on said highway. Just south of the Town of Sumner, the cars collided. Mrs. Denman, Miss Tanner and Ross were killed. Betty, nearly seven years of age at the time, and Mrs. Haining were injured. Neither had any recollection of what had happened at the time of the collision. * * *

Plaintiff's father, Stuart Denman, who went to the scene shortly after the collision, described the situation substantially as follows: The Ford car was about seven yards off the paved surface on the east side in a bar pit "heading back towards the railroad track, which is in an easterly direction." The engine and transmission were on the opposite side of the road, out of the car and about fifty yards apart. The Plymouth was also on the east side, facing west, about fifteen yards north of the Ford.

No proof was offered as to skid marks, or other evidence to show the point of contact between these two vehicles. Eleven photographs of the damaged Plymouth, taken from various positions, and thirteen pictures of the damaged Ford, also taken from various positions, other than being mute evidence of a terrible tragedy, depict no reasonable or plausible explanation as to why this collision occurred, or who was responsible for it. * * *

Over objection by the defendant, John Barnett testified that he was driving a Dodge pickup north of highway 49E on his way to Tutwiler; that he was traveling at a speed of fifty or fifty-five miles per hour; that the Plymouth, which was in the wreck, passed him about three-fourths of a mile south of where the collision occurred, going at a speed of about seventy miles per hour; that when it passed, it got back in its lane, and neither wavered nor wobbled thereafter; that he followed and observed it for a distance of forty or fifty yards, and that it stayed in its proper lane as long as he saw it. Although another car was on the road ahead of him, he could have seen as far as the place of the accident except for the rain and fog.

Over objection by the defendant, Hal Buckley, a Negro man, testified that he was also traveling north on 49E on his way to Tutwiler at a speed of forty to fifty miles per hour. About two hundred yards south of the place where the collision occurred, a light green Plymouth, which he later saw at the scene of the accident, passed him at a speed of seventy-five or eighty miles an hour. He could see its taillights after it passed, and "he was just steady going; he wasn't doing no slowing up." He saw it until it ran into the other car. On cross-examination, he said that, after this car passed him, it got back on its side of the road, drove straight, and he did not notice that it ever went back over the center. Also on cross-examination, in an effort at impeachment, a part of the transcript in [an earlier] * * * trial [brought unsuccessfully against the estate of plaintiff's grandmother] containing this question and answer, was read to him as follows: "What do you estimate the speed of that car was when it passed you—the one that was going the same direction that you were?," and the answer was: "Well, I don't have no idea." * * * He then admitted that when the car passed him, it got back on its side and drove straight ahead, and that he could see the accident, but he could not tell anything about it or on which side of the road it happened. He also did not notice the other car, which came from the other direction.

Since Barnett did not see the car any more after it had gone forty or fifty yards beyond him, and his knowledge of speed was based on what he saw about three-fourths of a mile south of the place where the collision occurred, this evidence was inadmissible * * *. On the contrary, since Buckley testified the speed of this car, when it passed him, was seventy-five to eighty miles an hour and that it did not slow down in the remaining distance of two hundred yards before the collision, such evidence was competent and admissible * * *. The attempted impeachment went to its credibility and not its admissibility.

From this evidence, the plaintiff reasons that the jury could, and did, find that the Ross car was being operated, under inclement weather conditions, at an unlawful and negligent rate of speed, and that, if Ross had had his car under adequate and proper control, in all probability the collision could have been avoided. She voices the opinion that the physical facts, including the pictures of the wrecked vehicles, indicated that the

Ford car was probably across the highway at an angle of perhaps forty-five degrees at the time of the collision.

But the testimony of Buckley showed only that the Plymouth was being operated at an excessive and negligent rate of speed. It otherwise showed that the car was in its proper lane. He did not notice it go over the center at any time, but it was driven straight down the road. No eyewitness claimed to have seen what happened. There was no evidence to indicate the place in the road where the vehicles came in contact with each other. There was no showing as to the speed of the Ford, whether fast or slow; or as to whether it was traveling on the right or wrong side of the road; or as to whether it slid or was suddenly driven to the wrong side of the road into the path of the Plymouth. The cars were so badly damaged that the pictures afford no reasonable explanation as to what person or persons were legally responsible for their condition. In other words, just how and why this grievous tragedy occurred is completely shrouded in mystery.

The burden was on the plaintiff to prove by a preponderance of the evidence, not only that the operator of the Plymouth was guilty of negligence but also that such negligence proximately caused or contributed to the collision and consequent damage. By the use of metaphysical learning, speculation and conjecture, one may reach several possible conclusions as to how the accident occurred. However such conclusions could only be classed as possibilities; and this Court has many times held that verdicts cannot be based on possibilities. At all events, there is no sound or reasonable basis upon which a jury or this Court can say that the plaintiff met that burden.

The judgment must be affirmed.

Affirmed.

NOTES AND QUESTIONS

1. Do you believe a jury properly could have found for plaintiff in the *Denman* case? What inferences would have to be drawn from the evidence to reach such a conclusion? How would you support the proposition that these inferences reasonably could be found to be stronger than other inferences that would not lead to a verdict for plaintiff?

2. Cases like *Denman,* which involve head-on vehicular collisions, present a difficult problem with regard to the control of jury verdicts. The circumstances of these collisions ordinarily suggest that at least one driver was negligent but may not indicate which driver it was, and direct evidence often is lacking because all witnesses are dead.

3. Under what circumstances, if any, may a court, on the basis of evidence presented at trial, decide that a party who has the burden of proof, must prevail? See Scott v. Harris and the Notes and Questions on pp. 503–05, infra.

CHAPTER 14

APPELLATE REVIEW

■ ■ ■

In this Chapter, we consider appellate review. First, there is the question of the purposes and aims of appellate review. Second, there is the question of timing. When can an aggrieved party obtain review of a court order? Must he or she await a final decision in the action or may the matter be reviewed at once? As we shall see, the basic rule limiting appeals in the federal courts to final judgments has a number of exclusions and exceptions. Third, there is the question of reviewability and the standard to be applied. How do the scope and timing of appellate review affect other aspects of the judicial proceeding that you have studied, such as discovery, case management, and the use of pretrial motions to resolve cases?

SECTION A.   THE PRINCIPLE OF FINALITY

Commentators point to the following justifications for maintaining an appellate system: "(1) to correct errors committed by the tribunal from which the appeal is taken; (2) to have a consistent, uniform declaration of what the law is, not only in the case on appeal, but also as it will be applied to similar cases in the future; and (3) to satisfy the public's demand for justice, which includes a demand that important grievances be heard and resolved by the highest possible governmental authority." See Kelso, *A Report on the California Appellate System*, 45 Hastings L.J. 433, 434–35 (1994) (citations omitted). To these traditional purposes commentators also point to the appellate court's lawmaking function and its role in preventing legal error. See Shavell, *The Appeals Process as a Means of Error Correction*, 24 J. Legal Stud. 379, 379–80, 416, 425–26 (1995). How does finality promote these purposes?

1.   APPLICATION OF THE BASIC CONCEPT

———

Read 28 U.S.C. §§ 1291 and 1292 in the Supplement.

———

COOPER, EXTRAORDINARY WRIT PRACTICE IN CRIMINAL CASES: ANALOGIES FOR THE MILITARY COURTS, 98 F.R.D. 593, 594–96 (1983):

A truly final judgment is one that marks the completion of all the events that will occur in a trial court. Nothing more remains to be done, unless it be execution of a judgment against the defendant.

The advantages that may be gained by deferring appeals until entry of a truly final judgment are familiar, and can be summarized in short order. Immediate review of every ruling made by a trial court could not be tolerated. Repeated interruptions and delays could put the trial process beyond any reasonable control, even if appeals were taken only when there was a good faith and reasonable belief that the court was wrong. The opportunities for less honorable delay and harassment of an adversary also would not go entirely unexploited. More limited opportunities for interlocutory review would not be so disastrous, but would carry some part of the same costs. The possible advantages to be set against these costs arise from the opportunity to correct a wrong ruling. These advantages, however, are reduced by the prospects that most trial court rulings are correct; that wrong rulings often are corrected by the trial court; and that uncorrected wrong rulings will not, in the end, taint the final judgment.

The price that is paid for a final judgment rule, however, can be high. An erroneous ruling may taint everything that follows. If appeal must be delayed until final judgment, it may become necessary to repeat the entire trial proceeding. The costs of repeating the trial go beyond the obvious costs of expense and anxiety. The further proceedings will be held later, and may suffer from lapses of memory, inconsequential inconsistencies that are blown into exaggerated importance, and actual loss of evidence. Beyond these defects, the retrial proceedings often will be affected by lessons learned at the first trial. * * * The problem is more than one of boredom; strategies have been revealed and must be revised, opportunities to sustain truth by impeachment are diminished, and so on.

* * *

Beyond the impact on individual cases, loss of the opportunity for interlocutory review means that some areas of law must develop without much opportunity for appellate guidance. Questions of discovery, for example, may confuse and divide trial courts for years without the guidance and uniformity that appeals could provide.

2. THE NEW YORK APPROACH

New York has taken a different approach than that followed by the federal courts, allowing appeals to the state's intermediate appellate court—the Appellate Division—in a great many situations in which no final judgment has been rendered. Read the New York provision, N.Y.C.P.L.R. 5701, which is found in the Supplement following 28 U.S.C.

§ 1292. What benefits and burdens does the New York system contain that the federal system does not?

KORN, CIVIL JURISDICTION OF THE NEW YORK COURT OF APPEALS AND APPELLATE DIVISIONS, 16 Buffalo L. Rev. 307, 332 (1967):

Today * * * it is well known that there is hardly a question of practice that cannot be appealed; and, if a matter is said to be addressed to the court's discretion or favor, this may mean a more limited scope of review but will rarely affect appealability. Appeals on practice matters are legion, ranging far and wide over questions of venue, parties, consolidation and joint trial, pleading and pre-trial disclosure. The only meaningful method of inquiry as to the content of the present standards is to examine the types of orders that have been held *not* to involve some part of the merits or affect a substantial right.

NOTES AND QUESTIONS

1. What are the advantages of freely allowing appeals from interlocutory orders? The disadvantages? Is it better to resolve the question of allowing an interlocutory appeal by weighing these advantages and disadvantages against each other in the abstract or by considering them as they apply in each case? See Scheffel, *Interlocutory Appeals in New York—Time Has Come for a More Efficient Approach*, 16 Pace L. Rev. 607 (1996).

2. In refusing to allow an appeal from an interlocutory order, an unnecessary appellate hearing may be avoided; in allowing an appeal, an unnecessary trial may be avoided, either by disposing of the case at that stage or by correcting in advance of trial an error that might otherwise require a new trial. Is there any basis for supposing that the appellate hearing is more likely to prove unnecessary than the trial? Is it relevant that the trial judge, hopefully, will be correct in his rulings more often than he is wrong?

Even if it is assumed that a reversal of the trial court's order by the appellate court is as probable as its affirmance and consideration is taken of the possibility that trial may demand more time of lawyers and judges than an appeal, does it follow that interlocutory appeals should be freely allowed? Consider the effect of the following factors. (1) In the course of a single lawsuit there may be many interlocutory orders from which one of the parties would like to appeal; thus, if finality is required, several appeals may be saved for every trial that would be saved under the other approach. (2) Not every reversal of an interlocutory order will terminate the case without trial. (3) The number of appellate courts cannot be increased as readily as can the number of trial courts in order to take care of heavier calendars. There will be a serious problem as long as it is the function of appellate courts not only to review trial-court decisions but also to establish and maintain a degree of uniformity in the law.

Is the trial judge's independence and discretion threatened by too frequent a review? Is a party who has been ordered to answer questions in a deposition interested in obtaining immediate review solely in order to save time or money? Moreover, the debate over the relative merits of a final-judgment rule and an interlocutory-appeal system is intertwined with the larger problem of court congestion at the appellate level. The attention given to crowding at the trial level has obscured the fact that a comparable problem exists in many reviewing courts.

3. DEPARTURES FROM THE FINAL JUDGMENT RULE IN THE FEDERAL COURTS

a. Defining "Finality"

(i) *Cases Involving Multiple Claims*

———

Read Federal Rule of Civil Procedure 54(b) and the accompanying materials in the Supplement.

———

SEARS, ROEBUCK & CO. v. MACKEY, 351 U.S. 427, 76 S.Ct. 895, 100 L.Ed. 1297 (1956). Mackey brought suit for damages against Sears, Roebuck under the Sherman Antitrust Act (Counts I and II) and under common law for unlawfully inducing a breach of contract (Count III) and unfair competition and patent infringement (Count IV). The District Court dismissed only those claims presented in Counts I and II. On appeal to the Court of Appeals for the Seventh Circuit, the court upheld its appellate jurisdiction under 28 U.S.C. § 1291. The Supreme Court affirmed.

The Court noted that before the promulgation of the Federal Rules, no appeal would have been allowed from the final determination of Counts I and II since the District Court's judgment was not a final decision of the whole case. However, with the adoption of the Federal Rules and the subsequent increase in multiple-claim actions, the promulgators recognized the need to ameliorate the standard that "*all* claims had to be finally decided before an appeal could be entertained from a final decision upon any of them." Id. at 434, 76 S.Ct. at 899, 100 L.Ed. at 1305. Consequently, Rule 54(b) was adopted.

> * * * [Rule 54(b), as amended in 1946,] does not relax the finality required of each decision, as an individual claim, to render it appealable, but it does provide a practical means of permitting an appeal to be taken from one or more final decisions on individual claims, in multiple claims actions, without waiting for final decisions to be rendered on *all* the claims in the case. * * *

To meet the demonstrated need for flexibility, the District Court is used as a "dispatcher." It is permitted to determine, in the first instance, the appropriate *time when each "final decision"* upon "one or more but less than all" of the claims in a multiple claims action is ready for appeal. This arrangement already has lent welcome certainty to the appellate procedure. Its "negative effect" has met with uniform approval. The effect so referred to is the rule's specific requirement that for "one or more but less than all" multiple claims to become appealable, the District Court must make both "an express determination that there is no just reason for delay" and "an express direction for the entry of judgment." A party adversely affected by a final decision thus knows that his time for appeal will *not* run against him until this certification has been made.

* * *

In the case before us, there is no doubt that each of the claims dismissed is a "claim for relief" within the meaning of Rule 54(b), or that their dismissal constitutes a "final decision" on individual claims. Also, it cannot well be argued that the claims stated in Counts I and II are so inherently inseparable from, or closely related to, those stated in Counts III and IV that the District Court has abused its discretion in certifying that there exists no just reason for delay. They certainly *can* be decided independently of each other.

* * *

* * * The District Court *cannot,* in the exercise of its discretion, treat as "final" that which is not "final" within the meaning of § 1291. But the District Court *may,* by the exercise of its discretion in the interest of sound judicial administration, release for appeal final decisions upon one or more, but less than all, claims in multiple claims actions. The timing of such a release is, with good reason, vested by the rule primarily in the discretion of the District Court as the one most likely to be familiar with the case and with any justifiable reasons for delay. * * *

* * * [Rule 54] does not supersede any statute controlling appellate jurisdiction. It scrupulously recognizes the statutory requirement of a "final decision" under § 1291 as a basic requirement for an appeal to the Court of Appeals. It merely administers that requirement in a practical manner in multiple claims actions and does so by rule instead of by judicial decision. By its negative effect, it operates to restrict in a valid manner the number of appeals in multiple claims actions.

We reach a like conclusion as to the validity of the amended rule where the District Court acts affirmatively and thus assists in properly timing the release of final decisions in multiple claims actions. The amended rule adapts the single judicial unit theory so that it better meets the current needs of judicial administration. Just as Rule 54(b), in its original form, resulted in the release of some decisions on claims in multiple claims actions before they otherwise would have been released, so amended Rule 54(b) now makes possible the release of more of such decisions subject to judicial supervision. The amended rule preserves the historic federal policy against piecemeal appeals in many cases more effectively than did the original rule.

Id. at 435–38, 76 S.Ct. at 899–901, 100 L.Ed. at 1306–07 (emphasis in original).

(ii) Decisions Involving "Collateral Orders"

In COHEN v. BENEFICIAL INDUSTRIAL LOAN CORP., 337 U.S. 541, 69 S.Ct. 1221, 93 L.Ed. 1528 (1949), Cohen brought a shareholder's derivative suit in a New Jersey federal court. The District Court denied Beneficial's motion to require Cohen to post security for costs pursuant to a New Jersey statute, holding the statute inapplicable to an action in a federal court. The Court of Appeals reversed, and the Supreme Court affirmed that decision. The Justices addressed the question of appealability in the following passage:

> * * * Appeal gives the upper court a power of review, not one of intervention. So long as the matter remains open, unfinished or inconclusive, there may be no intrusion by appeal. But the District Court's action upon this application was concluded and closed and its decision final in that sense before the appeal was taken.

> Nor does the statute permit appeals, even from fully consummated decisions, where they are but steps towards final judgment in which they will merge. The purpose is to combine in one review all stages of the proceeding that effectively may be reviewed and corrected if and when final judgment results. But this order of the District Court did not make any step toward final disposition of the merits of the case and will not be merged in final judgment. When that time comes, it will be too late effectively to review the present order and the rights conferred by the statute, if it is applicable, will have been lost, probably irreparably. We conclude that the matters embraced in the decision appealed from are not of such an interlocutory nature as to affect, or to be affected by, decision of the merits of this case.

> This decision appears to fall in that small class which finally determine claims of right separable from, and collateral to, rights asserted in the action, too important to be denied review and too independent of the cause itself to require that appellate consideration be deferred until the whole case is adjudicated. The Court has long given this provision of the statute this practical rather than a technical construction. * * *

> We hold this order appealable because it is a final disposition of a claimed right which is not an ingredient of the cause of action and does not require consideration with it. * * * Here it is the right to security that presents a serious and unsettled question. If the right

were admitted or clear and the order involved only an exercise of discretion as to the amount of security, a matter the statute makes subject to reconsideration from time to time, appealability would present a different question.

Id. at 545, 69 S.Ct. at 1225, 93 L.Ed. at 1536.

NOTES AND QUESTIONS

1. There are numerous other examples of situations where a party's interlocutory appeal based on the collateral order doctrine has been rejected despite hardship for the appealing party and the potential waste of resources:

(a) In LAURO LINES S.R.L. v. CHASSER, 490 U.S. 495, 109 S.Ct. 1976, 104 L.Ed.2d 548 (1989), defendant argued that the case, brought in a United States court, should have been filed in Italy in accordance with a contract between plaintiffs and defendant. The Supreme Court held that the issue would be reviewable at the end of the case.

(b) In VAN CAUWENBERGHE v. BIARD, 486 U.S. 517, 108 S.Ct. 1945, 100 L.Ed.2d 517 (1988), defendant, who had been extradited to the United States, argued that he was immune from civil process. Again, the Supreme Court held that the issue would be reviewable at the end of the civil case.

(c) In RICHARDSON–MERRELL, INC. v. KOLLER, 472 U.S. 424, 105 S.Ct. 2757, 86 L.Ed.2d 340 (1985), the Supreme Court held that an order to disqualify a party's attorney is not subject to immediate appeal regardless of how difficult and costly it might be for a substitute attorney to "catch up."

(d) In DIGITAL EQUIP. CORP. v. DESKTOP DIRECT, INC., 511 U.S. 863, 114 S.Ct. 1992, 128 L.Ed.2d 842 (1994), the Supreme Court held that immediate review was not available from an order rejecting a party's claim to immunity from suit under a private settlement agreement.

(e) In CUNNINGHAM v. HAMILTON COUNTY, 527 U.S. 198, 119 S.Ct. 1915, 144 L.Ed.2d 184 (1999), the Supreme Court held that an order imposing sanctions for discovery violations under Federal Rule 37 on an attorney who no longer represented the client in the ongoing matter could not be immediately appealed.

2. On the other hand, the Supreme Court has stated that when a party refuses to obey a court order and has been held in criminal contempt, the issue is so distinct from the underlying case, and so important, that an appeal will be permitted. See, e.g., United States v. Ryan, 402 U.S. 530, 91 S.Ct. 1580, 29 L.Ed.2d 85 (1971). Indeed the Court went even further in UNITED STATES v. NIXON, 418 U.S. 683, 690–92, 94 S.Ct. 3090, 3098–99, 41 L.Ed.2d 1039, 1053–55 (1974), where the President of the United States had been ordered to produce certain tape recordings for examination by a federal judge. The Court found that an appeal was appropriate even though the President had not refused to comply and thus had not been held in contempt. It explained that "the traditional contempt avenue to immediate appeal is peculiarly inappropriate due to the unique setting in which the question arises. To require a President of the United States to place himself in the posture of disobeying an order of a court merely to trigger the procedural

mechanism for review of the ruling would be unseemly, and would present an unnecessary occasion for constitutional confrontation between two branches of Government."

(iii) Decisions Based on "Pragmatic Finality"

In BROWN SHOE CO. v. UNITED STATES, 370 U.S. 294, 82 S.Ct. 1502, 8 L.Ed.2d 510 (1962), the District Court found defendant had violated the antitrust laws and directed divestiture of a subsidiary, but it reserved its ruling on a specific plan of divestiture. On a direct appeal by the shoe company under the Expediting Act, 15 U.S.C. § 29, the Supreme Court held the divestiture decree was sufficiently final to be appealable even though a specific plan had not been formulated. Its own past practice, said the Court, had been to hear such appeals in antitrust cases; the substantive aspects of the case had been fully determined and to delay decision on the merits would chill the "careful, and often extended, negotiation and formulation" of the final divestiture order.

———

In 1992, Congress amended Section 1292(e) of the Judicial Code to authorize the Supreme Court to prescribe rules providing for appeals of interlocutory decisions not otherwise covered by that statute. As of this writing, the Supreme Court has promulgated only one new provision, Rule 23(f), under either Section 2072(c) or Section 1292(e), which permits plaintiffs or defendants to petition the Court of Appeals to review a grant or denial of class certification.

b. Avoidance or Evasion of the Basic Concept—Mandamus

———

Read 28 U.S.C. § 1651(a) in the Supplement.

———

NOTES AND QUESTIONS

1. In SCHLAGENHAUF v. HOLDER, 379 U.S. 104, 85 S.Ct. 234, 13 L.Ed.2d 152 (1964), the substantive aspects of which are set out at p. 451, supra, the Court upheld the use of mandamus to review an order requiring defendant to submit to a physical and mental examination:

> It is, of course, well settled that the writ is not to be used as a substitute for appeal * * * even though hardship may result from delay and perhaps unnecessary trial * * *. The writ is appropriately issued, however, when there is "usurpation of judicial power" or a clear abuse of discretion * * *.

> [T]he challenged order * * * appears to be the first of its kind in any reported decision in the federal courts under Rule 35 * * *.

* * * It is thus appropriate for us to determine on the merits the issues presented and to formulate the necessary guidelines in this area. * * *

This is not to say, however, that following the setting of guidelines in this opinion, any future allegation that the District Court was in error in applying these guidelines to a particular case makes mandamus an appropriate remedy.

Id. at 110–12, 85 S.Ct. at 238–39, 13 L.Ed.2d at 156–60.

2. Many of the Supreme Court's decisions regarding mandamus concern discovery disputes. Consider WILL v. UNITED STATES, 389 U.S. 90, 88 S.Ct. 269, 19 L.Ed.2d 305 (1967), a criminal case in which the government sought mandamus to overturn a District Court order granting discovery for the defendant. The Court of Appeals granted the writ. The Supreme Court reversed, stating that the facts did not reveal an extraordinary situation for which the writs must be reserved. The Court did not discuss the fact that without mandamus the government cannot obtain guidance on discovery matters since it cannot appeal an acquittal. Relying heavily on *Will,* the Supreme Court in KERR v. UNITED STATES DISTRICT COURT, 426 U.S. 394, 96 S.Ct. 2119, 48 L.Ed.2d 725 (1976), affirmed a denial of mandamus by a court of appeals in a civil case in which the trial judge ordered defendants, state correction officers, to turn over to plaintiff a number of prisoner personnel files. Defendants argued that such discovery should be compelled only after a determination by the trial judge that plaintiff's need for the information outweighs its confidentiality. The Court reiterated the reasons for limiting use of writs to avoid piecemeal appeals and also recognized that restricting the use of writs to matters of "jurisdiction" in the technical sense would be too narrow. The Court "assumed" that the trial judge would now accept its "suggestion" to review each of the personnel files *in camera* to determine if discovery should be permitted, thus making a writ unnecessary.

3. The writ of mandamus has been invoked in discovery disputes involving separation-of-powers concerns and inter-branch conflict. In NIXON v. SIRICA, 487 F.2d 700 (D.C. Cir. 1973), a district judge ordered the President of the United States to produce certain tape recordings for the judge's inspection prior to a determination whether the recordings were subject to a grand jury subpoena. The President petitioned for a writ of mandamus, and the Court of Appeals, although denying the petition on the merits, held that mandamus was an appropriate mode of review "particularly in light of the great public interest in prompt resolution of the issues * * *." Id. at 707.

4. In CHENEY v. UNITED STATES DISTRICT COURT, 542 U.S. 367, 124 S.Ct. 2576, 159 L.Ed.2d 459 (2004), the Vice President sought a writ of mandamus to halt discovery of the National Energy Policy Development Group, an Executive Branch task force charged with making policy recommendations to the President. The Court of Appeals declined to issue the writ because, relying on *Nixon,* it regarded the possible assertion of executive privilege as an available avenue of relief. The Supreme Court reversed, holding that it was error to treat the assertion of the privilege as a "necessary precondition" to mandamus, and remanded to permit the appeals court to consider whether the writ should issue. In *Cheney,* the Supreme Court set out a three-part test for issuance of the writ of mandamus: there must be "no

other adequate means" to attain the relief sought; the movant bears the burden of showing that the right to relief is "clear and indisputable"; and the issuing court in its discretion "must be satisfied that the writ is appropriate under the circumstances." Id. at 380–81, 124 S.Ct. at 2587, 159 L.Ed.2d at 477–78 (internal quotations and citations omitted). Why would the issuance of mandamus in a discovery dispute ever meet this test? See Fullerton, *Exploring the Far Reaches of Mandamus*, 49 Brook. L. Rev. 1131, 1152 (1983). For a discussion of this issue in the context of privilege claims, see Robertson, *Appellate Review of Discovery Orders in Federal Court: A Suggested Approach for Handling Privilege Claims*, 81 Wash. L. Rev. 733, 756–58 (2006).

5. Before *Cheney*, federal appeals courts had articulated various multi-factor tests for determining whether the writ should issue. In IN RE CEMENT ANTITRUST LITIGATION, 688 F.2d 1297 (9th Cir. 1982), the Ninth Circuit refused to issue a writ of mandamus compelling the district judge to revoke his order granting the defendants' motion that the judge recuse himself, relying on a flexible "analytic framework":

> In order to confine the use of mandamus to its proper office, we enunciated five general guidelines * * * to assist in the determination of whether mandamus is the appropriate remedy in a particular case. The guidelines are: (1) whether the party seeking the writ has no other adequate means, such as direct appeal, to attain the relief he desires; (2) whether the petitioner will be damaged or prejudiced in a way that is not correctable on appeal; (3) whether the district court's order is clearly erroneous as a matter of law; (4) whether the district court's order is an oft repeated error or manifests persistent disregard for the federal rules; and (5) whether the district court's order raises new and important problems or issues of law of first impression. * * * Related considerations include: whether the injury alleged by petitioners, although not correctable on appeal, is the kind that justifies invocation of our mandamus authority; whether the petition presents an issue of law which may repeatedly evade appellate review; and whether there are other compelling factors relating to the efficient and orderly administration of the district courts.

Id. at 1301. How do these factors compare to *Cheney*'s three-part approach? Although the Ninth Circuit held that the exercise of supervisory mandamus authority was appropriate in this case because the issue raised was an important issue of first impression capable of evading review given its collateral nature, it also held that the grant of the recusal motion was not erroneous and that, even if erroneous, it was harmless error. Because only five Justices of the Supreme Court were not disqualified from hearing the appeal, a quorum of the Court did not exist and the Ninth Circuit's decision was affirmed summarily under 28 U.S.C. § 2109. Arizona v. United States District Court, 459 U.S. 1191, 103 S.Ct. 1173, 75 L.Ed.2d 425 (1983).

c. Displacement of the Basic Concept—Discretionary Appeals and Appeals of Orders Regarding Injunctions

———

Read 28 U.S.C. §§ 1292(a)(1), and 1292(e) in the Supplement.

———

ATLANTIC CITY ELECTRIC CO.
v. GENERAL ELECTRIC CO.

United States Court of Appeals, Second Circuit, 1964.
337 F.2d 844.

PER CURIAM. The district court has certified pursuant to section 1292(b) * * * that its order, sustaining objections to interrogatories designed to discover whether damages were actually sustained by plaintiffs who may have shifted such damages, if any, to their customers of electricity, involves a controlling question of law in these litigations and that there is substantial ground for differences of opinion. * * *

In sustaining the objections to the interrogatories posed, the district court has, in effect, foreclosed defendants from pre-trial discovery of facts relating to a defense that plaintiffs have "passed-on" to their customers any damages incurred by plaintiffs and hence are not entitled to recover to the extent that defendants can prove such passing-on.

Upon this application for leave to appeal it would not be appropriate to isolate and endeavor to decide before an appeal from any final judgment this particular question of law. Pre-trial leave to appeal applications must be decided against the background of the entire case. Many important questions of law will undoubtedly arise in these cases but the problem now confronting us is the feasibility and advisability of trying to decide this particular question in advance of trial.

If pre-trial discovery were allowed as defendants request it could easily develop into a multitude of full scale rate cases which could dwarf in time and testimony the already extensive pre-trial proceedings. If the district court is in error * * * defendants will have full opportunity in the event of an adverse judgment, if based in whole or in part upon this error, to have it corrected upon appeal together with any other errors which may be urged. It is doubtful that any discoveries or hearings required to establish the extent of any damages, if the passing-on-doctrine applies, would be more burdensome then than now. Since defendants' rights to this defense are not being taken away or prejudiced on any ultimate appeal by denial of the pre-trial appeal now sought, we believe that the ultimate disposition of these cases would be delayed rather than advanced by granting this application.

Application denied.

NOTE AND QUESTIONS

What justification is there for Section 1292(a)(1)? Why does it extend to decisions denying temporary injunctive orders as well as to those granting such relief? To what extent could a litigant provide for an interlocutory appeal of her case merely by requesting a temporary injunction along with a demand for damages?

SECTION B.   THE TIME TO APPEAL

Read Federal Rule of Civil Procedure 58 and Rules 3, 4, and 5 of the Federal Rules of Appellate Procedure in the Supplement.

The time limit for appeal is treated as a matter of jurisdiction and cannot be altered by consent of the parties. See 16A Wright, Miller, Cooper & Struve, Federal Practice and Procedure: Jurisdiction and Related Matters 4th § 3949.6. It may be extended by the district court only, not by an appellate court, for thirty days upon a showing of "excusable neglect." The time limitation is triggered when the district court clerk enters a judgment conforming to the requirements of Federal Rule 58. The clerk is required to mail notice of entry of judgment to the parties but a party may elect to serve notice formally on his opponent. Federal Rule 77(d).

In BOWLES v. RUSSELL, 551 U.S. 205, 127 S.Ct. 2360, 168 L.Ed.2d 96 (2007), an inmate who had been imprisoned for life for his involvement in the beating death of an individual, unsuccessfully challenged his conviction on habeas corpus and failed to file a timely notice of appeal. The District Court granted petitioner's motion to reopen the period in which he could do so and extended the time by seventeen days, although fourteen days is the period set out in statute. Relying on the District Court's order, petitioner filed a notice of appeal within the period set out in the judicial order. The Court of Appeals dismissed the appeal for lack of jurisdiction, and the Supreme Court affirmed, holding that timely filing is jurisdictional and that a court lacks power to create equitable exceptions. Justice Souter dissented. He insisted that the timely notice requirement is not jurisdictional. Emphasizing counsel's reliance on the trial court's order, he found "not even a technical justification for condoning this bait and switch," calling it "intolerable for the judicial system to treat people this way." Id. at 215, 127 S.Ct. at 2368, 168 L.Ed.2d at 107. Under what circumstances should a filing deadline be treated as a jurisdictional limit?

SECTION C. THE AMBIT OF APPELLATE REVIEW

1. ISSUES SUBJECT TO REVIEW

There are a number of well-defined limits on the scope of appellate review. First, the alleged errors must appear in the trial-court record. Thus it is vital during the course of pretrial preparation as well as during trial itself that an attorney make certain that all rulings and evidence that might form the basis for an appeal be formally recorded. Second, an aggrieved party must have objected promptly to the trial court regarding rulings or events that the judge could have corrected or ameliorated. Normally an error is waived unless a proper objection was taken. Third, even if the issue that the appellant seeks to have reviewed has been presented properly below and has not been waived, it must not constitute "harmless error"—that is, it must have affected substantial rights. Finally, an alleged error must be presented to the appellate court in appellant's brief and the relevant portions of the trial-court record must be brought to the appellate court's attention. Even when the issues have been preserved properly in the trial court and presented to the appellate court for review, there is another aspect of the scope of appellate review that must be considered—whether, and in what circumstances, an appellate court may entertain an appeal by the party who, at least ostensibly, won below.

2. SCOPE OF REVIEW OF FACTS

a. The Power to Order a New Trial in a Case Decided by a Jury

In 1957, Professor Charles Alan Wright stated "that, so far as I can find, there is not a single case in which a federal appellate court has ever reversed and ordered a new trial on the ground that the trial court did abuse its discretion in denying a motion [for a new trial on the weight of the evidence] * * *." Wright, *The Doubtful Omniscience of Appellate Courts*, 41 Minn. L. Rev. 751, 760 (1957). At the time he was criticizing a dictum of the Court of Appeals for the District of Columbia Circuit claiming the existence of the power to reverse; but, he observed, "today's dictum claiming extended power for appellate courts is frequently the prelude to tomorrow's holding to that effect." Id. at 763. Two years later, a court of appeals acted as Professor Wright prophesied, see Georgia–Pac. Corp. v. United States, 264 F.2d 161 (5th Cir. 1959), but cases following suit remain "extremely few." 11 Wright, Miller & Kane, Federal Practice and Procedure Civil: 2d § 2819.

The power to reverse denials of new trials on the ground that the verdict is excessive or to condition affirmance upon a remittitur is not precluded by the Seventh Amendment, see Gasperini v. Center for Humanities, Inc., p. 257, supra, in spite of the extremely strong doubts thrown on the subject by Justice Brandeis's opinion in FAIRMOUNT GLASS WORKS v. CUB FORK COAL CO., 287 U.S. 474, 53 S.Ct. 252, 77 L.Ed. 439 (1933).

b. The Power to Set Aside a Trial Judge's Findings in a Non-jury Case—Rule 52(a)

Federal Rule 52(a) was amended in 1985 to apply the "clearly errone-ous" standard to a trial court's findings of fact, even if they are based on documentary evidence. The logic of the change also would apply to other situations in which the findings do not involve the credibility of witnesses. What is the justification for the amendment? If an appeals court is in the same position as the trial court to ascertain the facts, why isn't a de novo review appropriate?

In ANDERSON v. CITY OF BESSEMER, 470 U.S. 564, 105 S.Ct. 1504, 84 L.Ed.2d 518 (1985), an employment discrimination case, the Supreme Court held that the Rule 52(a) clearly erroneous test applies even to findings of historical fact—physical or documentary evidence or inferences from other facts—that do not depend on the credibility of witnesses. The Supreme Court emphasized:

> The trial judge's major role is the determination of fact, and with experience in fulfilling that role comes expertise. Duplication of the trial judge's efforts in the court of appeals would very likely contrib-ute only negligibly to the accuracy of fact determination at a huge cost in diversion of judicial resources. In addition, the parties to a case on appeal have already been forced to concentrate their energies and resources on persuading the trial judge that their account of the facts is the correct one; requiring them to persuade three more judges at the appellate level is requiring too much.

Id. at 575, 105 S.Ct. at 1512, 84 L.Ed.2d at 529.

CHAPTER 15

THE BINDING EFFECT OF PRIOR DECISIONS: RES JUDICATA AND COLLATERAL ESTOPPEL

■ ■ ■

In this Chapter, we focus on the twin doctrines of res judicata and collateral estoppel—now known as claim preclusion and issue preclusion—and explore the binding effect of prior judgments. We look at the history, the doctrine, and the policies that support the concept of finality. "Courts can only do their best to determine the truth on the basis of the evidence, and the first lesson one must learn on the subject of res judicata is that judicial findings must not be confused with absolute truth." Currie, *Mutuality of Collateral Estoppel: Limits of the* Bernhard *Doctrine*, 9 Stan. L. Rev. 281, 315 (1957). The Chapter opens by examining the reach of claim and issue preclusion within a single court system and closes by widening the scope to the inter-system effects of a judgment, surely one of the most difficult and vexing questions in the entire Procedure course. As you study these materials, notice how attitudes toward this defense have changed over the years and consider how preclusion rules might best be adapted to balance competing values of efficiency, repose, deterrence, dignity, and compensation.

SECTION A. TERMINOLOGY

Although the doctrine of former adjudication is complex, four common sense principles explain it. First, a party, ordinarily, gets only one chance to litigate a "claim"; if a party litigates only a portion of a claim the first time around, she risks losing the chance to litigate the rest. Second, a party ordinarily gets only one chance to litigate a factual or a legal "issue"; once litigated, she cannot ask a second court to decide it differently later. Third, a party is entitled to at least one "full and fair" chance to litigate before being precluded. And fourth, preclusion may be waived unless it is claimed at an early stage of the litigation.

The effects of a former adjudication have been discussed in varying and occasionally conflicting terminology. Although the time has not yet come when courts will use a single vocabulary, substantial progress has been made toward a convention.

> "Res judicata" has been used * * * as a general term referring to all of the ways in which one judgment will have a binding effect on another. That usage is and doubtless will continue to be common, but it lumps under a single name two quite different effects of judgments. The first is the effect of foreclosing any litigation of matters that never have been litigated, because of the determination that they should have been advanced in an earlier suit. The second is the effect of foreclosing relitigation of matters that have once been litigated and decided. The first of these, preclusion of matters that were never litigated, has gone under the name, "true res judicata," or the names, "merger and bar." The second doctrine, preclusion of matters that have once been decided, has usually been called "collateral estoppel."

Wright & Kane, Federal Courts § 100A (6th ed. 2002) (footnotes omitted).

Another useful summary is the following:

> * * * "Res judicata" is the term traditionally used to describe two discrete effects: (1) what we now call claim preclusion (a valid final adjudication of a claim precludes a second action on that claim or any part of it), see Restatement (Second) of Judgments §§ 17–19 (1982); and (2) issue preclusion, long called "collateral estoppel" (an issue of fact or law, actually litigated and resolved by a valid final judgment, binds the parties in a subsequent action, whether on the same or a different claim), see *id.*, at § 27.

Baker v. General Motors Corp., 522 U.S. 222, 233 n.5, 118 S.Ct. 657, 664 n. 5, 139 L.Ed.2d 580, 592 n.5 (1998). For excellent and comprehensive discussions of claim preclusion, see 18 Wright, Miller & Cooper, Federal Practice and Procedure: Jurisdiction and Related Matters 2d §§ 4401–15; Shapiro, Civil Procedure: Preclusion in Civil Actions (2001).

SECTION B.   CLAIM AND DEFENSE PRECLUSION

1.   CLAIM PRECLUSION

It is difficult to give a precise definition of the doctrine of claim preclusion, but it is possible to sketch its general form. One formulation is: In certain circumstances, when a second suit is brought, the judgment in a prior suit will be considered conclusive, both on the parties to the judgment and on those in privity with them, as to matters that actually were litigated or should have been litigated in the first suit. Justice Field has provided a more detailed formulation of the same basic rule:

> * * * [A] judgment, if rendered upon the merits, constitutes an absolute bar to a subsequent action. It is a finality as to the claim or demand in controversy, concluding parties and those in privity with

them, not only as to every matter which was offered and received to sustain or defeat the claim or demand, but as to any other admissible matter which might have been offered for that purpose. Thus, for example, a judgment rendered upon a promissory note is conclusive as to the validity of the instrument and the amount due on it, although it be subsequently alleged that perfect defences actually existed, of which no proof was offered, such as forgery, want of consideration, or payment. * * * The judgment is as conclusive, so far as future proceedings at law are concerned, as though the defences never existed. * * *

CROMWELL v. COUNTY OF SAC, 94 U.S. (4 Otto) 351, 352–53, 24 L. Ed. 195, 197–98 (1876).

Another helpful explanation is the following:

* * * [T]he preclusive scope of a judgment * * * depends on defining the breadth of the claim or cause of action hazarded in the first suit. If the plaintiff wins, the entire claim is merged in the judgment; the plaintiff cannot bring a second independent action for additional relief, and the defendant cannot avoid the judgment by offering new defenses. If the plaintiff loses, the entire claim is barred by the judgment, even as to evidence, theories, arguments, and remedies that were not advanced in the first litigation. The process of defining the claim or cause of action is thus aimed at defining the matters that both might and *should* have been advanced in the first litigation. * * * If the second lawsuit involves a new claim or cause of action, the parties may raise assertions or defenses that were omitted from the first lawsuit even though they were equally relevant to the first cause of action. * * *

18 Wright, Miller & Cooper, Federal Practice and Procedure: Jurisdiction and Related Matters 2d § 4406 (emphasis in original).

———

Only judgments of a certain quality will give rise to preclusion. The traditional words used to describe a judgment of sufficient quality to create preclusion are that the judgment must be valid, final, and on the merits. These terms are not unambiguous, however; indeed, they are somewhat misleading. Courts often enter judgments that are considered "on the merits," despite the fact that the judgment resulted from less than a full adjudicatory proceeding. In addition, courts increasingly are faced with the prior determinations of state or federal administrative agencies that act in a quasi-judicial capacity. In addition, the parties in the subsequent action must be identical to those in the first. This requirement is one of the most important distinctions between claim preclusion and its sister doctrine, issue preclusion. And, third, the claim in the second suit must involve matters properly considered included in the first action.

Clearly, this last requirement turns on what the first action decided or should have decided.

———

RUSH v. CITY OF MAPLE HEIGHTS

Supreme Court of Ohio, 1958.
167 Ohio St. 221, 147 N.E.2d 599, certiorari denied
358 U.S. 814, 79 S.Ct. 21, 3 L.Ed.2d 57.

[Plaintiff was injured in a fall from a motorcycle. She brought an action in the Municipal Court of Cleveland for damage to her personal property; that court found that defendant city was negligent in maintaining its street and that this negligence was the proximate cause of plaintiff's damages, which were fixed at $100. Defendant appealed and the judgment was affirmed by the Ohio Court of Appeals and Supreme Court. Plaintiff also brought this action in the Court of Common Pleas of Cuyahoga County for personal injuries she incurred in the same accident; her motion to set trial on the issue of damages alone was granted on the ground that the issue of negligence was res judicata because of the Municipal Court action; judgment was entered on a verdict for $12,000, and the Court of Appeals affirmed.]

HERBERT, JUDGE. The eighth error assigned by the defendant is that "the trial and appellate courts committed error in permitting plaintiff to split her cause of action * * *."

In the case of Vasu v. Kohlers, Inc., 145 Ohio St. 321, 61 N.E.2d 707, 709, 166 A.L.R. 855, plaintiff operating an automobile came into collision with defendant's truck, in which collision he suffered personal injuries and also damage to his automobile. At the time of collision, plaintiff had coverage of a $50 deductible collision policy on his automobile. The insurance company paid the plaintiff a sum covering the damage to his automobile, whereupon, in accordance with a provision of the policy, the plaintiff assigned to the insurer his claim for such damage.

In February 1942, the insurance company commenced an action * * * against Kohlers, Inc., * * * to recoup the money paid by it to cover the damage to Vasu's automobile.

In August 1942, Vasu commenced an action in the same court against Kohlers, Inc., to recover for personal injuries which he suffered in the same collision.

In March 1943, in the insurance company's action, a verdict was rendered in favor of the defendant, followed by judgment.

Two months later an amended answer was filed in the Vasu case, setting out as a bar to the action * * * the judgment rendered in favor of defendant in the insurance company case. A motion to strike that defense * * * [was] sustained * * *. A trial of the action resulted in a verdict for plaintiff, upon which judgment was entered.

On appeal to the Court of Appeals the defendant claimed that the Court of Common Pleas erred in sustaining plaintiff's motion to strike from the defendant's answer the defense of *res judicata* claimed to have arisen by reason of the judgment in favor of the defendant in the action by the insurance company.

The Court of Appeals reversed the judgment of the Court of Common Pleas and entered final judgment in favor of defendant.

This court reversed the judgment of the Court of Appeals, holding in the syllabus, in part, as follows:

* * *

4. Injuries to both person and property suffered by the same person as a result of the same wrongful act are infringements of different rights and give rise to distinct causes of action, with the result that the recovery or denial of recovery of compensation for damages to the property is no bar to an action subsequently prosecuted for the personal injury, unless by an adverse judgment in the first action issues are determined against the plaintiff which operate as an estoppel against him in the second action.

* * *

6. Where an injury to person and to property through a single wrongful act causes a prior contract of indemnity and subrogation as to the injury to property to come into operation for the benefit of the person injured, the indemnitor may prosecute a separate action against the party causing such injury for reimbursement for indemnity monies paid under such contract.

7. Parties in privy, in the sense that they are bound by a judgment, are those who acquired an interest in the subject matter after the beginning of the action or the rendition of the judgment; and if their title or interest attached before that fact, they are not bound unless made parties.

8. A grantor or assignor is not bound, as to third persons, by any judgment which such third persons may obtain against his grantee or assignee adjudicating the title to or claim for the interest transferred unless he participated in the action in such manner as to become, in effect, a party.

* * * The sixth, seventh and eighth paragraphs deal with the factual situation which existed in the Vasu case, i.e., a prior contract of indemnity and subrogation. Although, as discussed infra, it was not actually necessary to the determination of the issue in that case, attention centers on the fourth paragraph.

* * * [Subsequent] cases, distinguishing and explaining the Vasu case, have not changed the rule established in paragraph four of the syllabus * * *.

However, it is contended here that that rule is in conflict with the great weight of authority in this country and has caused vexatious litigation. * * *

Upon examination of decisions of courts of last resort, we find that the majority rule is followed in the following cases in each of which the action was between the person suffering injury and the person committing the tort, and where insurers were not involved, as in the case here. * * * [The court cited cases from 20 states forming the majority and 5 states forming the minority.]

The reasoning behind the majority rule seems to be well stated in the case of Mobile & Ohio Rd. Co. v. Matthews * * * [115 Tenn. 172, 91 S.W. 194 (1906)], as follows:

> The negligent action of the plaintiff in error constituted but one tort. The injuries to the person and property of the defendant in error were the several results and effects of one wrongful act. A single tort can be the basis of but one action. It is not improper to declare in different counts for damages to the person and property when both result from the same tort, and it is the better practice to do so where there is any difference in the measure of damages, and all the damages sustained must be sued for in one suit. This is necessary to prevent multiplicity of suits, burdensome expense, and delays to plaintiffs, and vexatious litigation against defendants. * * *

The minority rule would seem to stem from the English case of Brunsden v. Humphrey (1884), 14 Q.B. 141. The facts in that case are set forth in the opinion in the Vasu case * * * concluding with the statement:

> The Master of the Rolls, in his opinion, stated that the test is "whether the same sort of evidence would prove the plaintiff's case in the two actions," and that, in the action relating to the cab, "it would be necessary to give evidence of the damage done to the plaintiff's vehicle. In the present action it would be necessary to give evidence of the bodily injury occasioned to the plaintiff, and of the sufferings which he has undergone, and for this purpose to call medical witnesses. This one test shows that the causes of action as to the damage done to the plaintiff's cab, and as to the injury occasioned to the plaintiff's person, are distinct."

The fallacy of the reasoning in the English court is best portrayed in the dissenting opinion of Lord Coleridge, as follows:

> * * * [I]t seems to me a subtlety not warranted by law to hold that a man cannot bring two actions, if he is injured in his arm and in his leg, but can bring two, if besides his arm and leg being injured, his trousers which contain his leg, and his coat-sleeve which contains his arm, have been torn.

There appears to be no valid reason in these days of code pleading to adhere to the old English rule as to distinctions between injuries to the person and damages to the person's property resulting from a single tort.

It would seem that the minority rule is bottomed on the proposition that the right of bodily security is fundamentally different from the right of security of property and, also, that, in actions predicated upon a negligent act, damages are a necessary element of each independent cause of action and no recovery may be had unless and until actual consequential damages are shown.

Whether or not injuries to both person and property resulting from the same wrongful act are to be treated as injuries to separate rights or as separate items of damage, * * * a plaintiff may maintain only one action to enforce his rights existing at the time such action is commenced.

The decision of the question actually in issue in the Vasu case is found in paragraphs six, seven and eight of the syllabus, as it is quite apparent from the facts there that the first judgment, claimed to be *res judicata* in Vasu's action against the defendant, was rendered against Vasu's insurer in an action initiated by it after having paid Vasu for the damages to his automobile. * * *

Upon further examination of the cases from other jurisdictions, it appears that in those instances where the courts have held to the majority rule, a separation of causes of action is almost universally recognized where an insurer has acquired by an assignment or by subrogation the right to recover for money it has advanced to pay for property damage.

* * *

In the light of the foregoing, it is the view of this court that the so-called majority rule conforms much more properly to modern practice, and that the rule declared in the fourth paragraph of the syllabus in the Vasu case, on a point not actually at issue therein, should not be followed.

* * *

Judgment reversed and final judgment for defendant.

STEWART, JUDGE (concurring). * * * If it had been necessary [in *Vasu*] to decide the question whether a single tort gives rise to two causes of action as to the one injured by such tort, I would be reluctant to disturb that holding. However, neither the discussion in the Vasu case as to whether a single or double cause of action arises from one tort nor the language of the fourth paragraph of the syllabus was necessary to decide the issue presented in the case, and obviously both such language and such paragraph are obiter dicta and, therefore, are not as persuasive an authority as if they had been appropriate to the question presented.

* * *

ZIMMERMAN, JUDGE (dissenting). I am not unalterably opposed to upsetting prior decisions of this court where changing conditions and the lessons of experience clearly indicate the desirability of such course, but, where those considerations do not obtain, established law should remain undisturbed in order to insure a stability on which the lower courts and the legal profession generally may rely with some degree of confidence.

* * *

NOTE AND QUESTION

The tests for determining the scope of claim preclusion have undergone a significant development since the beginning of the century. The Restatement (Second) of Judgments summarizes this transition:

> * * * In defining claim to embrace all the remedial rights of the plaintiff against the defendant growing out of the relevant transaction (or series of connected transactions), * * * [Section 24 of the Restatement Second] responds to modern procedural ideas which have found expression in the Federal Rules of Civil Procedure and other procedural systems.

> "Claim," in the context of res judicata, has never been broader than the transaction to which it related. But in the days when civil procedure still bore the imprint of the forms of action and the division between law and equity, the courts were prone to associate claim with a single theory of recovery, so that, with respect to one transaction, a plaintiff might have as many claims as there were theories of the substantive law upon which he could seek relief against the defendant. Thus, defeated in an action based on one theory, the plaintiff might be able to maintain another action based on a different theory, even though both actions were grounded upon the defendant's identical act or connected acts forming a single life-situation. In those earlier days there was also some adherence to a view that associated claim with the assertion of a single primary right as accorded by the substantive law, so that, if it appeared that the defendant had invaded a number of primary rights conceived to be held by the plaintiff, the plaintiff had the same number of claims, even though they all sprang from a unitary occurrence. There was difficulty in knowing which rights were primary and what was their extent, but a primary right and the corresponding claim might turn out to be narrow. Thus it was held by some courts that a judgment for or against the plaintiff in an action for personal injuries did not preclude an action by him for property damage occasioned by the same negligent conduct on the part of the defendant—this deriving from the idea that the right to be free of bodily injury was distinct from the property right. Still another view of claim looked to sameness of evidence; a second action was precluded where the evidence to support it was the same as that needed to support the first. Sometimes this was made the sole test of identity of claim; sometimes it figured as a positive but not as a negative test; that is, in certain situations a second action might be precluded although the evidence material to it varied from that in the first action. Even so, claim was not coterminous with the transaction itself.

> The present trend is to see claim in factual terms and to make it coterminous with the transaction regardless of the number of substantive theories, or variant forms of relief flowing from those theories, that may be available to the plaintiff; regardless of the number of primary rights

that may have been invaded; and regardless of the variations in the evidence needed to support the theories or rights. The transaction is the basis of the litigative unit or entity which may not be split.

Restatement (Second), Judgments § 24, comment *a* (1982). Consider how the different tests for determining a claim would affect the reasoning in the case that follows.

MATHEWS v. NEW YORK RACING ASSOCIATION, INC.

United States District Court, Southern District of New York, 1961.
193 F.Supp. 293.

MacMahon, District Judge. Defendants move for summary judgment, pursuant to [Federal] Rule 56(b), * * * on the ground that a judgment in a prior action in this court is res judicata as to the claim alleged in the complaint.

New York Racing Association Inc. is a New York corporation which operates Jamaica Race Track. It employs defendant Thoroughbred Racing Protective Association Inc., a private detective agency, for security purposes.

Plaintiff brings this action against the Association and Thoroughbred alleging that on April 4, 1958, at Jamaica Race Track, he was "assaulted," "kidnaped," "falsely arrested," and "falsely imprisoned" by employees of Thoroughbred. He further alleges that the defendants charged him with disorderly conduct and maliciously caused him to be prosecuted and convicted in the Magistrate's Court of the City of New York on April 10, 1958. He prays for relief in the form of money damages and an injunction restraining the defendants from interfering with his attendance at race tracks, from publication of libelous statements, and from acting as peace officers.

The prior judgment on which defendants rely was entered in this court on June 30, 1960 following a trial before Judge Palmieri sitting without a jury. The complaint in that action alleged, among other matters, that plaintiff was assaulted by the defendant's private investigators at Jamaica Race Track on April 4, 1958. It also alleged that the employees of the defendants had made libelous statements concerning the plaintiff on several occasions, including plaintiff's trial for disorderly conduct on April 10, 1958. The relief prayed for in that action was also money damages and an injunction from further interference with plaintiff's attendance at race tracks within the United States. The earlier action named three individuals as defendants. The only two properly served were employees of the defendants named in the present suit.

* * *

* * * [T]he question is whether the claim alleged in this complaint is the same as that in the suit concluded earlier. The term "claim" refers to

a group of facts limited to a single occurrence or transaction without particular reference to the resulting legal rights. It is the facts surrounding the occurrence which operate to make up the claim, not the legal theory upon which a plaintiff relies. * * *

* * *

The facts relevant to [plaintiff's current lawsuit] * * * along with three other separate claims based on different facts, were tried to a conclusion in the earlier suit. There, the plaintiff relied on the acts of the agents occurring on April 4, 1958 as the basis of a claim against them on the theory of assault. Now, he asserts these same acts as the basis of a claim against the agents' principals on the theory of false arrest. In the earlier action, plaintiff relied on the statements of the agents made on April 10, 1958 as the basis of a claim against them on the theory of libel. Now, he asserts those same statements as the basis of a claim against their principals on the theory of malicious prosecution. Clearly, any liability of the defendants for the acts or statements of their agents must be predicated upon the familiar principle of respondeat superior. Thus, if the agents committed no actionable wrong against the plaintiff, neither did their principals. * * *

* * *

The plaintiff cannot be permitted to splinter his claim into a multiplicity of suits and try them piecemeal at his convenience. * * * "The plaintiff having alleged operative facts which state a cause of action because he tells of defendant's misconduct and his own harm has had his day in court. He does not get another day after the first lawsuit is concluded by giving a different reason than he gave in the first for recovery of damages for the same invasion of his rights. The problem of his rights against the defendant based upon the alleged wrongful acts is fully before the court whether all the reasons for recovery were stated to the court or not." * * *

* * *

The court is cognizant of the fact that plaintiff appears pro se, but as the law provides a beginning for litigation, it must also provide an end. * * *

Notes and Questions

1. *Rush* and *Mathews* illustrate one of the primary purposes of the claim preclusion doctrine: to prevent the splitting of a single claim into two separate suits. In *Rush*, plaintiff won her first suit for property damage, and the court held that any claims she had for personal injuries were "merged"—in other words, extinguished—in the first suit. In *Mathews*, plaintiff had lost the first suit. Since the basic factual setting of the claim in the second suit was the same as in the first, the court held that the allegations were "barred" by the earlier judgment. By using a different definition of a "claim," could you make an argument that the second suit should not have been precluded?

2. *Rush* and *Mathews* used the transaction approach to determine the scope of the first suit's preclusive effect. One of the greatest advantages of this test is its flexibility. Yet, flexibility comes at a price. Because a court may interpret the claim presented in the first lawsuit more broadly than a litigant does, the litigant unknowingly may forfeit parts of his action by failing to raise them. For this reason litigants will learn "by trial and error in the harsh school of experience" of the need to raise all possibly connected allegations in the first proceeding. Cleary, *Res Judicata Reexamined*, 57 Yale L.J. 339, 340 (1948). This well may mean that they will advance claims that they otherwise might not have brought to court. Recall that in *Mathews*, plaintiff was appearing pro se. Should the sophistication of the litigant be considered in deciding issues of claim preclusion?

3. In the federal system, the transaction test governs whether counterclaims are compulsory and implicates whether supplemental jurisdiction may be exercised. See p. 203 and p. 349, supra. Is the concept of a "transaction" the same in these two contexts? In defining what a transaction is, should it matter whether a judge is using supplemental jurisdiction to open the court to litigants, or invoking compulsory counterclaim and preclusion rules to shut litigants out of court?

4. Consider how the transaction test would affect the preclusive effect of a judgment in the following situations:

(a) An abused spouse sues for divorce. Does the divorce judgment bar her from filing a later tort action for spousal abuse? Should it matter whether the abuse was claimed as the basis for the divorce in the earlier suit? Compare McCoy v. Cooke, 165 Mich.App. 662, 419 N.W.2d 44 (Mich. Ct. App. 1988), with Shelar v. Shelar, 910 F.Supp. 1307 (N.D. Ohio 1995). See Dalton, *Domestic Violence, Domestic Torts and Divorce: Constraints and Possibilities*, 31 New Eng. L. Rev. 319, 378–94 (1997).

(b) An individual who was exposed to toxic chemicals sues for damages and seeks reimbursement for the expense of ongoing medical monitoring. Years later, plaintiff learns that she has suffered greater physical injury than initially anticipated or diagnosed. Can she bring a new lawsuit? See In re St. Jude Medical, Inc. Silzone Heart Valves Prods. Liability Litigation, 2004 WL 45504 (D. Minn. 2004). For a discussion of the impact of the transaction approach in cases of latent medical injury, see Note, *Claim Preclusion in Modern Latent Disease Cases: A Proposal for Allowing Second Suits*, 103 Harv. L. Rev. 1 989 (1990); Comment, *Medical Monitoring Plaintiffs and Subsequent Claims for Disease*, 66 U. Chi. L. Rev. 969 (1999).

———

FEDERATED DEPARTMENT STORES, INC. v. MOITIE, 452 U.S. 394, 101 S.Ct. 2424, 69 L.Ed.2d 103 (1981). Respondents Moitie and Brown were two of seven plaintiffs to file separate antitrust actions against petitioner (*Moitie I* and *Brown I*). The actions were consolidated in the District Court after which they were dismissed for failure to allege an "injury" to their "business or property" within the meaning of Section 4 of the Clayton Act. The other five plaintiffs appealed to the Ninth Circuit.

Moitie and Brown, however, did not appeal, but, instead, refiled their actions in state court (*Moitie II* and *Brown II*). The actions were removed to federal court and then dismissed on res judicata grounds. Meanwhile, the five appeals cases were reversed and remanded to the District Court to be reconsidered in light of an intervening Supreme Court opinion. When *Moitie II* and *Brown II* reached the Ninth Circuit on appeal, the court held that, although a strict application of res judicata would preclude the second action, an exception should be made where the dismissal rested on a case that had been effectively overruled. The Supreme Court disagreed:

> The Court of Appeals * * * rested its opinion in part on what it viewed as "simple justice." But we do not see the grave injustice which would be done by the application of accepted principles of res judicata. "Simple justice" is achieved when a complex body of law developed over a period of years is evenhandedly applied. The doctrine of res judicata serves vital public interests beyond any individual judge's ad hoc determination of the equities in a particular case. There is simply "no principle of law or equity which sanctions the rejection by a federal court of the salutary principle of *res judicata.*" * * * The Court of Appeals' reliance on "public policy" is similarly misplaced. This Court has long recognized that "[p]ublic policy dictates that there be an end of litigation; that those who have contested an issue shall be bound by the result of the contest, and that matters once tried shall be considered forever settled as between the parties." Baldwin v. Iowa State Traveling Men's Association, 283 U.S. 522, 525, 51 S.Ct. 517, 518, 75 L.Ed. 1244 (1931). We have stressed that "[the] doctrine of *res judicata* is not a mere matter of practice or procedure inherited from a more technical time than ours. It is a rule of fundamental and substantial justice, 'of public policy and of private peace,' which should be cordially regarded and enforced by the courts. . . ." Hart Steel Co. v. Railroad Supply Co., 244 U.S. 294, 299, 37 S.Ct. 506, 507, 61 L.Ed. 1148 (1917). * * *

Id. at 401–02, 101 S.Ct. at 2429–30, 69 L.Ed.2d at 110–11.

NOTES AND QUESTIONS

1. In spite of the harsh language of *Moitie,* there are situations in which considerations of justice and fairness dictate that prior judgments not be given preclusive effect. When the prior judgment was obtained by the use of fraud, courts generally will not consider it binding. See, e.g., McCarty v. First of Georgia Ins. Co., 713 F.2d 609 (10th Cir. 1983). Should preclusive effect be given to a judgment that rests on a clear and fundamental jurisdictional defect that should have prevented the rendering court from hearing the suit?

2. What impact should an appeal have on the preclusive effect of a trial court's judgment? See, e.g., Crawford v. Chabot, 202 F.R.D. 223 (W.D. Mich. 1998), affirmed without opinion 229 F.3d 1151 (6th Cir. 2000). Federal courts grant preclusion pending appeal of an underlying judgment, but state rules vary. Suppose the appeals court remands the initial judgment for retrial. Does

the initial judgment retain any preclusive effect? What if the appellate opinion overrules the legal basis underlying the initial judgment? See Federal Rule 60(b)(5); 18A Wright, Miller & Cooper, Federal Practice and Procedure: Jurisdiction and Related Matters 2d § 4433.

3. In *Moitie*, defendants removed the actions to federal court on the basis of federal question jurisdiction, and the cases subsequently were dismissed due to the preclusive effect of the prior judgment. In a similar case, Rivet v. Regions Bank, 522 U.S. 470, 118 S.Ct. 921, 139 L.Ed.2d 912 (1998), the dispute involved only state issues, but defendants, relying on *Moitie*, sought to remove the case to federal court on the ground that plaintiff's action was precluded by a prior federal judgment. The United States Supreme Court rejected this interpretation of *Moitie*, holding that claim preclusion does not create an exception to the rule that defendant cannot remove on the basis of a federal defense under Section 1441(b). On *Moitie*, see generally Miller, *Artful Pleading: A Doctrine in Search of Definition*, 76 Texas L. Rev. 1781 (1998).

————

JONES v. MORRIS PLAN BANK OF PORTSMOUTH

Supreme Court of Appeals of Virginia, 1937.
168 Va. 284, 191 S.E. 608.

GREGORY, JUSTICE.

William B. Jones instituted an action for damages against the Morris Plan Bank of Portsmouth for the conversion of his automobile. * * *

After the plaintiff had introduced all of his evidence and before the defendant had introduced any evidence on its behalf, the latter's counsel moved to strike the evidence of the plaintiff and the court sustained the motion. A verdict for the defendant resulted.

The facts are that the plaintiff purchased from J.A. Parker, a dealer in automobiles, a Plymouth sedan, agreeing to pay therefor $595. He paid a part of the purchase price by the delivery of a used car to Parker of the agreed value of $245 and after crediting that amount on the purchase price and adding a finance charge of $78.40, there remained an unpaid balance due the dealer of $428. This latter amount was payable in 12 monthly installments of $35.70 each and evidenced by one note in the principal sum of $428.40. The note contained this provision: "The whole amount of this note (less any payments made hereon) becomes immediately due and payable in the event of nonpayment at maturity of any installment thereof." The note was secured by the usual conditional sales contract * * * in which it was agreed that the title to the car would be retained by the dealer until the entire purchase price was paid in full. * * * [T]he contract was assigned to the defendant * * * and the note was indorsed by Parker and delivered to the defendant at the same time.

Installment payments due on the note for May and June were not made when payable and for them an action was instituted in the civil and police court of the city of Suffolk. No appearance was made by the defendant (Jones) in that action and judgment was obtained against him for the two payments. Execution issued upon the judgment and it was satisfied * * * by Jones * * *.

Later the defendant instituted another action against Jones in the same court for the July installment which had become due and was unpaid, and to that action Jones filed a plea of res adjudicata, whereupon the * * * [Bank] took a nonsuit.

* * * [T]he defendant * * * took possession of the automobile without the consent of the plaintiff and later sold it and applied the proceeds upon the note.

Afterwards, the plaintiff instituted the present action for conversion to recover damages for the loss of the automobile. His action in the court below was founded upon the theory that when the May and June installments became due and were unpaid, then under the acceleration clause in the note, the entire balance due thereon matured and at once became due and the defendant having elected to sue him for only two installments instead of the entire amount of the note, and having obtained a judgment for the two installments and satisfaction of the execution issued thereon, it waived its right to collect the balance. He also contends that the note was satisfied in the manner narrated and that the conditional sales contract, the sole purpose of which was to secure the payment of the note, served its purpose and ceased to exist, and, therefore, the title to the automobile was no longer retained, but upon the satisfaction of the note, passed to the plaintiff and was his property when the agent of the defendant removed it and converted it to its own use.

The position of the defendant is that * * * the title to the automobile, which was the subject of the alleged conversion, was not vested in the plaintiff at the time of the action, nor since, because the condition in the contract was that the title should be retained by the seller (whose rights were assigned to the defendant) until the entire purchase price was paid, and that the purchase price had never been paid * * *.

The defendant also contends that the note and conditional sales contract were divisible; that successive actions could be brought upon the installments as they matured; and that it was not bound, at the risk of waiving its right to claim the balance, to sue for all installments in one action.

* * *

We decide that under the unconditional acceleration provision in the note involved here and in the absence of the usual optional provision reserved to the holder, the entire amount due upon the note became due and payable when default was made in paying an installment. * * *

Was it essential that the defendant here institute an action for all of the installments then due, or could it institute its action for only two of the installments and later institute another action for other installments?

The answer to that question depends upon the nature of the transaction. If a transaction is represented by one single and indivisible contract and the breach gives rise to one single cause of action, it cannot be split into distinct parts and separate actions maintained for each.

On the other hand, if the contract is divisible giving rise to more than one cause of action, each may be proceeded upon separately.

Was the contract here single and indivisible or was it divisible? Our answer is that the note and conditional sales contract constituted one single contract. The sole purpose of the conditional sales contract was to retain the title in the seller until the note was paid. When that condition was performed, the contract ended.

One of the principal tests in determining whether a demand is single and entire, or whether it is several, so as to give rise to more than one cause of action, is the identity of facts necessary to maintain the action. If the same evidence will support both actions, there is but one cause of action.

In the case at bar, all of the installments were due. The evidence essential to support the action on the two installments for which the action was brought would be the identical evidence necessary to maintain an action upon all of the installments. All installments having matured at the time the action was begun, under well-settled principles, those not embraced in that action are now barred.

* * * At the time the defendant lost its right to institute any action for the remaining installments, the title to the automobile passed to the plaintiff. He was the owner at the time the agent of the defendant took possession of it and exposed it to sale.

It follows that the judgment of the court below will be reversed, and the case will be remanded for the sole purpose of determining the quantum of damages.

Reversed and remanded.

NOTES AND QUESTIONS

1. When a debt is secured by a series of notes or when a bond includes a number of interest coupons, an action on one of the notes or coupons, even though others are due, does not bar a subsequent action on those others. Restatement, Judgments § 62, comment *i* (1942); Restatement (Second), Judgments § 24, comment *d* (1982). Cf. NESBIT v. INDEPENDENT DISTRICT OF RIVERSIDE, 144 U.S. 610, 619, 12 S.Ct. 746, 748, 36 L.Ed. 562, 565 (1892):

> Each matured coupon is a separable promise, and gives rise to a separate cause of action. It may be detached from the bond and sold by itself. Indeed, the title to several matured coupons of the same bond may be in as many different persons, and upon each a distinct and separate action be maintained. So, while the promises of the bond and of the coupons in

the first instance are upon the same paper, and the coupons are for interest due upon the bond, yet the promise to pay the coupon is as distinct from that to pay the bond as though the two promises were placed in different instruments, upon different paper.

2. It is difficult to define the scope of a prior judgment in controversies involving continuing or renewed conduct. The Restatement (Second) of Judgments lists some considerations relevant to determining whether a factual grouping constitutes a single transaction, and suggests evaluating "whether the facts are related in time, space, origin, or motivation, whether they form a convenient trial unit, and whether their treatment as a unit conforms to the parties' expectations or business understanding or usage." See Restatement (Second), Judgments § 24 (1982).

There are some other useful rules of thumb to be used in cases of continuing or renewed conduct. For example, if the conduct that is the subject of the first action continues after judgment in the first action, claim preclusion would not prevent a second suit. Issue preclusion may apply, however, to matters of status or to issues of fact resolved in the first action. When the purpose of the first suit is to establish general rules of legality, such as when the first suit is a declaratory judgment action, subsequent claims involving the same conduct are precluded. Nuisance suits commonly involve continuing conduct. Judgments involving "permanent" nuisances are considered to have full preclusive effect; those involving "temporary" nuisances are not considered to preclude later litigation involving the same behavior. Courts are not always consistent in their classification of nuisances. For a further discussion of claims that involve continuing and renewed conduct, see 18 Wright, Miller & Cooper, Federal Practice and Procedure: Jurisdiction and Related Matters 2d § 4409.

3. As the previous Notes suggest, often the underlying substantive law will affect the definition of the claim for the purposes of preclusion. For example, if one party to a contract commits a material breach that is neither accompanied nor followed by a repudiation, the law of contracts teaches that the other party is free, on the one hand, to treat the contract as binding and sue for the damages or, on the other hand, to treat the contract as ended. If the aggrieved party chooses the former option and then suffers further material breaches, she will not be barred from suing for damages not sought in the first suit. See Restatement (Second), Judgments § 26, comment *g* (1982).

4. The expectations of the parties also may be decisive in determining the scope of the prior judgment. Imagine that a wholesale distributor regularly ships goods to a retailer on credit. If the parties conceive of their relationship as a series of discrete transactions, a suit by the creditor seeking to recover any one of the payments would not bar subsequent suits for other payments. If, however, the parties believe they have a single running account, the creditor would have to seek to recover the entire balance then due.

2. DEFENSE PRECLUSION

Thus far we have looked at claim preclusion from the perspective of plaintiff. However, defendants also need to take the doctrine into account, typically in one of three situations:

> The first two situations involve a second action in which a former defendant seeks to advance a claim against the original plaintiff. In one, the claim involves matters that were not advanced in the first action; in the other, the claim involves matters that were advanced in the first action but are not foreclosed by issue preclusion. The third situation involves a second action by the original plaintiff in which the defendant seeks to raise defenses that were equally available in the first action but were not advanced there.

18 Wright, Miller & Cooper, Federal Practice and Procedure: Jurisdiction and Related Matters 2d § 4414. "The third situation" is referred to as "defense preclusion," and the scope of the doctrine is implicated in the case that follows.

_____

MITCHELL v. FEDERAL INTERMEDIATE CREDIT BANK

Supreme Court of South Carolina, 1932.
165 S.C. 457, 164 S.E. 136.

[An action for an accounting against defendant bank for proceeds of a crop of potatoes. Plaintiff alleged that in order to obtain loans from defendant he had—at the behest of defendant's agent—sold his potatoes through a growers' association and assigned the proceeds as security for two notes, totalling $9,000, which had been discounted with defendant; that the potatoes had netted $18,000, but that he had never received any of this, and that the proceeds had been received by defendant or an agent of defendant. In a previous action by defendant on the notes, plaintiff had pleaded in the answer the same facts now the basis of an affirmative claim, but had not counterclaimed or asked relief; judgment had been for him in that action. In the present suit, defendant contended that plaintiff's claim was merged in the earlier judgment. This contention was upheld by the trial court.]

STABLER, J. * * *

We now come to the main question presented by the appeal, namely, Was the circuit judge in error in sustaining the plea in bar to plaintiff's action? Turning to appellant's answer in the federal court case * * * we find that the facts there pleaded by him as a defense to the bank's recovery on its notes are the same as those set out by him in his complaint as the basis of his action in the case at bar, it being alleged that the total amount paid to the bank was in excess of all sums advanced to him on the notes or otherwise, and as a result of the transaction the notes sued upon were fully paid and discharged. In addition, we find in the record of the case before us the following statement by appellant as an admission of fact on his part: " * * * The indebtedness of the bank to Mitchell arising from the embezzlement of the proceeds of the crop was used pro tanto as an offset to the claim of the bank in the Federal Court. The case at bar seeks recovery of the surplusage, over the offset, of the proceeds of the same crop lost by the same embezzlement. The appellant, however, is not seeking to recover in this action the same money that has already been used as an offset."

* * *

In support of his position * * * appellant cites certain decisions of this court, which he claims to be conclusive of the issue, relying especially upon Kirven v. Chemical Co., 77 S.C. 493, 58 S.E. 424, 426.

* * * [T]he record shows that Kirven had bought from the Chemical Company $2,228 worth of fertilizers and had given his note for that amount. The company, upon maturity of the note, brought action against him on his obligation. He at first filed an answer setting up three defenses, the third of which was that the fertilizers furnished were deleterious and destructive to the crops, and that there was an entire failure of consideration for the note. Later, he was permitted to file a supplemental answer in which he withdrew the third defense. On trial in the federal court, the jury rendered a verdict for the Chemical Company. Thereafter, Kirven brought an action against the company * * * alleging that the defendant caused damage to his crop in the sum of $1,995 by reason of the deleterious effect of the fertilizers furnished. The company set up the defense that the issues in this action were or could have been adjudicated in the [first] suit * * *. A verdict was given Kirven in the amount prayed for, and on appeal * * * it was pointed out that the question raised in the state court was not *actually* litigated and determined in the federal action, and it appears that the court, for that reason, took the view that a bar or estoppel did not exist. Mr. Justice Woods, in his concurring opinion, took the view that, as Kirven elected not to use, as a defense, the fact of *worthlessness,* which might have been available in the action of the company against him, "he was not precluded from using the very different facts of deleteriousness and positive injury caused by appellant's alleged negligence in the manufacture of the fertilizer as the basis of an independent cause of action."

We think the facts of the case at bar, however, present a different situation. * * *

O'Connor v. Varney, 10 Gray (Mass.) 231, was an action on contract to recover damages for Varney's failure to build certain additions to a house according to the terms of a written agreement between the parties. The defendant set up as a defense "a judgment recovered by O'Connor in an action brought by Varney against him on that contract to recover the price therein agreed to be paid for the work, in defence of which O'Connor relied on the same nonperformance by Varney, and in which an auditor to whom the case was referred * * * found that Varney was not entitled to recover under the agreement," as the work had been so imperfectly done that it would require a greater sum than the amount sued for to make it correspond with the contract. At the trial of the second action, the trial judge ruled that the judgment in the first suit was a bar, and directed a verdict for the defendant. The plaintiff O'Connor thereupon appealed.

Chief Justice Shaw, who rendered the opinion of the court, said: "The presiding judge rightly ruled that the former judgment was a bar to this action. A party against whom an action is brought on a contract has two modes of defending himself. He may allege specific breaches of the contract declared upon, and rely on them in defence. But if he intends to claim, by way of damages for nonperformance of the contract, more than the amount for which he is sued, he must not rely on the contract in defence, but must bring a cross action, and apply to the court to have the cases continued so that the executions may be set off. He cannot use the same defence, first as a shield, and then as a sword. * * * "

It will be noted that Varney was not entitled to recover in the first suit because his dereliction amounted to more than he sued for. This would seem to be exactly the situation in the case at bar.

* * * When the bank sued * * * [Mitchell] on his two notes, amounting to about $9,000, he had the option to interpose his claim as a defense to that suit or to demand judgment against the bank, by way of counterclaim, for the amount owing him by it. * * * The transaction out of which the case at bar arises is the same transaction that Mitchell pleaded as a defense in the federal suit. He might, therefore, "have recovered in that action, upon the same allegations and proofs which he there made, the judgment which he now seeks, if he had prayed for it." He did not do this, but attempted to split his cause of action, and to use one portion of it for defense in that suit and to reserve the remainder for offense in a subsequent suit, which, under applicable principles, could not be done. * * *

The judgment of the circuit court is affirmed.

NOTE AND QUESTION

Federal Rule 13(a) defines when a counterclaim is compulsory. See Peterson, *The Misguided Law of Compulsory Counterclaims in Default Cases*, 50 Ariz. L. Rev. 1107, 1108–09 (2008). Can a party raise the omitted claim in a separate action? Professor Wright has written that "it has never been doubted in any of the jurisdictions which have adopted such a rule that the pleader who fails to comply therewith is prohibited from subsequent assertion of his claim." Wright, *Estoppel by Rule: The Compulsory Counterclaim Under Modern Pleading*, 38 Minn. L. Rev. 423, 449 n.121 (1954). See, e.g., May v. Exxon Corp., 256 Ark. 865, 867, 512 S.W.2d 11, 12 (1974) ("Failure to plead the counterclaim is res judicata."). Is the preclusion a result of waiver or res judicata?

SECTION C. ISSUE PRECLUSION

One of the most frequently quoted descriptions of what once was called collateral estoppel and now is referred to as issue preclusion was provided by the first Justice Harlan in SOUTHERN PACIFIC RAILROAD CO. v. UNITED STATES, 168 U.S. 1, 48–49, 18 S.Ct. 18, 27, 42 L.Ed. 355, 377 (1897):

> The general principle announced in numerous cases is that a right, question, or fact distinctly put in issue and directly determined by a court of competent jurisdiction, as a ground of recovery, cannot be disputed in a subsequent suit between the same parties or their privies; and, even if the second suit is for a different cause of action, the right, question, or fact once so determined must, as between the same parties or their privies, be taken as conclusively established, so long as the judgment in the first suit remains unmodified.

As this passage reveals, there is a critical difference between claim preclusion and issue preclusion. Under the doctrine of claim preclusion, a claim may be "merged" or "barred" by a party's failure to raise the claim in a prior action. Issue preclusion, however, applies only to matters argued and decided in an earlier lawsuit.

For issue preclusion to exist, a proceeding must involve the same issue as a previous suit. The term "issue," like the term "transaction" in the context of claim preclusion, is ambiguous and subject to interpretation. And, the application *vel non* of doctrines of issue preclusion sometimes will turn on the ability of advocates to manipulate the definition of this crucial term.

To trigger the doctrine of issue preclusion, however, more than a mere duplication of issues is required. It is necessary to examine the nature of the first action and the treatment that the issue received in it. Just as for claim preclusion, the judgment in the first action must have been of a certain "quality"—that is, it must have been valid, final, and on the merits (the "on the merits" requirement does not apply if the issue being precluded is exclusively a procedural issue). Moreover, the issue raised in a second suit must have been actually litigated in the first action, and must have been decided by the first court. And, determination of that issue must have been necessary to the court's judgment.

Some courts require still more before they will allow a party to invoke issue preclusion. For example, some demand that the issue have occupied a high position in the hierarchy of legal rules applied in the first action— that it was important. Others require "mutuality"—that is, that the party invoking preclusion would have been bound by an unfavorable judgment in the first suit. Fewer and fewer courts now impose these latter two conditions, however, and the mutuality requirement in particular is now widely disregarded depending on the context.

1. ACTUALLY LITIGATED

CROMWELL v. COUNTY OF SAC

Supreme Court of the United States, 1876.
94 U.S. (4 Otto) 351, 24 L.Ed. 195.

Error to the Circuit Court of the United States for the District of Iowa.

MR. JUSTICE FIELD delivered the opinion of the court.

This was an action on four bonds * * * each for $1,000, and four coupons for interest, attached to them, each for $100. The bonds were issued in 1860, and were made payable to bearer, in the city of New York, in the years 1868, 1869, 1870, and 1871, respectively, with annual interest at the rate of ten per cent a year.

To defeat this action, the defendant relied upon the estoppel of a judgment rendered in favor of the county in a prior action brought by one Samuel C. Smith upon certain earlier maturing coupons on the same bonds, accompanied with proof that the plaintiff Cromwell was at the time the owner of the coupons in that action, and that the action was prosecuted for his sole use and benefit.

* * *

In considering the operation of this judgment, it should be borne in mind * * * that there is a difference between the effect of a judgment as a bar or estoppel against the prosecution of a second action upon the same claim or demand, and its effect as an estoppel in another action between the same parties upon a different claim or cause of action. In the former case, the judgment, if rendered upon the merits, constitutes an absolute bar to a subsequent action. [The Court's description of claim preclusion appears at p. 570, supra.] * * * The language * * * which is so often used, that a judgment estops not only as to every ground of recovery or defence actually presented in the action, but also as to every ground which might have been presented, is strictly accurate, when applied to the demand or claim in controversy. * * *

But where the second action between the same parties is upon a different claim or demand, the judgment in the prior action operates as an estoppel only as to those matters in issue or points controverted, upon the determination of which the finding or verdict was rendered. In all cases, therefore, where it is sought to apply the estoppel of a judgment rendered upon one cause of action to matters arising in a suit upon a different cause of action, the inquiry must always be as to the point or question actually litigated and determined in the original action, not what might have been thus litigated and determined. Only upon such matters is the judgment conclusive in another action.

The difference in the operation of a judgment in the two classes of cases mentioned is seen through all the leading adjudications upon the doctrine of estoppel. Thus, in the case of Outram v. Morewood, 3 East, 346, the defendants were held estopped from averring title to a mine, in an action of trespass for digging out coal from it, because, in a previous action for a similar trespass, they had set up the same title, and it had been determined against them. In commenting upon a decision cited in that case, Lord Ellenborough, in his elaborate opinion, said: "It is not the recovery, but the matter alleged by the party, and upon which the recovery proceeds, which creates the estoppel. The recovery of itself in an action of trespass is only a bar to the future recovery of damages for the same injury; but the estoppel precludes parties and privies from contending to the contrary of that point or matter of fact, which, having been once distinctly put in issue by them, or by those to whom they are privy in estate or law, has been, on such issue joined, solemnly found against them."

* * *

Various considerations, other than the actual merits, may govern a party in bringing forward grounds of recovery or defence in one action, which may not exist in another action upon a different demand, such as the smallness of the amount or the value of the property in controversy, the difficulty of obtaining the necessary evidence, the expense of the litigation, and his own situation at the time. A party acting upon considerations like these ought not to be precluded from contesting in a subsequent action other demands arising out of the same transaction. * * *

If, now, we consider the main question presented for our determination * * * its solution will not be difficult. It appears from the findings in the original action of Smith, that the county of Sac, by a vote of its people, authorized the issue of bonds to the amount of $10,000, for the erection of a court-house; that bonds to that amount were issued by the county judge, and delivered to one Meserey, with whom he had made a contract for the erection of the court-house; that immediately upon receipt of the bonds the contractor gave one of them as a gratuity to the county judge; and that the court-house was never constructed by the contractor, or by any other person pursuant to the contract. It also appears that the plaintiff had become, before their maturity, the holder of twenty-five coupons, which had been attached to the bonds, but there was no finding that he had ever given any value for them. * * * The case coming here on writ of error, this court held that the facts disclosed by the findings were sufficient evidence of fraud and illegality in the inception of the bonds to call upon the holder to show that he had given value for the coupons; and, not having done so, the judgment was affirmed. Reading the record of the lower court by the opinion and judgment of this court, it must be considered that the matters adjudged in that case were these: that the bonds were void as against the county in the hands of parties who did not acquire them before maturity and give value for them, and that the plaintiff, not having proved that he gave such value, was not entitled to recover upon the coupons. * * * The finding and judgment upon the invalidity of the bonds, as against the county, must be held to estop the plaintiff here from averring to the contrary. But as the bonds were negotiable instruments * * * they would be held as valid obligations against the county in the hands of a *bona fide* holder taking them for value before maturity * * *. If, therefore, the plaintiff received the bond and coupons in suit before maturity for value, as he offered to prove, he should have been permitted to show that fact. There was nothing adjudged in the former action in the finding that the plaintiff had not made such proof in that case which can preclude the present plaintiff from making such proof here. The fact that a party may not have shown that he gave value for one bond or coupon is not even presumptive, much less conclusive, evidence that he may not have given value for another and different bond or coupon. The exclusion of the evidence offered by the plaintiff was erroneous * * *.

Judgment reversed, and cause remanded for a new trial.

[The dissenting opinion of JUSTICE CLIFFORD is omitted.]

NOTES AND QUESTIONS

1. Section 27 of the Restatement (Second) of Judgments (1982) adopts the "actually litigated" requirement as a condition for according issue preclusive effect to a judgment. What are the reasons supporting this approach? Are you persuaded that these justifications are sound? Consider this criticism of the doctrine:

> * * * [One argument made in favor of the actually litigated requirement is] that an action may involve "so small an amount that litigation of the issue may cost more than the value of the lawsuit." [Restatement (Second), Judgments § 27, comment *e* (1982).] * * * This is a rather curious rationale. It does not support the "actually litigated" requirement; rather it supports a rejection of issue preclusion under any circumstances. If there is insufficient incentive to litigate a matter, then there should be no issue preclusion. Litigation in small claims courts or prosecutions for misdemeanors cannot give rise to issue preclusion because often those actions provide litigants with inadequate incentive to litigate. Although the line is not clearly defined, it seems reasonable to conclude that prosecutions for felonies and civil litigation involving substantial amounts will give rise to issue preclusion. The burden properly falls on the presumably precluded party to show why issue preclusion should not apply.

> * * * [A second argument used to justify the actually litigated requirement is] that "the forum may be an inconvenient one in which to produce the necessary evidence or in which to litigate at all." [Id.] If a valid judgment is going to be handed down, then this forum must have jurisdiction over the defendant and it is the forum of choice of the plaintiff. As the forum of choice of the plaintiff, it is proper to hold that

the plaintiff should be bound by any adverse decision reached by the court. It is only in the case of the defendant that he might be able to assert that he should not be bound because it is inconvenient.

In light of (a) the present constitutional limitations on the exercise of jurisdiction over defendants, (b) the fact that the suit by definition involves a substantial interest, and (c) the availability of procedures to get and present the relevant evidence, this justification is not very persuasive. Would it not be better to hold for issue preclusion, and then permit the apparently precluded party to explain why preclusion should not apply?

The [Restatement's] Comment also gives as a reason for the "actually litigated" rule that a rule to the contrary "might serve to discourage compromise, to decrease the likelihood that the issues in an action would be narrowed by stipulation, and thus to intensify litigation." Id. This litigation, where there is the incentive to litigate, must involve substantial interests on the part of the parties. The issue preclusion that may flow from the judgment does not change the suit from unimportant to important. The suit is, by definition, important. If a compromise is going to be discouraged, it probably will be by the size of the present suit. If there is going to be a refusal to stipulate and thus narrow issues, in all probability it will be because of the importance of the instant suit and not because of the issue preclusion that may flow from the decision.

Vestal, *The Restatement (Second) of Judgments: A Modest Dissent*, 66 Cornell L. Rev. 464, 473–74 (1981).

2. Consider the following criticism of Professor Vestal's approach to the "actually litigated" requirement:

A good case can be made for saying that if a matter is distinctly put in issue and formally admitted, the party making the admission should be bound by it in subsequent litigation. This was the old formulation of the rule of "judicial estoppel," as it was then called: "The former verdict is conclusive only as to facts directly and distinctly put in issue * * *." But how can a matter be "directly and distinctly put in issue"? Obviously, by actual litigation. * * *

* * *

Professor Vestal says there should be an estoppel because, where there is an incentive to deny, failure to deny constitutes an admission. This turns the notion of incentive to litigate on its head. The "incentive to litigate" formula, as used in most of the cases and in the *Restatement Second*, allows a party who *did* litigate an issue to relitigate it if the party can show that the original litigation was a side show rather than a struggle to the finish. [See Restatement (Second), Judgments § 28, comment *j* (1982).] The *Restatement Second* allows a party to rebut the inference naturally drawn from the fact that the issue was actually litigated—the inference that the party had treated the issue with entire seriousness in the first litigation. In Professor Vestal's system, however, "incentive to litigate" allows a court to conjecture that the party probably had reason to litigate the issue in the first action, and to conjecture further that the failure to litigate is an admission of a proposition not litigated. Professor Vestal's "opportunity" theory allows the court to infer that the issue was important to a party whose behavior indicates he thought the issue was unimportant, and, having done that, to convict the party by his silence. * * *

Hazard, *Revisiting the Second Restatement of Judgments: Issue Preclusion and Related Problems*, 66 Cornell L. Rev. 564, 577–79, 584 (1981). What is your response to this argument?

3.   How should a court determine what was decided in a prior litigation? Will the difficulty of this task be affected by whether the case was tried to a judge or to a jury? Are there any procedural rules that can play a role in defining what a suit has decided? Consider, in particular, Rule 49 and Rule 52. When the prior decision is ambiguous on what it actually decided, doubts should be resolved against the party seeking to assert preclusion. But it sometimes will be necessary to conduct a hearing to determine what was decided. Is it possible to use the record of the prior trial to help ascertain what issues actually were decided? Is it permissible to introduce extrinsic evidence to prove what issues were litigated? There is some authority for permitting both of these methods of proof. How should the court determine whether an issue was actually litigated in the following situations?

(a) In the course of a divorce proceeding, the court determines that a child has been born of the marriage and orders the husband to pay child support. Does the decree collaterally estop the child when she seeks to litigate the question of paternity? If paternity is disproved, does the divorce decree issue preclude the husband from seeking reimbursement for child support payments already made? See Tedford v. Gregory, 125 N.M. 206, 959 P.2d 540 (Ct. App. 1998). What additional information would you want to know about the divorce proceeding?

(b) In the course of a *"Markman"* proceeding, see p. 534, supra, the court construes the meaning of a patent claim. Is the trial court's construction binding on the patent holder in a subsequent infringement suit? E.g., In re Freeman, 30 F.3d 1459 (Fed. Cir. 1994). See Van Over, *Collateral Estoppel and* Markman *Rulings: The Call for Uniformity*, 45 St. Louis U. L.J. 1151 (2001).

4.   For a general discussion of this topic, see 18 Wright, Miller & Cooper, Federal Practice and Procedure: Jurisdiction and Related Matters 2d § 4420. See also Heiser, *California's Confusing Collateral Estoppel (Issue Preclusion) Doctrine*, 35 San Diego L. Rev. 509, 535–58 (1998).

2. NECESSARILY DECIDED

RIOS v. DAVIS

Court of Civil Appeals of Texas, Eastland, 1963.
373 S.W.2d 386.

Collings, Justice.

Juan C. Rios brought this suit against Jessie Hubert Davis in the District Court to recover damages * * * alleged to have been sustained as a result of personal injuries received * * * in an automobile collision. Plaintiff alleged that his injuries were proximately caused by negligence on the part of the defendant. The defendant answered alleging that Rios was guilty of contributory negligence. Also, among other defenses, the defendant urged a plea of res judicata and collateral estoppel based upon the findings and the judgment entered * * * in a suit between the same parties in the County Court at Law of El Paso County. The plea of res judicata was sustained and judgment was entered in favor of the defendant * * *.

It is shown by the record that * * * Popular Dry Goods Company brought suit against appellee Davis * * * seeking to recover for damages to its truck in the sum of $443.97, alleged to have been sustained in the same collision here involved. Davis answered alleging contributory negligence on the part of Popular and joined appellant Juan C. Rios as a third party defendant and sought to recover from Rios $248.50, the alleged amount of damages to his automobile. The jury * * * found that Popular Dry Goods Company and Rios were guilty of negligence proximately causing the collision. However, the jury also found that Davis was guilty of negligence proximately causing the collision, and judgment was entered * * * denying Popular Dry Goods any recovery against Davis and denying Davis any recovery against Rios.

Appellant Rios in his third point contends that the District Court erred in sustaining appellee's plea of res judicata based upon the judgment of the County Court at Law because the findings on the issues regarding appellant's negligence and liability * * * were immaterial because the judgment entered in that case was in favor of appellant. We sustain this point. * * * The sole basis for the judgment * * * as between Rios and Davis was the findings concerning the negligence of Davis. The finding that Rios was negligent was not essential or material to the judgment and the judgment was not based thereon. On the contrary, the finding * * * that Rios was negligent proximately causing the accident would, if it had been controlling, * * * [lead] to a different result. Since the judgment was in favor of Rios he had no right or opportunity to complain of or to appeal from the finding that he was guilty of such negligence even if such finding had been without any support whatever in the evidence. The right of appeal is from a judgment and not from a finding. * * * In the case of Word v. Colley, Tex. Civ. App., 173 S.W. 629, at page 634 of its opinion (Error Ref.), the court stated as follows:

> It is the judgment, and not the verdict or the conclusions of fact, filed by a trial court which constitutes the estoppel, and a finding of fact by a jury or a court which does not become the basis or one of the grounds of the judgment rendered is not conclusive against either party to the suit.

* * *

The judgment is, therefore, reversed, and the cause is remanded.

Notes and Questions

1. The verdict in the earlier action in *Rios* reflects the practice of submitting a case to the jury on "special issues." Does *Rios* offer a reason for using special verdicts more frequently?

2. In *Rios,* even though the jury gave a special verdict, certain issues were not given preclusive effect because the outcome did not depend upon those findings. Should preclusive effect be given where the jury could not have arrived at the same judgment without each of those finding? See, e.g., Patterson v. Saunders, 194 Va. 607, 74 S.E.2d 204 (1953).

3. The court in *Rios* held that the judgment in the earlier case did not estop Rios from denying his own negligence. Should the earlier judgment estop Davis from denying his own negligence?

4. The court in *Rios* supports its view by noting that Rios could not appeal the finding of his negligence in the earlier action. See also Restatement (Second), Judgments § 28(1) (1982). Should the prevailing party in the earlier action be permitted in a later action to attack a finding that was necessary to the judgment in the earlier action? Such a situation will not be common.

5. How would you justify each of these statements?

(a) When a judgment is supported by multiple independent grounds, all of the grounds may be relitigated. See Halpern v. Schwartz, 426 F.2d 102, 106 (2d Cir. 1970).

(b) When a judgment is supported by multiple independent grounds, none of the grounds may be relitigated. See In re Westgate-California Corp., 642 F.2d 1174 (9th Cir. 1981).

(c) When a judgment is supported by multiple independent grounds, the primary issue may not be relitigated, but secondary issues are not barred. See National Satellite Sports, Inc. v. Eliadis, Inc., 253 F.3d 900 (6th Cir. 2001).

SECTION D. THE REQUIRED QUALITY OF JUDGMENT

Only judgments of a certain quality will give rise to preclusion. The traditional words used to describe a judgment of sufficient quality to create preclusion are that the judgment must be valid, final, and on the merits. These terms are not unambiguous, however; indeed, they are somewhat misleading. Courts often enter judgments that are considered "on the merits," despite the fact that the judgment resulted from less than a full adjudicatory proceeding. In addition, courts increasingly are faced with the prior determinations of state or federal administrative agencies that act in a quasi-judicial capacity. This Section is designed to highlight some of the difficult questions the "quality of judgment" requirement raises.

1. JUDGMENTS OF JUDICIAL TRIBUNALS

HANOVER LOGANSPORT, INC. v.
ROBERT C. ANDERSON, INC.

Court of Appeals of Indiana, Third District, 1987.
512 N.E.2d 465.

STATON, JUDGE.

[Hanover Logansport, Inc. ("Hanover") and Robert C. Anderson, Inc. ("Anderson") entered into an agreement pursuant to which Hanover agreed to lease certain property to Anderson for use as a liquor store. Hanover failed to deliver the premises on the agreed upon date, and Anderson filed suit for breach of the lease. Before trial, Hanover offered to deliver the real estate to Anderson, and Anderson accepted with the following reservation: "[T]he offer is only accepted for purposes of mitigation of damages and not in settlement of damages arising to Plaintiff caused by Defendants' breach of contract."

The parties filed a stipulation that "the judgment as stipulated to by the Defendants herein should be recorded of record in the judgment record book of the County of St. Joseph." Anderson took possession of the premises, and, after several months, Hanover moved to dismiss the earlier breach of contract action. The trial court denied the motion, and Hanover appealed, arguing that the prior consent judgment precluded any further litigation based on the same cause of action.]

* * *

Hanover makes the following argument:

1. The complaint seeks specific performance of the lease or *in the alternative* money damages for loss of profits *over the term of the lease.*

2. Hanover made an offer of real estate pursuant to [Indiana Trial Rule 68] consistent with one of the alternatives—specific performance—in the complaint.[a]

3. Anderson accepted the offer.

4. Under T.R. 68, the clerk is required to enter judgment.

5. Anderson took possession of the real estate.

6. By accepting the offer of real estate and taking possession of the premises, Anderson chose its remedy and is now barred by law from continuing the litigation.

Anderson argues that (1) an offer of judgment under T.R. 68 may be in part or in whole; and (2) both Hanover and the trial court were on notice that the offer of judgment did not address and dispose of the whole of its claim. Anderson points to the portion of its acceptance which states:

---

a. Indiana Rules of Procedure, Trial Rule 68, is similar to Federal Rule 68, and is set out in the Supplement.

" . . . Further, the offer is only accepted for purposes of mitigation of damages and not in settlement of damages arising to Plaintiff caused by Defendants' breach of contract." In its brief, Anderson states: "The acceptance of said offer specifically states that the lease between the parties would be as contracted, subject to the conditions in the lease, but that the Plaintiff did not waive damages for breach of contract which arose due to the failure of Defendant to honor its contract *between the date the offer was signed and the date the Court entered an Order approving the [settlement] as to possession.*" (Emphasis added.)

Thus, we address the following issue: Whether, by law, a plaintiff, who accepts an offer of judgment which conforms to one of the alternative prayers for relief contained in his complaint, may then seek additional damages arising from the same cause of action.

* * *

A consent judgment has a dual aspect. It represents an agreement between the parties settling the underlying dispute and providing for the entry of judgment in a pending or contemplated action. See James, *Consent Judgments as Collateral Estoppel*, 108 U. Pa. L. Rev. 173, 175 (1959). It also represents the entry of such a judgment by a court—with all that this means in the way of committing the force of society to implement the judgment of its courts. Id.

As a result of this dual aspect, some courts and commentators focus on the contractual aspect of a consent judgment, thus determining whatever its preclusive effect may be by ascertaining the intent of the parties—in the same way courts construe other agreements. * * *

Yet, other courts and commentators focus on the entry of a consent judgment by a court and argue that such a judgment possesses the same force with regard to *res judicata* and collateral estoppel as a judgment entered after a trial on the merits. * * *

Proponents of the consent-judgment-as-contract theory argue that if consent judgments are given preclusive effect regardless of the intent of the parties, such a rule would lessen the chance of compromise between them. This, they argue, is true for two reasons. First, in many cases, the application of such a rule (at least in regard to the collateral estoppel aspect of the rule) would be unforeseeable—it would reach into all possible future disputes among the parties, no matter how hard it may be to predict them at the outset of the first litigation. Second, if all issues and claims must be negotiated and dealt with in a consent judgment or foregone forever, parties will be reluctant to enter into such an agreement for fear that they will "miss" something.

But, proponents of the consent-judgment-as-final judgment theory counter that the preclusive effect of a consent judgment serves several objectives. Among them, economy is achieved in the use of judicial resources, the harassment of parties avoided, and the possibility of inconsistent results is eliminated. * * *

* * *

We note that T.R. 68 is intended to encourage settlements, discourage vexatious suits, and avoid protracted litigation. See 12 Wright & Miller, *Federal Practice and Procedure*, § 3001. Therefore, the result we reach should serve those purposes.

Because we agree that if all issues and claims must be negotiated and dealt with in a consent judgment or foregone forever, parties will be reluctant to enter into such agreements, we adopt the consent-judgment-as-contract theory and hold that the preclusive effect of a consent judgment must be measured by the intent of the parties. However, it must be clear that *both* parties have agreed to reserve an issue or claim. *And,* it must be precisely stated what issues or claims are being reserved.

* * *

* * * [I]n order to insure that both parties have agreed to reserve a claim or issue[9] and that the reserved claim or issue is clearly apparent to both parties, we hold that (1) the reservation must be incorporated into the offer of judgment itself and (2) it must be an inherent part of the original complaint. Thus, for example, before a party may reserve an additional cause of action in a consent judgment, that cause of action must have been originally set out on the face of the complaint. Because Anderson did not include a claim for damages for delay in tendering the real estate in its Complaint, it is precluded from reserving such a claim in the consent judgment.[10]

* * *

* * * [T]his rule will avoid protracted litigation, since it requires plaintiffs to reserve a claim or issue both in the complaint and in the consent judgment. If we were to require such a reservation only in the consent judgment (as Anderson asks us to do here), the potential for protracted litigation would be too great. For example, in a situation where A and B have entered a consent judgment and B thinks the controversy has ended, such a rule would allow A: (1) to argue that it had no intention of ending the controversy and (2) to proceed on the alleged balance of its

---

9. Here, we are dealing with the reservation of a claim for damages. However, there may be cases where a party desires to reserve an issue or another cause of action. The same rule would apply in those situations.

10. Indiana Rules of Procedure, Trial Rule 12(B) states, in part:

" * * * When a motion to dismiss is sustained for failure to state a claim under subdivision (B)(6) of this rule the pleading may be amended once as of right pursuant to Rule 15(A) within ten [10] days after service of notice of the court's order sustaining the motion and thereafter with permission of the court pursuant to such rule. * * * "

However, Anderson may not take advantage of this rule by amending the complaint, then arguing it has met the requirements set out by this opinion. Obviously, the claim or issue must be in the complaint at the time the parties reach an agreement or enter a judgment.

claim. This could potentially allow the litigation to continue on and on through the years.

But, under the rule we have set forth here, A would not be allowed to make such a claim unless it was shown that a reservation was made in A's complaint and in the consent judgment. In this way, courts can be assured it was also B's intention to continue the litigation.

Therefore, we reverse and remand to the trial court, with instructions to enter a judgment on the offer of judgment and to grant Hanover's motion to dismiss.

Reversed and remanded.

Notes and Questions

1. Should the agreement between Hanover and Anderson be considered a court judgment, or is it more properly characterized as a contract? If it is merely a contract, should the intent of the parties as to its preclusive effect be dispositive? Did the parties require the approval of the court in the form of a judgment to make a new contract? Do you agree that a rule that did not make the intent of the parties dispositive would have the effect of discouraging consent judgments? For a discussion of consent judgments, see Easterbrook, *Justice and Contract in Consent Judgments*, 1987 U. Chi. Legal F. 19.

2. Even if a consent decree has claim preclusive effect, should it also have issue preclusive effect? Doesn't collateral estoppel doctrine require that an issue be "actually litigated"? In ARIZONA v. CALIFORNIA, 530 U.S. 392, 120 S.Ct. 2304, 147 L.Ed.2d 374 (2000), the Supreme Court explained:

> * * * [S]ettlements ordinarily occasion no *issue preclusion* (sometimes called collateral estoppel), unless it is clear * * * that the parties intend their agreement to have such an effect. "In most circumstances, it is recognized that consent agreements ordinarily are intended to preclude any further litigation on the claim presented but are not intended to preclude further litigation on any of the issues presented. Thus consent judgments ordinarily support claim preclusion but not issue preclusion."
> * * * This differentiation is grounded in basic res judicata doctrine. It is the general rule that issue preclusion attaches only "[w]hen an issue of fact or law is actually litigated and determined by a valid and final judgment, and the determination is essential to the judgment." Restatement (Second) of Judgments, § 27 * * * (1982). "In the case of a judgment entered by confession, consent, or default, none of the issues is actually litigated. * * *."

Id. at 414, 120 S.Ct. at 2319, 147 L.Ed.2d at 395–96 (internal citation omitted).

3. Should a final judgment be stripped of its preclusive effect if both parties consent to that result on appeal? A stipulated reversal allows parties seeking to facilitate settlement during the pendency of an appeal to join together in asking the appellate court to set aside a trial court judgment, rather than dismissing the appeal, thereby avoiding the preclusive effect of a final judgment. In U.S. BANCORP MORTGAGE CO. v. BONNER MALL

PARTNERSHIP, 513 U.S. 18, 115 S.Ct. 386, 130 L.Ed.2d 233 (1994), the Supreme Court unanimously denied petitioner's motion to vacate a court of appeals judgment in a case that had become moot by reason of settlement after certiorari was sought, but the Court recognized that vacatur could be granted in "extraordinary circumstances." Id. at 29, 115 S. Ct. at 393, 130 L. Ed. 2d at 244. What circumstances might count as "extraordinary"?

Two years earlier, in NEARY v. REGENTS OF THE UNIVERSITY OF CALIFORNIA, 3 Cal.4th 273, 10 Cal.Rptr.2d 859, 834 P.2d 119 (1992), the California Supreme Court had held that stipulated reversals are consistent with the policy of peaceful settlements and should be granted *absent* a showing of extraordinary circumstances warranting an exception to this general rule. What did the California court mean by "extraordinary circumstances"? Why is it appropriate to permit a losing defendant to cloak himself against collateral estoppel in later cases, thereby denying subsequent plaintiffs the benefit of having complex liability issues resolved in the initial litigation? The California legislature during its 1999–2000 session modified California Code of Civil Procedure § 128(a)(8) to provide that an appellate court shall not permit a stipulated reversal absent a finding of two specified conditions:

> unless the court finds both of the following: (a) there is no reasonable possibility that the interests of nonparties or the public will be adversely affected by the reversal; and (b) that the reasons of the parties for requesting reversal outweigh the erosion of public trust that may result from the nullification of a judgment and the risk that the availability of stipulated reversal will reduce the incentive for pretrial settlement.

See Martin & Schatz, *Reverse Course*, 25 L.A. Law. 24 (Feb. 2003) (discussing trend in denial of stipulated reversal requests post-amendment of Section 128(a)(8)). Are there other circumstances that might support vacatur?

For a discussion of *Bancorp* and *Neary*, see Resnik, *Whose Judgment? Vacating Judgments, Preferences for Settlement, and the Role of Adjudication at the Close of the Twentieth Century*, 41 UCLA L. Rev. 1471 (1994).

4. Suppose that rather than settling the dispute in *Hanover*, the parties merely stipulated most of the material facts concerning the lease agreement. The case went to trial, further factual findings were made, and a decision was rendered for Hanover against Anderson. Should the admissions in those stipulations be available in a subsequent suit between the parties? What if the suit is between another plaintiff and Hanover, and the complaint is based upon the same alleged breach of the lease? What light does the last sentence of Rule 36(b) shed on this problem? Do stipulated facts constitute an "adjudication on the merits"?

5. Modern rules of procedure allow courts to dismiss an action and enter judgment at various stages of a litigation prior to a final verdict. See, e.g., Federal Rule 12. These dismissals are not based upon the agreement of the parties, and, indeed, usually are opposed vigorously. Should a judgment consented to by the parties be considered more "on the merits" than an involuntary dismissal or judgment? Why?

2. JUDGMENTS OF NONJUDICIAL TRIBUNALS

HOLMBERG v. STATE, DIVISION OF RISK MANAGEMENT

Supreme Court of Alaska, 1990.
796 P.2d 823.

MOORE, JUSTICE.

Karen Holmberg asks us to reverse the Alaska Workers' Compensation Board ("AWCB") decision denying her permanent total disability benefits on the ground that a later decision of the Public Employees Retirement Board ("PERB") conclusively determined that she was not physically able to perform her duties as an employee of the State of Alaska. * * *

* * *

I.

Karen Holmberg began working for the State of Alaska, Division of Risk Management ("Risk Management") in 1979. She has a history of back injuries dating to the early 1960s. * * *

* * *

* * * On February 18, 1988, AWCB awarded Holmberg temporary total disability benefits, but denied her claim for permanent total disability benefits. Holmberg appealed AWCB's denial of permanent total disability benefits to the superior court in March 1988.

Holmberg also sought disability benefits from [the Public Employees Retirement System ("PERS")]. The Division of Retirement and Benefits ("Retirement and Benefits"), which administers PERS, awarded her non-occupational disability benefits. However, the Disability Review Board denied her claim for occupational disability benefits. Holmberg appealed this initial decision to PERB. On April 20, 1988, after AWCB had denied her claim for permanent total disability benefits, PERB found that Holmberg was permanently and totally disabled as a result of accidents at work, and accordingly, awarded her occupational disability benefits.

Holmberg supplemented the record in her appeal from the prior AWCB decision with the new PERB decision. In the proceedings before the superior court, Holmberg argued that the AWCB decision should be reversed because of the preclusive effect of the later PERB decision. The superior court affirmed the AWCB decision and Holmberg appealed.

II.

Holmberg's primary contention is that PERB's factual determination that she was physically unable to perform her duties at Risk Management should be given binding effect in this appeal of the AWCB decision against her.[2] * * *

* * *

Although res judicata principles were developed in judicial settings, they "may be applied to adjudicative determinations made by administrative agencies." Jeffries v. Glacier State Tel. Co., 604 P.2d 4, 8 (Alaska 1979) * * *. Of course, "[a]n administrative decision commands preclusive effects only if it resulted from a procedure that seems an adequate substitute for judicial procedure." * * * [18 Wright, Miller and Cooper, Federal Practice and Procedure § 4475].

Recently, we held that AWCB decisions may have preclusive effect. * * * We see no reason why PERB decisions should not also be given preclusive effect. First, like AWCB proceedings, PERB hearings include many of the procedural safeguards of a judicial hearing including the right to introduce evidence, call witnesses, and cross-examine opposing witnesses. * * * Second there is no indication in the PERS enabling statute * * * that a PERB determination should not preclude an independent judicial determination.

The state does not contend that PERB decisions should not be given preclusive effect. Rather, the state argues that preclusive effect should not be given to PERB determinations in AWCB proceedings. We have not addressed the question how res judicata principles apply between different agencies. The Supreme Court has held that litigation conducted before one agency or official is generally binding on another agency or official of the same government because officers of the same government are in privity with each other. Sunshine Anthracite Coal Co. v. Adkins, 310 U.S. 381, 402–03, 60 S. Ct. 907, 916–17, 84 L. Ed. 1263 (1940). The Court stated that "[t]he crucial point is whether or not in the earlier litigation the representative of the United States had authority to represent its interests in a final adjudication of the issue in controversy." 310 U.S. at 403, 60 S. Ct. at 917. * * *

The United States Court of Appeals has applied this authority principle in appropriate cases. In Safir v. Gibson, 432 F.2d 137 (2d Cir.), cert. denied, 400 U.S. 850, 91 S. Ct. 57, 27 L. Ed. 2d 88 (1970), the court relied on the authority principle in holding that the Federal Maritime Commission's determination that the rates of a conference of common carriers were unfair and unjustly discriminatory precluded the independent Maritime Administration from relitigating the issue. * * * In Porter & Dietsch, Inc. v. FTC, 605 F.2d 294 (7th Cir. 1979), cert. denied, 445 U.S. 950, 100 S. Ct. 1597, 63 L. Ed. 2d 784 (1980), the court refused to give preclusive

---

2. * * * Holmberg recognizes that the question whether she was disabled for purposes of PERS is not the same question as whether she was disabled for purposes of the Alaska Workers' Compensation Act. * * * Holmberg limits her collateral estoppel claim to the narrower factual question whether she was physically able to work at Risk Management. However, she maintains that the resolution of this factual issue in her favor is tantamount to a finding that she was permanently and totally disabled for purposes of workers' compensation because the state conceded as much in the AWCB proceeding.

effect to a Postal Service factual determination concerning the safety of a diet pill in a Federal Trade Commission proceeding. The court found that there was "a clear and convincing need for a new determination of the issue ... because of the potential impact of the determination on the public interest or the interests of persons not themselves parties to the initial action." 605 F.2d at 300.

The court's holding in *Porter & Dietsch* illustrates the principle that preclusion may be defeated by finding such an important difference in the functions of different agencies that one does not have authority to represent the interests of the other. * * *

* * *

In this case, it does not appear that PERB has any more expertise than AWCB in making factual determinations of a person's physical ability to work at a particular job. Therefore, there is no affirmative reason why the PERB decision should be given preclusive effect as * * * [the agency's] decision was in *Safir*. The state makes several arguments why granting PERB determinations preclusive effect in AWCB proceedings would be inconsistent with the Alaska Workers Compensation Act * * * [but this argument] stems from the false premise that Holmberg seeks to preclude AWCB's ultimate disability determination instead of its factual determination that Holmberg was physically able to perform her job duties.[3]

The state argues that the different functions of the workers compensation system and PERS prevent the application of collateral estoppel. * * * [The court noted that the disability standards for PERB and AWCB decisions differ, but went on to state] * * * they provide no substantial reason why AWCB should be allowed to relitigate the narrow factual question whether Holmberg is physically able to continue performing her job with Risk Management. Although the value of collateral estoppel may be low in light of the [different] * * * disability inquiry under AWCA, that is not a substantial reason to allow relitigation.* * *

* * *

III.

[The court then determined whether the two agencies are in privity with each other as to allow issue preclusion against a nonparty to a judgment.]

* * *

---

3. For example, the State's argument that collateral estoppel is not properly invoked between two independent tribunals which have statutory discretion to fashion separate remedies confuses issue preclusion with claim preclusion. * * * AWCB's authority to fashion a separate remedy is no argument against precluding the relitigation of identical factual issues decided in an earlier PERB proceeding. * * *

B.

Our holding that the state is not in privity with PERS is sufficient to deny affording any preclusive effect to the PERB decision as against the state. However, even if the state and PERS were in privity, the PERB decision would not preclude any issues raised in the earlier AWCB proceeding because the PERB decision was not the first final judgment addressing those issues. Holmberg observes that "[t]his case presents the collateral estoppel issue in a somewhat unusual procedural context." AWCB reached its decision first. While that decision was on appeal, PERB entered a contrary decision which was not appealed. Holmberg argues that the PERB decision was the first final judgment for the res judicata purposes and therefore precludes AWCB's contrary decision because the AWCB decision was appealed.

We disagree. A final judgment retains all of its res judicata effects pending resolution of an appeal of the judgment. * * * This rule respects the principle of repose inherent in the doctrine of res judicata. If a judgment was denied its res judicata effects merely because an appeal was pending, a litigant could refile an identical case in another trial court creating duplicative litigation. This case well illustrates the point. Having lost on the issue whether she was physically able to perform her job duties in the AWCB proceeding, Holmberg appealed the decision and then successfully relitigated the issue before PERB. Retirement and Benefits did not argue that PERB was precluded from relitigating the issue that AWCB already had decided. Now Holmberg asks us to reverse the earlier AWCB determination simply because of the later PERB determination. * * * To reward relitigation of an issue by reversing the original determination is completely at odds with the purpose of collateral estoppel to prevent relitigation of issues that already have been decided.

* * *

In this case, the AWCB decision was the first final judgment even though it was appealed. The later PERB determination that Holmberg was not physically able to perform her duties at Risk Management cannot preclude AWCB's earlier contrary determination. Indeed, if the other requirements of collateral estoppel were satisfied, Retirement and Benefits could have precluded Holmberg from relitigating the issue already decided by AWCB.

* * *

The decision of the superior court is AFFIRMED.

NOTE AND QUESTION

In evaluating whether to give preclusive effect to the PERB judgment, is it significant that the agency used "judicial" procedures to reach its decisions?

What procedures might be considered critical to ensure the quality of judgment deserving of issue preclusive effect?

SECTION E.   PERSONS BENEFITTED AND PERSONS BOUND BY PRECLUSION

1.   THE TRADITIONAL MODEL

The traditional rule of issue preclusion was that persons benefitted from a prior judgment only if they also were bound by it. "This rule, known as the rule of mutuality, established a pleasing symmetry—a judgment was binding only on parties and persons in privity with them, and a judgment could be invoked only by parties and their privies." 18A Wright, Miller & Cooper, Federal Practice and Procedure: Jurisdiction and Related Matters 2d § 4463. The modern trend has been an erosion in the requirement of mutuality—"followed more recently by second thoughts about whether the erosion is sufficiently justified." Shapiro, Civil Procedure: Preclusion in Civil Actions 102–03 (2001).

Indemnification relations provided the earliest basis for an exception from the rule of mutuality. See First Nat. Bank v. City Nat. Bank, 182 Mass. 130, 65 N.E. 24 (1902). The policy rationale was rooted in the indemnification obligation:

> * * * [D]enial of preclusion would force an impossible choice between unacceptable alternatives. If a second action can be maintained against the indemnitee, either the indemnitee must be allowed to assert his right of indemnification or the right must be defeated by the judgment in favor of the indemnitor. To allow the right of indemnification would be to destroy the victory won by the indemnitor in the first action. To deny the right of indemnification would be to destroy the indemnitee's right by the result of an action in which he took no part.

18A Wright, Miller & Cooper, Federal Practice and Procedure: Jurisdiction and Related Matters 2d § 4463. As you read the remainder of this Section, consider whether it is appropriate in circumstances other than the indemnification relation to allow a nonparty to take advantage of a favorable judgment when that nonparty would not have been subject to preclusion if the prior judgment had been unfavorable to him. Courts have shown an increasing willingness to permit preclusion (often referred to as nonmutual estoppel) in various other circumstances. Conversely, would it ever be appropriate to bind nonparties by an unfavorable judgment?

2. THE DECLINE OF THE MUTUALITY DOCTRINE

BERNHARD v. BANK OF AMERICA NAT. TRUST & SAV. ASS'N
Supreme Court of California, 1942.
19 Cal.2d 807, 122 P.2d 892.

TRAYNOR, JUSTICE.

In June, 1933, Mrs. Clara Sather, an elderly woman, made her home with Mr. and Mrs. Charles O. Cook in San Dimas, California. Because of her failing health, she authorized Mr. Cook and Dr. Joseph Zeiler to make drafts jointly against her commercial account in the Security First National Bank of Los Angeles. On August 24, 1933, Mr. Cook opened a commercial account at the First National Bank of San Dimas in the name of "Clara Sather by Charles O. Cook." * * * Thereafter, a number of checks drawn by Cook and Zeiler on Mrs. Sather's commercial account in Los Angeles were deposited in the San Dimas account * * *.

On October 26, 1933, a teller from the Los Angeles Bank called on Mrs. Sather at her request to assist in transferring her money from the Los Angeles Bank to the San Dimas Bank. In the presence of this teller, the cashier of the San Dimas Bank, Mr. Cook, and her physician, Mrs. Sather signed by mark an authorization directing the Security First National Bank of Los Angeles to transfer the balance of her savings account in the amount of $4,155.68 to the First National Bank of San Dimas * * * "for credit to the account of Mrs. Clara Sather." The order was credited by the San Dimas Bank to the account of "Clara Sather by Charles O. Cook." Cook withdrew the entire balance from that account and opened a new account in the same bank in the name of himself and his wife. * * *

Mrs. Sather died in November, 1933. Cook qualified as executor of the estate and proceeded with its administration. After a lapse of several years he filed an account at the instance of the probate court accompanied by his resignation. The account made no mention of the money transferred by Mrs. Sather to the San Dimas Bank; and Helen Bernhard * * * [and other] beneficiaries under Mrs. Sather's will, filed objections to the account for this reason. After a hearing on the objections the court settled the account, and as part of its order declared that the decedent during her lifetime had made a gift to Charles O. Cook of the amount of the deposit in question.

After Cook's discharge, Helen Bernhard was appointed administratrix with the will annexed. She instituted this action against defendant, the Bank of America, successor to the San Dimas Bank, seeking to recover the deposit on the ground that the bank was indebted to the estate for this amount because Mrs. Sather never authorized its withdrawal. In addition to a general denial, defendant pleaded two affirmative defenses: (1) That the money on deposit was paid out to Charles O. Cook with the consent of

Mrs. Sather and (2) that this fact is res judicata by virtue of the finding of the probate court * * *. The trial court * * * gave judgment for defendant on the ground that Cook's ownership of the money was conclusively established by the finding of the probate court. * * *

Plaintiff contends that the doctrine of res judicata does not apply because the defendant who is asserting the plea was not a party to the previous action nor in privity with a party to that action and because there is no mutuality of estoppel.

* * *

Many courts have stated the facile formula that the plea of res judicata is available only when there is privity and mutuality of estoppel. * * * Under the requirement of privity, only parties to the former judgment or their privies may take advantage of or be bound by it. * * * A party in this connection is one who is "directly interested in the subject matter, and had a right to make defense, or to control the proceeding, and to appeal from the judgment." * * * A privy is one who, after rendition of the judgment, has acquired an interest in the subject matter affected by the judgment through or under one of the parties, as by inheritance, succession, or purchase. * * * The estoppel is mutual if the one taking advantage of the earlier adjudication would have been bound by it, had it gone against him. * * *

The criteria for determining who may assert a plea of res judicata differ fundamentally from the criteria for determining against whom a plea of res judicata may be asserted. The requirements of due process of law forbid the assertion of a plea of res judicata against a party unless he was bound by the earlier litigation in which the matter was decided. * * * He is bound by that litigation only if he has been a party thereto or in privity with a party thereto. * * * There is no compelling reason, however, for requiring that the party asserting the plea of res judicata must have been a party, or in privity with a party, to the earlier litigation.

No satisfactory rationalization has been advanced for the requirement of mutuality. Just why a party who was not bound by a previous action should be precluded from asserting it as res judicata against a party who was bound by it is difficult to comprehend. * * * Many courts have abandoned the requirement of mutuality and confined the requirement of privity to the party against whom the plea of res judicata is asserted. * * * The commentators are almost unanimously in accord. * * * The courts of most jurisdictions have in effect accomplished the same result by recognizing a broad exception to the requirements of mutuality and privity, namely, that they are not necessary where the liability of the defendant asserting the plea of res judicata is dependent upon or derived from the liability of one who was exonerated in an earlier suit brought by the same plaintiff upon the same facts. * * * Typical examples of such derivative liability are master and servant, principal and agent, and indemnitor and indemnitee. Thus, if a plaintiff sues a servant for injuries caused by the servant's alleged negligence within the scope of his employment, a judgment against the plaintiff of [sic] the grounds that the servant was not negligent can be pleaded by the master as res judicata if he is subsequently sued by the same plaintiff for the same injuries. Conversely, if the plaintiff first sues the master, a judgment against the plaintiff on the grounds that the servant was not negligent can be pleaded by the servant as res judicata if he is subsequently sued by the plaintiff. In each of these situations the party asserting the plea of res judicata was not a party to the previous action nor in privity with such a party * * *. Likewise, the estoppel is not mutual since the party asserting the plea, not having been a party or in privity with a party to the former action, would not have been bound by it had it been decided the other way. The cases justify this exception on the ground that it would be unjust to permit one who has had his day in court to reopen identical issues by merely switching adversaries.

In determining the validity of a plea of res judicata three questions are pertinent: Was the issue decided in the prior adjudication identical with the one presented in the action in question? Was there a final judgment on the merits? Was the party against whom the plea is asserted a party or in privity with a party to the prior adjudication?

* * * Since the issue as to the ownership of the money is identical with the issue raised in the probate proceeding, and since the order of the probate court settling the executor's account was a final adjudication of this issue on the merits * * *, it remains only to determine whether the plaintiff in the present action was a party or in privity with a party to the earlier proceeding. The plaintiff has brought the present action in the capacity of administratrix of the estate. In this capacity she represents the very same persons and interests that were represented in the earlier hearing on the executor's account. In that proceeding plaintiff and the other legatees who objected to the executor's account represented the estate of the decedent. They were seeking not a personal recovery but, like the plaintiff in the present action, as administratrix, a recovery for the benefit of the legatees and creditors of the estate, all of whom were bound by the order settling the account. * * *

The judgment is affirmed.

———

Bernhard focuses on whether defendant can bar plaintiff from relitigating an issue that was decided against plaintiff in an earlier lawsuit involving a different defendant. Commentators call this use of preclusion "nonmutual defensive collateral estoppel." For a classic discussion, see Currie, *Civil Procedure: The Tempest Brews*, 53 Cal. L. Rev. 25, 38–46 (1965). See also Currie, *Mutuality of Collateral Estoppel—Limits of the* Bernhard *Doctrine*, 9 Stan. L. Rev. 281 (1957).

———

In BLONDER–TONGUE LABORATORIES, INC. v. UNIVERSITY OF ILLINOIS FOUNDATION, 402 U.S. 313, 91 S.Ct. 1434, 28 L.Ed.2d

788 (1971), a patent infringement action, the Supreme Court first began to abrogate the mutuality requirement in the federal system. The Court expressed the following views on the propriety of nonmutual preclusion:

> The cases and authorities discussed * * * connect erosion of the mutuality requirement to the goal of limiting relitigation of issues where that can be achieved without compromising fairness in particular cases. The courts have often discarded the rule while commenting on crowded dockets and long delays preceding trial. Authorities differ on whether the public interest in efficient judicial administration is a sufficient ground in and of itself for abandoning mutuality, but it is clear that more than crowded dockets is involved. The broader question is whether it is any longer tenable to afford a litigant more than one full and fair opportunity for judicial resolution of the same issue. The question in these terms includes as part of the calculus the effect on judicial administration, but it also encompasses the concern exemplified by Bentham's reference to the gaming table in his attack on the principle of mutuality of estoppel. In any lawsuit where a defendant, because of the mutuality principle, is forced to present a complete defense on the merits to a claim which the plaintiff has fully litigated and lost in a prior action, there is an arguable misallocation of resources. To the extent the defendant in the second suit may not win by asserting, without contradiction, that the plaintiff had fully and fairly, but unsuccessfully, litigated the same claim in the prior suit, the defendant's time and money are diverted from alternative uses—productive or otherwise—to relitigation of a decided issue. And, still assuming that the issue was resolved correctly in the first suit, there is reason to be concerned about the plaintiff's allocation of resources. Permitting repeated litigation of the same issue as long as the supply of unrelated defendants holds out reflects either the aura of the gaming table or "a lack of discipline and of disinterestedness on the part of the lower courts, hardly a worthy or wise basis for fashioning rules of procedure." Kerotest Mfg. Co. v. C-O-Two Co. Fire Equipment Co., 342 U.S. 180, 185, 72 S.Ct. 219, 222, 96 L.Ed. 200 (1952). Although neither judges, the parties, nor the adversary system performs perfectly in all cases, the requirement of determining whether the party against whom an estoppel is asserted had a full and fair opportunity to litigate is a most significant safeguard.

Some litigants—those who never appeared in a prior action—may not be collaterally estopped without litigating the issue. They have never had a chance to present their evidence and arguments on the claim. Due process prohibits estopping them despite one or more existing adjudications of the identical issue which stand squarely against their position. * * * Also, the authorities have been more willing to permit a defendant in a second suit to invoke an estoppel against a plaintiff who lost on the same claim in an earlier suit than they have been to allow a plaintiff in the second suit to use offensively a judgment obtained by a different plaintiff in a prior suit against the same defendant. But the case before us involves neither due process nor "offensive use" questions. Rather, it depends on the considerations weighing for and against permitting a patent holder to sue on his patent after it has once been held invalid following opportunity for full and fair trial.

Id. at 328–33, 91 S.Ct. at 1442–43, 28 L.Ed.2d at 799–800.

The Court emphasized that the district court retained discretion to accept or reject a plea of collateral estoppel:

> * * * [W]e do not suggest, without legislative guidance, that a plea of estoppel by an infringement or royalty suit defendant must automatically be accepted once the defendant in support of his plea identifies the issue in suit as the identical question finally decided against the patentee or one of his privies in previous litigation. * * * Rather, the patentee-plaintiff must be permitted to demonstrate, if he can, that he did not have "a fair opportunity procedurally, substantively and evidentially to pursue his claim the first time." * * * This element in the estoppel decision will comprehend, we believe, the important concerns about the complexity of patent litigation and the posited hazard that the prior proceedings were seriously defective.

> Determining whether a patentee has had a full and fair chance to litigate the validity of his patent in an earlier case is of necessity not a simple matter. In addition to * * * considerations of choice of forum and incentive to litigate * * *, certain other factors immediately emerge. For example, if the issue is nonobviousness, appropriate inquiries would be whether the first validity determination purported to employ the [appropriate legal] standards * * *; whether the opinions filed by the District Court and the reviewing court, if any, indicate that the prior case was one of those relatively rare instances where the courts wholly failed to grasp the technical subject matter and issues in suit; and whether without fault of his own the patentee was deprived of crucial evidence or witnesses in the first litigation. But as so often is the case, no one set of facts, no one collection of words or phrases will provide an automatic formula for proper rulings on estoppel pleas. In the end, decision will necessarily rest on the trial courts' sense of justice and equity.

Id. at 332–34, 91 S.Ct. at 1445, 28 L.Ed.2d at 802.

The Court underscored that although relaxing the mutuality requirement in patent cases would produce cost savings for the federal courts, this factor alone would not be dispositive of the question:

> * * *[A]lthough patent trials are only a small portion of the total amount of litigation in the federal courts, they tend to be of disproportionate length. * * *

> * * * [I]t is clear that abrogation of [the mutuality rule in patent cases] * * * will save *some* judicial time if even a few relatively lengthy patent suits may be fairly disposed of on pleas of estoppel.

More fundamentally, while the cases do discuss reduction in dockets as an effect of elimination of the mutuality requirement, they do not purport to hold that predictions about the actual amount of judicial time that will be saved under such a holding control decision of that question.

Id. at 348–49, 91 S.Ct. at 1452–53, 28 L.Ed.2d at 810–11.

————

PARKLANE HOSIERY CO. v. SHORE

Supreme Court of the United States, 1979.
439 U.S. 322, 99 S.Ct. 645, 58 L.Ed.2d 552.

Certiorari to the United States Court of Appeals for the Second Circuit.

Mr. Justice Stewart delivered the opinion of the Court.

* * *

The respondent brought this stockholder's class action against the petitioners in a federal district court. The complaint alleged that the petitioners * * * had issued a materially false and misleading proxy statement in connection with a merger. * * * The complaint sought damages, rescission of the merger, and recovery of costs.

Before this action came to trial, the SEC filed suit against the same defendants in a federal district court, alleging that the proxy statement that had been issued by Parklane was materially false and misleading in essentially the same respects as those that had been alleged in the respondent's complaint. Injunctive relief was requested. After a four-day trial, the District Court found that the proxy statement was materially false and misleading in the respects alleged, and entered a declaratory judgment to that effect. * * * The Court of Appeals for the Second Circuit affirmed * * *.

The respondent in the present case then moved for partial summary judgment against the petitioners, asserting that the petitioners were collaterally estopped from relitigating the issues that had been resolved against them in the action brought by the SEC. The District Court denied the motion on the ground that such an application of collateral estoppel would deny the petitioners their Seventh Amendment right to a jury trial. The Court of Appeals for the Second Circuit reversed * * *. Because of an intercircuit conflict * * * we granted certiorari.

I

The threshold question to be considered is whether, quite apart from the right to a jury trial under the Seventh Amendment, the petitioners can be precluded from relitigating facts resolved adversely to them in a prior equitable proceeding with another party under the general law of collateral estoppel. Specifically, we must determine whether a litigant who was not a party to a prior judgment may nevertheless use that judgment "offensively" to prevent a defendant from relitigating issues resolved in the earlier proceeding.[4]

* * *

B

The *Blonder-Tongue* case involved defensive use of collateral estoppel * * *. The present case, by contrast, involves offensive use of collateral estoppel—a plaintiff is seeking to estop a defendant from relitigating the issues which the defendant previously litigated and lost against another plaintiff. In both the offensive and defensive use situations, the party against whom estoppel is asserted has litigated and lost in an earlier action. Nevertheless, several reasons have been advanced why the two situations should be treated differently.

First, offensive use of collateral estoppel does not promote judicial economy in the same manner as defensive use does. Defensive use of collateral estoppel precludes a plaintiff from relitigating identical issues by merely "switching adversaries." * * * Thus defensive collateral estoppel gives a plaintiff a strong incentive to join all potential defendants in the first action if possible. Offensive use of collateral estoppel, on the other hand, creates precisely the opposite incentive. Since a plaintiff will be able to rely on a previous judgment against a defendant but will not be bound by that judgment if the defendant wins, the plaintiff has every incentive to adopt a "wait and see" attitude, in the hope that the first action by another plaintiff will result in a favorable judgment. * * * Thus offensive use of collateral estoppel will likely increase rather than decrease the total amount of litigation, since potential plaintiffs will have everything to gain and nothing to lose by not intervening in the first action.[13]

A second argument against offensive use of collateral estoppel is that it may be unfair to a defendant. If a defendant in the first action is sued for small or nominal damages, he may have little incentive to defend vigorously, particularly if future suits are not foreseeable. * * * Allowing offensive collateral estoppel may also be unfair to a defendant if the judgment relied upon as a basis for the estoppel is itself inconsistent with one or more previous judgments in favor of the defendant. Still another situation where it might be unfair to apply offensive estoppel is where the second action affords the defendant procedural opportunities unavailable in the first action that could readily cause a different result.[15]

---

4. In this context, offensive use of collateral estoppel occurs when the plaintiff seeks to foreclose the defendant from litigating an issue the defendant has previously litigated unsuccessfully in an action with another party. Defensive use occurs when a defendant seeks to prevent a plaintiff from asserting a claim the plaintiff has previously litigated and lost against another defendant.

13. The *Restatement (Second) of Judgments* (Tent. Draft No. 2, 1975) § 88(3), provides that application of collateral estoppel may be denied if the party asserting it "could have effected joinder in the first action between himself and his present adversary."

15. If, for example, the defendant in the first action was forced to defend in an inconvenient forum and therefore was unable to engage in full scale discovery or call witnesses, application of

C

We have concluded that the preferable approach for dealing with these problems in the federal courts is not to preclude the use of offensive collateral estoppel, but to grant trial courts broad discretion to determine when it should be applied. The general rule should be that in cases where a plaintiff could easily have joined in the earlier action or where, either for the reasons discussed above or for other reasons, the application of offensive estoppel would be unfair to a defendant, a trial judge should not allow the use of offensive collateral estoppel.

In the present case, however, none of the circumstances that might justify reluctance to allow the offensive use of collateral estoppel is present. The application of offensive collateral estoppel will not here reward a private plaintiff who could have joined in the previous action, since the respondent probably could not have joined in the injunctive action brought by the SEC even had he so desired.[17] Similarly, there is no unfairness to the petitioners in applying offensive collateral estoppel in this case. First, in light of the serious allegations made in the SEC's complaint against the petitioners, as well as the foreseeability of subsequent private suits that typically follow a successful government judgment, the petitioners had every incentive to litigate the SEC lawsuit fully and vigorously. Second, the judgment in the Commission action was not inconsistent with any previous decision. Finally, there will in the respondent's action be no procedural opportunities available to the petitioner that were unavailable in the first action of a kind that might be likely to cause a different result.[19]

We conclude, therefore, that none of the considerations that would justify a refusal to allow the use of offensive collateral estoppel is present in this case. Since the petitioners received a "full and fair" opportunity to litigate their claims in the SEC action, the contemporary law of collateral estoppel leads inescapably to the conclusion that the petitioners are collaterally estopped from relitigating the question of whether the proxy statements were materially false and misleading.

* * *

---

offensive collateral estoppel may be unwarranted. Indeed, differences in available procedures may sometimes justify not allowing a prior judgment to have estoppel effect in a subsequent action even between the same parties, or where defensive estoppel is asserted against a plaintiff who has litigated and lost. The problem of unfairness is particularly acute in cases of offensive estoppel, however, because the defendant against whom estoppel is asserted typically will not have chosen the forum in the first action. See *Restatement (Second) of Judgments* (Tentative Draft No. 2, 1975) § 88(2) and Comment *d*.

17. SEC v. Everest Management Corp., 475 F.2d 1236, 1240 (CA2) ("[T]he complicating effect of the additional issues and the additional parties outweighs any advantage of a single disposition of the common issues"). Moreover, consolidation of a private action with one brought by the SEC without its consent is prohibited by statute. 15 U.S.C. § 78u(g).

19. It is true, of course, that the petitioners in the present action would be entitled to a jury trial of the issues bearing on whether the proxy statement was materially false and misleading had the SEC action never been brought—a matter to be discussed in Part II of this opinion. But the presence or absence of a jury as factfinder is basically neutral, quite unlike, for example, the necessity of defending the first lawsuit in an inconvenient forum.

The judgment of the Court of Appeals is

Affirmed.

[A dissenting opinion by MR. JUSTICE REHNQUIST is omitted.]

NOTES AND QUESTIONS

1. Offensive nonmutual collateral estoppel is the term used to describe a case in which "a plaintiff seeks to preclude a defendant from relitigating an issue which the defendant previously litigated and lost against a different plaintiff." 47 Am Jur. 2d Judgments § 647 (2d ed. 2004). How does this situation differ from the defensive use of collateral estoppel in *Bernhard* and *Blonder-Tongue*?

2. *Parklane* permits the offensive use of nonmutual issue preclusion by a nonparty against a party, but limits its application. One limitation involves prior judgments that are inconsistent with each other. See Hynes, *Inconsistent Verdicts, Issue Preclusion, and Settlement in the Presence of Judicial Bias*, 2 U. Chi. L. Sch. Roundtable 663, 664 (1995). Consider the justification for this limitation in the context of the following problem: A train accident injures fifty passengers. Each of these passengers files a separate negligence action against the railroad. The railroad prevails in the first twenty-five suits to reach judgment, but loses the twenty-sixth. How should the twenty-sixth judgment affect the remaining suits? See Currie, *Mutuality of Collateral Estoppel: The Limits of the* Bernhard *Doctrine*, 9 Stan. L. Rev. 281 (1957).

How might your answer to this question change if the prior twenty-five cases all had been litigated in a court of limited jurisdiction, such as a small-claims court, and if the twenty-sixth judgment was rendered by a court of general jurisdiction? How does this variation on the hypothetical differ from the issue of whether a judgment by a court of limited jurisdiction should itself preclude the relitigation of certain issues?

Currie's hypothetical was designed to highlight the aberrant quality of the twenty-sixth judgment. Yet there is no reason that this "aberrant" result might not have been reached in the first trial rather than the twenty-sixth. If the holding against the railroad had been rendered in the first case, nonmutual estoppel would have been available to the remaining forty-nine passengers. In short, although any single decision may be an anomaly, a single decision still can have preclusive effect. See, e.g., Harrison v. Celotex Corp., 583 F.Supp. 1497 (E.D. Tenn. 1984).

3. What factors other than a prior inconsistent judgment might persuade a court not to accept a plea of offensive nonmutual issue preclusion?

(a) What if before a case settles it yields a judicial finding that conflicts with a prior adjudication of the same issue? Such a finding may result, for example, when a motion to dismiss is denied before a settlement is reached. Can that finding create sufficient inconsistency to block offensive issue preclusion? See Jack Faucett Assocs., Inc. v. American Telephone & Telegraph Co., 744 F.2d 118 (D.C. Cir. 1984), certiorari denied 469 U.S. 1196, 105 S.Ct. 980, 83 L.Ed.2d 982 (1985).

(b) What if a prior judgment has been affirmed on appeal, but in the course of its affirmance, the Circuit Court holds that one of the trial judge's evidentiary rulings was erroneous, but harmless? Should the presence of even "harmless" error in the rulings upon whose findings a second court was being urged to rely be an obstacle to offensive issue preclusion?

(c) What if the prior judgment is a guilty verdict? Obviously, since plaintiff in a subsequent civil action did not have the opportunity to join in the criminal case, the concern that plaintiff will bring repetitious litigation is not present. On the other hand, are the issues necessary to resolve the civil case the same as those that are central to the criminal case? Does the criminal defendant have the same range of discovery as a civil litigant?

(d) What if the prior judgment reflects a compromise verdict?

4. Suits against the federal government represent an important exception to the extension of offensive nonmutual collateral estoppel. See United States v. Mendoza, 464 U.S. 154, 104 S.Ct. 568, 78 L.Ed.2d 379 (1984). What are the policy reasons for not applying offensive nonmutual issue preclusion against the government? Should the government be able to invoke offensive nonmutual issue preclusion against a private party?

3. BINDING NONPARTIES

In MONTANA v. UNITED STATES, 440 U.S. 147, 99 S.Ct. 970, 59 L.Ed.2d 210 (1979), the Supreme Court held that when nonparties assume control over litigation in which they have a direct financial or pecuniary interest, they may be precluded from relitigating issues that the earlier suit resolved. Montana gave contractors different tax treatment depending on whether they contracted to build public or private projects. A contractor on a federal construction project brought a state-court action challenging the constitutionality of this practice. The United States directed and financed the litigation for the contractor, but it also brought a federal court action challenging the practice. After the Montana Supreme Court upheld Montana's system of taxation, the United States continued with its federal action. But Montana argued that the federal government was bound by the state-court judgment. When the case reached the United States Supreme Court, Justice Marshall, writing for the Court, observed that "although not a party, the United States plainly had a sufficient laboring oar in the conduct of the state-court litigation to actuate principles of estoppel." Id. at 154–55, 99 S.Ct. at 974, 59 L.Ed.2d at 217–18.

Montana thus accorded preclusive effect to an adverse judgment against a nonparty that had controlled the prior adjudication. Another exception arises where an individual agrees by contract to be bound by a judgment. See Restatement (Second) of Judgments § 40 (1982). For example, an individual might agree to accept a test case as preclusive of further litigation. See Lahav, *Bellwether Trials*, 76 Geo. Wash. L. Rev. 576 (2008). In addition, certain substantive proceedings, such as bankruptcy and probate actions, as well as class actions, will bind nonparties. These actions use special procedures to make sure due process is satisfied. See, e.g., Begleiter, *Serve the Cheerleader—Serve the World: An Analysis of Representation in Estate and Trust Proceedings and Under the Uniform Trust Code and Other Modern Trust Codes*, 43 Real Prop. Tr. & Est. L.J. 311 (2008). Should a nonparty be precluded if he stays on the sidelines of an action but his interests are litigated through an agent or proxy? Does due process require the court to make sure that the nonparty's interests have been represented adequately? What factors are relevant to that assessment?

———

TAYLOR v. STURGELL

Supreme Court of the United States, 2008.
__ U.S. __, 128 S.Ct. 2161, 171 L.Ed.2d 155.

Certiorari to the United States Court of Appeals for the District of Columbia.

JUSTICE GINSBURG delivered the opinion of the Court.

[Petitioner filed a lawsuit under the Freedom of Information Act against the Federal Aeronautics Administration ("FAA") in the District Court for the District of Columbia seeking documents related to a vintage airplane manufactured by the Fairchild Engine and Airplane Corp. Greg Herrick, petitioner's friend, had previously filed an unsuccessful suit seeking the same documents. Petitioner and Herrick had no legal relationship, and there was no evidence that petitioner controlled, financed, participated in, or had notice of Herrick's lawsuit. The District Court granted summary judgment to defendants, holding that petitioner was barred by the judgment against Herrick because his interests had been virtually represented by a party. In reaching this result, the District Court relied on the Eighth Circuit's seven-factor test that requires an identity of interests between the nonparty and the party to the judgment, and six other factors that are relevant but not required: (1) a close relationship between the present party and a party to the judgment alleged to be preclusive; (2) participation in the prior litigation by the present party; (3) the present party's apparent acquiescence to the preclusive effect of the judgment; (4) the present party's deliberate maneuvering to avoid the preclusive effect of the prior judgment; (5) adequate representation of the present party by a party to the prior adjudication; and (6) a suit raising a public law (such as a constitutional question) rather than a private law issue. The Eighth Circuit's multifactor balancing test differed from the narrower approach used by the Fourth Circuit, which precludes a nonparty only where the court has given tacit approval to a party to act on the nonparty's behalf and the party is accountable to the nonparty.]

* * *

Rejecting * * * [the approach of both the Eight and the Fourth Circuits], the D.C. Circuit announced its own five-factor test. The first two factors—"identity of interests" and "adequate representation"—are necessary but not sufficient for virtual representation. * * * In addition, at least one of three other factors must be established: "a close relationship between the present party and his putative representative," "substantial participation by the present party in the first case," or "tactical maneuvering on the part of the present party to avoid preclusion by the prior judgment." * * *

Applying this test to the record in Taylor's case, the D.C. Circuit found both of the necessary conditions for virtual representation well met. * * *

We granted certiorari * * * to resolve the disagreement among the Circuits over the permissibility and scope of preclusion based on "virtual representation." * * *

* * *

II

* * *

A person who was not a party to a suit generally has not had a "full and fair opportunity to litigate" the claims and issues settled in that suit. The application of claim and issue preclusion to nonparties thus runs up against the "deep-rooted historic tradition that everyone should have his own day in court." Richards [v. Jefferson County, 517 U.S. 793, 798, 116 S.Ct. 1761, 1766, 135 L.Ed.2d 76, 82 (1996)] * * *.

B

Though hardly in doubt, the rule against nonparty preclusion is subject to exceptions. For present purposes, the recognized exceptions can be grouped into six categories. * * *

[The Court summarized the exceptions as (1) a nonparty may agree to be bound by a judgment; (2) certain substantive relationships, traditionally referred to by the term privity, may justify preclusion of a nonparty; (3) a nonparty may be bound if its interests are represented adequately by a party to the suit, citing as examples class actions and suits by trustees and guardians; (4) a nonparty who has assumed control over a lawsuit may be precluded; (5) a nonparty who has colluded to avoid the preclusive effect of a judgment by litigating through a proxy may be bound; and (6) special statutory schemes, such as bankruptcy, or other suits that are brought only on behalf of the public at large may bind a nonparty.]

* * *

III

Reaching beyond these six established categories, some lower courts have recognized a "virtual representation" exception to the rule against nonparty preclusion. * * *

The D.C. Circuit, the FAA, and Fairchild have presented three arguments in support of an expansive doctrine of virtual representation. We find none of them persuasive.

A

[The D.C. Circuit argued that] * * * a person may be bound by a judgment if she was adequately represented by a party to the proceeding yielding that judgment. * * * But the D.C. Circuit's definition of "adequate representation" strayed from the meaning our decisions have attributed to that term.

* * * [Our precedent has] established that representation is "adequate" for purposes of nonparty preclusion only if (at a minimum) one of * * * two circumstances is present. [The Court described the two circumstances as cases in which (1) the court uses "special procedures to protect the nonparties' interests" or (2) there is "an understanding by the concerned parties that the first suit was brought in a representative capacity."] * * *

* * *

B

Fairchild and the FAA do not argue that the D.C. Circuit's virtual representation doctrine fits within any of the recognized grounds for nonparty preclusion. Rather, they ask us to abandon the attempt to delineate discrete grounds and clear rules altogether. Preclusion is in order, they contend, whenever "the relationship between a party and a non-party is 'close enough' to bring the second litigant within the judgment." * * * Courts should make the "close enough" determination, they urge, through a "heavily fact-driven" and "equitable" inquiry. * * * Only this sort of diffuse balancing, Fairchild and the FAA argue, can account for all of the situations in which nonparty preclusion is appropriate.

We reject this argument for three reasons. First, our decisions emphasize the fundamental nature of the general rule that a litigant is not bound by a judgment to which she was not a party. * * * Accordingly, we have endeavored to delineate discrete exceptions that apply in "limited circumstances." * * * Respondents' amorphous balancing test is at odds with the constrained approach to nonparty preclusion our decisions advance.

* * *

Our second reason for rejecting a broad doctrine of virtual representation rests on the limitations attending nonparty preclusion based on adequate representation. A party's representation of a nonparty is "adequate" for preclusion purposes only if, at a minimum: (1) the interests of the nonparty and her representative are aligned * * * and (2) either the party understood herself to be acting in a representative capacity or the original court took care to protect the interests of the nonparty * * *. In addition, adequate representation sometimes requires (3) notice of the original suit to the persons alleged to have been represented * * *. In the class-action context, these limitations are implemented by the procedural safeguards contained in Federal Rule * * * 23.

An expansive doctrine of virtual representation, however, would "recogniz[e], in effect, a common-law kind of class action." Tice [v. American Airlines, Inc., 162 F.3d 966], * * * 972 [(7th Cir. 1988)] * * *. That is, virtual representation would authorize preclusion based on identity of interests and some kind of relationship between parties and nonparties, shorn of the procedural protections [that are grounded in due process and] prescribed in *Hansberry* [, p. 410, supra,] * * * and Rule 23. * * *

Third, a diffuse balancing approach to nonparty preclusion would likely create more headaches than it relieves. Most obviously, it could significantly complicate the task of district courts faced in the first instance with preclusion questions. An all-things-considered balancing approach might spark wide-ranging, time-consuming, and expensive discovery tracking factors potentially relevant under seven- or five-prong tests. And after the relevant facts are established, district judges would be called upon to evaluate them under a standard that provides no firm guidance. * * * Preclusion doctrine, it should be recalled, is intended to reduce the burden of litigation on courts and parties. * * * * "In this area of the law," we agree, " 'crisp rules with sharp corners' are preferable to a round-about doctrine of opaque standards." Bittinger v. Tecumseh Products Co., 123 F.3d 877, 881 (C.A. 6 1997).

C

Finally, * * * the FAA maintains that nonparty preclusion should apply more broadly in "public-law" litigation than in "private-law" controversies. To support this position, the FAA offers two arguments. First, the FAA urges * * * the plaintiff has a reduced interest in controlling the litigation "because of the public nature of the right at issue." * * *

Taylor's FOIA action falls within * * * the [public-law] category * * *, the FAA contends, because "the duty to disclose under FOIA is owed to the public generally." * * * The Act, however, instructs agencies receiving FOIA requests to make the information available not to the public at large, but rather to the "person" making the request. * * * Thus, in contrast to * * * public-law litigation * * *, a successful FOIA action results in a grant of relief to the individual plaintiff, not a decree benefiting the public at large.

Furthermore, * * * States are free to adopt procedures limiting repetitive litigation [of public law controversies]. * * * It hardly follows, however, that *this Court* should proscribe or confine successive FOIA suits by different requesters. Indeed, Congress' provision for FOIA suits with no statutory constraint on successive actions counsels against judicial imposition of constraints through extraordinary application of the common law of preclusion.

But we are not convinced that this risk [of repetitive public law litigation] justifies departure from the usual rules governing nonparty preclusion. First, *stare decisis* will allow courts swiftly to dispose of repetitive suits brought in the same circuit. Second, even when *stare decisis* is not dispositive, "the human tendency not to waste money will deter the bringing of suits based on claims or issues that have already been adversely determined against others." * * * [Shapiro, Civil Procedure: Preclusion in Civil Actions 97 (2001)]. This intuition seems to be borne out by experience: The FAA has not called our attention to any instances of abusive FOIA suits in the Circuits that reject the virtual-representation theory respondents advocate here.

IV

For the foregoing reasons, we disapprove the theory of virtual representation on which the decision below rested. * * *

Although references to "virtual representation" have proliferated in the lower courts, our decision is unlikely to occasion any great shift in actual practice. Many opinions use the term "virtual representation" in reaching results at least arguably defensible on established grounds. * * *

In some cases, however, lower courts have relied on virtual representation to extend nonparty preclusion beyond the latter doctrine's proper bounds. We now turn back to Taylor's action to determine whether his suit is such a case, or whether the result reached by the courts below can be justified on one of the recognized grounds for nonparty preclusion.

A

It is uncontested that * * * [there] is no indication that Taylor agreed to be bound by Herrick's litigation, that Taylor and Herrick have any legal relationship, that Taylor exercised any control over Herrick's suit, or that this suit implicates any special statutory scheme limiting relitigation. Neither the FAA nor Fairchild contends otherwise.

It is equally clear that preclusion cannot be justified on the theory that Taylor was adequately represented in Herrick's suit. Nothing in the record indicates that Herrick understood himself to be suing on Taylor's behalf, that Taylor even knew of Herrick's suit, or that the Wyoming District Court took special care to protect Taylor's interests. Under our pathmarking precedent, therefore, Herrick's representation was not "adequate." * * *

That leaves only the * * * [possibility of] preclusion because a nonparty to an earlier litigation has brought suit as a representative or agent of a party who is bound by the prior adjudication. Taylor is not Herrick's legal representative and he has not purported to sue in a representative capacity. He concedes, however, that preclusion would be appropriate if respondents could demonstrate that he is acting as Herrick's "undisclosed agen[t]." * * *

Respondents argue here, as they did below, that Taylor's suit is a collusive attempt to relitigate Herrick's action. * * * The D.C. Circuit considered a similar question in addressing the "tactical maneuvering" prong of its virtual representation test. * * * The Court of Appeals did not, however, treat the issue as one of agency, and it expressly declined to reach any definitive conclusions due to "the ambiguity of the facts." * * * We therefore remand to give the courts below an opportunity to determine whether Taylor, in pursuing the instant FOIA suit, is acting as Herrick's agent. Taylor concedes that such a remand is appropriate. * * *

We have never defined the showing required to establish that a nonparty to a prior adjudication has become a litigating agent for a party to the earlier case. Because the issue has not been briefed in any detail, we do not discuss the matter elaboratively here. We note, however, that courts should be cautious about finding preclusion on this basis. A mere whiff of "tactical maneuvering" will not suffice; instead, principles of agency law are suggestive. They indicate that preclusion is appropriate only if the putative agent's conduct of the suit is subject to the control of the party who is bound by the prior adjudication. * * *

B

On remand, Fairchild suggests, Taylor should bear the burden of proving he is not acting as Herrick's agent. * * *

We reject Fairchild's suggestion. Claim preclusion, like issue preclusion, is an affirmative defense. * * * Ordinarily, it is incumbent on the defendant to plead and prove such a defense, * * * and we have never recognized claim preclusion as an exception to that general rule * * *. We acknowledge that direct evidence justifying nonparty preclusion is often in the hands of plaintiffs rather than defendants. * * * But "[v]ery often one must plead and prove matters as to which his adversary has superior access to the proof." * * * In these situations, targeted interrogatories or deposition questions can reduce the information disparity. We see no greater cause here than in other matters of affirmative defense to disturb the traditional allocation of the proof burden.

* * *

For the reasons stated, the judgment of the United States Court of Appeals for the District of Columbia Circuit is vacated, and the case is remanded for further proceedings consistent with this opinion.

It is so ordered.

NOTES AND QUESTIONS

1. Why might nonparty preclusion apply more broadly in public law cases than in private law cases? Hasn't the law traditionally recognized an exception for certain public law cases by characterizing them as in rem actions? Are there some substantive areas of law in which the need for finality and predictability ought to outweigh an individual's autonomy interests? See

Headwaters Inc. v. United States Forest Service, 399 F.3d 1047 (9th Cir. 2005). In such circumstances, does due process require the use of special procedures to ensure adequate representation of individuals who do not appear in the action but whose interests will be affected by it?

2.   So far, issue preclusion has been applied defensively or offensively only against persons who were parties to the prior litigation. See Tidmarsh & Transgrud, Complex Litigation: Problems in Advanced Civil Procedure 177 (2002). Does *Taylor* bar issue preclusion against a nonparty? In LYNCH v. MERRELL-NATIONAL LABORATORIES DIV. OF RICHARDSON-MER- RELL, INC., 646 F.Supp. 856 (D. Mass. 1986), affirmed on other grounds 830 F.2d 1190 (1st Cir. 1987), plaintiff sought damages for injuries sustained by her child's exposure during gestation to a prescription drug manufactured by defendant. Plaintiff had elected not to participate in earlier consolidated trials raising identical claims against the drug company. The court held that plaintiff was issue precluded by the earlier judgment from proving causation. Is *Lynch* at odds with the day-in-court ideal that informs the Court's decision in *Taylor*?

3.   Hasn't the day-in-court ideal been compromised by such trends as summary disposition, aggregate litigation, and mass settlement? See Miller, *The Pretrial Rush to Judgment: Are the "Litigation Explosion," "Liability Crisis," and Efficiency Clichés Eroding Our Day in Court and Jury Trial Commitments?*, 78 N.Y.U. L. Rev. 982 (2003). Why draw the line at nonparty issue preclusion?

SECTION F.   INTER-SYSTEM PRECLUSION

Read Article IV, § 1 of the United States Constitution and 28 U.S.C. § 1738 in the Supplement.

The preceding discussion of preclusion assumed that both the original and subsequent courts were in the same judicial system. Often, however, questions of preclusion are presented to a court that is part of a judicial system different from the court that rendered the prior judgment. Should this affect the preclusive effect given the prior judgment? The materials in this section are designed to introduce you to a very complicated area of the law that many of you will choose to study in advanced courses on judgments and federal jurisdiction.

1.   STATE-STATE AND STATE- FEDERAL PRECLUSION

The Full Faith and Credit Clause of the Constitution requires one state to honor the final judgment of a sister state to the same extent that the courts of the rendering state would honor it. This is true even though the decision was clearly against the policy of the second state which would not have given the same judgment had the case been brought there initially. See Fauntleroy v. Lum, 210 U.S. 230, 28 S.Ct. 641, 52 L.Ed. 1039 (1908). It follows, of course, that if the initial decision is modifiable in the rendering state, such as in the case of a child support order, then it is subject to modification in the second state.

It generally is agreed that the Full Faith and Credit Clause applies only to state courts. However, Congress in enacting 28 U.S.C. § 1738 (known as the Full Faith and Credit Statute) has imposed the same general principles on the federal courts, requiring them to accord full faith and credit to the judgments of state courts. Because the requirement is statutory and not constitutional, it may be supervened. Moreover, the writ of habeas corpus, which is authorized by the federal Constitution and by statute, 28 U.S.C. §§ 2241–55, provides a federal forum in which people who have been convicted of crimes in state court may litigate constitutional claims arising out of their prosecutions. Under traditional rules of preclusion, this subsequent action would be prevented.

What other circumstances might justify departing from the usual rules of inter-system preclusion? Consider, for example, cases involving federal issues. Should a federal court give preclusive effect to a state-court determination of federal law? What about circumstances in which the federal claim arises only by way of defense, and thus the original action could not have been removed to federal court? What if that issue was an area, such as copyright, which is within the exclusive jurisdiction of the federal courts?

2. FEDERAL-STATE PRECLUSION

Must a state court grant preclusive effect to a prior federal-court judgment? The general requirement that federal judgments be given full faith and credit in state courts never has been challenged seriously, even though the Full Faith and Credit Clause does not apply to the situation, and even though most courts agree that Section 1738 is inapplicable as well. Commentators invoke various provisions of the Constitution (including the Supremacy Clause and the "case or controversy" doctrine of Article III of the Constitution) to support binding state courts to federal court judgments. The lack of any express provision may reflect the constitutional compromise that relegated to Congress the decision of whether to establish inferior federal courts.

The conclusion that state courts are obliged to grant preclusive effect to federal court judgments does not determine which rules of preclusion the state should apply. There is almost universal agreement that federal preclusion rules usually apply in a state court when the prior federal-court judgment involves a federal question. But should federal preclusion rules define the effect in a subsequent action of a prior federal judgment deciding state law claims? Consider this question as you read the case that follows:

―――――

SEMTEK INTERNATIONAL INC. v. LOCKHEED MARTIN CORPORATION

Supreme Court of the United States, 2001.
531 U.S. 497, 121 S.Ct. 1021, 149 L.Ed.2d 32.

[Petitioner sued respondent in California state court, alleging breach of contract and various business torts. After removal to the United States District Court for the Central District of California on the basis of diversity of citizenship, the action was dismissed "on the merits and with prejudice" because it was barred by California's two-year statute of limitations. The Ninth Circuit affirmed. Petitioner also brought suit against respondent in the Circuit Court for Baltimore City, Maryland, alleging the same causes of action, which were not time barred under Maryland's three-year statute of limitations. Respondent asked the California federal court to enjoin this action; it also removed the Maryland state court action on federal-question grounds (diversity grounds were not available because Lockheed "is a Maryland citizen"). The California federal court denied the requested relief, and the Maryland federal court remanded the case to state court because the federal question arose only by way of defense. The Maryland state court granted Lockheed's motion to dismiss on the ground of res judicata. Petitioner appealed the Maryland trial court's order of dismissal to the Maryland Court of Special Appeals. That court affirmed, holding that, regardless of whether California would have accorded claim-preclusive effect to a statute-of-limitations dismissal by one of its own courts, the dismissal by the California federal court barred the Maryland complaint since the res judicata effect of federal diversity judgments is prescribed by federal law, under which the earlier dismissal was "on the merits" and claim preclusive. The Maryland Court of Appeals declined to review the case.]

Certiorari to the Court of Special Appeals of Maryland.

MR. JUSTICE SCALIA delivered the opinion of the Court.

* * *

It is * * * true * * * that no federal textual provision addresses the claim-preclusive effect of a federal-court judgment in a federal-question case, yet we have long held that States cannot give those judgments merely whatever effect they would give their own judgments, but must accord them the effect that this Court prescribes. * * * The reasoning of that line of cases suggests, moreover, that even when States are allowed to give federal judgments * * * no more than the effect accorded to state judgments, that disposition is by direction of *this* Court, which has the last word on the claim-preclusive effect of *all* federal judgments * * *. In short, federal common law governs the claim-preclusive effect of a dismissal by a federal court sitting in diversity. * * *

It is left to us, then, to determine the appropriate federal rule. * * * Since state, rather than federal, substantive law is at issue there is no need for a uniform federal rule. And indeed, nationwide uniformity in the substance of the matter is better served by having the same claim-preclusive rule (the state rule) apply whether the dismissal has been ordered by a state or a federal court. This is, it seems to us, a classic case for adopting, as the federally prescribed rule of decision, the law that would be applied by state courts in the State in which the federal diversity court sits. * * * As we have alluded to above, any other rule would produce the sort of "forum-shopping ... and ... inequitable administration of the laws" that *Erie* seeks to avoid * * * since filing in, or removing to, federal court would be encouraged by the divergent effects that the litigants would anticipate from likely grounds of dismissal. * * *

This federal reference to state law will not obtain, of course, in situations in which the state law is incompatible with federal interests. * * * No such conflict with potential federal interests exists in the present case. Dismissal of this state cause of action was decreed by the California federal court only because the California statute of limitations so required; and there is no conceivable federal interest in giving that time bar more effect in other courts than the California courts themselves would impose.

* * *

Notes and Questions

1. Do you agree with the Court's conclusions regarding the relevance of *Erie* and *Hanna*, the Rules Enabling Act, and federal common law, all subjects you encountered in Chapter 6, supra? See Degnan, *Federalized Res Judicata*, 85 Yale L.J. 741 (1976); Note, Erie *and the Preclusive Effect of Federal Diversity Judgments*, 85 Colum. L. Rev. 1505 (1985).

2. The rule in *Semtek* requires courts to apply the law of the forum state of the prior action to determine the preclusive effect of prior diversity actions. Will this rule, as Justice Scalia claims, really reduce forum shopping? The *Semtek* decision, of course, is completely consistent with the principles espoused in *Erie* and *Klaxon*, p. 265, supra. Although preclusion doctrines vary from state to state, and state preclusion rules are part and parcel of each state's law, note that if the California preclusion rules had been applied by the Maryland court, that court's dismissal on res judicata grounds might well have been sustained. Did the Maryland court's failure to do so justify reversal?

3. Will there be situations in which the Supreme Court might conclude that a federal interest would be "incompatible" with the application of a state preclusion standard? What would they be? When could a federal court craft its own rule of federal common law of claim preclusion?

4. What happens if a state court, in attempting to apply federal preclusion rules to a prior federal judgment, makes a mistake? If the parties

subsequently return to federal court to correct the error, is the federal court bound under Section 1738 to give preclusive effect to the state court's prior decision on the issue of preclusion?

In PARSONS STEEL, INC. v. FIRST ALABAMA BANK, 474 U.S. 518, 106 S.Ct. 768, 88 L.Ed.2d 877 (1986), the Supreme Court held that a state court's rejection of a claim that an earlier federal judgment precludes the state action is itself res judicata in the context of a later federal action to enjoin the enforcement of the state-court judgment.

CHAPTER 16

ALTERNATIVE DISPUTE RESOLUTION

■ ■ ■

In this Chapter, we examine nonadversarial approaches to dispute resolution and the ways in which they are reshaping civil litigation. The materials explore the critiques of adversarial justice, the variety of alternative dispute resolution ("ADR") procedures, their integration into civil litigation, and the advantages and disadvantages of ADR. Although nonadjudicative processes have existed for centuries, a movement arose in the 1970s to promote ADR in place of or as a complement to litigation. Since then, ADR has become not only a common element of most lawyers' practices, but also a mandatory feature of many court systems. The institutionalization of ADR means that it no longer can be understood entirely as a voluntary, private, nonlaw-based alternative to the adversary system of justice. As you read the materials in this Chapter, consider the implications of having ADR constitute both a parallel "private" system of dispute resolution and an integrated element of the public court system. Are ADR mechanisms qualitatively different from litigation or merely different points on a spectrum of binding civil dispute resolution? To the extent that ADR programs represent instances of state-sponsored dispute resolution, should they be subject to the constitutional guarantees of due process? What new problems, as well as new possibilities, does ADR present for the fair and efficient resolution of disputes?

SECTION A. THE CRITIQUE OF ADVERSARIAL JUSTICE

The preceding Chapters focused on one important mode of dispute resolution: civil litigation. As you have seen, courts are highly structured institutions in which technically trained representatives (lawyers) present arguments on behalf of their clients before a fact-finding body (judge and/or jury). And, of course, a court's decisions are enforced by the state. The formality that is characteristic of courts offers many advantages in terms of public accountability, enforcement of rights, and opportunities for individual participation. But formality also carries a number of disadvantages, which have led some to conclude that court-based solutions are not always the best or even an appropriate approach to dispute resolution.

A primary criticism of litigation is that it takes too long and costs too much. See Priest, *Private Litigants and the Court Congestion Problem*, 69 B.U. L. Rev. 527 (1989). However, the extent and even the existence of a "litigation crisis" remain controversial. See Galanter, *The Day After the Litigation Explosion*, 46 Md. L. Rev. 3 (1986). Professor Miller has warned "that the supposed litigation crisis is the product of assumption; that reliable empirical data is in short supply; and that data exist that support any proposition." Miller, *The Pretrial Rush to Judgment: Are The "Litigation Explosion," "Liability Crisis," and Efficiency Clichés Eroding Our Day in Court and Jury Trial Commitments?*, 78 N.Y.U. L. Rev. 982, 996 (2003).

How much delay might be attributable to the rules of procedure, evidence, and appellate review that govern formal adjudication? These rules, while protecting litigants, might invite strategic behavior by lawyers that contribute to delay. In addition, because delay might increase the cost of litigation, some individuals with meritorious claims may perceive them as too small to pursue or may find themselves "out litigated" by an opponent with greater resources and experience. On the other hand, these procedures provide important protections to the parties and help to ensure integrity in the court's decision making process.

Another criticism of adversarial justice is that court-centered dispute resolution deprives lay parties from direct control of the decision making process and the crafting of solutions, and instead substitutes lawyers and judges who have legal expertise and professional skill. Moreover, instead of providing for maximal disclosure of relevant facts, the litigation process may create incentives for adversaries to hide those facts. Finally, litigation in some settings may tend to polarize the parties, decreasing opportunities for future cooperation and straining the social fabric. This is particularly problematic when disputants have an ongoing relationship, as in the case of neighbors or family members and even in commercial settings. All of these factors may combine in some situations to obstruct disputants from reaching optimal outcomes.

Finally, some commentators criticize litigation for its law-based focus, which aims at the enforcement of rights and entitlements. As Professor Menkel–Meadow has explained:

> * * * The "culture of adversarialism" and the rules that enforce this culture often (not always) distort how we think about legal and human problem solving by assuming there are only two sides to an issue or question, that "truth" about either what happened factually or what is correct legally can best be resolved by vigorous contestations between two fully armed advocates and decided by a third-party judge who is separate from the parties and appointed by the state. * * * Often, what is most important to parties may be excluded from consideration, as irrelevant or inadmissible, according to our well-worn legal principles, which may protect other important interests

(like privileges, trade secrets, bias and prejudice, or constitutional rights).

Menkel–Meadow, *The Lawyer as Problem Solver and Third–Party Neutral: Creativity and Non–Partisanship in Lawyering*, 72 Temple L. Rev. 785, 788–89 (1999).

SECTION B. ALTERNATIVE DISPUTE RESOLUTION PROCESSES

The push toward alternative dispute resolution responds to some of the criticisms of adversarial justice. At the start of the ADR movement, commentators suggested establishing a Dispute Resolution Center that would match disputes to the decision making mechanism "best suited for the resolution of the particular controversy":

> Take, for example, a case involving a minor assault by one neighbor against another growing out of increasing anger over a trespassing dog. Presently such a dispute would probably wind up in criminal court because that is the tag society has placed on this type of conflict. But since the parties really want help in resolving this interpersonal problem, not a determination of whether A struck B, the case might well be sent to mediation, at least in the first instance. Similar treatment might be accorded to a landlord-tenant dispute over the adequacy of the services provided by the landlord. But if the landlord sought to raise questions about the constitutionality of the rent-control law, then obviously that case would have to be sent to the regular court. * * *

> The notion thus is that a sophisticated intake officer would analyze the dispute and refer it to that process, or sequence of processes, most likely to resolve it effectively. The potential benefits of such a multi-faceted mechanism are increased efficiency, possible time and cost savings, and the legitimization of various alternative dispute-resolution processes, thus decreasing citizens' frustration in attempting to locate the most appropriate mechanism. An additional benefit is that it would help us to gain a better understanding of the peculiar advantages and disadvantages of particular dispute-resolution processes for specific types of disputes. Perhaps the intake official could also refer disputants' associated nonlegal problems to appropriate social service agencies.

Sander, Varieties of Dispute Processing, in The Pound Conference: Perspectives on Justice in the Future 65 (Levin & Wheeler eds. 1979); see also Sander, *The Multidoor Courthouse*, National Forum, Vol. LXIII, No. 4, Fall 1983.

In contrast to the principle of transsubstantivity that defines the Federal Rules of Civil Procedure, see p. 30, supra, commentators emphasize that ADR is not a single system but rather a multiplicity of approaches to dispute resolution. Professor Resnik refers to ADR as "an umbrella term that encompasses a range of processes * * * and of places." Resnik, Processes of the Law: Understanding Courts and Their Alternatives 97 (2004). Other commentators have referred to ADR as a continuum or spectrum of processes. E.g., Dessem, Pretrial–Litigation: Law, Policy, and Practice 569 (1991). Overall, however, commentators emphasize ADR's "informality, its focus on interpersonal relationships, its low cost or speed, or its ability to foster personal growth and awareness * * *." Sternlight, *Is Binding Arbitration a Form of ADR?: An Argument That the Term "ADR" Has Begun To Outlive Its Usefulness*, 2000 J. Disp. Resol. 97, 99.

The following description of ADR processes is designed to introduce you to the variety of approaches that are possible. As you read the materials, keep in mind the different questions a policymaker might need to consider in designing a fair and efficient dispute resolution system.

- **Who resolves the dispute?** Possibilities include a judge, an officer of the state with professional education in the law; a lawyer with similar professional training; an expert in the field in which the dispute arose with no legal training; a representative of the community; the disputants with the help of a neutral third party; the disputants themselves.

- **What is the source of the standard for resolution?** Possibilities include rules established by legislatures and courts ("law"); the prior practice of those similarly situated; community values; standards developed by the disputants themselves.

- **Who speaks for the disputants?** Possibilities include lawyers; persons without professional legal training (including friends, relatives, experts, business associates, or neighbors); the disputants themselves.

- **What is the nature and extent of fact-finding and standard-finding?** Possibilities include no fact-finding or standard-finding; monopolization of these tasks by a third party; the sharing of these tasks by a third party and the disputants and their representatives; responsibility in the disputants and their representatives alone.

- **Who decides the dispute?** Possibilities include a third party privately chosen by the disputants; a third party mandated by the state; the parties themselves.

- **What is the binding effect of any resolution?** Possibilities include binding on the parties through coercive sanctions; binding on the parties in an advisory or precatory sense; binding on nonparties; binding on the parties in ways that they decide themselves.

By combining answers to these and other questions in various ways, ADR offers a menu of procedural options that can supplement or supplant litigation. The following description of different ADR processes is designed to introduce you to the basic themes and concepts. However, keep in mind that ADR is in a state of transition, with processes evolving in response to institutional and other pressures.

1. NEGOTIATION

Negotiation is perhaps the most familiar form of dispute resolution. See generally Fischer & Ury, Getting to Yes (1981). In a negotiated settlement, the disputants themselves resolve the conflict under whatever standards they choose. Some commentators, however, argue that knowledge of legal rules plays a strategic role in negotiation strategy. See Mnookin & Kornhauser, *Bargaining in the Shadow of the Law: The Case of Divorce*, 88 Yale L. J. 950 (1979); Jacob, *The Elusive Shadow of the Law*, 26 L. & Soc'y Rev. 565 (1992). In addition, studies indicate that standards of fairness often associated with due process are important to the success and acceptance of negotiated solutions. See Hollander-Blumoff & Tyler, *Procedural Justice in Negotiation: Procedural Fairness, Outcome Acceptance, and Integrative Potential*, 33 L. & Soc. Inq'y 473 (2008).

Although in the early stages the disputants may represent themselves, once lawyers become involved they tend to handle the negotiations as well. There is no need for fact-finding or standard-finding as such, since the only facts and standards that matter are those that the disputants choose to recognize. One commentator distinguishes between negotiation and adjudication as follows:

> In contrast [to adjudication], the universe and operation of norms in dispute-negotiation is typically open-ended. Thus it is characteristic of dispute-negotiation that when norms collide account is taken of both, although the eventual settlement may reflect an adjustment for relative applicability and weight. Similarly, the parties in dispute-negotiation may accord partial or even full recognition to a norm that is generally deemed subordinate or even legally invalid, so that a negligent plaintiff who has no "right" to prevail in a tort action because of the doctrine of contributory negligence may nevertheless make a favorable settlement by reason of the legally invalid but socially real principle of comparative negligence. Finally, parties to dispute-negotiation can and frequently do take person-oriented norms into account as freely as act-oriented norms.

Eisenberg, *Private Ordering through Negotiation: Dispute-Settlement and Rulemaking*, 89 Harv. L. Rev. 637, 644–45 (1976). Commentary also distinguishes between problem-solving and adversarial negotiation. See Hurder, *The Lawyers Dilemma: To Be or Not To Be a Problem-Solving Negotiator*, 14 Clinical L. Rev. 253 (2007). What do you think are the important differences between these two negotiation approaches?

2. MEDIATION

Mediation is a process in which a neutral third party, who is often but not always a human-relations professional, assists the disputants in reaching a negotiated settlement of their differences. The mediator is not empowered to render a decision. Thus the decision makers are the disputants themselves. Since mediation ultimately seeks agreement between the disputants, a mediator, at least in theory, does not evaluate the strengths and weaknesses of each side's evidence and arguments. Instead, she seeks common ground between the disputants concerning facts and standards. One commentator explains: "[M]ediation goes beyond * * * 'lawyers only' bargaining sessions and brings in a third party with no personal interest in the outcome of the case to serve as a 'neutral'— literally, a go-between for the parties." Tarpley, *ADR, Jurisprudence, and Myth*, 17 Ohio St. J. on Disp. Resol. 113, 116 (2001). See also Daiker, *No J.D. Required: The Critical Role and Contributions of Non-Lawyer Mediators*, 24 Rev. Litig. 499 (2005). There are, however, different forms of mediation, and mediators have differing conceptions of their proper role. Some mediators are simply communication facilitators. Others are more active, suggesting possible grounds for settlement and attempting to persuade the disputants to do so. Mediators of the former type are more likely to conduct all sessions with both disputants present; mediators of the latter type are more likely to conduct both joint sessions and private sessions with each disputant.

Parties in mediation do not have a discovery mechanism to force the opposing side to reveal information (about such topics as financial condition or mental health information) that may be critical to a full and fair evaluation of the dispute. Although the source of the standard for resolution is the disputants, when a mediator attempts persuasion, other values, such as those of the mediator or the community, also come into play. Disputants often but not always represent themselves; some mediators actively discourage the presence of lawyers and witnesses. Mediation is considered to be most appropriate when the disputants have equal bargaining power. This ordinarily occurs when the conflict is between individuals, rather than a conflict between an individual and a private institution or government. If successful, mediation results in a signed agreement that defines the parties' future behavior. This agreement may be an enforceable contract. Mediation often is used when the disputants have a continuing relationship that is important to preserve. Rather than attempting to assess blame for past conduct, mediation focuses the disputants' attention on the future and the desirability of maintaining an amicable relationship. In its early years, mediation often was seen as an appropriate way to resolve disputes between neighbors or family members, and mediation programs were established for domestic-relations cases. These programs have evolved from a voluntary court-connected process to one that sometimes is judicially mandated. Mediation is also used for corporate and commercial disputes. See Brazil, *Hosting Mediations as a Representative of the System of Civil Justice*, 22 Ohio St. J. on Disp. Resol. 227 (2007).

3. NEUTRAL FACTFINDING
AND OMBUDSPERSONS

Neutral fact-finding is a generic term for the use of a third party to gather information relevant to the settlement of a dispute. One of the most common institutional instances of a neutral fact finder is the ombudsperson. An ombudsperson is a third party who receives and investigates complaints aimed at an institution by its constituents, clients, or employees. She may take actions such as bringing an apparent injustice to the attention of high-level officials, advising the complainant of available options and resources, proposing a settlement of the dispute, or proposing systemic changes in the institution. A neutral fact finder often is employed by the institution against which the complaint is made. In government, an ombudsperson can serve the important function of steering a complaint through a tangled bureaucracy.

Ombudspersons are most likely to be hired in closely regulated institutions, those in which customer satisfaction is critical, and in institutions concerned with resolving disputes internally. Universities frequently use ombudspersons to enforce a set of university rules that may be different from those applicable to people generally. Some independent ombudspersons are employed by local media and use publicity as their major tool. The disputants are responsible for resolving the dispute, although the ombudsperson can pressure them to settle. The source of the standard for resolution is either internal policy or commonly shared values. The ombudsperson acts as representative of the complainant, investigating and presenting the facts for her as well as reminding the high-level officials of the policies they have set or the community's shared values.

4. EARLY NEUTRAL EVALUATION

It has been observed that parties often do not settle at an early stage in the litigation process because they fail to evaluate the case adequately until the trial process requires them to do so. Early neutral evaluation ("ENE") is a mechanism designed to respond to this problem. ENE involves the factual and legal presentation of a dispute to a neutral selected by the parties or a court. On the basis of this presentation the neutral, often an experienced lawyer, arbitrator, or former judge, provides the parties with an open assessment of their respective positions. This can have the effect of encouraging settlement, but at the very least it should help to focus the issues for the litigation process and assist in its efficient management.

5. MINI–TRIALS

Similar to early neutral evaluation, but procedurally more complex, the mini-trial is a privately developed method of helping to bring about a negotiated settlement in lieu of protracted corporate litigation. The procedural contours of mini-trials are tailored individually in accordance with the desires of the disputants. A typical mini-trial is a confidential process that entails a period of limited discovery after which attorneys for each side present an abbreviated version of the case before a panel consisting of managers with authority to settle and a neutral advisor. The neutral advisor is often a retired judge or respected lawyer. The managers then enter settlement negotiations.

Thus the parties resolve the dispute aided by the assessment of the neutral advisor as to the likely outcome should the matter go to court. The advisor's impartial appraisal of the conflict encourages the parties to adopt more realistic goals in negotiating a settlement. The source of the resolution standard is the disputants, despite the presence of the neutral legal advisor. Both sides are represented by lawyers, but the key to the process is that the managers see the other side's best case directly, in addition to the filtered version provided by their own lawyer. Facts and standards are researched and presented by the disputants' lawyers, although in an abbreviated way. Mini-trials have been used successfully in disputes that were bogged down in discovery and motion practice by reconverting what had become a lawyer's problem back into a business problem. See *Recent Developments in Alternative Forms of Dispute Resolution*, 100 F.R.D. 512 (1984).

6. SUMMARY JURY TRIAL

A summary jury trial is similar in some respects to a mini-trial, but is used for cases ready to be tried before a jury. Instead of presenting a formal case before a full jury panel, the lawyers for the parties present an abbreviated case before a panel of six jurors. The presentations usually last less than a week and the resulting "verdict"—although not binding on the parties—provides a basis for settlement. The summary jury trial has proven to be helpful when each party has a very different view regarding the likely outcome of the case, and prior settlement attempts have been unsuccessful. See Posner, *The Summary Jury Trial and Other Alternative Methods of Alternative Dispute Resolution: Some Cautionary Observations*, 53 U. Chi. L. Rev. 366 (1986).

7. ARBITRATION

Arbitration is the method of alternative dispute resolution with which the American legal system has had the longest experience. The parties select an arbitrator or arbitrators, who conduct hearings and then reach a decision. The arbitration hearing is an adversary proceeding, in which each of the parties presents its case, with full opportunity for cross-examination and rebuttal. Lawyers often represent the disputants, and are responsible for gathering and presenting evidence and arguments. Frequently, the decision of the arbitrator, called an "award," is then entered in court, much as a judgment in a formally adjudicated case is entered. In each case, both parties are bound to abide by the award, even though in certain limited circumstances, either or both parties may seek to challenge, modify, or even vacate the award.

As a general matter, arbitration is contractual: either the parties must have agreed in writing, before the dispute in question arose, to submit disagreements to arbitration, or they must have entered into an agreement to submit an existing dispute to arbitration. Arbitration first developed in the commercial context and, in the latter half of the nineteenth century, extended to labor-management relations. The practice achieved widespread acceptance after World War II, although initially the practice was confined to commercial contexts where the parties shared roughly equal bargaining power, such as securities broker agreements and construction contracts. More recently, arbitration has become a tool for resolving a broad range of disputes involving employment, consumer transactions, and hospital care, and contracts in these fields typically include binding arbitration clauses. Federal and state statutes play a significant role in shaping the context in which arbitration occurs. The Federal Arbitration Act, 9 U.S.C. §§ 1 et seq., and Article 75 of New York's Civil Practice Law and Rules are the most notable statutes of this type, and both have served as models for other states' arbitration statutes.

Although arbitration is a form of adversary adjudication, its procedural structure depends largely on the pre-dispositions of the arbitrator or arbitrators conducting a given hearing. The arbitrator is relatively free to shape the hearing as he sees fit. The arbitrator has three broad areas of responsibility: (1) the pre-hearing phase; (2) the hearing; and (3) the award and the opinion (if an opinion is thought necessary). Patterns of practice tend to become associated with particular types of arbitration. For example, commercial arbitrators frequently receive written briefs. By contrast, labor arbitrators tend to discourage them. Pre-hearing discovery is often limited to what the parties voluntarily disclose. However, arbitrators are empowered at the request of either party to subpoena documents and persons for the hearing, and counsel generally can agree on a procedure to review the subpoenaed documents in advance of the hearing. Further, arbitration in the securities industry offers formalized discovery proceedings in the pre-hearing phase that permit the parties themselves to serve written requests for information or documents on other parties to the arbitration. The arbitrator is the sole judge of the relevance and materiality of evidence offered and need not conform to the legal rules of evidence. However, some arbitrators believe that at least some compliance with traditional rules of evidence is both necessary and beneficial. Because the arbitrator has such broad discretion to choose to admit or exclude evidence or to hear or refuse to hear witnesses, his or her power to find facts and decide questions of law virtually is unlimited. The final phase of arbitration produces the award. The arbitrator's award of a dispute need not contain anything more than a statement of the rights and obligations of the parties to that dispute. However, the parties may request a written statement of decision.

In addition to standard arbitration, there are several other forms, including final-offer and one-way arbitration. Final-offer arbitration is much like standard arbitration but is used typically to set the terms of contracts (such as the salaries of major league baseball players and some public employees) rather than to interpret and apply contractual provisions. Each party proposes a final offer of settlement, and the neutral must choose between the two. This process encourages parties to be reasonable in the positions they advocate and is designed to encourage serious negotiation in contexts in which it is important that the disputants' dealings not be interrupted. Fact-finding can be more limited because the arbitrator need only choose between two positions rather than find and justify one particular result out of many that are possible. In one-way arbitration only one party agrees to be bound.

Court-annexed arbitration builds upon the standard model of arbitration described above except that the parties have not previously agreed to arbitrate their dispute. Instead, certain disputes, usually those in which the amount in controversy is less than a certain dollar figure, must be referred to an arbitrator before the court will hear them. The arbitrator thus is less likely to have expertise in the subject area in which the conflict arose. Moreover, since the source of the standard for resolution is the law, the arbitrator typically will be a lawyer. The nature and extent of fact-finding and standard-finding are not substantially different from adjudication, although discovery may be limited and the rules of evidence may be relaxed. If a disputant is dissatisfied with the arbitrator's decision, he can demand a trial *de novo*, but if the disputant fails to obtain a better result at trial, he may be required to pay the costs of the opposing party.

8. PRIVATE JUDGING

Disputants who can afford it may utilize private judging in order to avoid the delays of the court system. The disputants agree, after the dispute has arisen and been filed in court, to hire a private judge. Often a private judge has retired from the public court system. The court then refers the case to that judge.

The source of the standard for resolution is the law and the proceedings are conducted in much the same manner as a bench trial, although in an expedited and simplified manner. Unlike an arbitrator's award, the decision can be appealed as if the court referring it to the private judge had made the decision itself. Thus the disputants can ensure that the resolution will be in accordance with the law, while bypassing the backlog in the trial courts.

NOTE AND QUESTIONS

Each form of dispute resolution has its own strengths and weaknesses. Mediation may provide an excellent forum for dealing with disputes involving an ongoing relationship, but may prove useless in a setting characterized by acute antagonism. Arbitration is designed as a quick and inexpensive method of resolving simple disputes, but may be inappropriate in complex multi-party disputes or when the disputants lack parity of bargaining power. Litigation is well-equipped to deal with complex issues requiring public adjudication, but demands sophisticated knowledge and legal expertise. What principles should guide selecting the best process for resolving a particular dispute?

SECTION C. ADR AND CIVIL LITIGATION

1. CHANGING ATTITUDES TOWARD ADR: THE EXAMPLE OF BINDING ARBITRATION

———

Read Federal Rules of Civil Procedure 16, 54(a), 54(d), and 68 and 28 U.S.C. § 1920 in the Supplement.

———

Both Congress and the Supreme Court have supported the integration of ADR into the civil justice system. Professor Sternlight thus refers to "an intertwining" of litigation and other dispute resolution devices. Sternlight, *ADR Is Here: Preliminary Reflections on Where It Fits in a System of Justice*, 3 Nev. L.J. 289, 295 (2002–2003). Faced with concerns about caseload pressure, Congress enacted the Civil Justice Reform Act of 1990, requiring federal courts to consider ADR mechanisms as a way to reduce litigation expense and delay. 28 U.S.C. §§ 471 *et seq.* In 1998, this "invitation" was upgraded to a requirement under the Alternative Dispute Resolution Act, 28 U.S.C. § 651, that federal courts implement ADR programs and mandate participation. In parallel developments, state courts incorporated ADR into their judicial systems. See, e.g., Dana, Jr., *Court-Connected Alternative Dispute Resolution in Maine*, 57 Me. L. Rev. 349 (2005). For a comprehensive assessment of court-annexed ADR, see Shestowsky, *Disputants' Preferences for Court-Connected Dispute Resolution Procedures: Why We Should Care and Why We Know So Little*, 23 Ohio St. J. on Disp. Resol. 549 (2008).

Administrative agencies also have established large-scale ADR programs, a development required by Congress through the enactment of the Administrative Dispute Resolution Act, 5 U.S.C. §§ 571–83. See Marcus & Senger, *ADR and the Federal Government: Not Such Strange Bedfellows*

After All, 66 Mo. L. Rev. 709 (2001). The private sector's use of ADR also has increased dramatically, with corporations and professional associations institutionalizing mediation and arbitration procedures for the resolution of both internal and external disputes. See *Developments—The Paths of Civil Litigation*, 113 Harv. L. Rev. 1851 (2000).

Courts also now include ADR options in the public justice system. Some have suggested that the "mainstreaming" of ADR, particularly in the context of court-annexed mediation, has subverted ADR's fundamental vision of flexibility, participation, and cooperative resolution. See Menkel-Meadow, *Pursuing Settlement in an Adversary Culture: A Tale of Innovation Co-Opted or "The Law of ADR,"* 19 Fla. St. U. L. Rev. 1 (1990). It is argued that ADR has become mass-produced and that it models itself too closely on procedural rules and evidentiary devices usually employed in litigation. These procedures include such familiar devices as notice requirements, "information exchanges" (discovery), party submissions to neutrals (briefs, motions), induced attendance of persons and production of things (subpoenas), consolidation, interim relief, and a number of others. See Welsh, *The Thinning Vision of Self-Determination in Court-Connected Mediation: The Inevitable Price of Institutionalization?*, 6 Harv. Negot. L. Rev. 1, 5 (2001); Sabatino, *ADR as "Litigation Lite": Procedural and Evidentiary Norms Embedded Within Alternative Dispute Resolution*, 47 Emory L.J. 1289 (1998). Commentators have expressed concern that ADR is increasingly expensive and complex, yet it fails to provide participants with adequate procedural protection. See Reuben, *Public Justice: Toward a State Action Theory of Alternative Dispute Resolution*, 85 Cal. L. Rev. 579 (1997).

Other commentators criticize court-annexed ADR programs as being no more than settlement conferences that push disputants to a quick disposition rather than a consensual working out of grievances. See Brown, *A Community of Court ADR Programs: How Court-Based ADR Programs Help Each Other Survive and Thrive*, 26 Just. Sys. J. 327, 330 (2005). In addition, commentators question whether ADR should ever be mandatory. For example, some states now mandate mediation for domestic disputes, and require mediation before permitting the filing of an action for divorce. Does mandating mediation in this setting violate due process? See King, *Burdening Access to Justice: The Cost of Divorce Mediation on the Cheap*, 73 St. John's L. Rev. 375 (1999).

Questions also are raised as to whether the private sector's increasing trend toward including mandatory ADR clauses in employment and consumer contracts promotes the values that ADR is intended to serve, namely, party control, informality, preservation of relationships, and nonadversarial justice. See Sternlight, *Rethinking the Constitutionality of the Supreme Court's Preference for Binding Arbitration: A Fresh Assessment of Jury Trial, Separation of Powers, and Due Process Concerns*, 72 Tul. L. Rev. 1 (1997). Critics warn that ADR is producing long-term deleterious effects on democratic life, hastening the elimination of jury trials, undermining the enforcement of statutory rights, and impeding the creation of judicial precedent. Is there an inevitable conflict between mandatory ADR and the day-in-court-ideal on which American justice is based? See Reuben, *Democracy and Dispute Resolution: The Problem of Arbitration*, 67 Law & Contemp. Probs. 279, 310 (Spring 2004).

Within twenty years of Professor Sander's "multi-door" suggestion, p. 628, supra, some commentators now argue that ADR, in practice, is closing the door to justice for many disputants who are remitted to non-judicial processes. See Resnik, *Many Doors? Closing Doors? Alternative Dispute Resolution and Adjudication*, 10 Ohio St. J. on Disp. Resol. 211 (1995). Changes in judicial attitudes toward arbitration reflect this trend. In WILKO v. SWAN, 346 U.S. 427, 74 S.Ct. 182, 98 L.Ed. 168 (1953), the Supreme Court ruled that claims arising under Section 12(2) of the Securities Act of 1933 were not subject to compulsory arbitration. Today, however, a strong presumption exists in favor of arbitration as an acceptable method of resolving disputes without litigation. See Resnik, *Procedure as Contract*, 80 Notre Dame L. Rev. 593, 620–21 (2005).

One step in this shift was SOUTHLAND CORP. v. KEATING, 465 U.S. 1, 104 S.Ct. 852, 79 L.Ed.2d 1 (1984). In *Southland*, appellant, the owner and franchisor of 7-Eleven convenience stores, entered into franchise agreements with over 800 franchisees located in California. Between September 1975 and May 1977, a class of these franchisees as well as several individual appellees sued appellant for breach of contract, fraud, misrepresentation, breach of fiduciary duty, and violations of the California Franchise Investment Law. The California courts consolidated the various actions. Pursuant to the terms of the franchise agreements, appellant sought arbitration of all the claims. However, the California Supreme Court held that appellees's claims under the Franchise Investment Law were not arbitrable under the arbitration clauses. The Court interpreted the California Investment Law to require judicial consideration of claims brought under the statute and concluded that the California statute did not contravene Section 2 of the Federal Arbitration Act, which provides that an arbitration provision relating to a transaction involving commerce "shall be valid, irrevocable, and enforceable, save upon such grounds as exist at law or in equity for the revocation of any contract."

The Supreme Court reversed, holding that "in enacting Section 2 of the federal Act, Congress declared a national policy favoring arbitration and withdrew the power of the states to require a judicial forum for the resolution of claims which the contracting parties agreed to resolve by arbitration. * * * Congress has thus mandated the enforcement of arbitration agreements." Id. at 10, 104 S.Ct. at 858, 79 L.Ed.2d at 12. The Court rejected the argument advanced in dissent by Justices O'Connor and Rehnquist that Congress intended the Act to be a procedural restraint only on federal courts; Chief Justice Burger's opinion for the Court maintained that the possibility of forum-shopping by litigants militated in favor of reading the statute as a source of substantive law binding both federal and state courts.

In SHEARSON/AMERICAN EXPRESS, INC. v. McMAHON, 482 U.S. 220, 107 S.Ct. 2332, 96 L.Ed.2d 185 (1987), the Court upheld compulsory arbitration under the Federal Arbitration Act of claims alleging violation of Section 10(b) of the Securities Exchange Act of 1934 and the Racketeer Influenced and Corrupt Organizations Act (RICO). The arbitration clause appeared in predispute brokerage customer agreements. Although a section of the Securities Exchange Act provided that "[t]he district courts of the United States * * * shall have exclusive jurisdiction" over violations of the Act, and another section declared void any agreement "to waive compliance with any provision" of the Act, the Court interpreted these provisions to prohibit only a waiver of compliance with the substantive provisions of the Act. Noting that the arbitration procedures of the various stock exchanges had been specifically approved by the Securities and Exchange Commission, the Court reasoned that arbitration tribunals are "fully capable of handling" claims of Securities Exchange Act violations. Id. at 232–34, 107 S.Ct. at 2341, 96 L.Ed.2d at 198–99. Similarly, the Court rejected the arguments that RICO claims are "too complex to be subject to arbitration"; "that the 'overlap' between RICO's civil and criminal provisions" precluded arbitration even of civil RICO claims; and that "the public interest in the enforcement of RICO precludes its submission to arbitration." Id. at 239–40, 107 S.Ct. at 2344, 96 L.Ed.2d at 202.

Two years later, in RODRIGUEZ de QUIJAS v. SHEARSON/AMERICAN EXPRESS, INC., 490 U.S. 477, 109 S.Ct. 1917, 104 L.Ed.2d 526 (1989), the Court held that a predispute agreement to arbitrate claims arising under the Securities Act of 1933 was enforceable. Going one step beyond its decision in the *McMahon* case, the Court concluded "that *Wilko* was incorrectly decided and is inconsistent with the prevailing uniform construction of other federal statutes governing arbitration agreements in the setting of business transactions." Id. at 484, 109 S.Ct. at 1921, 104 L.Ed.2d at 536. In both *McMahon* and *Rodriguez*, Justices Stevens, Brennan, Marshall, and Blackmun dissented, asserting that the policy arguments presented were not sufficient to "overturn an interpretation of an Act of Congress that has been settled for many years." Id. at 487, 109 S.Ct. at 1923, 104 L.Ed.2d at 539.

In GILMER v. INTERSTATE/JOHNSON LANE CORP., 500 U.S. 20, 111 S.Ct. 1647, 114 L.Ed.2d 26 (1991), the Court held that claims arising under the Age Discrimination in Employment Act (ADEA) are subject to compulsory arbitration. The Court explained that the purpose of the Federal Arbitration Act "was to reverse the longstanding judicial hostility to arbitration agreements that had existed at English common law and had been adopted by American courts, and to place arbitration agreements upon the same footing as other contracts." Id. at 24, 111 S.Ct. at 1651, 114 L.Ed.2d at 36.

The Court went on to reject the arguments that arbitration would fail to address the "important social policies" embodied in ADEA and would "undermine the role of the * * * [Equal Employment Opportunity Commission] in enforcing the ADEA." After dismissing a number of arguments directed against the fairness of arbitration proceedings, the Court found that the arbitration agreement in *Gilmer* did not result from "unequal bargaining power between employers and employees." It reasoned that there was no indication "that Gilmer, an experienced businessman, was coerced or defrauded into agreeing to the arbitration clause." Id. at 29–30, 111 S.Ct. at 1656, 114 L.Ed.2d at 41–42.

Justices Stevens and Marshall dissented. They pointed to a provision contained in Section 1 of the Federal Arbitration Act: "Nothing herein contained shall apply to contracts of employment of * * * any * * * class of workers engaged in foreign or interstate commerce." This exclusion, they argued, "should be interpreted to cover any agreements by the employee to arbitrate disputes with the employer arising out of the employment relationship" even where—as was the situation in *Gilmer*— the arbitration agreement was not a part of the contract of employment. Id. at 32, 111 S.Ct. at 1659, 114 L.Ed.2d at 46. The dissenters also contended that compulsory arbitration "conflicts with the statutory purpose animating the ADEA." Id. at 33, 111 S.Ct. at 1660, 114 L.Ed.2d at 47.

In ALLIED-BRUCE TERMINIX COMPANIES, INC. v. DOBSON, 513 U.S. 265, 115 S.Ct. 834, 130 L.Ed.2d 753 (1995), the Court held that a predispute agreement to arbitrate trumped a state statute invalidating such agreements. The Court explained that the Federal Arbitration Act's grant of enforcement of written arbitration provisions in contracts "evidencing a transaction involving commerce" extends the Act's federal supremacy to the limits of Congress's Commerce Clause power. Id. at 270– 72, 115 S.Ct. at 837–38, 130 L.Ed.2d at 756–57. The Court acknowledged that the statute's basic purpose, to put arbitration provisions on the same footing as a contract's other terms, was consistent with that broad interpretation of the Act's language. Id. at 272–274, 115 S.Ct. at 838–39, 130 L.Ed.2d at 758. Justices Thomas and Scalia dissented, reiterating the view advanced by Justices O'Connor and Rehnquist in dissent in *Southland* that Congress intended that the Act be a procedural restraint only in federal court.

The trend in favor of arbitration continued in GREEN TREE FINANCIAL CORP. v. RANDOLPH, 531 U.S. 79, 121 S.Ct. 513, 148 L.Ed.2d 373 (2000), in which the Court held that an arbitration agreement is not unenforceable merely because it fails to address the question of arbitration costs; arbitral procedures need not "affirmatively protect a party from potentially steep arbitration costs." Id. at 82, 121 S.Ct. at 517, 148 L.Ed.2d at 378. Although recognizing that "the existence of large arbitration costs could preclude a litigant such as * * * [the consumer in this case, the purchaser of a mobile home] from effectively vindicating her federal statutory rights in the arbitral forum," the Court nevertheless held that "the party resisting arbitration bears the burden of proving that the claims at issue are unsuitable for arbitration." Id. at 90–92, 121 S.Ct. at 522–23, 148 L.Ed.2d at 383–84.

The Court's endorsement of binding arbitration continued in CIR-CUIT CITY STORES, INC. v. ADAMS, 532 U.S. 105, 121 S.Ct. 1302, 149 L.Ed.2d 234 (2001), holding that Section 1 of the Federal Arbitration Act, exempting from its scope contracts of employment of workers engaged in interstate or foreign commerce, applies only to contracts involving transportation workers. Thus other workers would be prohibited from filing a discrimination suit in court and instead would be compelled to submit their claims to binding arbitration.

The Supreme Court also has shown an increasing willingness to accord broad power to arbitral decision making. In GREEN TREE FINANCIAL CORP. v. BAZZLE, 539 U.S. 444, 123 S.Ct. 2402, 156 L.Ed.2d 414 (2003), the Court held that the question whether an arbitration contract forbids class arbitration is one for the arbitrator and not the court to decide. In BUCKEYE CHECK CASHING, INC. v. CARDEGNA, 546 U.S. 440, 126 S.Ct. 1204, 163 L.Ed.2d 1038 (2006), the Court held that an arbitrator, and not a federal or a state court, should consider a claim that a contract containing an arbitration provision is void for illegality. The decision in *Buckeye Check Cashing* was followed by the decision of the Court in PRESTON v. FERRER, 552 U.S. 346, 128 S.Ct. 978, 169 L.Ed.2d 917 (2008), in which it was held that an agreement between parties to arbitrate all aspects of an employment dispute under the Federal Arbitration Act superseded a state statutory provision requiring the particular dispute to be heard first by a state designed tribunal (in this case, the state Labor commissioner).

However, in HALL STREET ASSOCIATES, L.L.C. v. MATTEL, INC., 552 U.S. 576, 128 S.Ct. 1396, 170 L.Ed.2d 254 (2008), the Court placed limits on the parties' authority to expand by contract the scope of judicial review of arbitral awards, holding that the grounds for prompt vacatur and modification set out in the Federal Arbitration Act may not be supplemented or compromised by contract. The decision presents an unresolved question involving the scope of a district court's Federal Rule 16 power to review an award on grounds beyond those in the FAA.

> * * * The Arbitration agreement was entered into in the course of district-court litigation, was submitted to the District Court as a request to deviate from the standard sequence of trial procedure, and was adopted by the District Court as an order. * * * Hence a question raised by this Court at oral argument: should the agreement be treated as an exercise of the District Court's authority to manage its cases under Federal * * * [Rule] 16?

Id. at 589, 128 S.Ct. at 1406, 170 L.Ed.2d at 266. The Supreme Court remanded to allow the Court of Appeals to consider "whether the District Court's authority to manage litigation independently warranted that court's order on the mode of resolving the * * * issues remaining in this case. Id. at 592, 128 S.Ct. at 1408, 170 L.Ed.2d at 268.

Finally, in VADEN v. DISCOVER BANK, ___ U.S. ___, 129 S.Ct. 1262, 173 L.Ed.2d 206 (2009), the Court considered the relation between

Section 1331's well-pleaded complaint rule, see p. 184, supra, and the District Court's jurisdiction to hear a petition to compel arbitration of a dispute under Section 4 of the Federal Arbitration Act. Defendant, a credit card company, sued a credit card-holder in state court under state law to recover arrearages. Petitioner answered and alleged counterclaims, styled as class actions, challenging defendant's finance and other charges as violative of state law. Relying on an arbitration provision in the credit card contract, defendant petitioned the District Court to compel arbitration of petitioner's counterclaims, arguing that they were completely preempted by federal banking law. The Fourth Circuit affirmed the District Court's order of arbitration, on the ground that the court has jurisdiction over a petition to arbitrate if the underlying dispute presents a federal question. The Supreme Court reversed, with Justice Ginsburg writing the Court's opinion. Although the Court agreed that a district court may "look through" the petition to determine whether it has Section 1331 jurisdiction to hear the underlying dispute, jurisdiction must be determined by plaintiff's well-pleaded complaint, and cannot rest on counterclaims. In dissent, Chief Justice Roberts, joined by Justice Stevens, Justice Breyer, and Justice Alito, agreed that a district court must "look through" the petition to determine whether Section 1331 jurisdiction exists over the underlying dispute, but insisted that the underlying dispute includes only the issue that the petition seeks to arbitrate, and not the entire controversy as set out in the state-court complaint.

NOTES AND QUESTIONS

1. In *Vaden*, Justice Ginsburg noted that petitioner's "preference for court adjudication is unsurprising," underscoring the fact that the arbitration clause that Discover Bank sought to enforce contained language that barred the card-holder from filing any claims as a representative or member of a class. Id. at ____, 129 S.Ct. at 1269 n.2, 173 L.Ed.2d at 215 n.2. Do you agree that a court must enforce a contractual provision that waives the protections of a Federal Rule of Civil Procedure? Compare Sternlight, *As Mandatory Binding Arbitration Meets the Class Action, Will the Class Action Survive?*, 42 Wm. & Mary L. Rev. 1 (2000), with Ware, *The Case for Enforcing Adhesive Arbitration Agreements—With Particular Consideration of Class Actions and Arbitration Fees*, 5 J. Am. Arb. 251 (2006). The circuit courts currently are divided on the answer to this question, as are the state courts. See Rice, *Enforceable or Not: Class Action Waivers in Mandatory Arbitration Clauses and the Need for a Judicial Standard*, 45 Hous. L. Rev. 215 (2008) (collecting cases). What would be the costs and benefits of permitting litigants to design their own procedures for federal court actions, rather than requiring them to conform to the Federal Rules? See Moffitt, *Customized Litigation: The Case for Making Civil Procedure Negotiable*, 75 Geo. Wash. L. Rev. 461 (2007).

2. Arbitrators do not receive any in-depth professional training or briefing on their task. Although they lack the protections of life tenure associated with Article III judges, arbitrators exercise broad discretion in their decision making. Is there a danger that their method of selection will create a potential

for bias, particularly among arbitrators who receive repeat appointments by one company or by one segment of a regulated industry? See Rossein & Hope, *Disclosure and Disqualification Standards for Neutral Arbitrators: How Far to Cast the Net and What Is Sufficient to Vacate Award*, 81 St. John's L. Rev. 203 (2007). An empirical study has found a perception of pro-industry bias among securities-industry arbitrators, leading customers to "express a consistently negative impression of the overall arbitration process * * *." Gross, *When Perception Changes Reality: An Empirical Study of Investors' Views of the Fairness of Securities Arbitration*, 2008 J. Disp. Resol. 349, 389 (2008). Is there also a danger that informality will permit gender bias or racial prejudice to operate unchecked? See Delgado, Dunn, Brown, Lee & Hubbert, *Fairness and Formality: Minimizing the Risk of Prejudice in Alternative Dispute Resolution*, 1985 Wis. L. Rev. 1359. Similar concerns have been raised about other forms of ADR. See, e.g., Bryan, *Women's Freedom to Contract at Divorce: A Mask for Contextual Coercion*, 47 Buffalo L. Rev. 1153 (1999); Lefcourt, *Women, Mediation and Family Law*, Clearinghouse Rev. 266 (July 1984).

3. In reaching her decision, the arbitrator is not required to apply rules of decision derived from federal or state statutes, common-law rules, or even from the decisions of other arbitrators, although she may draw on such sources for guidance in reaching a decision. For this reason, many commentators refer to arbitration as "lawless." E.g., Black & Gross, *Making It Up As They Go Along: The Role of Law in Securities Arbitration*, 23 Cardozo L. Rev. 991 (2002). Yet it has become common practice for parties to arbitration proceedings to circulate arbitration awards and decisions. Considering the legal system's reluctance to disturb arbitration awards and decisions except in certain narrowly defined circumstances, is this use of arbitration awards and decisions as nonbinding precedent sound? Conversely, might the diversion of disputes to arbitration proceedings make it more difficult for the courts to create precedent in important fields of law? See Scodro, Note—*Arbitrating Novel Legal Questions: A Recommendation for Reform*, 105 Yale L. J. 1927 (1996)

2. ADR AND THE JUDICIAL PREFERENCE FOR SETTLEMENT

———

Read Federal Rules of Civil Procedure 54(d) and 68 in the Supplement.

———

DELTA AIR LINES, INC. v. AUGUST, 450 U.S. 346, 101 S.Ct. 1146, 67 L.Ed.2d 287 (1981). Rosemary August filed suit against Delta Air Lines seeking $20,000 in back pay for violation of Title VII of the Civil Rights Act of 1964. Delta made a formal settlement offer of $450, which August rejected. At trial, judgment was for Delta and the District Court directed that each party bear its own costs. The court held that Federal Rule 68, which directs that a plaintiff who rejects a formal settlement offer must pay post-offer costs if the "judgment that the offeree finally obtains is not more favorable than the unaccepted offer," was not applicable since Delta's offer of $450 was not a reasonable, good-faith attempt to settle the case. The Court of Appeals for the Seventh Circuit affirmed on the same grounds.

The Supreme Court affirmed the result, although it rejected the reasoning of the lower courts. In an opinion written by Justice Stevens, the Court held that "the plain language, the purpose, and the history of Rule 68" made clear that the words, in Rule 68 as it then existed, "judgment * * * obtained by the offeree" do not encompass a judgment against the offeree:

> Our interpretation of the Rule is consistent with its purpose. The purpose of Rule 68 is to encourage the settlement of litigation. In all litigation, the adverse consequences of potential defeat provide both parties with an incentive to settle in advance of trial. Rule 68 provides an additional inducement to settle in those cases in which there is a strong probability that the plaintiff will obtain a judgment but the amount of recovery is uncertain. Because prevailing plaintiffs presumptively will obtain costs under Rule 54(d), Rule 68 imposes a special burden on the plaintiff to whom a formal settlement offer is made. If a plaintiff rejects a Rule 68 settlement offer, he will lose some of the benefits of victory if his recovery is less than the offer. Because costs are usually assessed against the losing party, liability for costs is a normal incident of defeat. Therefore, a nonsettling plaintiff does not run the risk of suffering additional burdens that do not ordinarily attend a defeat, and Rule 68 would provide little, if any, additional incentive if it were applied when the plaintiff loses.

> Defendant argues that Rule 68 does provide such an incentive, because it operates to deprive the district judge of the discretion vested in him by Rule 54(d). According to this reasoning, Rule 68 is mandatory, and a district judge must assess costs against a plaintiff who rejects a settlement offer and then either fails to obtain a judgment or recovers less than the offer. * * *

> * * * If, as defendant argues, Rule 68 applies to defeated plaintiffs, any settlement offer, no matter how small, would apparently trigger the operation of the Rule. Thus any defendant, by performing the meaningless act of making a nominal settlement offer, could eliminate the trial judge's discretion under Rule 54(d). We cannot reasonably conclude that the drafters of the Federal Rules intended on the one hand affirmatively to grant the district judge discretion to deny costs to the prevailing party under Rule 54(d) and then on the other hand to give defendants—and only defendants—the power to take away that discretion by performing a token act. Moreover, if the Rule operated as defendant argues, we cannot conceive of a reason why the

drafters would have given only defendants, and not plaintiffs, the power to divest the judge of his Rule 54(d) discretion. * * * When Rule 68 is read literally, however, it is evenhanded in its operation. As we have already noted, it does not apply to judgments in favor of the defendant or to judgments in favor of the plaintiff for an amount greater than the settlement offer. In both of those extreme situations the trial judge retains his Rule 54(d) discretion. * * * Thus unless we assume that the Federal Rules were intended to be biased in favor of defendants, we can conceive of no reason why defendants—and not plaintiffs—should be given an entirely risk-free method of denying trial judges the discretion that Rule 54(d) confers regardless of the outcome of the litigation.

The Court of Appeals, perceiving the anomaly of allowing defendants to control the discretion of district judges by making sham offers, resolved the problem by holding that only reasonable offers trigger the operation of Rule 68. But the plain language of the Rule makes it unnecessary to read a reasonableness requirement into the Rule. * * *

Id. at 352–55, 101 S.Ct. at 1150–52, 67 L.Ed.2d at 292–95.

————

MAREK v. CHESNY, 473 U.S. 1, 105 S.Ct. 3012, 87 L.Ed.2d 1 (1985). Three police officers, in answering a call on a domestic disturbance, shot and killed Alfred Chesny's son. Chesny, on his own behalf and as administrator of his son's estate, filed suit against the officers in federal district court under 42 U.S.C. § 1983 and state tort law. Prior to trial, the police officers made a timely offer of settlement of $100,000, expressly including accrued costs and attorney's fees, but Chesny did not accept the offer. The case went to trial and Chesny was awarded $5,000 on the state-law claim, $52,000 for the Section 1983 violation, and $3,000 in punitive damages. Chesny then filed a request for attorney's fees under 42 U.S.C. § 1988, which provides that a prevailing party in a Section 1983 action may be awarded attorney's fees "as part of the costs." The claimed attorney's fees included fees for work performed subsequent to the settlement offer. The District Court declined to award these latter fees pursuant to Rule 68. The Court of Appeals reversed, but the Supreme Court agreed with the District Court.

The Court held first that the officers' offer was valid under Rule 68. As the Court read it, the Rule does not require that a defendant's offer itemize the respective amounts being tendered for settlement of the underlying substantive claim and for costs. In reaching this result, Chief Justice Burger, writing for the majority, asserted that the drafters' concern was not so much with the particular components of offers, but with the judgments to be allowed against defendants. Whether or not the offer recites that costs are included or specifies an amount for costs, the offer allows judgment to be entered against the defendant both for damages caused by the challenged conduct and for costs. In Chief Justice Burger's view, this construction of Rule 68 furthers its objective of encouraging settlements.

Chief Justice Burger next noted that the drafters of Rule 68 were aware of the various federal statutes that, as an exception to the "American Rule," authorize an award of attorney's fees to prevailing parties as part of the costs in particular cases. From this, he concluded that the term "costs" in the Rule was intended to refer to all costs properly awardable under the relevant substantive statute. Thus, when the underlying statute defines "costs" to include attorney's fees, the fees are to be included as costs for purposes of Rule 68. Since Section 1983 expressly includes attorney's fees as "costs" available to a prevailing plaintiff in a suit under the statute, those fees are subject to the cost-shifting provision of Rule 68. As Chief Justice Burger saw it, rather than "cutting against the grain" of Section 1983, applying Rule 68 in the context of a Section 1983 action is consistent with Section 1988's policies and objectives of encouraging plaintiffs to bring meritorious civil rights suits; Rule 68 simply encourages settlements.

Justice Brennan filed a vigorous dissent for himself and Justices Marshall and Blackmun.

NOTES AND QUESTIONS

1. Implicit in the attempt to encourage settlement is an assumption that a negotiated resolution of a dispute is more desirable than that of a judicial disposition. See Menkel-Meadow, *Whose Dispute Is It Anyway?: A Philosophical and Democratic Defense of Settlement (In Some Cases)*, 83 Geo. L.J. 2663 (1995). Consider the contrary position of Professor Fiss, who has emphasized the public role of litigation as "an institutional arrangement for using state power to bring a recalcitrant reality closer to our chosen ideals":

> * * * I do not believe that settlement as a generic practice is preferable to judgment or should be institutionalized on a wholesale and indiscriminate basis. It should be treated instead as a highly problematic technique for streamlining dockets. Settlement is for me the civil analogue of plea bargaining: Consent is often coerced; the bargain may be struck by someone without authority; the absence of a trial and judgment renders subsequent judicial involvement troublesome; and although dockets are trimmed, justice may not be done. Like plea bargaining, settlement is a capitulation to the conditions of mass society and should be neither encouraged nor praised.

Fiss, *Against Settlement*, 93 Yale L.J. 1073, 1075, 1089 (1984) (footnotes omitted).

2. Settlement terms may be drafted to protect the privacy of the parties to the contract. Retaining the confidentiality of information may be desirable for the parties, but is it desirable for society as a whole? See Macklin, *Promoting Settlement, Foregoing the Facts*, 14 N.Y.U. Rev. L. & Soc. Change

579 (1986) (stressing the value of judicial fact-finding as "a source of tested facts" for use in public policy discussion and planning).

3. How does judicial participation in the settlement process affect the judge's traditional role as decision maker? Some judges delegate the task of negotiating a settlement to an extrajudicial officer. Other judges may conduct a mediation conference with the goal of settling the dispute. See Brunet, *Judicial Mediation and Signaling*, 3 Nev. L.J. 232 (2002–03). Is there a danger that judicial mediation might undermine the judge's ability to be a neutral decision maker if the dispute later goes to trial? See Shweder, *Judicial Limitations on ADR: The Role and Ethics of Judges Encouraging Settlements*, 20 Geo. J. Legal Ethics 51 (2007).

D. ASSESSING ADR AND THE ROLE OF CIVIL LITIGATION IN AMERICAN SOCIETY

Does ADR deliver the benefits it promises in terms of speed, cost, participation, and flexibility? Data are limited, show mixed results, and are difficult to assess given the variety of ADR mechanisms. Moreover, because many ADR services are private and the proceedings are closed to the public, it is difficult to obtain information that a proper assessment would require. See Landsman, *ADR and the Cost of Compulsion*, 57 Stan. L. Rev. 1593 (2005). For a summary of available, recent data on mandatory federal court-annexed ADR, see Ward, *Mandatory Court-Annexed Alternative Dispute Resolution in the United States Federal Courts: Panacea or Pandemic?*, 81 St. John's L. Rev. 77 (2007).

NOTE AND QUESTIONS

What impact might ADR be having on the role of courts in democratic governance? Professor Hensler has stated:

> The public spectacle of civil litigation gives life to the "rule of law." * * *
> In a democracy where many people are shut out of legislative power either because they are too few in number, or too dispersed to elect representatives, or because they do not have the financial resources to influence legislators, collective litigation in class or other mass form provides an alternative strategy for group action. Private individualized dispute resolution extinguishes the possibility of such collective litigation. Conciliation has much to recommend it. But the visible presence of institutionalized and legitimized conflict, channeled productively, teaches citizens that it is not always better to compromise and accept the status quo because, sometimes, great gains are to be had by peaceful contest.

Hensler, *Our Courts, Ourselves: How the Alternative Dispute Resolution Movement Is Re-Shaping Our Legal System*, 108 Pa. St. L. Rev. 165 (2003). A noted federal judge likewise has expressed concern that ADR might adversely affect the operation of the public courts:

> Widespread privatization of dispute resolution has the potential to stunt the common law's development as entire areas of law are

removed from the courts; deprive the public of important information, such as news of a product's harmful effects; deny plaintiffs the therapeutic benefit of having their "day in court;" degrade constitutional guarantees of the right to a jury trial; and prevent public debate and consensus-building in cases with national public policy implications.

Weinstein, *Some Benefits and Risks of Privatization of Justice through ADR*, 11 Ohio St. J. on Disp. Resol. 241, 246 (1996). Compare Main, *ADR: The New Equity*, 74 U. Cin. L. Rev. 329 (2005), with Sternlight, *Is Alternative Dispute Resolution Consistent with the Rule of Law? Lessons from Abroad*, 56 DePaul L. Rev. 569 (2007).

Recall the question posed at the beginning of your study of civil procedure: "What is the test of a good system of procedure?" What is the relevance of this question to your assessment of ADR? How has your answer changed over the course of your study of Civil Procedure?

INDEX

References are to Pages

†